WOODROW WILSON CENTER SERIES

The state and economic knowledge

Other books in the series

The state and economic knowledge

The American and British experiences

Edited by
MARY O. FURNER and BARRY SUPPLE

WOODROW WILSON INTERNATIONAL CENTER
FOR SCHOLARS

AND

CAMBRIDGE UNIVERSITY PRESS
Cambridge
New York   Port Chester   Melbourne   Sydney

Published by the Press Syndicate of the University of Cambridge
The Pitt Building, Trumpington Street, Cambridge CB2 1RP
40 West 20th Street, New York, NY 10011, USA
10 Stamford Road, Oakleigh, Melbourne 3166, Australia

First published 1990

Printed in the United States of America

Library of Congress Cataloging-in-Publication Data
The State and economic knowledge.
(Woodrow Wilson Center series)
"The result of a symposium organized by
the . . . Center's Program on American Society and
Politics"—Fwd.
1. United States—Economic policy—Congresses.
2. Economics—United States—History—Congresses.
3. Administrative agencies—United States—History—
Congresses.   4. Great Britain—Economic policy—
Congresses.   5. Economics—Great Britain—History—
Congresses.   6. Administrative agencies—Great Britain—
History—Congresses.   I. Furner, Mary O.   II. Supple,
Barry.   III. Series.
HC103.S74   1990   338.973   90-1541

British Library Cataloging in Publication applied for

m.R   ISBN 0-521-39424-4 hardback

WOODROW WILSON INTERNATIONAL CENTER FOR SCHOLARS

BOARD OF TRUSTEES

The Center is the "living memorial" of the United States of America to the nation's twenty-eighth president, Woodrow Wilson. The U.S. Congress established the Woodrow Wilson Center in 1968 as an international institute for advanced study, "symbolizing and strengthening the fruitful relationship between the world of learning and the world of public affairs." The Center opened in 1970 under its own presidentially appointed board of trustees.

In all its activities, the Woodrow Wilson Center is a nonprofit, nonpartisan organization, supported financially by annual appropriations from the U.S. Congress and contributions from foundations, corporations, and individuals. Conclusions or opinions expressed in Center publications are those of the authors and do not necessarily reflect the views of the Center staff, fellows, trustees, advisory groups, or any individuals or organizations that provide financial support to the Center.

Woodrow Wilson International Center for Scholars
1000 Jefferson Drive, S.W.
Washington, D.C. 20560
(202) 357-2429

Contents

vii

Part III. Industrial maturity and economic policy

Foreword

This volume is the result of a symposium organized by the Woodrow Wilson Center's Program on American Society and Politics. It represents one element in a long-term project designed to reexamine in historical and comparative perspective relations between government activity and the development of knowledge in the domains of society, economy, and culture. The project began with the recognition that of all the activities undertaken by the modern state, the most neglected as a subject of study is the subtle and multifaceted role played by its agencies in helping to elicit, organize, assess, augment, employ, refine, and conserve in many fields the knowledge base upon which in complex ways contemporary life has come to depend. It is the hope of those who have supported and worked on the project that this volume and subsequent volumes will deepen understanding of the processes behind the development of knowledge itself, its diffusion, and its impact on changing social and cultural life. And so far as the agendas of the scholarly disciplines themselves are concerned, the hope is to highlight once again the usefulness of a historical approach to public affairs and to encourage closer collaboration of those concerned with the history of ideas and those who work on the administrative history of public institutions.

The project grew out of the daily life of the Woodrow Wilson Center, and a word of thanks is due to those former Center fellows and advisers who began these discussions and helped organize the program. The late Warren Susman, a gifted historian and interpreter of emerging trends in scholarship, was especially important in getting things started. This volume's editors, Mary O. Furner and Barry Supple, not only brought into being the present collection of essays but contributed importantly to the formulation of other aspects of the total project as well. Robert Cuff, Hugh Heclo, Don K. Price, and the late Jack L. Walker also assisted at key points in the course of things. Finally the Center gratefully acknowledges the support of the Ford Foundation, the Nuffield Foundation, and the Shell Oil Company Foundation for helping to make the work possible.

Michael J. Lacey, *Director*
Program on American Society and Politics
Woodrow Wilson International Center for Scholars

Part I

The state and the uses of economic knowledge

1

Ideas, institutions, and state in the United States and Britain: an introduction

MARY O. FURNER and BARRY SUPPLE

This book is about the relation between political institutions, economic change, and economic knowledge. In one sense, therefore, it is part of the recent renewal of interest among historians and sociologists in the position, structure, and role of the state.[1] More specifically, we are concerned

As editors, we express our warm thanks to everyone who participated in the conference that gave rise to this volume. More particularly, we are aware of our great debt to Michael J. Lacey for his organizational and intellectual contributions. Participants who presented papers were exemplary in meeting deadlines and (even more significant) in tolerating our editorial advice. We would also like to emphasize our debt to the various commentators, especially Donald Winch, whose introductory paper at the conference and subsequent comments on this chapter were most helpful, and to Robert Cuff and Hugh Heclo, who were responsible at the end of the conference for summary comments highlighting what they observed as important themes, and whose overviews of the subject matter were masterpieces of systematic analysis and academic tact. We have drawn on their comments extensively—and not always with direct attribution. Finally, the conference greatly benefited from a keynote address by Janet Norwood (commissioner, U.S. Bureau of Labor Statistics), whose remarks provided rare and valuable firsthand insight into the operation and problems of a government agency concerned with the accumulation of economic knowledge.

[1] See Theda Skocpol, "Bringing the State Back In: Strategies of Analysis in Current Research," in Peter B. Evans, Dietrich Rueschmeyer, and Theda Skocpol, eds., *Bringing the State Back In* (Cambridge, Eng.: Cambridge University Press, 1985); Theda Skocpol, "Political Response to Capitalist Crisis: Neo-Marxist Theories of the State and the Case of the New Deal," *Politics and Society* 10 (1980): 155–201; Theda Skocpol and Kenneth Finegold, "State Capacity and Economic Intervention in the Early New Deal," *Political Science Quarterly* 97 (1982): 255–78; Thomas K. McCraw, "Regulation in America: A Review Article," *Business History Review* 49 (1975): 159–83; Thomas K. McCraw, ed., *Regulation in Perspective: Historical Essays* (Cambridge, Mass.: Harvard University Press, 1981); William E. Nelson, *The Roots of American Bureaucracy, 1830–1900* (Cambridge, Mass.: Harvard University Press, 1982); William R. Brock, *Investigation and Responsibility: Public Responsibility in the United States, 1865–1900* (Cambridge, Eng.: Cambridge University Press, 1984); Louis Galambos, ed., *The New American State: Bureaucracies and Policies Since World War II* (Baltimore: Johns Hopkins University Press, 1987). For a

with the relation between the rise of the modern state, with special reference to the institutions responsible for the formulation of public economic policy, and the generation and uses of economic knowledge.[2]

THE PROBLEM

In an economic system that is sensitive to political decisions regarding such matters as interest rates, taxes, trade rules, and investment policies, it is not difficult to recognize that the state must have a large interest in economic knowledge—in the practical perception of facts and relationships, in the discovery and deployment of data concerning the operation of the economy and economically based social relations, and in the articulation of systematic theories that may bear on the state's policies or influence its critics. Yet relatively little is known about the relation between the state and economic knowledge over time.

Frequently, the scholarly literature has portrayed governments as passive consumers of whatever ideas economists in the private sector and professions have offered. As a result, the infiltration into government of externally generated economic ideas and the pace and processes that characterize the state's acceptance and implementation of them have been studied fairly extensively. There is a sizable literature, for example, on the "influence of" Benthamite and Keynesian theories. In contrast, the state's own role in the growth of economic knowledge has only recently begun to receive systematic recognition. Although the contributors to this volume deal with the state as both consumer and producer of knowledge, this collection's most distinctive feature is perhaps the assessments it provides of the multidimensional influence of the state and policy formation on the substance and structure of economic knowledge. We hope that this new emphasis has been achieved without falling into a crude instrumentalism in explaining the links between policies and theories, and also without denying the possibility of a significant degree of autonomy in the evolution of ideas.

recent discussion of the varying significance of the political realm, see Charles Maier, ed., *The Changing Boundaries of the Political: Essays on the Evolving Balance Between the State and Society, Public and Private in Europe* (Cambridge, Eng.: Cambridge University Press, 1987).
[2]This specific focus falls within the more general theme of the connection between modern states and the entire range of knowledge, a topic treated perceptively by Gianfranco Poggi, "The Modern State and the Idea of Progress," in Gabriel Almond, ed., *Progress and Its Discontents* (Berkeley, Calif.: University of California Press, 1982), 337–60.

The state's unavoidable concern with economic knowledge derives from the fact that governments in modern societies have been obliged to come to terms with a number of related developments: violent fluctuations in the performance of national and international economies, structural changes and pressures from interest groups, the sharpened focus of class structures in the nineteenth century and the intermittent pressure of class conflicts, and the emergence of new organizational forms, such as large-scale business corporations and mass-membership trade unions. In this process, governments have had to draw on or generate basic information about economic conditions. For a general orientation to these conditions, they have relied on systematic theory already existing or have encouraged its development within or outside the state. Governments have also been forced to take account of and perhaps attempt to neutralize or modify conventional wisdom, to the extent that widely held beliefs about the workings of the economy have served as catalysts or impediments to policy decisions. More than this, the gathering of information and the analysis of principles and policies have led to the creation of state institutions—statistical agencies, registration offices, committees of inquiry, and permanent departments devoted to monitoring and regulating discrete aspects of economic activity, such as labor or trade—that have themselves reshaped the nature and capacities of government. This quest for economic knowledge to be used for public purposes figures as one of the important building blocks of the modern state.

The dependence of government on economic knowledge expanded with the emergence of the modern industrial state. Perhaps the most important development in this connection has been the assumption by the modern state of ultimate responsibility for the economic well-being of its citizens and for the country's competitive position in the international economy. Throughout modern history, capitalist societies have relied heavily on private initiatives, accumulation, and investment to stimulate economic growth; yet for two centuries, and with increasing intensity, the public sector has acted, often with the approval of other interest groups, but sometimes over their opposition, to facilitate and coordinate private activity, and to deal with serious problems and frictions in the market economy.

The expectation of some public oversight and coordination has been a constant in industrial states. Even during the middle third of the nineteenth century, when laissez-faire was recognized as the dominant ideology in Britain, such national economic goals as the provision of an adequate food supply for a rapidly growing population, the removal of obstacles to labor mobility, and the strengthening of the country's international trading position were in part addressed by the adoption of *public* policies, including free trade, a sound monetary system, and a reformed Poor Law. In the United States in the nineteenth century, to take another set of examples, the pursuit of economic development and the response to interest-group pressures involved national and state governments in an array of positive measures, such as a liberal land policy, public investment in the transportation infrastructure, and the manipulation of tariffs and credit. And in each case, whether for inspiration or justification, public officials frequently made explicit use of economic knowledge (in one of its various forms), and helped to shape it.

Given that states were active in these ways when societies were in the relatively early stages of modern economic development, it is hardly surprising that the role of government became even more important as capitalist development under a regime of competition brought acute economic and social dislocation. In part for this reason, the chapters in this book are primarily, though not exclusively, devoted to the experience of the past hundred years. They are also confined to the experience of the United States and Britain. Such a choice provides an opportunity to compare two industrial societies with many common features, but at the same time to learn from a contrast of cultures and institutions. Britain and the United States developed industrially at different times and in different ways; when, in the 1880s, Britain began to experience the first symptoms of relative decline, or at least maturity, and the associated intensification of competition, America—by then a rapidly industrializing society—was, in effect, part of the problem, with consequences addressed by Barry Supple in Chapter 10 of this volume. Later, in the 1930s and 1940s, as Barber and Collins show in Chapters 4 and 5, the American state and American economists were compelled to consider the problems of the United States's own apparent maturity. Concurrently, between roughly the 1920s and 1950s, British economic policymakers faced a new supply of stubborn crises and dislocations that challenged existing strategies and incited conflict between competing paradigms within and outside government, as described by Clarke, Peden, and Supple in Chapters 6, 7, and 10.[3]

---

[3] "Maturity" can, of course, mean either of two distinct conditions: a flowering or development of a system and its institutions (such as American industrial maturity in the 1890s) and a condition of actual or threatened decadence or stagnation (as in the United States in the 1930s and perhaps the 1970s).

The ways in which the two societies responded to these experiences and their parallel patterns in the evolution of economic knowledge were, of course, shaped by the societies themselves, as well as by the problems they faced. Thus, many of the differences in the relations between the state and knowledge in the United States and Britain stemmed from differences in their constitutional and political structures and cultures. Federalism, the presidential system, and the very organization of political institutions and debate in the United States made for more diversity and less continuity in policy discussions and in the elaboration of certain kinds of economic knowledge. As a result, attitudes to industrial structures and competition, trade and labor policy, and even the perceived role of the market varied markedly between the two countries. Obviously, some of these differences also derived from the nature of the two economies: Trade policy, for example, is not simply the product of interest groups and political structures, but is based in large part on a country's position in and dependence on the international economy. Nevertheless, the broader differences in institutions and outlook had a vital role to play—not simply in the articulation of political economy and public policies, but also in the degree of accessibility of state institutions to new ideas, the potential for diversity within official opinion, and the extent to which state agencies could act as arenas for economic investigation and debate and as devices for effective management. (For a fuller discussion of the role of institutions, see the final section of this chapter.)

Much can be learned, therefore, from the contrasts between the United States and Britain. But much, too, can be learned from their similarities, for the two industrial societies have clearly confronted a common range of practical problems and have inherited what, for these purposes, may be considered a common body of political and economic theory. Despite their different histories, the United States and Britain also share a number of important institutional characteristics—not the least of which is the relative permeability of the boundary between the public and private spheres, as compared with more statist forms and traditions in some continental European societies. This greater permeability has allowed the American and British states both to devolve responsibilities more easily and to be relatively receptive to policy initiatives that reflect the perceived needs of particular interests—which may be self-consciously organized into pressure groups, but which may also be more informal or less politicized associations.

The lack of a sharp and enduring distinction between public and private in these two societies has implications that merit careful consideration. Some students of the subject interpret it as a vulnerability of the state to control by private groups, a weakness in "governing institutions" when confronted with vested interests—particularly capitalist vested interests. From this perspective, the state escapes "hegemony" only when the economic system is in crisis, and the threat of civil disorder overrides the reluctance of officials to oppose the wishes of powerful business supporters.

No serious student would deny that economic (and social) policy in both countries has very often been greatly influenced, and sometimes even determined, by the needs and appetites of particular groupings in civil society. Yet it is surely as important to recognize the limits to private control over public action as it is to understand the historical boundaries of state interference. For example, it is hardly surprising that governments that in some sense arise from society at large (and not, by contrast, from a hereditary or self-perpetuating governing class) should be disinclined to act against the interest of any powerful social group whose constructive endeavors are judged to be essential to stability and growth. Since the Enlightenment at least, states have been regarded as servants rather than masters, in the sense that they have been expected to govern rationally, in the public interest, and they have often been called to account when their actions seem irresponsibly to favor a privileged group. In both the United States and Britain, although development has been encouraged by state policies, the state has been unwilling to put the demands of any particular interest consistently first, given the necessity to consider each issue in terms of the total situation. And for the same reason even capitalists as a class have not always had their way. They have benefited, to be sure, from state assistance in repressing or diverting protest movements, and in circumscribing the role of labor unions. But the states under consideration here have also, in their different ways, and often over capitalist protest, backed far-reaching welfare programs, and more generally, capitalists have had cause for complaint against extensive interference with market forces. The state has also been unwilling to put specifically economic interests consistently ahead of other considerations, including highly respected cultural values. In the United States, for example, a reverence for competition and an animus toward monopoly were sufficient to override considerations of mere efficiency in the development of antitrust policy. An awareness of contingency and contextuality in all these forms suggests caution in assessing the role of the state in policy and "reform." Clearly the state's unwillingness to override capitalist interests in these countries has operated within a framework of culturally embedded commitments to liberal values and institutions, in which the necessity for private accumulation and investment was always recognized, even when public ownership in specific industries and public oversight of economic performance were considered appropriate and necessary. Yet the proof of the state's subservience (or, in stricter methodological parlance, of the claim that the state generally operates as a *dependent* variable in policy formation) must rest on something other than government support for measures demonstrably necessary to promote the *legitimate* interests of private groups.

One approach to this problem of the state's relationship to private interests has been to stress the independence, or autonomy, of the state—even in nonstatist societies such as those considered here. As Patricia Thane pointed out at our conference, there was a powerful étatist tradition in nineteenth-century Britain, whose "leaders sought and to a high degree created a strong, flexible state," and were therefore able to fight successful wars against more bureaucratized nations and establish and administer a huge empire. Politicians and civil servants were part of a broader culture that generated ideas and information, yet were skeptical in their approach to new ideas and data, and were positive and purposeful in deciding what sorts of knowledge to use and when it was appropriate to use them. Politicians ultimately "called the tune," guided by independently selected political ideas, social priorities, and institutional constraints. To this extent, economic policy can be said, in the last resort, to have been determined by the governing institutions.

An alternative to viewing the state as either subordinate or autonomous—and perhaps in the longer term a better analytical framework—is an approach that recognizes powerful bonds of interaction and interdependence between a variety of political institutions and the more self-conscious and better organized groups in civil society, with the state often containing even within itself conflicting currents of opinion, and speaking with different voices to various traditions and constituencies. In the American case, for example, political democracy has permitted a variety of "hegemonic" movements, and the state has been as much exposed to expectations from republican, antimonopolist, populist, and democratic, as from purely capitalist quarters. As Robert Cuff suggests in a companion volume to this one, for example, the American state in World War I was open to and indeed dependent on the managerial skills and policy initiatives of corporate executives who headed the emergency agencies that managed mobilization; but during the New Deal, agencies with an anticorporate animus developed their own claims to managerial competence and asserted their right to participate in managing World War II mobilization.[4] To take another example of these conflicting currents within the state: As Brownlee reminds us in Chapter 13, the Treasury under McAdoo endorsed and advanced the long-term goals of antimonopolists who hoped to achieve a more equitable society through redistributive tax policies, only to lose out in the Mellon years to groups supporting taxation theories and policies that stressed accumulation and investment rather than redistribution.

This capacity of the democratic state to provide an arena for contesting views is a powerful stimulus to the development of a knowledge base adequate for making and defending policy decisions. The traditions and institutions of representative government enable, and indeed compel, public officials to define a civic purpose larger than the ambitions of any particular interest. In sum, both hegemony and autonomy theories encompass altogether too monolithic a view of the state in the context of either the American or the British historical setting.[5]

In these societies, policy initiatives have come from both public and private sources, in a multifaceted structure of parallel investigations that allows both collaboration and confrontation. Of course, various private groups are unequal in terms of their resources or access to authority. Yet, while a constant flow of "interested" information has been available, so has a supply of somewhat more "disinterested" data and theory, including a good deal of that proffered by professional economists, reflecting theoretical developments somewhat removed from policy considerations. The advantaged position of the state with respect to information gathering has allowed various state agencies—in America, often working at cross-purposes with one another, and even in Britain, usually reflecting more than a single official view—to seek their own data. Occasionally, as Barber shows in Chapter 4, when existing theory has failed to cope with unforeseen circumstances, state-based economists have progressed more rapidly than academic economists in developing new theories to deal with

[4]Robert Cuff, "War Mobilization, Social Teaming, and State Building: 1917–1941," in Michael Lacey and Mary O. Furner, eds., *The State and Social Investigation in Britain and the United States* (forthcoming).
[5]On the question of autonomy, in addition to the works cited in note 2, see a recent symposium in the *American Political Science Review* 82 (1988): 853–901, with a lead essay by Gabriel Almond and rejoinders by Eric Nordlinger, Theodore Lowi, and Sergio Fabbrini.

immediate policy problems. Similarly, the privileged position of the state when it comes to policy formation has left public officials of one sort or another with the authority, finally, to decide what knowledge to apply.

How does all this relate to the state's role in formulation of economic knowledge? To perform its various functions effectively, as well as to maintain legitimacy, a government must have bases for its actions and be able to justify its policies, especially when these policies conflict with the pressures of private interests. On the one hand, this entails marshaling accurate empirical information about the condition and operations of the economy; on the other, it means having to rely on explanatory models of its operations. These models are not necessarily empirically based, or always fully articulated as analytical constructs, but they nevertheless amount to a specific form of economic knowledge, even when (as is almost invariably the case) they incorporate potent political assumptions and values. (See the next section for a discussion of the concept of economic knowledge.)

It is also important to emphasize that the state's accumulation of information and application of models are related to the performance of functions that no private interest can adequately undertake, namely, adjusting or at least recognizing different sectional interests, pursuing general objectives, and assessing particular policies in light of their consequences for society as a whole. The state, after all, *is* different.

As already implied, the state's concern with economic knowledge in its various manifestations can be considered from two perspectives. One involves the relationship between policy and knowledge: Is knowledge policy-driven, or is policy knowledge-driven? Do people know in order to act or act in order to know? How do specific situations, contexts, and historical conditions affect the knowledge-policy relationship? The other involves the role of institutions in the development of ideas and of the state: To what extent do acts of inquiry and management transform the very agency that initiated them and the knowledge they were designed to identify? These broad topics are discussed in the next two sections, as a general prelude to the substantive chapters following in this book.

SOME CATEGORIES OF ECONOMIC KNOWLEDGE

This is not the place to enter deeply into philosophical discussion of the nature and status of knowledge in general, or of the criteria for judging progress (or, for that matter, retrogression) in economic knowledge in particular.[6] It does seem useful, nevertheless, to specify what we mean, in the present context, by "economic knowledge." It may also be helpful at this stage to draw attention to the different types of economic knowledge that have some claim, with other types of knowledge and belief, to determine policy, and to the different ways in which such knowledge has been made available to politicians and bureaucrats for purposes of state.

As Robert Cuff's penetrating summary comments at the conference suggested, the categories of economic knowledge exemplified in this volume[7] largely reflect the various ways in which that knowledge has entered political debate and policy-making.[8] Taking Cuff's taxonomy as the basis for our approach, we can identify the following distinct types: *professional, or disciplinary, knowledge; informed opinion, or practical knowledge;* and *cultural beliefs and values* regarding the economic order. The first category, professional, or disciplinary, knowledge, refers to knowledge based on organized inquiry or research, including both the systematic collection of relevant empirical data and the formulation of general, middle-range and specific theories and models. Such knowledge passes through a system of professional evaluation and criticism. Economic discourse at this level incorporates both debates about macroeconomic models of overall economic performance and more empirical analytical questions having to do with the problems of specific economic stages, industries, or sectors.

Informed opinion, or practical knowledge, includes the whole structure of quasi-technical rules and operating assumptions possessed and used by administrators, politicians, economic journalists, business people, labor leaders, and others who, although not actively engaged in formal, structured economic inquiry, find themselves more or less constantly involved in assessing economic performance and making decisions with economic consequences. Their understanding of economic relationships is normally based both on formal instruction in economics, often

---

[6]See Daniel M. Hausman, ed., *The Philosophy of Economics: An Anthology* (Cambridge, Eng.: Cambridge University Press, 1984); Terence Hutchinson, *On Revolutions and Progress in Economic Knowledge* (Cambridge, Eng.: Cambridge University Press, 1978).

[7]Our categorization was derived from the discussion in the conference itself, and in this respect we were particularly dependent on the provocative and detailed synthesis offered by Robert Cuff in his concluding remarks. Cuff identified four different uses of "knowledge" in the papers presented at the conference: formal disciplinary knowledge; informed or lay opinion; general "folklore"; and practical knowledge. These, with some adaptation, have become the basis for our approach, although for heuristic purposes we have conflated the second and fourth categories.

[8]Thus, the categorization contains a tautological element, in that the categories are derived from the very issues to which we apply them.

limited to popularized versions of "masterworks" such as those by Smith or Keynes or Friedman, and on intermittent, problem-focused reading in various types of economic literature, including trade publications, government reports, financial journals, and the like. This category of economic knowledge is also, of course, derived from their own direct experience of the performance and vicissitudes of the economic system.

The third form of policy-relevant economic knowledge, cultural beliefs and values, embraces moral precepts, political convictions, social expectations, and customary maxims that people draw on when making judgments regarding economic questions. Derived from a wider range of experiences and sources than the purely economic, these guiding principles and assumptions about what is right or wrong, natural or unnatural, beneficial or dangerous to the public good provide a basis for general conceptions of the economic system as an element in the total social order. Such designs for national life and progress are, in the widest sense, models of political economy. They encompass the economic elements in the system of beliefs and values—the "civic culture"—that operates more or less coherently in any modern society, and on whose most fundamental elements there is often widespread agreement ("the laborer is worthy of his hire"; "each tub must stand on its own bottom"; "good times follow bad").

But this category of knowledge also includes opinions and expectations that are peculiar to particular subcultures (e.g., a habitual distrust of big business or of big government; contempt for welfare recipients or a conviction that the rich cannot possibly deserve their wealth). Such myths and values comprise, at the most general and unscientific (but not necessarily irrational or false) level, the "economic mind" of the nation or group. This is the kind of economic knowledge any person is first exposed to, and most people, including economists and bureaucrats, maintain such beliefs alongside or underneath more sophisticated forms of economic knowledge all their lives, except when a major crisis cuts the ground from under their system, as was the case for many Americans and Britons who lived through the Great Depression.

Policymakers often base their economic decisions more on established principles drawn from earlier experiences that have shaped the national culture (the "lessons" of the Poor Laws, for example), or on traditional sociopolitical values, such as individual responsibility, than on the empirical or theoretical findings of economists. Even if persuaded by new data, politicians understand that people hold such bedrock values and often refuse expert advice that points in a different direction.

Yet, as we said at the start, modern states do require a base of theory and information for their policies, and they turn to specialists for much of it. Most of the chapters in this volume are concerned with the state's role in developing and applying what we have called professional knowledge. Such disciplinary knowledge provides what is, in essence, a culturally accepted and privileged discourse, which has become more sharply defined, more abstracted from other social phenomena, and, therefore, more isolated and limited in its applicability to certain kinds of social problems as the social sciences have been increasingly fragmented in the twentieth century (a point Harris takes up in Chapter 12).

In this context, "professional" does not necessarily mean academic, for, as Winch (Chapter 2) notes, for long periods there were few important academic economists. Frequently, the form and medium of professional knowledge are determined by who the intended audience is, what the historical circumstances are, and who needs to be persuaded. These considerations also affect the positioning of professional spokesmen and professional arguments. In the following pages, for example, a striking contrast in the use of professional knowledge is offered by Collins's (Chapter 5) description of Keyserling's contempt, even as chairman of the Council of Economic Advisers, for academe and by Clarke's (Chapter 6) discussion of Keynes, some of whose most telling influence was exercised through polemical journalism—which the Treasury's civil servants thought outrageous, but were nevertheless obliged to answer.

Because our ultimate interest is in the role of the state in the process by which knowledge is formed, we must also be alert to the dangers of an instrumentalism that sees the "advance" of "useful" knowledge or theory as the simple outcome of "pragmatic" needs and practical problems. The development of theoretical knowledge has a certain autonomy; although not insulated from outside influences, it is driven by the internal logic or dynamic of ideas, a point Winch discusses with some force in Chapter 2.

The perspectives adopted in most of the chapters in this volume—including those by Supple on British industrial and regional policy (Chapter 10), Furner and Hawley on economic inquiry and industrial policy in the United States (Chapters 8 and 9), Barber, Clarke, and Peden on Keynesianism (Chapters 4, 6, and 7), Collins on growthmanship (Chapter 5), and Brownlee on taxation theory and policy in the United States (Chapter 13)—necessarily entail a legitimate concentration on the other side, the extent to which the needs and pressures of government, particularly at moments of crisis, engendered new thinking, or the reformulation and acceptance of old thinking. Nevertheless, we must remember that this is merely one perspective, and that ideas—even the ideas to which the state resorts in crisis—have a social, cultural, and intellectual history of their own, independent of immediate policy considerations. Indeed, new theories in economics often develop in advance of, or without regard to, economic changes or crises; conversely, as Harris shows (in Chapter 12), important innovations in social policy, such as social insurance, were often adopted with only the most haphazard inputs from economists, or none at all.

Of course, whatever the autonomy of ideas or the primacy of policy needs, there remains an intimate relationship between ideas and politics. Economic knowledge does not come unheralded and self-motivated into the political marketplace; occasionally, indeed, the demand for ideas is so pressing that the result is both institutional adaptation (a Macmillan Committee on Finance and Industry or an Economic Advisory Council in Britain, or a National Bureau of Economic Research or a Council of Economic Advisers in the United States) and elicitation of an enhanced supply. More than this, however, the formulation of economic ideas helps shape the political debate itself: in modern societies, economic theory not only provides the lion's share of the meanings and vocabulary of that debate; it also structures the conceivable alternatives, establishing what Collini calls the "context of refutation."[9]

This dependency explains in part the way in which policy discourse has been progressively "economized." As industrial societies became more politically modern, as economic problems became politically visible and policy debates more public and democratic, so the use of economics, in the sense of professionally sanctioned styles of economic argumentation, ensured that assertions concerning policy, no matter by whom they were made, had to be defended and answered. Increasingly in the twentieth century, political argument concerning economic policy has necessarily become a public act; policy recommendations and enactments have had to be explained, justified, and made consistent. Consequently, civil servants and politicians have been increasingly obliged to seek an explicit rationale for their brand of economic knowledge. And, to the extent that economic efficiency or material well-being supersedes other, perhaps conflicting values, economic theory provides the best, conceivably the only, level at which a persuasive rationale for state policies can be found. As a

[9] Stefan Collini, *Liberalism and Sociology: L. T. Hobhouse and Political Argument in England, 1880–1914* (Cambridge, Eng.: Cambridge University Press, 1979), 9.

result, while economics has been politicized, politics has had to acknowledge the domain of economics, even though politicians often assert the primacy of noneconomic values and therefore do not confine their argumentation to disciplinary economic knowledge. Examples of this include the Macmillan Committee and Barlow Commission in Britain and the Industrial Commission, the Commission on Industrial Relations, and the Committee on Recent Economic Changes in the United States. (See Chapters 5, 8, and 10.)

As many of the chapters make clear, variety and disputation exist even *within* the disciplinary realm of discourse. Whatever the degree of autonomy in the evolution of economic ideas, they are by no means monolithic. On the one hand, different aspects of professional economic knowledge attain contrasting levels of sophistication or generality. For example, in this collection, the chapters in Part II concerned with debates about macroeconomic, and particularly Keynesian, models of overall economic performance contrast sharply with the first three chapters in Part III, which discuss the growth of empirical and analytical knowledge concerning industrial structures and sectoral performance.

On the other hand, there are outright disagreements about the purposes and operations of economic systems. Such cleavages within professional opinion are often related to differing views on the practical role of politics and the state—embodying differences in fundamental, even ideological, assumptions about the way in which society works, or ought to work. Thus, in the late nineteenth and early twentieth centuries, when neoclassical economists tended to favor a regime of laissez-faire and free trade, institutional and historical economists, taking a different view of human motives and market efficiency, looked to intervention, state building, and "positive" policies—a view that was clearly related to the methodological assumption that "economics is not a branch of logic or mathematics, but belongs to the art of managing public affairs by the application of sound reasoning to the whole corpus of existence."[10] Such differences were far more embodiments of funda-

[10] J. M. Keynes, "H. S. Foxwell," *Economic Journal* 46 (1936): 593, quoted in Stefan Collini, Donald Winch, and John Burrow, *That Noble Science of Politics: A Study in Nineteenth-Century Intellectual History* (Cambridge, Eng.: Cambridge University Press, 1983), 275. Compare the verdict of the historical economist William Cunningham (quoted in ibid., 268): "Economic development has been consciously and deliberately controlled in the supposed interest of the polity." For an assessment of the split between deductive economics and the historical school, see ibid., 249–75; Gerard M. Koot, *English Historical Economics, 1870–1926: The Rise of Economic History and Neomercantilism* (Cambridge, Eng.: Cambridge University Press, 1987).

mentally different views of economic society and the relations between economic institutions and political culture than they were technical disagreements about logical constructs. (See the discussion of cultural beliefs below.)

Disagreements within the ranks of professional economists become most visible during episodes of political dislocation. In such periods of crisis economic knowledge has often been mobilized institutionally in new and effective ways. Although an "organizational revolution" was under way generally in the United States during the late nineteenth century, it is no accident that the professionalization of American economics coincided with the demise of laissez-faire as a coherent, reputable system. Depression and mass violence in the 1870s and 1880s engendered a kind of social fear. "New School" economists responded by offering a charter for the American Economic Association (AEA) in 1885 that made expansive claims for economists in policy formation, at the same time rejecting laissez-faire and endorsing a larger moral and regulatory role for the state. Woodrow Wilson's well-known plea for an American science of public administration, as well as Henry Carter Adams's less recognized but equally significant call for research and instruction in public finance as a preparation for public service, was related to the broader crisis of public authority that accompanied the economic crisis. The economists who seized this opportunity to put laissez-faire into play, so to speak, were mostly German-trained; yet the shrewdest of them were careful to distance themselves from German statism as well as from English individualism, and to announce the intention of developing a new economics (and by implication a new state) true to American civic traditions, especially early republican precedents, which, on their reading, allowed for a much larger public presence in economic regulation and planning. From these events, there followed in the United States a competitive development of economics graduate programs and journals, a détente between the warring schools of economists, a strategic retreat from the militancy of the early AEA, and increased involvement of economists as experts in government service.[11]

---

[11]Louis Galambos, "The Emerging Organizational Synthesis in Modern American History," *Business History Review* 44 (1970): 279–90; idem, "Technology, Political Economy, and Professionalization: Central Themes of the Organizational Synthesis," ibid., 57 (1983): 471–93; Mary O. Furner, *Advocacy and Objectivity: A Crisis in the Professionalization of American Social Science, 1865–1905* (Lexington: University of Kentucky Press, 1975), esp. Chs. 3 and 4; A. W. Coats, "The Educational Revolution and the Professionalization of American Economics," *Breaking the Academic Mould: Economists and American*

In Britain, similarly, although more ambiguously, economists such as John Ingram and W. J. Ashley attempted to link historical and institutional economics with the movement toward New Liberalism. At the same time, as Winch shows in Chapter 2, Alfred Marshall sought to upgrade university instruction in economics as a means of informing elite opinion, promoting civic consciousness among business leaders, and shaping the views of future civil servants regarding economic issues, while—distrusting bureaucracy as he did—preserving a more minimalist state. On the whole, the historical economists were less successful in establishing their view of economics and the state in Britain than in the United States; even though New Liberals such as Hobson and Hobhouse had considerable influence, the neoclassical tradition remained more central in Britain, at least in policy circles. In the United States, on the other hand, reflecting deeply ingrained tensions in American political culture, the opposition between the two approaches continued to divide economists, providing theoretical support for conflicting visions of the role of the state in economic management.[12]

But the important point of our analysis is simply that in *both* countries there was a relationship between crisis—the long depression, its social consequences, its challenge to authoritative systems—and the development of new directions in economic theory, professional organization, and education. The chapters that follow repeatedly emphasize this connection between the role of economic or social crisis or disjunction and the evolution of knowledge as well as policy. Barber, Collins, Clarke, and Peden call attention to fundamental differences regarding macroeconomic issues; Furner, Hawley, and Supple, to opposing approaches to questions of industrial economics; and Brownlee, to conflicting theories of income distribution and social policy. These various accounts confirm the historical and disciplinary significance of strains in the economy and the political society. Although dependence on system-

---

Higher Learning in the Nineteenth Century, ed. William J. Barber (Middletown, Conn.: Wesleyan University Press, 1988), 340–75; Thomas L. Haskell, *The Emergence of Professional Social Science: The American Social Science Association and the Nineteenth Century Crisis of Authority* (Urbana: University of Illinois Press, 1977), 75–91, 166–67; Woodrow Wilson, "The Study of Administration," *Political Science Quarterly* 2 (1887): 197–222; Henry Carter Adams, "Relation of the State to Industrial Action," *Two Essays by Henry Carter Adams,* ed. Joseph Dorfman (New York: Augustus Kelley Reprints, 1969), 57–133; Thomas Haskell, ed., *The Authority of Experts: Studies in History and Theory* (Bloomington, Ind.: Indiana University Press, 1984), passim.
[12]Koot, *English Historical Economics;* John Maloney, *Marshall, Orthodoxy, and the Professionalization of Economics* (Cambridge, Eng.: Cambridge University Press, 1985).

atic knowledge is profound even in relatively prosperous and stable periods, the availability of new knowledge and theories becomes critical at moments of tension. Such tensions arise most readily in two sorts of circumstances. First, strains occur toward the ends of cycles of economic growth and decline, when conventional relationships between economic interests are breaking down and old policy assumptions and structures seem to have run their course. Such a breakdown occurred when foreign competition threatened some of Britain's most important industries in the late nineteenth and early twentieth centuries and led to a challenge to free-trade doctrines. A similar moment arrived when "ruinous competition" in late-nineteenth-century America undermined faith in market mechanisms for allocating investment capital, leading to a wave of giant mergers, justified by many economists, which paved the way for changes in antitrust policies, while a simultaneous escalation of labor radicalism provoked an extensive review of public policy toward industrial relations.

Second, new or neglected knowledge also becomes especially important when an abrupt threat (a war or a sudden slump) presents a "life-threatening" challenge to the existing order. All crises are capable of force-feeding change, but wars in particular compel national audits, even while they enhance the state's capacity by transforming official controlling institutions, recruiting managers to the task of public oversight, and stimulating the production of more systematic information about the size, structure, and workings of the economy. Wars therefore leave a legacy of social learning, and this learning frequently takes the form of new elements in professional as well as practical opinion. Major depressions have been the equivalent of war in this regard; in both countries, the Great Depression undermined the theoretical justification of the "self-regulating market" and paved the way, either immediately before or after the next war, for elaborate experiments in national economic stabilization and embryonic planning based on Keynesian assumptions.

And yet, despite the tendency of emergencies to foster new approaches and perceptions, the fact remains that events need to be interpreted, and the meanings they take on are largely constructed from what is available in the battery of existing ideas. (For a discussion of the noninstrumental role of ideas and their critical relationship to action, see Chapter 2.) Although crises do occasionally generate completely new knowledge, more often they bring to light new and better data on subjects not featured prominently earlier, focus attention on alternative theories not previously in favor, and/or change the priorities applied to the political choice between existing models for improving economic performance.

Of course, once doubts about inherited ideas arise, new empirical data, or data that can be seen from a new perspective, can be a potent force to undermine hitherto dominant professional opinion as well as conventional wisdom. For example, the increasingly "visible" evidence of sticky wages helped erode the theoretical case for the gold standard and the Treasury model of the economy (see Chapter 6); the awareness of declining real wages fueled the transformation of labor economics in the early twentieth century (Chapter 8); and the growing sense of the immobility of labor enforced new perceptions of regional and industrial economics in interwar Britain (Chapter 10). Yet there is a sense in which ostensibly "new" information is *always* present. It only waits for conceptual apparatus or doubt to make more sense of it. And it is, indeed, through such processes of verification and falsification, rather than the more cynical process of rationalization, that, even in crisis, knowledge and events come together—each, if one prefers to phrase it so, from its own "separate" sphere.

In effect, then, governments are neither purely consumers nor purely producers of economic knowledge. The relationship is essentially symbiotic. In this sense, the state is a player like other players (although one with distinctive capacities, responsibilities, and interests). This point is brought out in this volume in Clarke's assessment of the coherence and standing of the rival Treasury and Keynesian models of the British interwar economy, and in Furner's references to competing public and private investigations. And this interaction is one reason for stipulating the need for informed opinion as a second category of economic knowledge.

As we have just implied, the many forms of interaction between pure and applied knowledge may tend to blur the distinction between the two. To the extent that disciplinary knowledge develops in response to crisis and political demand, the two categories overlap. Yet it is also clear that a body of practical information, observations, and use-tested principles about how the economy works, or ought to work, which is *not* directly related to or derived from professional or disciplinary economic knowledge, has always existed. Prior to the professionalization of economics, accumulated wisdom of this sort was the starting point for systematic theorizing about the economy; the authors of what Winch (Chapter 2) refers to as the "four synoptic gospels" of modern economics (Adam Smith, Thomas Malthus, David Ricardo, and John Stuart Mill), in addition to being intellectuals, all in one way or another, as civil servants, teachers of civil servants, or men of affairs, dealt with practical problems.

This form of knowledge is practical in two senses: It derives from actual experience in or oversight of economic activity, and it is oriented toward solving immediate problems, usually by attacking or defending specific policies through selectively mobilizing evidence and principles, rather than, in the customary professional manner, by relating technically sophisticated inquiries to the theoretical issues under consideration in the discipline. Informed opinion in this sense embraces the heterogeneous backgrounds and outlooks of civil servants, politicians, capitalists, managers, labor leaders, economic journalists, and others who find themselves involved in framing, implementing, or assessing economic policies.

The difference between disciplinary knowledge and informed opinion has been cast as one between amateurs and professionals, partisanship and scientific neutrality, and advocacy and objectivity, with an invidiousness that can cut either way. To Keynes, the distinction could be blurred to the demerit of both kinds of knowledge ("Practical men, who believe themselves to be quite exempt from any intellectual influences, are usually the slaves of some defunct economist").[13] But economists in government have also been contemptuous of ivory-tower theorists, as Collins (Chapter 5) demonstrates, for example, in his account of Leon Keyserling's animus toward academics when he was head of the Council of Economic Advisers. And within the discipline itself, a closely related tradition—valuing historical and statistical investigation of practical problems over abstract theorizing—runs from the historical-institutional economists of the past century, such as Richard Ely and William Ashley, to much more modern figures, such as Ely Devon and Wassily Leontieff, who also favored the empirical over the theoretical, approaching economic inquiry from a relativistic perspective that emphasized the importance of the linkage between economic knowledge and administrative technique.

Despite the tendency toward convergence, practical knowledge differs from the disciplinary variety in various respects. First, it is not directly based on elaborate and explicit logical analysis and argumentation (although, as already suggested, increasingly in modern democracies it has to be justified by some reference to such argumentation, and in the course of time is vulnerable to indisputable empirical information that contra-

[13] Austen Robinson and Donald Moggridge, eds., *The Collected Writings of John Maynard Keynes* (London: Macmillan, 1971), VII, 383.

dicts its models).[14] Second, it is frequently much more explicitly related, often in an unabashedly partisan way, to social and cultural values or ideological commitments, expressed, for example, in assumptions about the efficiency or inefficiency of markets, or the virtues of thrift or competition. Third, and in large part because of the first two characteristics, it is likely to exhibit selectivity and considerable lags in accepting adaptations in theoretical reasoning. Fourth, the reason that persons who deploy informed opinion think of themselves as having practical knowledge is that they frequently occupy positions where they cannot deal with technical problems in isolation. Rather, they have to take some account of the effects of specific policies on political processes and the interests of many constituencies—hence the sense of the superiority of practicality and the contempt for professors and theoretical knowledge. This attitude has existed on both sides of the Atlantic: in Winston Churchill's defense of the return to the gold standard in 1925 as the outcome of advice from Bank of England and Treasury officials, whose opinions "count more than the clever arguments of academic theorists,"[15] and in one American congressman's argument that legislation to regulate the coal industry in the 1930s was made possible by "practical, hard-headed businessmen and hard-working miners—not fanciful theoretical college professors bent on conducting some new social or economic experiment."[16]

At the same time, the ambiguous nature of systematic ideas in the practical sphere of informed opinion means that there is considerable scope for the influence of individuals and the pressures of groups in the formulation of "knowledge," and even more in its application. This point is exemplified a number of times in the chapters that follow—most notably, perhaps, in Collins's chapter (Chapter 5) on growthmanship. Collins implies that particular bodies of official thought about the workings and prospects of the American economy were associated with the presence, in such positions of authority as the Council of Economic Advisers, of particular individuals and groups. Similarly, analyzing the use of theory

[14]Differences in political institutions and political culture meant that the process of intellectual challenge and amendment was quicker in the United States than Britain. See Chapters 4–7.

[15]Churchill's comment, made in the House of Commons, was particularly ironic in view of the lengths to which he had gone to confront his officials with Keynes's arguments against the return to the gold standard. (We are indebted to Donald Winch for drawing our attention to this quotation and its implications.)

[16]Quoted in Barry Supple, "The Political Economy of Demoralisation: The State and the Coalmining Industry in America and Britain between the Wars," *Economic History Review*, 2d ser., 41 (1988): 566–91.

concerning taxation policy, Brownlee (Chapter 13) implies that an important role was played by a specific individual—Thomas Sewell Adams—who was able to bend theory to the changing policy requirements of financial mobilization in World War I, monetary reconversion, and the great expansion of the 1920s. Such possibilities for penetrating the world of policy invite academics' cultivation of officials and increase the possibility for cross-fertilization between the two types of knowledge.

Although the importance of strategic position for the bearer of a particular set of ideas counters the simplistic view that all is attributable to impersonal forces, ideas are not less important than people. The significance of individuals is in large part the significance of their ideas and theories. Also, the role of individuals illustrates the interaction and overlaying of different categories of knowledge. In Brownlee's history of taxation policy (Chapter 13), Adams appears not simply as a pioneer in tax theory and administration, but also as the bearer of a cultural vision of society related to a nineteenth-century tradition of republicanism and egalitarianism, to be achieved through income redistribution and antimonopoly policies. In this light, Adams's seeming opportunism fades into the background.

Just as in the case of formal disciplinary economic knowledge, informed opinion on economic questions can embody competing and clashing viewpoints. (Such a conflict surfaced in the different approaches to the American labor question adopted by the Industrial Commission and the Commission on Industrial Relations, and in the hearings before an important British commission of inquiry into regional economies in the late 1930s. See Chapters 8 and 10.) In the resulting debates, or when a government is genuinely undecided about a course of action in the face of a pressing problem, disciplinary knowledge becomes more directly relevant. Indeed, analysis of the relations between the state and economic knowledge raises the twin questions of how far professional knowledge enforces shifts in informed opinion (an issue addressed directly in various chapters in Part II on Keynesian economics and its acceptance) and how much governments seek to incorporate disciplinary considerations—or how developed the market for ideas is. (The former issue is specifically discussed in Clarke's Chapter 6; the latter, in Barber's and Collins's Chapters 4 and 5.) Indeed, in some fields and at some periods, as Harris (Chapter 12) and Winter (Chapter 14) show, the urgency and confidence with which objectives are sought means that informed opinion and policymakers neglect economic theory almost entirely.

When technical knowledge *is* needed (as for the sort of modern industrial policy considered by Hannah in Chapter 11), its transmission takes place either by the movement of professional economists into government or by the acceptance of their theories by administrators and politicians. In either case, the effects on the state are far-reaching; they involve creating new departments and agencies, taking expert testimony, recruiting in-house capabilities, using private or ad hoc research bodies, and institutionalizing professional advice (see the following section of this chapter). And at an even more general level, one of the characteristics of modern societies (albeit exemplified to different degrees in the two countries) has been the augmentation of the supply of economists by the quasi-official support of formal education in their subject matter—a development obviously facilitated where a close relationship between the state and universities already existed.

The third category of knowledge, cultural belief, is as much ideological as analytical in the ordinary scientific sense. It involves large, culturally based "visions" of the economic order, commonsense conceptions that relate economic processes and institutions to desirable political and social ends, which may include the preservation of the fundamental characteristics of the political system or the active promotion of sociopolitical values by economic means, with economic matters subordinated to these larger political goals.

Although not always directly addressed in the following chapters, this concept of knowledge, operating on the borderlands of economics and politics, was an underlying element in all our discussions at the conference. Economic knowledge is, after all, an element in political culture: Economic knowledge—those things that people "know" in the sense of believing them—embraces theories or assumptions about the ways in which different types of economic structures promote or hamper civic progress, equality, and welfare; the relations between economic expansion and individual liberty (and, indeed, the very nature of liberty); and the links that unite particular forms of government and prosperity. This type of economic knowledge is the main, perhaps the only kind, possessed by ordinary people, but it is also a contributing factor, and often the decisive one, along with more systematically organized disciplinary and practical knowledge, in the judgments made by professional economists and policymakers.

From the standpoint of the state, perhaps the most important elements in cultural beliefs and expectations are those that have to do with the relations between market processes and the political goals, and even the identities, of peoples. Implicit in much of the political and intellectual history of the United States and Britain is a debate about the nature and social role of the market as a force shaping national development. Thus, many people in nineteenth-century America saw market competition as a means of fulfilling the social possibilities of the American Revolution, unleashing energies, realizing the potential of individual citizens, and escaping the grip of monopolists or autocrats. As Larson (Chapter 3) suggests, with the market perceived as an essentially liberating force, John Quincy Adams's attempt to revive a "commonwealth" vision of national development failed, largely because democratizing and commercializing forces were already undercutting this vision. Across the Atlantic and in later periods in America, however, a different and sometimes conflicting valuation was placed on the market. For dominant groups in British society (including not only officials at the Treasury but most business-men), free trade, the gold standard, and financial rectitude were means of restraining political irresponsibility, or rendering society "knave-proof." At another level, American corporatists between the Progressive Era and the 1970s recognized a tendency to instability in market society, which they preferred to correct as much as possible through private, associative efforts; whereas more statist, social-democratic contemporaries frequent-ly envisaged the market as the major source of both monopoly and social injustice and favored government intervention. But at a more popular level, the linkage between free enterprise and a broader conception of liberty survived, to be revived subsequently at higher levels of authority. Such contrasting, culturally rooted perspectives on market institutions have continued to influence American and British conceptions of the proper sphere of government action through the years. In the 1980s, these perspectives were subtly embodied in differences in the appeals by Reagan and Thatcher to the objectives of freer markets.

As the modern state has evolved, the chapters in this book implicitly attest, so such visions of culturally and politically essential economic processes and state roles have also been transformed. The most general instance of such an evolution is obviously the changing attitude toward laissez-faire and the managed economy. This change serves to emphasize two important points. First, politicians and civil servants are not the only people whose understanding of economic processes is conditioned by ideologically laden cultural beliefs. Disciplinary economics, too, has shared such visions and been shaped by basic moral and political values.

(Can one conceive of a classical economics in Confucian China?) Second, as with knowledge in general, ideological presumptions are neither mono-lithic nor uncontroversial. Clashes and divisions, evolution and disrup-tion, are ever present. In the last resort, the contested terrain is, of course, the battleground of politics, but even debates within professional theory can be influenced by such large, controversial issues, falling out-side its everyday arena. And on the other side, economic (disciplinary) theory itself, although a potent method of articulating alternative policy strategies and outcomes, can also be effective in sorting out the means and ends of larger visions of economic society, and lending them intellec-tual force. Thus it was that the New Liberalism involved not simply a particular vision of social and political relationships, but also detailed analyses of the economic processes of society;[17] and thus, too, demo-cratic socialism's alternative vision of Western society in the interwar years was handicapped by the lack of a distinctive economic analysis.[18] Knowledge itself—in all its manifestations—is ultimately as permeable as state institutions.

KNOWLEDGE AND INSTITUTIONS

Any discussion of the state and economic knowledge must take account of the mediating role of institutions. Indeed, it is probably impossible to discuss the state and ideas in isolation from the institutional structures that bring them into contact. Although the concept of the state in conti-nental European societies has certain Hegelian overtones, representing a mystical unity or an evolutionary Idea, in the Anglo-American context the state has usually been regarded operationally. It is perceived as a single institution in one sense, but more practically as an evolving struc-ture or collection of specialized governing institutions. In this interpreta-tion, the state is not monolithic or poised above civil society, but diverse, and composed of elements that interact more or less independently with the changing structure of private groups and institutions, differing from them mainly by virtue of the monopoly of coercion and authoritative control it possesses over all sorts of resources.[19]

[17]See Peter Clarke, *Liberals and Social Democrats* (London: Cambridge University Press, 1978).
[18]See Elizabeth Durbin, *New Jerusalems: The Labour Party and the Economics of Demo-cratic Socialism* (London: Routledge & Kegan Paul, 1985).
[19]On the conceptions of the state embodied in various systems of political theory, see Patrick Dunleavy and Brendan O'Leary, *Theories of the State: The Politics of Liberal Democracy*

This interpenetration of state and civil society facilitates the two-way traffic between the state and the development of economic knowledge mentioned earlier. On the one hand, the process of gathering and using economic knowledge influences the structure of the state by promoting the creation of new agencies and capacities in government; on the other hand, existing state capacities and the existing structure of institutions also have a determining effect on the structure of economic knowledge. The difference in constitutional forms between the United States and Britain implies contrasts at other levels. Thus, there is a greater degree of policy unity among the various institutions of government in Britain, leading to official encouragement for economic inquiry mainly along lines that reflect the needs of the party in power. In contrast, federalism and the constitutional separation of powers in the United States allow for greater ideological diversity and more policy conflict among the various organs within government, and consequently there is official support for economic inquiries, and receptiveness to economic theories, that point in diverse and often conflicting directions.[20]

In the evolving relations between the state and economic knowledge, institutions perform three distinctive and related functions: They serve as contexts for "social learning,"[21] as mechanisms for state building,[22] and as vehicles for the mediation of ideas that permit exchanges between the worlds of learning and public affairs and make economic theories and their policy implications available to a wider public. Institutions with a role in the formation and political application of knowledge come in a variety of types, including all the permanent and temporary agencies, commissions, and inquiries that have responsibility for gathering data,

---

(London: Macmillan, 1987); Martin Carnoy, *The State and Political Theory* (Princeton, N.J.: Princeton University Press, 1984); Gianfranco Poggi, *The Development of the Modern State: A Sociological Introduction* (Palo Alto, Calif.: Stanford University Press, 1978).

[20] On the theme of conflicting visions in American political culture, there is a developing literature, too extensive to indicate here, concerning the conflicts and tensions within and between liberalism and republicanism. This literature begins, for historiographical purposes, with Bernard Bailyn, *The Ideological Origins of the American Revolution* (Cambridge, Mass.: Harvard University Press, 1967); Gordon Wood, *The Creation of the American Republic, 1776–1787* (Chapel Hill: University of North Carolina Press, 1969). For different perspectives on this theme in the present volume, see Chapters 3, 8, and 9.

[21] We follow the usage of Hugh Heclo, *Modern Social Politics in Britain and Sweden* (New Haven, Conn.: Yale University Press, 1974), 304–22.

[22] On state building in Britain, see Gillian Sutherland, ed., *Studies in the Growth of Nineteenth-Century Government* (London: Routledge and Kegan Paul, 1972); for the United States, see Stephen Skowronek, *Building a New American State: The Expansion of National Administrative Capacities, 1877–1920* (Cambridge, Eng.: Cambridge University Press, 1982).

monitoring performance, and inquiring into the causes of problems; for reacting to the demands of interest groups and coordinating the activities of different economic sectors; and for responding to unforeseen challenges and planning for foreseeable ones, such as economic stabilization in a recession, reconversion from a war economy, and stimulation of economic growth. Some of the most important examples of these knowledge-gathering, integrating, and interpreting arms of government figure prominently in the chapters in this volume. In particular, Chapter 8 by Furner and Chapter 10 by Supple discuss investigating commissions and inquiries that responded to economic and social emergencies, such as the U.S. Industrial Commission and Commission on Industrial Relations in the United States, and Britain's Royal Commission on the Depression in Trade and Industry in the 1880s, (Balfour) Committee on Industry and Trade of the 1920s, and Royal (Barlow) Commission on the Geographical Distribution of the Industrial Population of the late 1930s; Chapter 8 by Furner and Chapter 9 by Hawley discuss permanent agencies for monitoring the performance of specific sectors and regions, including the U.S. Bureaus of Labor Statistics and Agricultural Economics; Chapter 5 by Collins and Chapter 6 by Clarke investigate ad hoc and permanent bodies for providing expert economic advice on macroeconomic problems, such as the Council of Economic Advisers in the United States and the Macmillan Committee in Britain; and Chapters 8 and 9 discuss special investigations by private and quasi-public agencies, such as the National Civic Federation and the National Bureau of Economic Research.

Much that these various bodies do is related merely to amassing data, for defending policies already in force or rationalizing new ones about to be adopted. But all these institutions have the capacity to contribute to a process of social learning whose essence Hugh Heclo has captured in the phrase "governments not only power, they also puzzle."[23] Seen in this light, politics has a function that goes beyond brokering the demands of conflicting interests. With a coherence and continuity not always matched in interest groups' more episodic approach to economic and social issues, government officials often play the leading role in deciding what conditions will be recognized as problems, how their causes and effects will be defined, and what policy alternatives will be considered.[24]

[23]Heclo, *Modern Social Politics*, 305.
[24]Jack L. Walker, "The Diffusion of Knowledge, Policy Communities and Agenda Setting: The Relationship of Knowledge and Power," in John E. Tropman, Milan J. Dluhy, and Roger M. Lind, eds., *New Strategic Perspectives on Social Policy* (New York: Pergamon Press, 1981), 75–96.

In Supple's account of British administrative responses to economic maturity and industrial decline (Chapter 10), for example, a new structural analysis of the economy and a new, theoretically based rationale for state action arose from a series of investigations that individually did little more than catalog the problems of declining industries and depressed areas and suggest specific steps to be taken, largely by private businesses. Such deep-seated problems as declining industrial efficiency, an erosion of living standards, or the perception of distributive inequity challenge existing economic paradigms and create a demand for information and theory. A process that Heclo calls "collective puzzlement" ensues, which may extend over several years or even decades. To satisfy the demand for new policy options, specialized institutions, sometimes staffed with experts from locations outside the state, are created. And these investigative institutions then serve as access points at which relevant theory and empirical findings can enter policy discourse and from which new ideas can be routed back to the wider public that is attentive to political argument, and interpreted in terms of deeper cultural values.

Not surprisingly, the capacity for social learning becomes critical at moments of crisis, when established structures of industrial and international relations are breaking down and states can no longer muddle through by merely refurbishing old policies. Emergencies such as wars and depressions are also the times when new institutions for inquiry and management proliferate, enlarging the state's capacity as well as knowledge. Not every change in economic conditions results in an aggrandizement of the state, of course. Economic dislocation and the necessity to provide an adequate food supply for a mobile population paved the way for the revision of the Poor Laws and the experiment with free trade that ushered in the era of laissez-faire in Britain.[25] And, as Larson suggests in Chapter 3, with the commercialization and democratization of American society in the early nineteenth century, John Quincy Adams's grand vision of coordinated national development became politically impossible (although "state withdrawal" was selective, and public promotion of development continued, especially at the state level).[26] We do not subscribe to

---

[25]J. R. Poynter, *Society and Pauperism: English Ideas on Poor Relief, 1795–1834* (London: Routledge and Kegan Paul, 1969); Boyd Hilton, *Cash, Corn, Commerce: The Economic Policies of the Tory Governments, 1815–1830* (Oxford: Oxford University Press, 1977).

[26]For an incisive reinterpretation of the role of national leadership in economic development, see Robert Wiebe, *The Opening of American Society* (New York: Alfred A. Knopf, 1984). See also George Rogers Taylor, *The Transportation Revolution, 1815–1860* (New York: Holt, Rinehart and Winston, 1951); Carter Goodrich, *Government Promotion of*

the Whiggish view that linked continuous growth of government with increased availability of scientific expertise for purposes of state.

In general, however, crises of all sorts—wars, class conflict, and depressions—have fed a process of inquiry, analysis, legislation, and administration that has enlarged the scope of state activities. As Brownlee (Chapter 13) shows, the unprecedented revenue needs created by World War I, linked with Progressive demands for redistributive taxes as a check on corporate power, produced a comprehensive system for taxing excess profits, and institutionalized in the American Treasury capacities necessary for administering this system, with economists in charge for the first time. Similarly, according to the accounts by Barber, Clarke, and Peden (Chapters 4, 6, and 7), intensified international competition in the twenties and high unemployment during the Great Depression were the forcing houses in which American and British economic policymakers began to depart from the neoclassical models that had guided policy earlier, preparing the ground for more interventionist strategies based on Keynesian-style macroeconomic conceptions. Here again, strategically placed economists, as bearers and builders of new knowledge, were important. They helped shape both the political dialogue that brought these changes and the new investigative and administrative agencies, such as the councils of economic advisers that appeared in both countries, and in the United States were assured an important role in the central coordination of economic activity. Barber's phrase "insider learning" highlights the way in which economists in government turned their practical experience with the gaps and failures in old theories to advantage and moved ahead of academics in developing new theories.

In recognizing the demand-pull of political necessity as a catalyst in the development of economic knowledge, we do not mean to suggest that economists were always centrally placed in the political debates and experiments that contributed to social learning, or that theory as such always plays an important part in policy formation. Until quite recently, the policy role of economists was circumscribed. As Harris notes in Chapter 12, prior to 1964 in Britain, "no *social* [emphasis added] policy department in British government employed any practicing economists as

American Canals and Railroads, 1800–1890 (New York: Columbia University Press, 1960); Richard L. McCormick, *The Party Period and Public Policy: American Politics from the Age of Jackson to the Progressive Era* (New York: Oxford University Press, 1984); L. Ray Gunn, *The Decline of Authority: Public Economic Policy and Political Development in New York State, 1800–1860* (Ithaca, N.Y.: Cornell University Press, 1988).

economic advisers," so the impact of economic theory on social policy was seldom immediate or direct. Rather, economic data and ideas combined with other forms of knowledge to bring about "gradual and often scarcely perceptible shifts in the wider climate of economic and political culture." Even in areas where economists were recognized as the significant experts, Collins (Chapter 5) finds, economic theory per se was of limited importance, as in the American Council of Economic Advisers in the Truman era; and Winter (Chapter 14) concludes that economic analysis of population trends in postwar Britain was invoked after the fact, as a rationalization for predetermined social and political goals.

Nevertheless, the nexus between a more inquiring and a more active state remains. The institutionalization of public processes for promoting and applying economic knowledge is indeed connected to state building. One can look at this association in a variety of ways. In his abstract model of relations between modern states and science, Poggi refers to regular stages in state development: With the "rationalization" and "functionalization" of rule, science and reason replace raw power and caprice as the bases for state action, and the state, seen as the container of social processes and the principal agency through which society can act upon itself, takes on an increasing array of functions that promote social and economic progress.[27] From another perspective, the modern state can be viewed as a Leviathan of immense proportions—one that Hobbes could hardly have imagined.

Our approach to the connection between investigation and state building is more historically specific, concentrating in the first instance on the expansion of official inquiry, which grew into systems for permanent state monitoring of various aspects of working conditions and industrial relations. A time came, in the latter part of the nineteenth century, when what Larson (Chapter 3) calls "the disintegration of credible sources of authority" in the United States was reversed. Amid a complex array of influences—the activist legacy of the Civil War era, the perceived failure of the market as a liberating and stabilizing mechanism, mobilization of reformist sentiment in voluntary organizations such as the American Social Science Association, the professionalization of knowledge, and conflicts over distribution and inequality—there arose the perception that government should play a role in economic and social policy beyond what could be accomplished in a regime of courts and parties (Stephen

[27]Poggi, "The Modern State and the Idea of Progress," 345–53.

Skowronek's apt construction of what went on before).[28] To some degree, this perception harked back to the vision of national development that John Quincy Adams had enunciated long before. In the construction of a state capable of "knowing" and acting responsibly in the face of economic and social crisis, investigation played a paramount role. Ad hoc investigations of persistent troubles became permanent agencies (for example, the bureaus of labor statistics); a continuous, permanent flow of information, systematically gathered and analyzed, provided a basis for standards and regulation; and public authority invaded areas formerly left to private dealings.[29] The process in Britain, although not so formalized, was similar; from the 1890s, the Labour Department, the Home Office, and the Ministry of Mines gathered information that laid the basis for continuous oversight of industrial and working conditions in selected industries—and from World War I, for a more continuous concern with the structure and performance of these industries.[30] Indeed, much of the meaning of the New Liberalism on both sides of the Atlantic was captured in this aggrandizement of the moral and social functions of the state.

The reconstruction of public authority met opposition, in the form of competing models for the role of the state in the ordering of the economy. In the United States, reflecting a persistent antistatism, corporatist organizations such as the National Civic Federation favored voluntary, associative action in most areas of economic dysfunction. Their view found official sanction in the Hoover years, when the investigative function itself was privatized in structures such as the National Bureau of Economic Research, in order, in Hoover's view, to remove investigation from partisan influences. In Britain, too, rival investigations originated outside the state, particularly in the 1930s, in structures such as Political and Economic Planning and the Next Five Years group. These developments

---

[28]Skowronek, *Building a New American State*, 24–35.

[29]Several chapters pertaining to this theme will appear in a companion volume to this one, Lacey and Furner, *The State and Social Investigation* (forthcoming). See also Nelson, *The Roots of American Bureaucracy;* Skowronek, *Building a New American State;* Mary O. Furner, *Advocacy and Objectivity: A Crisis in the Professionalization of American Social Science* (Lexington: University Press of Kentucky, 1975); Thomas Haskell, *The Emergence of Professional Social Science* (Urbana: University of Illinois Press, 1977).

[30]Roger Davidson, *Whitehall and the Labour Problem in Late-Victorian and Edwardian Britain: A Study in Official Statistics and Social Control* (Dover, Eng.: Croom Helm, 1985); Jose Harris, *Unemployment and Politics: A Study in English Social Policy, 1886–1914* (New York: Oxford University Press, 1972).

underline our earlier point about the blurring and permeability of the line between public and private in Anglo-American culture.[31]

Still, the liberal response to the new conditions of industrial society was statist as well as associationist, and it produced an inescapable proliferation of agencies. Faced by war and depression and the resulting needs for increased revenue, by crises in troubled industries and regions, and ultimately by a slump that dragged down whole economies, politicians in both countries gave new powers to existing agencies, such as the Bureau of Agricultural Economics (BAE) and the Board of Trade; created new ones, such as the Industrial Transference Board and the National Recovery Administration; and were obliged to assume greater powers over economic structure and management. Ultimately, although in large part only after another war had intervened, politicians asserted public authority in the area of macroeconomic policy, which rested heavily, as several of the chapters in this book suggest, on newly constructed national income accounts, and called for new quasi-planning agencies in both countries. Although the trend was somewhat spotty and not comprehensive (no "Bureau of Industrial Economics" in either country became permanent), these impulses toward government intervention eventually created the modern regulatory and managerial state, and rested the defense of it largely on proto-Keynesian or Keynesian theory.

This reference to legitimation directs our attention to the third function of institutions—the mediation of ideas. We have already emphasized that ideas are not self-interpreting, but rather are interpreted in relation to the structures of meaning that every culture generates as a way of organizing experience and orienting action (see Chapter 2).[32] To have an impact, to become effective as elements in policy formation, ideas must come in contact with these larger structures of meaning. They must become in some sense public, and register with the body politic in a way that makes the connection between ideas and the everyday reality of social existence clear. Many people in nineteenth-century Britain and

[31]On this theme, see James Weinstein, *The Corporate Ideal in the Liberal State, 1900–1918* (Boston: Beacon Press, 1968); Ellis Hawley, "Herbert Hoover, the Commerce Secretariat, and the Vision of an 'Associative State,' 1921–1928," *Journal of American History* 61 (1974): 116–40; Guy Alchon, *The Invisible Hand of Planning: Capitalism, Social Science, and the State in the 1920s* (Princeton: Princeton University Press, 1985). See also Chapters 8, 9, and 10 in this volume.

[32]See also Clifford Geertz, chapter on "Ideology as a Cultural System," *The Interpretation of Cultures* (New York: Basic Books, 1973), 193–233; J. G. A. Pocock, *Politics, Language and Time* (New York: Atheneum, 1971).

America, whether they liked the implications or not, could see a relationship between the laissez-faire of classical economics and both the dirty, desperate realities of the poorhouse and the burgeoning farms and booming industries of a youthful America. By the same token, for large numbers in the depression-ridden 1930s, the futility of private charity and the helplessness of individual businessmen were palpable, and the call for immediate government action, justified in structural terms, made some kind of analytical sense.

Ideas connect with reality and achieve political effect through institutions. Agencies and inquiries concerned with specific or general structural problems provide the arenas in which ideas can be articulated, debated among experts, and tested. At one level, of course, this point underlines the conservative function of public institutions: shaping a receptive climate for the goals and purposes of the people in power—in a word, hegemony. Yet even the most cynical view of public opinion grants that, in democracies at least, a lack of public support falling far short of organized opposition can still frustrate government policies. As Heclo and others have pointed out, unless political institutions are to be treated simply as mechanisms for aggregating individual preferences, it must also be recognized that they are capable of performing a didactic function. With reference to economic policy, this means that certain government agencies are not only deliberative institutions, informing themselves and providing access for data and arguments from interest groups. They also enter a wider discussion, informing and educating preferences, often in competition with other public and private organizations. Agencies with an economic portfolio not only gather information about economic conditions but also disseminate it in usable form; they explain events in terms of existing theory, offer prognoses and predictions, and engage generally in high-level popularization. In this process of politicizing knowledge, institutions act as intermediaries, translating relevant theory, data, and experience into the many "languages" of political discourse. In the course of political debate, enduring cultural beliefs and values are tested against disciplinary knowledge and empirical data based on experience—a process that, not infrequently, leads to the adjustment of traditional beliefs, as happened with the abandonment of free trade, the gold standard, and the balanced budget, or the overturning of conventional wisdom concerning scarcity and industrial maturity in Britain from the 1880s and America in the 1930s.

At more specific levels, however, there are obvious differences between the United States and Britain with respect to the role of institutions in relating knowledge and power. Such differences can be approached by comparing the institutional configurations in both countries. Thus, the contrast between the openness of the American institutional structure and the more elitist, monolithic British structure can be used to draw attention to the different degrees of accessibility of government in the two countries and to an important difference in the extensiveness—in terms of participating social groups—of political argument and policy debate. In Britain, Winch (Chapter 2) suggests, the parliamentary system is more unitary, ministerial control is greater, and there is a stronger tradition of filling the administrative ranks of the civil service from the elite universities where liberal economics forms an important part of the curriculum. These characteristics help explain the more homogeneous official perspective on matters of economic doctrine and on the proper role of government in managing the economy, and the greater uniformity of educated opinion regarding economic policy.

In contrast, America exhibits a more fragmented, freewheeling structure of power, decentralized control in many areas of economic policy, a commitment to popular sovereignty rooted in the revolutionary tradition, and a greater skepticism toward expertise—all of which permit diverse and conflicting perspectives and groups to have far easier access to government. Another relevant feature of America's institutional structure is the diversity of perspectives *within* government. At the most fundamental level, the different branches of government oppose each other not merely out of institutional jealousy, but because they embody different principles: popular sovereignty in the legislative branch, due process in the judicial, and rational management in the executive. Unlike the parliamentary system, in which government departments and agencies are expected to reflect the positions of the minister and party in power, an American president frequently faces a congressional majority of the other party, and congressional committees and executive agencies handling the same subjects remain in different hands, often reflecting close ties to opposing, politically conscious groups in society. The sources of official authority are therefore less obvious in the United States, and a policy campaign lost with one agency can be begun anew with another one with overlapping jurisdiction. Both the state itself and institutions such as think tanks that intend to staff the state's agencies after the next election function as holding areas for many different and contrasting viewpoints and visions, reflecting fundamental tensions in the political culture that have never been resolved.

In the American case, investigations and commissions that sought the structural causes of economic problems in the early twentieth century also helped promote the creation of permanent bureaucratic structures, both public and private, for sustained investigation as a tool of economic management. And both types of institutions also reflected different visions of national development, grounding their policy choices in different segments or versions of grand theory. The Industrial Commission and the Commission on Industrial Relations described in Chapter 8 represented opposing interests within their memberships and introduced conflicting viewpoints on the key issue of public versus private ordering of the economy. In the less open, less accessible British system, as Chapter 10 shows, royal commissions were more Establishment-minded, although the membership of each contained disparate elements, and influential heretical ideas, inspiring real debate, were more likely to come from witnesses (or occasionally even from commission members *acting* as witnesses). This was not invariably the case, of course, as the examples of the Poor Law Commission and the Macmillan Committee illustrate, and nineteenth-century select committees could be "packed" by more than one group. But it was generally harder for heterodoxy to get a hearing in Britain than in the United States, as Keynes's long and unsuccessful effort to persuade the Treasury reveals.

All this leads to a second point of contrast between the two institutional structures: the difference in their "capacity for continuity." Britain has a greater capacity for maintaining one design—one pattern of ideas and coordinating policies—through time. (We have already identified the reliance on the market and the desire to knave-proof institutions.) The United States has a greater predilection for entertaining competing designs: republicanism versus liberalism, individualism versus majority rule, federalism versus localism, popular sovereignty versus bureaucratic efficiency, moralism versus materialism, and voluntarism versus government control. Thus, in the American case, there is less continuity, but a greater tendency toward recurrence of ideas and policies that were once in power and rejected, not finally, but for a time, remaining available for restoration. Historians have recognized these persistent tensions in American public culture as a tendency toward visionary ideas, dualism, and a cyclical politics in which liberal and conservative eras alternate at intervals of about a generation. In Britain, although more radical measures have been possible, via class politics and a Labour party, than have been taken in the United States, these challenges have generally been absorbed as the structure of power and dominant outlook adapted and incorporated critics. Labor militance and a socialist critique were elements in the New Liberalism in both countries, but achieved less in structural terms in the United States; even in Britain, Labour's claims were mainly distributive, because socialism, for all the power of its moral criticism, was unable at the time to offer a distinctive and convincing set of policy alternatives in the context of the British system.

Turning from the social structure of politics to the established institutions of government, one finds another noteworthy contrast between the two systems regarding the scope for participation by bureaucratic agencies in highly partisan debates. In the United States, it can be argued, the price of survival for investigative bodies such as the Bureau of Labor Statistics has been dissociation from most controversial aspects of political debate, and especially from overt partisanship in the great debate over distribution. Thus, Carroll Wright was drawn toward the official view when he headed the national agency, although, in the special circumstances of the New Deal, Isador Lubin could be more partisan as Bureau of Labor Statistics chief. In Britain, the bureaucracy is generally allowed a higher profile because its viewpoint is expected to change with the administration. There is a much clearer distinction in Britain between the opposition and the government, and agencies are permitted to engage in the distributive controversies of the day as servants of the government. This pattern is buttressed by the British conception of the Higher Civil Service and by the tradition of ministerial responsibility and oversight. The situation is different in the United States. Admittedly, agencies that have powerful constituencies in both Congress and the country (e.g., the Bureau of Agricultural Economics) can readily attain continuity in policy, as Hawley (Chapter 9) shows. But this is continuity at the sectoral level, not at the level of grand national design.

A final observation concerns the state's bargaining capacity, that is, its ability to win cooperation, extract concessions, and make deals in order to control situations and implement policies. Obviously, the level of control that a state can exercise over society and the economy depends on a number of factors, including the availability of technical expertise and the role the political culture or ideology specifies for the state. But here again, the configuration of institutions embedded in the national life can strengthen or weaken a state's capacity to influence the behavior of other players. By comparison with more bureaucratic, statist societies, both the United States and Britain have a relatively limited deal-making capacity, as is attested by the relative lack of permanence and success in their corporatist experiments. As Chapter 10 indicates, in Britain, the government has shown a greater capacity to influence distribution, largely through social policies, than to promote greater industrial efficiency. There has simply been no quid pro quo that the parties to industrial production would accept, in contrast to Japan or continental Europe, where the state has more to offer and more power to entice or compel cooperation.

The United States may be even less well equipped along these lines than Britain, given the tradition of voluntarism, the easy penetrability of American government, the resourcefulness of interest groups and their ability to compete with government for attention and expertise, the resilience of pluralism, and the failure of even the most liberal administrations to legitimate and sustain a public capacity for comprehensive national planning. In such conditions, it is not surprising that courts and agencies with quasi-legal authority generally become important disciplinary mechanisms, because they are less open to influence and more immediately effective than either administrative or parliamentary institutions.

These differences were exemplified in the 1980s, both in the relatively stable, doctrinaire, and monolithic pattern of Thatcherism, as it approached economic restructuring, and in the more pluralistic, shifting, and unstable character of Reaganism. Of course, continuity and consensus on the British model can be disabling if governments refuse to recognize social realignment or market failure, as the Treasury did in the interwar period. And openness to democratic influences, an investigative and policy pluralism that enriches the flow of information, and an adaptability in institutions themselves can be strengths, especially when they increase participation in the intellectual aspects of politics and verify the claim that policy is based on reputable, tested theory.

These various themes dealt with in this chapter are enlarged upon and exemplified in the chapters that follow. The following chapter, which concludes Part I, "The State and the Uses of Economic Knowledge," provides further general guidance on the complex issue of the relations between knowledge and policy, stressing the active role of the state in the formation of economic knowledge. Part II, "The State and Economic Performance," explores the evolving role of the state in assessing and encouraging economic development and, in general, in macroeconomic planning and coordination. Larson and Collins discuss aspects of the American experience. Larson's chapter portrays the conflict between John Quincy Adams's activist, republican conception of the public role in national development and the minimalist conception of the state's role during the nineteenth-century heyday of democratic capitalism. Collins draws attention to a major shift in thinking about the role of government in economic performance, from the scarcity economics of the 1930s to an economics of abundance and growth after World War II. Barber, Clarke, and Peden explore the development and adoption of Keynesian theory and policy in the two countries, with particular emphasis on the role of government officials in the formation and reception of macroeconomic insights.

In Part III, "Industrial Maturity and Economic Policy," the contributors explore the changing uses of official investigation and inquiry for influencing economic policy in the era of American economic maturity and British industrial decline. Furner and Hawley describe the expansion of public and private investigative capacities in the United States between the late nineteenth century and the 1930s, stressing the persistent tension between opposing visions of the American system and between public and private control over direction of the economy. Supple surveys economic inquiries between the 1880s and the 1930s, when Britain first experienced symptoms of decline, concluding that the policy problems raised by practical political necessity often drove knowledge. Hannah's chapter assesses the knowledge-policy interface in the postwar era. In Part IV, "Economic Knowledge and Social Action," Harris provides a broad overview of the relationship between economic knowledge and British social policy, contrasting the situation in the nineteenth and twentieth centuries. Brownlee and Winter offer detailed case studies of the role of economic knowledge and economists in the major restructuring of tax policy in America during the post–World War I era and in the formulation of a population policy for Britain in the post–World War II period. Taken together, the thirteen chapters that follow offer convincing evidence of an active role for the state in the growth of economic knowledge.

2

Economic knowledge and government in Britain: some historical and comparative reflections

DONALD WINCH

Economic knowledge—chiefly but not solely as embodied in the four synoptic gospels written by Adam Smith, Robert Malthus, David Ricardo, and John Stuart Mill—came to play a major part in the reordering of political and economic life in nineteenth-century Britain. Or so it could be argued on the basis of some familiar facts: the gradual victory of free trade, culminating in the abolition of the Corn Laws in 1846; the reform of the old Poor Law along Malthusian—or, more properly, Benthamite—lines in 1834; the annulment of exclusive trading privileges, epitomized by the removal of the East India Company's trading monopoly; the revocation of the Combination Acts; the return to currency convertibility in 1819 and the enshrinement of orthodox central banking ideas in the Bank Charter Act of 1844; and the official endorsement of principles of public finance in what became known as their Gladstonian form.

In each of these cases, of course, there was considerable debate as to the precise role played by articulated economic ideas as opposed to interests, functional imperatives, "high politics," alternative "public" philosophies, and the dogged adjustment of policies and institutions to everyday developments by pragmatic means. In the final section of this chapter, I suggest that this debate has often been based on a misconception of the nature of economic ideas and the extent to which their "influence" needs to be proved. For the present, however, I bypass such

I am grateful for the advice and friendly criticism offered by John Burrow, Stefan Collini, Jennifer Platt, Julia Stapleton, and Barry Supple on the first draft of this chapter. I have also benefited from the discussions that took place at the conference at the Wilson Center in September 1988.

matters by noting the height at which claims on behalf of the influence exerted by political economy could be pitched by the first generation of retrospective commentators.

THE NINETEENTH-CENTURY LEGACY

Consider, for example, the following statement made by John Elliot Cairnes in a lecture at University College in 1870:

Great Britain, if not the birthplace of Political Economy, has at least been its early home, as well as the scene of the most signal triumphs of its manhood. Every great step in the progress of economic science . . . has been won by English thinkers; and while we have led the van in economic speculation, we have also been the first to apply with boldness our theories to practice. Our foreign trade, our colonial policy, our fiscal system, each has in turn been reconstructed from the foundation upwards under the inspiration of economic ideas; and the population and the commerce of the country, responding to the impulse given by the new principles operating through these changes, have within a century multiplied themselves manifold.[1]

Walter Bagehot was hardly less enthusiastic a few years later, when celebrating the achievements of political economy in the hundred years since the *Wealth of Nations* was published:

In that time [political economy] has had a wonderful effect. The life of almost every one in England—perhaps of every one—is different and better in consequence of it. The whole commercial policy of the country is not so much founded upon it as instinct with it. Ideas which are paradoxes everywhere else in the world are accepted axioms here as results of it. No other form of political philosophy has ever had one thousandth part of the influence on us; its teachings have settled down into the common sense of the nation, and have become irreversible.[2]

Although, as we shall see, it would be rash to conclude that such confidence in the influence of economic ideas was entirely misplaced, these examples of intellectual chauvinism are memorable chiefly because they were made in the midst of what could be seen more clearly in retrospect as a profound crisis in the intellectual fortunes of classical political economy. The crisis was partly internal to the orthodox version of the discipline, and later led to the reformulation of its central theoretical propositions along marginalist or neoclassical lines, and partly external, a challenge to the

[1] "Political Economy and Laissez-Faire," reprinted in *Essays on Political Economy: Theoretical and Applied* (London: Macmillan, 1873), 232.
[2] "The Postulates of English Political Economy," in *Economy Studies* (London: Longmans, 1908), 1.

methodology and authority of the science as a guide to public affairs. This challenge came from a formidable combination of opponents, which included Comtian-style positivists, Christian political economists, idealists, socialists, post-Darwinian or Spencerian evolutionists, and the upholders of fashionable forms of historical, institutionalist, and inductive modes of social and economic inquiry.[3] In fairness to Cairnes and Bagehot, however, it should be pointed out that their remarks were made as a prelude to posing the question why the science, in the latter's words, "lies rather dead in the public mind," and why the successes achieved on its native heath had not so far been replicated abroad.

Neither Cairnes nor Bagehot felt it necessary to investigate or document in any detail the processes by which political economy had transformed British economic policy and public life—the ways in which a reciprocal relationship between the needs of state and economic knowledge had been established and sustained. This relationship was something that could, apparently, be taken for granted—an assumption that becomes more significant when it is noted how widely it was shared, and continued to be shared throughout the nineteenth century and beyond, by opponents of as well as apologists for political economy. For example, Coleridge, Carlyle, and many others in the first half of the century denounced the baleful influence exerted by the "dismal science,"[4] but the later testimony of successive generations of historical economists is more impressive, precisely because they set out to be historians of economic institutions and policies, and because they were eager to promote forms of economic knowledge capable of supporting an alternative conception of the role of the nation-state in economic affairs.[5]

To interpret this literature appropriately, some allowance must be made for artificial enlargement of the polemical target in view. This need for allowance is clear from Arnold Toynbee's famous but hardly neutral

---

[3]Although there have been many studies of this episode, that by T. W. Hutchison in Chapter 1 of his *Review of Economic Doctrines, 1870–1929* (Oxford: Clarendon Press, 1953) is still authoritative; see also his *On Revolutions and Progress in Economic Knowledge* (Cambridge, Eng.: Cambridge University Press, 1978), Chapter 3.

[4]For a recent compendium, see E. Jay and R. Jay, eds., *Critics of Capitalism: Victorian Reactions to "Political Economy"* (Cambridge, Eng.: Cambridge University Press, 1986).

[5]For treatment of this from a political perspective, see "Particular Polities: Political Economy and the Historical Method," in S. Collini, D. Winch, and J. Burrow, *That Noble Science of Politics: A Study in Nineteenth-Century Intellectual History* (Cambridge, Eng.: Cambridge University Press, 1983); see also D. C. Coleman, *History and the Economic Past: An Account of the Rise and Decline of Economic History in Britain* (Oxford: Clarendon Press, 1987); and G. Koot, *English Historical Economics, 1870–1926* (Cambridge, Eng.: Cambridge University Press, 1988).

pronouncement in his *Lectures on the Industrial Revolution,* given in 1881–2, that "the bitter argument between economists and human beings has ended in the conversion of the economists."[6] But what also seems remarkable about Toynbee's lectures is the attention devoted to the doctrines of orthodox political economy, and to the most esoteric of its exponents, David Ricardo, in particular.[7] Of the latter's *Principles of Political Economy,* for example, Toynbee asserted that "no other book, not even the *Wealth of Nations,* obtained the same immediate ascendancy over men of intellectual eminence": After only four years in Parliament, "Ricardo revolutionized opinion there on economic subjects."[8]

The nearest equivalent to such sweeping conclusions was uttered fifty or so years later, when John Maynard Keynes told readers of the *General Theory* that "Ricardo conquered England as completely as the Holy Inquisition conquered Spain."[9] Keynes was referring to certain dogmatic macroeconomic propositions, summarized as Say's Law, that had been a prominent part of Ricardo's dispute with Malthus over the self-equilibrating properties of capital accumulation and the role of "effective demand." The same macroeconomics of employment and output levels was, of course, to provide the rationale for the more extensive employment of economists within government in both Britain and the United States during and after World War II.

Long before Keynes had fully worked out the underlying theory and policies now associated with the Keynesian revolution, however, he had delivered his opinion on the nineteenth-century legacy of political economy. In a pair of lectures given in 1924 and 1926, and later published as "The End of Laissez-Faire," he considered the issues that had lain at the heart of the previous century's debate on the role of the state. It was an exercise in *Ideengeschichte* conducted in the grandest of manners, ranging widely over the eighteenth- and nineteenth-century sources of individualism and laissez-faire, and attributing influence to these ideas by invoking such vague, possibly circular, and probably erroneous connections as "conformity with the needs and wishes of the business world of

---

[6]*Lectures on the Industrial Revolution of the Eighteenth Century in England* (London: Longmans, 1923), 137.
[7]For a reconstruction of Toynbee's aims and motives, see Alon Kadish, *Apostle Arnold: The Life and Death of Arnold Toynbee, 1852–1883* (Durham, N.C.: Duke University Press, 1986), especially Chapter 5.
[8]*Lectures on the Industrial Revolution,* 140.
[9]*General Theory of Employment, Interest and Money,* in D. Moggridge, ed., *The Collected Writings of John Maynard Keynes* (London: Macmillan for the Royal Economic Society, 1971–1989), VII, 32. (This series is abbreviated hereafter as *J.M.K.*)

the day."[10] The scholarship on which Keynes based his conclusions with regard to the intellectual provenance and influence of laissez-faire doctrines belonged exclusively to the nineteenth century, with especially heavy borrowings from work by Cairnes, Cliffe Leslie, Arthur Oenken, Henry Sidgwick, and Leslie Stephen. As D. H. MacGregor pointed out when discussing the origins of laissez-faire, Keynes might well have noticed that he had been preceded by Mill (1833), Cairnes (1870), and G. J. Goschen (1883) in announcing the demise of the doctrine. MacGregor himself endorsed Oenken's conclusion "qu'on laisse passer laissez-faire": The doctrine had long lost whatever meaning it had possessed as a description of economic policy dispositions.[11] Jacob Viner and Lionel Robbins later gave similar answers in works that mark a kind of historiographic watershed in the scholarly treatment of the qualifications that need to be made to simple laissez-faire interpretations.[12]

Even if it had suited Keynes's limited purpose to dig deeper, it is not clear where he could have dug in 1926. He might, for example, have cited A. V. Dicey's account of the influence of Benthamite individualism, as superseded after 1870 by the growth of collectivism, in his *Law and Public Opinion in England During the Nineteenth Century* (first edition, 1905; second edition, 1914). Yet, as later students of the nineteenth-century revolution in government have shown, Dicey's book—the work of someone who, true to the Benthamite spirit, regarded historical research as the enemy of reform—was largely responsible for many of the misunderstandings that have bedeviled work in this field.[13] Dicey treated influence in terms of tautologous appeals to the zeitgeist and maintained that when Benthamite individualism was in the ascendant, everybody was a commonsense utilitarian without knowing it. Elie Halévy's *Growth of Philosophical Radicalism*, first published in French in 1901–3, would have provided more of a challenge, as it still does, even when the fundamental distinction between natural and artificial harmony on which much of the argument rests has been controverted. Halévy's work is an example of the well-known value of the outsider's perspective, but the book on which much of his reputation as one of the most acute analysts of British society rests was

---

[10]*J.M.K.*, IX, 286.
[11]*Economic Thought and Policy* (Oxford: Clarendon Press, 1949), Chapter 3.
[12]See J. Viner, "Bentham and J. S. Mill: The Utilitarian Background," in *The Long View and the Short* (Glencoe, Ill.: The Free Press, 1958), 306–31; and L. Robbins, *The Theory of Economic Policy in English Classical Political Economy* (London: Macmillan, 1953).
[13]See H. Parris, "The Nineteenth-Century Revolution in Government: A Reappraisal Reappraised," *Historical Journal* 3 (1960): 17–37; and Richard A. Cosgrove, *The Rule of Law: Albert Venn Dicey, Victorian Jurist* (London: Macmillan, 1980), Chapter 8.

not translated into English until a couple of years after Keynes's lectures on the end of laissez-faire, and its absorption into scholarly debate in the anglophone world did not occur until much later.[14]

Indeed, it was not until the 1950s that the process of detailed investigation got under way, giving rise to a large body of monograph literature on the influence of classical political economy and its Benthamite associate on official policy thinking in Britain in the nineteenth century. Moreover, particularly since the relaxation of the rules of access to public archives, there is also a burgeoning literature on the role of economists in economic policy-making in the twentieth century.[15] We have certainly come a long way since the days when all that was thought necessary to establish influence was to relate biographical anecdotes, an approach that is still epitomized, perhaps, by persistent references to William Pitt's expressions of discipleship to the ideas of Adam Smith ("We will stand till you are seated, for we are all your scholars").[16]

The decline in interest in policy heroes has been accompanied by an equivalent, though still incomplete, move away from the search for scapegoats or evil geniuses on whom the blame can be pinned for policies that fall short of the historian's moral and political standards.[17] Sober and detailed studies of the part played by economic spokesmen in Parliament and as members of and expert witnesses before Select Committees and Royal Commissions are now available.[18] There are also impressive studies of the genesis of free-trade policies under both Tory and Whig governments

---

[14]See Myrna Chase, *Elie Halévy: An Intellectual Biography* (New York: Columbia University Press, 1980), Chapter 2.

[15]For bibliographic and other information on this theme, see A. W. Coats, ed., *Economists in Government: An International Comparative Study* (Durham, N.C.: Duke University Press, 1981).

[16]For recent treatments of Smith's influence and the early reception given to the *Wealth of Nations*, see K. Willis, "The Role in Parliament of the Economic Ideas of Adam Smith," *History of Political Economy* 11 (1979): 505–44; D. Winch, "Science and the Legislator: Adam Smith and After," *Economic Journal* 93 (1983): 501–20; and R. Teichgraeber, "Less Abused than I Had Reason to Expect: The Reception of the *Wealth of Nations* in Britain, 1776–90," *Historical Journal* 30 (1987): 337–66.

[17]Malthus has been one of the main scapegoats, but for evidence of a change of tone, see especially E. A. Wrigley, "Elegance and Experience: Malthus at the Bar of History," in D. Coleman and R. Schofield, eds., *The State of Population Theory: Forward from Malthus* (Oxford: Blackwells, 1986), 46–64; and D. Winch, *Malthus* (Oxford: Oxford University Press, 1987). Similarly, a shift from the accusatory stance toward the Poor Law Amendment Act was first evident in J. R. Poynter, *Society and Pauperism: English Ideas on Poor Relief, 1795–1834* (London: Routledge, 1969).

[18]See B. J. Gordon, *Political Economy in Parliament, 1819–23* (London: Macmillan, 1976), and *Economic Doctrine and Tory Liberalism, 1824–30* (London: Macmillan, 1979); F. W. Fetter, *The Economist in Parliament, 1760–1870* (Durham, N.C.: Duke University Press, 1980).

in the decades after 1815.[19] The background to almost every major new legislative initiative in the social and economic field has been studied in the literature on the growth of government and the origins of the Victorian administrative state;[20] and some distinguished work has been done on the role played by economic ideas in the governance of Ireland and India.[21]

ACADEMIC RECOGNITION AND PUBLIC SERVICE

In the light of these detailed studies of the political and institutional context within which economic knowledge relating to government has been cultivated and disseminated, it may be worth recalling a paradox that lies behind Bagehot's and Cairnes's expansive claims on behalf of political economy. Despite a lingering tendency to speak as though the opposition to classical political economy faced a powerful *academic* orthodoxy, in fact, the development of the science in Britain took place largely without benefit of academic or other forms of official recognition. Malthus's Chair of Political Economy at Haileybury was unusual both because of the importance it accorded political economy and because it incorporated political economy in a program designed exclusively to produce civil servants destined for India.[22] In contrast, the chairs created at University College, London, and at Oxford offered employment to their holders for a few years only, requiring merely an annual lecture series that was not integrated within the general curriculum. At Cambridge, two men, George Pryme and Henry Fawcett, held the Chair of Political Economy for nearly sixty years after 1828, but their part-time professorial

[19]See L. Brown, *The Board of Trade and the Free Trade Movement* (Oxford: Clarendon Press, 1958); and Boyd Hilton, *Corn, Cash, Commerce: The Economic Policies of the Tory Governments, 1815–30* (Oxford: Oxford University Press, 1977).

[20]See William C. Lubenow, *The Politics of Government Growth: Early Victorian Attitudes toward State Intervention, 1833–1848* (Newton Abbott: David and Charles, 1971); G. Sutherland, ed., *Studies in the Growth of Nineteenth-Century Government* (London: Routledge, 1972); and O. MacDonagh, *Early Victorian Government, 1830–1870* (London: Weidenfeld, 1977).

[21]See R. D. C. Black, *Economic Thought and the Irish Question, 1817–70* (Cambridge, Eng.: Cambridge University Press, 1960); E. Stokes, *The English Utilitarians and India* (Oxford: Clarendon Press, 1959); W. J. Barber, *British Economic Thought and India, 1650–1858* (Oxford: Clarendon Press, 1975); and S. Ambirajan, *Classical Political Economy and British Economic Policy in India* (Cambridge, Eng.: Cambridge University Press, 1978).

[22]India remained unusual in the sense that competitive examinations were first introduced in 1855 for entry into the Indian Civil Service and were only followed, and partially followed at that, as a system for recruiting home civil servants fifteen years later; see J. Roach, *Public Examinations in England, 1850–1900* (Cambridge, Eng.: Cambridge University Press, 1971), 25–6, Chapter 8.

duties were incidental to their professional and political careers. Throughout much of the nineteenth century, academic recognition did not match public significance. As Cairnes complained in the lecture cited earlier,

In this vast London, so energetic, so enterprising, so enlightened; in this great centre of the world's commerce; in this metropolis of the country which has produced Adam Smith, Ricardo, Malthus, Mill; which has produced, again, Pitt and Huskisson, Peel, Cobden and Gladstone; in this focus of economic activity and power; the systematic study of economic science is almost without practical recognition.[23]

By "practical recognition," it is important to note, Cairnes meant inclusion of political economy within an existing liberal scheme of higher education; he was not making a case for the vocational training of future civil servants. Indeed, as he maintained during the controversy over university reform in Ireland in 1866, he could conceive of nothing "better calculated to correct *the evils of the bureaucratic spirit* [emphasis added] than the liberalizing effects of an university education."[24] Cairnes's opinion mirrors the position adopted in the Northcote-Trevelyan report of 1853, which recommended competitive examination as the alternative to patronage in recruiting to the permanent civil service. Northcote-Trevelyan stated that they hardly needed to "allude to the important effect that would be produced upon the general education of the country, if proficiency in history, jurisprudence, political economy, modern languages, political and physical geography, and other matters, besides the staple of classics and mathematics, were made directly conducive to the success of young men desirous of entering into the public service."[25] But political economy was officially endorsed as a desirable component of university education in order to widen the field of potential recruits and to "quicken the progress of our Universities" in incorporating the subjects listed within existing curricula. The recommended changes were not intended to equip entrants with any of the specific practical skills they would need as civil servants. As Mill said in supporting testimony, the examination system was to be viewed "as a test of powers and habits of mind, still more than of acquirements."[26] Overcoming aristocratic favoritism by means of a

[23]"Political Economy and Laissez-Faire," 233.
[24]*Political Essays* (London: Macmillan, 1873), 274.
[25]Report on the Organization of the Permanent Civil Service, *Parliamentary Papers*, XXVII, 1854, 14.
[26]See Papers Relating to the Reorganization of the Civil Service, *Parliamentary Papers*, XX, 1854–5, 98; see also A. Ryan, "Utilitarianism and Bureaucracy: The Views of J. S. Mill," in G. Sutherland, ed., *Studies in the Growth of Nineteenth-Century Government* (London: Routledge, 1972), 33–62.

device that raised general standards of cultural attainment was the main goal in view.

Mill's position is perhaps all the more remarkable in light of his views on the role of the state as a (if not *the*) locus of knowledge in social affairs:[27] At various stages in his life, he supported, with qualifications, St. Simonian managerialism, Comte's notion of *un pouvoir spirituel*, and Coleridge's concept of a clerisy. Speaking simply as a philosophic radical, Mill could hardly be accused of underplaying the necessity for legislative expertise; and in direct opposition to St. Simon, Comte, and Coleridge, he considered a knowledge of political economy to be one of the essential ingredients in this expertise. When defending the need under democracy for the people to "choose for their rulers the most instructed and ablest persons who can be found," he chose political economy as his illustration:

Many of the truths of politics (in political economy for instance) are the result of a concatenation of propositions, the very first steps of which no one who has not gone through a course of study is prepared to concede; there are others, to have complete perception of which requires much meditation, and experience of human nature. How will philosophers bring these home to the perceptions of the multitude? Can they enable common sense to judge of science, or inexperience of experience?[28]

In his methodological writings and in the *Principles of Political Economy*, Mill made many concessions to the radical and conservative critics of political economy, largely by stressing that many of its conclusions with respect to policy were hypothetical. But he also held that political economy "approaches nearer to the rank of science, in the sense in which we apply that name to the physical sciences, than anything else connected with politics yet does"; and as Stefan Collini has pointed out, Mill "was not . . . called as an expert witness before five Parliamentary Select Committees on economic questions between 1850 and 1861 because he had made clear the purely hypothetical character of the conclusions of political economy."[29]

[27]See, for example, *On Liberty*, in *Essays on Politics and Society*, in J. M. Robson and A. Brady, eds., *The Collected Works of John Stuart Mill* (Toronto: University of Toronto Press, 1977), XIX, 306: "What the State can usefully do, is to make itself a central depository, and active circulator and diffuser, of the experience resulting from many trials. Its business is to enable each experimentalist to benefit by the experiments of others; instead of tolerating no experiments but its own."

[28]For a discussion of the esoteric quality of knowledge of political economy, see "Tocqueville," in *Essays on Politics and Society*, in J. M. Robson and A. Brady, eds., *Collected Works*, XVIII, 73.

[29]"The Tendencies of Things: John Stuart Mill and the Philosophic Method," *That Noble Science of Politics*, 141–2.

Specialized knowledge by an intellectual elite, however openly recruited, was undoubtedly a central feature of Mill's notion of how progress could be reconciled with the less desirable aspects of democratic institutions and mores. The university was to be one of the prime means of satisfying this public need, and since "the cultivation of speculative knowledge . . . is a service rendered to a community collectively, not individually," provision of higher education was a prime example of an exception to the general rule of laissez-faire.[30] But a liberal concept of education continued to provide the general framework within which this case was made, and political economy took its place alongside classics.[31] In this respect, Mill's confidence in the knowledge associated with political economy did not separate him from any of the leading advocates of liberal education in nineteenth-century Britain. Moreover, Mill fully endorsed the general attitudes that differentiate British and American views on knowledge and government from more bureaucratic state traditions elsewhere; that is, he was an opponent both of a completely state-run (as opposed to state-supported and -regulated) educational system and of any move that would confer on the state a monopoly in the employment of "high talent."[32]

The revival of interest in "stateness" in recent years has focused on Britain and the United States as examples of countries possessing "weak" or nonautonomous state traditions.[33] As Patricia Thane pointed out during the conference that gave rise to this volume, however, the nineteenth-century British state not only strove for autonomy, but aimed at strength by deliberately limiting, through delegation to other institutions, what it attempted to achieve. This pattern is evident in the relations between the

[30]W. J. Ashley, ed., *Principles of Political Economy* (London: Longmans, 1909), 976.
[31]See *Inaugural Address Delivered to the University of St. Andrews,* in *Essays on Equality, Law and Education,* in J. M. Robson and S. Collini, eds., *Collected Works,* XXI, 215–57. For a more detailed examination of the respects in which Mill belongs to the dominant tradition favoring a liberal concept of education, see B. Knights, *The Idea of the Clerisy in the Nineteenth Century* (Cambridge, Eng.: Cambridge University Press, 1987), especially Chapters 5 and 6.
[32]Mill's opposition to state-run schools is apparent in *Principles of Political Economy,* 953–6. For his view on the dangers of a state monopoly of "high talent" and a Chinese mandarin style of bureaucracy, see *On Liberty* in *Collected Works,* XIX, 308.
[33]See, for example, P. Evans, D. Rueschemeyer, and T. Skocpol, eds., *Bringing the State Back In* (Cambridge, Eng.: Cambridge University Press, 1985). The associated comparative-historical perspective has also led to studies of the processes by which social scientific knowledge is both sponsored and adopted by states or political systems. For a collection of essays focusing on the Keynesian revolution from this point of view, see P. Hall, ed., *The Political Power of Economic Ideas* (Princeton, N.J.: Princeton University Press, 1989).

state and economic knowledge, where, compared with Germany and, to a lesser extent, with France, this relationship could be portrayed as "weak" in academic and institutional terms. Again, though, the arm's-length methods used did not require a "strong" relationship—a relationship that would have conflicted with more important goals. What has been said here about lack of academic recognition, therefore, conforms with the British state's well-known lack of direct involvement in the provision of higher education during the nineteenth century.

A clear contrast could be made with the German university system. Although its permanent denizens came to enjoy a larger measure of freedom from political interference than their French counterparts, the nineteenth-century development of the system "was intimately connected with the evolution of the German bureaucracy."[34] Whether one looks back to the incorporation of economic topics within university syllabuses covering *Cameralwissenschaft* and later *Staatswissenchaft,* or forward from the establishment of the *Verein für Sozialpolitik* in 1872, the German story links the teaching of forms of economic knowledge and the structuring of economic debate among academics to the administrative concerns of the German states or, later, state.[35]

The German academic model, with its strong tradition of scholarly and scientific research, was the focus of a good deal of envy on the part of English university reformers in the nineteenth century,[36] and as trade rivalry grew toward the end of the century, this envy extended to German technical and commercial education.[37] In 1894, the British Association for the Advancement of Science, in a report on "Methods of Economic Training in This and Other Countries," painted a gloomy picture of the state of economic studies in Britain. With the possible exception of Oxford and Cambridge, "it is difficult to imagine a more complete indifference to the *scientific study* of Economics than that displayed at the present time."[38] The report unfavorably compared Britain with America and

---

[34]F. Ringer, *The Decline of the German Mandarins: The German Academic Community, 1890–1933* (Cambridge, Mass: Harvard University Press, 1969), 34.

[35]See K. Tribe, "Cameralism and the Science of Government," *Journal of Modern History* 56 (1984): 263–4, and his *Governing Economy: The Reformation of German Economic Discourse, 1750–1840* (Cambridge, Eng.: Cambridge University Press, 1988).

[36]See S. Rothblatt, *Tradition and Change in English Liberal Education: An Essay in History and Culture* (London: Faber, 1976), 157, 165–7.

[37]See M. Sanderson, *The Universities and British Industry, 1850–1970* (London: Routledge, 1972), 21–4, 187, 215.

[38]See *Report of the Proceedings of the British Association for the Advancement of Science,* London, 1894, 365–91. For quotation, see 391.

the Continent, where economics was a regular part of the qualifying examinations for entry into the civil service and other professions. C. F. Bastable, in his presidential address to the British Association in the same year, complained about the insularity of British economics and the failure, compared with "German economic investigation," to study economic phenomena as part of a wider grouping of social and historical subjects, including "political science, jurisprudence and the scientific principles of administration."[39]

French observers who were eager to achieve greater recognition for economics as a university discipline also looked enviously across the Rhine, but the social sciences in France owed more to institutions such as the Collège de France and the Ecole Pratique des Hautes Etudes, which were established alongside and in competition with the universities. A chair of political economy, whose first incumbent was Jean-Baptiste Say, existed at the Collège de France from 1831 onward, and although the establishment of a section devoted to the economic sciences within the Ecole des Hautes Etudes was long delayed, the very existence of a system of *grandes écoles* capable of being expanded in response to the emerging needs of the state is a symbol of the wider differences between the political cultures of France and Britain, and hence between the resulting relationships of the states to organized knowledge of all kinds.

The rigidities and political vicissitudes of a centrally controlled university system were counterbalanced by the existence of such institutions as the Ecole des Ponts et Chaussées, which, from the time of Jules Dupuit in the 1840s onward, acted as a congenial home for several generations of economist-engineers dedicated to forms of analysis capable of dealing with preeminently public forms of investment in railways, roads, and bridges.[40]

What was perhaps the most significant of the French schools for our theme, the Ecole Libre des Sciences Politiques, began in 1872 as a private institution with a distinct bias toward modern subjects that would prepare its students for public life, and with the explicit aim of acting as an elitist counterweight to the dangers inherent in democracy. It rapidly

[39]For quotation see ibid., 720, 725. Ibid., 719–28; see also Sanderson, *Universities and British Industry*, Chapter 7.
[40]On the general situation of the social sciences in France, see T. N. Clark, *Prophets and Patrons: The French University and the Emergence of the Social Science* (Cambridge, Mass.: Harvard University Press, 1973). On economics in particular, see R. B. Ekelund and R. F. Hebert, "Public Economics at the Ecole des Ponts et Chaussées, 1830–1850," *Journal of Public Economics* 2 (1973): 241–56.

became the dominant institution both for educating public and private functionaries and for conducting related research, proving to be more flexible in its response to changing circumstances, intellectual and political, than its main competitors, the university law faculties within which the teaching of economics was housed, frequently under intellectually cramping conditions.[41]

The Ecole Libre and the British Association report of 1894 were twin inspirations to Beatrice and Sidney Webb when they "resolved to make an attempt to start a centre of economic teaching and research in London on the lines of that in Paris."[42] Ironically, however, the institution that emerged as the London School of Economics (LSE) in 1895, in its early years at least, was more like a business school than a training ground for budding public administrators destined to play a part in furthering the cause of bureaucratic collectivism.[43] This outcome serves as a reminder that from at least the 1890s onward, commerce and business often made more insistent claims on the British university system than did government—a reminder that is more welcome perhaps in view of the current tendency to regard the universities as having a large share in producing the antienterprise culture from which Britain is now having to be rescued.[44]

At Cambridge, Alfred Marshall's interest in recruiting potential businessmen into his newly autonomous Economics Tripos after 1903 went beyond fashion and finance, although the curriculum that emerged was less vocationally oriented than that of LSE and that required for William Ashley's commerce degree at Birmingham.[45] Marshall did not wish to

---

[41]See P. Favre, "Les sciences d'état entre déterminisme et libéralisme: Emile Boutmy et la création de l'Ecole libre des Sciences politiques," *Revue Française de Sociologie* 22 (1891): 429–65.

[42]N. Mackenzie, ed., *The Letters of Sidney and Beatrice Webb* (Cambridge, Eng.: Cambridge University Press, 1978), II, 176.

[43]See Sanderson, *Universities and British Industry,* 192: "What had begun as a political school floated by money avowedly for the propagation of Socialist, anti-capitalist ideas was turning into a school for predominantly commercial subjects for young men entering business, with the hearty encouragement and support of the City." In fairness to Beatrice and Sidney Webb, it should also be pointed out that they, too, hoped London University would "show that there is no incompatibility between . . . the most practical professional training and genuine cultivation of the mind." *Our Partnership* (Cambridge, Eng.: Cambridge University Press, 1975), 239; see also Sanderson, 168.

[44]The crucial document here is M. Wiener's influential study of *English Culture and the Decline of the Industrial Spirit, 1850–1980* (Cambridge, Eng.: Cambridge University Press, 1981).

[45]Alfred Marshall, *A Plea for the Creation of a Curriculum in Economics and Associated Branches of Political Science* (1902), reprinted in C. W. Guillebaud, ed., *Principles of Economics* (London: Macmillan, 1961), II, 161–81.

have accountancy part of the curriculum, or to follow the city-based universities in offering overt training to businessmen, but his own commitment to the theoretical and inductive study of modern industrial organization could hardly be faulted. Moreover, Marshall's suspicion of the state's entrepreneurial capacities, dislike of political jobbery, and belief that "bureaucratic methods are alien from the genius of democracy" led him to place great stress on the importance of the "captain of industry" and on the possibilities of building on what he described as the "latent chivalry in business life."[46] Nevertheless, he did not ignore the needs of the civil service, and like Mill and others before him, Marshall believed that the Indian service offered great opportunities for those with "a good grounding in economics who have already got to understand the main bearings of those modern economic forces which are revolutionizing the West, and are making great changes in the East."[47]

A number of excellent studies of Marshall's contribution to the professionalization of British economics now exist, and they all indicate the limitations of his success when judged in terms of the number of serious students attracted to the new prospectus.[48] Had he been more successful in this respect, however, he would not so much have equipped a more intelligent state with economic experts as produced a generation or two of economists who had "cool heads but warm hearts" and were capable of educating the public, encouraging "social responsibility" among business and trade union leaders, and mobilizing "the moral pressure of social opinion in constraining and directing individual action in those economic relations in which the rigidity and violence of government interference would be likely to do more harm than good."[49] Although the tone is characteristically a moralizing one, it is perhaps best interpreted as giving the economist a social or permeationist, rather than administrative, role in furthering the rational "deliberateness" Marshall believed to be the chief characteristic of modern economic life.

[46]See the preface to *Industry and Trade* (London: Macmillan, 1919), and "Social Possibilities of Economic Chivalry," in A. C. Pigou, ed., *Memorials of Alfred Marshall* (London: Macmillan, 1925), 323–52.
[47]See J. M. Keynes, ed., *Official Papers of Alfred Marshall* (London: Macmillan, 1926), 274–5, 325–6.
[48]See A. W. Coats, "Sociological Aspects of British Economic Thought, 1880–1930," *Journal of Political Economy* 75 (1967): 706–29; A. Kadish, *The Oxford Economists in the Late Nineteenth Century* (Oxford: Clarendon Press, 1982); and J. Maloney, *Marshall, Orthodoxy and the Professionalization of Economics* (Cambridge, Eng.: Cambridge University Press, 1985).
[49]See A. C. Pigou, ed., *Memorials of Alfred Marshall* (London: Macmillan, 1925), 174; and *Principles of Economics*, variorum edition, ed. C. W. Guillebaud for the Royal Economic Society (London: Macmillan, 1890), vol. 1, 42.

THE INTERWAR STATE AND ECONOMIC KNOWLEDGE: TECHNOCRATIC POSSIBILITIES AND HOPES

Before World War I, supporters of the permeationist strategy could point to one or two promising examples of success. In the case of the Tariff Reform controversy, there was much effort to mobilize the support of economic experts on both sides of the public debate, with Marshall's confidential "Memorandum on the Fiscal Policy of International Trade" (1903, published in 1908), written at the behest of the chancellor of the Exchequer, probably proving more effective than an ill-fated public letter to the *Times* signed by a prominent group of free-trade economists in 1903.[50] Hubert Llewellyn Smith's achievements in the Labour Department of the Board of Trade illustrate what could happen in a department that was extraordinarily permeable by those who had established their credentials in statistical and other types of social investigation during the late-nineteenth-century period of enthusiasm for quantitative estimates of the nature and extent of poverty.[51] The activities of the Webbs, too, in relation to the Report of the Royal Commission on the Poor Laws, 1905–9, furnish another example of the same type of activity by outside experts, following, in this case, the pressure tactics of their Benthamite predecessors.[52]

During and immediately after World War I, it was the Webbs' original hopes when founding the LSE, rather than Marshall's when creating the Cambridge Economics Tripos, that looked most likely to be fulfilled. Beatrice Webb became involved in the activities of the Ministry of Reconstruction, and especially with one of its progeny, the Haldane Committee on the Machinery of Government, which she had high hopes would usher in a new era of scientific administration. Building on the experiment begun by Llewellyn Smith, the report of the Haldane Committee recommended in 1918 that "in the sphere of civil government the duty of investigation and thought, as a preliminary to action, might with great advantage be more definitely recognized."[53] Not only should every exist-

---

[50]See A. W. Coats, "Political Economy and the Tariff Reform Campaign of 1903," *Journal of Law and Economics* 11 (1968): 181–229.

[51]See R. Davidson, "Llewellyn Smith, the Labour Department and Government Growth, 1886–1909," in Sutherland, ed., *Growth of Nineteenth-Century Government*, 227–62; and R. Davidson and R. Lowe, "Bureaucracy and Innovation in British Welfare Policy, 1870–1945," in W. J. Mommsen, ed., *The Emergence of the Welfare State in Britain and Germany* (London: Croom Helm, 1981), 263–91.

[52]See G. R. Searle, *The Quest for National Efficiency: A Study in British Politics and Political Thought, 1899–1914* (Oxford: Blackwell, 1971), 235–56.

[53]*Report of the Committee on the Machinery of Government, Reports from Commissioners, Inspectors, and Others,* vol. XII, Cd. 9230, 1918, 6.

ing department provide for research, but the report envisaged the need for a separate official body devoted to economic intelligence working on problems outside the range of the departments. As a result of the rapid and wholesale dismantling of the apparatus of wartime planning after the war, very little came of these recommendations. Nevertheless, they provided the foundation for the idea of an economic general staff, the case for which was frequently rehearsed in the 1920s, and the idea was eventually implemented in the form of the Economic Advisory Council (EAC) created by the second Labour government in 1930.

With the dramatic expansion in the wartime role of the state, many graduates of the reformed university system were recruited into the civil service.[54] Among those who were later to play an important role as economists in government were Keynes and Hubert Henderson, both of whom entered the civil service on a temporary basis, joining other economists and statisticians such as William Beveridge, Ralph Hawtrey, Arthur Salter, Llewellyn Smith, and Josiah Stamp, all of whom had more regular prewar experience as civil servants. Keynes and Henderson were to become major figures on the EAC and later on its subcommittees throughout the 1930s, at the end of which the body gave way to a more extensive system for employing economists in government.[55]

The EAC provided Keynes with another platform, along with his serious and journalistic writings and appearances before the Macmillan Committee on Finance and Industry, from which to launch his ideas on economic diagnosis and policy. When the EAC was being established, and at other points in its deliberations, Keynes expressed some of his most optimistic sentiments concerning the technocratic possibilities opened up by the employment of economists in government:

A move along these lines would indeed be an act of statesmanship, the importance of which cannot easily be exaggerated. For it would mark a transition in our conception of the functions and purposes of the State, and a first measure towards the deliberate and purposive guidance of the evolution of our economic life. It would be a recognition of the enormous part to be played in this by the scientific spirit as distinct from the sterility of the purely party attitude, which is never more out of place than in relation to complex matters of fact and interpretation involving technical difficulty. It would mean the beginning of ways of doing and thinking about political problems which are probably necessary for the effi-

---

[54]See Sanderson, *Universities and British Industry*, 213.
[55]For further details, see S. K. Howson and D. Winch, *The Economic Advisory Council, 1930–39: A Study in Economic Advice during Depression and Recovery* (Cambridge, Eng.: Cambridge University Press, 1977).

cient working of modern democracy. For it would be an essay in the art of combining representative institutions and the voice of public opinion with the utilization by Governments of the best technical advice in spheres, where such advice can never, and should not, have the last word or the power, but must be a necessary ingredient in the decision of those entrusted by the country with the last word and with the power.[56]

The reference to "deliberate and purposive guidance" is a reminder of one of Keynes's main preoccupations during the 1920s and relates to another feature of his essay on "The End of Laissez-Faire." Keynes's attack on what he took to be nineteenth-century presumptions is of interest as a guide to the development of his own thinking and that of other New Liberals in seeking a middle path between uninhibited private capitalism and state socialism during the interwar period.[57] As hinted earlier, there was little that was novel in the generalities of Keynes's diagnosis: "The important thing for government is not to do things which individuals are doing already, and to do them a little better or a little worse; but to do those things which at present are not done at all." Nor was there much that was new in the idea that many economic evils were the "fruits of risk, uncertainty, and ignorance" that could not be avoided or minimized by individual prudence. Some of his solutions also had nineteenth-century precedents; for example, his suggestion that the state should be active "in the collection and dissemination on a great scale of data relating to the business situation, including the full publicity, by law if necessary, of all business facts which it is useful to know" could be traced back to Marshall, Mill, and Bentham.[58]

The chief departures in Keynes's position lie in the political instrumentalities and some of the goals that he believed it was now the responsibility of the state to promote. Thus, one of the instrumentalities he favored was the establishment of "semi-autonomous bodies within the state" that could be made "subject in the last resort to the sovereignty of the democracy expressed through Parliament"—a solution that could be justified on grounds of the separation of ownership from control in large corporations, where there was already "a tendency of big enterprise to socialise itself." In

---

[56] Ibid., 21.
[57] M. Freeden in *Liberalism Divided: A Study in British Political Thought, 1914–39* (Oxford: Clarendon Press, 1986) argued that the contributions of Keynes and other interwar economists to liberal theory were "marginal and indirect," 154–73. For an interpretation that places Keynes more firmly within the context of New Liberalism, see P. Clarke, "The Politics of Keynesian Economics, 1924–31," in M. Bentley and J. Stevenson, eds., *High and Low Politics in Modern Britain* (Oxford: Clarendon Press, 1983), 175–80.
[58] See *J.M.K.*; IX, 288–94.

calling for "deliberate control of the currency and of credit by a central institution" and for "some coordinated act of intelligent judgement" on the level and direction of national savings and investment, Keynes was preparing the agenda most often associated with his name today.[59]

Given the relative lack of official recognition accorded to economic expertise in the 1920s, Keynes's emphasis on the need for "directive intelligence" prompts questions concerning the recruitment, education, and social location of those who would exercise it. Marshall's hero, the farsighted captain of industry whose deliberative capacities had been honed in the competitive struggle to survive, was now a "tarnished idol": "We grow more doubtful whether it is he who will lead us into paradise by the hand."[60] Where was the alternative to be found? Keynes hinted that the answer lay in the universities when he took up H. G. Wells's contrast—as expressed in *The World of William Clissold* (1926), a semi-autobiographical novel of prophecy—between Brahma and Siva, representing the creative and destructive principles at work in British society. Keynes agreed with Wells that Brahma was still too committed to the service of science and business, rather than politics or government, and that Siva's power to frustrate the creative principle could be detected in "the passionate destructiveness of labour awakening to its now needless limitations and privations." But Keynes also felt that in dealing with the universities, Wells "underestimates altogether their possibilities—how they may become temples of Brahma which even Siva will respect."[61]

Apart from isolated observations of this kind, however, Keynes had relatively little to say about the universities—although he can hardly be accused of underplaying the need for "the collaboration of all the bright critical spirits of the age," or of underestimating the role of rational debate, up-to-date statistics, and technical expertise in public affairs. Indeed, much criticism of Keynes centers on the excessive optimism of his belief in the power of economic intelligence, not to mention the overtly elitist claims that accompany this position: "I believe that the right solution will involve intellectual and scientific elements which must be above the heads of the vast mass of more or less illiterate voters."[62] He was at

[59]Ibid., for a discussion of the duty of government with respect to "the wholesale collection and dissemination of industrial knowledge," see *J.M.K.*, XIX, 643–4.
[60]*J.M.K.*, VIII, 287.
[61]Ibid., 320.
[62]Ibid., 295. For recent comment and criticism, see W. Parsons, "Keynes and the Politics of Ideas," *History of Political Thought* 4 (1983): 367–92; and Freeden, *Liberalism Divided*, 158–64.

one with Marshall in thinking "that it is a mistake for the universities to attempt vocational training" for businessmen;[63] but he also discerned the beginnings of a "scientific age in economics and business" that would allow the Northcote-Trevelyan principle, one might say, to be extended to industrial management.[64] Not only would economic advice and intelligence need to be available at the highest levels of decision making in government, therefore, but the new semiautonomous public corporations would require a salariat recruited by education rather than the "mere accident of circumstance and parentage and locality": "I do not see why we should not build up in this country a great public service running the business side of public concerns recruited from the whole population with the same ability and the same great traditions as our administrative Civil Service."[65]

The civil service model can be thought of as a subspecies of a more general ideal associated with professionalism.[66] In this respect, there are interesting similarities between Keynes's position and that of R. H. Tawney, the Christian socialist who was, for a time at least, a fellow member of the EAC. As a leading twentieth-century upholder of the Ruskin-Morris train of moral thought, Tawney regarded the claims of an objective science of economics with great suspicion, if not scorn.[67] In common with Keynes, he was unimpressed by Marshall's faith in an enlightened and chivalrous breed of business leader as an alternative to collectivist control.[68] Despite maintaining close personal relations with the Webbs, Tawney remained suspicious of their bureaucratic vision of

---

[63]*J.M.K.*, XIX, 654.

[64]Ibid., 726.

[65]Ibid., 646, 697.

[66]On the attractions of professionalism in this period, see T. L. Haskell, "Professionalism versus Capitalism: R. H. Tawney, Emile Durkheim, and C. S. Peirce on the Disinterestedness of Professional Communities," in T. L. Haskell, ed., *The Authority of Experts* (Bloomington: Indiana University Press, 1984), 180–225.

[67]This attitude is reflected in Tawney's unqualified rejection of even the heavily moralized form of the discipline proffered by Marshall in his arguments for the Cambridge Economics Tripos: "There is no such thing as a science of economics, nor ever will be. It is just cant, and Marshall's talk as to the need for social problems to be studied by the same order of mind which tests the stability of a battleship in bad weather is twaddle"; see J. M. Winter, ed., *R. H. Tawney's Commonplace Book* (Cambridge, Eng.: Cambridge University Press, 1972), 11, 26, 72. Tawney also opposed the teaching of "technical" economics at the London School of Economics; see R. Terrill, *R. H. Tawney and His Times* (Cambridge, Mass.: Harvard University Press, 1973), 66.

[68]For Tawney's political thought, see J. M. Winter, *Socialism and the Challenge of War* (London: Routledge, 1974), especially Chapters 3 and 6.

socialism. During World War I, however, he became enthusiastic about "the erection of a vast wartime state with unparalleled powers and authority,"[69] and he later wrote the obituary of this episode as a warning against precipitate dismantling of the machinery of economic control after World War II.[70]

In *The Acquisitive Society* (1921), Tawney hoped it would be possible to harness a disinterested professional ethic among "brain workers" and industrial managers by encouraging them to adopt public service rather than material gain as their reward—an idea that was also endorsed by the Webbs in *A Constitution for the Socialist Commonwealth of Great Britain* (1920).[71] Although Keynes would not, of course, have shared Tawney's dismissal of economics, and had a healthy respect for economic self-seeking as an alternative to more destructive forms of power seeking, the two men were closer to one another than perhaps might be expected. The agreement extended to the subservience of economics to morality and art, to the transitory nature of the public obsession with economic issues, to the implications of the separation of ownership from management, and even to what Keynes later described as the "euthanasia of the rentier."[72]

It is no secret that—with the limited exception of the EAC and several privately funded research bodies, notably Political and Economic Planning, and despite a number of significant extensions of the role of the state in economic life—none of the optimistic hopes considered here came to fruition in interwar Britain. Beatrice Webb's gloomier diagnosis of the relationship between the state, economic knowledge, and public service, confided to her diary during World War I, proved nearer the mark:

The British governing class, whether aristocratic or bourgeois, has no abiding faith in the concentrated and disinterested intellectual toil involved in the scientific method. Science to them is a sort of intellectual adventure to be undertaken by a rare type of man. The adventure may or may not turn out worth while, but in any case it is silly to expect this adventurous spirit from ordinary men in the

[69]Ibid., 168.
[70]See "The Abolition of Economic Controls, 1918–21," in J. M. Winter, ed., *History and Society: Essays by R. H. Tawney* (London: Routledge, 1978).
[71]See R. H. Tawney, *The Acquisitive Society* (London: Fontana, 1961), 128–31, 152–75; and S. Webb and B. Webb, *A Constitution for the Socialist Commonwealth of Great Britain* (Cambridge, Eng.: Cambridge University Press, 1975), Chapters 6 and 7.
[72]For other respects in which Tawney remained a representative of "socialism with a liberal face," see Freeden, *Liberalism Divided*, 313–20. For "euthanasia of the rentier," see *J.M.K.*, VII, 376.

conduct of daily life. Indeed, applied to social, economic and political questions the scientific method is to be shunned as likely to lead to experiments dangerous to liberty and property and the existing order of society. . . . The Englishman hates the impersonality of science.[73]

The despair over prevailing attitudes to expertise, together with disillusionment with the fate of the Labour party, increasingly drove the Webbs to find consolation in Soviet communism; they claimed to find among the party cadres the right mix of administrative expertise and a quasi-Comtian religious dedication to public service.

Keynes's lack of success in gaining lasting official recognition for his theoretical and policy ideas during the interwar period is equally well known.[74] In view of his high opinion of the civil service tradition and his unrivaled experience of its internal workings (among economists and hence, a fortiori, among social scientists), it is ironic that so much of the resistance to his ideas came from the civil service in general and the Treasury in particular. On the eve of World War II, Keynes recorded his disillusionment:

The Civil Service is ruled today by the Treasury school, trained by tradition and experience and native skill to every form of intelligent obstruction. . . . Great as is my admiration for many of the qualities of our Civil Service, I am afraid that they are becoming a heavy handicap in our struggle with the totalitarian states and in making ourselves safe from them. They cramp our energy, and spoil or discard our ideas.[75]

That he was quickly to be proved wrong when the outbreak of war created more propitious circumstances for the implementation of his views on a wide variety of economic policy issues, domestic and international, does not alter the fact that the relationship between economic knowledge and the state in Britain has only for relatively brief periods approximated the technocratic models sometimes favored by economists and other social scientists.

[73] The Diary of Beatrice Webb (Cambridge, Mass.: Harvard University Press, Belknap Press, 1983), III, 304–5. I am grateful to Julia Stapleton for drawing this entry to my attention.
[74] See D. Winch, "Keynes, Keynesianism and State Intervention," in Hall, ed., The Political Power of Economic Ideas, 107–27; see also the large body of literature on the "Treasury view": for example, G. C. Peden, "The 'Treasury View' on Public Works and Employment in the Interwar Period," Economic History Review, 2d ser., 37 (1984): 167–81; R. Middleton, Towards the Managed Economy: Keynes, the Treasury and the Fiscal Policy Debate of the 1930s (London: Methuen, 1985); and A. Booth and M. Pack, Employment, Capital and Economic Policy: Great Britain, 1918–39 (Oxford: Basil Blackwell, 1985).
[75] J.M.K., XXI, 496–7.

SOME ANGLO-AMERICAN COMPARISONS

An ample body of literature on social science and government compares Britain unfavorably with the United States and seeks explanations not merely in the differing constitutional structures but in cultural attitudes that encouraged early academic professionalization and have consistently granted higher social and political status to the policy scientist in the United States.[76] On every possible count, the resources that continue to be available for the support of social scientific research in the United States dwarf those available in Britain—with differences in quality probably paralleling the differences in quantity. In Britain, the period from the mid-1960s to the mid-1970s seems a positive bonanza compared with the past decade, with its austerities and the government's indifference, if not downright hostility, toward universities in general and the social sciences in particular.[77] Powerful ideological sea changes have ended the long period of postwar consensus. Intellectual and policy failures have also played a part in generating this outcome, and there are clear signs that frustration is giving way to productive appraisal of the lessons that can be learned from the slow rise and rapid fall of what looked like a relatively stable relationship between government and social science. Against this backdrop, this section mentions in almost headline fashion some points suggested by the longer historical view.

The Anglo-American literature on the Keynesian revolution as well as other branches of what might be called applied social science points to a paradox that has been expressed by one observer as a "puzzling disparity between the scale and quality of American social science research and its access to government on the one hand, and the effectiveness of American government on the other."[78] What can be learned, for example, from the contrast between the early acceptance yet delayed implementation of

[76]For an acute summary of the various differences, see L. J. Sharpe, "The Social Scientist and Policy-Making: Some Cautionary Thoughts and Transatlantic Reflections," *Policy and Politics* 4 (1975): 7–34; see also M. Bulmer, ed., *Social Science Research and Government: Comparative Essays on Britain and the United States* (Cambridge, Eng.: Cambridge University Press, 1987).

[77]The firm evidence for hostility centers on the attack by the then minister of education, Sir Keith Joseph, on the Social Science Research Council. For an account of this episode, see " 'Pulling Through': Conspiracies, Counterplots, and How the SSRC Escaped the Axe in 1982," in Bulmer, ed., *Social Science Research and Government*, 353–72. For a sober summary of the facts concerning the recent cycle affecting funding, see C. S. Smith, "The Research Function in the Social Sciences," in G. Oldham, ed., *The Future of Research* (London: Society for Research into Higher Education, 1982), 150–68.

[78]Sharpe, "The Social Scientist and Policy-Making," 20.

Keynesian ideas in America and the delayed acceptance yet earlier implementation of the same ideas in Britain?[79] The answers to such questions seem to lie as much in differences of political culture as in the better-known contrast between a unitary state where the executive controls the legislature and commands (or is commanded by) the resources of the bureaucracy and a state characterized by the separation of powers and numerous competing government agencies, each with its own internal and external sources of expertise.

Despite the well-established comparisons between British and American attitudes toward the use of economic and social knowledge in government, one should not minimize the effectiveness, especially within Britain's more homogeneous political culture, of two well-established modes of influence. The first of these, and the one that is more difficult to document in short order, involves the publication of seminal work that alters the basic categories according to which economic and social life is perceived. The second mode involves deliberately creating and employing social networks designed to connect academic or outside expert thinking with bureaucratic practice and deliberation.[80]

The claims of Cairnes and Bagehot rest on the first of these modes, and the detailed application and extension of Adam Smith's work by his followers over a lengthy period bear out the view that in significant areas British policy had become "instinct with" his fundamental approach. The authority acquired by this approach, its success in shifting the onus of disproof onto the opposition, can be judged from the fact that much of late-nineteenth-century economic debate still turned either on outright attacks on the methods and categories of political economy or on attempts to show why the circumstances that had made it apposite to an earlier era no longer reigned. A twentieth-century example of a similar long-drawn-out process is the way in which economists, with Keynes at their head, succeeded during the interwar period in delineating something that could be called economic policy—centering on the connections between employment levels and monetary, exchange rate, and fiscal conditions—out of elements that had previously been treated

---

[79]For an attempt to answer this question, see M. Weir, "Ideas and Politics: The Diffusion of Keynesianism in Britain and the United States," in Hall, ed., *The Political Power of Economic Ideas*, 53–86.

[80]See D. Donnison, "Research for Policy, "*Minerva* 10 (1972): 519–36; C. S. Smith, "Networks of Influence: The Social Sciences in Britain Since the War," in Bulmer, ed., *Social Science Research and Government*, 61–76; and J. Platt, "Research Dissemination: A Case Study," *Quarterly Journal of Social Affairs* 3 (1987): 181–98.

separately as questions of social administration on the one hand or narrow technical matters of banking and fiscal management on the other.[81] As enshrined, albeit somewhat ambivalently, in the 1944 White Paper on Employment Policy, and when combined with the Beveridge report on social security, these ideas, as Paul Addison has pointed out, epitomized "the thought of the upper-middle class of socially concerned professional people, of whom Beveridge and Keynes were the patron saints."[82]

The mere existence of such modes of influence, of course, provides no guarantee that what is advanced at any given time as new social or economic knowledge will determine, or even modify, the dispositions of representative or bureaucratic government. But these kinds of influence could help to explain the rapidity with which ideas, once accepted as relevant to the agenda of state, are developed and implemented. As observers recognize anew with the disappearance of the Keynes-Beveridge axis, it did provide the basis for an extraordinarily high degree of bipartisan agreement in postwar Britain—a level of agreement lacking in postwar America. Around it, powerful supportive networks linking economists in government with academics outside were constructed. Hence, too, the extent of the postmortem needed to account for the current success of what look like pre-Keynesian ideas, the revival of mid-Victorian attitudes toward the provision of social welfare, and the mushrooming of new policy-forming institutions and social networks designed to give them reformist purchase.

In light of the capacity of seminal works to shift the focus of public debate, it may be necessary to qualify the implied criticisms of Dicey and Keynes in the early sections of this chapter for failing to pay attention to the processes of conversion and dissemination. We now know far more about the ways in which Benthamites and liberal economists established networks for influencing opinion and permeating public agencies.[83]

[81]See, for example, Jose Harris's conclusion, in *Unemployment and Politics: A Study in English Social Policy, 1886–1914* (Oxford: Clarendon Press, 1972), that "throughout this period the history of unemployment policy at all levels . . . is . . . primarily concerned with problems of social administration; it is only rarely concerned with the regulation or elimination of unemployment by methods of economic, fiscal, or monetary control" (p. 6). Although there is much I would wish to change in my own early and now largely outdated work *Economics and Policy* (London: Fontana, second edition, 1972), I stand by its treatment of the emergence of economic management as a theme.

[82]P. Addison, *The Road to 1945: British Politics and the Second World War* (London: Quartet Brooks, 1977), 277.

[83]See, for example, S. E. Finer, "The Transmission of Benthamite Ideas, 1820–50," in Sutherland, ed., *Growth of Nineteenth-Century Government*, 11–32. For a study of

These findings reinforce criticisms of the vacuousness of Dicey's definition of "true" public opinion as something confined to the majority "of those citizens who have at any given moment taken an effective part in public life."[84] Similar, perhaps, was Keynes's response to Friedrich von Hayek's dire predictions about planning in *The Road to Serfdom:* The experiment in Britain, Keynes argued, "will be safe if those carrying it out are rightly orientated in their own minds and hearts to the moral issue."[85] But behind the circularity and complacency of this view of the effective public there lies the following possible justification: One does not need to demonstrate the currency of ideas if it is obvious to any member of the relevant subculture that these ideas have become the means by which governing elites attempt to comprehend economic reality. Whether the minds and hearts of the people implementing ideas were likely to perceive the possibilities of misuse could seem equally obvious.

The comparative evidence about Britain's weak academic institutionalization, the nonvocational emphasis of nineteenth-century proponents of political economy, and the lack of official recognition of the discipline as a technical preparation for the bureaucracy can be reinterpreted in the same light. Comparisons with societies possessing longer traditions of centralized bureaucracy, especially those with national university systems, obscure the real sense in which the preparation of students to meet the growing need for civil servants, including those destined for local government as well as imperial service, was a prominent aim of the spokesmen for "modern" subjects at Cambridge, Oxford, and the London School of Economics.[86] The call for curriculum reform occurred long before the technocratic mood fostered by World War I had its brief efflorescence; and because Oxbridge curricula formed the basis for meritocratic recruitment into the civil service, the potential conflict between the liberal and vocational aims of education was minimized.[87] Behind the liberal disclaimers, therefore, lay confident, if only half-articulated, as-

overlapping social scientific communities in the nineteenth century, see L. Goldman, "The Social Science Association, 1857–1886: A Context for Mid-Victorian Liberalism," *English Historical Review* 101 (1986): 95–134.

[84] *Law and Public Opinion in England* (London: Macmillan, 1930), 10.

[85] *J.M.K.*, XXVII, 385–7.

[86] For studies of this in relation to political science, see "A Place in the Syllabus: Political Science at Cambridge," in Collini et al., *That Noble Science of Politics*, 341–63; and J. Stapleton, "Academic Political Thought and the Development of Political Studies in Britain, 1900–1950" (Ph.D. diss., University of Sussex, 1985).

[87] On this point, Collini et al., *That Noble Science of Politics*, 354; and S. Rothblatt, *Tradition and Change in English Liberal Education*, 203.

sumptions about the nature of the elites likely to be recruited into the higher realms of the civil service, and this confidence could be extended to the way in which specific forms of knowledge, once accepted, were likely to be deployed, not simply within government, but in that larger arena surrounding and conditioning government, educated opinion.

Given the preponderance of Oxbridge entrants into the administrative grades of the civil service between the wars, describing the situation in terms of the old-boy network does not do too much injustice to the facts, but it ignores the caste consciousness that accompanied the creation of a professional civil service, especially when the Treasury's close control over the system meant that prospects for promotion could be enhanced by following priorities internal to the service. The concomitant resistance to the outside expert helps explain why Keynes's sustained knowledge-based attempts to alter the agenda and instrumentalities of the state proved unsuccessful. In 1936, after nearly two decades of attempts to influence official and public opinion, Keynes concluded that "it is my fellow economists, not the general public I must first convince."[88] Although this shift of tactics can be defended, the number of academic economists in Britain, the rudimentary nature of their professional organization, and the prevailing distrust of knowledge separated from practical experience and responsibility (Beatrice Webb's complaint cited earlier) meant that, even if successful, Keynes's move could hardly have mobilized a powerful battalion capable of acting as a counterweight to the civil service's priorities.

Official recruitment of economists during World War II brought them into closer contact with the civil service, and it is a sign of Keynes's acceptance of the small-scale, commanding-heights view of the economic adviser that he (like other economists with wartime experience) was not willing to support more ambitious, and potentially more *dirigiste,* schemes for employing economists in government after the war.[89] During the late 1960s and early 1970s, the number of economists employed as career civil servants, or on short-term contracts and consultancies, by a

[88]*J.M.K.,* VII, vi.
[89]On the wartime system, see R. Stone, "The Use and Development of National Income and Expenditure Estimates," in D. N. Chester, ed., *Lessons of the British War Economy* (Cambridge, Eng.: Cambridge University Press, 1951), 83–101; D. N. Chester, "The Central Machinery for Economic Policy," in ibid.; and R. Sayers, *Financial Policy 1939–45* (London: 1956), 5–33. See also A. Booth and A. W. Coats, "Some War-Time Observations on the Role of Economists in Government," *Oxford Economic Papers* 32 (1980): 177–99.

variety of ministries and advisory bodies expanded. The underlying system, therefore, still used economists as in-house civil servants—with the exception of occasional free-floating and overtly political appointments by the prime minister.

Judgments on the Thatcher era are bound to be partial in every sense of the word, but it seems as though the predominant associations of economics with Keynesianism in all its varieties and the belief that Keynesianism represents a prostatist ideology rather than a technocratic form of knowledge may have reduced the part played by economists as civil servants, in the macroeconomic field at least, while increasing the part played by ad hoc advisers and partisan think tanks.[90] The professional organization of academic and other economists is showing signs of reacting defensively to this state of affairs, but the erosion of the publicly funded academic base, taken in conjunction with cuts in Economic and Social Research Council funding, means that the counterweights to prevailing government attitudes are still unconvincing at present.

Comparisons with the United States are relevant at this juncture: The lack of multiple points of entry into the legislative process and the virtual monopoly of access to ministers by the civil service are the other side of the British coin. The elaboration of the Treasury view as a complete internal diagnosis of what could or could not be attempted by government in the economic sphere, and the tenacity with which this view was defended for more than a decade, provides a well-documented example of how changes of objective, and hence of the kinds of knowledge needed, could be resisted within such a system. Moreover, exceptions also seem to prove the rule, as is clear from the equally well-documented achievements of Llewellyn Smith at the Board of Trade mentioned earlier; an unusual policy of external recruitment of statistical and other experts proved advantageous to a department that was embarking on new courses of action in uncharted fields.[91] Most of the typical cases of policy innovation based on alternative theoretical diagnoses probably fall somewhere between the extremes marked out by the interwar Treasury and the prewar Board of Trade. They fall into the

[90]Leslie Hannah presents a more optimistic picture of the microeconomics of industrial policy in his contribution to this volume (Chapter 11).

[91]See Searle, *Quest for National Efficiency*. R. Lowe's *Adjusting to Democracy: The Role of the Ministry of Labour in British Politics, 1916–39* (Oxford: Clarendon Press, 1986) contains a great deal on the interwar civil service ethos and places Keynes's campaign and the Treasury response in the broader perspective provided by the Ministry of Labour's deliberations.

learning-by-doing category; that is, novel problems presented them-selves, often in the form of crises of one kind or another, forcing inquiry by officials, by royal commissions, and by the large number of private and philanthropic bodies that continued to operate during the interwar period, generating new information for interpretation.[92]

IDEAS AND ACTION

In conclusion, it seems worth returning to the question of what kind of influence the historian should expect to establish. Is the very word *influence* misleading? Does it not suggest that action by the state is usually knowledge-driven, rather than, as must be the case, that politicians and administrators are highly selective in their use of ideas produced by "out-siders"; that knowledge can be used mainly for justifying choices if not simply for legitimizing choices post hoc? What, indeed, constitutes *economic* knowledge? The introductory chapter to this volume offers a use-ful classification, suggested by a typology proposed by Robert Cuff at the conference from which this book arises. As presented there, economic knowledge covers a spectrum that ranges from the most rarefied discipline-based, theoretical understanding to the most commonplace, persistent, culturally embedded values and beliefs concerning the work-ings of the economy, where the latter form a kind of economic folklore. It also includes all of the informed opinion and practical knowledge pos-sessed by public officials and other economic decision makers, an amal-gam that embraces the ability to learn by doing—to combine the selection of goals with the choice of practical means of attaining them.

In the discussion provoked by the conference, a number of dichoto-mies, explicit and implicit, were invoked: between rhetoric and reality, between persuasion and proof, between opportunistic and sincere uses of knowledge. Yet all such binary distinctions conceal strong claims to knowledge beneath their denial of, or skepticism toward, the claims of others. As in the classic example of false consciousness, true conscious-ness is implied.

This chapter stresses discipline-based knowledge, the ideas of profes-sional economists produced either in the quietness of the study or in

---

[92]This is one of the main conclusions to emerge from Barry Supple's paper given at the conference "The State and Social Investigation: An Historical Overview," sponsored by the Woodrow Wilson Center, Washington, D.C., September 10–12, 1986; see also Martin Bulmer's comment on that paper.

response to the more immediate demands of official and public life. Once the importance of such knowledge is posited, the way is open to counter-suggestions that other kinds of ideas may have been more influential because they were more in tune with the social and political beliefs of political decision makers. But must other kinds of ideas be set up as alternatives? It does not seem to matter greatly whether the Treasury view is described as a form of practical knowledge based on the informed opinion of a group of senior civil servants, or even as a sophisticated form of economic folklore. In all cases, once introduced into the public realm, the ideas warrant description as claims to economic knowledge—to a knowledge, that is, of how economic variables are related and how accepted goals can best be achieved by economic means. One of the functions of professional knowledge is not to trump some practitioner's ace but to force articulation, to bring hidden assumptions into the light—as Keynes patently did in confronting the Treasury view in newspaper articles, books, and public testimony.[93] The process also works in reverse: As economists have made claims to guide policy, so they have been forced to provide practicable solutions, engaging with people whose chief responsibility lies in implementation rather than conceptualization.

Many of the historical studies cited in this chapter have registered doubts as to the feasibility or even validity of establishing causal links between theory and practice, ideas and action.[94] But in seeking an alternative to mechanical and monocausal analyses and conclusions, observers need not limit their scope to opaquely holistic notions of zeitgeist or to pure pragmatism, on the one hand, or circumstantial determinism, on the other. Nor do they need to employ functionalist interpretations of ideology that leave little scope for the free-spirited advocacy of change based on new knowledge of how society actually works or ought to work. Ideas do not have to be treated instrumentally. Ideas, theories, and professed principles are the only way people can confer meaning on action; they can be fruitfully yet straightforwardly treated as the reasons that make best sense of our actions and recommendations for action by others.[95] In

---

[93]This has been established most conclusively by Peter Clarke's reconstruction of the history of the private and public debate surrounding Keynes's evolving position; see P. Clarke, *The Keynesian Revolution in the Making, 1924–1936* (Oxford: Clarendon Press, 1988).

[94]See especially Alan Ryan's opening paragraphs in "Utilitarianism and Bureaucracy: The Views of J. S. Mill," in Sutherland, ed., *Growth of Nineteenth-Century Government*, 33–62.

[95]The scholar who has done most to establish this position in recent years is Quentin Skinner; see, for example, "Some Problems in the Analysis of Political Thought and Action," *Political Theory* 2 (1974): 277–303; and "The Principles and Practice of Opposi-

societies that regularly require reasons to be given for public actions; in societies that have inherited a rich vocabulary of principles that can be invoked when discussing public affairs; in societies that possess elaborate forums and procedures for examining the adequacy of the reasons supplied by public actors, the history of ideas in relation to practice requires no special commitment or prior act of faith. It becomes no more (or less) than an extension of the rules of everyday conduct to the study of past beliefs, actions, and debates. Differences of opinion between historians are not, therefore, about whether ideas have played a large or negligible role in history, but about what kinds of ideas—elaborate, conventional, explicit, or otherwise—have to be invoked to make sense of which past actions.

There is more scope than has so far been exploited, especially by those who write the history of economic thinking in relation to policy, for applying such insights to the problems considered here. Their implications are sufficiently clear, however, to provide additional support for those who prefer the "clarifactory" model to the "sociotechnic" model of the deployment of social scientific knowledge by governments.[96] The latter is strongly wedded to the search for policy solutions to whatever problems arise in the everyday conduct of public affairs, and it depends for its effectiveness on a degree of both professional and political consensus that may be decidedly fragile and fickle, leading to overreaction when the error of overselling the technocratic approach becomes apparent. The clarifactory model derives its priorities more from the internal imperatives of social scientific investigation, and it places more emphasis on explanation than immediate prescription. It is less prone to politicization in the form of overidentification with the fortunes of this or that party program, and its effect on policy, if any, is more indirect and long term.

In Britain today, however, the delicate balance among universities as

tion: The Case of Bolingbroke Versus Walpole," in N. McKendrick, ed., *Historical Perspectives: Studies in English Thought and Society* (London: Europa, 1974), 93–128. See also G. Wood, "Intellectual History and the Social Sciences," in J. Higham and P. K. Conkin, eds., *New Directions in American Intellectual History* (Baltimore: Johns Hopkins University Press, 1979), 27–41.

[96] This distinction is employed, alongside others, by P. Abrams in his chapter "The Uses of British Sociology, 1831–1931," in M. Bulmer, ed., *Essays on the History of British Sociological Research* (Cambridge, Eng.: Cambridge University Press, 1985), 181–205; the distinction also underlies Abrams's earlier work *Practice and Progress: British Sociology 1950–1980* (London: Allen and Unwin, 1981). See also M. Bulmer, *The Uses of Social Research: Social Investigation in Public Policy-Making* (London: Allen and Unwin, 1982); and P. Thomas, "The Use of Social Research: Myths and Models," in Bulmer, ed., *Social Science Research and Government*, 51–60.

self-governing public institutions, as respondents to market incentives, and as direct emanations of the state is being altered in ways the outcome of which is currently difficult to predict. Under these circumstances, the clarifactory model is running into difficulties. It requires, for example, a degree of intellectual confidence and public esteem that is hard to sustain, particularly when the nonvocational aspects of the publicly supported system are under suspicion, and private sources of finance are difficult to find or move in harmony with the priorities set by government. Here again, American pluralism may be more genuinely pluralistic, less subject to synchronized swings of attention.

Finally, although it is easy to mock the naiveté of earlier visions of a social scientific utopia, the idea of a progressive march of mind led by well-meaning professional groups working in the national interest, skepticism should not lead to nihilism—a temptation to which a post-Vietnam generation, and one that takes a more cynical view of the self-seeking qualities of all organized groups, is perhaps particularly prone. Claims to knowledge, especially those that conflate goodness with truth and imply a privileged role for an intellectual class, always deserve to be treated with caution. But, as the example of Keynes shows, science does not have to mean scientism. And even the ordinary, nonpositivist meaning of science as organized knowledge, subject to public debate and criticism, contains an inescapable esoteric element: Science entails, at a minimum, notions of novices, initiates, and bearers who are inevitably separated from the general public in the early stages of dissemination. Whether economic knowledge at any given time is firm enough to be treated as the independent variable in the relationship with the state, whether it is generated in some sphere enjoying relative autonomy or in response to political signposting, covert or explicit, its cultivators cannot abandon responsibility for it as a form of knowledge without forsaking claims to have any special contribution to make to public debate.

Part II

The state and economic performance

3

Liberty by design: freedom, planning, and John Quincy Adams's American System

JOHN LAURITZ LARSON

Historically, the relationship between the American national state and systems of economic thought has been paradoxical. The United States stands today as the largest modern state without an explicit industrial policy or a central ministry of economic management. Since the middle of the nineteenth century, it has been the rhetorical champion of laissez-faire and a more or less consistent enemy of national economic planning. Yet the United States was created by self-conscious designers working with the most sophisticated models of political economy and moral philosophy known to the eighteenth century. Their republican principles imposed on the general government a responsibility for the welfare and happiness of the *whole* people, but these same principles also guaranteed liberties that stubbornly resisted that government in its pursuit of national objectives.

For the first fifty years of national existence, and again in the most recent half century, the American national government has acted in various ways to protect and promote the interests of the whole people; individual states have played a more sustained if sometimes less effective role. But for the century between the administrations of Andrew Jackson and Franklin Delano Roosevelt, the national government and the national culture sustained a rough-and-tumble capitalist system that denied the sovereign government practically any authority to infringe on the rights of property. Admittedly, policies were never truly laissez-faire, and gov-

This research was funded in part by a grant from the Indiana Committee for the Humanities. For critical advice and commentary, I am indebted to Robert Cuff, Mary O. Furner, L. Ray Gunn, Hugh Heclo, Michael A. Morrison, and Barry Supple.

73

ernment at all levels frequently wrestled with matters of general welfare; but rhetoric and values usually returned to the classical liberal position. Even in the declining years of the Keynesian age, Americans who utterly depend on the management of a welfare economy have embraced Ronald Reagan's neoclassical Gilded Age rhetoric as the pure milk of the founders' intent. Enjoying liberty and riches because of structures and policies that owe much to economic knowledge, most Americans cherish values that admit no legitimate role for the state in planning or design.

The source of this irony lies in the unique connection between systematic knowledge and liberty embodied in the founding of the American Republic and in the policy struggles that dominated its first fifty years. Revolution did not happen accidentally, and the American Revolution offers one of the most extraordinary examples of self-conscious revolutionaries striving to erect a new society according to principles of design. The relationship between purpose and action has been scrutinized in countless studies of the intellectual and ideological origins of the American Revolution, and the demise of authority has been demonstrated in equally numerous histories of democratization and the triumph of Andrew Jackson. The change itself is usually portrayed as either the triumph of democracy or the corruption of republicanism, depending on which face of the Revolution one prefers. The purpose of this chapter is to explore the connection between liberty by design and the rise of democratic politics and laissez-faire.[1]

The confrontation between these two elements of America's Revolutionary culture came sharply into focus in 1825, in the first annual message to Congress of President John Quincy Adams.[2] This incredible document, with its tragic plea for energetic leadership, national development, and

[1] On the revolutionary tradition, see Bernard Bailyn, *The Ideological Origins of the American Revolution* (Cambridge, Mass.: Harvard University Press, 1967); Gordon S. Wood, *The Creation of the American Republic, 1776–1787* (Chapel Hill: University of North Carolina Press, 1969); J. G. A. Pocock, *The Machiavellian Moment: Florentine Political Thought and the Atlantic Revolutionary Tradition* (Princeton, N.J.: Princeton University Press, 1975); and Forrest McDonald, *Novus Ordo Seclorum: The Intellectual Origins of the Constitution* (Lawrence: University of Kansas Press, 1985). On Jacksonian democracy, see Arthur M. Schlesinger, Jr., *The Age of Jackson* (Boston: Little, Brown and Company, 1945); Robert V. Remini, *Andrew Jackson and the Course of American Freedom, 1822–1832* (New York: Harper & Row, 1981); Richard P. McCormick, *The Presidential Game; Origins of American Presidential Politics* (New York: Oxford University Press, 1982); and Edward Pessen, *Jacksonian America: Society, Personality, and Politics*, rev. ed. (Homewood, Ill.: Dorsey Press, 1978).

[2] John Quincy Adams, "First Annual Message," in James D. Richardson, ed., *A Compilation of the Messages and Papers of the Presidents* (New York: Bureau of National Literature, 1897), II, 865–77.

high moral purpose, marked the culmination of the founders' efforts to impose design on the new Republic. It immediately served as well as the instrument of its author's political destruction and hastened the acceptance of freewheeling competition in politics and enterprise. Adams's message reflected the concern for design and good order that had guided the framers' work and attracted men of property and standing to the 1787 Constitution. He condensed and magnified their sense of purpose and control, until the authority inherent in design could be sustained no longer. Confronted with the barefaced claim that "liberty is power,"[3] Americans recoiled—but not instinctively, as historians have long believed. Opposition to Adams's sentiments, many of them echoes of Washington, John Adams, Jefferson, Madison, and Monroe, matured gradually and strategically as the majority of people, aided by Adams's political enemies, realized that his design contradicted their new understanding of liberty.

The ultimate failure of Adams's vision was the failure of all unified design in a time and country especially congenial to expansive personal liberty. The promise of the American Revolution released unimaginable popular energies in a rich field of resources. One by one, all familiar sources of authority collapsed in the early Republic. Good order and improvement, concepts from a world of scarcity and limits, no longer were required for individual success in the new United States. The very assumption of human corruption—a central premise alike of traditional religion and enlightened moral philosophy—faltered. Thinking about natural rights slipped into romantic assumptions that human nature was good. Republicanism evolved from a system designed to improve *and then* empower virtuous citizens into a system that empowered a populace already innately virtuous. These tendencies, unleashed by the Revolution itself, were precisely the forces supposed to be checked by the founders' designs; but by John Quincy Adams's day, liberation had changed irrevocably—and by the time of the Jackson administration, which followed, it was success in the market, not the elegance of systematic logic, that rendered true things true. Thus began a divergence between science or philosophy and democratic thought that was often taken by observers to be the hallmark of American culture.[4]

[3]Ibid., II, 882.
[4]The classic discussion is in Alexis de Tocqueville, *Democracy in America*, ed. J. P. Mayer (Garden City, N.Y.: Anchor Books, 1969), II, Part I, 429–65. See also James Willard Hurst, *Law and Markets in United States History: Different Modes of Bargaining among Interests* (Madison: University of Wisconsin Press, 1982).

ADAMS'S MESSAGE

On Tuesday, December 6, 1825, John Adams, Jr., son and private secretary of President John Quincy Adams, read his father's first annual message to Congress. The event was conventional yet heavy with anticipation, for the elder Adams knew that his claim to the presidency seemed uniquely illegitimate. Elected in 1824 by the House of Representatives, in an electoral process almost nobody respected, over Andrew Jackson who had more so-called popular votes, Adams had accepted the office with a painful acknowledgment of his questionable mandate, but at the same time felt he had a mission. "I may not be destined to send another message," he told his worried cabinet, and, as the duly elected president, he felt an "indispensable duty" to express his ideas. At stake, he believed, was the success of the American experiment in government.[5]

In this annual message the president invoked guidance from the "Disposer of all Good" (Adams's ultimate source of knowledge) and then reviewed with satisfaction the state of the Union. The cause of South American independence was progressing. The treasury at home was flourishing. The Board of Engineers for Internal Improvement, created by Congress one year previously under the 1824 General Survey Act, was energetically exploring routes for roads and canals all across the land. The national government kept busy fulfilling the demands of Congress for all kinds of public works aimed at improving the country through economic development. Much work remained to be done, but Adams thought the course and proper means of development were beginning to become clear.[6]

This flurry of activity in the realm of internal improvement inspired the president to recommend "the general principle in a more enlarged extent":

The great object of the institution of civil government is the improvement of the condition of those who are parties to the social compact. . . . Moral, political, intellectual improvement are duties assigned by the Author of Our Existence to social no less than to individual man. For the fulfillment of those duties governments are invested with power, and to the attainment of the end—the progressive improvement of the condition of the governed—the exercise of delegated powers is a duty as sacred and indispensable as the usurpation of powers not granted is criminal and odious.[7]

[5]John Quincy Adams, *Memoirs,* ed. Charles Francis Adams (Philadelphia: J. B. Lippincott, 1874–77), VII, 63. See McCormick, *Presidential Game,* 117–26.
[6]Adams, "First Annual Message," II, 865–77.
[7]Ibid., II, 877.

Employing both the style and the vocabulary of eighteenth-century moral philosophers such as John Locke, David Hume, Adam Smith, and Thomas Reid (all of whom he studied as a youth), Adams thus opened his message to Congress with a short lecture on the nature of the Republic and its mission on earth. Carefully distinguishing the exercise of "delegated powers" from the usurpation of those "not granted," the president emphasized the obligation of republican governors to lead just as surely as they must not oppress their people.[8]

In theory, republics depended on the virtue of their citizens. Steeped as they were in Protestant religion or faculty psychology—or both—many leaders of the American Revolution had worried that their fellow Americans might not inherently possess sufficient virtue to sustain the Republic. Still, most of these republican enthusiasts at least hoped that liberty would foster improvement, that citizens would cultivate their "higher faculties" once they enjoyed the freedom and encouragement to do so.[9] This was the first assumption on which Adams erected his grand design. The first instrument of improvement was knowledge, and to the acquisition of knowledge "public institutions and seminaries of learning" were essential. So convinced of this was President Washington, Adams continued, that he had often recommended to Congress the creation of a national university; but that "spot of earth which he had destined and bequeathed" for the university remained "still bare and barren."[10]

Shielded by the name of Washington, Adams proceeded with a stinging critique of a nation that he thought partook of the common stock of human knowledge but did not labor to contribute its share. For the voyages of discovery that gave birth to America, the nation owed "a sacred debt." Great Britain and France spared no expense in patronizing research into weights and measures, latitude and longitude, and astronomical observation. For example, "with no feeling of pride as an American," Adams counted in Europe "upward of 130 of these light-houses of

[8]See Drew R. McCoy, *The Elusive Republic: Political Economy in Jeffersonian America* (Chapel Hill: University of North Carolina Press, 1980), 13–104.

[9]See Daniel Walker Howe, "The Political Psychology of *The Federalist*," *William and Mary Quarterly*, 3d ser., 44 (July 1987), 485–509; and Roger H. Brown, " 'May We Hope for a Reformation of Manners': The Founding Fathers and the Improvability of Man" (Paper delivered at the Society for Historians of the Early American Republic Conference, Worcester, Mass., July 22, 1988) (thanks to Professor Brown for permission to use his unpublished work). For different views, see Joyce Oldham Appleby, *Capitalism and a New Social Order: The Republican Vision of the 1790s* (New York: New York University Press, 1984), and John R. Nelson, Jr., *Liberty and Property: Political Economy and Policymaking in the New Nation, 1789–1812* (Baltimore: Johns Hopkins University Press, 1987).

[10]Adams, "First Annual Message," II, 879–80.

the skies, while throughout the whole American hemisphere" there was "not one." If knowledge laid the footing for moral, political, and economic progress, Americans were not constructing foundations. Supposedly corrupt and decaying, the Old World surged ahead; but America had "neither observatory nor observer upon our half of the globe," and the earth revolved "in perpetual darkness to our unsearching eyes."[11]

Astronomy was just an example of what worried the president. His countrymen's lack of scientific interest reflected a preoccupation with selfish gain, private ambition, and jealous individualism, qualities their fathers had associated with corruption and dissipation. People might object that patronizing science and exploration was unconstitutional, but Adams could not believe that his father's generation intended to prohibit such responsibilities of sovereignty in cases where local and private authorities had failed. In fact, Adams reasoned, if the powers enumerated in the Constitution *might* effect internal improvements, then to "refrain from exercising them for the benefit of the people themselves would be to hide in the earth the talent committed to our charge—would be treachery to the most sacred of trusts."[12]

Having explained that Americans' exceptional freedom did not exempt them from their duty to humankind (or to God), Adams closed with a soaring peroration that pressed his argument and his rhetoric to a splendid consummation:

The spirit of improvement is abroad upon the earth. It stimulates the hearts and sharpens the faculties not of our fellow-citizens alone, but of the nations of Europe and of their rulers. While dwelling with pleasing satisfaction upon the superior excellence of our political institutions, let us not be unmindful that *liberty is power* [emphasis added]; that the nation blessed with the largest portion of liberty must in proportion to its numbers be the most powerful nation upon the earth, and that the tenure of power by man is, in the moral purposes of his Creator, upon the condition that it shall be exercised to ends of beneficence, to improve the condition of himself and his fellow-men. While foreign nations less blessed with that freedom which is power . . . are advancing with gigantic strides in the career of public improvement, were we to slumber in indolence or fold up our arms and proclaim to the world that we are palsied by the will of our constituents, would it not be to cast away the bounties of Providence and doom ourselves to perpetual inferiority?[13]

Here is a picture of liberty rich with the cautions of the founding elites, rooted in Protestant theology, the classics, Locke, and Smith. Perhaps

[11]Ibid.
[12]Ibid., II, 882.
[13]Ibid.

because of his enduring faith in the presence of God and the final judgment, Adams (like Locke) connected liberty with obligations to the Creator. All freedoms were contingent, and all people would be required to account for their use of such gifts. The close connection in Adams's mind between human improvement and economic development emerged in his final illustrations of the "spirit of improvement": the opening of Jefferson's University of Virginia and the completion of New York's Erie Canal. Each represented a single state's accomplishment of objectives Washington once had placed on the national agenda. Advocates of states' rights often cited these examples as proof that the federal government should not engage in such activities, but Adams drew just the opposite conclusion. If such achievements could be won "by the authority of single members of our Confederation, can we, the representative authorities of the whole Union, fall behind our fellow-servants" in pursuit of "works important to the whole and to which neither the authority nor the resources of any one State can be adequate?"[14]

Since the critical period of the Confederation Congress, broad-minded individuals had admitted that competing local interests produced jealousy and pettiness that easily perverted the decisions of lawmakers. "Disinterested" statesmen or the multiplicity of interests might transcend such passions, but only if the Union's sovereignty at least matched the power of the states (Madison's point in *Federalist*, no. 10). Consciously referring to the separate spheres that made dual sovereignty comprehensible at all, Adams challenged his listeners in the Nineteenth Congress to perform for the *whole* people the sovereign function that these two model states had performed for their particular inhabitants.[15]

ADAMS'S MEANING

What was Adams trying to say as his first year in office closed? First, he was arguing that the American national government had real work to do. Despite more than three decades' experience under the new Constitution,

[14]Ibid. See also John Quincy Adams to George Washington Adams, September 11, 1811, in Adrienne Koch and William Peden, eds., *Selected Writings of John Adams and John Quincy Adams* (New York: Alfred A. Knopf, 1946), 279.
[15]See Wood, *Creation*, 391–468; also Wood, "Interests and Disinterestedness in the Making of the Constitution," in Richard Beeman, Stephen Botein, and Edward C. Carter II, eds., *Beyond Confederation: Origins of the Constitution and American National Identity* (Chapel Hill: University of North Carolina Press, 1987), 69–109; and Robert H. Wiebe, *The Opening of the American Society from the Adoption of the Constitution to the Eve of Disunion* (New York: Random House, 1984), 7–109.

the issue of federal power still generated heated debate. As foreign threats subsided, Americans who had accepted the Union only to protect the states from annihilation sought an ever-declining role for what they called the "general government." Others envisaged a sharp functional distinction between "domestic" government within the states and "foreign" (interstate and international) affairs.

Adams rejected such narrow views, claiming instead that within its proper sphere as the whole people's government, federal sovereignty was intended by the framers to be competent and complete. Desperate to pacify localists and preserve the Union, he believed, early presidents usually had limited their reach to matters of national defense, the public credit, and foreign affairs. Changing conditions now required energetic leadership to design and construct interstate roads and canals, to establish national standards of weights and measures, to encourage inventors through patent protection, to support universities and scientific institutions, and to patronize explorations of the national domain. So much work stood ready to be done that Adams thought a home department, first suggested by Madison in 1817, desperately was needed to direct these undertakings efficiently.[16]

Second, Adams wished to recover the legitimate use of power within a republican frame of government. The genius of republicanism lay in its potential for circumscribing power within a government that depended for its authority on the frequent suffrages of a free people. Republicanism did not mean powerless government. Almost nobody in the founders' generation had wished to see anarchy, simple democracy, or radical individual autonomy—even Painite artisans respected a commonwealth tradition. Constitutions written at both the state and federal levels almost always sought to balance liberty with power.[17] The classical critique, recycled by English "Real Whig" radicals such as John Trenchard and Thomas Gordon, that power was the mortal enemy of liberty, had helped Americans destroy the legitimacy of Britain's imperial government. After independence, however, local and federal officials sought protection from these potent solvents of authority by claiming the inherent legitimacy of republi-

---

[16]John Quincy Adams to Christopher Hughes, June 22, 1818, in *Writings of John Quincy Adams*, ed. Worthington Chauncy Ford (New York: Macmillan Company, 1913–17), VI, 354.
[17]See Wood, *Creation*, 125–256, and Patrick T. Conley and John P. Kaminski, eds., *The Constitution and the States* (Madison, Wis.: Madison House, 1988); on artisans, see Sean Wilentz, *Chants Democratic: New York City and the Rise of the American Working Class, 1788–1850* (New York: Oxford University Press, 1984), 61–106.

can forms of government. Washington's 1797 "Farewell Address" begged for political quiescence, but it never came. The Whig attack crept back into practical politics whenever men who opposed an administration felt compelled to condemn it as corrupt. Jefferson did as much to Alexander Hamilton and John Adams; New England Federalists and other state particularists crippled Jefferson and Madison in turn. Repeated assaults on federal power, whether cynical or sincere, gradually undermined the legitimacy of power itself. Eventually, postwar nationalists such as Henry Clay, John C. Calhoun, and John Quincy Adams encountered what seemed to them absurd: a federal government unable to do great works for the people because some politicians insisted it had no authority to act.[18]

It was partly to answer the frustration of thirty years in public service that Adams now pronounced his views on the power of the national government. Power was not inherently corrupt, he argued, but it could be corrupted by false purposes, like the disunionist plots that once drove him from the old Federalist party. Similarly, liberty was not exclusively virtuous: If it resulted in nothing more than the immediate gratification of base passions, then it was surely as corrupt as the indulgence of voluptuous aristocrats. Liberty *is* power! Adams's phrase was an equation deduced from logical steps similar to those by which Jefferson originally explained independence: (1) All men were created free and equal; (2) they were endowed by their Creator with certain inalienable rights; and (3) to secure these rights, governments were instituted, deriving their just powers from the consent of the governed. If Adams placed greater emphasis on the duties of republican citizens, he differed in degree, not in kind, from Jefferson's position. Governments instituted merely to protect private ambitions or to frustrate the exercise of human ingenuity failed to serve their greatest purpose. Adams's term "improvement" implied an upward moral trajectory; so did Jefferson's "happiness." Nobody wanted liberty that did not promise betterment. For Adams, the founders' gift of freedom belonged not to selfish individuals who sharpened their wits in trade and competition, but to those who pushed the architecture of human achievement ever higher, that the edifice might better shelter all who dwelled within.[19]

[18]George Washington, "Farewell Address," in Richardson, eds., *Messages*, I, 207–12. On the fragmentation of federal authority, see James Sterling Young, *The Washington Community* (New York: Harcourt, Brace and World, 1966); Wiebe, *Opening*, 110–209; and J. C. A. Stagg, *Mr. Madison's War* (Princeton, N.J.: Princeton University Press, 1983).

[19]See George A. Lipsky, *John Quincy Adams: His Theory and Ideas* (New York: Thomas Y. Crowell, 1950), 69–77, 150–66.

Adams also was saying that improvement was the highest object that legitimized the exercise of power. Freedom ultimately derived from a jealous God who judged the merit of a life by the amount it had improved. Liberty did not license the ignorant and slothful to wallow in their leisure; it enjoined them to excel. To an 1809 Harvard class, Adams spoke of "the moral obligation, which a liberal education imposes upon those, to whom it is given; . . . a deposit, of which the fruits belong not exclusively to yourselves, but in common to your fellow-citizens and your fellow-men."[20] In 1822, he wrote to a friend: "Our improvements of physical nature seem to realize the enchantments of a fairy tale." Could it be that "moral existence" was "advancing with equally gigantic strides"? Adams knew that moral improvement probably trailed material improvement, but he took great comfort in the belief that the "first *duty* of a nation" was "bettering its own condition by internal improvement," and that somehow the individual liberty that made material advancement possible must soon affect morals, too.[21]

The physical improvement of which Adams spoke could be found by the 1820s in steam power, mechanization, and, most dramatically, the conquest of time and space through innovations in transportation. Much progress in these areas originated in the field, from the practical inventions of self-taught entrepreneurs, but Adams recognized the parallel rise of scientific inquiry and technical education, which alone could regularize innovation, rendering it cumulative and reproducible. Similarly, he accepted what Adam Smith called the "third and last duty of the sovereign or commonwealth," that is, "erecting and maintaining those public institutions and those public works" that are "advantageous to a great society" but are too costly to "repay the expense" to one or a few investors.[22] Especially in a new country (Smith's term was "barbarous"), government must intervene to encourage formation of capital and provide essential facilities. Following Smith's formulation almost exactly, Adams stressed education and public works, coupling in his closing illustration for Congress the Erie Canal and the University of Virginia.

[20]John Quincy Adams, *Lectures on Rhetoric and Oratory* (1810; repr., New York: Russell & Russell, 1962), II, 399.
[21]John Quincy Adams to James Lloyd, October 1, 1822, in *Writings*, VII, 311–12.
[22]Adam Smith, *An Inquiry into the Nature and Causes of the Wealth of Nations,* ed. Edwin Cannan (New York: Modern Library, 1937), 681. See also Brooke Hindle and Steven Lubar, *Engines of Change: The American Industrial Revolution, 1790–1860* (Washington, D.C.: Smithsonian Institution Press, 1986), 9–58, 74–93, 109–124; and A. Hunter Dupree, *Science in the Federal Government* (Cambridge, Mass.: Harvard University Press, 1957), 1–90.

Finally, Adams claimed that his vision was little different from the programs of Monroe, Madison, Albert Gallatin, and Jefferson, all reflecting at bottom a common commitment to the "federalism of Washington, Union, and Internal Improvement." These had been the "three hinges" on which Adams's own political life had turned, and, he thought, they provided to the American experiment a thread of continuity that survived the corruption of partisan intrigue.[23]

Adams's view that these men shared important common ground was unusual, but not so preposterous as his enemies insisted. The areas of congruence were genuinely large: republican structures, moral and material improvement, the importance of the Union as a check on disintegrative forces, and the obligations of government to promote the general welfare. Except for Monroe, who advocated almost nothing, each of Adams's predecessors had favored many of his objectives, even if they spoke differently once out of office. Arguments about the relative powers of state and national governments obscured their common interests. But constitutional bickering was used so strategically by all Adams's contemporaries that it indicated very imperfectly their theories about government.[24] At bottom, Adams's reasons for seeking energy in government, although clearer and more forceful, were not fundamentally different from the reasons offered by every previous chief executive faced with national disintegration.

It was Adams's compulsion to reach the logical limits of his theories, instead of seeking the blurry middle ground of "practical" politics, that made him an easy mark for less philosophical politicians. But for Adams, blurring for practical advantage was the real problem. He pressed, not his own peculiar design for American liberty, but a design that originated in the sacred founding of the nation and had been articulated and adapted by each succeeding administration in legitimate succession. Ambivalence and popular accommodation yielded drift and reinterpretation, a process exaggerated by excessively partisan rhetoric and the popular game of faction. By claiming to follow the original republicanism of Washington *and* Jefferson, Adams tried to cut through partisan rhetoric that had

[23]Samuel Flagg Bemis, *John Quincy Adams and the Union* (1956; repr., Westport, Conn.: Greenwood Press, 1965), 64; see also Ralph Ketcham, *Presidents above Party: The First American Presidency, 1789–1829* (Chapel Hill: University of North Carolina Press, 1984).

[24]For a detailed illustration, see John Lauritz Larson, "A Bridge, a Dam, a River: Liberty and Innovation in the Early Republic," *Journal of the Early Republic* 7 (Winter 1987): 351–75.

divided those two presidents and to reestablish continuity in American history. Given his keen sense of the workings of an active God, he may have seen his extraordinary election as a prophetic opportunity.

INHERITING THE REVOLUTION

Blessed with the overwhelming force of hindsight, historians have almost universally rejected Adams's claim to the Jeffersonian lineage. "It was really a reversion to Federalism," wrote Samuel Flagg Bemis in 1956, in what has stood for thirty years as the most authentic portrait of this difficult man. Bemis could account for the urgency with which Adams made his case only by reference to his insular and towering ego: "John Quincy Adams seemed to think that this whole program, little of which was popular with the people, hung on the thread of his own life!"[25] Mary Hargreave's 1985 account of Adams's presidency repeated the asssertion that "he had not, in renouncing his Federalist antecedents, rejected that party's governmental philosophies," which may be true but is misleading.[26] In 1977, Clyde N. Wilson, introducing a volume of Calhoun's papers, gave full force to the standard line: "Adams's assumption, or presumption, that he was the legitimate heir to the Jeffersonian Republicans (an assumption often adopted tacitly if not consciously by historians) was simply not correct." As if the lid would not stay down, Wilson insisted that "Adams's style, program, and rise to power raised the 'fear of constitutional degeneration' with which Americans were deeply imbued."[27]

Beneath this assessment of Adams and his presidency lies a tendency to believe that the Federalists were what their Jeffersonian enemies said, namely, counterrevolutionaries and monarchists, whereas the Jeffersonians were what they claimed to be, that is, "true republicans." But for twenty years now, historians of the revolutionary period have more or less agreed that the federalists who made the Constitution remained thoroughgoing republicans, and that there was no fixed correlation between the

---

[25]Bemis, *Adams and the Union*, 68.

[26]Mary W. M. Hargreaves, *The Presidency of John Quincy Adams* (Lawrence: University of Kansas Press, 1985), 29.

[27]*The Papers of John C. Calhoun*, ed. Robert L. Meriwether, W. Edwin Hamphill, and Clyde N. Wilson (Columbia, S.C.: 1959–85), X, xvi. See also Paul Nagel, *Descent from Glory: Four Generations of the John Adams Family* (New York: Oxford University Press, 1983), 144–5; and Marie B. Hecht, *John Quincy Adams: A Personal History of an Independent Man* (New York: Macmillan Company, 1972), 425–7.

ratification parties of Federalists and Antifederalists and the later parties of Hamilton and Jefferson. "Constitutional degeneration" haunted everybody in this critical transitional period. Each practical adaptation of theories or structures imperiled the delicate balance between nature and design that gave revolutionary Americans any hope for success. Yet rapidly changing conditions required constant innovations from a people who had never completely agreed on constitutional principles or their underlying philosophical tenets. Hamilton disappointed Madison with his distortions of their collaborative arguments in *The Federalist*. Jefferson frequently adapted his reading of the republican experiment, from the libertarian "Spirit of '98" to the authoritarian Embargo of 1807–8, and back again. Adams, who had opposed Virginia's "faction" in the 1790s, reversed himself over the embargo, when Jefferson stood for the national interest and "factious" New England screamed. In this swirling ideological environment, Adams's interpretations were no less legitimate (and often more consistent) than those of his contemporaries. In light of the many new studies of ideological conflict, drift, and change in the republicanism of the founders and their immediate successors, it seems appropriate to examine Adams's claim to be a republican anew.[28]

No single thread better united Adams's amazing life experiences, from his boyhood trip to Europe in 1778 to his inauguration as president in 1825, than his participation in the continuing struggle of disciplined, rational minds against the passions and intrigues of politics. Demagoguery, he believed, posed the greatest threat to America's republican experiment, and Adams's first publication in 1791 leveled just such a charge at Tom Paine. Embarrassed by Jefferson's endorsement of Paine's latest radical tract, *The Rights of Man*, Adams denounced the pamphlet as "historical, political, miscellaneous, satirical, and panegyrical," but not logical. Paine's majoritarian views ignored the "eternal and immutable laws of

---

[28]In addition to works already cited, see John F. Hoadley, *Origins of American Political Parties, 1789–1803* (Lexington: University of Kentucky, 1986); Richard Buel, Jr., *Securing the Revolution: Ideology in American Politics, 1789–1815* (Ithaca, N.Y.: Cornell University Press, 1972); Lance Banning, "Jeffersonian Ideology Revisited: Liberal and Classical Ideas in the New American Republic," *William and Mary Quarterly*, 3d ser., 43 (January 1986): 3–19; John M. Murrin, "The Great Inversion, or Court Versus Country: A Comparison of the Revolution Settlements in England (1688–1721) and America (1776–1816)," in J. G. A. Pocock, ed., *Three British Revolutions: 1641, 1688, 1776* (Princeton, N.J.: Princeton University Press, 1980), 368–453; Andrew R. L. Cayton, *Frontier Republic: Ideology and Politics in the Ohio Country, 1780–1825* (Kent, Ohio: Kent State University Press, 1986); and Peter S. Onuf, *Statehood and Union: Jurisdictional Controversies in the United States, 1775–1787* (Philadelphia: University of Pennsylvania Press, 1983).

justice and of morality" and made liberty the "sport" of tyranny in the "party-colored garments of democracy."[29]

Here was the start of a quarrel with Jefferson that later would help destroy Adams's claim to Republican views. Denounced as a monarchist and apologist for his father, the vice-president, Adams was marked as an enemy of what Jefferson then called popular government. But Adams's argument, if less radical than Jefferson's, nevertheless stood well within the Revolution's enlightened intellectual tradition. Time and again, Adams wrote or spoke of a "common property" or a "treasure of public liberty" that resulted when free individuals joined themselves within the social compact.[30] A social duty originating in the natural "union of the sexes" that underlay all society, obligated individuals to use their "rational faculties in the service of the Lord, to release the energy stored in nature, and to raise all men above the level of want."[31] Adams believed the 1787 Constitution marked the advent of a new era of perfection in human government. Reason and the "incomparable energies of the human intellect" promised to reveal truth, and the new frame of government ought to encourage discipline and improvement, lifting mankind above "brute creation." For Adams, mere liberation of the unreformed masses promised the worst excesses of democracy or mobocracy, a perversion of the gift of liberty. This fear of freedom without discipline separated him from Jefferson in the 1790s and from Jackson Democrats after 1824, giving credence to charges of monarchism; but once it had united republican nationalists such as Jefferson, Madison, and the elder Adams against antifederalists in the states.[32]

Adams based his hopes for the Republic on his truly startling faith in the "improvement of the physical, moral, and intellectual condition of man upon earth," and here his harmony with Jefferson was obvious. In his 1821 rhapsody on the French metric system, he claimed for weights and measures the power to advance "the object of a Savior's mission" and produce a "foretaste here of man's eternal felicity."[33] It is little won-

[29] John Quincy Adams, "Letters of Publicola," in Koch and Peden, Selected Writings, 228–30.

[30] John Quincy Adams, "Columbus," in ibid., 238.

[31] John Quincy Adams, Report of the Secretary of State upon Weights and Measures (1821; repr., New York: Arno Press, 1980), 9; JQA to Charles W. Upham, February 2, 1837, quoted in Lipsky, JQA: His Theory and Ideas, 77.

[32] Quoted in Lipsky, JQA: His Theory and Ideas, 69, 150. For a new view of discipline, see Paul A. Gilje, The Road to Mobocracy (Chapel Hill: University of North Carolina Press, 1988).

[33] Adams, Weights and Measures, 90, 48. I am indebted to A. Hunter Dupree for important advice on Adams's understanding of measurement.

der, then, that Adams placed enormous stock in education and works of public improvement: The rising glory of the United States and the salvation of humankind depended on it. President Washington had cherished similar (if less apocalyptic) hopes for internal improvement, especially of the Potomac route to the West. In the 1780s, Jefferson ardently supported Washington's scheme to get the states of Maryland and Virginia to charter a Potomac Canal Company in which the "monied gentry" (Washington's phrase) would invest their capital for their own and the nation's benefit. In those critical early days of the Republic, all efforts calculated to bind the Republic together received the warmest approbation of constitutional nationalists like Jefferson, Madison, and Hamilton. The memory of that unity was the bedrock of Adams's triad of "Washington, Union, and Internal Improvement."[34]

Although Jefferson harbored great fears that public works might be the instruments of legislative corruption or executive influence, after 1800 he developed enough confidence in his own "purified" administration to inaugurate the Cumberland Road. By 1805, when domestic peace and profits from Europe's wars handed Jefferson a treasury surplus, he called for a "repartition" of money among the states, to support the improvement of "rivers, canals, roads, arts, manufactures, education, and other great objects within each state." Characteristically, Jefferson preferred to direct resources into state hands rather than inflate the operations of the general government, but this did not mean he surrendered all pretense to design, guidance, or control. During the location of the Cumberland Road, for instance, he insisted that his national project should not be diverted to satisfy the swarms of local interests. A constitutional amendment, Jefferson thought, might clarify federal authority to build roads and canals and thereby minimize the dangers of reliance on implied powers. But nowhere did Jefferson indicate a fear of improvements themselves or the integrative forces they might generate in national life.[35]

In 1806, in response to Jefferson's encouragement for works of improvement, the advocates of several projects pressed Congress for grants of financial aid. Immediately, the specter of pork barrel politics emerged, and it was to prevent such a corruption of the president's desires that then-Senator Adams introduced a resolution calling for a plan for a na-

---

[34]John Lauritz Larson, " 'Bind the Republic Together': The National Union and the Struggle for a System of Internal Improvements," *Journal of American History* 74 (September 1987): 371–2.

[35]Ibid., 371–87; see also Joseph H. Harrison, Jr., "*Sic et Non:* Thomas Jefferson and Internal Improvements," *Journal of the Early Republic* 7 (Winter 1987): 335–49.

tional system of roads and canals. "*Under another's name,*" he recalled bitterly in 1837, the Senate adopted his resolution, and the cornerstone of his grand design was laid.[36] Subsequently in 1808 Treasury Secretary Gallatin's report on roads and canals sought to integrate Jefferson's republicanism with national planning for internal improvement. A great barrier to major works, Gallatin explained, lay in the patchwork of jurisdictions that did not correspond to physical geography and natural routes of travel. Improvements in one state required corresponding works in another; sometimes, as in the case of the Chesapeake and Delaware Canal, projects of great interest to one state lay entirely in others where jealous interests sought to obstruct development. "The national legislature alone," Gallatin argued, "embracing every local interest, and superior to every local consideration, is competent to the selection of such national objects."[37]

Gallatin conceived such a national legislature in republican terms, not as a marketplace for competing interests, but as a forum for the whole people. Unfortunately, Jefferson's political style and rhetoric, if not all his actions, seriously eroded this kind of national authority. Jefferson had masked the loss of institutional power inherent in many of his principles by managing the business of government with his forceful personality and influence. Endowed with less charisma, Madison inherited a government he could not govern, and power in Washington declined dramatically. In 1817, when Calhoun's "Bonus Bill" for promoting national internal improvements came before the president, Madison vetoed what he saw as a pork barrel system of legislative usurpation that invited corruption, and he called for an amendment to clarify federal authority. Seven more years of vigorous debates in Congress finally produced the 1824 General Survey Act, which Adams took to be at least a binding assertion of Congress's right to plan and promote public works in the states.[38]

---

[36] John Quincy Adams to Charles W. Upham, February 2, 1837, in "Ten Unpublished Letters of John Quincy Adams, 1796–1837," ed. Edward H. Tatum, Jr., *Huntington Library Quarterly* 5 (1941): 383.

[37] Albert Gallatin, *Report of the Secretary of the Treasury on the Subject of Roads and Canals* (1808; repr., New York: A. M. Kelley, 1968), 75; see Nelson, *Liberty and Property*, 100–33.

[38] For surveys on national legislation, see Joseph H. Harrison, Jr., "The Internal Improvement Issue in the Politics of the Union, 1783–1825" (Ph.D. diss., University of Virginia, 1954); Carter Goodrich, *Government Promotion of American Canals and Railroads, 1800–1890* (New York: Columbia University Press, 1960); Douglas Clanin, "Internal Improvements in National Politics," in *Transportation and the Early Nation* (Indianapolis: Indiana Historical Society, 1982), 30–60; and Daniel Feller, *Public Lands and Jacksonian Politics* (Madison: University of Wisconsin Press, 1984).

From George Washington to John Quincy Adams, the presidents' internal improvement policies had differed primarily on the issue of amending the Constitution. Even Jefferson believed that the national government ought to have the power to promote internal improvement and that the people readily would grant it. Unfortunately, after Jefferson's "Revolution of 1800," politicians increasingly used constitutional objections for strategic as well as fundamental purposes, so that any grant of new power in Washington, however popular or intelligent, became unobtainable. During the 1824 campaign, Adams privately explained that to ask for the power in Congress to make internal improvements would be to admit not only "that they *do not* but that they never will possess it. A great majority of the people of this Union now think with me that Congress do possess the power. Why should they beat about the bush for the bird which they have in hand?"[39] Perhaps more to the point, Adams preferred the reasoned assumptions of the original founders to the corrupt and noisy politics of his own day as a source for constitutional truth. "Constitutional degeneration" had arrived. In and out of Congress, politics had become frankly competitive and factious, delivering liberty without improvement.

REACTION IN 1825

Was Adams correct that a "great majority" of the American people shared his confidence that Congress possessed the power to make internal improvements? Historians resoundingly say no, but contemporary evidence is not so conclusive. Admittedly, popular opinion in the early Republic is impossible to test accurately, especially because the very idea of popular opinion was just shedding its coat of illegitimacy. Yet political candidates and the editors of newspapers seemed more concerned than ever with articulating "popular" positions, pitching their rhetoric less to the learned gentry and more to the common man. Therefore, contemporary evidence sustaining Adams is at least as valid as retrospective evidence condemning him.

If the issue orientation of the leading candidates for president in 1824 offers any guidance, Adams may well have judged popular opinion correctly. He, Calhoun, Clay, and William H. Crawford all shared the common partisan heritage of Republican nationalism coming out of the War of

[39]John Quincy Adams to Jno. Hampden Pleasants, June 25, 1824, quoted in Bemis, *Adams and the Union*, 26.

1812. Together, Clay and Calhoun had constructed the new Bank of the United States, the 1816 protective tariff, and the 1817 Bonus Bill for national roads and canals. From 1817 through 1824, Calhoun evaded constitutional scruples (with President Monroe's blessing) by pursuing federal improvements in the War Department. There, appropriations could be garnered in the name of defense—a pork barrel business, too, but not a new and splendid cask of spoils. Through it all, Calhoun insisted that Congress had the power "to commence and complete such a system of internal improvements as it may deem proper."[40] Clay fought bitterly to gain through open legislation what the War Department did by executive finesse, until the 1824 General Survey Bill apparently resolved the conflict. At the State Department, Adams supported all schemes of national improvement. Only Crawford kept his distance from the nationalists' work, not by open disagreement, but by allowing his "friends" to pour a steady fire of opposition into Monroe's house of "good feelings."[41]

Crawford was the least popular contender, nominated by a legislative caucus composed almost entirely of Virginia's henchmen. The disgraceful nature of Crawford's nomination became the common theme of all his opponents, at a stroke giving novel importance to popular support instead of endorsement by the existing elites. The change was permanent and set the stage for Andrew Jackson's claim that he was cheated out of popular election by a corrupt bargain between Adams and Clay. Jackson was a wild card in this game of faction, running as a virtuous outsider unstained by office or intrigue, concerned only that the voice of the people be heard. On internal improvements, Jackson agreed with Monroe's 1822 rejection of national roads and canals; yet when pressed further, Jackson acknowledged full power to apply public funds "to such objects as may be deemed National." In other words, Jackson did not wish to be seen as the friend or the enemy of national improvement.[42]

To the voters who tried in various ways to choose among these candidates, there was never any doubt where Clay stood on issues of national

[40]John C. Calhoun to James Monroe, December 3, 1824, in *Papers of Calhoun*, IX, 424–9.
[41]See Hargreaves, *Presidency*, 19–40, for a good summary of the campaign; see also George Dangerfield, *The Awakening of American Nationalism, 1815–1828* (New York: Harper and Row, 1965), 212–30. Adams's diary (*Memoirs*, VI) is full of detail on the cabinet. Calhoun's letters (*Papers of Calhoun, IX*) clearly support my reading of his position until they abruptly change after February 9, 1825, the date of Adams's election.
[42]For quotation, see Andrew Jackson to James Lanier, n.d. (May 15?, 1824), in *The Correspondence of Andrew Jackson*, ed. John Spencer Bassett (Washington, D.C.: Carnegie Institution, 1928), III, 253. See also Andrew Jackson to James Monroe, July 26, 1822, ibid., 253; McCormick, *Presidential Game*, 118–20. Monroe's long message on internal improvements can be found in Richardson, ed., *Messages*, II, 713–52.

development, and little question about Adams or Calhoun. Their three names were intimately connected with what Clay and Adams each called the "American System," and all three drew fire from Crawford's "Old Republican" allies for their contributions to the "consolidation" of the Union. They were, charged one Kentucky commentator, "Federalists" addicted to "power and patronage" rather than liberty and the people's will. Uncanny in his choice of disastrous phrases, Adams insisted that the Constitution's authors could not have been "*so ineffably stupid,* as to deny themselves the means of bettering their own condition."[43] If some Republicans thought Adams a neo-Federalist, many Federalists feared him as a ruthless enemy. Still others believed that he, like Jackson, might be a nonpartisan alternative to either the "caucus" candidate Crawford, or to that unrestrained nationalist, Clay. How people finally voted cannot be traced to this or any other single issue, but given the ambiguity of Jackson's position, it seems impossible to treat the election as a referendum against national internal improvements. Only forty-one electoral votes went to the candidate who clearly opposed improvements under national authority, and about three times as many votes went to Adams and Clay.[44]

A brief look at the public prints, responding to Adams's pronouncements, further supports his reading of the public's position. The leading Republican daily in the nation's capital, Joseph Gales, Jr., and William W. Seaton's *National Intelligencer,* understood by its readers to be Crawford's mouthpiece, nevertheless took a conciliatory view of the incoming Adams administration. The editors commended the new president for outlining for his constituents, in the March 4 inaugural address, "the leading principles" that would govern his conduct.[45] Nine months later, this same newspaper, never friendly enough to be an organ of the administration, reviewed the December 6 message to Congress:

The part of the Message, in anticipation of which, we believe, more curiosity was felt by politicians, and which has certainly excited a greater sensation than

[43]"Consolidation," by "An Anti-Federalist," Lexington *Kentucky Gazette,* December 30, 1824, and January 6, 15, 1825. Adams is quoted in this piece.
[44]See Henry Warfield to Daniel Webster, February 3, 1825, and Webster's reply, February 5, 1825, in *The Papers of Daniel Webster: Correspondence,* ed. Charles M. Wiltse and Harold D. Moser (Hanover, N.H.: Dartmouth College Press, 1974–1984), II, 18, 21–2; see also Albert Ray Newsome, *The Election of 1824 in North Carolina* (Chapel Hill: University of North Carolina Press, 1939) for a surprising view of Adams. In the Electoral College, Jackson received 99 votes, Adams 84, Crawford 41, and Clay 37. Electoral votes were meaningless indicators of popularity, however, because in six states, including New York, the legislature appointed electors.
[45]Washington *National Intelligencer* (daily), March 17, 1825.

any other, is that which concerns Internal Improvement. . . . The President has not left to conjecture, or inference, what his opinion is of the power of the General Government to appropriate money for the construction of Roads and Canals of that description "to which neither the authority nor the resources of any one State can be adequate."

Having the honor to concur in this view of the Constitution, it will not be deemed surprising that we take no exception to the assertion of this power.[46]

These influential editors, close to the center of the Republican establishment, granted Adams his claim as heir to Monroe and the Virginia nationalists. "Judging the Message without fear, favor, or affection— trying it in the crucible of analysis—we find it to propose, as we understand it, nothing for which precedent" could not be found in the "administration of the illustrious men who have preceded Mr. Adams," in the "columns of this print," and in the "sanction of public approbation."[47] Strongly pro-Adams papers, such as the *United States Gazette* of Philadelphia, edited by James G. Watts, praised the high tone of the message as befitting the "enlightened chief magistrate of a free people."[48]

Obviously, some readers found Adams's scholarship reassuring, but the rhetoric raised a flag of panic in Richmond, Virginia, where the long-time head of the Old Republican junto, Thomas Ritchie, turned his partisan pen against the new president with unrestrained fury.[49] Ritchie's determination to oppose Adams was clear from the start. In the Richmond *Enquirer,* he criticized the inaugural address for being "too loose" toward the landmarks in the Constitution. Denouncing the president as a "complete Latetudinarian," Ritchie asked a loaded question: What did Adams include in his interpretation of the "rights and interests of the *federative fraternity*" (Adams's term)? Apparently roads and canals qualified. "Does a system of emancipation?" For some time, states' rights radicals like Nathaniel Macon and John Randolph had been warning that power to build roads suggested power to free slaves, as if the purpose of internal improvement was tyranny followed by emancipation. The issue had become a rhetorical trigger.[50]

[46]*National Intelligencer* (Washington daily), December 14, 1825.
[47]Ibid.
[48]*United States Gazette* (Philadelphia daily), December 9, 1825.
[49]*Enquirer* (Richmond) March 8, 11, and December 10, 13, 1825. See Joseph H. Harrison, Jr., "Oligarchs and Democrats—The Richmond Junto," *Virginia Magazine of History and Biography* 78 (1970): 184–98.
[50]Two-part editorial, Richmond *Enquirer,* March 8, 11, 1825. Nathaniel Macon first warned Bartlett Yancey on February 18, 1818, that if Congress could make canals, they could "with more propriety emancipate." It was an instructional analogy, not a prophecy,

Discussing the December speech, Ritchie headlined his column: "The President's Message. Splendid Government!" What "friend to the real principles of the Constitution" could read the last part of the president's message "without a species of indignant astonishment?" Ritchie belittled the reference to lighthouses of the skies: "Are we really reading a state paper, or a school boy's Thesis?" He denounced the recommendation of a home department (once Madison's idea) as nothing more than executive aggrandizement. But he inevitably returned to what he considered the "wildest construction" of the Constitution, the "extraordinary ground that *Liberty is Power*."[51]

Ritchie's great fear was usurpation, not improvement itself; but usurpation was becoming a code word for authority in government whenever different interests in the states collided. As the *National Intelligencer* and other newspapers immediately protested, Ritchie's tantrum repudiated years of southern toleration of precisely the same exercise of national authority under the Virginia Dynasty. Hezekiah Niles, who as Baltimore editor of *Niles' Weekly Register* had given his "hearty approbation" to Adams's "plain, republican, practical" message, opened fire on Ritchie in turn: The *Enquirer* "teemed with some of the most extraordinary essays and doctrines that were ever promulgated since the invention of printing— with the sole apparent object of whipping up an opposition about something—*anything*, to cause a rallying 'round the opinions and dogmas of 'imperial Rome' as in the days that are passed."[52]

The charge of imperial pretensions in Virginia found its mark. Some contemporaries thought Virginia's patriotism had acquired a narrow and selfish cast. Adams and Clay felt betrayed by men they took to be their mentors. Editor Niles ridiculed the Virginians for proclaiming the "end of the world" because their fears of roads and canals were not shared by "a majority of the people."[53] For nationalists like Niles, Adams's position on internal improvement placed him squarely in the line of succession from Jefferson through Monroe. In Virginia, however, men like Ritchie deduced right principles from character, from nature, trusting only their

---

but the connection acquired import during the Missouri debates, and by 1824, John Randolph was hurling it in Congress against the General Survey Bill. See Edwin Mood Wilson, *The Congressional Career of Nathaniel Macon* (Chapel Hill: University of North Carolina Press, 1900), 51.

[51] *Enquirer* (Richmond), December 10, 13, 1825.

[52] *Niles' Weekly Register*, 3d ser., V (December 10, 1825): 224; V (December 17, 1825): 241.

[53] Ibid., V (December 17, 1815): 241; V (December 31, 1825): 274.

own kind with the delicate task of construing American republicanism. Adams's articulation of popular programs threatened to establish the legitimacy of his voice in general, and his voice was not theirs.

Here a grain of truth formed the nucleus of a partisan attack, for Adams was never an Old Republican. Men like Ritchie clung to the libertarian edge of the revolutionary tradition, as suspicious earlier of Jefferson and Madison as they were now of Adams. They sometimes tolerated boldness in Virginia presidents because at least they pursued "correct" regional interests, but New Englanders by definition harbored dangerous intentions. Adams's nationalism was not tempered with a love of Old Dominion. Anticipating the dynasty's fall, Jefferson dusted off his theory of natural parties, first heard at the turn of the century: "The parties of Whig and Tory are those of nature. . . . The sickly, weakly, timid man, fears the people, and is a tory by nature. The healthy, strong and bold cherishes them, and is formed a Whig by nature." The old enemies of freedom were back, he fretted, "openly marching by the road of construction in a direct line to that consolidation which was always their real object." One month before Adams's election, Jefferson marked him as a thoroughgoing monarchist: "J. Q. Adams, the son, was more explicit than the father, in his answer to Paine's *rights of man*."[54]

Ghosts of a revolutionary life haunted Jefferson's fading vision as he resurrected the partisan "Spirit of '98." But things were not as they appeared to the Sage of Monticello, and Madison urged the old man not to join in Ritchie's agitation. Madison himself blamed the "obnoxious career of Congress, or, rather, of their constituents" for the encroachments of the nation on the states, recognizing a fact Jefferson never liked to admit, that a majority of the people might freely choose to do wrong things! The "great temptation of 'utility,' brought home to local feelings," wrote the author of the national Union, was the "most dangerous snare for Constitutional orthodoxy." Madison now wondered whether the judiciary, of all things, might be a "safer expositor of the power of Congress" than the outdoor political process. Fearing always for the maintenance of balance, Madison urged surrender on the question of roads and canals,

---

[54]Thomas Jefferson to the Marquis de Lafayette, November 4, 1823, in *The Works of Thomas Jefferson,* ed. Paul Leicester Ford (New York: G. P. Putnam's Sons, 1905), XII, 323. Thomas Jefferson to Robert Garnett, February 14, 1824, in ibid., XII, 341. Thomas Jefferson to William Short, January 8, 1825, in ibid., XII, 394–5. On the tradition of regionalism, see Drew R. McCoy, "James Madison and Visions of American Nationality in the Confederation Period: A Regional Perspective," in Beeman et al., eds., *Beyond Confederation,* 226–58.

using a constitutional amendment to acknowledge what the people now demanded, while still closing the door to further use of the Constitution's elastic clauses.[55] Jefferson immediately agreed: "A Majority of the people are against us on this question," he wrote in January 1826, and if "we can make such a compromise" amendment "we shall save and at the same time improve our constitution."[56]

So Jefferson and Madison privately conceded what Adams claimed, that a popular national consensus backed an American System of internal improvements. Private correspondence daily reinforced the optimistic Clay and the brooding Adams in their belief that they spoke for the people. Savage attacks had greeted Clay's elevation to secretary of state in March 1825, but by summer, triumphal dinners and speeches studded his tour of the West. Clay's correspondents assured him that only intriguing politicians spoke against the administration, and by October, Clay predicted Adams's reelection three years hence by "a majority of two thirds of the Union."[57] Sustained by this evidence that his sentiments were not just right but even popular, Adams drafted his bold message hoping to outflank politicians in Congress, speak to the people outdoors, and perhaps restore forever the energy of the Union. "The Administration appear (to my mind) *'venturing upon wisdom'* with great boldness," wrote a Chillecothe man, which to Adams was the whole point.[58]

There was no spontaneous outpouring of shock or dismay in response to Adams's first message to Congress because the message promised popular programs. The storm of opposition built slowly from a center in Virginia, spreading through local political establishments in states that had opposed Adams's election. This opposition coalesced in the Nineteenth Congress, in the Senate, precisely where the president-elect had predicted: The "system of opposition" would form, Adams confided in his diary two days after his election, "to bring in General Jackson as the next President, under the auspices of Calhoun. To this end the administration must be rendered unpopular and odious, whatever its acts and mea-

---

[55]James Madison to Thomas Jefferson, December 28, 1825; Madison to Thomas Ritchie, December 18, 1825; Madison to Jefferson, February 17, 1825; Madison to Martin Van Buren, September 20, 1826; in *Letters and Other Writings of James Madison*, Congress ed. (New York: R. Worthington, 1884), III, 512–14, 506–10, 483, 528–30.

[56]Thomas Jefferson to William Gordon, January 1, 1826, in *Works of Jefferson*, XII, 430.

[57]Henry Clay to John Quincy Adams, July 21, 1825; Clay to Amos Kendall, October 18, 1825; Clay to Amos Kendall, October 18, 1825; in *The Papers of Henry Clay*, ed. James F. Hopkins and Mary W. M. Hargreaves (Lexington: University of Kentucky Press, 1959–1988), IV, 547, 758.

[58]Richard Douglas to Henry Clay, December 19, 1825, ibid., 924.

sures may be."[59] For the first time in the history of the government, the vice-president, Calhoun, actually took up the gavel of the Senate, appointing committee chairmen and presiding daily over debates. From this novel vantage point, Calhoun began to work against his president.[60]

To the astonishment of both Adams and Clay, the Senate erupted almost at once in opposition to the appointment of ministers to the Panama Congress—an issue both men thought was popular and harmless. Weeks of spleenful oratory, cloaked in the secrecy that enhances credibility, tortured the objectives and motives of the president with the most sordid fantasies, until rumors had the whole nation boiling with curiosity and doubt. Usurpation of power, executive pretension, monarchism, internationalism, and a sympathy for Haitian-style slave rebellion were the charges leveled at Adams. The more preposterous the insults to executive authority, the more he felt compelled to defend his office. A pointless pamphlet war with Calhoun lured the president into elaborate discussions of authority and order, each sounding more like his besieged father's pleas for relief from organized dissent. By the end of the session, the Adams administration was self-destructing.[61]

Public confidence in Adams's intentions deteriorated under the steady assault of Calhoun, the Virginians, Jackson, Martin Van Buren, and others. The rhetoric of leadership, discipline, and unity contained in the December 1825 message looked increasingly like the alien and dangerous pretension Ritchie originally called it. Congress proceeded to endorse specific works of internal improvements, but lawmakers simultaneously backed away from the systematic vision and central authority embodied in Adams's view. Each time a city, state, or interest group got substantially what it wanted from national legislation without submitting to the discipline of national direction, the case for power in Washington grew weaker. By the time Jackson drove Adams from the White House, Adams looked to a majority of voters like the arrogant, alien, neo-Federalist enemy of popular democracy historians continue to portray. With the collapse of his reputation expired as well the likelihood that a designing and energetic national government would ever shape and direct the ambitions of a people most blessed with that "freedom which is power."

[59] Adams, *Memoirs*, VI, 507.
[60] For Calhoun's role in the Senate, see *Papers of Calhoun*, X, xxxi.
[61] See "Patrick Henry" and "Onslow," in *Papers of Calhoun*, X, 92–232. Adams's authorship of "Patrick Henry" is not certain, but if he did not write these essays, he customordered them. See also Andrew R. L. Cayton, "The Debate over the Panama Congress and the Origins of the Second Party System," *The Historian* 47 (February 1985): 219–38.

LIBERTY WITHOUT DESIGN

John Quincy Adams's design for an American System of national development drew from the finest economic knowledge and social science known to his generation. It was a blueprint for political liberty and human progress that reflected the order, reason, and benevolence of Enlightenment idealism. Adams wished to encourage formal inquiry and education to refine and perfect the design as progress itself unfolded. Expertise designed systems that encouraged expertise, perpetually spiraling upward toward the perfection of human society. To all who accepted his original premises, Adams's arguments proved attractive, even compelling, but they depended absolutely on believing what the experts said at that time about power, liberty, and the human condition on earth.

Once "these truths" had been "self-evident," but the success of the Revolution and the promise of individual liberty began quickly to change the culture from which Adams's principles derived. Experience with freedom and self-government led ordinary people to assume the qualities of citizenship they once ascribed to men of high station, while persistent conflicts over policies and interests fed their suspicions of men wielding power. The result was a dynamic of empowerment that steadily democratized the American Republic while it eroded Enlightenment beliefs about the baseness of human beings and their need for improvement.

The transformation of the culture can be seen in the subtle decay of the idea of a system of internal improvement (singular) into many demands for internal improvements (plural).[62] The grand designs of the founders, whose intent Adams purposefully recalled, incorporated many projects and programs in a single common purpose: the elevation of the human condition. By 1825, however, Adams's listeners clamored for particular works of capital improvement valued exclusively in economic or utilitarian terms. The components were practically the same—universities and schools, roads and canals, and scientific expeditions—but the connections among them had disappeared. Grand designs proposed environmental changes for the purpose of disciplining human behavior. Random collections of capital projects simply altered physical nature according to human convenience.

For the purpose of promoting grand designs, George Washington had sought the aid of the moneyed gentry of the 1780s, and elites in every

---

[62]I am indebted to Joseph H. Harrison, Jr., for introducing to me the significance of this subtle difference.

state had once encouraged systematic improvement. Fearing corruption in the hands of these private promoters, men like Adams, Madison, and Jefferson had tried to republicanize the authority of designs, bringing them under political control in a national blueprint like the Gallatin Plan. Reactionaries frightened of all infringements on their liberties worked diligently against any scheme or institution that would mold, determine, or "improve" the individual at home. At the same time, ambitious individuals in many cities and states expected great gains from immediate local development and worked to block nationwide or comprehensive programs. Together, these interested and ideological enemies of systematic improvement frustrated grand designs until their cultural foundations disintegrated.

The authority of grand designs could be no better than the authority of the persons who made them, but who in the new American Republic had the right to impose his design? Dissatisfaction with particular authorities had caused revolutionary Americans and their children to tear down institutions of control one after the other, and the philosophy of liberation made it impossible to reestablish limits or bring the explosion to a finish. Patients denounced physicians, clients sued their lawyers, schoolchildren grasped the barest rudiments of learning and immediately offered themselves as teachers. Jefferson himself complained that modern students lacked "the article of discipline." "Premature ideas of independence," he explained in 1822, "too little repressed by parents, beget a spirit of insubordination," which was "the great obstacle to science with us, and a principal cause of its decay."[63] Only the Constitution enjoyed unquestioned authority, yet even common men reserved to themselves (if not to their enemies) the right to interpret it definitively. In this democratizing culture, governments that really tried to *govern* their constituents failed at the next election.

In the field of internal improvement, the question of authority was crucial. Jefferson lost confidence that the monied gentry would submerge their private interest in the public good, and he moved to undercut their power. Reflecting Jefferson's fear of corruption at work on the local level, Gallatin lodged the power of design in the national legislature. Ten years later, Madison found that body hopelessly corrupted by interest group brokers and the rising demands of the constituents outdoors. Calhoun tried to usurp authority in the name of national defense, while Clay

---

[63]Thomas Jefferson to Thomas Cooper, November 2, 1822, in *Works of Jefferson*, XII, 273.

sought whatever imperfect foundations he could win through ordinary congressional legislation. When the General Survey Bill of 1824 finally authorized the creation of a Board of Engineers, Adams took refuge in the hope that scientific expertise might resurrect design despite the shallowness of politics. Then, poised at the threshold of success, he was struck down by his own political enemies, who used his dedication to intelligence, improvement, order, and authority to portray him as a power-mad consolidationist bent on saddling the people with a "splendid" central government and riding them to national glory. Because it *was* his purpose to guide, discipline, and improve the people, Adams could not deflect the charge. Democratization had rendered unrepublican one of the fundamental assumptions of American republicanism.

Not even men of science could establish their authority in Adams's day. After all, appointments to West Point (where American engineers were trained) came through political preferment. When the Army Corps estimated costs for the Chesapeake and Ohio Canal at more than twice the sum suggested by promoters, friends of the improvement denounced the engineers and sought new estimates more in line with their resources. There were too few American experts for the work to be done, yet Europeans were generally proscribed. Ferdinand Rudolph Hassler, a competent Swiss scientist once in charge of the United States coastal survey and a friend of Adams, fell repeatedly from grace as jealous Americans declared their independence from his foreign expertise.[64] Only free competition in the marketplace—the metaphor originated in economics but quickly spread to all aspects of American culture—seemed capable of sorting out the clash of interests without vesting in the winners some enduring, illegitimate authority over parallel or future contests.

Depending as it did on higher and external authorities, Adams's American System belonged to a republican vision of improvement of humankind through the use of virtuous authority speeding on the day of universal enlightenment. To his father's generation, improvement explained liberation, made it rational, excusable, endurable. The most conservative among the old Federalists desired to make improvement a prerequisite to freedom, excluding from participation in republican self-government individuals not yet improved. Others hoped the grant of freedom would encourage men (and gradually women, too) to cultivate their own improvement, grateful for the opportunity liberty provided. The founders

[64]See Hargreaves, *Presidency,* 178, and Adams, *Memoirs,* VII, 190–1; VIII, 48–9. On Hassler, see Dupree, *Science in the Federal Government,* 29–33, 52–5.

looked for truths that were permanent and timeless, and their constitutional convictions were never theoretically divorced from the goals and objectives they personally cherished; but liberation by its own dynamic energy fostered impatience in the face of all gradual designs. As long as men in power chose to foster liberation as a strategy for conquering their rivals, the momentum of empowerment continued, until the only fixed principle surviving was the principle of mass participation.

Eventually, democratic politics and freedom of the markets established invisible systems of self-regulation that Americans proved willing to accept. Both concepts found roots in natural law—the source of American liberty as well. Both placed the hand of authority out of view, untraceable and unassailable. Both reflected responsibility back on the individual for whatever came to pass. If democracy alone protected Americans from false doctrines and tyrants in politics, a laissez-faire approach might save them from state-sponsored errors in economics as well. Reflecting each other eternally, these parallel liberal doctrines eliminated forever (or so it seemed) the designs of men like Adams to govern or control American liberty.

In 1828, Andrew Jackson resoundingly defeated Adams for the presidency. More romantic than rational, not a founder but a product of the revolutionary Republic, Jackson seemed to symbolize for many Americans the political and economic liberation they craved. Within a decade of Jackson's election, after the Panic of 1837 drove many state systems of public works to insolvency, leading businessmen began to claim that private interests alone were competent to carry on America's internal improvement. By the middle 1840s, the capital markets of New York and Boston were doing just that. Gradually, the triumph of laissez-faire, coupled with new tools of capital formation such as the modern business corporation, produced accelerating national improvement.[65] Without question, this was progress, but it was liberty without design, progress charted on a course determined not by popular governments or scientific experts, but by investors and speculators in a rough-and-tumble game of capitalism.

Two generations later, after the Civil War and Reconstruction had tested the Constitution, and after unprecedented power had accumulated

---

[65]See R. Carlyle Buley, *The Old Northwest* (1950; repr. Bloomington: Indiana University Press, 1978), II, 260–325; Goodrich, *Government Promotion*, 51–120, 265–97; and Ralph D. Gray, "The Canal Era in Indiana," in *Transportation in the Early Nation*, 121–9.

in the hands of the business elite, Americans began to reconsider the triumph of laissez-faire and look for alternative sources of authority in the marketplace of ideas. By then, the capitalists claimed for themselves complete immunity from the interfering hand of government. At the same time, they labored tirelessly to defeat in the market the forces of competition they had long celebrated as natural and immutable. The "visible hand of management"[66] displaced the invisible hand of Smithian theory; then, once established as masters of material prosperity, these industrialists subdued liberty in politics as well. Thus, the consolidation and arbitrary power that were predicted as a consequence of Adams's conceptions of energetic government came to pass despite his defeat.

For the last thirty years of the nineteenth century, grass-roots movements for economic reform—farmer-railroad struggles in the East and Middle West, agitation by Alliancemen and Populists in the South and far West, "good government" campaigns of urban reformers in nearly every city, labor movements concerning wages, hours, and safety—all shared a common reference to designs that were *supposed* to guide American development but somehow had been misplaced.[67] Study Robert La Follette's "Wisconsin Idea," or Carroll Wright's Bureau of Labor Statistics, alongside Adams's first message to Congress, and you will hear the voice whose echo these reformers heard, when they stopped to get their bearings in the late Gilded Age. Once again, people turned hopefully to notions of scientific government, virtuous leadership, and designs for shaping liberty. Not surprisingly, the problem of authority once more clothed these policy designs in "party-colored garments," often leading people to confound their interests with their liberties in ways that drove serious reformers to distraction. Only when the Great Depression of the 1930s destroyed popular confidence in the automatic working of the marketplace did a clear majority of Americans concede the importance of national designs for economic policy. Even then, they grudgingly adopted

[66]The phrase is Alfred D. Chandler, Jr.'s. See *The Visible Hand: The Managerial Revolution in American Business* (Cambridge, Mass.: Harvard University Press, 1977).

[67]See Lee Benson, *Merchants, Farmers, and Railroads: Railroad Regulation and New York Politics, 1850–1887* (Cambridge, Mass.: Harvard University Press, 1955); John Lauritz Larson, *Bonds of Enterprise: John Murray Forbes and the Burlington Route in America's Railway Age* (Cambridge, Mass.: Harvard University Press, 1984); Lawrence Goodwyn, *Democratic Promise: The Populist Moment in America* (New York: Oxford University Press, 1976); John L. Thomas, *Alternative America: Henry George, Edward Bellamy, Henry Demarest Lloyd and the Adversary Tradition* (Cambridge, Mass.: Harvard University Press, 1983); Mark W. Summers, *Railroads, Reconstruction, and the Gospel of Efficiency* (Princeton, N.J.: Princeton University Press, 1984); as well as chapters in this volume by Robert Collins, Mary O. Furner, and Ellis W. Hawley (Chapters 5, 8, and 9).

indirect tools for stimulating growth, again dodging the bullet of planning. In the context of the modern American economic and welfare policy system, people still do not talk confidently, as Adams did, of using knowledge or the power of government to improve the condition of "man upon earth."

4

Government as a laboratory for economic learning in the years of the Democratic Roosevelt

WILLIAM J. BARBER

> I have no sympathy for the professional economists who insist that things must run their course and that human agencies can have no influence on economic ills. One reason is that I happen to know that professional economists have changed their definition of economic laws every five or ten years for a very long time.
>
> Franklin D. Roosevelt, third fireside chat,
> July 24, 1933

As president of the United States, Franklin D. Roosevelt was a major architect of the American "mixed economy." In that capacity, he worked with a considerable mix of economists. These were years of fundamental redefinition of the role of government in the economy and of the role of economists in government. From this ferment, new insights into the functioning of the economic system emerged. Indeed, the discipline of economics itself underwent a transformation.

This chapter is concerned with the contributions to learning made by economists who served in official capacities during this period. One of the things we owe to John Maynard Keynes is the suggestion that the thought processes of high policymakers are ultimately controlled by the "academic scribblers."[1] There are moments in history when the academy

I am indebted to John W. M. Barber and Peter Sallick for assistance in gathering material for this essay. I am also grateful for comments on the initial draft provided by participants in the Wilson Center Conference (at which the papers being prepared for this volume were discussed) and for the careful reading of the manuscript by Craufurd D. Goodwin and William Emerson.
[1] The *locus classicus* of this view is the peroration in the concluding paragraph of *The General Theory*: "the ideas of economists and political philosophers, both when they are right and when they are wrong, are more powerful than is commonly understood. Indeed

does indeed have primacy in the production of what is accepted as economic knowledge, but it would be extreme to insist that this should always and necessarily be the case. It may thus be instructive to reexamine the manner in which the boundaries of economic understanding were extended during the Roosevelt years, with particular attention to the work of the "insiders."

This phase of American economic history presented no lack of challenges to economic analysis, among them, the problem of the persistence of the Great Depression, the perplexities presented by a major downturn in economic activity (in 1937–8) which the received learning could not readily account for, and the urgencies of mobilizing the economy for war while restraining runaway inflation. This period is singular in another respect: never before had so many economists been attracted to Washington. In more normal times, many who then entered the bureaucracy would probably have elected instead to pursue full-time careers in academic life. Circumstances of depression, however, had diminished employment opportunities in academe: government employment was one of the few growth sectors in an otherwise depressed labor market for white-collar professionals. The public service then enjoyed an extraordinary advantage in the competition for the ablest in the nation's talent pool. For economists, Washington was where the most interesting jobs were. It was also where the action was.

THE ADMINISTRATION AND THE STATE OF THE ART, 1933–1936

Thirty-six long years ago I began a more or less intensive study of economics and economists. The course has continued with growing intensity, especially during the last four years. As a result I am compelled to admit—or boast—whichever way you care to put it, that I know nothing of economics and that nobody else does either! (Franklin D. Roosevelt to Joseph Schumpeter, professor of economics at Harvard University, December 19, 1936, president's personal files, Franklin D. Roosevelt Library)

Roosevelt's agnosticism about the truth-value of alleged economic knowledge, as expressed in December 1936, might be regarded as reflecting the

the world is ruled by little else. Practical men, who believe themselves to be quite exempt from any intellectual influences, are usually the slaves of some defunct economist. Madmen in authority, who hear voices in the air, are distilling their frenzy from some academic scribbler of a few years back." See John Maynard Keynes, *The General Theory of Employment, Interest, and Money* (London: Macmillan, 1936), 383.

kernel of truth in Keynes's remark about the captivity of statesmen to the "academic scribblers." To be sure, Roosevelt was never enslaved to any single body of economic advice: on the contrary, he regularly exercised his rights as a sovereign consumer to pick selectively, to discard and to repackage the policy recommendations presented to him. Even so, the policy "mix" of the opening years of the first Roosevelt administration was significantly influenced by the thinking of two strands of heterodox academic economics.

The representative spokesman for the first of these strands was Rexford Guy Tugwell, professor of economics at Columbia University and one of the original "Brains Trusters." In his prolific academic writings before coming to Washington, Tugwell had sounded a consistent theme. Laissez-faire—which stood for "competition and conflict"—was bankrupt and out of touch with the reality of modern industrial life. Bigness was the order of the day in the manufacturing sector of the economy, and this meant that producers were price-makers not price-takers. When resource allocation was governed by the profit motive, waste, inefficiency, and instability were inevitable. For Tugwell, the formula for recovery could be found in "concentration and control." Bigness per se and the economies of scale that went with it were not to be shunned: here Tugwell forcefully differentiated his position from the more orthodox body of economic thought calling for revitalization of a competitive order through more vigorous enforcement of the antitrust laws. Concentration, in his judgment, should survive, but the basic decisions on the direction of capital spending and on the volume of production should be taken out of private hands and placed under the jurisdiction of public authorities.

In short, this was a call for planning on a grand scale. Public ownership of the means of production was not part of this program, but government direction of their use was. Similarly, in the agricultural sector of the economy, there was no alternative to invoking the visible hand of the state to coordinate supply and demand.[2] Strictly speaking, there was nothing new in this line of argument. Among critics of the automaticity of the "invisible hand," similar doctrines had been taking shape in American economic debate for several decades. Never before, however, had advocates of this point of view enjoyed such access to the corridors of power.

---

[2] For specimens of Tugwell's thought, see "The Principle of Planning and the Institution of Laissez-Faire," *American Economic Review Supplement* (March 1932): 75–92, and *The Industrial Discipline and the Governmental Arts* (New York: Columbia University Press, 1933).

Tugwell's writings gave some academic underpinning to the programs of structural intervention that were enacted in the National Industrial Recovery Act (NIRA) and in the Agricultural Adjustment Act (AAA) during the first hundred days. (At the same time, it should be noted that the ultimate shaping of these pieces of legislation was, in large measure, a response to the lobbies for trade associations and organizations of aggrieved farmers.) Tugwell's conception of essential economic knowledge, however, was less than complete. He could be eloquent, as well as highly repetitive, in denouncing the unrealism of models of competitive equilibrium presented in the textbooks and in insisting that the guidance they offered was bound to produce the wrong policy answers. But he could never offer a detailed blueprint of the way his planners should proceed to get the right answers. His distaste for formal microeconomic theorizing precluded him from entering the analytic territory that was shortly to be explored, for example, by a number of Britain's Labour party economists who were working with such concepts as marginal-cost pricing to guide resource allocation in a socialist state.[3] For Tugwell, the planners would learn from experience and should have the wit to correct their own mistakes.[4]

Academic scribblers of a quite different persuasion informed what passed for a conscious macroeconomic strategy in the early days of the New Deal. Roosevelt had come into office proclaiming his belief in balanced budgets and denouncing Hoover as a reckless deficit spender. All this had the ring of old-fashioned fiscal orthodoxy—with the qualification that extraordinary emergency spending for unemployment relief should not be counted against his pledge to balance the budget. Nevertheless, the administration was committed to restoring purchasing power, and the instrument chosen for that purpose was a heterodox version of monetarism. The objective was to raise the general level of prices by increasing the money supply. This action, it was believed, would relieve debt burdens and, in turn, stimulate spending. Yale's Irving Fisher was an ardent advocate of this approach, which he urged insistently on the president and his advisers as well as on congressional committees. The doc-

---

[3]The works of E. F. M. Durbin and James Meade are cases in point. This approach to "planning" is reviewed by Elizabeth Durbin, *New Jerusalems: The Labour Party and the Economics of Democratic Socialism* (London: Routledge and Kegan Paul, 1985), especially Chapters 8 and 9.

[4]For Tugwell, the determination of prices and of the volume of production would "have to be worked out in conjunction with careful factual surveys of situations; and facts cannot be anticipated." Tugwell, *The Industrial Discipline and the Governmental Arts*, 210–11.

trine on which Roosevelt acted, however, was shaped more by two Cornell economists, George F. Warren and Frank Pearson. Their statistical investigations suggested that the behavior of commodity prices generally was highly correlated with the price of gold. The route to "reflation" was thus to be sought through raising gold prices. Roosevelt's gold purchase program, initiated in October 1933, was designed to do precisely that.[5]

If movement of the economy toward full recovery were to be taken as the criterion of success, these early experiments were signal failures. Three months of the program to purchase gold raised its price to $35 per ounce— the point at which the dollar was stabilized in January 1934. This level amounted to an increase of some 75 percent in the price of gold, but there was precious little to show for this effort in the movement of commodity prices. Many economists shared Keynes's judgment that the application of the "Professor Warren theory" resembled a "gold standard on the booze," rather than a genuinely managed currency.[6] By mid-1934, the performance of the National Recovery Administration (NRA) was the source of further disenchantment. Intense criticism displaced the wave of ballyhooed enthusiasm of the summer of 1933 as it became increasingly evident that its "codes of fair competition" were really a form of legalized collusion. Thomas Blaisdell, whom Tugwell had brought to Washington from Columbia University, captured the prevalent mood. As he reported to a Senate committee in April 1935, his investigations into the workings of the mackerel-fishing code had been revealing. Although this industry was hardly a major component of overall economic activity, the effects of code making there exemplified a pervasive phenomenon. As far as Blaisdell could determine, the "only individuals who benefited were the mackerels themselves": the agreement among fishermen to restrict output in order to raise prices meant that fewer mackerel were caught![7] Irving Fisher was even more outspoken in his assessment: "NRA," he wrote to the president, "has *retarded* recovery and especially retarded re-employment."[8]

[5]For Irving Fisher's position at this time, see "The Debt-Deflation Theory of Great Depressions," *Econometrica* (1933): 337–57. Warren's argument is set out in G. F. Warren and F. A. Pearson, "The Future of the General Price Level," *Journal of Farm Economics* (January 1932): 23–46.

[6]John Maynard Keynes, "Open Letter to President Roosevelt," December 31, 1933.

[7]Testimony of Thomas Blaisdell, director, Consumers' Division, National Emergency Council, Hearing before the Senate Committee on Finance (74th Cong., 1st sess.), April 1, 1935, vol. 44, 841.

[8]Fisher to the president, August 30, 1934, Franklin D. Roosevelt Library. In 1935, Fisher asserted that "the middle letter in 'NRA' could more properly stand for 'Retardation' than for 'Recovery.'" See his memorandum, " 'Deflation' from the Dissolution of N.R.A.," transmitted to Roosevelt on June 3, 1935.

Although the observable flow of events was disappointing, it did not follow that the "theorists" who helped to shape policy lost faith in the soundness of their "models." The champions of structural intervention could still argue that the shortcomings in performance were attributable to deficiencies in administrative execution, not to imperfections in their original analyses. Tugwell and his former Columbia colleague, Gardiner C. Means (who had joined the research staff of the Department of Agriculture), adopted this posture. The mistake in NRA, they maintained, arose from the fact that the administrator had allowed business interests to exercise too much authority. The outcome would have been much different if NRA had been structured as a proper vehicle for planning with public officials in the paramount positions.[9] Similarly, the confidence of the monetarists in their doctrines was unshaken. "Reflation" had not occurred, but the administration should be faulted for this failure. As Irving Fisher, for example, read the situation, monetary expansion had simply not been pressed on a scale sufficient to do the job.[10]

If he had not known it already, Roosevelt by mid-1935 was conscious of the pertinence of John R. Commons's observation that "the authoritative faculty of political economy" in the United States was the Supreme Court.[11] The president did not share the economic doctrine underlying the Court's decisions in striking down the NRA and the AAA. At the same time, he had adequate grounds for reacting cautiously to "experts" who claimed to command economic "truth." There may have been ambiguity about the appropriate lessons to draw from the First New Deal's experiments in manipulating the economy. But one point was clear: the deliberate interventions in those years were linked with doctrines worked out by academics before they made contact with Roosevelt's Washington. No novel contributions to economic theory emerged from hands-on work in the laboratory itself. The failure of the economy to respond to treatments prescribed by the planners and the monetary manipulators did, however, reinforce the confidence of the more orthodox—who had been suspicious of extraordinary government intervention all along—in the rightness of their views.

[9]Gardiner C. Means developed this argument in a document titled "NRA and AAA and the Reorganization of Industrial Policy Making," October 15, 1934, which Tugwell forwarded to the White House with his endorsement.

[10]See Fisher's "Revised Report on Stopping Unemployment," October 22, 1934, Franklin D. Roosevelt Library.

[11]John R. Commons, *Legal Foundations of Capitalism* (Madison: University of Wisconsin Press, 1968), 7. This volume was originally published in 1924.

Latent in the body of the first Roosevelt administration were the germs of an alternative approach to the stimulation of a depressed economy—one that called for a deliberate and aggressive program of deficit spending. The leading advocates of this position—Marriner Eccles, chairman of the Board of Governors of the Federal Reserve System, and Lauchlin Currie, his research assistant—had also brought their ideas to Washington with them. By background, Eccles was a Mormon banker from Utah and untutored in technical economic theory.[12] He had, however, absorbed the teachings of two amateurs, William Trufant Foster and Waddill Catchings, who had proclaimed in popular writings in the 1920s that the economy was exposed to chronic underconsumption. This tendency might be suppressed temporarily by special stimulants to total demand, such as credit-financed spending on consumer durables, and by lending abroad. But ultimately the instability of the system, arising from what they termed the "dilemma of thrift," would be exposed. High levels of production and employment could no longer be maintained, they asserted, without an injection of additional net spending, that is, through government outlays financed by borrowing.[13] Eccles found these ideas congenial, and the Roosevelt administration, delighted to find a banker whose views did not fit the standard mold, found a niche for him in Washington.

Currie had arrived at similar conclusions about the importance of stimulative fiscal policy, via a different route. As a student of monetary theory and policy while a junior member of the Harvard economics faculty, he had concluded that monetary policies were ineffective as depression remedies: a fiscal spur to spending was required. These doctrines were at odds with the prevailing orthodoxy at Harvard. Denied a tenured position there, he migrated to Washington in 1934 as an academic "displaced person."[14]

Spokesmen for a fiscal approach to macroeconomic strategy were thus absorbed into the Roosevelt administration, although they made little headway. The secretary of the treasury, Henry Morgenthau, Jr., had no time for such heresies, and the president, although he ran deficits of

---

[12]See Marriner S. Eccles, *Beckoning Frontiers: Public and Personal Recollections,* Sidney Hyman, ed. (New York: Alfred A. Knopf, 1951).

[13]The views of Foster and Catchings are most fully set out in *The Road to Plenty* (Boston: Houghton Mifflin, 1928).

[14]For background on Currie's early career, see Alan Sweezy, "The Keynesians and Government Policy, 1933–39," *American Economic Review Papers and Proceedings* (May 1972): 116–33, and the accompanying comments by Currie.

unprecedented peacetime magnitude, remained a fiscal conservative at heart. Politically, it was important to rationalize the existence of deficits as the unfortunate consequence of a diminished revenue base. The president was not, however, prepared to endorse deficit spending as a positive good in times of massive unemployment.

At a quite different level—that of empirical investigation—the first Roosevelt administration did make some impressive contributions to the enlargement of economic knowledge. One of its significant achievements was the institutionalization of machinery to produce national income accounts routinely. In the early 1920s, proposals had been in circulation that an arm of the federal government should perform this function. Herbert Hoover, as secretary of commerce, rejected them. Although himself an enthusiast for strengthening the statistical services provided by government, he held that national income accounting was properly the responsibility of research institutes (such as the National Bureau of Economic Research) or of private scholars. Such inquiries, he maintained, involved "interpretive questions" and thus could not "adequately be undertaken by the Government."[15] For a brief period in the 1920s, the Federal Trade Commission did prepare a national income series, but this effort was soon abandoned for lack of funding.[16]

In June 1932, the United States Senate, on the motion of Senator Robert M. La Follette, took the initiative to fill this void by passing a resolution requesting that the secretary of commerce report estimates of the national income for the years 1929 through 1931. Simon Kuznets of the National Bureau of Economic Research was engaged to direct this work and took up his duties at the Department of Commerce in January 1933. Even before this Senate-inspired study was completed—it was published in 1934 under the title *National Income, 1929–1932*—arrangements were under way to make national income reporting a continuing function of the Department of Commerce. This time it was argued that a government agency (as opposed to a private organization) was uniquely qualified to perform this task because of its superior access to primary data. Robert R. Nathan, a former student of Kuznets, was ultimately charged to head this organization. Its research results, which appeared periodically in the Commerce

[15]Secretary of Commerce Herbert Hoover to Edwin F. Gay, president of the National Bureau of Economic Research, October 20, 1921, Commerce Papers, Herbert Hoover Library.

[16]Carol S. Carson, "The History of the United States National Income and Product Accounts: The Development of an Analytical Tool," *Review of Income and Wealth* (June 1975): 153–81.

Department's *Survey of Current Business,* thereafter provided a systematic barometer of the performance of the macroeconomy.[17]

Allied with this work was a pioneering attempt to identify the part played by the government's fiscal activities in movements of the national income. This line of investigation was launched in 1935 by Lauchlin Currie and Martin Krost of the research staff of the Federal Reserve Board. The task they set themselves was to measure the "net income-increasing expenditures of the Federal government." This expression was taken to mean "all income received directly from Government agencies and from persons and institutions which are financing their expenditures by borrowing from Government agencies, minus all deductions from income paid over to the government as taxes, fees, etc." The results of this exercise were first circulated in November 1935, still in fairly rough form. Even so, the preliminary use of this technique suggested that the net stimulus to spending arising from government activities was not necessarily closely linked to the size of the federal deficit (as reported in accordance with the Treasury's accounting conventions). In three of the four calendar years investigated in this initial study, the magnitude of the net impact was substantially less than the officially reported deficit. This was a type of knowledge that could have been generated only by "insiders" with privileged access to information, and it invited a new way to look at fiscal policy.[18]

These types of data generation enlarged the role of government as a patron of empirical economic studies—a practice that had been pioneered at the Bureau of Labor Statistics and at the Bureau of Agricultural Economics (see Chapters 8 and 9 of this volume). Such initiatives in the United States stand in arresting contrast to the British rejection of official sponsorship of empirical economic studies. As Peter Clarke has observed, those committed to the "Treasury view" were persuaded that they knew how the economy should work in a "knave-proof" system. From this perspective, systematic study of the observables had low priority and, at least potentially, could be disruptive to "sound" policy should the results suggest that self-adjusting properties of an ideal system were not demonstrable in reality (see Chapter 6 of this volume).

---

[17]Ibid.

[18]Lauchlin Currie and Martin Krost, "Federal Income-Increasing Expenditures," circa November 1935, reprinted in *History of Political Economy* (Winter 1978): 534–40. See also Byrd L. Jones, "Lauchlin Currie, Pump Priming, and the New Deal Fiscal Policy, 1934–1936," 509–24, and commentary by Currie in the same issue.

The American government tradition, in contrast, provided far more encouragement to empirical work in economics—even when the findings of the investigators suggested shortcomings in the policies of their political masters. The Roosevelt administration did not launch this tradition but gave it fresh momentum.

THE RECESSION OF 1937–1938
AND ITS INTELLECTUAL FALLOUT

The programs inaugurated during the last four years to combat the depression and to initiate many new reforms have cost large sums of money, but the benefits obtained from them are far outweighing the costs. We shall soon be reaping the full benefits from these programs and shall have at the same time a balanced Budget that will also include provision for redemption of the public debt. (Franklin D. Roosevelt, annual budget message for the fiscal year 1938, submitted in January 1937)

The second Roosevelt administration opened on a note of optimism about the prospects for the economy. There seemed to be adequate ground for believing that soon the momentum of the economy would be sufficient to generate recovery and that the elusive goal of a balanced budget would be in sight. The year 1936 had been a good one, the best since the start of the Depression. But there was still a cloud on the horizon: price increases in certain sectors, particularly those producing materials for the construction industry (such as steel, copper, lumber), might put a brake on capital spending. Writing in March 1937, Leon Henderson, who had earlier directed the NRA's Research and Planning Division and who then served as a consulting economist with the Works Progress Administration (WPA), noted that wholesale prices had risen almost 10 percent since September 1936, and he perceived a "real danger of runaway prices." He then argued that, in the absence of "firm action" against inflated prices, "the expected boom may never materialize."[19]

Those who expected that the country would shortly be back to business as usual were rudely jolted in the second half of 1937. The recession that began in August was, in fact, more precipitous than the downturn immediately following the crash of October 1929. But, as a challenge to economic analysis, there was an important difference. The upper turning point in 1929 had occurred when the economy was operating at a high level of capacity utilization, when a cyclical adjustment might have been

[19]Leon Henderson, "Boom and Bust," March 29, 1937, Franklin D. Roosevelt Library.

regarded as part of the normal order of things. In 1937, in contrast, the collapse set in when the economy was still far short of full employment. This turn of events did not mesh with anyone's prior conception of the way the system ought to behave.

When interpreted ex post, the observable evidence could be given a variety of readings. Critics of the administration were inclined to treat it as a damning indictment of its policies and as testimony to the bankruptcy of deficit financing or to the mischief of tax policies that "harassed" business (such as the controversial undistributed corporate profits tax). Alternatively, the Federal Reserve could be faulted for its decisions to raise reserve requirements in 1937—moves taken to give the central bank greater leverage should monetary restraint ultimately be needed. Within the bureaucracy, the events of 1937 also gave fresh ammunition to those calling for policies to discipline the "administered price-makers," although differences remained about whether this should be done through more direct planning or through investigations and prosecutions by the Justice Department's Antitrust Division.

By late 1937, the administration was adrift with no consensus in sight about the diagnosis of the recession or about appropriate remedies. Harry Hopkins, director of the Works Progress Administration, urged the president to "talk to the boys who actually write the heads of department's memos and get some first hand dope on what is after all a highly technical matter."[20] Roosevelt acted on this suggestion by convening a White House session involving Currie, Leon Henderson, and Isador Lubin, commissioner of labor statistics in the Department of Labor. At this point, the conceptual scheme that Currie and Krost had begun to work on in 1935 came into its own. When data for 1936 and 1937 on the "net contribution of government to spending" were analyzed, they produced an arresting finding. In 1936, government had stimulated spending in substantial measure by the payout of the final installment of the World War I Veterans Bonus (a measure mandated by Congress over the president's veto). But the 1936 bonus stimulant was nonrepeatable, and nothing replaced it in 1937. Meanwhile, the payment of payroll taxes into the Social Security Trust Fund began. These collections withdrew income from the potential expenditure stream; that income would not be replenished until payments to Social Security beneficiaries began, which was not scheduled until 1942. In light of these findings, the recession of 1937

[20] As quoted in Byrd L. Jones, "Lauchlin Currie and the Causes of the Recession of 1937," *History of Political Economy* (Fall 1980): 303–15.

no longer seemed so mysterious. Primary responsibility could be assigned to an unfortunate shift in fiscal operations between 1936 and 1937.[21]

This finding was indeed new learning, with the government economists in the vanguard. It had long been recognized that fluctuations in the level of the national income were a potent determinant of budgetary outcomes. Now the facts seemed to demonstrate that changes in tax receipts and government spending were potent determinants of aggregate income. This conclusion synchronized with the analysis Keynes had presented in *The General Theory,* published in 1936. The fiscal expansionists in Washington were certainly familiar with this work and welcomed the reinforcement it provided. Even so, they had produced a "home-grown" product, and it would have been available if there had been no *General Theory.*[22] There can be little question that the indigenous quality of their arguments, based as they were on American data and expressed in an American idiom, enhanced the prospects of their ultimate acceptability to official Washington. The appeals that Keynes personally directed to the president, in letters in February and March 1938, received only perfunctory attention.[23]

Currie and his colleagues were satisfied that they had advanced "the state of the art" in their studies of the 1937–8 recession. They had

---

[21]Currie subsequently elaborated this argument at considerable length in a memorandum entitled "Causes of the Recession," April 1, 1938. This document has been published in *History of Political Economy* (Fall 1980): 316–35.

[22]Currie, for example, was certainly not uncritical of the content of *The General Theory.* In a review prepared in 1937 and published as "Some Theoretical and Practical Implications of J. M. Keynes' General Theory," *The Economic Doctrines of John Maynard Keynes* (New York: National Industrial Conference Board, 1938), he wrote, "Here, perhaps, at last, is the answer to an economist's prayer—the key that will enable him to make accurate interpretations and predictions. Such expectations, I am afraid, are doomed to disappointment. Certain aspects of our big problem are illuminated here and there, but all too often we find that familiar things are being described in unfamiliar language, that concepts cannot be given statistical meaning and that precision and definiteness are being purchased at the expense of reality" (p. 15). Currie found it a "peculiarity of Keynes' work that he appears always to think of an increase in income as being generated by an increase in investment and never by an increase in consumption" (p. 18). Nor did he find Keynes's conception of the multiplier to be convincing. Currie's attempts to calculate the value of this coefficient—using Kuznets's data for net income and net investment in the United States from 1919 through 1934—revealed that "on five occasions net investment and income moved in opposite directions: on two other occasions the increase in income was less than the increase in investment" (p. 21).

[23]In February 1938, for example, Keynes wrote to Roosevelt urging, among other things, a major program of deficit spending on public works. The president asked Morgenthau, whose antipathy to this strategy was undisguised, to draft a response for his signature. Morgenthau's reply simply ignored this component of Keynes's programmatic recommendations. See John Morton Blum, *From the Morgenthau Diaries: Years of Crisis 1928–1938* (Boston: Houghton Mifflin, 1959), 402–5.

produced an explanation of this unexpected turn of events that seemed to be analytically persuasive.[24] On the basis of these findings, they pushed their policy recommendations with a strengthened sense of confidence. What the economy needed was a stronger dose of deficit spending to enhance purchasing power. But it took the intervention of Harry Hopkins, Leon Henderson, and Beardsley Ruml (treasurer of Macy's Department Store and an adviser to the National Resources Committee) to move Roosevelt to action. In April 1938, they presented the case for deficit spending in a more homely fashion, rather than in its more technical form. The federal government, they maintained, had long been in the business of creating purchasing power, notably, through the alienation of the national domain to private ownership. With the closing of the frontier, this technique was no longer available. In modern conditions, government was obliged to support purchasing power through its own spending.[25]

In April 1938, over the objections of the secretary of the treasury, the Roosevelt administration committed itself for the first time to a deliberate strategy of fiscal stimulation. This program was explicitly designed to raise aggregate income, and it was announced without apology for the deficits it entailed.[26]

The postmortem on the causes of the 1937–8 recession thus marked a turning point in the "fiscal revolution" in American economic thinking. The capacity of the "new" line of analysis to account for the observable facts enhanced its credibility. And it was crucial in winning converts to a Keynesian style of thinking, not least among some who had expressed major reservations about the message of *The General Theory*. The debates over this episode, for example, had a major influence on Harvard's Alvin Hansen (who was soon to become a leading American apostle of Keynesian doctrine, although he had started out as a skeptic).[27] But the fallout had still wider implications. It increased substantially the demand

[24]Although the analysis of the "net contribution of government to spending" was indeed a step forward, it was still a step short of what would now be regarded as the proper measure of "fiscal thrust" or "fiscal drag." The latter concepts are based on the deficits or surpluses that would arise from a high-employment level of income.
[25]This memorandum, undated and untitled, is in the Hopkins Papers, Franklin D. Roosevelt Library.
[26]This episode has been well covered by Herbert Stein, *The Fiscal Revolution in America* (Chicago: University of Chicago Press, 1969), in a chapter aptly titled "The Struggle for the Soul of FDR, 1937–1939."
[27]See William J. Barber, "The Career of Alvin H. Hansen in the 1920s and 1930s: A Study in Intellectual Transformation," *History of Political Economy* (Summer 1987): 191–205.

within government for the services of economists who could think in a new mode.

One of the key figures in widening the presence in Washington of economists sympathetic to Keynesian doctrines was Harry Hopkins, appointed by the president to be secretary of commerce on December 24, 1938. On the face of it, Hopkins would seem to have been an unlikely choice to head a department that historically had been expected to be the representative of the business viewpoint within the administration. Hopkins lacked the usual credentials for the job. He had never met a payroll; on the contrary, as a relief administrator, he had specialized in dispensing handouts. Nevertheless, he regarded direct relief as repugnant and insulting to human dignity, even though, in some circumstances, a dole was unavoidable. The real remedy for worklessness was work. By the time he took up his assignment at the Commerce Department, Hopkins was convinced that action, informed by the macroeconomic insights then emerging, held the key to reemployment.

Hopkins aspired to make the Department of Commerce a focal point for the analysis and dissemination of the "new" economic knowledge. Since the days when Herbert Hoover had occupied the post of secretary, the department had played a role as an economic "educator," but now its mission was redefined. Hoover's conception of economic education was preoccupied with the collection and publication of current market intelligence—for example, data on production, sales, changes in inventories—to enhance the rationality of business decisions. Hopkins's vision of economic intelligence emphasized instead analyses of the macroeconomic variables determining the behavior of aggregate income. The department's national income accountants already had in hand much of the material required for this work. What was needed was a richer understanding of its significance.[28]

Among Washington economists of the new breed in 1939, the standard view was that a national income of $80 billion to $85 billion was necessary to achieve a high level of employment. Numbers of this order of magnitude were in circulation not only at the Department of Commerce but also at the Federal Reserve Board and at the National Resources

---

[28]The change in approach was signaled in an internal Commerce Department memorandum of April 10, 1939, titled "Policy and Program." It was argued therein that priority should be assigned to "the interpretation of information assembled by the Department and to its prompt dissemination," rather than to "the publication and wholesale distribution of a multitude of items whose place is really in a reference or handbook." (Department of Commerce Records, National Archives.)

Planning Board. There could be no doubt that the economy was operating far short of this target at the time Hopkins assumed his new duties. As Robert Nathan (then styled as the chief of the National Income Section of the department's Division of Economic Research) informed him, preliminary estimates indicated a national income of $61 billion to $62 billion for 1938, a shortfall from $69.8 billion in 1937.[29] There was clearly work to be done.

But although Hopkins and his associates recognized the importance of fiscal measures, they were also persuaded that government alone could not fill the spending gap. It was thus important to create an environment in which capital spending in the private sector would be substantially increased. This meant that government needed to establish better rapport with the business community.[30]

Hopkins devised a three-part approach to this issue. The first component involved expansion and elaboration of the department's studies of the behavior of the national income. Although the department had pioneered in the regular official preparation of national income accounts, its work to date had been concentrated on estimating aggregate income by industrial source and type of payment, supplemented by studies of income that individuals received by type of payment and by analysis of individual incomes by state. As Nathan pointed out to the secretary in June 1939, this material, valuable though it was, left many important questions unanswered. Nathan assigned priority to developing a capability to break down the national product into categories of output (producers' goods, durable consumers' goods, perishable consumers' goods, services), to identify flaws and sources of savings, and to measure the size distribution of income. Reliable data of this type, he emphasized, would enrich understanding of the behavior of aggregate consumption, saving,

[29]Robert R. Nathan to Hopkins, "The National Income in 1938," January 20, 1939, Hopkins Papers, Franklin D. Roosevelt Library.
[30]The attention given to this point at this time—although not necessarily inspired directly by Keynes—is consistent with views Keynes had transmitted to Roosevelt in February 1938. He had then written, "Businessmen have a different set of delusions from politicians; and need, therefore, different handling. They are, however, much milder than politicians, at the same time allured and terrified by publicity, easily persuaded to be 'patriots,' perplexed, bemused, indeed terrified, yet only too anxious to take a cheerful view, vain perhaps but very unsure of themselves, pathetically responsive to a kind word. You could do anything you liked with them, if you would treat them (even the big ones), not as wolves and tigers, but as domestic animals by nature. . . . If you work them into the surly, obstinate, terrified mood, of which domestic animals, wrongly handled, are so capable, the nation's burdens will not get carried to market" (Keynes to the president, February 1, 1938, Franklin D. Roosevelt Library).

118   WILLIAM J. BARBER

and investment.[31] Shortly thereafter, Nathan's jurisdiction was enlarged and his title upgraded to chief of the National Income Division. A major step in the direction of creating new knowledge about the behavior of the Keynesian macroeconomic variables was thus taken.

A second prong of the Hopkins strategy called for a major strengthening in the department's analytic capabilities, and for that purpose he created a Division of Industrial Economics. To staff it, he wanted economists sympathetic to the new macroeconomic way of thinking. This initiative, however, had controversial aspects. As the undersecretary, Edward J Noble (formerly chairman of Life Savers Corporation), noted: "There is a very widespread impression among businessmen that economists are very theoretical and often impractical." Noble recommended an "infusion of genuine business experience," adding that he saw "no reason why we should not use a good many young men from the graduate schools of business and other men who have something more than a passing acquaintance with economic theory."[32] As matters worked out, the lineup of the Division of Industrial Economics included a mix of theorists and practical men, although the former were clearly dominant. The person selected to head it, Richard V. Gilbert of Harvard, had already come into prominence as coauthor of one of the first American manifestos proclaiming Keynesian demand-management, spurred by expansionary fiscal policy as the solution to the nation's problems.[33] Others recruited to the new division included Gerhard Colm, a German immigrant brought to Washington from the New School for Social Research; V. Lewis Bassie, a junior colleague of Currie's on the research staff of the Federal Reserve Board; Walter Salant, one of the unidentified contributors to *An Economic Program for American Democracy;* Donald Humphrey, formerly on the research staff of the Works Progress Administration; and Roderick Riley, a former research assistant to Senator La Follette. The original team also

[31]Nathan to Hopkins, "Proposed Expansion in the Work of the Department of Commerce in National Income and Related Fields," June 15, 1939, Hopkins Papers, Franklin D Roosevelt Library.
[32]Edward J. Noble to Hopkins, July 20, 1939, Hopkins Papers, Franklin D. Roosevelt Library.
[33]This document, titled *An Economic Program for American Democracy* (New York: Vanguard Press, 1938), was billed as the product of the discussions of seven Harvard and Tufts economists. The collaborators identified were Richard V. Gilbert, George H. Hildebrand, Jr., Arthur W. Stuart, Maxine Yaple Sweezy, Paul M. Sweezy, Lorie Tarshis, and John D. Wilson. Walter Salant, Emile Despres, and Alan Sweezy also participated, but in their capacities as government employees, they elected to remain anonymous. Alan Sweezy, "The Keynesians and Government Policy, 1933–1939," *American Economic Review Papers and Proceedings* (May 1972): 116–33.

included Paul Truitt, who had worked his way up to a senior position with Sears, Roebuck, & Co., and Dudley P. K. Wood, a business executive with experience in the machinery industries.[34]

Hopkins thus provided a nest in the Department of Commerce for economists of the new persuasion, but their job involved more than packaging macroeconomic data in novel forms and interpreting their significance for policy-making. They were also expected to develop a liaison with business and to encourage private investment. This was the third ingredient of the strategy. Various mechanisms of communication were available. A familiar one was the department's monthly publication, *The Survey of Current Business*, which began to present data in formats that drew attention to the determinants of macroeconomic activity: the magnitudes of business capital spending, aggregate consumer outlays, inventory accumulation, and the net contribution of government to spending. This publication helped to educate the business community to a new way of perceiving both the performance of the economy and its prospects. But another mechanism was called into play as well: a revitalized Business Advisory Council. This organization, structured as an informal consultative body, had been in place for a number of years and had been conceived as a vehicle through which business leaders could communicate their views or grievances to government. Hopkins saw it as a two-way channel through which economists on his staff could enlighten members of the business community on the insights of macroeconomics. It is perhaps no accident that a substantial number of the members of Hopkins's Business Advisory Council were later to be associated with the Committee on Economic Development, a business-sponsored organization that championed compensatory fiscal policies.[35]

Concurrent with these developments was missionary work for the macroeconomic perspective in hearings of the Temporary National Economic Committee (TNEC). This inquiry was the creature of Congress and had been part of its response to Roosevelt's request for extraordinary appropriations in April 1938. The original charge to the committee—which was composed of three members of the Senate, three members of the House, and six representatives of executive departments and agencies—

[34]Willard L. Thorp to Hopkins, August 17, 1939, Hopkins Papers, Franklin D. Roosevelt Library.
[35]Among them were Henry Dennison, Ralph Flanders, and Lincoln Filene. Of the twenty original trustees of the Committee on Economic Development in 1942, fourteen had served or were serving on the Business Advisory Council. See Robert M. Collins, *The Business Response to Keynes, 1929–1964* (New York: Columbia University Press, 1981), 84.

called for investigations of the impact of monopolistic practices. Under the guidance of Leon Henderson, executive secretary of the TNEC, the focus of its work took a different turn. By the spring of 1939, the TNEC hearings had been transformed into a platform for the propagation of a Keynesian-style gospel. Lauchlin Currie and Alvin Hansen of Harvard appeared as star witnesses, armed with charts and graphs to demonstrate that the fundamental problem facing the economy was a deficiency in total demand. To achieve and maintain high employment, they argued, it was essential to find "offsets" to savings. Savings were withdrawals from the expenditure stream, and—unless they were absorbed by capital spending by business, outlays for residential housing construction, lending abroad, or loan-financed expenditures by government—the economy was doomed to a chronic state of underemployment.

This line of argument had a distinctly Keynesian ring, but there was something American in the accents as well. Hansen, in particular, maintained that the problems of the American economy had special characteristics. In the nineteenth and early twentieth centuries the country's economic performance had been buoyed by the investment opportunities associated with the taming of a continent. With the closing of the frontier, big capital outlays for social infrastructure spending were no longer required on a comparable scale. Meanwhile, declining rates of population growth—which, among other things, diminished the prospective demand for residential housing—compounded the problem of finding sufficient outlets for a high-employment level of saving.[36] This situation defined the challenge to government. In the questioning before the TNEC, Hansen and Currie acknowledged that tax reduction might pay dividends in stimulating private spending. But their central argument was that government could better manipulate aggregate demand by other means.[37]

CONSOLIDATION OF THE KEYNESIAN BEACHHEADS IN 1940

I have come to suspect that you are somewhat bothered by the apparent conflict between the humanitarian and social aims of the New Deal and the dictates of "sound economics." I feel convinced that in place of conflict there is really complete harmony and for that reason only the New Deal can solve the economic

---

[36]Hansen had earlier presented this argument, which came to be known as the "secular stagnation thesis," in his presidential address to the American Economic Association in December 1938; see Hansen, "Economic Progress and Declining Population Growth," *American Economic Review* (March 1939): 1–15.

[37]See the testimony of Hansen and Currie, Hearings before the Temporary National Economic Committee, 76th Cong., 1st Sess., May 1939.

problem. . . . After having had to interview and read the outpourings of number-less cranks and crack-pots, I feel a little abashed at coming forward and saying, "I know the answer." I trust, however, that you will make a distinction! (Lauchlin Currie to the president, March 18, 1940, Franklin D. Roosevelt Library)

There was certainly a note of triumphant self-confidence in the "Memo-randum on Full Employment" that Currie submitted to the president in March 1940. It represented, he wrote, "the line of investigation I initiated at the Reserve Board and which is today being carried on by the brilliant group of young economists in Harry Hopkins' office." He added, "The basic analysis is that of J. M. Keynes."[38]

Although he acknowledged a debt to Keynes, Currie's argument was less pure Keynes than "Curried" Keynes. The apparatus for the analysis of the components of aggregate demand was deployed, a Keynesian con-sumption function was explained, and an investment-income multiplier introduced. Moreover, standard conclusions of Keynes's analysis were derived: that the achievement of full employment depended on a volume of nonconsumption spending sufficient to absorb the savings generated at a full-employment level of income and that the dimensions of this prob-lem would be magnified as income rose and the ratio of savings to income increased.

But the primary remedy Currie offered for a deficiency in aggregate demand was not the one that Keynes had emphasized. Currie down-played deficit spending on public works in his recommendations for ac-tion. There was still a place for such public investment—financed, if possible, outside the budget—but it should not play the major role. Fur-ther increases in the national debt presented politically sensitive issues in the American context and should be constrained. The main weight in the strategy Currie proposed to the president was assigned to government programs to shift the consumption function upward. The objective was to achieve a "high-consumption and low-saving" economy. This goal could be reached by combining a "truly progressive" tax system with redistributive transfer payments and enlarged public outlays for health, education, and welfare. Thus the "humanitarian and social aims of the New Deal" could be reconciled with "sound economics."[39]

The Keynesian style of thinking had advanced in official favor by the time this analysis was produced. Currie had been appointed to the White

[38]Currie to the president, "Memorandum on Full Employment," March 18, 1940, Franklin D. Roosevelt Library.
[39]Ibid.

House staff as the economic adviser to the president, and he was the first to hold this title. But there were also some temporary setbacks for economists of the new breed. Hopkins's Division of Industrial Economics, which had begun with such promise, was terminated in mid-1940 when Congress balked at further funding of its operations. Congressional ire had been aroused by a comment comparing businessmen with savages in *An Economic Program for American Democracy*, the book Gilbert had written with several other authors while still at Harvard.[40] This crisis was short-lived. Veterans of the defunct Division of Industrial Economics were quickly reabsorbed elsewhere in government. Some, including Gerhard Colm, joined the recently reorganized Bureau of the Budget. Others, including Gilbert and Walter Salant, moved to the newly created Office of Price Administration (OPA).

Although there were some bumps along the way, proponents of a new "learning" on the role of government in the management of aggregate demand had arrived near the commanding heights of economic policymaking by 1940. The form in which they articulated their arguments was adapted to the American political environment and economic conditions, but there was an arresting irony here. A Keynesian-style perspective on the role of fiscal policy in the promotion of full employment in a peacetime economy had come to be better represented within the American bureaucracy than in the British one. As George Peden has noted, deficit spending, in the conventions of the British Treasury, was typically regarded not as an instrument for demand management but as finance for capital expenditures for public services, the cases for which would have to be defended on their respective merits (see Chapter 7 of this volume).

GIRDING FOR WAR IN 1941

I agree with what you say about the danger of a "school," even when it is one's own. There is great danger in quantitative forecasts which are based exclusively on statistics relating to situations that are by no means parallel. I have tried to persuade Gilbert and Humphrey and Salant that they should be more cautious. I have also tried to persuade them that they have tended to neglect certain theoretical considerations which are important in the interests of simplifying their statisti-

[40]The passage that gave offense read as follows: "The truth is that the businessman, caught in the toils of events he does not understand, is merely seeking to lay the blame on something he thinks he does understand, just as the savage in the face of the mysterious forces of nature seeks to make them more intelligible by inventing a host of gods and devils. But business is afflicted with a disease far more serious than government intervention in economic affairs." See Richard V. Gilbert et al., *An Economic Program for American Democracy*, 90.

cal task. (J. M. Keynes to Professor J. M. Clark, July 26, 1941, in *The Collected Writings of John Maynard Keynes,* XXIII, Donald Moggridge, ed. [London: Macmillan, 1979], 192)

Keynes's observations on the work of members of the Keynesian cadre in Washington were occasioned by his visit to the United States in the late spring and early summer of 1941 as a member of the British delegation negotiating Lend-Lease arrangements with American officials. This trip afforded him a number of opportunities to meet with American colleagues, among them, Lauchlin Currie, Alvin Hansen, Leon Henderson, Gerhard Colm, in addition to Richard Gilbert, Walter Salant, and Donald Humphrey. The focus of their conversations was the threat of inflationary pressures arising from the American defense build-up. In the discussion of this issue, Keynes found himself at odds with a number of his American followers.

For his part, Keynes had already set out his views on the management of economic mobilization in the British context in *How to Pay for the War,* published in 1940. This document had called for stringent fiscal constraints, through tax increases and compulsory savings, to reduce private demand. Rationing and control over prices and wages also formed part of this program. But, Keynes had insisted, the effectiveness of such measures of direct control ultimately depended on shrinking private purchasing power through fiscal interventions.[41]

The predominant view among Washington's "new school" economists in mid-1941, however, was that the United States could still have both guns and butter. Richard Gilbert had articulated this view forcefully a year earlier, when a serious American preparedness program had been launched, by maintaining that the economy still suffered altogether too much from unemployment and idle capacity and that the stimulus to demand from debt-financed defense spending posed no threat.[42]

By mid-1941, Gilbert conceded that there was some inflationary danger, but argued that it could be contained with controls over prices and inventory accumulations, supplemented by a scheme of allocation priorities for commodities in short supply.[43] For Keynes's benefit, Walter Salant summarized the prevailing view of the American Keynesians:

---

[41]Keynes, *How to Pay for the War: A Radical Plan for the Chancellor of the Exchequer* (New York: Harcourt, Brace, 1940).

[42]Richard Gilbert, "National Defense and Fiscal Policy," June 1940, as reported by Joseph P. Lash, *Dealers and Dreamers* (New York: Doubleday, 1988), 400–1.

[43]As reported by Gerhard Colm in his summary of a meeting of American economists with Keynes on July 23, 1941; see Colm to J. Weldon Jones, "Discussion of Anti-inflationary Measures," July 24, 1941, Records of the Bureau of the Budget, National Archives.

We do not say that the expansive efforts of the defense program upon income will die out before full utilization of all capacity is reached. If there is a "gap" at the point of full utilization (or in practice somewhat before that point is reached), we are perfectly willing to take whatever special measures are necessary to close it. But we are strongly opposed to taking those measures long before full utilization is reached. Such a policy would retard further expansion. . . . If the choice were between a 50 percent rise of prices and several hundred thousand unemployed, no doubt we would regard the latter as the preferable alternative. I think, however, that the actual alternatives for 1942 are closer to a 15 percent rise of prices or 6 million unemployed. Faced with that choice we would prefer the former alternative.[44]

The Americans, who were not yet at war, still saw the achievement of full employment as the overriding priority. Some of them were inclined to read Keynes's disappointment with their position as reflecting a different priority: positioning the U.S. economy to be of maximum support to the British war effort.

But a more technical issue underlay this intrafamilial disagreement. Salant and Gilbert had appropriated tools from the conceptual kits of *The General Theory* in preparing their estimates of the likelihood of inflationary pressures. Their procedure involved these steps: (1) estimating the volume of investment spending and net government spending expected in a future period; (2) forecasting the level of income associated with these magnitudes, taking into account multiplier and acceleration effects; and (3) calculating aggregate consumption on the basis of a presumed value for the marginal propensity to consume.

To be sure, this was the Keynesian way of approaching the problem, but Keynes had two quibbles with the results produced in the mid-1941 American exercise, hence, the "cautions" that he urged. The first concerned what he read as an implicit assumption of perfect elasticity in the supply of nondurable consumer goods (which he regarded as unrealistic). The second turned on the presumed value of the marginal propensity to consume (which he feared was too low). Salant estimated that only 39 percent of the anticipated increment in national income for 1942 would be allocated to consumption. In support of this calculation, he argued that it was consistent with historical values for the marginal propensity to consume: in other words, the underlying consumption function was normally taken to have stable and predictable properties. This was the basis for the initial approximation. The "normal" consumption-income rela-

---

[44]Walter S. Salant to Keynes, June 12, 1941, as reproduced in *The Collected Writings of John Maynard Keynes*, XXIII, 186.

tionships were then adjusted to take account of special factors expected to prevail in 1942. Salant identified three such factors: (1) increases in consumption were expected to lag behind increases in income; (2) shortages of consumers' durable goods were anticipated, and they were expected to lower the marginal propensity to consume (on the ground that frustrated spending on durables would not be fully reallocated to the purchase of nondurables); and (3) the effects of increased tax rates, which would reduce the consumption share of pretax household income, were estimated. Keynes applauded the way in which "various disturbing factors" were built into the analysis, but his doubts were not fully put to rest. As he wrote to Salant in July 1941: "Whether your assumptions about the marginal propensity to consume are correct is another matter which experience will test."[45]

Considerable scope for argument thus remained about how solidly based the findings from the new learning on the size of the "inflationary gap" really were. At least there was consensus that this problem should be at the top of the research agenda. And, as not infrequently happens in Washington, bureaucratic in-fighting provided an extra stimulus to discussion. In the first phase of "inflationary gap" analysis, economists associated with the Office of Price Administration set the pace. Competitors for leadership soon appeared. Economists at the Bureau of the Budget, for example, perceived "gap analysis" as an opportunity to enhance their organization's status. As Gardiner Means saw matters in August 1941, the experts in the operating agencies had better access to the resources needed to analyze specific tax and price control measures. In one field, he observed, "the other agencies have made such little progress that the Bureau could easily place itself in a position of practical authority, namely the determination of the 'gap' which needs to be closed by policy adjustment." It was important, he then argued, that the deflationary effect to be sought through fiscal measures be determined with reasonable precision. Otherwise, "as in 1937, it would be possible to produce too much as well as not enough deflationary effect."[46] Means subsequently proposed that the problem should be approached by estimating the "hypothetical discrepancy" between saving and investment at the

[45]Salant to Keynes, July 15, 1941; Keynes to Salant, July 24, 1941, in *The Collected Writings*, XXIII, 188–90.
[46]Gardiner C. Means to J. Weldon Jones, "The Gap Problem and Bureau Leadership in Developing Fiscal Policy," August 14, 1941, Records of the Bureau of the Budget, National Archives.

targeted future level of national income.[47] This line of argument had a Keynesian flavor. It also presupposed that consumption and saving functions would be well behaved.

Yet another department of government, the Treasury, had an obvious stake in the analysis of counterinflationary strategies. But there, under the leadership of Secretary Morgenthau, anything that smacked of Keynesianism was immediately suspect. As an aid to organizing its thinking on counterinflationary strategies, the Treasury drew on a study, begun in June 1941, by Carl Shoup of Columbia University, assisted by Milton Friedman and Ruth Mack. Shoup was nominally the senior member of the team, but Friedman developed the technique of analysis. This group was charged to consider the magnitude of tax increases necessary to prevent inflation. Its preliminary findings were presented to the Treasury in October 1941.[48]

This study was distinctly different, both in method and in conclusions, from other attempts then under way to calculate the magnitude of the "gap." Friedman, the architect of its methodology, wanted to start from the data to which a reasonable degree of confidence could be assigned: for example, observable consumption spending in the base period and prospective increases in defense spending (based on projections supplied by the military authorities). Insofar as possible, he sought to avoid working with multiplier concepts, the coefficients of which he regarded as highly problematic at best. Various assumptions were introduced about possible growth in real GNP during the next period. These magnitudes were then compared with projected increases in claims arising from the defense budget. Four possible combinations were considered, but in none of them could the increased claims for defense be satisfied from the increment in real output. It followed that the private sector's share of the total product would need to shrink. To accomplish this result without an increase in prices, private spending would obviously have to be reduced. If tax measures were used for this purpose, however, the increase in tax revenues would have to exceed the value of resources diverted from civilian to military purposes. This conclusion could be derived from the

[47]Means, "Statistical Bases for Anti-inflation Policy," August 15, 1941, Records of the Bureau of the Budget, National Archives.

[48]The preliminary mimeographed report, completed on October 15, 1941, was titled "Amount of Taxes Needed in June, 1942, to Avert Inflation." An expanded version of this study later appeared in book form as Carl Shoup, Milton Friedman, and Ruth P. Mack, Taxing to Prevent Inflation: Techniques for Estimating Revenue Requirements (New York: Columbia University Press, 1943).

fact that a reduction of private disposable income by one dollar would not reduce private spending by the same amount because part of what was taxed away would otherwise have been saved. By how much then should taxes rise to avert inflation by mid-1942? The authors offered not one answer, but four, ranging from $4.6 billion to $8.4 billion.[49] In their view, it would be unscientific to claim greater precision. Nevertheless, they regarded this experiment as a constructive contribution. The framework it provided for organizing thinking about tax policy was a decided improvement over untutored intuition and "guesses of what Congress or the public at large would be willing to accept."[50]

The differences between these approaches to inflation containment were publicly aired in exchanges between Salant and Friedman at the December 1941 meetings of the Econometric Society. Salant criticized the Shoup-Friedman-Mack study because it failed to measure secondary effects of changes in spending and because "it does not deal with the curves of the propensity to consume. It deals with those points on the curves that correspond to the consumer disposable income of the base period." The OPA method, on the other hand, was built around a "logically complete system of interdependent quantitative relations" designed to provide forecasts of the components of aggregate demand in a future period.[51]

From Friedman's perspective, what the Keynesians had to offer was less fact than fiction. He preferred to concentrate on the observables: only they could actually be measured. The attempt to specify future consumption-income relationships, for example, was an exercise in speculation. Much depended on the way in which income was redistributed in the movement from one income to another. A variety of possibilities could be entertained; for example, a shift in the income distribution between profit and wage incomes would certainly alter the marginal propensity to consume. Friedman concluded that "at the present stage of our knowledge of the functioning of the economic system, estimating the gap is a presumptuous undertaking." In December 1941, he added a caution to those who might "suppose that a new technique has been developed for guiding public policy in peacetime. . . . Gap analysis has added nothing to our understanding of economic change."[52]

[49]Ibid., 67.
[50]Ibid., 75.
[51]Walter S. Salant, "The Inflationary Gap: Meaning and Significance for Policy Making," *American Economic Review* (June 1942): 308–20.
[52]Milton Friedman, "Discussion of the Inflationary Gap," *American Economic Review* (June 1942): 319, 320.

Friedman's skepticism was informed, at least in part, by his own experience as an economist in government. Between 1935 and 1937 he had cut his professional teeth as a technical adviser to the National Resources Planning Board, which had conducted studies of household consumption behavior. Subsequently, he had worked with Simon Kuznets in research on the income and expenditure patterns of professionals. As an empirical investigator into the raw material on which calculations of the aggregate consumption function were based, he was sensitized to the fallibility of the data and to the hazards of forecasts that presupposed high predictability in spending behavior.[53]

The gap between the participants in this discussion did not close. Their exchanges, however, did focus attention on another question: What should legitimately count as an advance in economic knowledge?

ECONOMIC ARGUMENT IN THE ENVIRONMENT OF ALL-OUT MOBILIZATION

They think that the Government can do the thing one day by pumping money in, and the next day they think the Government can do the thing by putting the brakes on the lower income groups, but I have yet to see a single one of them make a success of anything they have undertaken. (Secretary of the Treasury Henry Morgenthau, Jr., on Keynesian economists in Washington, as quoted in John Morton Blum, *From the Morgenthau Diaries: Years of War 1941–1945* [Boston: Houghton Mifflin, 1967], 37–8)

The truth is [the Secretary of the Treasury] is avoiding facing the real issues in fiscal policy. I am beginning to think he doesn't even understand them. (Harold D. Smith, director of the Bureau of the Budget, April 16, 1942, Harold D. Smith Papers, Franklin D. Roosevelt Library)

American involvement in the war reordered the agenda. No longer was the question of achieving full employment part of the discussion, as it had been in 1941. The central problem became one of managing the allocation of resources between civilian and military demands when capacity was stretched to its limits. No one questioned the importance of curbing civilian spending, but councils within government were divided on how that could best be accomplished. The division reflected, in part, the differences in the social and political convictions of senior policymakers. But

---

[53]These points are well covered in a forthcoming volume by Neil de Marchi and Abraham Hirsch on Friedman's methodology and practice, which I have benefited from reading in manuscript.

they were also reflections of divergent perspectives about the way the economic mechanism could work. These intramural controversies, in turn, sparked fresh thinking on points of economic theory and policy.

The issues dividing the Keynesians at the Bureau of the Budget and the Office of Price Administration from Secretary of the Treasury Morgenthau and his economic advisers were joined in earnest in April 1942. Although all parties to the discussion agreed that stringent economic control measures were necessary in wartime, they did not share a common reading of what the optimal mix should be. The Keynesians supported fiscal constraints through tax increases and were sympathetic toward tax measures that were specifically aimed at reducing consumption, such as a general sales tax. In addition, they called for a universal compulsory savings program: a scheme to absorb 5 percent of after-tax income, later to be increased to 10 percent, was then mooted. These forced savings would be placed in "non-negotiable bonds payable after the war when hard times begin."[54]

In presenting the Treasury's position, Morgenthau informed the president that "there are radical points of difference between our conclusions and those of Harold Smith's group." He registered strong objection to the use of sales taxes on the grounds that they would bring hardship to the lower-income groups, adding that a presidential recommendation for such legislation would probably encourage Congress "to make drastic cuts in the Administration's proposals for increases in personal and corporate incomes and profits [taxes]." He also took strong exception to proposals for compulsory savings. In his judgment, they were misguided for two reasons: they would kill the Treasury's voluntary saving program and would probably lead to liquidations of war bonds already sold to the public. The Treasury supported a program of "strict rationing" to frustrate potential consumption spending and to swell the volume of funds flowing into voluntary purchases of bonds.[55]

Economists at the Bureau of the Budget found all these arguments to be flawed. From a Keynesian perspective, a central task of wartime eco-

---

[54]These proposals were presented to Roosevelt in "A Memorandum for the President Urging an Anti-inflation Program" on April 18, 1942, signed by Claude R. Wickard (secretary of agriculture), Leon Henderson, Marriner Eccles, Harold D. Smith, and Henry Wallace (vice-president), Franklin D. Roosevelt Library. Morgenthau, who had been appointed to this interdepartmental group to devise an anti-inflation program, refused to endorse these recommendations.

[55]Morgenthau to the president, April 3, 1942, and April 10, 1942, Franklin D. Roosevelt Library.

nomic management was to reduce private demand, and reduction of private demand meant that tax policy should bite the incomes of those with the highest propensity to consume. In normal circumstances, progressive taxation might be desired. But, "in the present situation . . . we must resort to the absorption of mass purchasing power because taxation of the upper-income brackets does not have the requisite anti-inflationary effect." Similarly, a compulsory universal saving plan had merit because it would "collect most of its receipts from the lower and middle bracket incomes while the voluntary savings originate largely in the higher income brackets." Nor was the Treasury's faith in general rationing well founded: rationing and price controls could not be effective unless fiscal constraints drained off excess demand.[56]

Two divergent intellectual perspectives shaped these exchanges. The Keynesians focused attention on aggregate demand management through the manipulation of the macroeconomic variables. In their analyses, it was self-evident that the task of suppressing consumption required targeting incomes of those with highest propensities to spend—and they were prepared to suspend some of the freedoms consumers normally enjoyed in order to accomplish their purpose. The Treasury position, in contrast, was rooted in a different philosophical tradition. Despite the urgencies of war, Morgenthau fought for minimal compromise in his vision of the New Deal's commitment to a progressive tax structure. And, despite his enthusiasm for direct controls, he sought to preserve a measure of individual freedom of choice in consumption-savings decisions. There were some overtones here of debates that had raged during World War I over excess profits taxes versus taxes on consumption and their respective implications for distributive "justice," on the one hand, and for inflation fighting, on the other (see Chapter 13 of this volume).

One of the by-products of this clash in perspectives in 1942 was a Treasury initiative in packaging an innovative approach to wartime fiscal management—an "expenditure tax." Strictly speaking, the analysis underlying it was not altogether new: in one form or another, the idea had been around since at least the early 1920s. The context of World War II, however, gave renewed vitality to this concept. The challenge facing Treasury's economists at that time was to devise a tax program that would minimize the burdens on the lower-income groups, while raising more

---

[56]Bureau of the Budget, "Comments on the Letter and Memorandum of the Secretary of the Treasury to the President," April 1942, Records of the Bureau of the Budget, National Archives.

revenue and discouraging consumption. An "expenditure tax" could be cut to these specifications. This scheme, intended as a supplement to the income tax, promised to raise tax receipts and to provide a deterrent to consumption and an incentive to saving. Spending on necessities would be exempt, and households in the higher consuming brackets would be assessed at higher rates than those in lower ones. Because savings would be immune from this levy, adoption of this tax program would also enhance the willingness of the public to purchase war bonds voluntarily. These attractive features notwithstanding, the "expenditure tax" proved to be a nonstarter when presented to the Senate Finance Committee in September 1942.[57] It was, however, kept alive for a bit in discussions among professional economists.[58]

Innovation of another type emerged from the work of economists in the Keynesian camp who were pondering the problems of wartime fiscal management. This contribution to theory, which has since entered the textbooks as the "balanced-budget-multiplier theorem," marked a distinct analytic advance. In effect, it said that a budget that was balanced, but at a higher level of taxation and expenditure than had previously prevailed, would not be "neutral." Instead it would have an expansionary impact on aggregate demand, a result arising because not all of the dollars taxed away would have been spent had they been left in private hands. This insight moved the analysis of the effect of fiscal policy to higher ground than had been reached with the Currie-Krost measurement of "the net contribution of government to spending." And, in the context of the discussions in 1942, it demonstrated that the "inflationary gap" was larger than the size of the budget deficit. This finding was set out in a memorandum of July 30, 1942, by William A. Salant (brother of Walter S. Salant), who was then an assistant to Lauchlin Currie on the White House staff.[59] Independently and concurrently, others were thinking along similar lines. Salant's pioneering theoretical formulation, however, was inspired by a governmental "insider's" concern to sharpen the analytical tools needed to address a pressing practical problem.

---

[57]The expenditure tax and its fate are summarized in Blum, *From the Morgenthau Diaries: Years of War 1941–1945* (Boston: Houghton Mifflin, 1967), 44–8.

[58]Milton Friedman, then working in the Division of Tax Research at the Treasury Department, argued the merits of this plan in "The Spendings Tax as a Wartime Fiscal Measure," *American Economic Review* (March 1943): 50–62.

[59]This paper, which was not published until 1975, appears to be the first exposition in English of the "balanced-budget-multiplier." See the discussion of the "Origins of the Balanced-Budget-Multiplier Theorem," with papers by Walter S. Salant, William A. Salant, and Paul A. Samuelson, in *History of Political Economy* (Spring 1975): 3–31, 43–55.

"Insider" learning thus helped refine an aspect of the Keynesian conceptual system. But on-the-job experience of one economist in Washington sowed the seeds for what would later become a counterrevolution in macroeconomic thinking. From his base as principal economist for the Federal Deposit Insurance Corporation (FDIC), Clark Warburton read the issues of the "inflationary gap" (and of price determination more generally) through quite different lenses. His assignment required him to make detailed investigations of banking statistics—initially with close attention to the distribution of bank failures and to the behavior of bank deposits—to inform the FDIC's determination of premiums to charge when insuring bank deposits.[60] One of the fruits of his continuing researches was the conclusion that the primary factor driving the behavior of the economy was the size of cash balances available to consumers. This position clearly separated him from the Keynesians: as he put it in 1944, there was a "gap between economists who approach the problem of price inflation from analysis of the use of income and those who approach it from monetary theory and the analysis of monetary statistics." The issue could be resolved by determining "which relationship—consumers' expenditures to individuals' incomes, or to their cash balances—past experience indicates to be the more stable."[61]

Warburton was convinced that his data gave empirical validation to the superiority of a monetary approach over an income approach.[62] Moreover, Warburton claimed that his findings on the "stability of the ratio of consumers' expenditures to individuals' cash balances" provided the proper foundation for policies to stabilize the economy. His version of recommended monetary "rules" took the following form: "(1) avoiding at any time a decrease in the per capita cash balances of individuals, and (2) increasing the cash balances of individuals at a rate approximately equal to the rate of increase in production of consumers' goods and services, adjusted for taxes paid by individuals."[63]

Warburton's anti-Keynesian monetarism had virtually no impact at

[60]For background on Warburton, see Thomas F. Cargill, "Clark Warburton and the Development of Monetarism since the Great Depression," *History of Political Economy* (Fall 1979): 425–49.

[61]Clark Warburton, "Monetary Expansion and the Inflationary Gap," *American Economic Review* (June 1944): 303–27.

[62]This analysis was sharply criticized by Keynesians. See, for example, Jacob L. Mosak and Walter S. Salant, "Income, Money, and Prices in Wartime," *American Economic Review* (December 1944): 828–39.

[63]Warburton, "Who Makes the Inflationary Gap?" *American Economic Review* (September 1943): 607–12.

this time. His status within the bureaucracy was remote from the nerve centers of high policy-making. In addition, circumstances of war were not congenial to probing discussions of monetary issues. With the Federal Reserve assigned the task of supporting the government bond market, monetary policy had no autonomy. What Warburton had to offer seemed to be beside the point.

THE AMERICAN KEYNESIANS AND THEIR VISION OF POSTWAR PLANNING

Fiscal policy will be one of our major weapons both in avoiding depressions and in combatting inflation. I believe that fiscal policy, both on the revenue and the expenditure sides, is the most potent weapon we have for influencing markets and employment, especially when we need quick results. It is also a means of action most consistent with free enterprise. Public finance must be our servant and not our master. (Harold D. Smith, director of the Bureau of the Budget, on the full employment bill before the House Committee on Expenditures in the Executive Departments, September 25, 1945)

By early 1944, victory in Europe seemed assured, and the Keynesians in Washington began to turn their attention to closing another kind of "gap." The prospective end of hostilities would necessarily lead to sharp reductions in government spending for military purposes, and demobilization would swell the civilian labor force. The central question would soon become whether aggregate demand would be sufficient to generate full employment in the postwar world. Economists recognized that the combination of pent-up consumer demand for durables and the extraordinary volume of household liquidity associated with wartime savings would provide a short-term stimulant to consumption spending. But what would happen when the force of this stimulus wore off? In light of the accumulated learning on income determination, the Keynesians were convinced that large-scale unemployment was a distinct threat, but also that it could be avoided.

At the Bureau of the Budget, the first phases of the discussion of the postwar employment problem involved preliminary studies of the possible size of a "deflationary gap." Arthur Smithies of the bureau's Fiscal Division made one such calculation in February 1944. Although he cautioned that his estimates of consumer spending out of disposable income were based on "pre-war relationships" (and thus might need to be revised), he was persuaded that they were solid enough to support a judgment that "there would be a large deflationary gap in the post-demobilization period."[64] Attention should thus be turned to measures to spur spending. Not surprisingly, many familiar possibilities were resurveyed: accelerated spending on useful public works; federal subsidies to the construction of residential housing; and federal guarantees to minimum income standards and social welfare programs. But a fresh note was also struck: generous provision of benefits to veterans was now seen as a device for easing the postwar employment problem.

By August 1944, thinking on these issues had entered a new phase. The Keynesians—encouraged by Eccles at the Federal Reserve Board and Smith at the Budget Bureau—set to work on an "American White Paper" on full employment, with Harvard's Alvin Hansen (then a consultant at the Federal Reserve Board) serving as coordinator of its drafting committee.[65] As this document evolved, some new emphases were introduced. Government was called on to make a formal commitment to responsibility for economic stabilization, which included attacking both deflationary and inflationary gaps. And when it needed to spur aggregate demand, it should not do so only as a spender. Attention should also be given to variations in tax rates to spur private spending. But to do the job properly a major reform in administrative machinery was needed. The draft report of August 17, 1944, proposed the following:

It will be necessary to set up . . . a national investment board or a fiscal authority to cooperate closely with a joint congressional fiscal committee. Under a broad legislative grant a program of public construction should be laid out for a period of 5 to 10 years. The national investment board or fiscal authority should be allowed to adjust and fluctuate the total expenditure so appropriated according to the requirements of economic stability. . . . The public investment board or fiscal authority should, moreover, operate within a broad grant of power by Congress and, within specified limits imposed by Congress, should be empowered to make variations in income tax rates and in social security pay roll taxes as a means to regularize the flow of total expenditures and to promote economic stability.[66]

This daring scheme amounted to a grand design for a "Fisc" with discretionary powers to execute fiscal policy analogous to the powers the Fed

[64]Arthur Smithies, "The Economic Problem in 1950," February 21, 1944, Records of the Bureau of the Budget, National Archives.
[65]Others participating in this exercise included Richard Gilbert, Gerhard Colm, Emile Despres, Arthur Smithies, and Walter Salant.
[66]Alvin H. Hansen to Weldon Jones, August 18, 1944, with attached draft of "Postwar Employment Program" (dated August 17, 1944). Records of the Bureau of the Budget, National Archives.

enjoyed over monetary policy. That it could be proposed at all reflected the confidence of the Keynesians that they now possessed the knowledge needed to manage the economy.

The fate of the "full employment bill" has been amply chronicled elsewhere.[67] The outcome was a distinct disappointment to the Keynesians who had set this ball rolling. Congress had no interest in delegating its jurisdiction over taxing and spending to "experts" in the executive branch. Even the adjective "full" was stripped from the language of the Employment Act passed in February 1946. The act did, however, create a new organization, the Council of Economic Advisers, but it denied its members any operational authority and charged them with no duties beyond preparing periodic reports. So great was the distance between the aspirations of the Keynesians and the congressional product that the Bureau of the Budget staff seriously contemplated advising President Truman to veto the bill. In the end, they did not: a statute that affirmed government responsibility for "maximum employment, production, and purchasing power" could be regarded as an achievement, even if a dismayingly limited one. But when Truman offered Budget Director Harold D. Smith the post of chairman of the Council of Economic Advisers, Smith declined. He perceived the job as "a very hazardous one." The public would expect much from the incumbent, yet he would lack the authority needed to meet those expectations. "I am willing to be expendable in a good enterprise," he told Truman, "but I want to be sure that the enterprise is a good one."[68]

THE EDUCATIONAL LEGACY OF A DOZEN YEARS

Government isn't infallible by any means. Government is only beginning to learn a lot of these new tricks. We are all going to school. (Franklin D. Roosevelt, remarks on his economic program during his sixty-sixth press conference, November 3, 1933)

The laboratory of government enriched economic understanding during the Roosevelt years. The president provided an environment for experimentation unlike anything the country had seen before. Some of the early experiments failed and were soon abandoned. Others, particularly those linked with the use of fiscal tools for economic management, seemed to

[67]See, for example, Stephen K. Bailey, *Congress Makes a Law: The Story behind the Employment Act of 1946* (New York: Columbia University Press, 1950).
[68]"Conference with President Truman," February 8, 1946, Harold D. Smith Papers, Franklin D. Roosevelt Library.

offer promising solutions to the nation's problems in both war and peace. By the time of Roosevelt's death, the Keynesian conceptual apparatus had come to shape the official macroeconomic agenda. This framework for policy was worlds removed from the fiscal orthodoxy Roosevelt had proclaimed when he first campaigned for the presidency.

Economists who served in government were catalysts to this fiscal revolution. Necessarily they were highly sensitive to the practical problems calling for analytical interpretation and to the importance of improving the data needed to inform policy-making. Through their efforts, the volume of hard information on the behavior of the economy was vastly enlarged. As contributors to the reformulation of theory, they also widened the domain of the discipline. In these years, there can be little question that "insiders" were pressing the frontiers far more than were their colleagues who remained in academe.

The assimilation of a Keynesian-style macroeconomics into American official thinking was a marked result of a dozen years of turbulence for the economy and for economists. But to treat the learning acquired in the "school" of government as a total victory for a Keynesian point of view would be incorrect. Government experience also provided some ammunition for a Keynesian critique and helped to give another twist to professional debate. Was the economic universe ordered around a stable consumption function with predictable properties that would permit "fine-tuning" through policy (as the more doctrinaire of the American Keynesians claimed)? Or should economists be more humble, acknowledging the limitations of their knowledge and resisting temptations to intervene (as critics of Keynesianism recommended)? These fundamental questions, which were later to receive sharper definition, had already been brought into focus in the "school" of Roosevelt's Washington. The points over which Friedman and Salant had parted company in their competing views of "gap" analysis soon resurfaced in postwar controversies.[69]

[69]Noteworthy in the immediate postwar years were the exchanges between Alvin Hansen and Arthur Burns. Hansen had attacked Burns's essay, *Economic Research and the Keynesian Thinking of Our Times* (National Bureau of Economic Research, 1946), and Burns replied as follows: "I suspect that Hansen is troubled because my essay conveys the impression that Keynesians are excessively mechanical in their thinking, that they gloss over the turbulent life that goes on within aggregates, that they give little heed to adjustment processes in our society, that they subject *ceteris paribus* to excessive strain, that they slight in particular the instability of the consumption function; and that while Keynes is guilty on all of these counts the Keynesians—among whom Hansen is outstanding—are guiltier still." See Burns, "Keynesian Economics Once Again," *Review of Economic Statistics* (November 1947): 252–68.

Researches conducted in the government laboratory also foreshadowed the controversy that was later to divide the profession between monetarists and Keynesians. Warburton's monetarism stirred few waves at the time it was first put forward. Indeed it passed largely unnoticed, even by some who later embraced this position. Friedman, although early in establishing himself as a critic of Keynesianism, came only later to monetarism. When he did so, the debt to Warburton was recognized. As Friedman and his collaborator on *A Monetary History of the United States* observed, "His detailed and valuable comments on several drafts have importantly affected the final version. . . . Time and again, as we came to some conclusion that seemed to us novel and original, we found that he had been there before."[70] Whereas debates among the "insiders" gave shape to a fiscal revolution in professional and official thinking, they also helped to spawn subsequent counterrevolutions.

How typical, or atypical, was the experience of these years for the relationships between government and the stimulation of economic learning? In important respects, this period has the markings of a "special case." In the crises of depression (and later of war), the American polity was prepared to suspend the historic ground rules on the respective jurisdictions of the public and private sectors. Roosevelt, by temperament, was eager to exploit that opportunity. Unlike his predecessor in the White House, he was unencumbered by principled convictions on the way the economic system functioned or could be made to function. Nor did he regard consistency and continuity as necessary when deciding on the approaches to economic policy that he chose to adopt. His administrations thus generated a lively demand for new ideas and for new data to reinforce them. Meanwhile, in the atmosphere of depression and war, service in government had an attractiveness to professional economists that was unprecedented. Many of those who migrated to Washington in these years experienced a life akin to a full-time graduate research seminar. Intellectual puzzles abounded amid the challenges of addressing practical issues. Indeed, their professional work-product within government frequently appeared, with little delay and without substantial modification, in the economic journals of the day. Convergence of these factors yielded an environment propitious for "insider learning."

[70]Milton Friedman and Anna Jacobson Schwartz, *A Monetary History of the United States, 1867–1960* (Princeton, N.J.: Princeton University Press, 1963), xxii.

5

The emergence of economic growthmanship in the
United States: federal policy and economic
knowledge in the Truman years

ROBERT M. COLLINS

The influence of the so-called Keynesian revolution on economic thought
and policy in the United States is beyond dispute. It is understandable and
indeed proper that this development has also loomed large in the histori-
ography of modern American political economy. But much else of consequence was happening beneath the gradually unfolding Keynesian um-
brella; and the very drama and impact of the Keynesian revolution must
not be allowed to obscure its own quite significant shadings, subtleties,
and ambiguities.

This chapter has two essential purposes. The first is to sketch the
landscape of post-1929 political economy in terms of the shifting goals
that guided and determined national economic policy and of the interplay
among such goals when several were held simultaneously. The emphasis
here is not on the means of Keynesianism but, rather, on the ends in the
service of which Keynesianism was harnessed. In charting the changing
objectives of macroeconomic policy, I single out for special attention the
emergence of economic growth as an overriding goal of postwar policy.
Analysis of this "growthmanship" is at the heart of my enterprise.

My other purpose, second in order of appearance but fully coequal in
analytic significance, is to ascertain the connections between this development in national economic policy—the emergence of growthmanship—
and developments in the realm of economic knowledge, particularly in
economic theory and measurement. The question that lies behind this
inquiry—does science push policy, or does policy pull science?—is un-

138

doubtedly simplistic in its phrasing and misleadingly dichotomous, but it is nonetheless compelling in its historical interest and contemporary relevance. The relationship between knowledge and policy is rich and multidimensional, and we need to understand its complexity in order to comprehend our past and shape our future.

THE POLICY CONTEXT: FROM THE ECONOMICS OF SCARCITY TO THE ECONOMICS OF ABUNDANCE, 1932–1946

Although quantitative measures can be used to gauge the swiftness and depth of the nation's economic collapse after 1929, it is more difficult to recapture the collapse of New Era optimism and the rise of the new pessimism in economic thought that accompanied the Great Depression. Whereas Herbert Hoover had in his 1929 inaugural address proclaimed, "I have no fears for the future of our country. It is bright with hope," his opponent in the 1932 presidential campaign spoke of a different new era, an epoch defined by economic maturity.[1]

Roosevelt's uncertainty about the future of the economy surfaced most clearly in his campaign address at the Commonwealth Club in San Francisco in September 1932. He noted at the outset that the world in depression seemed "old and tired and very much out of joint." In contrast, he observed, "America is new. It is in the process of change and development. It has the great potentialities of youth." But this proclamation of vigor immediately gave way to a portrait of a mature, indeed sclerotic, economy:

Our industrial plant is built; the problem just now is whether under existing conditions it is not overbuilt. Our last frontier has long since been reached, and there is practically no more free land. . . . We are not able to invite the immigration from Europe to share our endless plenty. We are now providing a drab living for our own people. . . . Clearly, all this calls for a re-appraisal of values. A mere builder of more industrial plants, a creator of more railroad systems, an organizer of more corporations, is as likely to be a danger as a help. . . . Our task now is not discovery or exploitation of natural resources, or necessarily producing more goods. It is the soberer, less dramatic business of administering resources and plants already in hand, . . . of adapting existing economic organizations to the service of the people.[2]

[1]U.S. President, *Public Papers of the Presidents of the United States: Herbert Hoover, 1929* (Washington, D.C.: U.S. Government Printing Office, 1974), 11.
[2]Franklin D. Roosevelt, *The Public Papers and Addresses of Franklin D. Roosevelt*, comp. Samuel Rosenman, 13 vols. (New York: Random House, 1938–50), 1:743, 750–2.

The theme of economic maturity would, Theodore Rosenof has argued, serve as "the primary divide" separating New Dealers, progressives, radicals, and conservatives in their approaches to the problems of the Great Depression.[3] The tension between the vision of the United States as a youthful, expansive economy, on the one hand, and an overbuilt, mature economy, on the other, reverberated throughout the Depression decade.

The specter of maturity bred a brand of scarcity economics that dominated the New Deal's initial policies for both industry and agriculture. Production controls that limited output were central to both the National Recovery Administration (NRA) and the Agricultural Adjustment Administration (AAA). The price-fixing provisions of the NRA's individual industrial codes inevitably had the effect of limiting production. *Balance* was a key word in discussions of early New Deal economic policy, and it implied a recovery that aimed to restore a previous level of prosperity but little more. The emphasis of so many New Deal programs on "security"—indeed, perhaps the single most important thread unifying what critics characterized as the New Deal hodgepodge—bespoke a similarly pessimistic reading of the nation's present condition and future chances.

Many liberals came to view massive unemployment as a permanent problem. Harry Hopkins, the New Deal's chief relief administrator, predicted in 1937 that "a probable minimum of 4,000,000 to 5,000,000" persons would remain without work "even in the future 'prosperity' periods."[4] In retrospect, the New Deal's pursuit of recovery, balance, and security provides a rather sober counterpoint to FDR's personal style of jaunty optimism.

The emergence late in the 1930s of a full-blown school of economic thought built on the idea of secular stagnation reinforced the New Deal's practical emphasis on balance and security. The classic formulation of the stagnationist analysis was Alvin Hansen's presidential address to the American Economic Association in December 1938. The United States, the Harvard economist told his colleagues, had reached economic maturity: Population increase had slowed dramatically, and territorial expansion was now a thing of the past. Technological innovation had produced no great industrial boom since the automobile, and it was doubtful that

---

[3]Theodore Rosenof, *Dogma, Depression, and the New Deal* (Port Washington, N.Y.: Kennikat Press, 1975), 113.
[4]Harry Hopkins, "The Future of Relief," *New Republic* (February 10, 1937): 8.

technological change could be counted on to stimulate the economy periodically. The result was secular stagnation—"sick recoveries which die in their infancy and depressions which feed on themselves and leave a hard and seemingly immovable core of unemployment."[5]

Hansen's fiscal policy seminar at Harvard, which attracted a large following, influenced both academe and government. In 1938, a group of young Harvard and Tufts economists influenced by Hansen published a stagnationist manifesto titled *An Economic Program for American Democracy*. The book appeared on Washington's best-seller list; and when, in February 1939, James Roosevelt discussed with his father the possibility of an educational film on the program and objectives of the New Deal, the president suggested the work of the Harvard-Tufts group as a good summation of the administration's economic philosophy.[6]

The New Deal's embrace of scarcity economics and stagnationism, however, was often a source of tension and contention. Some New Dealers spoke longingly of the day when they would be able to ease off on the economic brakes and step on the gas. "Rationalize it any way we have to," said Rexford Tugwell, "we can't make a religion out of growing or making fewer goods with this whole country and the whole world in bitter need."[7]

As secretary of agriculture, Henry A. Wallace became perhaps the nation's most visible restrictionist and a prime example of the New Deal's ambivalence. In two short months in 1933, Wallace oversaw the plowing under of 10 million acres of cotton already in the fields and the slaughter of 6 million piglets whose existence threatened a future glut in the hog market. The uproar was immediate. "To hear them talk," Wallace complained, "you would have thought that pigs were raised for pets." But he felt keenly the obscenity of attacking poverty in the midst of plenty by eliminating the plenty. "We of this administration," he wrote the next year, "are not committed indefinitely to crop control or to NRA codes." It was a matter of playing the hand you were dealt; the failures of the past made scarcity economics necessary. Agriculture had to be brought into some sort of balance with industry. But Wallace remained uncertain

---

[5]Alvin Hansen, "Economic Progress and Declining Population Growth," *American Economic Review* 29 (March 1939): 4.
[6] Richard Gilbert et al., *An Economic Program for American Democracy* (New York: Vanguard Press, 1938); Elliot Roosevelt, ed., *F.D.R.: His Personal Letters*, 4 vols. (New York: Duell, Sloan and Pearce, 1947–50), 4:857–8.
[7]Quoted in Arthur M. Schlesinger, Jr., *The Age of Roosevelt: The Coming of the New Deal* (Boston: Houghton Mifflin, 1958), 64.

whether the goal was "balance and continuous stability" or "a continually moving but balanced state."[8]

Skepticism and outright opposition to scarcity economics grew over the course of the Depression. In 1938, Philip La Follette, the governor of Wisconsin, tried to found a new political party based on a philosophy of increased production. At the same time, a group of congressional liberals led by Maury Maverick, Jerry Voorhis, and Tom Amlie fought for an industrial expansion bill that would use NRA-type mechanisms to plan for abundance rather than scarcity. But the bill went nowhere, and as the 1930s came to an end a combination of government policies and economic theory built around the themes of scarcity, security, and stagnation remained ascendant.[9]

The coming of World War II finally tipped the balance decisively away from the economics of scarcity and toward economic expansion. The goals of balance and recovery gave way to the pursuit of all-out production and full employment. The reorientation was more difficult and uneven than our social memory of the war suggests, but the forces behind expansion were ultimately overpowering. Defense orders from Europe followed by the necessity of arming the nation's own military forces created demand and energized the economy in a way that the New Deal's necessarily more limited spending for civilian purposes never could. Once the process was under way, the expansionist tendencies of the administration's growing cadre of Keynesian economists became clear, and they worked to keep the fire that had been lit under the economy at a white heat. They were determined to use the opportunity presented by the defense buildup to attack the persistent stagnation that had afflicted the economy for over a decade. Consequently, once the armament program was set in motion, they worried far less about the danger of overheating the economy and the risk of inflation than did Keynes himself. In 1940–1 the American Keynesians sought simultaneously to maintain New Deal programs, sustain civilian consumption, and arm the nation, thereby pushing the economy to full employment at a new, higher level of output.[10]

In their battle to push the pace of economic expansion, the "all-

[8]Schlesinger, *Coming of the New Deal*, 62–3; Henry A. Wallace, *New Frontiers* (New York: Reynal and Hitchcock, 1934), 28–9, 34, 47.

[9]Rosenof, *Dogma, Depression, and the New Deal*, 91–4.

[10]Keynes to J. M. Clark, July 26, 1941; and Walter Salant to Joseph Dorfman, June 8, 1971, both in Box 1, Walter Salant MSS, Harry S. Truman Presidential Library (hereafter HSTL).

outers" gained an important advantage by virtue of their expertise in national income analysis.[11] The expansionists were also aided by the belief of many New Dealers that the real obstacle to recovery was the system of administered markets that allowed firms in highly concentrated industries to maintain or raise prices while limiting output. Expansion would eliminate these bottlenecks by creating new capacity, increasing output, and inducing price reductions.

Thus, expansion was viewed as a means as well as an end, and it appealed both to the structural reformers and to the fiscalists among the New Dealers. The "sit-down strike by the capital" would finally be broken. Anything less than maximum expansion, warned Marriner Eccles, head of the Federal Reserve Board, would result in "a static economy frozen at a level of underemployment."[12] Some businessmen, however, viewed stasis as preferable to expansion. The automobile, electric power, petroleum, and railroad industries all shared a reluctance to expand capacity, and the struggle to get the nation's steelmakers to expand proved particularly difficult.[13]

The all-outers, from FDR on down, alternately badgered, bribed, and reassured the hesitant business leaders, and in the end the expansionists prevailed. Their efforts contributed to the expansion of capacity in steel and other basic industries, to the development of the government's all-out "Victory Program" for mobilization in 1941, and to FDR's proclamation of even more ambitious production goals in January 1942. And in the end, the productivity of the American economy counted heavily on what one military historian has characterized as a "gross national product war"—a contest that turned largely on the matter of which coalition could outproduce the other.[14]

In the last years of the war, the steady movement away from scarcity

---

[11]See Byrd L. Jones, "The Role of Keynesians in Wartime Policy and Postwar Planning, 1940–1946," *American Economic Review* 62 (May 1972): 125–33; John Kenneth Galbraith, "The National Accounts: Arrival and Impact," in U.S. Bureau of the Census, *Reflections of America: Commemorating the Statistical Abstract Centennial* (Washington, D.C.: U.S. Government Printing Office, 1980), 75–80; and John Brigante, *The Feasibility Dispute: Determination of War Production Objectives for 1942 and 1943* (Washington, D.C.: Committee on Public Administration Cases, 1950).

[12]Quoted in Richard A. Lauderbaugh, *American Steel Makers and the Coming of the Second World War* (Ann Arbor, Mich.: UMI Research Press, 1976), 78.

[13]The best account is ibid., 87–107. See also Gerald T. White, *Billions for Defense: Government Financing by the Defense Plant Corporation During World War II* (University: University of Alabama Press, 1980); and Bruce Catton, *The War Lords of Washington* (New York: Harcourt, Brace, 1948).

[14]Russell Weigley, *The American Way of War* (New York: Macmillan, 1973), 146.

economics toward a new economics of abundance gathered momentum. Hansen gravitated to an increasingly optimistic assessment of economic maturity. In suggesting that an abbreviated "White Paper on Employment Policy" be prepared for inclusion in the 1944 Democratic platform, he directed, "The draft should make a clear declaration that the government accepts as a primary responsibility the maintenance of full employment; and the prevention of depression and deflation on the one side and of inflation on the other." If such steps were taken, Hansen was, he wrote to a colleague in 1945, "really very optimistic about our prospects." America was not "through": "We can make adjustments to the changed situation [described in his theory of economic maturity] and go on to higher living standards and as great, if not greater, opportunities for private enterprise as we have had in the past." Such confidence, he reported, set him apart from Keynes himself, who had, in two seminars in 1944 and 1945, taken a much dimmer view of America's prospects for full employment.[15]

The new goals of abundance, high or full employment, and economic stability appeared in a number of different political guises. Liberals planned for a further extension of the New Deal, based on expansion instead of balance and security. In the 1944 election campaign Roosevelt sketched out the vision of a full-employment economy offering 60 million jobs. Henry A. Wallace's call for a postwar Century of the Common Man amplified the themes of abundance and full employment. Walter Reuther, a leading expansionist throughout the war, proclaimed, "The road leads not backward but forward, to full production, full employment and full distribution in a society which has achieved economic democracy within the framework of political democracy."[16]

Few businessmen favored a resurgent, hyperactive New Deal, but the optimism that inspired liberal visions of a new political economy encouraged many executives as well. Paul Hoffman, head of the Studebaker

---

[15]Hansen to Gerhard Colm, July 11, 1944, in Box 1, Gerhard Colm MSS, HSTL; Hansen to David McCord Wright, July 30, 1945, HUG (FP)-3.50, Box 2, Alvin Hansen MSS, Harvard University.

[16]Roosevelt, *Public Papers*, 12:574–5; 13:369–78; Theodore Rosenof, "The Economic Ideas of Henry A. Wallace, 1933–1948," *Agricultural History* 41 (April 1967): 143–53; John Morton Blum, "Portrait of the Diarist," in Blum, ed., *The Price of Vision: The Diary of Henry A. Wallace, 1942–1946* (Boston: Houghton Mifflin, 1973), 3–49; Henry A. Wallace, *Sixty Million Jobs* (New York: Simon and Schuster, 1945); Walter P. Reuther, "Reuther Challenges 'Our Fear of Abundance,' " *New York Times Magazine* (September 16, 1945): 8.

Corporation and chairman of the Committee for Economic Development, recalled that the Depression had given birth to "some strange thinking on the part of business, labor, agriculture, and government—thinking which in turn found expression in weird policies." These policies, he declared, had been "designed to fasten upon us an economy of scarcity." But the war had changed all that, and had opened the way to a "peacetime economy of abundance."[17] General Robert E. Wood of Sears, Roebuck, who in the late 1930s had quoted Hansen's stagnation theory approvingly—"It means," he observed rhapsodically, "that the sun has passed its zenith and the shadows of afternoon have begun to fall"—would backtrack soon after the war and declare the idea of economic maturity to be "the greatest of the many fallacies enunciated in the 1930's by the New Deal."[18]

The emergent consensus on the economics of abundance was tested during the debate over full employment in 1945 and ratified by the enactment of the Employment Act of 1946. Despite the significant dilution of the bill over the course of its passage, the Employment Act's final declaration of the government's "continuing policy and responsibility . . . to promote maximum employment, production, and purchasing power" signaled the formal recognition of "high" employment and economic stability as the chief aims of macroeconomic policy. The Employment Act represented both an extension of the developments of the Great Depression and a departure from them. With its passage, the focus of national economic policy formally shifted from the problem of curing a gravely, perhaps permanently, sick economy to maintaining a healthy one.

In addition to its declaration of policy, the Employment Act also established the Council of Economic Advisers (CEA) as a mechanism to ensure that the president would in the future benefit from expert economic advice provided routinely. Created at the point when the economics of abundance, with its goals of high employment and economic stability, superseded the Depression's stress on recovery, balance, and security, the CEA would, in its first years of existence, add to the dominant constellation of goals a fresh, self-conscious emphasis on economic growth, an emphasis that itself became a hallmark of the postwar political economy.

[17]Paul Hoffman, speech to the National Association of Manufacturers, December 6, 1944, in Box 2, Edwin Nourse MSS, HSTL.
[18]Quoted in Herman E. Krooss, *Executive Opinion* (Garden City, N.Y.: Doubleday, 1970), 306–7.

THE COUNCIL OF ECONOMIC ADVISERS AND THE EMERGENCE
OF ECONOMIC GROWTHMANSHIP, 1946–1952

Although focused and articulated most clearly by the new CEA, the postwar interest in economic growth per se was not the CEA's unique discovery or intellectual property. Even before the war's end, an informal committee that included Hansen and Gerhard Colm of the Bureau of the Budget's Fiscal Division had noted that "after the war, the volume of demand and production . . . will have to increase steadily from year to year in order to sustain full employment as the productive power of our country expands."[19] But in such thinking, growth remained more the by-product of sustained full employment than a primary end in itself. In a similar fashion, the Committee for Economic Development recognized in 1947, when developing its significant "stabilizing budget policy," that "reasonable stability of total demand at an adequate level . . . means a steadily rising level of demand as our productive capacity grows."[20] Here, too, however, growth remained subordinate to economic stability as the focus of policy.

Chester Bowles, the wartime head of the Office of Price Administration, viewed economic growth as a central matter. The New Deal, he recalled subsequently, had been "only half a success," and "many frustrated economists told us that there was little more that we could do about it. . . . We must learn to live with a certain amount of scarcity in the midst of plenty." Such was "a recipe for class warfare," Bowles believed, "and for a dog-eat-dog society in which no group could prosper except at the expense of some other group."[21] In the context of such concerns, Bowles in 1946 published *Tomorrow Without Fear*, a liberal tract that had at its heart the question, "Where is our productive capacity going to be ten years hence, twenty years from now?" The answer was optimistic:

Our population isn't going to stop growing, technology isn't going to stand still, and all these new plants and machines, bought by an average of 30 billion dollars a year in business investment spending, will steadily increase our ability to produce. . . . By the late 1960's our national production . . . will have grown to the breathtaking total of 400 billions of dollars a year![22]

[19]Memo, "Postwar Employment," October 9, 1944, Box 1, Colm MSS, HSTL.
[20]Committee for Economic Development, *Taxes and the Budget: A Program for Prosperity in a Free Economy* (New York: Committee for Economic Development, 1947), 10.
[21]Chester Bowles, *Promises to Keep: My Years in Public Life, 1941–1969* (New York: Harper and Row, 1971), 161–2.
[22]Chester Bowles, *Tomorrow Without Fear* (New York: Simon and Schuster, 1946), 44.

Significantly, Bowles shifted the discussion from economic expansion—that is, the putting to work of idle resources, the elimination of economic slack, and the achievement of full employment—to what economists regard as pure economic growth—the long-term growth of economic potential, of potential output. Still, it remained for Truman's new CEA to develop fully the concept of growth and give it a place of primacy among the other goals—notably, full employment and economic stability—that guided postwar economic policy.

The CEA began operation in August 1946 with a membership diverse in background, temperament, and politics. Edwin G. Nourse was a moderate conservative with excellent professional credentials; he had headed both the American Economic Association and the Social Science Research Council and was a vice-president at the Brookings Institution when selected to lead the CEA. Leon H. Keyserling had been in the vanguard of the New Deal; a graduate of the Harvard Law School, he did not hold a doctorate in economics but had proved himself a brilliant student of political economy during his long government service, most notably as a trusted adviser to New York's Senator Robert F. Wagner. John D. Clark had made a fortune in the oil business, then retired while in his early forties to study economics and undertake an academic career; he was serving as dean of the business school at the University of Nebraska when Truman tapped him to serve on the CEA.

The CEA members were an unusual mix in terms of economic philosophy as well. Although not strict Keynesians, all were familiar with Keynesian analysis and ready to accept many of the basic Keynesian prescriptions. Indeed, an early memorandum to the president spoke of the "wise policy of deficits under adverse business conditions."[23] But the three also had strong institutionalist leanings and a keen interest in microeconomic phenomena.[24] As Keyserling subsequently observed:

The whole basis of economic analysis is to analyze where your resource maladjustments are, where allocations are going wrong, where your income flows are going wrong. And you correct it by applying the stimulus or the restraint at the right points, which really gets back to what I said in 1948. . . . We don't have the kind

[23]CEA to Truman, December 13, 1946, in Box 1, John D. Clark MSS, HSTL.
[24]Craufurd D. Goodwin, "Attitudes toward Industry in the Truman Administration: The Macroeconomic Origins of Microeconomic Policy," in Michael J. Lacey, ed., *The Truman Presidency* (Cambridge, Eng.: Woodrow Wilson International Center for Scholars and Cambridge University Press, 1989), 89–127. See also Edwin Nourse, "The Professional Background of the First Chairman of the Council of Economic Advisers," August, 1963, Box 1, Nourse MSS, HSTL.

of economy where you can just throw a blunderbuss at the whole thing. Here again, economists are beginning to say that we need micro economic as well as macro economic policies.[25]

Thus it was out of what can only be described as a unique brand of economic eclecticism that the CEA forged the new emphasis on goal as the nation's foremost economic task.

A gradual but clearly perceptible quickening of interest in growth can be traced in the unusually philosophical year-end reports submitted by the CEA between 1946 and 1950. The first such report in December 1946 recognized the legitimacy of stabilization as a fundamental policy aim but also cautioned that mere stability was not by itself a wholly satisfactory criterion of success. Indeed, the "greatest danger of recent years" had been "a more or less permanent equilibrium at a low or 'stagnation' level."[26] Nor was high employment a completely trustworthy end in itself. The CEA warned in 1947:

Maximum *employment* may be achieved in a rich economy or in a poor economy, in a static economy or in a dynamic and growing economy. . . . The inadequacy of the goal of mere number of jobs . . . has been demonstrated during the first year of operation of the Employment Act. For we were astonished to find, after the country had reached the idealized figure of 60 million jobs, that the volume of production still was disappointing.[27]

At the end of 1947, the CEA suggested that the attention already given to economic stability and full employment be complemented by an increased emphasis on "maximum production," the "belatedly added phrase" in the Employment Act's declaration of policy that "should be kept foremost in our analysis of conditions and trends and in our efforts toward betterment." The CEA's view of production was rich and complex. It favored a proactive rather than reactive approach: "Government economic activities should be carefully designed to add to the resourcefulness, the productivity, and the growth of our business system as a whole instead of being regarded mainly as a device for applying poultices to that system when it becomes infected." But, the CEA warned in picturesque language, maximum production should not be interpreted to mean a life

[25]Erwin C. Hargrove and Samuel A. Morley, eds., *The President and the Council of Economic Advisers: Interviews with CEA Chairmen* (Boulder, Colo.: Westview Press, 1984), 79.

[26]U.S. Council of Economic Advisers, *First Annual Report to the President* (Washington, D.C.: U.S. Government Printing Office, 1946), 9, 12.

[27]U.S. Council of Economic Advisers, *Second Annual Report to the President* (Washington, D.C.: U.S. Government Printing Office, 1947), 7.

of grinding toil and deprivation so that "Pa can raise more corn to feed more hogs to buy more land to raise more corn to feed more hogs *ad infinitum.*" Instead, the report presented the vision of a redistributive mass consumption society in which "the enlarging production" would "go increasingly to filling in the consumption deficiencies of the erstwhile poor."[28]

The direction of the CEA's thinking during its first two years under Nourse's leadership was clear: The full-fledged growthmanship—a newly focused, newly self-conscious, newly single-minded emphasis on growth as the overriding (but not sole) national economic goal—that emerged when Leon Keyserling took over the effective leadership of the Council in 1949 was not a sudden departure in its thinking but rather the culmination of a trend already well under way.

Written under Keyserling's direction, the CEA's 1949 report constituted growthmanship's declaration of principles. In it, the CEA sought to offer "new ideas" to a "new generation," thereby distinguishing the liberalism of Truman's Fair Deal from its New Deal predecessor and from conservative alternatives. Accordingly, the report stressed that "the doctrine of secular stagnation no longer finds place in any important public circle with which we are familiar." In its stead, the CEA offered "the firm conviction that our business system and with it our whole economy can and should continue to grow." Equally significant was the contention that economic growth deserved priority over efforts to redistribute the nation's current product. In the CEA's view, such an emphasis on growth promised to reduce "to manageable proportions the ancient conflict between social equity and economic incentives which hung over the progress of enterprise in a dynamic economy." Indeed, the report found in growth the standard or criterion that could be applied to the vexing problem of "balance" in the economy, balance between production and consumption and balance among wages, profits, and prices.[29]

Here was a macroeconomic goal that contained a key to the solution of society's most vexing relational problems. Growth provided an economic yardstick that would allow factual economic analysis to be applied to the contending claims of consumers, labor, management, capital, agriculture, and government. For the CEA, it promised the opportunity to take issues of social strife out of the political arena and into the court of

---

[28]Ibid., 7, 10, 19, 27.
[29]U.S. Council of Economic Advisers, *Business and Government: Fourth Annual Report to the President* (Washington, D.C.: U.S. Government Printing Office, 1949), 3, 5, 6.

"scientific analysis": "It then becomes possible, albeit not easy, for businessmen, workers, and farmers to seek that share of the total product which is most conducive to the progress of the whole economy and thus to their own best interests in the long run." Daring in its conception and articulate in its presentation, the 1949 CEA report came close to raising growth from an overriding economic goal (first among equals) to a new organizing principle for a neo-corporatist political economy.[30]

Keyserling believed strongly that the CEA's emphasis on growth was indeed a departure, and he stressed the point repeatedly. The emphasis on economic growth was, he later observed, "the one really new thing" in Democratic programs since the New Deal, the "one really innovating factor." It was a departure as well from Keynesianism, "really a static economics" that "doesn't deal with economic growth at all."[31] Keyserling also took pains to contrast growthmanship with the updated restrictionism which held that a truly healthy economic readjustment after the war and the immediate postwar boomlet necessitated "not only a shrinkage of the price level but also a shrinkage of markets, also a shrinkage of employment, . . . also a somewhat lower level of production and distribution than we had in 1948."[32]

The CEA distinguished between the new goal of growth, now primary, and the longer-standing, but now decidedly secondary, aim of economic stability. In May 1950, Gerhard Colm, now a senior economist with the CEA, assessed the United Nations' Report on National and International Measures for Full Employment, which had been produced by a staff of experts appointed by the UN secretary general. The UN economists, he reported, placed their greatest stress on compensatory measures to offset fluctuations, whereas the Truman administration gave "primary attention" to "measures that promote steady expansion and [thereby] increase the shock resistance of the economy." Compensatory stabilization programs, while closely related, "should be kept in readiness as a second line of defense."[33]

The difference in priority had important analytical origins and policy consequences. The CEA believed that "economic disturbances originate in maladjustments, not of the aggregate, but of economic relationships."

[30]Ibid., 7.
[31]Leon Keyserling Oral History Memoir, HSTL. See also Keyserling, "New Economics for New Problems," December 4, 1951, OF 396, Box 1076, HSTL.
[32]Leon Keyserling, "Economic Outlook for Sales Management," May, 1949, General File/ Keyserling, President's Secretary's File, HSTL.
[33]Gerhard Colm, Memo, May 4, 1950, in OF 396, Box 1076, HSTL.

A countercyclical policy aimed at cushioning booms and declines necessarily "accepts defeat" in the primary effort to establish and maintain healthy relationships between consumption and investment and among wages, prices, and profits. The "more affirmative policy" of "promoting sustained expansion" led to "the necessity of focusing on crucial economic relationships as much [as] if not more than on the development of aggregates." In the CEA's view, growthmanship was not a retreat from microeconomic complexities but rather a way of merging and engaging a variety of macro- and microeconomic problems and objectives.[34]

By 1949 the emergent growth orientation was exerting a strong influence in discussions of economic policy both within the CEA and outside it. The president's economic messages sounded the battle cry of economic expansion and growth throughout the year, with a constancy that was particularly striking in light of the fact that the concern with inflation that had dominated the start of the year was soon replaced by worry about deflation as the recession of 1949 was belatedly recognized.[35] Similarly, in Congress economic expansion and growth appeared the keynote in a variety of legislative initiatives that claimed to address the problems of both inflation and recession. At the beginning of the year, the Spence Economic Stability Bill of 1949 (H.R. 2756) offered expansion as a weapon against inflation, following closely the lines of draft legislation prepared under the direction of the CEA. The Economic Expansion Bill of 1949 (S.281), introduced in July by Senator James Murray (after much redrafting) as an amendment to the expansionary Full Employment Bill of 1950 originally proposed by the National Farmers Union, used a similarly ambitious growth approach, which its supporters claimed would address the problem of deflation. This measure, too, was actively supported by Keyserling, although Truman withheld administration support from it for reasons that are not entirely clear. Both the Spence and Murray bills died aborning, but growth, it seemed, was in the air—a cure for all ills.[36]

[34]Ibid.

[35]Compare, for example, the State of the Union Message and the Special Message to Congress on the President's Economic Report in January with July's Report to the American People on the State of the National Economy. U.S. President, *Public Papers of the Presidents of the United States: Harry S. Truman, 1949* (Washington, D.C.: U.S. Government Printing Office, 1964), 1–7, 13–26, 369–74.

[36]Edwin G. Nourse, *Economics in the Public Service: Administrative Aspects of the Employment Act* (New York: Harcourt, Brace, 1953), 243–8; CEA to Truman, January 14, 1949, and "Draft of Interagency Working Group: A Bill," January 15, 1949, both in OF 396, Box 1076, HSTL; diary entries for June 18 and July 6, 1949, in Box 6, Nourse MSS, HSTL.

The CEA's influence on events increased dramatically in 1950. The January 1950 *Economic Report to the President* declared, "Maximum production and maximum employment are not static goals; they mean more jobs and more business opportunities in each succeeding year. If we are to attain these objectives, we must make full use of all the resources of the American economy."[37] Within months, the nation's national security policymakers, working under Keyserling's tutelage, incorporated the doctrine of growthmanship into cold war strategy. In the wake of the "loss" of China and the Soviet development of an atomic bomb, the policymakers undertook a sweeping reassessment of America's cold war stance. Truman first read the resulting document, the famous NSC-68, in April; after it appeared to have been validated by the outbreak of fighting in Korea in June, Truman finally approved it in September 1950.

NSC-68 suggested that economic growth could be used to generate the funds required for a massive rearmament and a redefinition of the nation's global responsibilities. Growth would provide the vast resources necessary for what the diplomatic historian John Lewis Gaddis has characterized as a "symmetrical version of containment," which would seek to give the United States a kind of perimeter defense against communism. All points on the perimeter would be equally important; in the words of NSC-68, "a defeat of free institutions anywhere is a defeat everywhere."[38] Thus was made a connection between unlimited means and unlimited ends that would bring another generation of liberals to grief in the late 1960s.

The combination of NSC-68 and the outbreak of the Korean War touched off a vigorous debate over economic mobilization policy later in 1950, and here, too, growthmanship played an important role. Keyserling later recalled the events in a fashion rather typically unencumbered by humility:

The really great issue that arose at the beginning of the Korean War was the balance between trying to finance the war out of diversion of resources, as against financing the war out of economic expansion. I think the greatest single decision made . . . was the decision to go for a program of very large economic expansion. This involved a very hot battle within the administration, and one which was won

---

[37]U.S. President, *The Economic Report of the President, 1950* (Washington, D.C.: U.S. Government Printing Office, 1950), 2.

[38]John Lewis Gaddis, *Strategies of Containment: A Critical Appraisal of Postwar American National Security Policy* (New York: Oxford University Press, 1982). On Keyserling's role, see Fred M. Kaplan, "Our Cold-War Policy, Circa '50," *New York Times Magazine* (May 18, 1980): 34ff.

completely by the growth people for the first part of the Korean war. I think that my initiation and participation in that was about as large as that of any one individual could be in influencing policy.[39]

Although self-serving, Keyserling's account was essentially correct.[40] The Defense Production Act signed into law on September 8, 1950, was, in the words of the CEA's executive secretary, Bertram Gross, "a third step in a series started by the Spence Bill and the Murray Economic Expansion Bill, particularly the third title, 'Expansion of Productive Capacity and Supply.' "[41] By the end of 1950, the growth orientation that had been developed gradually since 1946 and articulated clearly in 1949 was firmly embedded in national policy.

The triumphs of 1949–50 did not last, however. In 1951, both Keyserling's expansionist approach and his concomitant preference for indirect controls suffered defeat. In January, the administration instituted a general price freeze, and later in the year it decided to "stretch out" military procurement programs into 1955 and 1956. Full mobilization of American productivity gave way to minimum mobilization. The CEA also found itself excluded from the Fed-Treasury Accord of March 1951 and generally supplanted by the Office of Defense Mobilization as the leading source of advice concerning economic mobilization.[42]

The return of the Republicans to presidential power in 1953 furthered the eclipse of growthmanship within the federal government. For the newly reconstituted Eisenhower CEA, under the leadership of both Arthur F. Burns (1953–6) and Raymond J. Saulnier (1956–61), the tension between the goals of economic growth and stability remained central, but with a decidedly different emphasis. A visceral fear of inflation and a keen sensitivity to the political dangers of recession combined to lay stress on the business cycle and on stability. The result, at least in the minds of growth-oriented Democrats such as Walter Heller, "kept policy thinking in too restrictive a mold in the late 1950's."[43] Under Heller's leadership, of course, the Kennedy CEA launched a new, second round of growth-

[39]Leon Keyserling Oral History Memoir, HSTL.
[40]See Edward S. Flash, Jr., *Economic Advice and Presidential Leadership: The Council of Economic Advisers* (New York: Columbia University Press, 1965), 39–61; Keyserling, "Production: America's Great Non-Secret Weapon," October 23, 1950; and CEA to Truman, September 12, 1950, and October 19, 1950, all in OF 985, Box 1564, HSTL.
[41]Quoted in Flash, *Economic Advice*, 45.
[42]Ibid., 62–99; Leon Keyserling Oral History Memoir, HSTL; and Hargrove and Morley, eds., *Interviews with CEA Chairmen*, 52–4, 77–84.
[43]Walter Heller, *New Dimensions of Political Economy* (Cambridge, Mass.: Harvard University Press, 1966), 29.

manship, with striking energy and success, building more than they cared to admit on the foundation established in the early postwar years.

The temporary eclipse of growthmanship should not blind us to the considerable achievement of the CEA under Truman in introducing, articulating, and incorporating the new orientation into policy. These achievements owed much to the efforts of Leon Keyserling. From the outset, he was the leading force in developing the administration's economic philosophy. His views were a powerful influence within the CEA, both while that agency was headed by Edwin Nourse and thereafter when Keyserling himself served as chairman; his intelligence, energy, single-mindedness, combativeness, and political skill made him a truly formidable advocate in CEA deliberations. In addition, Keyserling served as a tireless publicist in the mass media, using the *New York Times* and national magazines to good advantage in popularizing the growth agenda.

At the same time, Keyserling operated more privately as an occasional writer of White House speeches and as a member of the so-called Wardman Park group, a weekly gathering of administration liberals who began meeting in 1947 in the hope of infusing Truman's presidency with a reformist identity and hence a political appeal all its own. Named for its meeting place—the apartment of Oscar Ewing, head of the Federal Security Agency—the group fed its ideas to Truman via two of its members, presidential advisers Clark Clifford and Charles Murphy. Keyserling's was the dominant voice on economic matters, and the refrain was economic growth.[44]

It would be a mistake, however, to view the turn to growth as simply the revelation of an individual or a political coup by a small group. The emergence of growthmanship was a response to broad currents in American life as well. Its roots ran deep in our culture and history. Its attractions were many: For the CEA, it provided the ultimate yardstick for macroeconomic management and the way to blend macro- and microeconomic objectives. For liberal activists, it offered a rationale and a vehicle for reform. For cold warriors, it made feasible a new, globalized and militarized containment policy. For Democratic partisans, it promised political appeal and electoral success. Most broadly, it expressed in the arena of political economy both the traditional ideals of the frontier experience and the ascendant values of the modern consumer culture.

[44] The Wardman Park group is discussed in Cabell Phillips, *The Truman Presidency* (New York: Macmillan, 1966), 162–5; and Leon Keyserling and C. Gerard Davidson Oral History Memoirs, HSTL.

Growthmanship and economic theory. If we grant the political and cultural roots of growthmanship, it remains to be seen what connections the emergence of the growth orientation had with the world of knowledge, the science of economics. To pursue such an inquiry, I have chosen to consider separately the theoretical and empirical dimensions of economic knowledge. In both dimensions, the interface between policy and knowledge proved to be richly textured but uneven and, given early aspirations, somewhat disappointing to those involved.

From the beginning, chairman Edwin Nourse conceived of the CEA as "a scientific agency of the Federal Government" that sought "to enlist economics in the public service."[45] The CEA, he recognized, was "not set up as a great research agency but as a very small synthesizing body." As a result, the CEA turned to the economics profession for help in bringing scientific research to bear on its efforts. In 1947, Nourse suggested optimistically that the American Economic Association's research committee "be organized and equipped to see that the scientific resources of economics are enlarged . . . and . . . brought to serve." In May 1948, he was still hopeful about "articulating our programs with research activities and interests of the profession through A.E.A."[46]

The relations between the CEA and the economics profession on matters of theory never fulfilled the early hopes and expectations of Nourse and others. John D. Clark noted the difficulties in bringing theory to bear on policy, using the example of business cycle theory. He observed that "there is no professional consensus upon business cycle theory, only professional agreement that each particular theory is inadequate." Moreover, he contended, "cycle theory has seemed to be almost irrelevant in the work the Council must perform. . . . Upon no occasion have the members of the council raised any point of cycle theory and no agreement upon any point under consideration . . . has ever been delayed while the Council members exchanged their views about the business cycle." The CEA's analysis, Clark added, "does not require resort to cycle theory but can be founded upon simple economic principles which are far more

---

[45]Nourse to Truman, July 29, 1946, quoted in Nourse, *Economics in the Public Service*, 106–7; Nourse "Economics in the Public Service," January 23, 1947, OF 985, Box 1564, HSTL.
[46]Nourse, "Economics in the Public Service," January 23, 1947, OF 985, Box 1564, HSTL; Nourse to Donald Wallace, May 3, 1948, Box 5, Nourse MSS, HSTL.

limited." And the situation concerning cycle theory was true more generally as well: "The Council has not found that its ability to reach a conclusion about the probable effect of various economic conditions or about
the correct government policy to meet observed problems has often been
seriously limited by the lack of a satisfactory economic theory."[47]

Keyserling found attempts to bring economic theory to bear on problems similarly unrewarding. In commenting on just such an effort by
Donald H. Wallace of Princeton, a study of "Price-Wage-Profits Relations" undertaken at the CEA's behest, Keyserling wrote, "It seems to me
that relatively little attention should be paid to [general theory], not
because it is unimportant, but because it is to be assumed that members
of the Council and staff are reasonably familiar with general economic
theory and kept abreast of it." Keyserling's preference for the empirical
over the theoretical was unmistakable:

> In the final analysis, we are fairly well in agreement here on general theory and
> need to get down to the brass tacks of some factual appraisals. While economists
> have long talked about prices and wages and profits in the refined atmosphere of
> theoretical techniques, we live in a world where prices and wages and profits are
> being *made*.[48]

In the real world of policy, Keyserling made it clear, theory played but a
small role at best.

It was undoubtedly with this perception in mind that Roy Blough, who
joined the CEA in 1950 as its third member after Nourse's resignation,
wrote shortly thereafter, "Economics in Washington is, in general, not at
the high level of intellectual intensity that is characteristic of the better
universities."[49] For the Truman CEA, theory did not inform policy in
general or the emergence of growthmanship in particular in any notable
way, if theory is taken to mean conceptualization of a specialized, technical sort beyond the general laws of textbook economics.

The growthmanship of the Truman CEA did, however, reflect a more
general intellectual influence: the broad economic tradition of American
institutionalism. The institutionalist school of economic analysis counted
among its adherents Thorstein Veblen, Wesley Clair Mitchell, John R.
Commons, and Rexford Tugwell. These rather diverse thinkers believed
that the U.S. economy was troubled by fundamental contradictions and

[47]John D. Clark, "The President's Economic Council," unpublished manuscript [1948],
    chapter 7, 44–5, 53, in Box 2, Clark MSS, HSTL.
[48]Keyserling to Nourse, August 14, 1948, Box 5, Nourse MSS, HSTL.
[49]Roy Blough to William Frank, September 23, 1950, Box 9, Roy Blough MSS, HSTL.

dislocations. To identify these structural defects, the institutionalists formulated a dynamic, strongly empirical, and inductive brand of economic analysis. They were skeptical of orthodox economic theory, emphasizing instead the urgency of practical problems, the complexity of the "real world," and the importance of institutional change. Both Mitchell and Tugwell taught at Columbia University when Keyserling studied there, and Tugwell's relationship with his young protégé was in many ways formative.[50]

The institutionalist approach left a lasting mark on Keyserling. Tugwell's own disregard for orthodox economic theory—"an abstraction of seriously limited use in the real world"—provided an intellectual inspiration for Keyserling's disdain of impractical academic economics.[51] More positively, the institutionalist orientation colored Keyserling's subsequent thought about economic matters. His concern for fundamental economic relationships and maladjustments, his appreciation of their institutional dimension, and his faith in the underlying productive power of the modern industrial system all echoed central elements of the institutionalist tradition. Keyserling's belief that institutional reform could help spark a new era of sustained economic growth reflected the influence of Thorstein Veblen and his followers more than that of Keynes or the more specialized theorists of economic growth.

Why was the relationship between policy and technical economic theory so underdeveloped, despite Nourse's early hopes? To answer this question, we need to look at the three factors that determined the nature and quality of the policy-knowledge interface:

1. The state of the scientific knowledge available for use and appropriation by policymakers
2. The desire and commitment of policymakers to tap this specialized knowledge
3. The existence of instruments and agencies for the exploitation of the interface

Weaknesses in each of these areas contributed to the CEA's theoretical impoverishment during the yeasty Truman years.

Leon Keyserling has noted the poverty of growth theory in the late 1940s. "There had been almost no interest in American economics in

---

[50]Leon H. Keyserling, "Introduction," in Rexford G. Tugwell, *To the Lesser Heights of Morningside: A Memoir* (Philadelphia: University of Pennsylvania Press, 1982), vii–xvii. Regarding institutionalism, see Joseph Dorfman, *The Economic Mind in American Civilization*, 5 vols. (New York: Viking, 1959), 4:352–98; and Wesley C. Mitchell, *Types of Economic Theory*, ed. Joseph Dorfman, 2 vols. (New York: Augustus M. Kelley, 1969), 2:599–736.

[51]Tugwell, *Lesser Heights of Morningside*, 78.

economic growth," he recalled.[52] It is true that growth had been of continuing interest to economists from the very beginning of economics as a science. As Paul Samuelson has pointed out, Adam Smith's *The Wealth of Nations* (1776) "can be read as a bible of economic development."[53] Whereas David Ricardo and Thomas Robert Malthus took a gloomy view of the prognosis for growth, and Karl Marx continued their preoccupation with distribution instead of growth, the later neoclassical writers retained rather more of Smith's optimism. Despite this continuing interest, however, the question of growth had over the years slipped out to the periphery of economic thought. To be sure, the landscape of growth theory was not quite so barren during the Truman years as Keyserling subsequently remembered. The work of R. F. Harrod in the late 1930s and Evsey D. Domar in the immediate postwar years would later serve as benchmarks for the beginning of "modern" growth theory.[54] But, as sweeping and ethnocentric as his judgment was, Keyserling exaggerated only a little.

When the American Economic Association undertook a review of the various fields of economics in the early 1950s, Moses Abramovitz wrote of the "fragmentary" and "rudimentary" state of the art in the economics of growth. "The theory of growth," he observed archly, "is an underdeveloped area in economics." Harold F. Williamson agreed, commenting that "economists generally have been too much concerned with static models and too culturally bound by a Western European framework of institutions to make the contributions to the subject of the economics of growth that might reasonably be expected from the profession." Simon Kuznets noted "a recent surge of interest in problems of economic growth," but added that it came "after decades during which the problem has been neglected in the traditional corpus of economic theory, and ruled out by some economists as not the proper concern of economics."[55]

[52]Leon Keyserling Oral History Memoir, HSTL.

[53]Paul Samuelson, "Economic Growth," in Robert C. Merton, ed., *The Collected Scientific Papers of Paul Samuelson*, 3 vols (Cambridge, Mass.: M.I.T. Press, 1972), 3:704.

[54]R. F. Harrod, "Scope and Method of Economics," *Economic Journal* 48 (September 1938): 405; Harrod, "An Essay in Dynamic Theory," *Economic Journal* 49 (March 1939): 14–33; Harrod, *Towards a Dynamic Economics* (London: St. Martin's Press, 1948); Evsey D. Domar, "Capital Expansion, Rate of Growth, and Employment," *Econometrica* 14 (April 1946): 137–47; Domar, "Expansion and Employment," *American Economic Review* 37 (March 1947): 34–55; and Domar, "The Problem of Capital Accumulation," *American Economic Review* 38 (December 1948): 777–94.

[55]Moses Abramovitz, "Economics of Growth," 133, 153; Harold F. Williamson, "Comment," 182; and Simon Kuznets, "Comment," 180, all in Bernard F. Haley, ed., *A Survey of Contemporary Economics, Volume II* (Homewood, Ill.: Richard D. Irwin, 1952).

A second reason for the underdevelopment of the relationship between policy and theory was the striking lack of interest in theory per se on the part of key CEA figures and, less surprising, on the part of the leader to whom they reported, President Truman. Nourse noted caustically in September 1949:

> Keyserling and Clark were quite impatient with my idea that, since we have to do a great deal of re-thinking of economic theory and business practices, the staff work is heavily weighted with refinement of issues and statements of pros and cons rather than setting forth dogmatic answers. Keyserling said that he knew it was quite possible to get prompt and definitive answers to the problems. When he was in the Housing Administration he had in two and a half months prepared a report that was a perfect example of the succinct laying out of a major economic problem with its proper solution.

He himself, Nourse concluded sardonically, was obviously handicapped in his CEA post "by my long experience as an independent research worker at Brookings and in the SSRC [Social Science Research Council]."[56] In fact, Nourse harbored his own reservations about economic theory. He both recognized the "blighting isolation of a great deal of the theorizing that economists have done" and was "mistrustful of the whole idea of a 'general theory' of employment, of money, of economic enterprise, or of any one of the significant segments of the economic process and still more of the idea that there could be a general theory of the economic process as a totality."[57]

Keyserling's war with academe was legendary even during his service on the CEA, and his antipathy for theory had both intellectual and psychological roots. Not possessing a doctorate, Keyserling felt put upon by academics, and he returned their supposed snubs and disdain with a highly developed and oft-expressed animus of his own. He loved to distinguish between "those who have been challenged by the responsibilities of practical action and particularly by the responsibilities of public office," on the one hand, and "the economist who has to maintain only a theoretical position, or to write his name imperishably (in his belief) into the literature of his profession," on the other.[58] Academic economists had fractured the discipline into esoteric subspecialties and "in that process came to regard those who wanted to take a general view of the economic

[56]Nourse, Daily Diary, September 2, 1949, Box 6, Nourse MSS, HSTL.
[57]Nourse to Bertram Gross, February 24, 1953, Box 1, Nourse MSS, HSTL.
[58]Keyserling, "Congressional Testimony of March 12, 1952," OF 985, Box 1564, HSTL.

problems of the nation as a whole and their relationship to one another as being almost apostates from the field of economics."[59] Such views made a disdain of theory into a defense of self.

As the CEA's "boss" and chief consumer of economic advice, Truman manifested no interest in the theory or even the reasoning behind CEA recommendations. Nourse could be devastating in his private assessment of the president's approach to economic problems. After one meeting, Nourse wrote, "I left with the feeling that his decisions were already pretty well taken, and this on the basis of information that comes to him casually from a variety of sources, with the final determinant his own political judgment. He seems to me quite quick and brittle in his reactions, not at all attracted by a contemplative analysis of basic issues."[60] Even Keyserling, who held Truman in considerable esteem, admitted, "He was not a technical economist, a formal economist. He had the level of understanding that one might expect, shaped by certain profound views that were fundamental to economics and public policy."[61]

Indeed, Truman's attitude regarding theory reflected less a lack of interest than actual resistance and antagonism. As presidential assistant Joseph Feeny expressed it (with the president's warm approval) in early 1950, "History has shown that the long-range theories of the past have sounded fine in theory but have rarely ever proved beneficial when applied. . . . Our country has reached the soundest and most stable era of prosperity by a realistic approach to each particular problem as it arose."[62] Thus the scientific weakness in growth theory was joined by a disinclination on the part of both adviser and policymaker to use whatever theory might nonetheless be available.

The final factor responsible for the uneven policy-theory relationship during the emergence of growthmanship in the Truman years was the condition of the primary instrument available to effect the interaction between policy and knowledge, the CEA. The CEA proved unequal to the task for a number of reasons. First, the press of current events and workaday routine exerted a stultifying influence on the intellectual work of the CEA. Donald Wallace complained to Nourse in mid-1947 of the CEA

---

[59]Keyserling, "New Economics for New Problems," December 4, 1951, OF 936, Box 1076, HSTL.
[60]Nourse, Daily Diary, November 26, 1946, Box 3, Nourse MSS, HSTL.
[61]Hargrove and Morley, eds., *Interviews with CEA Chairmen*, 58.
[62]Joseph Feeny to Truman, January 26, 1950; and Truman to Secretary of the Treasury, January 31, 1950, both in OF 396, HSTL.

staff's inability to find the time to do or even to oversee basic research, and the problem proved intractable.[63]

In 1949, Nourse wrote to Senator Paul Douglas that "the resources of the Council and its small staff are fully taxed by the continuing task of furnishing economic judgments upon concrete problems as they arise. . . . Therefore we have rigorously restricted our discussion of general problems in an abstract setting to a very few that we have dealt with in the Council's annual reports to the president."[64]

The next year, when Roy Blough joined the CEA, Blough wrote to a friend:

I suppose there are ways to make this job of mine a nice quiet study of economics, but I do not seem to have learned them. There are a lot of very difficult problems that we get drawn into; many conferences with the leading lights . . . ; newspapermen who want to get "background," or at least to satisfy their curiosity about what I look like; speeches to write and deliver.[65]

The next month, Blough wrote to another colleague, "I am enjoying the work, but find there is a good deal of pressure."[66] Moreover, all such pressures of daily routine, recurrent bureaucratic deadlines, and occasional policy crises were exacerbated by the "start-up" problems that inevitably troubled an entirely new agency like the CEA.

Compounding the deadening influence of workaday routine and the press of short-run problem solving were the budget and staffing difficulties that plagued the CEA during the Truman years, some the result of political pressure by conservatives and Republicans. The cuts were more than a mere annoyance. According to Nourse, they "precluded our holding topical conferences of academic, business, and labor economists that we had in mind as a means of mobilizing professional thinking on national economic problems."[67]

Finally, the effectiveness of the CEA's exploitation of the policy-theory interface was limited by the disunity that characterized the CEA during Nourse's tenure. The conflicts that separated Nourse from Keyserling and, to a slightly lesser extent, from Clark were real, encompassing professional (i.e., economic), political, and philosophical disagreements and

[63]Donald Wallace to Nourse, July, 1947, Box 1, Nourse MSS, HSTL. See also Nourse to Wallace, May 3, 1948, Box 5, Nourse MSS, HSTL.
[64]Nourse to Paul Douglas, August 2, 1949, in Daily Diary 1949–81, Box 6, Nourse MSS, HSTL.
[65]Roy Blough to William Hewett, November 1, 1950, in Box 9, Blough MSS, HSTL.
[66]Blough to Paul Parker, December 26, 1950, in Box 9, Blough MSS, HSTL.
[67]Nourse, *Economics in the Public Service,* 210.

personality clashes. In retrospect, Keyserling believed that the long-run cost of this disunity affected both the emergence and the staying power of the growth orientation. He recalled:

I think that President Truman was completely sold on the general idea of economic growth . . . ; but I cannot say that I was ever fortunate enough to have at any time, the kind of understanding and support and breadth of support which I think existed, let us say for the policies of the Kennedy economic advisers. . . . It was always a hard battle; it was a hard battle initially because the Council was divided on how it should behave.[68]

In the end, work pressures, budget constraints, and disunity all compromised the CEA's ability to exploit economic theory fully in the reorientation of policy around the overriding goal of growth.

In summary, growth theory itself was impoverished, the will to use it was feeble, and the instrument designed to foster the application of theory to policy—the CEA—was handicapped in significant ways. In its last year of operation, the Truman CEA continued to seek ways "to bring the thinking of the economics profession to bear upon the work of the Council."[69] This task had originally been undertaken with some optimism in 1946. That the effort seemed to be virtually starting anew six years later is testimony to the fact that the early hope for a blending of economic science and national policy remained unfulfilled.

If technical economic theory contributed little to the reorientation of policy around the goal of growth, what about influence running the other way, from policy to theory? Here judgment is more difficult and more speculative. It is true that the decade after 1952 witnessed, in the words of W. W. Rostow, "a most remarkable surge of thought centered on the process of economic growth."[70] As Simon Kuznets observed, this surge of interest was "clearly *not* an organic outgrowth of continuously and increasingly effective work on the problem leading to a scientific discovery, the latter stirring interest and stimulating research on a new foundation," but instead was the result of current events.[71] Among these events, the emergence of a "third world" of modernizing nation states and the continuation of a Soviet-U.S. cold war competition for military, economic, and propaganda dominance were undoubtedly central. It is possible, indeed

---

[68]Leon Keyserling Oral History Memoir, HSTL.
[69]J. L. Fisher to Keyserling, February 14, 1952, in Box 11, Blough MSS, HSTL.
[70]W. W. Rostow, *The Process of Economic Growth*, 2d ed. (New York: W.W. Norton, 1962), v.
[71]Simon Kuznets, "Comment," 180.

probable, that the prominence the Truman CEA accorded economic growth also contributed to the renewal of interest in the field of growth theory, but unfortunately this contribution cannot be measured precisely.

Growthmanship and the management of economic data. Although the development of growthmanship relied little if at all on technical economic theory, the CEA operated more effectively in the realm of scientific data management, borrowing and contributing in significant ways. Here, too, the relationship between policy and knowledge was governed by the state of the science, the will to use scientific knowledge, and the instruments at hand. All these factors were, on balance, stronger for the exploitation of empirical research and statistical science than for the appropriation of specialized theory.

Stuart Rice, the long-time chief statistician in the Bureau of the Budget, has observed that "statistics, like education, are pervasive in their influence."[72] He might have added that they are omnipresent as well. But for the formulators of growthmanship in the CEA, one field of statistical knowledge stood above all others in significance—the concept of national income. National income and its statistical relation the gross national product (GNP) have long served as the fundamental measure of economic change and, in the minds of many, of national welfare and progress as well.[73] The concept of national income took shape slowly in the 1920s and 1930s and was institutionalized in its modern form just as the Truman CEA began its work.

The modern era of national income accounting began with the efforts of the National Bureau of Economic Research in the 1920s. The Federal Trade Commission ventured into the field in 1926, but its work was terminated when funding for such general research was cut off. Ultimately, three developments—the Great Depression, the advent of Keynesian economic theory, and World War II—combined to propel national income accounting to the forefront of statistical science and economic policy-making. All three placed a premium on measuring aggregate in-

---

[72]Stuart Rice to Henry A. Wallace, December 22, 1944, Box 32, Stuart Rice MSS, HSTL.
[73]The discussion of national income accounting that follows is based on Paul Studenski, *The Income of Nations, Part I, History* (New York: New York University Press, 1961); Edgar Z. Palmer, *The Meaning and Measurement of the National Income and of Other Social Accounting Aggregates* (Lincoln: University of Nebraska Press, 1966); John W. Kendrick, "The Historical Development of National-Income Accounts," *History of Political Economy* 2 (Fall 1970): 284–315; and Carol S. Carson, "The History of the United States National Income and Product Accounts: The Development of an Analytical Tool," *Review of Income and Wealth* 21 (June 1975): 153–81.

come, outlays, and production. The Department of Commerce began to prepare national income estimates in the mid-1930s, and introduced quarterly estimates of GNP and national income in 1942. Finally in 1947 there appeared an expanded, double-entry set of income and product accounts by sector, which gave these measures their wholly modern form. Thus, at the beginning of its operations the CEA found available a set of highly sophisticated statistical data and an array of analytical tools. The CEA quickly incorporated these into its economic analysis and, by its public pronouncements and published reports, placed them in the national spotlight.

The CEA, divided and deeply ambivalent about the utility of sophisticated economic theory, appeared much more willing to grant the central importance of statistical fact finding—"the foundation of the work of this Council."[74] The CEA, John Clark reported in 1948, sought "to improve and expedite statistical service, and it has worked to this end with the several fact-gathering agencies."[75] Nor was the CEA's interest merely that of a voracious but passive consumer of data. Staff economist Walter Salant wrote to his colleagues regarding statistical matters:

Speaking for myself alone, I feel that if I do not know the parts that go into the analysis and also how they are put together, I am merely indulging in a kind of informal chatter when I discuss the outlook. . . . Each of us owes it to the Council to use scientific procedures in formulating our independent individual judgments as well as our collective judgment, and that requires that we see everything that goes into the pot.[76]

Whereas the CEA stood alone as the premier federal agency expected (by some if not by all) routinely to bring economic theory to bear on the formulation of policy, in the realm of economic measurement it joined a long-standing, multifaceted federal effort. The Departments of Agriculture, Commerce, Labor, and the Interior, as well as the Federal Reserve Board and the National Recovery Administration, were already engaged in data collection when Roosevelt in 1933 established the Central Statistical Board to coordinate the federal government's statistical services.[77] The coordinating function was subsequently transferred to the Bureau of the Budget under the Reorganization Act of 1939.

[74]CEA to Truman, April 4, 1947, Box 1, Clark MSS, HSTL.
[75]John D. Clark, "The President's Economic Council," unpublished manuscript [1948], Chapter 3, p. 23, in Box 2, Clark MSS, HSTL.
[76]Walter Salant to Staff, April 16, 1947, Box 2, Walter Salant MSS, HSTL.
[77]On the history of federal statistical programs, see Bureau of the Budget, Office of Statistical Standards, "Functions and Operations," November, 1952, Box 12, Rice MSS, HSTL.

World War II necessitated a dramatic expansion of the federal government's statistical capability: Just to mention the alphabet agencies such as WPB (War Production Board) and OPA (Office of Price Administration) is to conjure up the vision of a statistical juggernaut.[78] Soon postwar planning provided a further spur. In August 1944, Roosevelt set off a flurry of activity when he asked the Bureau of the Budget to prepare a comprehensive program of statistics for reconversion.[79] But Stuart Rice warned his superiors, "It is easier to ask for such a program than to develop it"; in the event, much of Roosevelt's proposed "Basic Statistics Program" failed to gain congressional funding.[80]

It would be a mistake, then, to paint too rosy a picture of the statistical tools and instruments available to the CEA as it set to work. The failure to fund Roosevelt's Basic Statistics Program was compounded by a further round of budget cutting in 1947; federal statistics programs of all kinds were attacked by conservatives who saw creeping socialism and intrusive bureaucracy everywhere.[81] By 1949, the Budget Bureau had simply stopped developing and submitting program proposals "in view of the congressional attitude toward statistics."[82] Despite such problems, the CEA inherited a legacy (however troubled) and a statistical arsenal (whatever the gaps) that served as a foundation for some noteworthy achievements on the policy-knowledge front.

The CEA's statistical activities did not usually include the actual gathering of data—other government and civilian agencies performed that service—but rather focused on the use of data collected by others. The CEA's contributions came in all three kinds of information found in the federal statistical system: indicators, frameworks, and basic research.[83] Some were fundamental to the task of policy-making and thus were unrelated to the emergence of growthmanship per se; others, however, were clearly linked to the CEA's growth orientation. One example of the former was the CEA's compilation of basic economic statistics published

---

[78] On the wartime use of statistics, see the correspondence in Box 32, Rice MSS, HSTL.

[79] Bureau of the Budget, Division of Statistical Standards, "Statistical Requirements in the Readjustment Period: Detailed Plans for a Government-wide Program," November 1, 1944, Box 13, Rice MSS, HSTL.

[80] Rice to Assistant Director, Bureau of the Budget, November 25, 1944, Box 7; Harold D. Smith to Truman, April 25, 1945, Box 8, both in Rice MSS, HSTL.

[81] See, for example, the memo "Integrity of Government Statistics: 1946 Controversy," Box 114, Rice MSS, HSTL.

[82] Rice to Frederick J. Lawton, February 2, 1949, Box 8, Rice MSS, HSTL.

[83] This trichotomy is borrowed from Milton Moss, "Changing Boundaries of Federal Statistics," March 1969, Box 164, Rice MSS, HSTL.

under the title *Economic Indicators*. The statistics had originally been published, in an abbreviated form, by the Bureau of the Budget, but at Keyserling's strong urging the CEA took over the effort, expanded its scope and distribution, and arranged for regular monthly publication under the auspices of the Joint Committee on the Economic Report.[84]

The CEA's development of statistical frameworks—systems for illuminating fundamental interrelationships between parts of the economic system—necessarily reflected the conceptual nature of its thinking over the years. The foremost statistical system adopted by the CEA, first for analytical and then increasingly for heuristic purposes, was the so-called Nation's Economic Budget. First used in the 1946 budget published in January 1945 and summarized in FDR's accompanying budget message, the Nation's Economic Budget was then incorporated into the full-employment proposals that led ultimately to the creation of the CEA. The CEA made it the statistical centerpiece of the yearly *Economic Report of the President*. In the words of Gerhard Colm, the Nation's Economic Budget

simply presents gross national income and gross national expenditures in the two columns of a national ledger. The totals of both sides must, of course, be equal. National income and national expenditures are allocated to consumers, business, international transactions, and government. . . . This presentation not only affords a check on the estimates but also shows the interrelation between transactions of consumers, business, and government.[85]

The Nation's Economic Budget concept combined an analysis of broad economic flows with a view of the interrelationships between profits, wages, and prices. It illuminated present conditions and offered a basis for projections into the future and hence for a degree of what might be called "economic planning." One reviewer of the CEA's initial reports was ecstatic: "This is not somebody's crackbrained theory; it is simple arithmetic."[86]

The CEA quickly attempted to extend the temporal range of its statistics. In October 1947, it began work on long-term projections of GNP, national income by demand category, and disposable income for 1950 and 1955 and on the development of "target" figures against which to measure its estimates. The CEA staff then planned to collaborate with the

[84]Nourse, *Economics in the Public Service*, 166–7.
[85]Gerhard Colm, "The Nation's Economic Budget: A Tool of Full Employment Policy," in National Bureau of Economic Research, *Studies in Income and Wealth* 10 (New York: National Bureau of Economic Research, 1947), 89.
[86]George Soule, *New York Times Book Review* (February 1, 1948): 29.

Bureau of Labor Statistics, using the latter's comprehensive input-output table in order to project investment needs for specific industries and public facilities.[87] The results of this project stirred controversy within the CEA when the staff tried to incorporate its ten-year projections into the 1949 *Economic Report* under the title "Basic Objectives for Balanced Economic Growth."

This was a daring use of statistical projections in support of just the sort of affirmative growth-oriented policy toward which the CEA had been moving, but the attempt proved too much for Nourse and Clark. Critical of the projections as "too highly speculative . . . whatever [their] exploratory value for scholars," the two CEA members at first sought to excise the offending section, then settled for its inclusion "in a more tentative and sketchy form."[88]

The next year, however, Keyserling, then serving as acting chairman and freed from Nourse's countervailing conservatism, included in the 1950 *Economic Report of the President* a full-employment model of the economy for 1954, which was considered by scholars a pioneering study. Under Keyserling, the CEA continued its work on "the preparation of economic objectives for 5- and 10-year periods," and it cooperated with the National Bureau of Economic Research to organize the Annual Conference on Research in Income and Wealth in 1951 on the subject of long-term projections.[89]

The growth orientation helped dictate another basic change in the framing of government statistics. When Keyserling assumed the chairmanship of the CEA, the Department of Commerce was reporting the GNP and its component figures only in current dollars. Keyserling recalled:

This was meaningless; you can't tell what the rate of growth has been; or what really happened in current dollars. You have to have constant dollars with different deflators. The Secretary of Commerce said this would cost too much and he didn't see why we should do it. I had to go to the President. The result was that the Secretary . . . was ordered to do it in constant dollars as well as in current dollars.

In this way, Keyserling has correctly observed, "the picture in constant dollars and in current dollars with the proper deflators" was made available to "economists and everybody else."[90]

---

[87]Gerhard Colm to Staff, October 14, 1947, Box 4, Nourse MSS, HSTL.
[88]Nourse, *Economics in the Public Service,* 233.
[89]"The Operations of the Council of Economic Advisers," May 15, 1950, Box 11, Blough MSS, HSTL; National Bureau of Economic Research, *Long-Range Economic Projection: Studies in Income and Wealth* 16 (Princeton, N.J.: Princeton University Press, 1954).
[90]Hargrove and Morley, eds., *Interviews with CEA Chairmen,* 73.

In the third area of statistics, basic research, the CEA's growthmanship fostered a major effort to study underdeveloped regions of the country. The regional development research program included studies of the Southeast (1949), New England (1950–1), and the Southwest (1951). Keyserling directed the local economists charged with the New England analysis to study carefully "the possibility that further self-development in this region may be encouraged and facilitated by some national action favorable both to that area and to national economic growth."[91] Thus, in the fields of statistical frameworks and basic research in particular, the CEA both borrowed from science and contributed significantly as well.

PERSPECTIVES AND CONCLUSIONS

To generalize about the interrelationships between policy and scientific knowledge in the emergence of economic growthmanship during the Truman years is not easy. In the areas of both economic theory and measurement, the interface between policy and knowledge was often murky and almost always hidden from public view. Clear, unambiguous patterns were the exception, not the rule. Technical economic theory contributed very little to the initial orientation of policy around the goal of growth. The prominence accorded growth quite possibly had a subsequent influence on the quickening of professional interest in growth theory, but it is impossible to specify this influence. The body of economic thought that most influenced CEA policy was the tradition of American institutionalism, which itself scorned the abstractions of professional theory and proposed a more practical brand of political economy. It is not surprising, therefore, that the reciprocal relationship between policy and knowledge was significantly stronger in the realm of data management. Advances in statistics made an important contribution to the development of growthmanship, and the CEA's growth orientation, in turn, added to the store of knowledge available to scholars and policymakers.

In its effort to add growth to the constellation of goals that determined postwar economic policy, the Truman CEA anticipated in crucial ways the intellectual revolution in U.S. economic policy-making so widely her-

[91]Keyserling to Committee of Experts on the New England Economy, May 15, 1950, OF 396, Box 1076, HSTL.

alded by its participants in the 1960s.[92] In many ways, the Truman CEA facilitated the development of a second stage of growthmanship under John Kennedy and Walter Heller. The CEA under Kennedy focused on the growth issue early in JFK's thousand days.[93] The CEA operated much more effectively and comfortably on the policy-knowledge interface than had Keyserling and his colleagues. Heller stressed the theoretical legitimacy of the emergent political economy of growth to a president who both welcomed and understood the intellectual rationale for action. The names of scholarly researchers such as Robert Solow, T. W. Schultz, Simon Kuznets, and Edward F. Denison began to appear in memos and speeches.[94] Heller announced proudly that the CEA was "engaged in both domestic studies and international comparative studies to push out the bounds of knowledge on economic growth."[95]

It is important to remember, however, that the CEA was able to operate so successfully in large part because Keyserling and the Truman CEA had put growth on the national agenda, and because Keyserling had then as a Democratic intellectual activist toiled indefatigably to keep growth alive as an issue. The first question JFK asked Walter Heller when they met was, "Well, now, if you're such a good economist, tell me, can we really achieve the 5 percent rate of growth that we promised in the Democratic platform?" Leon Keyserling was responsible both directly and indirectly for that platform pledge.[96]

[92]Walter S Salant, "Some Intellectual Contributions of the Truman Council of Economic Advisers to Policy-Making," *History of Political Economy* 5 (Spring 1973): 36–49. The developments of the 1960s have been treated by Walter Heller, *New Dimensions;* Heller, ed., *Perspectives on Economic Growth* (New York: Random House, 1968); James Tobin, *The Intellectual Revolution in U.S. Economic Policy-Making* (London: Longmans, 1966); Tobin, *National Economic Policy: Essays* (New Haven, Conn.: Yale University Press, 1966); Tobin, *The New Economics One Decade Older* (Princeton: Princeton University Press, 1974); and Arthur M. Okun, *The Political Economy of Prosperity* (Washington, D.C.: Brookings Institution, 1970).

[93]See, for example, Walter Heller to JFK, July 14, 1961, Box 5; Heller, "The American Economy: Progress, Prospects, and Policies," November 13, 1961, Box 17; Heller to Cabinet Committee on Economic Growth, September 25, 1962, Box 17, all in Walter Heller MSS, John F. Kennedy Presidential Library (hereafter JFKL).

[94]See, for example, Heller to Robert Solow, May 11, 1961, Box 17; Heller to JFK, March 3, 1962, Box 5; and Heller, "Economic Growth: Challenge and Opportunity," May 18, 1961, Box 17, all in Heller MSS, JFKL.

[95]Heller, "Economic Growth: Challenge and Opportunity," May 18, 1961, Box 17, Heller MSS, JFKL.

[96]Heller's account of his first meeting with Kennedy is in Hargrove and Morley, eds., *Interviews with CEA Chairmen,* 173. On Keyserling's post-CEA activities, see Herbert S. Parmet, *The Democrats: The Years after FDR* (New York: Macmillan, 1976); Sidney Hyman, "Can a Democrat Win in '60?" *Reporter* (March 5, 1959): 11–15; Leon Keyserling Oral History Memoir, HSTL.

Thus, it was in placing growth on the nation's political and intellectual agenda that the original authors of growthmanship had their greatest influence. This agenda setting did not flow ineluctably from the natural progress of economic science. Rather, it resulted from essentially political decisions, which, in turn, reflected the intellectual, ideological, experiential, and institutional influences at work on both policymakers and their expert advisers. For example, in the case of Leon Keyserling, the broad intellectual tradition of institutionalism was filtered through the historical experiences of the Great Depression, the New Deal, and World War II. The resultant outlook was then applied to a host of both general problems and specific decisions in the particular political, economic, and institutional environment of the Truman years. In the final analysis, the growth orientation was more politically determined than it was knowledge-driven.

To return to our initial question of does science push policy or policy pull science, the emergence of growthmanship suggests yet another image: Policy and science often marched in tandem, moving farther and faster together than either would have moved alone, and moving closer and closer together as time passed. But it was policy—an assertion of political will in the most fundamental sense—that caused the crucial first step to be taken. The lesson is an important one, both historically and politically.

6

The Treasury's analytical model of
the British economy between the wars

PETER CLARKE

The first question posed in this chapter is concerned with "practical knowledge"—how did Treasury officials understand the British economy to work in the 1920s and 1930s? A second question is, How far was that understanding influenced and modified over time by professional, discipline-based knowledge, on the one hand, and by general cultural values and beliefs, pertaining to the way the economy works, or was supposed to work, on the other?[1] The protean issue of the role of ideas in the process of government can thus be posed in a highly general way, but it arises also in forms that are specific to this particular topic.

It has, no doubt, often been easy to form an exaggerated view of the importance of "ideas," especially those expressed in "classic texts" written by "great thinkers." Such an account, in fact, can serve as a retrospective rationalization that tidies up more messy and complex developments, gaining in intellectual coherence what it lacks in historical verisimilitude. There are possible sub-Hegelian overtones and variations here, but let us restrict our attention to a rationalist model of purposive intellectual influence. Politics thus comprises little more than a unilinear logic of realized intentions—in this case, the supposed intentions of an articulate elite who are assigned a unique, if vaguely specified, importance.[2]

[1] I refer, of course, to distinctions between different types of economic knowledge articulated by Robert Cuff at the conference that preceded this volume, as they were adapted and enlarged by Mary Furner and Barry Supple in the Introduction to this volume.
[2] A populist variant of this account of politics as realized intentions would be to interpret public policy as the people's voice. For this taxonomy, see Peter Clarke, "Political History in the 1980s," in Theodore K. Rabb and Robert I. Rotberg, eds., *The New History* (Princeton, N.J.: Princeton University Press, 1982), 45–7.

Nowadays, it is easy to mock this view; yet it may be equally mis-guided to swing, in one irresistible sweep, to the conclusion that it must inevitably be wholly erroneous. If it implies a fallacious account of policy-making, its fallacy surely lies in supposing that a *sufficient* explana-tion can be derived from an examination of prevailing theories or doc-trines. So a more inclusive, comprehensive, multicausal account of policy is clearly required. But the question remains, what sorts of ideas are a *necessary* part of the explanation?

The specific topic with which this chapter deals—British economic policy in the interwar period—has seen fashion scuttle from one extreme interpretation to its opposite. The era of Keynesian triumphalism after World War II led to the great man's own view of the matter being ac-cepted at face value. In 1929 Keynes had characterized existing Treasury policy as not just practically ill-advised but theoretically misconceived. "Certainly this dogma is not derived from common sense," he wrote. "On the contrary, it is a highly sophisticated theory." He pilloried a leading Conservative cabinet minister for propagating it by saying that "he half understands an ancient theory, the premises of which he has forgotten."[3] An echo of the same charge is to heard in the well-known final passage of the *General Theory:* "Practical men, who believe them-selves to be quite exempt from any intellectual influences, are usually the slaves of some defunct economist."[4]

Recently, some historians have reacted, or overreacted, against what they see as Keynes's influentially misleading intellectualization of the problems faced by policymakers in this period.[5] Indeed, it may now seem tempting to say flatly that the Treasury simply did not have anything that can be described as an analytical model of the economy as a whole. At any rate this chapter questions whether British economic policy in the interwar period should be seen in terms of a dichotomy between Treasury orthodoxy and an alternative Keynesian agenda, with the one eventually being overturned by the force of the other. Keynes's image of the Treasury mandarins—"a few old gentlemen tightly buttoned-up in their frock coats, who only need to be treated with a little friendly disrespect and

---

[3] *The Collected Writings of John Maynard Keynes,* Austin Robinson and Donald Mogg-ridge, eds. (London: Macmillan for the Royal Economic Society, 1971–89; henceforth *J.M.K.*), XIX, 809, 811 (*Evening Standard,* April 19, 1929).
[4] *J.M.K.,* VII, 383.
[5] See J. Tomlinson, *Problems of British Economic Policy, 1870–1945* (London: Macmillan, 1981); and A. Booth and M. Pack, *Employment, Capital and Economic Policy* (Oxford: Basil Blackwell, 1985).

bowled over like ninepins"[6]—is indelible but blatantly partisan. The starting point must be how they saw themselves.

THE ROLE OF THE TREASURY

It is true that the Treasury remained fundamentally Gladstonian in outlook. It did not conceive its role in terms of general economic responsibilities but rather of particular tasks in the field of public finance. It saw itself as the national housekeeper, not the national breadwinner. It had to balance the accounts and do so in a way that did not prejudice the creation of wealth; but its responsibilities had conventionally been held to end there. The Treasury, in short, did not view the way the economy worked as its problem; it was defined as a nonproblem.[7] Indeed, the role of "the authorities"—the Treasury and the Bank of England—was seen as that of servicing a self-acting system. As long as the principles of sound finance were upheld, there was no need for the Treasury to become involved in a task of economic management for which it was unsuited. It maintained a self-denying ordinance against assuming the functions of an economic ministry.[8]

The self-acting system was founded on three interlocking principles. The balanced-budget convention defined the Treasury's essential task as that of raising sufficient revenue from the public to cover government expenditure, or rather of reining back public spending to a level that long-suffering taxpayers felt they could afford. Any fiscal impact upon the economy was unintended; indeed, it should be obviated so far as possible. The second principle was free trade, which merely extended the same precept to the international sphere, seeking to avoid distortion in the play of market forces. The third principle was the gold standard, envisaged as the pursuit of unimpeachable ends by inviolable means. The ends were those of sound money, riveting the parity of the pound to gold by a solemn and binding fiat (the obligation to convert sterling at a fixed value). The means were circumscribed by this prior commitment, leaving the Bank of England with only the barest margin for maneuver in operating a domestic credit policy dictated by its defense of sterling. Well might

[6]*J.M.K.*, IX, 125 (*Can Lloyd George Do It?*).
[7]The analogous position of the Bank of England is well stated in Henry Clay, *Lord Norman* (London: Macmillan, 1957), 167.
[8]See the helpful account in G. C. Peden, "The Treasury as the Central Department of Government, 1919–39," *Public Administration* 61 (1983): 371–85; and Roger Middleton, *Towards the Managed Economy* (London: Methuen, 1985), especially Chapters 3 and 5.

Sir John Bradbury, with the authority of a former permanent secretary to the Treasury (1913–19), commend this system on the ground that it was "knave-proof"—a phrase embalmed for posterity by his disciple, P. J. Grigg, who served as private secretary to successive chancellors of the Exchequer for nearly ten years from 1921. The merit of a knave-proof system was precisely that it was self-acting and that government was insulated from its economic consequences.

That the system nonetheless had economic consequences was in many ways the salient lesson of the 1920s, and learning this lesson was one way in which the economic knowledge of government grew. As chancellor of the Exchequer in Baldwin's Conservative government, Churchill recognized the decision on the gold standard as one that involved crucial choices, with no guarantee of an easy transition. His expert committee, under the successive chairmanship of Austen Chamberlain and Sir John Bradbury, and including the economist A. C. Pigou, was ultimately unanimous in favor of an early return to the gold standard. Grigg was later adamant that Churchill's advisers never concealed from him "that a decision to return might involve adjustments which would be painful, and that it would certainly entail a more rigorous standard of public finance than any system of letting the exchanges go wherever the exigencies of a valetudinarian economic and financial policy took them."[9] Churchill was to respond to the taunt "that the gold standard will shackle us to the United States" by saying, "For good or ill, it will shackle us to reality."[10] But there was no doubt about the grand object of the policy, whatever its immediate side effects. In the long run it was surely designed to restore the health of the British economy and thus to cure unemployment.

The self-acting system had been legitimated by the object lesson of British prosperity in the prewar era. Britain's return to the gold standard in 1925 can be seen as an attempt to reenter the Garden of Eden, to recover and recapture a prelapsarian innocence compromised by the war and its aftermath. With the restoration of the gold standard, the circle of sound finance was virtually complete. Despite the burdens of the war debt, the balanced-budget convention was not to be effectively challenged

---

[9] P. J. Grigg, *Prejudice and Judgment* (London: Jonathan Cape, 1948), 182; for the decision to return, see D. E. Moggridge, *British Monetary Policy, 1924–31* (Cambridge, Eng.: Cambridge University Press, 1972), Chapter 3.
[10] Quoted in Robert Rhodes James, *Churchill: A Study of Failure, 1900–39* (London: Weidenfeld and Nicolson, 1970), 160.

until the 1930s. Nor, once the Conservatives had burned their fingers over tariffs in the 1923 election, was free trade in immediate danger from governments of left or right. The late 1920s thus saw a consistent effort to re-create the conditions associated with prewar prosperity. Because the medicine notoriously failed to effect the cure, it thereby provoked a natural skepticism over the diagnosis. In the 1880s, as Barry Supple in Chapter 10 of this volume has shown, foreign competition, declining profits, and mounting unemployment promoted a more introspective mood; in the 1920s, similar adverse changes in the real world led to a more searching economic analysis of the problem.

TREASURY PERSONNEL

Questions of policy rested in very few hands. Without entering into a full account of the structure of the Treasury until its internal reorganization of 1932, two posts can be summarily identified as crucial: the controller of finance and the deputy controller. The first post was occupied in the early 1920s by Sir Otto Niemeyer, who was succeeded in 1927 by Sir Richard Hopkins; and the post of deputy was filled by F. W. Leith-Ross (later Sir Frederick) from 1925 to 1932, when he was, in effect, succeeded by (Sir) Frederick Phillips.[11] The thinking of the Treasury between the return to gold in 1925 and the outbreak of war in 1939 was thus dominated by these four Treasury knights. In the years up to 1931 their viewpoint was sympathetically interpreted to the chancellor by Grigg, as his private secretary.

Grigg, like Leith-Ross, looked back on the era of Bradbury and Niemeyer as truly a golden age, and the changing of the guard may itself be significant. Churchill had rankled under the tutelage of the doctrinaire Niemeyer and shed no tears over his premature departure to the Bank of England. To Niemeyer's lieutenant Leith-Ross, who obviously nurtured his own expectations of the succession, the appointment of the outsider Hopkins to the top post in the Treasury (from the Board of Inland Revenue) was a heavy blow. Although the accommodating temperament and political dexterity of "Hoppy" made him many friends, including Keynes, these did not appease the testy "Leithers," who took the opportunity to leave the Treasury at the beginning of 1932 for another post (nominally as economic

[11]For an authoritative account, see G. C. Peden, *British Rearmament and the Treasury, 1932–1939* (Edinburgh: Scottish Academic Press, 1979), 20–3 and appendix 1, 203.

adviser to the government). By this point, Bradbury's praetorian guard had been replaced; Hopkins and his taciturn adjutant Phillips were left to set their stamp on the Treasury in the changed conditions of the 1930s.

None of these men was trained as an economist, but then, as President Reagan once reminded us, neither was John Maynard Keynes. Niemeyer earned first-class honors in classics ("Greats") at Balliol College, Oxford, and was in top place in the civil service examinations in 1906 (Keynes came second). Leith-Ross trod exactly the same path three years later. Hopkins studied classics in part I of the tripos at Emmanuel College, Cambridge, and history in part II, with first-class honors in both parts. Phillips was also at Emmanuel, earning "Firsts" in the mathematical and natural sciences triposes; he placed first in the civil service examinations in 1908. Grigg was at St. John's College, Cambridge; another mathematician, he earned "Firsts" in both parts of the tripos, and placed first in the civil service examinations in 1913. These men were part of a small, self-conscious elite, largely self-taught in economics, but owing intellectual deference to nobody.

The nearest thing to a professional economist, in the modern sense, within the Treasury was the director of financial inquiries, a post created to accommodate the peculiar talents of R. G. Hawtrey. Hawtrey took his degree in mathematics at Trinity College, Cambridge. Within the First Class, called "Wranglers" in the Mathematics Tripos, he was placed nineteenth in the formal order of merit in 1901; his friend Keynes, following a closely comparable career from Eton to Cambridge, a member of the same small social coterie, and a candidate for the same specialized tripos, was to be Twelfth Wrangler in 1905. In the Treasury, Hawtrey was customarily regarded as rather a joke, and there is a vivid oral tradition depreciating his role.[12] It is easy to see that the herbivorous Hawtrey was no match for full-fledged carnivores like Niemeyer and Leith-Ross. But even Grigg's cameo of Hawtrey can be read as a veiled acknowledgment that ultimately he could not be ignored:

Mr. Churchill, when he became Chancellor, used to accuse us of giving Hawtrey too little scope. I remember his demanding from time to time that the learned man should be released from the dungeon in which we were said to have immured him, have the chains struck off and the straw brushed from his hair and clothes and be

---

[12]See Susan Howson, "Hawtrey and the Real World," in G. C. Harcourt, ed., *Keynes and His Contemporaries* (London: Macmillan, 1985), 142–88 and especially 176–8, for a well-considered appraisal of Hawtrey's influence, concluding that it was small in the 1930s.

admitted to the light and warmth of an argument in the Treasury board room with the greatest living master of argument.[13]

In becoming the house economist for the Treasury, Hawtrey acquired an expertise that busy administrators themselves lacked and, in the late 1920s and 1930s, thus exerted an insidious influence that is masked by the heavy banter Hawtrey had to endure from his colleagues. Although his direct advice on policy was often discounted, his pattern of thought helped determine Treasury perceptions, and hence policy, in more indirectly pervasive ways.

THE ORTHODOX THEORY

The gold standard. In April 1925, when Britain returned to the gold standard, the official unemployment figure stood at 10.9 percent. During the following twelve months the figure climbed above 12 percent before dropping back to 9.1 percent in April 1926. At this point there was a sudden jump upward to more than 14 percent from May to August 1926—which could be satisfactorily explained by the impact of the General Strike and the prolonged coal dispute. By the summer of 1927 the figure had dipped below 9 percent; taking the most optimistic view of the trend, one could point to a reduction from 14.6 percent to 8.7 percent in the twelve months to May 1927. The government's story up to this point was thus fairly plausible: the return to gold had laid the foundation for a return to prosperity that had been temporarily impeded by the industrial disputes of 1926.[14] From this point onward, however, the record no longer spoke for itself as an endorsement of sound finance. With a tendency for unemployment to rise rather than fall, so that it fluctuated around 10 or 11 percent throughout 1928 and 1929, the situation cried out for explanation, if not action. Moreover, the Treasury was specifically prompted to defend itself and its prognosis in response to a series of proposals for state intervention, chiefly linked with the names of Keynes and Lloyd George.

The Treasury position is therefore expounded in a loosely linked series of documents dating from 1928–9, drafted in the main by Leith-Ross but incorporating arguments derived from Hawtrey. The chief documents are as follows:

[13]*Prejudice and Judgment*, 82.
[14]For example, *Election Notes for Conservative Speakers and Workers* (London: National Union of Conservative and Unionist Associations, 1929), 141–2.

1. Leith-Ross's paper of August 1928 for the chancellor, criticizing Keynes's proposals published in the *Evening Standard* under the title "How to Organize a Wave of Prosperity"[15]
2. The Cabinet Paper CP 53 (29) of February 1929, reaffirming Treasury policy in face of internal dissension within the Conservative cabinet, notably from the home secretary, Sir William Joynson-Hicks, and the minister of labor, Sir Arthur Steel-Maitland[16]
3. Leith-Ross's drafts of a statement of the Treasury view, finally incorporated by Churchill into his budget speech in April 1929 (the background to this statement is illuminated by the contents of a hitherto inaccessible file [T 172/2095] that also highlights the importance of CP 53 [29] just cited, as the foundation text on the Treasury view)[17]
4. The Treasury memorandum, published as the final section of the government's white paper of May 1929, in criticism of the Liberal proposals on unemployment (i.e., Lloyd George's pledge as contained in the manifesto *We Can Conquer Unemployment*, subsequently supported by Keynes and H. D. Henderson in their pamphlet *Can Lloyd George Do It?*)[18]

Although all these documents addressed the same problem and manifested essentially the same outlook, in one respect the Treasury shifted ground in the course of the argument. This shift is apparent in the Treasury's response to Keynes's claim (in "How to Organize a Wave of Prosperity") that "the fundamental blunder of the Treasury and of the Bank of England has been due, from the beginning, to their belief that if they looked after the deflation of prices the deflation of costs would look after itself."[19] This statement questioned the crucial postulate that wages were in fact flexible, as required by the adjustment mechanism.

When Britain had returned to the gold standard, the parity adopted for sterling—the only one considered—was $4.86. There has always been controversy over whether this was the right rate, as measured by compara-

---

[15]F. Leith-Ross, memorandum, August 9, 1928, T. 172/2095, Public Record Office; first draft, August 3, 1928, also in T. 175/26. "How to Organize a Wave of Prosperity" is printed in *J.M.K.*, XIX, 761–6.

[16]CP 53 (29), "Unemployment," February 25, 1929, CAB 24/202; also in T. 172/2095. For this otherwise unrecorded episode, see Peter Clarke, *The Keynesian Revolution in the Making, 1924–36* (Oxford: Oxford University Press, 1988), 54–62.

[17]"Cure for Unemployment Memoranda of 1928 and 1929," T. 172/2095, had been kept in the library of the Treasury instead of the archive and was therefore not released to the Public Record Office until the summer of 1986. It forms the documentary spine of my chapter, "The Formulation of the Treasury View, 1925–9," in *Keynesian Revolution in the Making*, 47–69. The fullest draft from it, quoted below, is undated (but April 1929), 215–29.

[18]*Memoranda on Certain Proposals Relating to Unemployment*, London: H.M.S.O., Cmd. 3331 (1929).

[19]*J.M.K.*, XIX, 762.

tive prices and purchasing power.[20] As far as the consequences of this demarche are concerned, however, the point is simple. If sterling had not been "overvalued" in the late 1920s, the Bank of England would not have needed to maintain a "dear money" policy in order to protect it. Yet it became increasingly apparent that this was indeed the position in which the bank found itself. It was, in the phrase used by its governor, Montagu Norman, "under the harrow" in resorting to a high bank rate as its only means of preventing a flight from sterling.

According to the rules of the game under the gold standard, the authorities would be prompted to intervene whenever there was a serious loss of gold. If the imbalance were due to lack of competitiveness in export prices, it could be remedied by a stiff dose of deflation, which would bring down production costs and thus correct the disequilibrium at its source. Bradbury, as one of the architects of the return to gold, explained the underlying theory to the Macmillan Committee in 1930:

The first effect—and this is rather important, because [it is] the normal effect of dear money, what I might call the curative effect towards the reduction of prices—depends to a large extent on its being the short and sharp application of the remedy. . . . The result is a slump in stocks and a rapid fall in prices. That is the normal way in which the gold standard works.

Yet, by the time Bradbury gave this account, it was apparent that normal working was in abeyance.

I have often thought that one of our troubles arises from the fact that we have had, owing to the exchange rate since the War, to apply this dear money consistently over a long period. . . . Its curative power is very largely inhibited unless it is exercised very rapidly.[21]

At what point did the Treasury acknowledge that the stickiness of wages, above all else, stood in the way of a successful adjustment under the gold standard? Not in 1928, to judge from Leith-Ross's paper for the chancellor. He had written to Hawtrey, querying Keynes's claim that wage costs had been stable in the years 1925–8 and adding: "I should have thought that the average wage rates showed a substantial decline during the past 4 years."[22] Hawtrey pointed out to him that the index constructed by the statistician A. L. Bowley bore out Keynes's point, but Leith-Ross's subsequent draft nonetheless read:

---

[20]For a recent statement of an anti-Keynesian case, see K. G. P. Matthews, "Was Sterling Overvalued in 1925?," *Economics History Review*, n.s., 39 (1986): 572–87.

[21]Unpublished minutes, October 24, 1930, 3–5: copy in T. 200/5.

[22]Leith-Ross to Hawtrey, August 1, 1928, T. 172/2095.

It is, of course, quite true that the reduction of money wages to correspond with the reduction of prices has been the outstanding difficulty since our return to the gold standard and that the Chamberlain-Bradbury Committee seriously underestimated this difficulty. Political influences have not only operated to mitigate the hardships of industrial depression but have been engaged to a large extent in a deliberate attempt to counteract economic forces by means of subsidies. As a result, the natural resistance of wages to falling prices has been seriously increased, with a corresponding prolongation of economic disturbances. But Mr. Keynes exaggerates the extent of this resistance. Apparently he bases his statement that labour costs have not declined during the past 3 years on Professor Bowley's Index of Wages. It only shows how fallacious such indices are.[23]

Leith-Ross's paper cited Ministry of Labour figures against Bowley showing that the aggregate sums paid out in wages had declined. The paper accordingly identified Britain's main problem not in excessive labor costs but in structural weaknesses in industrial organization which could be remedied by "a bold industrial concentration policy."

Foreign lending and exports: a fluid model. The Treasury viewed the restoration of the export trade as the fundamental objective, to which all other aims had to be subordinated. This priority helps explain not only the Treasury's skepticism about schemes for domestic development but also its relaxed attitude toward capital flows. The Treasury regarded the export of capital as instrumental in stimulating other exports, and argued that the Keynes–Lloyd George proposals on public works would entail a diversion of capital from foreign to domestic investment, with deleterious consequences. Leith-Ross claimed in 1928 that the level of foreign investment over the previous three years was less than the regular income from the past lending; so although the historic capital had not been raided, the income had not, as in the prewar period, constituted a surplus that could finance further accumulation. (He pointed also to an offsetting increase in British short-term indebtedness.) The rationale of foreign investment lay in his further contention that "what we invest in foreign loans must, sooner or later, be exported; and insofar as it is sunk in development schemes for the Empire, it is probably exported almost at once in the form of capital goods."[24]

Now Leith-Ross was really stating two propositions: one a dogmatic assertion of a necessary effect on exports (albeit neither immediate nor direct) and the other an immediate, direct, pragmatic point about how

---

[23]Leith-Ross, memorandum, August 9, 1928, T. 172/2095.
[24]Ibid.

the close links between the empire and the mother country actually operated. It is noticeable that in 1929 the Treasury was more easily shifted on the pragmatic than on the dogmatic point. For in February of that year it was faced—in anticipation of the Liberal proposals for domestic development—with a rival proposal, launched within the Conservative cabinet, for a scheme of imperial development. It is illuminating to observe how the Treasury analyzed foreign lending in this context. Here, it might seem, were the very sorts of loans—to be "sunk in development schemes for the Empire"—that the Treasury might regard with special favor. Yet CP 53 (29) declares:

It should be borne in mind, however, in considering the *immediate* effects of development loans to the Dominions and Colonies upon employment in this country that on the average rather more than one half of the money will be spent on colonial labour, land and materials (thus further turning the exchanges against us), and it is only that portion of the money which is spent on the purchase of British materials which *directly* helps our own industry. The effect of such expenditure in stimulating British industry, even assuming that it is not merely a diversion of resources, is less than is often supposed. It is estimated that a loan of £10 million for overseas railway development, the expenditure of which would probably take about five years, would only involve an increase of about 1 percent in annual exports of iron and steel from this country and about 3 percent in the exports of rolling-stock.[25]

This remarkable disparagement of the very process that the Treasury was otherwise inclined to laud as beneficial probably betokens its determination, for more deep-seated reasons, to resist state expenditure rather than signaling a significant change of view. With the launching of the Liberal plan for home development, overseas loans were once more seen as clearly alternative to state intervention, and their immediate assistance to the domestic economy was suddenly glimpsed anew. Thus the Treasury memorandum wrote of the historic dependence of British export trades on foreign loans, as opposed to the more limited impact of domestic schemes:

The additional work that they might put in hand for bridges, etc., at home would be a poor substitute for the construction contracts of whole railways in foreign countries which they would have to forfeit. Admittedly, in the exceptional economic circumstances of the present time, these arguments must not be over-stressed, but the reactions to which they draw attention should not be overlooked.[26]

[25]CP 53 (29), paragraph 12; emphasis in original.
[26]Cmd. 3331, 51.

In the real world the Treasury was well aware of the immediate dangers of excessive lending abroad and was not always content to leave the scale of such lending to be determined by market forces. Bradbury himself had written in 1924, "I believe there is a real risk that the success of the policy we recommend may be jeopardised by excessive foreign lending." And Niemeyer advised Churchill in 1925 that "we want to go as slow with overseas loans as we can." As a result, the authorities repeatedly attempted to use moral suasion to restrain the volume of capital exports. Yet the prevailing attitude of the Treasury knights continued to rest on a series of assumptions neatly explicated by Moggridge: "that the mechanism involved was classical (i.e., that the loan increased foreign expenditure and reduced domestic expenditure while leaving the level of income unchanged), that if London did not make the loan no one else would, and that the transfer was perfectly effected in such a short period as to rule the financial deterioration out of court."[27] Thus although the empirical point about the relation between loans and exports was from time to time subject to different emphases, it found more consistent favor and expression when generalized as a theoretical proposition.

CP 53 (29) attributed postwar depression in the export staples to the development of competitors abroad, which implied excess supply, and to the wartime impoverishment of former customers, which implied deficient demand. "Meanwhile," it argued, "our own people had grown accustomed to consuming more and saving less than before the war, so that the capital available for investment abroad was limited. It is little wonder, therefore, that our exports have not yet reached the pre-war volume (after adjustment of prices)."[28] The implication here is that a higher level of investment abroad, out of a higher level of domestic saving, constituted a crucial means of stimulating British exports. The Treasury's contribution to the Conservative government's white paper, published in May 1929, reaffirmed this position. "On the ordinary view there is an intimate relation between the export of capital and of goods," the memorandum concluded. "If the [Liberal] plan were successful in diverting money from investment abroad that change would be accompanied by a great decrease in our exports or increase in imports, either of these things being highly prejudicial to important branches of industry."[29]

Apart from the appeal to history, the Treasury did not elaborate this

[27]Moggridge, *British Monetary Policy*, 205, 207, 217.
[28]CP 53 (29), paragraphs 25–6.
[29]Cmd. 3331, 52; cf. Leith-Ross's draft, T. 172/2095, f. 220.

argument on any of the occasions when it was advanced. Presumably, it felt no need to do so, because the process was implied by the working of the gold standard. International outgoings and receipts had to balance. They were substantially balanced by their relative price level (expressed in gold) and compensated or corrected at the margin by transfers of gold itself. These transfers, by augmenting or depleting the gold reserves, prompted the central bank to inflate or deflate the domestic price level, thus equilibrating the relative prices of exports and imports. This process, once completed, removed the need for the compensation or correction that had instigated it, with a tendency toward perfect equilibrium in the inward and outward flow of goods and services at compatible prices. Foreign investment complicated this picture only to the extent that it represented current exports for which payment (in the form of current imports) was deferred. In this light, therefore, foreign investment appeared as a means whereby the country accumulated a stock of wealth abroad for future benefit, by allowing it in the present to maintain an export surplus. Indeed, foreign loans, by *requiring* an export surplus, could be seen as a major stimulus to exports. This seems to have been the Treasury's understanding of the relationship, at least in the period up to 1929.

Rigidities. An alternative model, as postulated by Keynes, is pithily outlined in an article on the German transfer problem:

Historically, the volume of foreign investment has tended, I think, to adjust itself—at least to a certain extent—to the balance of trade, rather than the other way round, the former being the sensitive and the latter the insensitive factor. In the case of German reparations, on the other hand, we are trying to fix the volume of foreign remittance and compel the balance of trade to adjust itself thereto. Those who see no difficulty in this—like those who saw no difficulty in Great Britain's return to the gold standard—are applying the theory of liquids to what is, if not a solid, at least a sticky mass with strong internal resistances.[30]

On this reading, a given level of transfer across the exchanges— whether German reparations or British investment abroad—might produce its own distortions on the domestic economy. To reduce domestic wages to the level necessary to generate an export surplus, deflationary measures would be necessary. But "dear money" orthodoxy—Bradbury's "short and sharp application of the remedy . . . a rapid fall in prices"—

---

[30] *J.M.K.*, XI, 458 ("The German Transfer Problem," *Economics Journal*, March 1929).

would be defeated by the viscosity of the real-world relationships. The result would be a position of disequilibrium in which not all resources were fully employed.

Keynes's critique of the Treasury in 1929–30 was essentially from this standpoint. His own theory, as expounded in the *Treatise on Money* (1930), did not cast doubt on the tendency toward equilibrium. But he outlined a special case, applicable to Britain, in which the process of adjustment was stuck. This was the thrust of his exposition to the Macmillan Committee, as his listeners did not fail to perceive.

MACMILLAN: Does it come to this—that because we are not a closed nation the Bank rate cannot achieve the results?
KEYNES: There is also another reason. It could if we were a *fluid* system. For in that case, when we had a surplus of home investments over savings, the bank rate could always force wages down to a level where exports would be adequate.
MACMILLAN: It would be the principle of hydraulics.
KEYNES: Yes; that is the beauty of the Bank rate.[31]

Keynes attributed the *cause* of disequilibrium to excessive or uncompetitive costs, and he was even ready to concede, if pressed, that this disequilibrium could be put down to the rigidity of wages. But the *remedy* for this problem in the real world was, in Keynes's opinion, to be found in two unorthodox proposals (public work and tariffs), which were justified under the special case.[32] The shift in the Treasury position in 1929 was, on second thought, to accept the accumulating evidence that Keynes was right about the *cause* and to argue that this implied the simple *remedy* of inverting the process in order to restore flexibility.

Thus in March 1929, following the publication of *We Can Conquer Unemployment,* Leith-Ross again sought clarification from Hawtrey: "Mr. J. M. Keynes says that, despite the general reduction of price levels since 1925, there has been no appreciable reduction during the same period in the rates of wages paid to labour in the United Kingdom. The general table published in the *Ministry of Labour Gazette* seems to confirm this, but it appears to be so surprising that I should be glad if you would go into it."[33] When Hawtrey reiterated his opinion of the previous

---

[31]*J.M.K.*, XX, 85 (February 21, 1930), emphasis in original.
[32]For the clear specification of the "special case" as the means of reconciling Keynes's views on cheap money with his advocacy of public works at the time of the *Treatise*, see D. E. Moggridge and Susan Howson, "Keynes on Monetary Policy, 1910–46," *Oxford Economic Papers*, n.s. 26 (1974): 226–47, at 236. I have extended this analysis, in line with the *Treatise*, to cover tariffs, too, in *Keynesian Revolution in the Making*, Chapters 8 and 9.
[33]Leith-Ross to Hawtrey, March 13, 1929, T. 175/26.

year, that Keynes was correct, and now confirmed that the official statistics told the same story, Leith-Ross was finally persuaded. This appears to mark the point at which the Treasury conceded that the adjustments required for the successful operation of the gold standard had simply not been forthcoming.

So long as the Treasury believed that British costs were only marginally out of line with those overseas, this was held to constitute an argument in favor of returning to the gold standard. True, it was conceded that the Chamberlain-Bradbury Committee might have underestimated the extent of the discrepancy; and events had shown that "the adjustment of prices has been a longer and more difficult process than was anticipated," albeit for reasons that were not fully foreseeable. "But it remains true," CP 53 (29) concluded, "that the process of adjustment did not impose an impossible strain on the national economy; and that the other factors in favour of reversion to the gold standard were so important as to outweigh the transitional difficulties."

Depreciation of the currency, on this reading, would not have avoided unemployment, which was preexisting, because although the lower pre-1925 parity had "no doubt constituted an artificial stimulus to some British industries," it had likewise masked defects of management and equipment. Moreover, it was important to remember "that depreciation is a drug, addiction to which must in the end undermine the economic prosperity of any country that indulges in it." Hence the conclusion: "Surely it would be unthinkable at this stage, when we have got over the unpleasant jolt necessitated by the reversion to the gold standard, for the Government to treat the question as if it were in any respect an open one."[34]

Once Leith-Ross had discovered that British wages had by no means overcome the transitional jolt, he merely acted out his own precepts by displaying a smooth flexibility in making the necessary adjustment to his argument:

The main trouble with our industrial situation at the present time is that our costs of production are not yet on a fully competitive level. This is admitted by all economists, however much they may differ in regard to the remedies. Only last year Mr. Keynes wrote that "the fundamental blunder of the Treasury and the

[34]CP 53 (29), paragraphs 22, 28. In this section I am, of course, reporting the Treasury's perceptions; for a sophisticated modern discussion of the real difficulties, see R. C. O. Matthews, C. H. Feinstein, and J. C. Odling-Smee, *British Economic Growth, 1856–1973* (Oxford: Oxford University Press, 1982), 314–15, 470–1.

Bank of England has been due to their belief, that if they looked after the deflation of prices, the deflation of costs would look after itself." If this diagnosis is correct, what we have to do is to reduce costs by improving the organization of our industries, the efficiency of management and the output of labour.

What, then, of unemployment?

The remedy is easy enough to find. If our workmen were prepared to accept a reduction of 10 percent in their wages or increase their efficiency by 10 percent, a large proportion of our present unemployment could be overcome. But in fact organized labour is so attached to the maintenance of the present standard of wages and hours of labour that they would prefer that a million workers should remain in idleness and be maintained permanently out of the Employment Fund, than accept any sacrifice. The result is to throw on to the capital and managerial side of industry a far larger reorganization than would otherwise be necessary: and until labour is prepared to contribute in larger measure to the process of reconstruction, there will inevitably be unemployment.[35]

When this line of analysis was developed in the Treasury memorandum, the diagnosis was the same: costs of production were the root of the problem and must be made internationally competitive. The prognosis, however, was less brutal. "There was a time perhaps when reduction of the costs of production was looked upon as largely synonymous with reduction of wages," read the memorandum as published in May 1929, looking back all of about six weeks. It then explained that improved organization and efficiency, not to mention "all that is implied in the term 'rationalization,' " were what the situation demanded.[36] These changes of emphasis, which may well reflect the difference between a Leith-Ross draft and a Hopkins draft, can be regarded as cosmetic. The point was that, by whatever means, British costs had to become competitive at prices set in gold.

The Treasury view. It is on public works that Keynes's differences with the Treasury have always attracted most attention, and with good reason. The Treasury view, conceived as a theoretical doctrine or dogma, was the butt of Keynes's criticism in *Can Lloyd George Do It?*, and this perspective is reflected in the subsequent Keynesian literature. Revisionist historians, exploiting the availability of the public records, have shown that administrative and political constraints helped determine the outlook of Whitehall as a whole; but whether the dogmatic Treasury view of 1929

---

[35]Draft for Churchill (April, 1929), T. 172/2095, 221–2.
[36]Cmd. 3331, 52.

can now be safely dismissed as a myth is another matter.[37] In fact, once CP 53 (29) is revealed as the master text, the evidence in the public records decisively confirms that the formulation of the Treasury view did indeed owe much to precepts of a theoretical character, rather than simply to pragmatic political economy. In particular, the analysis Hawtrey developed, notably in a learned article published in *Economica* in 1925, exerted a demonstrable influence. It was Hawtrey's rigorous academic specification of the conditions under which "crowding-out" took place that reinforced the policy advice of Niemeyer and Leith-Ross.[38]

Churchill's budget speech of April 1929 is the *locus classicus* for the dogmatic promulgation of the Treasury view, just as the Treasury memorandum, published in the government's white paper the following month, offers the most authoritative amplification. The memorandum, it is worth noting, was already in its final form before Churchill uttered it in the House, so there is no need to scrutinize each statement successively for possible changes in the official line. Both, in fact, derive substantially from the statement in CP 53 (29), where, in four taut paragraphs, Leith-Ross distilled what he took to be Hawtrey's doctrine. The conclusion was that "in all cases the question is whether £1,000 spent by the Government would give more employment than if the £1,000 had been left to the public to spend. This will be so only if the Government is skillful enough to find ways of spending £1,000 which give more employment than the spending of £1,000 by the public would do." Such skill was notoriously unlikely to be forthcoming, and the effect of loan expenditure, therefore, was likely to be "quite nugatory as regards the general employment position."[39]

[37] Roger Middleton uses the term *myth* in his recent essay, "Treasury Policy on Unemployment," in Sean Glynn and Alan Booth, eds., *The Road to Full Employment* (London: Allen and Unwin, 1987), 115. This seems an incautious extension of his earlier well-argued points, especially *Towards the Managed Economy*, Chapter 8, building on his article, "The Treasury in the 1930s: Political and Administrative Constraints to Acceptance of the 'New' Economics," *Oxford Economic Papers*, n.s., 34 (1982): 48–77. The best general account is in G. C. Peden, "The 'Treasury View' on Public Works and Employment in the Inter-war Period," *Economic History Review*, 2nd Ser., 37 (1984): 167–81, although in my view this account needs some modification, especially in the light of the new evidence in T. 172/2095.
[38] R. G. Hawtrey, "Public Expenditure and the Demand for Labour," *Economica* 5 (1925): 38–48. There is thus now documentary support for earlier suggestions about the significance of this article, especially K. J. Hancock, "Unemployment and the Economists in the 1920s," *Economica*, n.s., 27 (1960): 311; and Susan Howson and Donald Winch, *The Economic Advisory Council* (Cambridge, Eng.: Cambridge University Press, 1977), 27. For the new evidence see Clarke, *Keynesian Revolution in the Making*, 51–4, 62–7.
[39] CP 53 (29), paragraphs 5, 7.

It is an illustration of the difficulty of deriving practical policy from theoretical analysis that the rigor of the Treasury view, which apparently owed so much to Hawtrey, depended on a proviso, the force of which was often subsequently overlooked. Hawtrey repeatedly stated that "crowding-out" took place only when there was no expansion of credit. If credit were expanded, however, there would indeed be room for new enterprise and for a net gain in employment. Hawtrey, it should be remembered, was arguing specifically against public works as such, and he clinched his case by noting that, once the proviso was relaxed, public works became unnecessary because creating the means to finance them would already have had the requisite expansionary effect. "To stimulate an expansion of credit is usually only too easy," Hawtrey argued. "To resort for the purpose to the construction of expensive public works is to burn down the house for the sake of the roast pig."[40]

In meeting the Liberal arguments for public works, the Treasury summarized the position fairly, categorizing it as "fundamental that the capital required must be raised without resort to inflation." The words of the Liberal manifesto itself about inflation—"It can be entirely ruled out"—were quoted in reaffirmation of this condition. If inflation were ruled out, the Treasury could draw only one inference. "It seems clear that in these circumstances a very large proportion of any additional Government borrowings can only be procured, without inflation, by diverting money which otherwise would be taken soon by home industry." This inference was fully in line with Hawtrey's logic and led to the conclusion, "The large loans involved, if they are not to involve inflation, must draw on existing capital resources."[41]

Whether Hawtrey himself had intended to bang, bar, and bolt the door against any move to expand credit, however, may be doubted. The notion of manipulating credit in a deflationary situation so as to stimulate the forces of economic expansion is, at any rate, a lurking possibility even in his 1925 statement of the case against public works. Hawtrey himself was not involved in the preparation of the main Treasury drafts dealing with public works in the early months of 1929, because he was on leave for the year at Harvard. He might well have sought to hedge the amateur doctrinal declarations of Grigg, Leith-Ross, and Churchill himself with proper academic caution.

At any rate, Hawtrey's own direct comment on the Liberal plan, writ-

[40]"Public Expenditure and the Demand for Labour," 44.
[41]Cmd. 3331, 45, 50–1, 53.

ten on his return from Harvard in June 1929, developed a suggestion for which his analysis had always allowed: If foreign lending were decreased (whether or not in aid of a public works loan), the immediate effect under the gold standard would be to inflate domestic credit. (The extent to which such inflation would be necessary posed an intellectual problem Hawtrey was to tackle by postulating what might be called a proto-multiplier.)[42] Hawtrey's schema, therefore, contained a possible pathway to expansion, the desirability of which he may not have normally recommended himself but the existence of which he never attempted to conceal. "Like a protective tariff, an import of capital is a device for bringing about inflation without depreciation," he wrote in 1925. "Here is a real tendency to improve employment, and it is remarkable that the advocates of public expenditure as a remedy for unemployment never seem to consider this point."[43]

The point was that, in a time of depression, one country could improve its employment position, in effect by reflating at home in ways that did not depreciate the gold reserves or the parity of sterling. Although such measures were technically compatible with the gold standard, they could be seen as clever dodges that flouted the spirit if not the letter of the "rules of the game." Just as it is unsurprising that the authorities frowned on such gamesmanship, so it is not wholly surprising that Keynes came to be associated with proposals that sought to exploit both these loopholes.

CHANGING THE PREMISES

Foreign lending and exports: a sticky model. By 1930 professional economic advice was being proffered to the government through two connected channels: the Economic Advisory Council and the Committee on Finance and Industry (the Macmillan Committee). The Economic Advisory Council, established by Ramsay MacDonald as Labour prime minister, and particularly its committee of economists, was set up on Keynes's recommendation in July 1930. "It may be that economics is not enough of a science to be able to produce useful fruits," he wrote to the prime minister. "But I think it might be given a trial, and that we might assume

---

[42]Hawtrey, "The Liberal Unemployment Plan," June 12, 1929, Hawtrey Papers, HTRY 1/41, Churchill College, Cambridge, also in T. 175/26. For further discussion in relation to the multiplier, see Clarke, *Keynesian Revolution in the Making*, 143–5.
[43]"Public Expenditure and the Demand for Labour," 46.

for a moment, if only as a hypothesis, that it can be treated like any other science, and ask qualified scientists in the subject to say their say."[44] The membership he suggested comprised, as well as himself, three current or former Cambridge colleagues (Professor A. C. Pigou, D. H. Robertson, and H. D. Henderson), the taxation expert Sir Josiah Stamp, Professor Henry Clay of the Bank of England, and Professor Lionel Robbins of the London School of Economics. All were leading figures in their field; all except Robertson and Clay actually served; and all except Robbins also gave evidence to the Macmillan Committee.

The Committee on Finance and Industry, under the chairmanship of Lord Macmillan, had been appointed by the Labour government in October 1929, and it took most of its evidence in the first half of 1930. When Keynes, as a member, gave his "private evidence" in February and March 1930, it was heard with close attention by the Treasury observer, Leith-Ross—the more so because the forthcoming Treasury evidence was being prepared, under Hopkins's direction, with considerable thoroughness and circumspection. Keynes was not the only academic economist whose advice counted, but it is not just in retrospect that he appears preeminent. What Keynes was giving the committee was an intelligent layman's guide to his *Treatise on Money*, published some six months later. This work, unlike the *General Theory*, had a direct and explicit bearing on current British economic policy, and it was cited by Keynes as analytical justification for his view both of the causes of the depression and of the appropriate remedies.

Leith-Ross produced an able twelve-page note on Keynes's evidence. He reproduced Keynes's explanation of how the bank rate should work to equilibrate a favorable balance on current receipts with an adverse balance on the capital account. Moreover, he endorsed it: "Mr. Keynes's diagnosis of our present difficulty, viz. that the normal Bank rate policy has 'jammed' owing to the difficulty of reducing wages is, broadly speaking, admitted. Certainly wages and costs tend to be more stereotyped than they were before the War—probably largely by reason of the existence of the Unemployment Insurance scheme."[45] On possible remedies—Keynes had outlined seven—Leith-Ross had his own preferences, acknowledging that there might be something in four of them but ruling out

---

[44] *J.M.K.*, XX, 368–9 (Keynes to MacDonald, July 10, 1930); and see Howson and Winch, *Economic Advisory Council*, 47ff.
[45] "Note on Mr. Keynes's exposition to the Committee on Finance and Industry" (n.d., but late February 1930), T. 175/26, 164–76.

the other three (devaluation, tariffs, and public works), which were actually those preferred at different times by Keynes. Leith-Ross's criticisms were subsequently encapsulated in a short paper called "The Assumptions of Mr. Keynes," which contested a number of "theoretic assumptions" before shifting the argument onto another footing:

The fact is that Keynes, like other economists, lives in a world of abstractions. He speaks of "Industry," "Profits," "Losses," "Price Level," as if they were realities. In fact, we have no such thing as "Industry." What we have is a series of different industries—some prosperous, some depressed and a number carrying on normally. The position of each has to be examined separately.[46]

This approach, relying much more on an empirical, multicausal disaggregation of the problem, became increasingly characteristic of the Treasury henceforward. It was applied in particular to the question of foreign lending, which Keynes was accused of treating "in too abstract a manner."[47] Leith-Ross appealed to experience on this point. He argued that the strain on the exchanges arose from paying off capital claims that had arisen from an earlier flight of European capital to London during the postwar era of currency instability. Moreover, he cited instances of the restriction of foreign loans leading to a reduction in exports. "This is the view of the FBI [Federation of British Industries] and it can be shown to be true in special cases, e.g., if Australia ceases to borrow, it certainly entails a reduction of our exports to that country." Thus Keynes's assumption "that our foreign loans do not create additional exports" was cautiously qualified, although not confidently overturned.[48]

Hopkins's brief for the Macmillan Committee, largely compiled within the Treasury itself, also included a series of notes prepared by the Board of Trade, one of which was devoted to the effects of lending abroad. This began with a short statement of the "broad theory" that overseas lending had no effect—neither one way nor the other—on employment "in the long run," because capital *either* "employs labour in making the goods that follow it (not necessarily to the same country)," *or*, if invested at home, would employ labor directly. A passage that evidently impressed Hopkins, however, turned to the particular application of this axiom:

---

[46]"The Assumptions of Mr. Keynes," revised draft, March 28, 1930, T. 175/26, 181; an earlier draft (in fact, February 27, 1930) is printed as Appendix 3 in Thomas Jones, *Whitehall Diary*, Keith Middlemas, ed., 3 vols. (Oxford: Oxford University Press, 1969), II, 288–9.
[47]"Note on Mr. Keynes's exposition," T. 175/26, f. 171.
[48]"The Assumptions of Mr. Keynes," T. 175/26.

If a country over a long period of years has been in the habit of sending considerable sums overseas, her industries get to be organized on such a relative scale that the necessary additional export of goods follows the money automatically, so to speak. In accordance with their comparative advantages, certain of its industries become dependent on exports or more dependent than they would be otherwise. This being the position, it is evident that, if the export of capital diminished considerably, employment in these industries must suffer. The serious thing is the shock of a sudden change.[49]

Here was an analysis of the beneficial role of foreign lending, which, far from being based on the premise of infinite flexibility, was based on the opposite assumption. Although providing a more realistic defense of the existing level—and channels—of overseas lending, it could not carry the further implication that an increase in lending would ease the difficulty of the export industries. The case for such remedial measures was largely hypothetical because of the difficulty in identifying such opportunities for productive investment; but here, too, the analysis pointed to the deficiencies of the gold standard adjustment process in effecting the sort of change on which its successful operation depended.

Advice reaching the governor of the Bank of England—although too late to reinforce his own evidence to the Macmillan Committee—was along similar lines, particularly a memorandum from Professor Henry Clay of Manchester, who was acquiring a position of considerable influence in the Bank of England. Clay argued that in "an economy that was both perfectly fluid and completely self contained," the balance of investment and consumption could be left to work out itself. Because the existing system was not fluid, however, the process of adjustment led to unemployment. Because the system was not self-contained, moreover, overloading domestic demand would be fruitless if productive resources were inadequate to satisfy that demand. It followed that "the spending that we have to stimulate, if we wish to relieve unemployment, is largely spending by overseas customers." The fact was "that unemployment is concentrated in industries which are specialized to export." Nor, under these conditions, would an increase in imports lead to an increase in exports, as it had in the prewar world, when relative costs were more finely attuned.

To relieve unemployment, therefore, by stimulating the complete spending of income, either on commodities or investments, it is necessary to ensure that the

---

[49]"Effects of Lending Abroad," section 4 of the papers sent by S. J. Chapman to Hopkins, April 16, 1930, T. 200/1.

allocation of expenditure will not diverge too much from the allocation to which industry is adjusted. Any sudden or large transfers of means of payment from home to foreign account, or vice versa, or from one class of purchasers to another, is likely to dislocate employment, and cause, not a general increase in employment, but overtime and rapid expansion in one part of the industrial field balanced by increased unemployment in another part.[50]

These comments reveal an appealing sense of realism; in hindsight, their appreciation of the constraints on expansion appears to be perceptive. Clay's firsthand knowledge of the Lancashire cotton industry gave him an insight into the structural problems of the old export staples. This pragmatism can be viewed, as it has in some of the recent literature,[51] as a wholesome corrective to the callow optimism of proposals to revitalize "industry" and turn "losses" into "profits" by manipulation of the "price level"—in short, the assumptions of Keynes. But the pragmatism exemplified by Clay can, by the same token, be seen as a repudiation of the assumptions on which the authorities had relied in brandishing the gold standard as the key to British prosperity. The rigidities that, as a matter of demonstrable fact, inhibited the flexible adjustment of the economy were coming to be acknowledged on all sides as integral to the problem. Although there was still room for more than one view on the appropriate response, the options constituted a matter of finely calibrated judgment rather than doctrinaire polarization of opinion.

The Labour government and public works. It is now often taken for granted that on public works there was little difference between the Labour government of 1929–31 and its Conservative predecessor.[52] Yet the two authoritative statements of the Treasury view on loan-financed capital expenditure had been in Churchill's budget speech—obviously a partisan statement in a preelection atmosphere—and in the white paper, published during the general election itself and regarded even by the *Times* as "no more and no less than the Conservative party's statement of its case."[53] The dogmatic Treasury view of 1929, in short, was used as a

---

[50]Clay, "Remedies," enclosed in Clay to Osborne, May 18, 1930, Bank of England archives, S. 44/1 (1).

[51]See especially Mark Casson, *Economics of Unemployment* (Oxford: Martin Robertson, 1983) for a sympathetic study of Clay (along with Edwin Cannan and Pigou).

[52]The challenging insight offered twenty years ago in Robert Skidelsky, *Politicians and the Slump* (London: Macmillan, 1967) has thus become stylized in a potentially misleading way.

[53]*The Times,* May 13, 1929.

plank in the Tory election platform and, like other policy commitments of a partisan character, lapsed on the change of government. In fact, within six months of taking office, the Labour government had approved schemes valued at £48 million, reaching £110 million within a year. (This compares with the program of £250 million within two years to which Lloyd George had been pledged.) Admittedly, less than half of these programs had actually come into operation. Even by June 1931, when the government had approved schemes worth £186 million, those in operation amounted to only £108 million. Roger Middleton has estimated that this money created jobs for 300,000 men (taking account of indirect and secondary employment).

These figures can be read in several ways. Middleton himself cites them as evidence of the inescapable delays involved and of "the exiguity of the employment generated relative to the magnitude of the unemployment problem"—work for only 10.9 percent of the total 2.74 million unemployed by June 1931.[54] The point about delay indicates a real constraint to which inadequate attention had been given. But the relatively small contribution of public works to mitigating the total unemployment figures is, of course, a function of the unprecedented rise in that total. Lloyd George's pledge was, in effect, that it was possible to create 600,000 jobs; and the Labour government eventually got halfway toward this. It is worth asking whether such results would have looked, in the perspective of 1929, like an unequivocal refutation or a limited vindication of the prospective claims.

A contemporary appraisal is provided by the white paper on unemployment, published in December 1930 as the Labour government's major statement of policy in this field. Its argument was that, although faced with a sudden and exceptional depression in world trade, the government could claim some success for its twofold policy. Its short-range policy, "designed to provide immediate employment by pressing forward development work of public utility with the utmost vigour," was combined with a long-range policy designed to increase efficiency. The latter included not only encouragement of industrial reorganization and moves toward cheap money but also interventionist steps to promote exports, to

---

[54]"The Treasury and Public Investment: A Perspective on Inter-War Economic Management," *Public Administration* 61 (1983): 351–70, at 361. See also, S. Howson, "Slump and Unemployment," in R. C. Floud and D. N. McCloskey, eds., *The Economic History of Britain Since 1700*, 2 vols. (Cambridge, Eng.: Cambridge University Press, 1981), II, 265–85, at 279–81.

expand electricity supply, to improve housing ("in a general programme of national development"), and to restore agricultural prosperity.[55]

Much of this, it should be said, was designed to take the wind out of the sails of proposals canvassed earlier that year by the Liberal party. Moreover, one section of the white paper was devoted to "The Quality of the Population," identifying improvements in welfare and training as an integral part of the government's long-range economic policy.

Beneficial results were naturally claimed for this policy, notably, that it would "provide employment to the extent of more than 500,000 man years" through "a programme which compares favourably with that which the Government of any other country has been able to frame to mitigate the unemployment problem resulting from the world depression of trade."[56] Whether this calculation was too optimistic is a question that can be left for further econometric investigation. But the claim that public works of an appropriate kind could exert a beneficial impact of this order on employment marks a sharp difference between this white paper and that of May 1929, which had branded such claims fallacious.

One man, at least, had reason to regard the 1930 white paper as having a different filiation altogether, not with the Treasury view of 1929 but with the critique of it in *Can Lloyd George Do It?* Hubert Henderson was a joint author of both documents. As editor of the Liberal paper the *Nation* and a former member of the Cambridge Economics Faculty, he was Keynes's close collaborator in 1929. As a civil servant, following his appointment as joint secretary of the Economic Advisory Council at the beginning of 1930, he then came to work alongside the leading Treasury officials. He and Hopkins, both of them products, as was Phillips, of Emmanuel College, Cambridge, quickly established a cordial working relationship, and their convergent views are evident in their joint drafting of the white paper.[57]

To Henderson, the abiding argument for public works was as "a means of facilitating a large readjustment of the national economy."[58] It was not an alternative to facing up to the structural problems of the declining staples but a necessary adjunct to the policy of transfer. Not

[55]*Statement of the Principal Measures Taken by H.M. Government in Connection with Unemployment* (London: H.M.S.O. Cmd. 3746, 1930), 3, 14.

[56]Ibid., 21.

[57]On this matter see the correspondence/drafts exchanged between them (December 1930) in T. 175/43.

[58]H. D. Henderson, "Do we want public works?" (May 1935) in *The Inter-war Years* (Oxford: Oxford University Press, 1955), 152.

only is this emphasis wholly consistent with the argument in *Can Lloyd George Do It?* but Henderson subsequently (1935) reaffirmed his confidence in it: "There is no doubt, I think, that an environment of prevailingly active trade makes the transfer problem easier to solve."[59]

The Treasury's objections to public works, of course, had not disappeared overnight, simply because Labour was now in office. But the sweeping claim that public works were capable only of displacing, not increasing, employment no longer carried conviction against Keynes's increasing stress on unused capacity, as developed during and immediately after the election campaign. Hawtrey's analysis had once seemed reassuring to the Treasury because it promised to be watertight; but with Hawtrey himself demonstrating a disconcerting propensity to redefine the premise, it looked as though the argument had, for all practical purposes, sprung a leak. Hopkins seems to have reasserted his authority in reformulating policy, especially in presenting the Treasury evidence to the Macmillan Committee along lines that took account of the changed ideological climate.[60]

The Treasury declined to bear the blame for thwarting initiatives designed to create work, which confronted enough obstacles in other quarters. The energetic commitment of ministers in pushing schemes forward was itself questionable, as was the appropriateness of the decision-making structure within government—criticisms mounted by Oswald Mosley during the course of his campaign for a more radical approach. What Hopkins stressed were the real administrative difficulties in implementing an effective program and the growing worries about confidence. Henderson, with his new responsibilities and new access to inside information, now felt that Keynes had made light of such considerations. Whereas in 1929 Keynes and Henderson had been allied as radicals against the Treasury orthodoxy of Hopkins and Leith-Ross, a year later Henderson had circumspectly distanced himself from Keynes's alleged irresponsibility, and Hopkins had adroitly freed himself from Leith-Ross's apparent inflexibility. The Hopkins-Henderson line on public works carried the day, with its professed readiness to entertain good schemes tempered by a pragmatic skepticism about achieving dramatic further improvement.

[59]Ibid., 159.

[60]On Hopkins, see G. C. Peden, "Sir Richard Hopkins and the 'Keynesian Revolution' in Employment Policy," *Economic History Review*, 2nd Ser., 36 (1983): 281–96. The argument for a crucial shift in perspective is developed in my chapter, "The reformulation of the Treasury View, 1929–30," *Keynesian Revolution in the Making*, 142–61.

After the fall. The "knave-proof" model of the economy, it should be remembered, relied heavily on free trade and on the self-adjusting mechanism of the gold standard to provide a necessary framework of financial discipline. Only when shackled to gold was the domestic economy shackled to the realities of a competitive world market. It is little wonder that those Treasury men who had sat at the feet of Sir John Bradbury in his prime regarded the abandonment of free trade, as he did himself, as an even greater disaster than going off gold. Bradbury had ruminated along these lines to the Macmillan Committee in the autumn of 1930:

I am afraid of tampering with Free Trade, and I am afraid of tampering with the gold standard. If I had to choose between tampering with the gold standard as a remedy and Protection, I should be solid for tampering with the gold standard.[61]

As it turned out, and as he had no doubt feared, the one was merely a prelude to the other. Looking back in retirement, Grigg saw that "our departure from the Gold Standard heralded the beginning of our repellent modern world." It was the final expulsion from the Garden. "At the end of it all we could see that the two great stabilizing forces of the nineteenth century had lost their influence—the British Navy and the International Gold Standard worked by and through the Bank of England and the City of London," Grigg concluded in 1947. "We are now adrift in a universe with no fixed criteria and no automatic regulators or indicators."[62]

The austere charm of the gold standard was as a closed and determinate system. It spoke with the purity of a dead language; it operated with the perfection of calculus; and as such it captivated minds that had been schooled to esteem elegance and rigor. But its appeal was not confined to the Oxford classicists and Cambridge mathematicians who staffed the Treasury. When Keynes expounded its workings to the Macmillan Committee, he concluded that "there is no need to wonder why two generations, both of theorists and of practical men, should have been entranced by it."[63] Even the romantic autodidact Churchill was not immune, reminiscing in later years about "the 'beautiful precision' with which Free Trade and the Gold Standard had worked 'not in this disastrous century but in the last.' "[64]

It was not simply an appraisal of the relevant empirical evidence that

[61]Unpublished minutes, November 7, 1930, 29 (T. 200/5).
[62]*Prejudice and Judgment*, 257, 260.
[63]*J.M.K.*, XX, 53 (February 20, 1930).
[64]Ben Pimlott, ed., *The Second World War Diary of Hugh Dalton* (London: Jonathan Cape, 1986), 578 (April 7, 1943).

had persuaded the authorities of the wisdom of returning to gold. The object lesson of prewar British prosperity, of course, weighed in its favor. The arguments about parity also could be joined on both sides, with technical appeals to rival index numbers expressing the relative price levels in Britain and the United States. But the verdict did not ultimately hinge on the adequacy of such proof. Nor was the unavailability of other possibly useful evidence crucial. The Treasury's sources of information may now seem seriously inadequate, but there is little evidence that this deficiency was keenly felt at the time, or that urgent measures were thought necessary to remedy it.

It was, significantly, Keynes who railed against the relative paucity of information about the British economy and the reluctance to make what information did exist properly available. "The secretiveness practiced by our business world, from the Bank of England downwards, would be excessive in criminals seeking to evade justice, and is, in fact, a major factor in British inefficiency," he declared in 1926.[65] Moreover, he was responsible for the composition of that part of the Liberal party's proposals on unemployment (the "Yellow Book") where, cheek by jowl, a chapter pleading for an economic general staff was followed by one on statistics. The "Yellow Book" denounced the "deficiency of vital information and the ineffective publication of the information which we have" as a scandalous inhibition on appropriate remedial action:

How can the State frame a policy or deal in a rational and scientific manner with the problem, for example, of unemployment, if we do not know the rates of growth and decay in different directions and the actual trends of the industrial system? How can economic science become a true science, capable, perhaps, of benefiting the human lot as much as all the other sciences put together, so long as the economist, unlike other scientists, has to grope for and guess at the relevant data of experience?

The Yellow Book thus disclosed the relations of means to ends: "The improvement of economic information is necessary for wise intervention or guidance by the State."[66]

A "hands-on" approach to the business of economic management might well require a radically improved form of expertise, but the Treasury's motto was "hands off." Indeed, the authorities gave the impression that they knew all they wanted to know. In 1925 they knew, as Norman

[65] *J.M.K.*, XIX, 597 (*Nation*, December 24 1926).
[66] *Britain's Industrial Future* (1928), 121–3; for authorship, see Roy Harrod, *The Life of John Maynard Keynes* (London: Macmillan, 1951), 393.

put it with self-deprecating humility, that "the Gold Standard is the best 'Governor' that can be devised for a world that is still human, rather than divine."[67] In the succeeding years, likewise, Niemeyer and Leith-Ross knew in their bones that Keynes was a quack doctor, peddling palliatives that might seem harmless in ministering to the immediate symptoms but were fallacious as a cure; and they turned to Hawtrey for a second opinion to confirm their intuition.

The authorities did not belie their name in upholding established doctrine and declaring it sound. A deep inner sense of conviction led them to cling so fervently to their theory of liquids even when they half-suspected that in practice they were confronted with "a sticky mass with strong internal resistances." A nineteenth-century positivist concept of "knowledge," striving for progress through the accretion of new facts, is inadequate here. Perhaps we can now improve on it and avoid being driven back—much further back—upon a mythopoeic account of how the mandarins, having resisted the temptations of the tree of knowledge, subsequently lived to regret eating its fruit. As it was, in the imperfect, indeterminate, fallen epoch that dawned in 1931, they ultimately seized on a synthesis that salvaged potent vestiges of the Eden they had lost.

New models for old. What had been the essential characteristics of "the historic doctrine of bank rate policy," as explained by Keynes to the Macmillan Committee?

You see what a very good doctrine it is, because the completely harmonious disposition of the economic forces of the world is preserved merely by the Bank of England changing the Bank rate from time to time in an appropriate way and leaving all the rest to the operation of *laissez faire.* And not only so; the Bank of England is set, in a sense, a very easy task, because movements of gold will always operate as a barometer to tell the Bank of England exactly when a change of bank rate has become necessary, so that the method, assuming that it works according to the way in which it is supposed to work, is as simple as possible. All you have to do is to watch those movements, change the bank rate accordingly and the economic system will then automatically grind out the proper levels of prices and wages at which everyone can be employed, at which business men can get normal profits and which furnishes the most advantageous division of the country's savings between investment at home and investment abroad, all owing to the fact that the Bank rate has this double influence.[68]

[67]Norman to Churchill, February 7, 1925, printed in Moggridge, *British Monetary Policy*, 272.
[68]*J.M.K.*, XX, 53 (February 20, 1930).

The efficacy of this process, if only it were allowed to operate, was not doubted at the time by Keynes, committed to the analysis of his *Treatise on Money,* any more than by Hawtrey. They were therefore unanimous in 1930 on a crucial feature of their policy advice over unemployment. They billed and cooed to one another before the Macmillan Committee in maintaining that cheap money would do the trick. When the more skeptical Clay, streetwise from Manchester, was asked by the bank for his critique of Keynes's proposals, he seized on this affinity, arguing that:

> Mr. Keynes's proposed method is open to doubt. His thesis is that the necessary stimulus to investment can be given by lowering the long-term rate of interest. This seems to me akin to Mr. Hawtrey's view that you can cure unemployment by keeping the Bank Rate low enough.[69]

On this reading, all the authorities had to do, when faced with deflation and depression, was to apply the appropriate monetary policy. According to Keynes, this delightfully simple remedy was barred in the real world because of Britain's obligation under the gold standard to bolster the parity of sterling by high interest rates, hence the expediency of "second-best" solutions like public works and tariffs under the "special case" of the *Treatise.* But the special case, of course, was rendered inoperative by Britain's departure from the gold standard in 1931, whereupon Keynes might have been expected to abandon his radical suggestions. In fact, within little more than a year, he was to discover other reasons to justify both tariffs and public works—the theory of effective demand.

The *Treatise* was a theoretical work, of high ambition, which Keynes submitted to Hawtrey, among others, for criticism. The nature of Hawtrey's criticisms, drawn together in a paper that was circulated to the Macmillan Committee in January 1931, were such as to cast considerable doubt on the validity of the definitions employed and hence on the theoretical rigor that Keynes claimed. Hawtrey's influence, indeed, was important in shifting Keynes toward the framework of what became the *General Theory.*[70] But Hawtrey himself resisted the allure of the theory of effective demand; instead he remained strikingly consistent both in his own theoretical analysis and in his policy conclusions. His book *The Art of Central Banking* (1932) expounded a theme that was "practical in that it teaches how to use a power of influencing events." He maintained that "there is no less scope for systematic reasoning in the study of means than

[69]Clay, "Remedies" (May 18, 1930), S. 44/1 (1).
[70]Clarke, *Keynesian Revolution in the Making,* 236–44.

in the study of causes. The pursuit of wisdom is as scientific as the pursuit of truth."[71]

The regulation of credit was the essential task, and in a deflationary world this meant an expansion of demand. "The inflation is desirable," he wrote, in these circumstances. "Indeed, people who regard the word inflation as necessarily having a bad sense would call this degree of expansion 'reflation.' "[72] He seems to have been among the first British economists to import this term from Hoover's America, for the obvious reason that it expressed his own conceptions so well. Although prepared to consider budget deficits if cheap money were to fail, Hawtrey still had no time for public works and would have relied, under those circumstances, on the reduction of taxation in itself to expand demand.

How far did the Treasury likewise come to condone policies of domestic expansion under the new conditions of the 1930s? Certainly, the Treasury view no longer stood as a formidable obstacle as it had in 1929, but this was already true by 1930, after Hopkins's reformulation of policy, admittedly under a Labour government that professed some sympathy for public works. It was the political color of the National government that ruled out interventionist measures after 1931, rather than the influence of the authorities. Indeed, with the end of the gold standard, the Bank of England was to become a source of discreet pressure for public works in a way that was perfectly consistent with Clay's long-standing skepticism about the efficacy of cheap money alone. In 1930 he had argued that "more direct and drastic influences on costs" were necessary as well.

> Again (he continued), it is admitted, when the conditions of profitable enterprise exist, and credit has been expanded beyond the point at which industry is fully and profitably employed, so that additional credit merely sends up prices, that restriction of credit or enhancing of its price by the banking system will be an effective brake or check on the boom. What is contended is only that it does not follow, because credit restrictions will check a boom, that credit expansion must create a boom. Taking off the brake is not the same thing as putting on the accelerator. Bank Rate is an excellent brake; but it will not necessarily serve also, by itself, as an accelerator.[73]

Because of this appraisal of the asymmetrical effects of monetary policy, the bank seems, from as early as 1933, to have been readier than the

[71]R. G. Hawtrey, *The Art of Central Banking* (London: Longmans, 1932), vi.
[72]Ibid., 271.
[73]Clay, "Bank Rate, Credit and Employment," May 17, 1930, EID 1/2.

Treasury to envisage direct intervention to stimulate recovery through public works.[74]

Keynes's new theory of effective demand had taken shape by the end of 1932. It was the basis on which he mounted his renewed pleas for expansion from the beginning of 1933, notably in a series of articles in the *Times* called "The Means to Prosperity" and a supporting piece in the *New Statesman* called "The Multiplier." The Treasury response to these articles, articulated chiefly by Phillips, has been well explained elsewhere, but the role of Henderson deserves special note here. It was he who disabused Phillips of the misconception that Keynes's argument depended on the existence of idle deposits in the banks. Henderson thus understood the force of Keynes's new theory: "His favourite theme is that the expenditure would serve to create most of the savings requisite to finance the public works," even if he could not accept it.[75]

The fact that Henderson was to remain skeptical about the multiplier is doubly suggestive. Retrospectively, it surely implies that the concept is not recognizable in *Can Lloyd George Do It?* and cannot properly be imported into the policy arguments of 1929. Prospectively, it shows that the multiplier was not essential to an advocacy of reflationary, or what he called at the time "frankly inflationary," measures.[76] For although Henderson did not believe major new public works to be warranted in the situation prevailing in the mid-1930s, he was in favor of "endeavouring to increase consumption" by higher social spending as an alternative means of administering "grease for the wheels of transfer" through economic expansion.[77] In fact, a relaxation of government policy over public works in 1935 waited on a change of tack by the chancellor, Neville Chamberlain, as an overtly political—indeed electoral—ploy. The slow tide of economic recovery, meanwhile, was no longer checked by tight credit, and the cheap money policy from 1932 brought the bank down to 2 percent.

There is more than one way to make sense of these cross-currents. Intellectual support for public works in the 1930s could, for example, be derived from the arguments of Clay, who believed that the structural problems of the economy demanded direct intervention by government,

[74]R. S. Sayers, *The Bank of England, 1891–1944* (Cambridge, Eng.: Cambridge University Press, 1976; 1986 edn.), 460–3.
[75]Henderson to Phillips, March 16, 1933, Henderson Papers, Box 10; for a full account of these exchanges, see Howson and Winch, *Economic Advisory Council*, 128–30.
[76]*J.M.K.*, XX, 164–6 (Henderson to Keynes, February 28, 1933).
[77]"Do We Want Public Works?" (May 1935), *The Inter-war Years*, 160.

now that the inhibitions of the gold standard had been removed. Henderson's line of argument demonstrated that there was scope for fiscal measures to reflate the economy, when appropriate, irrespective of the merits of either public works or the multiplier. Finally, it was Hawtrey who continued to argue that public works in themselves made very little difference and that the logical way to control trade fluctuations was by resorting to cheap money in a slump and applying a credit squeeze when boom conditions developed.

When it came to practical judgment on what to do and when to do it, Phillips was perfectly ready to override Hawtrey's immediate advice; and at this executive level it has to be conceded that the learned man was left immured in his dungeon throughout the 1930s. Yet, surveying Treasury policy in 1937, an observer in the bank could note wryly, "Whatever they may say about Hawtrey, his theories in fact fill the vacuum left in their minds by the lack of economic theories on this subject of their own."[78] A further speculation is tempting. For the sort of monetary policy favored by the Conservatives in the 1950s, in the heyday of the so-called Keynesian consensus, was to leave the Bank of England pulling the levers of inflation and deflation in a manner for which its operation of the gold standard might have served as an apprenticeship, although the bank now responded to a more complex range of signals. The outcome was a modification of the art of central banking, justifiably hailed as "pure Hawtrey,"[79] for which the appropriate handbook was not necessarily the *General Theory*.

CONCLUSION

This chapter has suggested that in the 1920s the Treasury held firmly to the self-acting model of the economy that minimized its own direct role. The gold standard was the highest expression of this model. It had been validated by years of experience, but it was also underpinned by theoretical axioms about equilibrium. It postulated a process of adjustment, once equilibrium was disturbed, so that another position of equilibrium, with optimal use of all resources, including labor, was quickly established. As long as such adjustments had been, if not wholly painless, then largely invisible, their operation gave rise to little introspection. It was the actual

[78]Memorandum for B. G. Catterns (Deputy Governor), February 12, 1937, G1 1/15 (authorship unknown).
[79]See George Peden, "Old Dogs and New Tricks," at n. 80.

breakdown of this adjustment process in the 1920s that provoked awkward questions. In the course of answering these, the authorities were forced to explain, and indeed to comprehend, the nature of the process much more thoroughly. These debates served to disclose an assumption of perfect flexibility or fluidity that was of fundamental importance in justifying Treasury policy. This assumption made sense of the high priority accorded to overseas investment and of the principled rejection of public works in 1928–9 (the Treasury view). The model was also of a kind that able administrators, with a traditional education at Oxford or Cambridge, could happily master and defend—a task relished by Niemeyer and Leith-Ross.

The reasons that rendered it indefensible between 1929 and 1931 were diverse. The direct influence of Keynes, albeit more as a publicist than as an academic economist, is demonstrably important. There are signs that the Treasury recognized the force of some of his arguments, especially about the actual state of disequilibrium in which the British economy appeared to be trapped. It may also have become apparent that the dogmatic Treasury view of 1929 rested on a misapprehension about the applicability of Hawtrey's rigorous assumptions to current conditions in Britain. Moreover, both the economic and the political contexts were changing, and were to change further.

The British economy was plunging deeper into depression under the impact of the world slump, which mocked hopes of an early return to equilibrium through normal trade recovery. Hitherto the lassitude of British exports could be attributed to wage rigidities, with the implication that price flexibility would unlock new markets abroad. But the inelastic world demand for British goods *at any price* was the immediate lesson of these years—a further demonstration that the theory of fluids was no longer relevant. In these conditions it is not surprising that a number of economists turned to analyzing the problems of disequilibrium; nor is it surprising that Treasury advice now took full account of the rigidities and imperfections of the economy. Such an approach, too, reflected the more open-minded outlook of the Hopkins-Phillips regime.

In politics, also, there were new pressures to which the Treasury had to adapt. True, the Liberal scheme to conquer unemployment dreamed up by Keynes and Lloyd George was sidetracked. But the election of a Labour government should be recognized as marking a significant departure in public works policy. The Treasury adapted to this departure, in a pragmatic and adroit way, just as it later accepted tariffs as a fact of life under the National government. Indeed, the end of the gold standard and the abandonment of free trade shifted policy onto a wholly new footing. If the self-acting model of the economy no longer exercised its own discipline, some kind of economic regulation was a task that the Treasury, however reluctantly, had to assume itself. Its concessions can be seen as minimal—preserving, so far as possible, the balanced-budget convention and operating a cheap money policy at arm's length. But alternative policies were seriously canvassed, by other economists as well as Keynes, and his distinctive theory of effective demand was not necessarily the touchstone by which such options were judged. The range of technical advice available to government was undoubtedly wider in the 1930s than it had been in the 1920s, and the work of the Economic Advisory Council, although abortive in producing big results, led to a variety of small results, notably through the Committee on Economic Information. Throughout this process, efforts to achieve a practical consensus on policy naturally took priority over any aspirations for doctrinal conversion, in a way that parallels the later American experience as reported by Robert Collins in Chapter 5 of this volume.

It was World War II that brought economists into the structure of government on a large scale, and this growth in expertise challenged the authority of the old mandarin class. Wilfrid Eady, as second secretary to the Treasury from 1942, had first-class honors in classics from Cambridge behind him but evidently felt himself at some disadvantage in discussions with the young professional adviser, James Meade, who records receiving from him "a most disarming letter saying that he had no training in economics but was trying to master the subject." As Meade commented in his diary: "When one looks at it objectively, what a state of affairs it is when the man chiefly responsible for internal and external financial policy has had no technical training. I am sure that in our grandchildren's days this will be considered very odd."[80]

In a series of recent studies by economic historians, skepticism has been voiced as to whether a genuine "Keynesian revolution" took place in Treasury policy before the late 1940s—or perhaps even the late 1950s.[81] The best conclusion here may be that the term *revolution* is itself inappropriate to describe policy changes that, by their nature, tend to be incremental, responding tentatively to a range of different pressures. Each

---

[80]James Meade diary, November 19, 1944, Meade Papers 1/3, London School of Economics.
[81]See, most recently, Neil Rollings, "British Budgetary Policy, 1945–54: A 'Keynesian Revolution'?" *Economic History Review*, 2d Ser., 41 (1988): 283–98.

historian, moreover, is ultimately at the mercy of his own concept of Keynesianism. Yet some definition is necessary, and one that simply stops at a commitment to countercyclical macroeconomic management of overall demand is too indiscriminate. Historians may thus have looked too exclusively to Keynes for the ideas that ultimately filtered into government; and this tendency has led to Keynes being credited/saddled with the praise/blame for shifts in policy of which he was by no means the only begetter. In addition to the sort of "Curried Keynes" that William Barber suggests was popular in New Deal America, the menu should perhaps also include various anglicized varieties of goulash, fricassee, and ragout, in which the ingredients were chopped, minced, and mixed to suit the customers' tastes.

In recognizing that the name of Keynes has been invoked too freely, however, it is not very illuminating to construct an alternative account in which the influence of ideas, of whatever kind, is systematically discounted as merely instrumental. There are other ways of appraising policy changes and analytical influences here than on a unilinear pro-Keynesian–anti-Keynesian scale; and there is no need to plump for naive Keynesian triumphalism, on the one side, or know-nothing administrative reductionism, on the other. For it should be acknowledged that the Treasury model of the 1920s had immense strengths, intellectual strengths not least. It was internally consistent; it could be grasped by educated lay minds; its postulates carried the academic authority of economic doctrine; its precepts were those that actually guided "the authorities" in the real world. As a self-acting model, moreover, it kept most economic issues out of politics except when its own premises (especially free trade) were challenged. This was the knave-proof fiscal constitution. It represented, then, economic knowledge of an analytical kind that made empirical knowledge, if not redundant, of secondary significance to government.

To some extent it was the purposive accumulation of economic information that called into question the applicability of this model to the real world. More crucially, however, the object lesson of economic depression brutally drove the point home. In the process of adjusting to these unprecedented changes, government may have learned from economists— but as much about the limitations of pure theory as anything else. The practical wisdom of an administrator like Hopkins was, in turn, a revelation to an economist like Henderson, and perhaps a salutary lesson to Keynes himself. Who learned most from whom is a question worth pondering. Much of this learning, moreover, was acquired "on the job." The state was called on to face more choices and possessed more information in making them. But if we ask in which way government learned most, the short answer is, "the hard way." The growth of economic knowledge in a technically more sophisticated sense was largely a product of an era when government had already become inescapably committed to unwonted tasks of economic management, confronting the Treasury with matters about which, left to itself, it had been happy not to know.

7

Old dogs and new tricks: the British Treasury and
Keynesian economics in the 1940s and 1950s

GEORGE C. PEDEN

This chapter explores various aspects of the relationship between government and the growth of economic knowledge:

1. To what extent did the British Treasury use Keynesian economics to solve new economic problems?
2. To what extent did the Treasury itself contribute to the generation of systematic economic knowledge?
3. Insofar as the Treasury did use Keynesian economics, did this use lead to a neglect of microeconomic variables in the formulation of economic policy?

The first section offers an explanation of what the Treasury's role in Whitehall was, who the "old dogs" in the Treasury were, and why they were open to new economic ideas in the 1940s and 1950s. Then comes a brief discussion of Keynes's ideas (the "new tricks") as these related to economic policy, and the way these ideas were interpreted by economists within, or with access to, Whitehall. The third, fourth, and fifth sections deal with policy-making in three periods: 1940–5, 1945–51, and 1951–9. The main emphasis here is on efforts to manage aggregate demand, especially through fiscal policy, because it is with the alleged Keynesian destruction of the doctrine of balanced budgets that some of the most trenchant criticisms of Keynes and his followers have been concerned. The sixth section assesses the Treasury's contribution to the compilation

The research on which this chapter is based was made possible through the generosity of the British Academy, the Leverhulme Trust, and the Wolfson Foundation. The author also wishes to thank Sir Alec Cairncross, Susan Howson, Roger Middleton, and Barry Supple for their comments on earlier drafts. The responsibility for any errors that remain is the author's alone.

of economic data. The seventh section argues that Treasury officials never allowed developments in macroeconomics to blind them to the importance of microeconomic variables. In particular, with reference to taxation, the adverse effects of heavy taxation on productivity are shown to have been a constant concern of the Treasury's.

The main conclusions to be drawn from the chapter are as follows:

1. The Treasury's responsibility for the control of public expenditure significantly influenced the way in which Keynesian theory was interpreted in the department.

2. The Treasury, while accepting elements of Keynesian analysis, continued to be concerned with what would now be called supply-side economics.

3. Not the least attraction of Keynesian analysis to the Treasury was that, in conditions of excess demand, as in the 1940s and 1950s, the chancellor of the Exchequer was justified in aiming at a budget *surplus* of revenue over current expenditure, whereas before the war financial orthodoxy had required no more than that the budget should balance. Thus, although Buchanan and Wagner may have correctly identified the long-term legacy of Keynes as inflation through deficit finance,[1] British experience in the 1940s and 1950s suggests that Keynesian economics could be used to reinforce sound finance.

It is true that in most years of the 1950s there was what would now be called a Public Sector Borrowing Requirement. Even then, however, in each budget expenditure "above the line"—that is, the expenditure of central government for which borrowing was not specifically authorized by Parliament—was more than matched by revenue. Deficits occurred "below the line," mainly on account of loans to local authorities, nationalized industries, and the Post Office,[2] but most of these loans were for capital expenditure that would produce a money return, in the form either of rents (from municipal housing) or of profits from public enterprise. Borrowing for such capital expenditure had been normal before the war, although the scale of "below the line" expenditure was much greater

---

[1] James M. Buchanan and Richard E. Wagner, *Democracy in Deficit: The Political Legacy of Lord Keynes* (New York: Academic Press, 1977). The Buchanan and Wagner thesis has been applied to Britain in J. M. Buchanan, John Burton, and R. E. Wagner, *The Consequences of Mr. Keynes* (London: Institute of Economic Affairs, 1978).

[2] (Radcliffe) *Committee on the Working of the Monetary System: Principal Memoranda of Evidence* (London: Her Majesty's Stationery Office [HMSO], 1960), 1:78. For discussion of the structure of the budget, see Sir Herbert Brittain, *British Budgetary System* (London: Allen and Unwin, 1959).

after the war. The point to be made here is that the explicit purpose of such expenditure was to improve public services, not to increase aggregate demand, although that may have been its effect because Britain enjoyed full employment after the war.

THE "OLD DOGS"

The Treasury is the central department of government in Britain. It is responsible for both international and domestic financial policy, including the budget and (in conjunction with the Bank of England) monetary policy. The Treasury is also responsible for the control of central government expenditure and, in the period in question, it was also responsible for the organization of the civil service.[3] Like the secretary of the treasury in the United States, the minister in charge of the British Treasury, the chancellor of the Exchequer, need not be an economic expert, although, as it happened, in the period in question two chancellors, Hugh Dalton (1945–7) and Hugh Gaitskell (1950–1), were professional economists, while another, Harold Macmillan (1955–7), had written on economic affairs.[4]

Normally, however, chancellors were highly dependent on their advisers in technical matters, even if ministers laid down broad political objectives. What might seem surprising today is that most of the chancellor's advisers had no formal training in economics. In the interwar years, only one of the Treasury's permanent officials, Ralph Hawtrey, had had a reputation as an economist, and he was self-taught.[5] Some economists, including Keynes, were taken on as advisers during World War II, and Keynes remained until his death in 1946. When Sir Stafford Cripps, who had been minister of economic affairs, became chancellor late in 1947, he brought with him a small Central Economic Planning Staff, including Austin Robinson and three young economists whom he had recruited in

---

[3]The best accounts of the Treasury and its role in this period are Samuel H. Beer, *Treasury Control* (Oxford: Oxford University Press, 1956) and Lord (Edward) Bridges, *The Treasury* (London: Allen and Unwin, 1966). Bridges was permanent secretary (official head) of the Treasury from 1945 to 1956.

[4]Dalton had been reader in economics, and Gaitskell had been reader in political economy, at London University. Macmillan's publications included *The Middle Way* (London: Macmillan, 1938), a book with extensive quotations from Keynes's *General Theory*.

[5]See Peter Clarke's contribution to this volume (Chapter 6). Hawtrey's influence in the Treasury waned in the 1930s to the point that he had none at all in the 1940s; see Susan Howson, "Hawtrey and the Real World," in G. C. Harcourt, ed., *Keynes and His Contemporaries* (London: Macmillan, 1985).

Cambridge. The major influx of economists, however, came in 1953, when the Economic Section of the Cabinet Office, under its director, Robert Hall, was transferred to the Treasury. The Economic Section itself was a wartime creation and, prior to the war, there had been no permanent presence of economists in Whitehall, although in the 1930s a number of "outsiders," including Keynes, had tendered advice periodically through the Cabinet Office.[6]

The Treasury's administrative officials learned about public finance on the job. Most had studied classics at university, this being the most common academic background of recruits even in the 1950s. Sir Horace Wilson, the permanent secretary (chief civil servant) of the Treasury from 1939 to 1942, was exceptional in having taken a B.Sc. (Econ.) at the London School of Economics after attending "night school" from 1904 to 1908.[7] His successors, Sir Richard Hopkins (1942–5) and Sir Edward Bridges (1945–56), were more conventional in having been classics scholars at Cambridge and Oxford, respectively. It should be said, however, that Hopkins had picked up plenty of expertise in public finance during twenty-five years on the Board of Inland Revenue before transferring to the Treasury in 1927, and by private study of economics. Sir Roy Harrod compared him to "an ancient sage" and credited him with the "unique distinction" of being able to match Keynes in an argument.[8] In general, however, administrative officials were not expected to be able to do more than take an intelligent layman's view of economic issues, and there was no formal instruction in economics for such officials before 1963.[9]

The Treasury's function of controlling public expenditure meant that officials had long been aware of the propensity of politicians to spend money. The traditional canons of public finance, as these had been developed in the nineteenth century, were designed to curb this tendency. Normally, all central government expenditure for current purposes had to be paid for from tax revenue; in other words, popularity to be gained by

[6]For the prewar position, see Susan Howson and Donald Winch, *The Economic Advisory Council, 1930–1939* (Cambridge, Eng.: Cambridge University Press, 1977). For the origins of the Economic Section, see Alan Booth, "Economic Advice at the Centre of British Government 1939–41," *Historical Journal*, 29 (1986): 655–75; and Sir Alec Cairncross, "An Early Think-Tank: The Origins of the Economic Section," *Three Banks Review* 144 (1984): 50–9.
[7]Wilson also had considerable experience of practical economic problems, having been permanent secretary of the Ministry of Labour, 1921–30, and chief industrial adviser to H. M. Government, 1930–9.
[8]R. F. Harrod, *The Life of John Maynard Keynes* (London: Macmillan, 1951), 422 and 529.
[9]Samuel Brittan, *The Treasury Under the Tories 1951–64* (Harmondsworth: Penguin Books, 1964), 25–30.

spending money was offset by unpopularity from raising taxes. Capital expenditure might be met by borrowing, but, at least as late as the 1930s, the orthodox Treasury doctrine was that such borrowing was permissible only when the expected money return would be sufficient to cover interest charges and to pay off the loan (Post Office investment in telephone exchanges being cited as an example). The Treasury also believed that British industry must maintain its competitiveness in world markets, if only because a densely populated island must be able to pay for essential imports of food and raw materials. Consequently, the Treasury was suspicious of policy proposals, such as those advocated by Keynes in 1929, for increasing domestic demand, for it was believed that such action would simply raise British domestic costs and make firms less willing to face up to foreign competition. As Peter Clarke's contribution to this volume (Chapter 6) shows, the Treasury developed sophisticated, theoretical objections to the use of public investment to create employment. Treasury objections to reflationary finance, however, also reflected a concern to preserve the traditional rules of public finance.[10]

Hopkins was very much the embodiment of this traditional wisdom of the Treasury until his retirement in 1945,[11] and even afterward (Dalton kept him on as an adviser in 1945–7). Most leading Treasury officials down to the late 1950s had entered the Treasury in the interwar period or even earlier, and had therefore been grounded in the same traditions of public finance as Hopkins. It was only toward the end of the 1950s that the generation of "old dogs"—represented by Bridges (Treasury service 1917–38 and 1945–56), or Sir Bernard Gilbert (1914–56) and Sir Herbert Brittain (1919–57), two of his leading lieutenants[12]—began to fade away. However, because, at the time of writing, the Treasury's records are available to researchers only down to 1957, it is difficult to know what impact changes in personnel had on the quality of advice reaching the chancellor thereafter. What is certain is that men like Hopkins and Bridges were not, by training or experience, inclined to be uncritical adherents of Keynesian economics. While there were differences of opinion within the Treasury, experience of controlling public

---

[10]G. C. Peden, "The 'Treasury View' on Public Works and Employment in the Interwar Period," *Economic History Review*, 2d Ser., 37 (1984): 167–81.

[11]See G. C. Peden, "Sir Richard Hopkins and the 'Keynesian Revolution' in Employment Policy, 1929–45," *Economic History Review*, 2d Ser. 36 (1983): 281–96.

[12]Both Gilbert and Brittain were members of the Treasury's Budget Committee in the 1940s and 1950s. Gilbert was joint second secretary of the Treasury from 1944, and Brittain became a second secretary in 1953.

expenditure and of raising revenue made officials exceedingly skeptical of the reflationary ideas of Keynes or his followers, especially as regards the ability of politicians to resist demands for increased expenditure or lower taxation once the traditional canons of public finance had been discarded.[13]

In the 1940s, however, British governments faced new challenges, to which the Treasury had to respond. The immediate problem was inflation during and after the war, and the Treasury was willing to adopt some of Keynes's ideas on how to curb excessive purchasing power. Moreover, strong political imperatives supported the adoption of some form of employment policy. Some 7 million out of a labor force of 23 million would have to be transferred from the armed forces or war work to civil production and services after the war,[14] and many of these 7 million would have cause to fear a return to the mass unemployment of the 1930s, when about 3 million had been unemployed. Moreover, in contrast to the position before the war, there was a widely held consensus in informed circles that governments could prevent unemployment, using Keynes's ideas.[15] In 1942 Keynes held that an unemployment rate of 5 percent (that is, half the official figure for the lowest level in the 1930s) would be about the highest the public would stand after the war. Beveridge, indeed, set a more ambitious target in 1944 of an annual average of 3 percent.[16] Moreover, it would be impossible for the enlarged social insurance scheme projected after the war to be actuarially sound if the average of postwar unemployment were to be higher than the lowest level in the 1930s (10 percent of the insured labor force or $8\frac{1}{2}$ percent of

---

[13]Sir David Waley, who had entered the Treasury in 1910 and rose to the rank of third secretary in 1946–7, was an exception that proves this rule. In 1942 he told Hopkins, "I hope that the war which kills so much will kill the superstition that there is any object in balancing budgets. Our object is for there to be enough purchasing power to secure full employment, but that beyond this point purchasing power should not be increased so as to avoid inflation." Waley to Hopkins, May 15, 1941, Treasury papers, series 273, file 258 (T273/258), Public Record Office (P.R.O.), London. However, Waley served in the Overseas Finance division of the Treasury, had no recent experience of controlling public expenditure, and was not a member of the Budget Committee. Hopkins resisted any idea of deficit finance for the purposes of employment policy, and even wanted a sinking fund after the war.

[14]*Employment Policy,* presented by minister of reconstruction, Cmd. 6527, paragraph 10, *British Parliamentary Papers (B.P.P.),* 1943–4, vol. VIII.

[15]*Times,* May 27, 1944, remarked that the government was able to accept responsibility for employment because the work of economists influenced by Keynes, and the accumulation of statistical knowledge, had "laid bare the essential mechanism of the national economy."

[16]*Collected Writings of John Maynard Keynes,* D. E. Moggridge, ed. (London: Macmillan, 1971–1989) (henceforth, *J.M.K.*) XXVII, 299; and Sir William Beveridge, *Full Employment in a Free Society* (London: Allen and Unwin, 1944), 128.

the total labor force).[17] The Treasury thus had strong political and fiscal reasons for tackling the problem of unemployment as well as inflation. The "old dogs" were willing to consider "new tricks," albeit with due departmental skepticism.

THE "NEW TRICKS"

It is hardly necessary here to describe at length the purely theoretical aspects of the Keynesian revolution. Moreover, our focus is on the policy implications of the *General Theory* because policy was the prime concern of senior Treasury officials (none of whom, it will be recalled, were trained economists). Treasury officials looked to professional economists for expert advice. Consequently, the theoretical bases for Treasury views on policy were bound to change as Keynes convinced his fellow economists of the validity of his analysis—the more so because Keynes himself was an adviser in the Treasury from 1940 to 1946, where he was a powerful advocate of his views. Nevertheless, professional advice was not accepted uncritically in the Treasury, and it was always related to the practicalities of policy implementation. The Treasury's acceptance or rejection of Keynes's theory can therefore best be measured by willingness to apply theory to policy. What follows is a summary of Treasury reactions to the policy implications of the *General Theory* in relation to domestic monetary policy, public investment, fiscal policy, and the compilation of national income data.

Even when the bank rate had remained at 2 percent from 1932 to 1939, the Treasury had been prepared to contemplate a rise to 4 percent to prevent a boom from getting out of hand.[18] But Keynes believed that the long-term rate of interest was a highly psychological phenomenon, determined by expectations of what future interest rates were likely to be, as well as by the maturity composition of people's portfolios, and that therefore nothing should be done to raise interest rates even in a boom, lest it then become impossible to reduce them in a slump.[19] It was also the case that the Treasury had taken advantage of low interest rates in the 1930s to fund the national debt, by converting Treasury bills into long-

---

[17]Sir William Beveridge, *Social Insurance and Allied Services*, Cmd. 6404, paragraph 441, B.P.P. 1942–3, vol. VI.

[18]Susan Howson, *Domestic Monetary Management in Britain, 1919–38* (Cambridge, Eng.: Cambridge University Press, 1975), 129–31.

[19]*J.M.K.*, VII, 202–3; XXI, 389.

term issues, a policy that tended to restrict bank lending because banks used Treasury bills as secondary reserves.[20] But Keynes argued that such funding (by which the Treasury and the Bank of England had hoped to gain control of the market) should be replaced by a series of tap issues with different terms and maturities. If the monetary authorities allowed the public to decide the degree of liquidity that it wanted, it should be possible, he believed, for the authorities to control the rate of interest.[21] There is no evidence that the Treasury accepted these arguments before World War II.

Although the Treasury had been prepared to concede in 1937 that modest variations in public investment could be used as a countercyclical device, it still believed that the principal means of combating a depression would be a reduction in interest rates.[22] Keynes, on the other hand, argued that changes in interest rates alone could not offset great changes in businessmen's expectations and that it would be necessary to use public investment to take up the slack in the economy if private investment fell. Keynes did, however, come to accept Hopkins's argument that, if a depression began through a fall in demand for British exports, an increase in public investment would simply worsen the trade balance, both by increasing imports and by raising British prices relative to other countries' prices, and thereby reducing exports still further. In 1945 Keynes said that in these circumstances it might be necessary to accept somewhat greater fluctuations in unemployment than those implied by Beveridge's average of 3 percent.[23]

As is well known, fiscal policy was barely mentioned in the *General Theory*. The chancellor of the Exchequer's budget at that time was a cash account for central government revenue and expenditure and did not cover such elements as local authority expenditure on roads or housing (other than central government grants to local authorities for these purposes) or the activities of public corporations like the Central Electricity Board, which was responsible for creating the national grid. In other words, all Keynes's favorite schemes for public investment were largely outside the chancellor's budget. Fiscal policy came to the fore in his policy recommendations only in 1939–40, when, with a view to counter-

[20] Howson, *Domestic Monetary Policy*, 90, 95–104, 133–5.
[21] National Debt Enquiry, 1945, notes of meetings of March 8 and March 22, and N.D.E. Paper 7, T233/158, P.R.O., London.
[22] Peden, "The 'Treasury View,' " 177–8.
[23] National Debt Enquiry, note of meeting on April 10, 1945, T233/158, P.R.O., London. See also Peden, "Sir Richard Hopkins," 283–4 and 295.

ing inflation, he advocated greater reliance on taxation rather than loans to finance the war.[24]

When Keynes came to consider postwar fiscal policy, he suggested a separation between a revenue budget, which would normally balance, and a capital budget, which would include not only such items as Post Office investment in telephone systems, which would produce a money return, but also major items, like school buildings, which had a social return. This capital budget, incorporating the investment of local authorities and public corporations as well as capital items in the chancellor's budget, would be financed by loans and would be varied according to the needs of employment policy.[25] A time for deficit finance for current expenditure might come, in Keynes's view, but only a generation or two hence, if opportunities for investment were insufficient to raise aggregate demand and it became necessary to raise consumption.[26]

The final strand in Keynes's ideas about management of the economy related to the use of a national income accounting framework. The Treasury had not bothered to have national income statistics compiled in the 1930s, although a pilot study by the Inland Revenue in 1929 had shown that this could be done.[27] It was only from 1940 that official national income statistics were compiled on a regular basis, and even then this work was done by economists and statisticians in the Cabinet Office, without the initial blessing of the Treasury, although Hopkins came to support the work.[28]

From 1940 there was a body of economists in Whitehall sympathetic to Keynes's ideas. Most were in the Economic Section of the Cabinet Office, and for the purposes of this chapter the most important Keynesians were James Meade, who served in the Economic Section during the war and was its director from 1945 to 1947, and Robert Hall, who was Meade's successor from 1947 to 1961. Neither, of course, was a carbon copy of Keynes. Meade, in particular, was far readier than Keynes to contemplate deficit finance to raise consumption in a depression, and he was far more prepared than Keynes to see a rise in interest rates to check

[24]*How to Pay for the War*, see *J.M.K.*, IX, 367–439.
[25]*J.M.K.*, XXVII, 405–13.
[26]Alan Booth, "The 'Keynesian Revolution' in Economic Policy-Making," *Economic History Review*, 2d Ser., 36 (1983): 115–6.
[27]G. C. Peden, "Keynes, the Treasury and Unemployment in the Later Nineteen-thirties," *Oxford Economic Papers*, new series, 32 (1980): 7–8.
[28]*J.M.K.*, XXII, 325–33.

investment, rather than to rely upon physical controls.[29] Circumstances in the 1950s were also to lead Hall to favor more active fiscal and monetary policy, with less emphasis on variations in public investment than Keynes had envisaged.

In addition to the economists in Whitehall, one other Keynesian merits our attention here. This was Roy Harrod, whom Macmillan described as an "old friend" and "a stalwart expansionist," in whose advice he had a greater belief than that of the Treasury or the Bank of England.[30] Such is the nature of the British establishment that a fellow of an Oxford college may influence political leaders.[31] Harrod, like other economists, was much concerned with inflation in the immediate postwar period, but from the autumn of 1956 his thoughts turned to the problems of expansion. At heart he was one of those Keynesians who objected to deflation to correct balance-of-payments problems, even if the amount of deflation required would have raised unemployment by as little as one percentage point (at a time when unemployment was below 2 percent).[32] This was, of course, quite different from Keynes's position in 1945 when, as already noted, he had been prepared, in the interests of balance-of-payments equilibrium, to accept greater fluctuations in unemployment than those implied by Beveridge's average of 3 percent. Harrod was also one of the economists responsible for shifting the objectives of Keynesian economics from being content with full employment to aiming at achieving the full growth potential of the economy. Moreover, to this end he was more willing than Keynes had been to contemplate budget deficits.[33] The fact

[29]On Meade and Keynes as regards unbalancing the current budget, see *J.M.K.*, XXVII, 317–20. On interest rates, Meade's disagreement with Keynes is recorded in National Debt Enquiry, note of meeting on April 5, 1945, T233/158, P.R.O., London. Meade's views on the relative merits of interest rates and physical controls are set out in his *Planning and the Price Mechanism* (London: Allen and Unwin, 1948), especially 26–33.

[30]Harold Macmillan, *Riding the Storm, 1956–1959* (London: Macmillan, 1971), 709, 728.

[31]Harrod was, in fact, a fellow of two colleges, Christ Church and Nuffield. In addition to his contacts with Macmillan, Harrod had earlier instructed Lord Cherwell in economics, while both were at Christ Church, and Cherwell in turn advised Churchill. See Sir Roy Harrod, *The Prof* (London: Macmillan, 1959), 32–3, 67–9, and 255–61.

[32]Roy Harrod, "The Arrested Revolution," *New Statesman*, December 5, 1969. (In this article Harrod made two of his less accurate forecasts, namely, that Keynes's influence would increase over the next twenty years and that the "curious revival" of the money supply theory under the influence of Friedman was "not likely" to "have a long life.") For examples of Harrod's economic advice in the 1950s, see his *Topical Comment* (London: Macmillan, 1961).

[33]Roy Harrod, "Are We Really All Keynesians Now?" *Encounter*, 22 (January 1964). For Harrod's contribution to "Keynesian" growth models, see Roger Backhouse, *A History of Modern Economic Analysis* (Oxford: Basil Blackwell, 1985), 318–20, 323–5, 347–8, and 362–4, and the references cited therein.

that Macmillan, who was chancellor from 1955 to 1957 and prime minister from 1957 to 1963, was inclined to listen to Harrod's expansionist ideas was to be of some significance when Treasury officials tried to curb the growth of public expenditure.

Given the spectrum of ideas from Keynes to Harrod, it is clear that the fallacy of ambiguity can creep into any argument using the term "Keynesian." In what follows, therefore, economic ideas and advice are related wherever possible to particular people: Keynes, Meade, Hall, Harrod, and various Treasury officials.

POLICY-MAKING, 1940–1945

I have divided my analysis of economic policy-making into three periods— 1940–5, 1945–51, and 1951–9—each representing a stage in the development of the managed economy. From 1940 to 1945 Britain had a coalition government and was engaged in a total war, with one clear objective, victory. Lend-Lease made it possible to acquiesce in a huge adverse balance of payments on current account. Fiscal policy was used to mop up purchasing power, but the principal instruments of economic policy were the government's extensive powers to control production and investment, to direct labor, to control imports and foreign exchange, to allocate raw materials, to fix prices, and to ration consumer goods. After the war the balance of payments, and especially the need to earn dollars, became the main focus of policy, with inflation proving to be a more immediate problem than unemployment. Although the Labour government of 1945–51 relaxed some wartime controls and made increasing use of fiscal policy to manage the level of aggregate demand, Labour ministers believed that some direct controls would always be necessary to maintain full employment without inflation.[34] Conversely, when the Conservatives came to power in 1951, direct controls were dismantled as quickly as possible, and instead monetary policy was used to supplement fiscal policy.[35]

Although inflation proved to be the more immediate problem, all parties were committed by the 1944 white paper on *Employment Policy* to maintaining a high and stable level of employment. The white paper

[34]Cabinet: Economic Policy Committee minutes, January 19, 1950, Cabinet Office papers, series 134, vol. 224 (CAB 134/224), P.R.O., London. For discussion of controls at this time, see Sir Alec Cairncross, *Years of Recovery: British Economic Policy, 1945–51* (London: Methuen, 1985), 329–53.
[35]For details see J. C. R. Dow, *The Management of the British Economy, 1945–60* (Cambridge, Eng.: Cambridge University Press, 1964), especially Chapters 3, 6, and 9.

had avoided any specific target for employment policy. In 1951, however, the Labour government told the United Nations Economic and Social Council that 3 percent was the maximum level of unemployment that would be tolerated,[36] and in fact the national rate of unemployment, measured as an annual average, did not rise above 3 percent until the 1970s. Even so, Whitehall gave much attention to employment policy in the 1940s and 1950s.

In the 1940–5 period, Keynes's ideas can be seen to have influenced the Treasury in three stages: (1) in the wartime budgets from 1941 on, (2) in the 1944 white paper *Employment Policy,* and (3) in the National Debt Enquiry of 1945. Keynes considered the 1941 budget to be "a revolution in public finance"[37] because, whereas previous budgets had been cash balances for central government only, the 1941 budget introduced a national income accounting framework. This framework was used to calculate the "inflationary gap" between total earnings and total output in the country, a gap that would have to be filled by increased taxation or savings. Keynes found that Wilson and Hopkins were willing converts to this macroeconomic approach, which was based on Keynes's pamphlet *How to Pay for the War* (1940).[38]

Keynes's macroeconomic ideas also found expression in the 1944 white paper *Employment Policy,* where aggregate demand was described as the sum of private consumption, public current expenditure, private investment, and public investment, plus or minus the foreign balance.[39] It is generally agreed that the white paper represented a compromise between Keynesian theory and traditional ideas about public finance.[40] A Keynesian might suppose that acceptance of the macroeconomic principles behind the 1941 budget would lead Treasury officials logically to accept expanding demand to prevent unemployment as the corollary of checking demand to prevent inflation. Although "by symmetry" is a powerful argument in mathematics, it is less than convincing in this area

---

[36]For an account of how the 3 percent figure emerged, see Jim Tomlinson, *Employment Policy: The Crucial Years 1939–1955* (Oxford: Oxford University Press, 1987), Chapter 7.

[37]*J.M.K.,* XXII, 354.

[38]Ibid., Chapter 4; and Hopkins, "The 1944 Budget: Structure of the Modern Budget," February 3, 1944, T171/367, P.R.O., London.

[39]*Employment Policy,* Cmd. 6527, paragraph 43, *B.P.P.* 1943–44, vol. VIII.

[40]See Booth, "The 'Keynesian Revolution,' " 103–23; Peden, "Sir Richard Hopkins," 281–96; Lord Roberthall, "The End of Full Employment," in Charles P. Kindleberger and Guido di Terra, eds., *Economics in the Long View* (London: Macmillan, 1982); and Tomlinson, *Employment Policy,* Chapter 3.

of political economy. As Keynes remarked in the *General Theory,* when there is full employment, as there was during the war, the differences between classical theory and his own theory disappear.[41] Even F. A. Hayek could agree with Keynes's analysis in *How to Pay for the War.*[42] It is one thing to use macroecomic analysis to reduce excess demand when supply is fixed, and quite another to assume that an increase in aggregate demand will somehow absorb the unemployed resources in the economy. Continued opposition within the Treasury after 1941 to the Economic Section's proposals for employment policy suggests that Treasury officials had not been converted to the expansionist implications of the *General Theory.*

In contrast to the interwar years, however, the Treasury did not attempt to argue against Keynes or the Economic Section at a theoretical level. Treasury objections between 1942 and 1945 to the Economic Section's proposals for employment policy were practical and largely microeconomic. Whereas the Economic Section, especially Meade, saw the problem as essentially one of maintaining aggregate demand, and assumed a sufficient mobility of labor to prevent structural unemployment, Treasury memoranda drew attention to the importance of particular causes of unemployment. These causes included a major loss of export trade or a major decline in an industry, owing to changes in demand or technology or to a lack of competitiveness.[43] Treasury arguments that the decline of particular industries would reduce purchasing power in the regions in which they were located reflected the experience of interwar Britain, where the regions most dependent on declining industries—such as South Wales (coal) or Lancashire (cotton)—had experienced the highest levels of unemployment. Consciously or not, Treasury arguments were also in line with Keynes's belief in 1937 that, once unemployment fell below about 10 percent, careful attention had to be paid to the direction as well as to the volume of demand.[44]

As in the 1930s, the Treasury drew attention to political and administrative problems of using fiscal policy, or variations in public investment, as means of maintaining employment without inflation. Even in 1945 Hopkins thought that it would be easy to reduce taxation when an expansion of demand was required, but that taxation would probably seldom

[41]*J.M.K.,* VII, 378.
[42]Ibid., XXII, 106.
[43]Peden, "Sir Richard Hopkins," 286–90.
[44]Peden, "Keynes, the Treasury and Unemployment," 11–14.

or never be increased when a budget surplus was required.[45] Consequently, the Treasury used its influence against the idea of deficit finance, and the 1944 white paper on *Employment Policy* stated that "none of the main proposals . . . involves deliberate planning for a deficit in the National Budget in years of sub-normal trade activity." As before the war, most of the public investment that is now included in the Public Sector Borrowing Requirement would be outside the chancellor's budget, although, in conformity with Keynes's ideas on a capital budget, there was to be a more complete analysis of savings and investment in the annual white paper on national income and expenditure.[46] Treasury influence was also used in drafting the white paper to modify the Economic Section's statement that the technique of varying public capital expenditure was familiar and certain.[47] Subsequently, Treasury officials strongly objected to a claim by the Economic Section that it had been decided that the main instrument of control over aggregate demand should be variations in public investment. In particular, Gilbert, who was in charge of the control of public investment, pointed to the problems of controlling variations in local government investment.[48]

Consequently, although the 1944 white paper on *Employment Policy* used a Keynesian analysis of aggregate demand, it does not follow that the Treasury followed Keynes as regards the *instruments* for varying these elements in the national income. Sir Wilfrid Eady, then in charge of the financial side of the Treasury, remarked in 1944 that the chief novelty of the white paper lay in the technique of national income accounting. This, he thought, could be used to raise the necessary revenue to deal with the national debt, which had greatly expanded during the war.[49]

This concern of Eady's brings us to the third stage of the penetration of the Treasury by Keynes's ideas during the war. In 1945 an enquiry was set up to consider, *inter alia,* the future management of the national debt. Initially Hopkins and then Bridges, when he became permanent secretary, was chairman. The members of the National Debt Enquiry included

[45]"Exchequer Capital Budget," June 27, 1945, T233/159, P.R.O., London.
[46]Cmd. 6527, paragraphs 74, 84.
[47]Peden, "Sir Richard Hopkins," 292.
[48]Gilbert to Bridges, June 6, and Sir Wilfrid Eady to Bridges, June 7, 1945, T273/319, P.R.O., London.
[49]Eady to Norman Brook, permanent secretary, Office of the Ministry of Reconstruction, April 26, 1944, CAB 124/215, P.R.O., London. Eady was a relative newcomer to the Treasury, having been in the Ministry of Labour for most of his career. He was chairman of the Board of Customs and Excise before becoming joint second secretary of the Treasury from 1942 to 1952.

Keynes, Lionel Robbins (the head of the Economic Section), and Meade, as well as Eady, Brittain, and senior officials from the Board of Inland Revenue. The fact that Hopkins, when drafting the National Debt Enquiry's report, used arguments and quotations from the *General Theory* has in the past been cited by Howson and Winch as evidence of the Treasury's apparent "conversion" to Keynes's ideas on economic management.[50] It is certainly true that Hopkins used Keynes's arguments, outlined earlier, in favor of cheap money and agreed that there should be no return to the prewar preoccupation with funding short-term and floating debt. However, Hopkins, like Keynes in 1945, assumed that there would be permanent control on external movements of capital, which would substantially insulate Britain from the effects of higher interest rates elsewhere, and that it would be possible to control investment through the Capital Issues Committee and to ration the volume of credit by influencing the volume of bank advances. In other words, policy would depend on what controls were possible as much as what theory was endorsed (and, in the event, the controls listed by Hopkins proved to be less effective than seemed possible in 1945).

Moreover, Hopkins was decidedly ambivalent in his references to the *General Theory*. He referred to the importance of low interest rates, if the burden on the budget of servicing the national debt was to be minimized, and he noted that members of the National Debt Enquiry knew of no other general theory that "began to hold out the same prospect" of achieving that objective. He also quoted the white paper on *Employment Policy* to the effect that "theory can be applied to practical issues with confidence and certainty only as experience accumulates and experiment extends over untried ground."[51]

Keynes's ideas on both fiscal policy and monetary policy seem to have been adopted by the Treasury more readily with regard to the control of inflation or reduction of the burden of the national debt than they were in the case of employment policy. Nevertheless, by 1945, insofar as the Treasury was guided by economic theory, the theory was Keynes's. For

---

[50]Howson and Winch, *The Economic Advisory Council*, 152. It is only fair to stress that Howson and Winch do no more than advance a tentative hypothesis as regards the "conversion" of the Treasury. For a more recent account by Howson of the National Debt Enquiry, see her "Origins of Cheaper Money, 1945–7," *Economic History Review*, 2d Ser. 40 (1987): 438–41.

[51]"Draft prepared by Sir R. Hopkins of an interim report for the Chancellor's eye only," n.d., T233/157, and "National Debt Enquiry—First Report: The Question of Future Gilt-Edged Interest Rates," May 15, 1945, T233/158, P.R.O., London.

much of the war there had been an economist within the Treasury, Sir Hubert Henderson, who had rejected Keynes's economics,[52] but with Henderson's departure at the end of 1944 Keynesians had a monopoly on professional advice within Whitehall. What is not certain, however, is how well officials other than Hopkins understood the *General Theory* or how willing they would be to apply its principles.

POLICY-MAKING, 1945–1951

As matters turned out, the sole threat to employment during Labour's term of office from 1945 to 1951 was only indirectly connected to management of demand. This threat concerned the availability of essential inputs for British industry—a threat that was exemplified by the coal crisis of 1947, when a coal shortage led to restrictions on the use of electricity, and almost 2 million workers had to be laid off temporarily. More generally, however, the threat to full employment came from the possibility that Britain might be unable to pay for sufficient imports of raw materials.[53] For a country like Britain, which is short of natural resources, certain imports, including oil, were essential inputs into the economic system, as well as leakages in a Keynesian model of aggregate demand. In the circumstances of postwar Britain, macroeconomic policy had to be geared to curbing demand at home, so that output could be diverted to export markets and the current-account balance of payments rectified. The balance-of-payments problem was exacerbated by Britain's continuing role as a world power, with large armed forces stationed abroad.[54] The Anglo-American Loan Agreement of 1945 and Marshall Aid could provide a breathing space, but ultimately full employment depended on Britain's ability to compete in international markets. Consequently, Treasury concern that public expenditure should not divert British industry away from export markets was no less than it had been in the interwar period.

[52]See Hubert Henderson, "Lord Keynes and Employment Policy" in *The Inter-war Years and Other Papers: A Selection from the Writings of Hubert Douglas Henderson,* Henry Clay, ed. (Oxford: Oxford University Press, 1955).
[53]Gilbert to E. Bamford, January 19, 1948, T161/1370/S.53555/011/2, and "Economic Policy in a Recession," note by officials, circulated by chancellor of the Exchequer, June 21, 1949, CAB 134/222, P.R.O., London.
[54]See G. C. Peden, "Economic Aspects of British Perceptions of Power on the Eve of the Cold War," in Josef Becker and Franz Knipping, eds., *Power in Europe?: Great Britain, France, Italy and Germany in a Postwar World 1945–1950* (Berlin and New York: de Gruyter, 1986), and "Economic Aspects of British Perceptions of Power 1952–1957" (forthcoming).

The role of fiscal policy, therefore, remained very much what it had been during the war. Not much was heard about the "inflationary gap," at least in public, in the first two years after the war. Part of the reason was that the figures were so uncertain. Meade, the head of the Economic Section, put forward estimates of an inflationary gap between national income and expenditure in an unpublished "Economic Survey for 1946," but Keynes attacked these figures on logical and statistical grounds.[55] Similarly, Dalton and his officials seem to have attached only limited importance to the Economic Section's arithmetic. In 1947 Hall, Meade's successor, estimated there would be a gap between prospective national money expenditure and real output of £600 million to £650 million, but increased taxation and other measures in the autumn budget of that year left more than £400 million—equivalent to 4 percent of gross domestic product—of the estimated gap apparently untouched.[56]

Even so, the fact that the Treasury aimed at a surplus in the autumn budget of 1947 has been hailed by Alan Booth as a "major milestone" on the Treasury's Damascus road to Keynesianism.[57] As Neil Rollings and Jim Tomlinson have pointed out, however, it required no intellectual conversion for the Treasury to accept the idea of budget surpluses as part of an anti-inflationary strategy.[58] Other elements in the strategy included direct controls on investment, rationing, food subsidies, and cooperation with the Trades Union Congress (TUC) to moderate wage increases.[59] Budget surpluses not only reduced the taxpayers' ability to spend but also offered the Treasury an opportunity to reassert its traditional control over public expenditure. Moreover, as already noted with respect to the 1941 budget, the crucial difference between Keynesian economics and classical economics related to a situation of demand deficiency, not to a situation of full employment.

In these circumstances, it is difficult to trace the influence of economic ideas on fiscal policy. The Treasury papers do indicate, however, that

[55]Keynes to Meade, January 15, 1946, T230/55, P.R.O. London. See Cairncross, *Years of Recovery*, 411–4 (where the reference is wrongly given as "1945 Economic Survey" ... T230/54).

[56]Neil Rollings, "British Budgetary Policy 1945–54: A 'Keynesian Revolution'?" *Economic History Review*, 2d Ser., 41 (1988): 289.

[57]Booth, "The 'Keynesian Revolution,' " 122–3.

[58]N. Rollings, "The 'Keynesian Revolution' and Economic Policy-making: A Comment," *Economic History Review*, 2d Ser., 38 (1985): 95–100, and "British Budgetary Policy 1945–54," 283–98; and Tomlinson, *Employment Policy*, Chapter 6.

[59]On wage policy, see Russell Jones, *Wages and Employment Policy 1936–1985* (London: Allen and Unwin, 1987), Chapter 4.

officials viewed the autumn budget of 1947 as a new departure in public finance. As Bridges observed at the time, the purpose of the budget was "not the old-fashioned one of extra taxation to balance the Budget, but a reduction in inflationary pressure."[60] The fact that the measures taken did not close the whole of the inflationary gap estimated by Hall reflected two factors. First, as Hall himself admitted, there was a good deal of uncertainty involved in his calculations of the foreign balance and voluntary private savings. In particular, the existence of large liquid balances in the personal and company sectors made the amount of voluntary saving, the most important item in Hall's calculation, "necessarily guess-work."[61] The second factor, which was reinforced by the first, was that cabinet ministers were reluctant to carry out some of the measures—especially a reduction in food subsidies—that Treasury officials thought necessary to close the inflationary gap.[62] Indeed, Treasury officials themselves recognized that the inflationary pressure of the late 1940s could not be removed by fiscal measures "within the realm of practical politics for, to remove it in this way, the real spending power of the people would have to be reduced to an amount sufficient, but no more than sufficient, to buy the necessaries of life."[63] In these circumstances, direct controls, and queues, were inevitable. Nevertheless, the budget was the main instrument for influencing the general balance of the economy. This itself represented a major departure from prewar practice for, when chancellors had merely balanced their budgets, monetary policy had been the main instrument for influencing the general balance of the economy.

Why did the Labour government stick to the "cheap money" policy recommended by the National Debt Enquiry in 1945? As the prime minister, Clement Attlee, himself observed in 1950, heavy taxation had not reduced consumption by as much as might have been expected, since people were spending savings they had accumulated during the war.[64] The fact was, however, that the Labour party and its economic advisers had a bias against the rentier and had faith in direct controls over invest-

[60]"Autumn Budget," by Bridges, September 23, 1947, T171/392, P.R.O., London.
[61]"The Inflationary Pressure," by Hall, September 1, 1947, ibid. There had been major changes in the propensity to save since before the war; see R. C. O. Matthews, C. H. Feinstein and J. C. Odling-Smee, *British Economic Growth 1856–1973* (Oxford: Oxford University Press, 1982), 143–8.
[62]"Autumn Budget," by Bridges, October 22, 1947, and "Cuts in Expenditure," by Dalton, n.d., T171/392, P.R.O., London.
[63]"Treasury Comment on BC(48)3," n.d., but January 1948, T171/394, P.R.O., London.
[64]Attlee to Cripps, March 11, 1950, and "Notes on Budget Proposals by The Lord Privy Seal" (Lord Addison), March 10, 1950, T171/400, P.R.O., London.

ment and prices. Dalton, acting on the advice of some Labour party economists as well as of Keynes and Treasury officials, had embarked on a policy of cheaper money in 1945–7, when he tried to reduce the long-term interest rate from 3 to $2\frac{1}{2}$ percent.[65] Even once it had become clear that inflationary pressures from 1947 had made it impossible to reduce interest rates further, those Labour ministers who had some training in economics had no wish to return to what they regarded as old-fashioned credit restriction.[66] The bank rate remained at 2 percent throughout Labour's term of office.

Official opinion within the Treasury had to take ministerial views into account. Moreover, two of the conditions that Hopkins had laid down in 1945 for a cheap money policy—exchange control and control over capital issues—were still reasonably effective, even if the Bank of England was reluctant to influence the volume of bank advances. In addition, interest rates abroad were low—the Federal Reserve Bank of New York discount rate, for example, was lower than bank rate in London.[67] In addition to these permissive factors, Treasury officials could see real advantages in cheap money. Eady thought in 1947 that the traditional check to investment of raising interest rates would be "a crude instrument," unless the government provided low-interest funds for essentials, such as housing, which would otherwise suffer as much as investment in nonessentials, such as greyhound racing tracks. Moreover, the inflationary pressure in the economy was such that, to be effective, the bank rate would have to be raised to 5 or 6 percent, which Eady regarded as "terribly dear" money.[68] The Treasury, of course, had its own interest in minimizing the cost to the Exchequer of servicing the national debt. Indeed, there is good reason to believe that this Treasury interest was a more powerful influence than the *General Theory* on Treasury thinking. Both in the *General Theory* and in the National Debt Enquiry, Keynes had argued against funding, but after 1945 the Treasury accepted the advice of the Bank of England to fund debt, the bank never having accepted Keynes's ideas on the techniques of debt management.[69] By 1949 some Treasury officials, including Bridges, had been persuaded that a rise in bank rate and higher interest rates generally were necessary to

[65]Howson, "Origins of Cheaper Money," 433–40.
[66]Cairncross, *Years of Recovery*, 443.
[67]Ibid., 428–9, 443.
[68]Eady to Bridges, July 9, 1947, T273/304, P.R.O., London.
[69]Howson, "Origins of Cheaper Money," 449.

restrict credit.[70] The Treasury's "conversion" to Keynes's ideas on monetary policy, as indicated by the National Debt Enquiry, seems to have been brief as well as tentative.

POLICY-MAKING, 1951–1959

In the third period of this analysis of policy-making, 1951–9, and later, Conservative governments maintained Labour's goals of full employment without inflation. Policy instruments, however, were somewhat different. In particular, whereas 54 percent of imports had been subject to some form of government controls in 1951, by 1955 this had been reduced to 22 percent. Other controls also were relaxed, and in 1954 building controls were abolished.[71] Conservative faith in market forces as the best means of allocating goods did not, however, mean a return to laissez-faire.

Dismantling direct controls on imports and investment increased the importance of managing demand to correct the balance of payments. Fiscal policy continued to be the principal means of managing demand, but in 1951 the chancellor of the Exchequer, R. A. Butler, unlike his Labour predecessors, accepted advice from Treasury officials and the Bank of England to reactivate monetary policy as a means of managing demand. The importance of demand management was also enhanced by the decision of the Conservative government in 1952 to reject a plan put forward by the Treasury and the Bank of England to have a floating exchange rate.[72] The decision to continue to peg sterling meant that, once import controls had been removed in the mid-1950s, domestic management of demand, rather than the exchange rate, would have to adjust to fluctuations in the international economy or shifts in confidence in sterling. There were, indeed, economists, of whom the most eminent was Robbins, who were prepared to make a virtue of this situation, by stating that balance-of-payments equilibrium should be regarded as the sole test of financial policy.[73] On this test financial policy was generally successful

[70]Alec Cairncross and Barry Eichengreen, *Sterling in Decline: the Devaluations of 1931, 1949 and 1967* (Oxford: Basil Blackwell, 1983), 121.

[71]Dow, *Management of the British Economy,* Chapter 6.

[72]See Cairncross, *Years of Recovery,* Chapter 9, and Donald MacDougall, *Don and Mandarin* (London: John Murray, 1987), Chapter 5.

[73]Lionel Robbins, *The Balance of Payments,* Stamp Memorial Lecture (London: Athlone Press, 1951), 17–18, 20–1. Robbins had been head of the Economic Section during the war, and his views continued to command respect thereafter. In the lecture Robbins criticized sole reliance on fiscal policy and urged the reactivation of monetary control.

in removing excess demand, except in the election years 1955 and 1959, when there was a current-account balance-of-payments deficit (1955) or a large reduction in the reserves (both years).

Tax changes were used to stimulate demand whenever unemployment threatened to rise to politically dangerous levels, but Butler and his officials resisted any suggestion of budget deficits in 1953, 1954, or 1955. What was under discussion in the 1950s was the chancellor's revenue budget, above the line, which, as before the war, did not include borrowing for capital expenditure, most notably by the nationalized industries. From 1952–3 onward, there was what would now be called a Public Sector Borrowing Requirement.

Robert Hall, whose Economic Section had been integrated into the Treasury in 1953, shared the view that the weak balance-of-payments position in these years, and the need to maintain confidence in sterling, made budget deficits inadvisable. Treasury officials, however, went further, in that they did not share Hall's belief that budget deficits were acceptable in principle. Instead, officials continued to express the views that Hopkins had held earlier: budget deficits not only would lead to a loss of confidence in financial markets, but also would be interpreted by other government departments as a sign that the Treasury was prepared to relax its control over public expenditure.[74] Because Hall himself seems to have considered that unemployment of up to 600,000 workers (about 2.7 percent of the labor force) was acceptable to correct an adverse balance of payments,[75] and because it was not necessary in this period to allow the national rate of unemployment to rise above this level for any length of time, the question of whether budget deficits were acceptable did not have to be resolved. There is, however, another test of the influence of Keynesian ideas on the Treasury: that is, how much did Keynesian ideas figure in Treasury discussions of macroeconomic policy?

The best case study is the year 1955, when an attempt was made to offset tax concessions by tightening monetary policy. By 1955 Britain had a more open economy than at any time since 1939: import controls were no longer an effective safeguard against a balance-of-payments crisis, and in February 1955 the Bank of England was allowed to support the rate for transferable sterling at about 1 percent below the official rate. This step was reckoned in the Treasury to have made sterling about 80 percent convertible at a pegged exchange rate, as officials believed that a fall in

[74]Tomlinson, *Employment Policy*, 146–8.
[75]"Economic Problems," by Hall, March 13, 1952, T273/315, P.R.O., London.

the transferable rate would be regarded by money markets as a major sign of weakness.[76] The maintenance of the value of sterling, therefore, depended essentially on foreign confidence in Britain's internal financial policies, and February also saw a rise in bank rate and the imposition of restrictions on credit transactions, so as to check a growth in imports and encourage exports. Nevertheless, Butler's budget in April was marked by a reduction in income tax (from nine shillings to eight shillings sixpence in the pound). Butler professed to believe that the February measures would continue to check internal demand sufficiently to leave a margin of production for increased exports; and he treated his anticipated budget surplus for 1955–6 (£282 million on the existing basis of taxation) as a sum from which concessions could be made, even though it was less than the realized surplus for 1954–5 (£423 million).[77]

Neither the approach to monetary policy nor fiscal policy reflected Keynes's ideas. Indeed Butler's belief that investment could be effectively controlled, particularly investment in stocks, by raising the bank rate, could have been pure Hawtrey.[78] Keynes, as we have seen, emphasized the importance of keeping the bank rate steady. The Treasury's belief that monetary policy could offset a reduction in the budget surplus suggests that Keynes's economics had come second to other considerations in framing fiscal policy. In the event, a credit squeeze applied in July failed to curb internal demand sufficiently to prevent a run on the pound, and an autumn budget subsequently raised taxes on consumers' expenditures although it did not reverse the reduction in the rate of income tax.

Unfriendly critics were quick to allege that the spring budget had been framed with electoral considerations in mind. However, although the fact that 1955 would be an election year was bound to be in the minds of the chancellor and his advisers, the Treasury's own records show there were

[76]"External Economic Policy," sent by Bridges to Butler, May 27, 1955, T273/317, P.R.O., London. The market for transferable sterling had arisen from transferable account arrangements Britain had made in 1946 with fourteen countries outside the sterling area. Under these arrangements a country's transferable account was made up of sterling accruing from current transactions or from existing balances that had not been blocked, and transferable sterling could be used for making current payments to other transferable account countries. By 1955 the scope of such arrangements had been extended so that there were only two major types of nonresident sterling: transferable and American account, the latter being freely convertible. Resident sterling was still subject to exchange controls.
[77]*Parliamentary Debates (Commons)*, 5th Ser., 1954–5, vol. 540, cols. 43, 50, 53–5.
[78]See R. G. Hawtrey, *A Century of Bank Rate*, 2d ed. (New York: Augustus M. Kelley, 1962), especially the introduction, where Hawtrey argued that, except in 1957, the bank rate was not raised high enough to check investment.

other considerations.[79] Foremost among these was that Treasury officials had long wished to improve incentives to increased production by reducing direct taxation, an ambition shared by Butler and the outgoing prime minister, Churchill.[80]

Second, the forecasts then available, both of economic trends and of revenue and government expenditure, were imperfect to a degree that made fiscal policy at best a crude instrument of demand management. The surplus anticipated in the 1954 budget had been £10 million, but the actual surplus proved to be £433 million, because revenue had been underestimated by £205 million and expenditure had been overestimated by £218 million.[81] This result seems to have encouraged officials to be less cautious about the prospects for 1955–6 than they might otherwise have been.

Finally, Treasury officials—although not some economists in the Treasury[82]—believed that experience since 1951 had shown that monetary policy was an effective means of reducing inflationary pressure. There were also those in the Treasury, including Hall and Bridges, who felt that monetary policy could have been more effective than it was in 1955, if the Bank of England had done more to restrict credit, instead of allowing bank advances to continue to rise.[83] Bank officials, for their part, believed that too little had been done to restrict public investment.

This analysis of policy-making in the 1950s can be concluded with a look at the problem of controlling public investment. The 1944 white paper on *Employment Policy*, following Keynes, had assumed that public investment could be slowed down as well as accelerated, to offset variations in private investment. As had been noted in the white paper, however, a large part of the capital expenditure of public authorities was dictated by urgent needs and could not be readily postponed to serve the

[79]What follows is largely based upon Budget Committee papers (T171/459; T171/468; T171/473); Economic Section papers on monetary policy (T230/384); and Bridges's papers (T273/316–317), P.R.O., London.
[80]R. A. Butler, *The Art of the Possible* (London: Hamish Hamilton, 1971) 160–1, 167–8, 176–9. The attitude of officials to incentives is dealt with in the last section of this chapter.
[81]*Parliamentary Debates (Commons)*, 5th Ser., 1954–5, vol. 540, col. 43.
[82]I. M. D. Little, for example, thought that "the fact that there is now such a large volume of Government debt makes it clear that a system which worked satisfactorily in the past may not be so satisfactory now," Little to Hall, "Control of Credit 1955," April 1, 1955, T230/384, P.R.O., London.
[83]Hall to Bridges and Chancellor of the Exchequer, "Monetary Policy," July 28, 1955, and Bridges to Chancellor, August 12, 1955, ibid.

purposes of smoothing out demand.[84] Thus, even though the economy was at full employment after the war, it was difficult to resist the many strong pressures tending to raise local authority spending on houses and schools.[85] The nationalized industries, like much of the rest of British industry, had suffered from neglect during the war and badly needed new investment. It was not easy to hold back public investment, although in Keynes's theory the combination of full employment and inflationary pressure in the economy dictated such action. Indeed, the reluctance of cabinet colleagues to agree to holding the total level of government spending in 1958–9 to the level of 1957–8 led to the resignation of the chancellor of the Exchequer, Peter Thorneycroft, and his two junior ministers, Nigel Birch and Enoch Powell.[86] There were reductions in public investment programs in 1955–6, but these did little, if anything, to offset the boom in private investment that had begun in 1954. Thorneycroft did have more success with the imposition of a ceiling on public investment in money terms in 1957.[87] Even so, his resignation early in 1958 was clear evidence that the chancellor believed that he was in less than complete control of the situation. In the autumn of 1957 Harrod was encouraging Macmillan to resist deflation,[88] and this fact may well explain why the prime minister failed to support his chancellor of the Exchequer a few months later. The influence of Keynesianism may have been limited within the Treasury, but public opinion was in tune with the expansionist aspects of Keynes's ideas. It is not surprising that in 1961 the Plowden report on *Control of Public Expenditure* concluded that social, political, and economic changes in the 1940s and 1950s had made the traditional system of Treasury control inadequate and that new ways must be found to control the growth of public expenditure.[89]

Quite apart from the political problems experienced in controlling public investment, experience showed that there were technical problems as well. At the microeconomic level, it had proved to be difficult to

[84]*Employment Policy*, Cmd. 6527, paragraphs 62–3.
[85]I discuss these matters in my *British Economic and Social Policy: Lloyd George to Margaret Thatcher* (Oxford: Philip Allan, 1985), 189–96.
[86]Macmillan's account, by no means an impartial one, of this episode is in his *Riding the Storm*, 366–72. Thorneycroft argued that the government must accept the same measure of financial discipline as it imposed on the private sector.
[87]Dow, *Management of the British Economy*, 217.
[88]Macmillan, *Riding the Storm*, 355–6.
[89]*Control of Public Expenditure*, presented by the chancellor of the Exchequer, Cmnd. 1432, B.P.P. 1960–61, vol. XX, paragraphs 6–14.

persuade local authorities to create a "reserve of works"—that is, to prepare plans and acquire land—so that public investment could be increased at short notice. Local authorities had many urgent needs to meet and were unwilling to bear the administrative and other costs of preparing a reserve of less urgent investment.[90] At the macroeconomic level, the experience of attempting to offset variations in private investment in 1957–8 with variations in public investment showed that, by the time policy took effect, the trend in private investment had changed and the direction of public investment policy was no longer appropriate. At least six to nine months passed before short-term changes in either direction took effect. In the words of the Plowden report, there had been "a tendency . . . to overestimate the possibilities of useful short-term action in public investment." In the light of experience the Treasury preferred to use monetary and fiscal instruments, complemented by only marginal adjustments in public investment.[91]

This preference can be compared with the Treasury's position in 1937, when it had believed that monetary policy was more important than variations in public investment in stabilizing employment. The difference between the Treasury's position in the late 1930s and at the end of the 1950s lay in the addition of fiscal policy to monetary policy and the use of a national income accounting framework. It is to the question of how the national income accounts were compiled that we now turn.

THE COMPILATION OF ECONOMIC DATA

As already noted, the Treasury played at best a passive role in the compilation of national income accounts during World War II. Indeed, economists entering Whitehall in 1940 found that statistics in many departments were in appalling shape for microeconomic as well as macroeconomic purposes[92]—a situation that was a reflection on the department whose permanent secretary was also head of the civil service. But once the Coalition government had committed itself in 1944 to an employment policy, the Treasury decided to establish a new division, with responsibility for collecting and collating information about capital

[90]"Economic Powers Bill," GEN. 324/5th meeting, January 10, 1951, item 3, and "Reserve of Works," GEN. 324/13, January 31, 1951, CAB 130/60, P.R.O., London.
[91]*Control of Public Expenditure,* Cmnd. 1432, paragraph 23. See also *Public Investment in Great Britain,* presented by the chancellor of the Exchequer, Cmnd. 1203, *B.P.P.* 1960–61, vol. XXVII.
[92]MacDougall, *Don and Mandarin,* 23, 28.

expenditure by local authorities, public utility companies, and, as far as practicable, private industry. The head of the new division, Dennis Proctor, collaborated with the Central Statistical Office and the Economic Section, and the Treasury gave its full support to collecting a wide range of statistics with a bearing on employment policy. These included better statistics than previously available on industrial activity, consumption, capital expenditure, stocks, wages and prices, shipping and foreign trade, and the balance of payments. Officials in Whitehall recognized from the beginning that the provision of all this information would impose a heavy burden on industry, especially small firms, and the Treasury agreed that the chancellor of the Exchequer would try to secure cooperation through meetings with trade associations, although compulsory powers also would be necessary. Departments such as the Board of Trade and the Ministry of Labour actually collected the statistics and forwarded them directly to the Central Statistical Office. Forecasts of national income and expenditure were the responsibility of the Economic Section. The Treasury itself handled the administrative and policy aspects of the work.[93]

Even ten years after the war, however, the economic statistics were very inadequate for the purposes of managing the economy. The shortcomings of Butler's first budget in 1955 could be attributed, in part, to a lack of information on current developments in the economy. It was still not possible to construct national income and expenditure figures quarterly, as was then being done in the United States. The British figures for fixed investment were a year out of date; information on stocks and work in progress was inadequate; full figures for industrial production were often four months or more late; there were serious gaps in the statistics on consumption; and very little was known about future plans for construction. At Robert Hall's behest in February 1955, Bridges encouraged the Central Statistical Office to be bolder in its demands for data, but a year later the lags in information meant that there was still much truth in Macmillan's remark that "we are always, as it were, looking up a train in last year's Bradshaw" (a well-known railway guide).[94]

Forecasts of the government's own revenue and expenditure were, on

[93]"Note for the Record," September 7, 1944, T273/318; Proctor to Bridges, May 2, 1945, Central Statistical Office, "Statistics for Employment Policy," May 1, 1948, and minutes of meetings on May 29 and June 1, 1945, T273/319, P.R.O., London.
[94]"Economic Statistics," by Hall, February 3, 1955, and Bridges to Hall, February 9, 1955, T273/317, P.R.O., London. *Parliamentary Debates*, (Commons), 1955–6, vol. 551, col. 867.

average, actually less accurate in the first ten postwar years than had been the case in the 1930s. In the case of forecasts by the Board of Inland Revenue, this state of affairs could almost entirely be accounted for by the introduction of more complex and less easily predictable taxes, notably, profits tax, purchase tax, and pay-as-you-earn income tax.[95] In the case of expenditure, part of the decline in accuracy can presumably be attributed to less strict Treasury control. Certainly the House of Commons' Select Committee on the Estimates expressed concern in 1958 about the fact that it had become far easier for spending departments to secure supplementary estimates in the course of a financial year than had been the case before the war.[96]

The Treasury's modest contribution to the overall compilation of economic data reinforces the impression that the "old dogs" were content with a fairly rough-and-ready form of economic management. It would be a great mistake to suppose that the British economy in the 1950s was subject to the degree of fine-tuning that Keynesian theory by then suggested was possible. But economic knowledge was advanced insofar as the use by the state of Keynesian techniques did lead to the provision of far more data for economists than had been available to Keynes when he wrote the *General Theory*.

MICROECONOMIC ASPECTS OF POLICY

One of the most telling criticisms that can be made of the British economics profession in the Keynesian era is that concentration on macroeconomic approaches to economic policy led to a neglect of crucial microeconomic variables.[97] It is, however, far from certain that this criticism can be fairly leveled at Treasury officials in the 1940s or 1950s. As has already been noted, during the wartime debate on employment policy, Treasury memoranda sought to balance academic theorizing about aggregate demand by drawing attention to the importance of microeconomic aspects of the problem, notably the need for British industry to be competitive. The theme of the need to compete in world markets was repeated in a further white paper, *The Economic Implications of Full*

---

[95]"Errors in Forecasting," August 1955, T171/473, P.R.O., London.
[96]*Treasury Control of Expenditure: Sixth Report from the Select Committee on Estimates*, B.P.P. 1957–8, vol. V, para. 19–22.
[97]Peter Sinclair, *Unemployment: Economic Theory and Evidence* (Oxford: Basil Blackwell, 1987), vii.

Employment in 1956.[98] Industrial matters were primarily the province of the Board of Trade, however, and the Treasury's attention to micro-economic matters is best studied in relation to taxation, for which the chancellor was directly responsible.

We are, of course, concerned here not with the effects of fiscal policy on aggregate demand, but with the effects of tax rates on incentives to producers to make greater efforts. The disincentive effects of high rates of income tax limited the scope for Keynesian fiscal policy even during the war. It will be recalled that, in the 1941 budget, taxes had been increased to mop up excess purchasing power, as calculated using a national in-come accounting framework. Six months later, however, the Ministry of Information was seriously concerned that the increase in income tax was reducing the willingness of workers to undertake overtime. Inland Reve-nue and Treasury officials were united in opposing any further increase in income tax, and even Keynes appears to have admitted that, with regard to major financial measures, the chancellor had shot his bolt.[99]

A similar problem was encountered with 100 percent excess profits tax ("excess" being defined as an increase over a firm's prewar level of profits). Government departments noted that this tax made firms reluc-tant to invest in new capacity, despite the prospect of a rebate of 20 percent on excess profits tax after the war.[100] Once direct taxation had reached such levels, the contribution that fiscal policy could make to management of demand in the immediate postwar period was largely limited to what reductions could be made in government expenditure.

The maintenance of high tax rates was not in accordance with the wishes of Treasury officials, who would rather have seen an even greater reduction in government expenditure than actually took place. Treasury officials believed that money in the hands of taxpayers was always likely to exert less inflationary pressure than money in the hands of the state. Taxpayers, they argued, would save part of their income, but the more they were taxed, the less they would save. The state, in contrast, spent its revenue on goods or services, or made transfer payments to people least likely to save.

Incoming Conservative ministers were told in 1951 that "one of the main faults of the last Government was to accept blithely extremely high

[98]Cmd. 9725, *B.P.P.* 1955–6, vol. XXXVI, paragraphs 3–6, 11, 19–23.
[99]*J.M.K.*, XXII, 355–7; "The Budget 1942," by H. Wilson Smith, November 5, 1941, and "Notes by the Board of Inland Revenue," n.d., T171/360, P.R.O., London.
[100]William Ashworth, *Contracts and Finance* (London: HMSO, 1953), 84–6, 231.

rates of taxation and to devote far too high a proportion of the national income to Government expenditure." This, in the opinion of Treasury officials, had created many vested interests in public expenditure, while leaving hardly any scope for removing disincentives from the taxation system.[101]

The Keynesians Meade and Hall shared the concern about incentives: one of Hall's early contributions to discussions on budget matters was to raise the question "of whether our present tax structure provides an adequate incentive to that part of the national economy which depends on private enterprise,"[102] and he returned to that theme frequently thereafter. It was because Bridges, Gilbert, and Hall believed that tax relief calculated to increase incentives and productivity would be valuable that they agreed not to advise against a reduction in income tax in 1955, despite anxiety about inflationary pressure in the economy.[103] Butler's spring budget in 1955 is open to considerable criticism from the standpoint of Keynesian demand management, but supply-siders may feel some sympathy for Treasury officials' microeconomic objective.

CONCLUSION

From the examination of these various issues it appears that the Treasury did use Keynesian economics, albeit imperfectly, to solve new economic problems in the 1940s and 1950s—the need to raise revenue to finance increased government expenditure and the need to dampen inflation. The "old dogs" of the Treasury, as represented by Hopkins, Bridges, and their immediate subordinates, seem never to have been wholly convinced by the Keynesian approach to unemployment, which remained a hypothetical problem during this period. The economists of the Economic Section were Keynesian as regards reflation as well as inflation, but there was little scope for experiments in reflation in the 1940s and 1950s. When there was reflation, as in the election years of 1955 and 1959, the effects on the external balance of payments only emphasized how little room for maneuver there was, given Britain's lack of foreign exchange reserves. Such unemployment as did occur prior to the 1970s was, as the Treasury had predicted in 1944, the result of the failure of particular industries to

[101]"Notes for Cabinet: Why Government Expenditure Should Be Reduced," December 20, 1951, T273/315, P.R.O., London.
[102]"Budget Committee," Hall to Plowden, March 19, 1948, T171/397, P.R.O., London.
[103]"Note for Record," March 8, 1955, T273/317, P.R.O., London.

maintain their competitive position in world markets, or the effects of the decline of particular industries on the districts in which they were located. Given these developments, it is hard not to agree with Treasury officials that the Keynesian aggregate demand approach could be only a partial solution to unemployment.

Down to the mid-1950s the Treasury's contribution to systematic economic knowledge, as represented by national income data, was modest and largely permissive. The Treasury also contributed some two hundred pages of evidence to the Radcliffe Committee's enquiry in 1957–9 into the working of the monetary system, a contribution that is beyond the scope of this chapter.[104] On that occasion, as usual, the Treasury avoided firm commitment to a particular theory.

One of the themes of this volume is the extent to which the traffic in knowledge between the economics profession and the state is a two-way one. Academic economists in Britain were glad to have more economic information from the state, but they were inclined to denigrate what they considered to be the "amateurism" of Treasury officials.[105] Although there was certainly a need to improve the training of officials, it is not clear that economic knowledge, in the widest sense, was advanced by the tendency of academic economists to ignore the traditional wisdom of the practitioners of public finance. Economists with experience of work in the Economic Section sometimes sounded a note of caution,[106] but Keynesian economists in general showed little awareness of some of the political problems involved in managing the economy. There was insufficient consideration among economists of how reflation created vested interests in public expenditure, or how these interests could obstruct demand management by resisting expenditure cuts even when deflation was called for.

As it happened, the Treasury's failure to persuade ministers to be more restrictive in public expenditure may be attributed in part to minis-

---

[104]*Committee on the Working of the Monetary System: Report,* presented by the chancellor of the Exchequer, Cmnd. 827, B.P.P. 1958–59, vol. XVII. Treasury evidence is reproduced in *Committee on the Working of the Monetary System: Minutes of Evidence* and *Principal Memoranda of Evidence,* vol. 1 (London: HMSO, 1960).

[105]The most famous attack by an economist on Treasury officials in the 1950s is Thomas Balogh's essay "The Apotheosis of the Dilettante" in Hugh Thomas, ed., *The Establishment* (London: Anthony Blond, 1959).

[106]See Sir Robert Hall, "The Place of the Economist in Government," *Oxford Economic Papers,* new series, 7 (1955): 119–35, and I. M. D. Little, "The Economist in Whitehall," *Lloyds Bank Review,* vol. 44 (April 1957): 29–40. Little was deputy director of the Economic Section from 1953 to 1955.

ters' willingness to listen to economists like Harrod, who believed that increasing public expenditure would promote economic growth. However, it is important not to credit economists with too much influence. After all, Keynesian economists can hardly be directly blamed for budget deficits in Reagan's America. The fact is that most politicians have a natural propensity to spend public money in ways that will win votes.[107] Treasury officials had long understood this fact, which is why they had compiled restrictive rules of public finance in the nineteenth century, and why they were still trying to apply such rules in the mid-twentieth century. Even Keynesian economics was applied by the Treasury in a restrictive way. Whereas before World War II chancellors had been content to balance the budget, after the war chancellors tried to achieve budget surpluses on current expenditure as part of an anti-inflationary strategy. Budget surpluses were difficult to achieve, however, in the postwar period, when there were strong political pressures for better welfare services, more investment in nationalized industries, and increased agricultural subsidies.

What is the significance of British experience in the 1940s and 1950s for our discussion of the state and economic knowledge? First, as the contributions by William Barber (Chapter 4) and Robert Collins (Chapter 5) to this volume also suggest, it seems that economists can expect the state and its agents to use theory in an eclectic way. Second, given sound rules of public finance, there would seem to be no reason why Keynesian analysis should not be used in formulating anti-inflationary policies. Third, if economic knowledge is defined as an amalgam of theory and the realities of political economy, we ought to be prepared to learn from "ancient sages" like Sir Richard Hopkins and the other "old dogs" of the Treasury.

[107]See David A. Stockman, *The Triumph of Politics* (New York: Harper and Row, 1985), for an account of how this propensity can run wild once the balanced-budget rule is relaxed.

Part III

Industrial maturity and economic policy

8

Knowing capitalism: public investigation and the labor question in the long Progressive Era

MARY O. FURNER

When Britain's economy was experiencing its first symptoms of industrial decline, between the 1880s and World War I, the United States was a rising industrial power whose enormous gains in productivity and wealth were offset, in human terms, by unprecedented social conflict and the waste and suffering caused by an unfamiliar business cycle. These economic changes threatened not only social harmony but also, indirectly, the political order itself, as a market-mediated system of contractual relations between freely competing equals in which many could realistically look forward to achieving economic independence gave way to market failure, collective action by labor and capital, and a class society. Under such conditions, the laissez-faire era in American history necessarily ended.[1]

I would like to express my warm appreciation to Michael J. Lacey for the many benefits of a fruitful collaboration over the past several years on all matters pertaining to the state as a factor in American culture. His insights and criticism contributed much to this essay. I am also grateful to Robert Cuff, Thomas K. McCraw, and John L. Thomas for helpful suggestions.

[1] On British industrial maturity, see Aaron L. Friedberg, *The Weary Titan: Britain and the Experience of Relative Decline, 1895–1905* (Princeton, N.J.: Princeton University Press, 1989); and Chapter 10 of this volume. On the economic transformation in America, see Jeffrey Williamson, *Late-Nineteenth-Century American Development* (Cambridge, Eng.: Cambridge University Press, 1974); Harold G. Vatter, *The Drive to Industrial Maturity: The U.S. Economy, 1860–1914* (Westport, Conn.: Greenwood Press, 1975); U.S. Bureau of Economic Analysis, *Long Term Economic Growth, 1860–1970* (Washington, D.C.: U.S. Department of Commerce, 1973). James Livingston, "The Social Analysis of Economic History and Theory: Conjectures on Late Nineteenth-Century American Development," *American Historical Review* 92 (February 1987): 69–95, provides a fresh approach to the connections between social history and economic theory in this period.

ECONOMIC KNOWLEDGE AND
THE AMERICAN NEW LIBERALISM

In response to the social and intellectual crisis produced by these changes, Americans faced a problem similar to the one their republican ancestors had confronted with the commercialization of a largely agrarian, peripheral society in the era of the Revolution. Forced again to reassess both private values and public ideology, the nation embarked on a complex process of adaptation and invention in which traditional cultural values and beliefs confronted the new realities and relations of an industrial society and were measured against important new developments in various fields of knowledge. The historical project of the long Progressive Era, stretching from the 1880s through World War I, was the reconstruction of American liberalism or, more precisely, the formation of an American "New Liberalism," capable of dealing with the pressing social, economic, and political issues of the day.

Because the social conflicts of this era were so entwined with economic changes and dislocations not anticipated by the American version of classical economics, it was clear that economic knowledge would be particularly important in this reconstruction. Less clear at the start was where the initiative for developing the economic knowledge needed to analyze and order an advanced industrial economy would come from. The elaborate structure of academic departments, government agencies, interest-group research bureaus, foundations, and think tanks that produces and evaluates economic knowledge today did not exist. But the discipline of economics was beginning to construct itself in modern form, and the new economists responded enthusiastically to a call from Henry Carter Adams, who proclaimed an "interregnum" in economic theory in the mid-1880s and challenged fellow economists to join him in constructing a political economy that addressed the problems of industrialism, while remaining faithful to American cultural traditions. Simultaneously, for both political and organizational purposes, business and labor groups began devising their own capacities for gathering data. Also, reflecting a long tradition of voluntary efforts in response to increased poverty and dependency, middle-class reformers such as the women at Hull House produced stunning early examples of the social surveys that would become such important weapons in the battle for decent urban conditions. Crusading journalists such as Henry George and Henry Demarest Lloyd invented another reformist genre, the muckraking exposé, which combined investigative reporting with economic analysis in devastating attacks on monopoly that also challenged the benign assumptions of the classical system.[2]

Most important for our purposes, the state itself played a major role, following a tradition of public economic inquiry dating back to the famous reports by Alexander Hamilton and Albert Gallatin. Because American federalism lodged control over many areas of economic performance and welfare at the state level, state legislatures and regulatory agencies became heavily involved in investigating economic and social conditions. Yet general problems such as economic instability and social conflict also required national action that could be defended on the basis of reliable data and theory. Through ad hoc investigations of the causes of depression, the problem of monopoly, and class conflict, and the formation of permanent investigative and regulatory bureaus such as the Bureau of Labor (later, the Bureau of Labor Statistics) and the Interstate Commerce Commission, the national government provided leadership in developing economic knowledge that became an element not only in specific policy debates but in the forming of a New Liberalism.

Although this process of ideological and policy reconstruction was a common pattern in all industrialized countries, there were national variations. As other chapters in this volume remind us, the New Liberalism in Britain took shape as a fairly unified body of theory and argumentation, culminating in Keynesianism, that justified a major role for the state in managing economic crisis and addressing the chronic problems of "sick industries" and "depressed areas." Opponents of New Liberalism rallied around the "Treasury view," which considered market discipline indispensable for maintaining character at home and competitiveness abroad.[3]

---

[2]Henry Carter Adams, "The Relation of the State to Industrial Action," *Publications of the American Economic Association* 1 (1887): 465–549. On Adams's liberalism, see Mary O. Furner, *Advocacy and Objectivity: A Crisis in the Professionalization of American Social Science, 1865–1905* (Lexington: University Press of Kentucky, 1975), 125–42 and passim; cf. Dorothy Ross, "Socialism and American Liberalism: Academic Social Thought in the 1880s," *Perspectives in American History* 11 (1977–8): 7–79. Theoretical developments in the emerging disciplines of psychology, sociology, and philosophy also played a role in the reconstruction of liberalism, in ways that are beyond the scope of this chapter. For examples of privately conducted surveys and muckraking, see *Hull House Maps and Papers* (New York: Thomas Y. Crowell, 1895); Henry Demarest Lloyd, *Wealth Against Commonwealth* (New York: Harper and Bros., 1894).

[3]There is now an extensive literature on British New Liberalism. See especially Michael Freeden, *The New Liberalism: An Ideology of Social Reform* (Oxford: Oxford University Press, 1978); Stefan Collini, *Liberalism and Sociology: L. T. Hobhouse and Political Argument in England, 1880–1914* (Cambridge, Eng.: Cambridge University Press, 1979); and Chapters 6 and 10 in this volume. On the transformation of liberalism generally, see Karl Polanyi, *The Great Transformation* (Boston: Beacon Press, 1957).

By contrast, through a process of "political learning" that involved public officials, capitalists, labor leaders, reformers, and middle-class professionals over an entire generation, reflecting tensions and ambiguities always present in their constituent ideologies, liberalism and republicanism, Americans identified *two* different and conflicting conceptions of their New Liberalism.

Both these competing visions of American development in the industrial era were collectivist, in that they rejected the natural law/natural rights individualism of classical political and economic theory and the laissez-faire policies of a Grover Cleveland. One was a voluntarist, associative collectivism that we have come to recognize as corporate liberalism. It was corporate, or perhaps more accurately corporatist, through its conception of modern society as an organic structure of functional, specialized, interdependent social segments or groups, each having legitimate needs and each entitled to representation. Corporate liberals looked on the modern corporation, with its rational, bureaucratic structure, its phenomenal productivity, and its capacity to administer markets, as a product of institutional evolution, justified by its superior efficiency and its capacity for providing new avenues of mobility to replace those foreclosed by the decline of proprietary capitalism. They linked progressive tendencies in civilization to commercial liberty and free contract. Thus they feared politicization of the market, opposed most forms of state action, and looked—for economic stabilization and class accommodation—to voluntary agreements between private parties, sometimes aided in noncoercive ways by government.[4]

The competing vision of an American New Liberalism was a more democratic and more statist collectivism. Although this variant resembled British New Liberalism, it took its central ethos and direction less from socialism than from a modernized version of the commonwealth tradition of early republicanism, with its expansive conception of the public sphere, its ingrained distrust of monopoly, and its ambiguous attitude to

---

[4]The pioneering works on corporate liberalism were Martin Sklar, "The Political Economy of Modern United States Liberalism," *Studies on the Left* 1 (1960): 17–47; James Weinstein, *The Corporate Ideal in the Liberal State: 1900–1918* (Boston: Beacon Press, 1968); and Ellis Hawley, "Herbert Hoover, the Commerce Secretariat, and the Vision of an 'Associative State,' 1921–1928," *Journal of American History* 61 (1974): 116–40. See also David Montgomery, *Workers' Control in America* (Cambridge, Eng.: Cambridge University Press, 1979); Jeffrey Lustig, *Corporate Liberalism* (Berkeley: University of California Press, 1982); Martin J. Sklar, *The Corporate Reconstruction of American Capitalism, 1890–1916* (Cambridge, Eng.: Cambridge University Press, 1988).

commerce.[5] Democratic collectivists attached great importance to political liberty, but they did not equate it with untrammelled freedom in economic matters. They appreciated the efficiencies of large-scale production, but they believed monopolistic corporations often sheltered inefficiencies that undermined progressive tendencies inherent in a more competitive order. More important, whatever their advantages, monopolies acquired attributes of sovereignty that were unacceptable in private hands, necessitating public control. Whereas corporate liberals identified the public interest with the long-term interests of capital, democratic collectivists rejected the identification of *any* private interest with the public good. In the early stages of this discourse, many of them held back on libertarian grounds from expanding *federal* power, but they considered the state, and not the corporation, the appropriate instrument for transcending selfish interests, on the grounds that voluntary associative arrangements would ordinarily favor the wealthy, whereas promoting social justice, equality, democracy, and balanced development would require increased state intervention, often redistributive in intent.

The elaboration of these alternative visions of a modern American liberalism was the project of a generation, as we have said. It confronted in a coherent, formative discourse the fundamental questions at the heart of modern political culture: the relations between individual and society; the labor question, with all its implications for welfare and virtue; and the role of the state in ordering the economy. This chapter addresses an aspect of this developing discourse, and more specifically the state's role in it, by examining the activities of those public agencies most directly responsible for analyzing the labor question. The most significant investigations at the national level, where this inquiry is focused, were done by the Bureau of Labor Statistics (and its predecessors, all designated here as the BLS) and by two special investigating commissions: the United States Industrial Commission (USIC) (1898–1902) and the Commission on Industrial Relations (CIR) (1912–15). As these examples will illustrate, state agencies and inquiries provided access for *both* the ideological alter-

---

[5] I discuss the earlier development of these ideologies, democratic collectivism and corporate liberalism, in "The Republican Tradition and the New Liberalism: Social Investigation, State Building, and Social Learning, 1865–1900," *The State and Social Investigation in Britain and the United States*, Michael J. Lacey and Mary O. Furner, eds. (Cambridge, Eng.: Cambridge University Press, forthcoming), and at greater length in a book manuscript titled "Redefining America: The Industrial Transformation and the American New Liberalism, 1870–1920" (in progress).

natives suggested here, and state-based investigations provided official
support for both points of view.

CARROLL WRIGHT, THE BUREAU OF LABOR STATISTICS, AND
THE LIMITS OF STATE POWER

In 1988 the Bureau of Labor Statistics had a budget of $228 million and
24,000 employees. The agency that Carroll D. Wright directed from its
inception in 1884 to his retirement two decades later was a far different
operation. Starting with a $25,000 budget, Wright was eventually able to
wring out of a frugal Congress the grand sum of $184,000 to support the
regular work of the bureau. Occasionally, Congress requested investigations, such as the study of wages and prices ordered by the Senate Finance
(Aldrich) Committee in 1890 and the World War I cost-of-living studies
that carried special appropriations. More typically, a special study of
women's and children's wages that consumed most of the bureau's time
from 1907 to 1911 came out of regular resources, compelling suspension
of important activities such as the vital wage and price series that offered
some hope for a scientific resolution of at least the factual issues in the
distribution conflict. By 1920, the bureau's regular budget was only
$322,000. Facing a chronic shortage of funds and qualified personnel,
the BLS of that era was never able to accomplish its full agenda.[6]

Yet, when the BLS opened in 1885 and for some time thereafter, the
American labor statistics movement was the most advanced in the world.
In the United States as in Britain, much of the early empirical work in labor
statistics was done by dedicated private investigators—heroic individuals
such as Charles Booth and Jane Addams, middle-class professionals in the
midcentury social science associations, and trade union officials. But
American conditions—most notably, a commonwealth tradition of investigation and reform that survived the mid-nineteenth-century ascendancy of
laissez-faire, pressure from politically mobilized labor organizations, and
the sizable labor vote (which existed nowhere else in the nineteenth

[6]Carroll D. Wright, "Value and Influence of Labor Statistics," U.S. Bureau of Labor, *Bulletin* 54 (1904): 1087–96; William T. Moye and Joseph P. Goldberg, *The First Hundred
Years of the Bureau of Labor Statistics*, Bureau of Labor Statistics, *Bulletin* 2235 (1985).
The bureau went through several incarnations: first, as the Bureau of Labor (1884–8), an
agency within the Department of Interior; next, as an independent subcabinet Department
of Labor (1888–1902); and later, as the Bureau of Labor Statistics in the Department of
Commerce and Labor (1903–13), and thereafter in the Department of Labor. The BLS
received a total of $700,000 for war-related work in 1918–19. See Moye and Goldberg,
First Hundred Years, 109.

century)—produced an early commitment to *public* investigation and responsibility on the labor question.

Labor bureaus existed in fifteen states by the mid-1880s. They were generally reformist, reflecting the labor republicanism of their main political constituency. The oldest bureau, founded in Massachusetts in 1869, campaigned openly for factory laws, shorter hours, and restrictions on child labor, and offered a lesson in republican values by comparing desperate conditions in the crowded tenements with the luxurious homes of Boston capitalists. Under Wright's management the Massachusetts Bureau of Statistics of Labor (MBSL) became less partisan, but his early reports, such as the famous 1882 study of living and working conditions in Massachusetts textile towns, left no doubt that the industrial system produced injustices requiring public attention. The MBSL started the earliest data series reporting average weekly wages, earnings, and employment by occupation, instituted reliable techniques for gathering data by field inspection, constructed a model of working-class consumption habits from actual family budgets, and began comparing wages and conditions in the United States with those of European competitors.[7]

There were no similar agencies in Europe until the 1890s. France established its Office du Travail in 1891, Germany formed an ad hoc Commission for Labor Statistics in 1892, and Belgium and Spain opened bureaus in 1894. Only in 1893 did Britain convert a small, poorly funded labor bureau in the Board of Trade, founded over Treasury opposition in 1886, into a reasonably competent, decently budgeted operation. American public statisticians set the model for official processing of labor statistics, and in 1892 Wright could proudly announce that the International Institute of Statistics had called for universal adoption of techniques pioneered in the United States for obtaining not only wage rates but actual earnings, and for analyzing mobility and turnover of labor. According to the American economist and statistician Charles Bullock in 1899, "In this department American investigators [had] less to learn from European examples than in many other branches of statistical science. Nowhere [had] official statistics of wages been more fully developed than in the United States."[8]

---

[7]MBSL, *Annual Report* 6 (1875), and 13 (1882); James Leiby, *Carroll Wright and Labor Reform: The Origins of Labor Statistics* (Cambridge, Mass.: Harvard University Press, 1960); Furner, "Republican Tradition and the New Liberalism."

[8]For comparative international data on bureaus, see Charles Bullock, "Contributions to the History of Wage Statistics," *Publications of the American Statistical Association* 6 (1899): 190–8; Wright, "Evolution of Wage Statistics," *Quarterly Journal of Economics* 6 (1892):

Charged with investigating class relations, monitoring the conditions and progress of labor, and making recommendations for legislation, the BLS provided both empirical data and theoretical analyses bearing on issues before the public. As founding commissioner, an internationally famous statistician who served as president of both the American Social Science Association and the American Statistical Association and as commissioner for the eleventh census, Wright conceived his role broadly, and despite occasional political reverses he established an independent agency with considerable influence, within the limits of aspiration he set. Although not a contributor to statistical theory, he was a practical innovator; and methods such as index numbers, as well as the major data series inaugurated in his tenure, remain the basis of current BLS practice. Although he avoided partisanship and valued his reputation for objectivity, like the midcentury social empiricists who populated the social science associations on both sides of the Atlantic, he understood social science as the knowledge basis of civic action, considered it his duty to inform and mobilize official and public opinion during policy debates, and shaped his own and the BLS's inquiries to that end. Furthermore, unlike labor bureaucrats of subsequent decades who were often hostile to academic discourse, as a self-taught economist Wright was close to the cutting edge of theoretical work in at least one important phase of economic theory— the causes of depressions and their effect on labor and capital—and attracted a number of prominent economists to the work of the BLS.[9]

The BLS's work was shaped by Wright's conception of its civic purpose, its relationship to other agencies, his changing sense of policy needs, and his own values and capacities, as well as by external pressures. Dur-

151–89; E. H. Phelps Brown and M. H. Brown, "Carroll D. Wright and the Development of British Labour Statistics," *Economica* 30 (1963): 279–80; E. R. L. Gould, "European Bureaus of Labor Statistics," *Yale Review* 2 (1893–4): 386–403; Roger Davidson, *Whitehall and the Labour Problem in Late-Victorian and Edwardian Britain: A Study in Official Statistics and Social Control* (London: Croom Helm, 1985), 79–103; Roger Davidson, "Llewellyn Smith, the Labour Department and Government Growth 1886–1910," *Studies in the Growth of Nineteenth Century Government,* Gillian Sutherland, ed. (London: Routledge and Kegan Paul, 1972), 227–62. This is not to say that the American public effort in this area remained the most effective. In other industrialized countries, data on sickness, accidents, unemployment, elderly indigence, and the distribution of income improved dramatically when social insurance and a broadly based income tax appeared, so in important areas the United States eventually fell behind countries that adopted more advanced social welfare programs.

[9]Carroll D. Wright, "Popular Instruction in Social Science," *Journal of Social Science* 22 (1887): 28–36; idem, *The Industrial Evolution of the United States* [1895] (New York: Charles Scribner's Sons, 1910); idem, *Outlines of Practical Sociology* (New York: Longmans, Green, 1899).

ing his twenty-year tenure, Wright consistently subordinated comprehensive and continuous statistical inquiries of the type he believed a general statistical agency such as the Census Bureau should do, to investigations that responded to public anxiety and the politically generated "market" for information on the divisive "social question" that arose during America's rapid industrial transformation. More generally, he supported investigations of the cultural as well as economic consequences of this huge reorganization of ownership and production in a society accustomed to measuring value by labor and thinking of proprietorship as something close to a natural right. Also, because there was no American Board of Trade—no Commerce Department until 1903—he shared responsibility with the Treasury and the consular service for keeping American producers and policymakers apprised of their competitive position in world trade, and for providing background data on political questions, such as tariff policy, that flowed from such developments.[10]

Wright consistently gave highest priority to improving the informational climate for policy decisions regarding the accelerating conflict between capital and labor. In his first annual report as national commissioner, he attacked the structural origins of the recent industrial depressions that had heightened class antagonism and provoked two congressional investigations, in which he had been an important witness. Focusing on the changing structure of industrial markets, Wright was one of the first to make a distinction between the regularly recurring slumps in trade that arrived simultaneously in all "the great manufacturing countries," and panics caused by speculation. Comparing price and production figures from the United States, Britain, France, Germany, and Belgium to demonstrate the similarity and interconnectedness of their trade cycles, he traced these cyclical fluctuations to the machine process itself and to the phenomenal productive capacity of industrialized nations. He argued that depressions resulted from competitive, unregulated expansion of productive capacity, eventually outstripping possible consumption under existing conditions, and leading to falling prices and profits, continued production at a loss, further glut, and widespread insolvency. Modern depressions were intensified by the

---

[10]Three different types of social investigation and a periodization of them are described in the introductory chapter of Lacey and Furner, eds., *The State and Social Investigation in Britain and United States* (forthcoming). On the BLS and other statistical agencies, see Leiby, *Carroll Wright and Labor Reform*, passim; and William F. Willoughby, "The Measurement of Unemployment: A Statistical Study," *Yale Review* 10 (1901): 188–202, 268–97.

"vast transference of floating to fixed capital" that had occurred in all industrial nations, in Wright's view, and therefore they were linked intrinsically to progress.[11]

Wright's version of the social implications of the business cycle gave a clue to his generally optimistic outlook on the labor question. Following David Ames Wells, a Republican financial guru, he reasoned that new technology created vastly more employment than it destroyed, while a general cheapening of consumer goods and the lag of wages behind falling prices offset the misfortune of occasional unemployment. He debunked the reformers' idyllic picture of the household production system of bygone days. Preindustrial workers were often drunken, disorderly, and superstitious, Wright argued; and the humble cottages where domestic industries flourished were "without comfort, convenience, good air, good food, and without much intelligence." The more disciplined regimen of machine production was a moral *and* an economic boon to the working class; and because progress depended on invention and accumulation, the fundamental interests of the industrial classes were, if not identical, clearly reciprocal.

Like Arthur Hadley, a Yale economist who did pioneering work on high–fixed cost industries, Wright believed that the structural problems of the new economy were a greater threat to capital than to labor. In the mid-1880s, he was fairly pessimistic about potential opportunities for profitable investment in the advanced countries, and he did not anticipate territorial and financial imperialism as major outlets for redundant capital, or foresee the full impact of urban growth. His analysis was an early example of "scarcity economics"—the sense that economic maturity was at hand, the preoccupation with stabilizing profits and wages—that characterized American economics between the 1880s and the 1930s.[12]

Although Wright lacked modern insights into techniques for coordinating supply and demand, he anticipated macroeconomic approaches to

[11]U.S. Bureau of Labor, First Annual Report, *Industrial Depressions* (1886). For a similar account, which may have influenced Wright's, see Arthur Hadley, "Over-production," *Lalor's Cyclopedia of Political and Social Science* (1884): 40–3; Arthur Hadley, *Railroad Transportation* (1885): 50–62. See also Carl Parrini and Martin J. Sklar, "New Thinking about the Market, 1896–1904: Some American Economists on Investment and the Theory of Surplus Capital," *Journal of Economic History* 43 (1983): 559–78.

[12]David Ames Wells, *Recent Economic Changes* (New York: D. Appleton, 1889); Wright, "Industrial Depressions"; Carroll D. Wright, *The Industrial Evolution of the United States* (New York: Charles Scribner's Sons, 1895), 323–52 (quotation, p. 346); Arthur Hadley, *Economics* (New York: G. P. Putnam's Sons, 1896), Chapters 9 and 10. On the preoccupation with scarcity in American economics between the 1890s and the 1930s, see Chapter 5 of this volume.

economic stabilization and endorsed a mix of public and private measures. He favored diverting land grants from corporations to homesteaders, restricting corporate privileges to check speculative investment, and outlawing contract immigration to protect American jobs and wages. The state might also promote arbitration or profit sharing to reduce wasteful conflict. But Wright saw voluntary organization of labor and capital as the only immediately effective means of "checking the tendency to overproduction, the manufacture of goods on demand only, less production, more even production, the equalization of supply and demand, and the reduction of the hours of labor."

In other words, the preferred approach to economic stabilization would be private planning and, more particularly, cooperative, cartel-like arrangements among capitalists to restrict supply and maintain prices at a profitable level. Again following Wells, Wright recognized increased efficiency, declining prices, and widening markets as natural consequences of machine production. He did not convert these observations into a strategy for centralized coordination of the types and volume of production as a means of sustaining economic growth. Instead, by offering scientific justification for private restraints on production, the BLS expressed its misgivings about the efficiency of freely running market forces and sanctioned, if not the form, at least the spirit of the trust movement of the 1880s.

Wright's enthusiasm for the trusts was fully matched by his approval of certain types of unions. His early regard for the moral value of labor organizations gradually matured into an appreciation for the stabilizing, harmonizing influence of conservative trade unions. In the early years of the bureau, the industrial strife intensified, leading to violent strikes, such as the railroad strikes of 1877 and 1885–6, which disrupted the economy, spurring both labor and capital to demand state intervention against the other side. In that era the BLS channeled resources into studies that presented strikes as a normal if regrettable part of a broader process of enlightenment and class accommodation, including equal organization, peaceful negotiation, voluntary arbitration, and a sharing of information and profits, which would limit the need for state intervention to cases of overriding public interest, such as transportation.

A series of reports on strikes and lockouts that appeared every few years between 1887 and 1904 recorded the frequency, causes, and outcomes of strikes and estimated their cost in lost wages and profits. Two arresting results revealed the change in the origin and character of strikes. It made a great deal of difference whether strikes were called by unions or not; if they were, they were likely to be larger, representing workers in more than a single firm, and, not surprisingly, they were more likely to be successful. Between 1881 and 1900, union strikes had a 53 percent total success rate and a 14 percent partial success rate, while spontaneous walkouts succeeded even partially only 45 percent of the time. Not surprisingly, the percentage of union strikes rose steadily. The most salient finding, now familiar from the work of David Montgomery, was a change in the cause of strikes. From the 1880s forward, wage strikes fluctuated slightly with the business cycle but steadily decreased, whereas strikes to win recognition and enforce union rules increased dramatically, from less than 10 percent to more than 30 percent by 1904. From less than 1 percent in 1881, sympathy strikes rose rapidly in the late 1880s to a peak in 1891 at 11.5 percent, fell back below 1 percent in the depression of the 1890s, and peaked again before the open shop and scientific management cut off their source in defensible craft skills.[13]

In its early years, the BLS emphasized the wastefulness of strikes. Reports on lost wages failed to recognize that even unsuccessful work stoppages might prevent future wage cuts or that the increase of strikes over recognition and work rules reflected capitalist efforts to eliminate union resistance to downward pressure on wages. Yet BLS research did constantly convey the impression that trade unions were a good thing, not only for their fraternal and uplifting character, emphasized in many studies, but also because, as they incorporated more workers and "matured," they would reduce the frequency of strikes, helping to pacify industrial relations. This trade union argument, made by Gompers and other labor chiefs since the 1880s, was confirmed by BLS data showing that unions exercised a restraining influence during depressions and actually helped stabilize disorganized industries such as bituminous coal by eliminating wage competition. The BLS made no direct effort to assess the impact of strikes on distributive equity, but consistently implied that organized action was necessary to achieve a just division, and that aggressive wage demands supported necessary consumption.[14]

[13]BLS, *Annual Report* 3 (1887); 10 (1894); 16 (1901); 21 (1906); Ira Cross, "Strike Statistics," *Publications of the American Statistical Association* 11 (1908–9): 168–94; G. W. W. Hanger, "Strikes and Lockouts in the United States," BLS *Bulletin* 54 (1904): 1097–117; Montgomery, *Workers' Control in America*, Chapter 2.

[14]Important reports on the functions of unions were BLS *Bulletin* 17 (1898), on the railroad brotherhoods; *Bulletin* 19 on the printing trade (1898); *Bulletin* 28 on wage determination in the iron and steel industry (1900); and *Bulletin* 51 on the union movement in coal mining (1904).

Healthy, growing, legally recognized unions were a key component in the private bargaining system that Wright increasingly understood as the ideal structure for resolving industrial disputes, without sacrificing efficiency or necessary profits. Throughout his tenure, BLS produced a steady flow of special reports on arbitration and conciliation, which required organization, as alternatives to strikes. In his own investigative reports on the politically explosive Pullman (1894) and Anthracite (1902) strikes, Wright commended unions for their conservatism, chastised capitalists for their intransigence, and strongly urged union recognition. He envisaged creation of a regular structure of class bargaining, including ever more workers—to be supplemented, in the special circumstances of the railroad industry, by compulsory state intervention. Active in drafting several arbitration bills, Wright made common cause with conservative union leaders who supported voluntary arbitration.

A sense of responsibility for forming public and official opinion on labor troubles initially attracted Wright to the statistical study of prices and wages. In the late 1880s Congress embarked on a long process of adjusting American protectionism to the new realities of international trade. In response to complaints that the McKinley tariff disadvantaged consumers, the Senate Finance Committee under Nelson Aldrich ordered a study of the change in prices between 1889 and 1891. Commissioned to conduct the study and prepare a report, known as the Aldrich report, the BLS took advantage of the special appropriation provided by Congress to construct the first continuous record of wages and prices in the United States, covering the entire period from 1840 to 1891. Using data taken directly from payrolls, trained investigators managed to generate 543 usable wage series for the 1860–91 period, covering laborers in 88 different establishments and 21 principal industries. Apparently for the first time, index numbers were used to chart the progress of wages, and the BLS reported a whopping increase—nearly 70 percent between 1860 and 1891.

To complement the wage series, the BLS constructed a wholesale price index for the same period covering more than 200 articles, prepared and analyzed by Roland Falkner, professor of economics and statistics at the University of Pennsylvania, and a retail price series for 1889–91 covering 215 commodities. The most significant product of the Aldrich report was a cost-of-living index that weighted items making up more than two-thirds of total family expenditures on the basis of a detailed study of the household budgets of 2,561 typical working-class families, which showed only a 5 percent rise in consumer prices since 1860. Although the report itself was cautious, citing limitations in the data, Wright concluded, "As wages had increased to a very large percentage during the same period[,] the relative purchasing power of wages, as indicated by the rates paid, becomes clearly apparent."[15]

This investigation lent support to Wright's contention that despite occasional hard times the conditions of American labor were steadily and inevitably improving. These findings were not universally accepted. A widely circulated report on the distribution of wealth in the United States and Europe charged that the Aldrich report was politically motivated. Linking the apparent rise in wages to monetary factors, Charles Spahr complained that the BLS study ignored high unemployment in depressions that made it impossible for labor, especially unorganized workers who were not well represented in the study, to resist wage cuts. In Spahr's view, the Aldrich report was contrary to everyday experience and common sense.[16]

In fact, the Aldrich study *was* methodologically flawed, and greatly exaggerated the increase in wages. The wage data used by the BLS were too narrowly based to indicate the general trend of wages in the country. They were exclusively northern, entirely urban, disproportionately drawn from skilled trades with higher-than-average wages, and often untypical of the occupations they represented. There were glitches in weighting; furthermore, the use of a single month in a single year as a base point instead of a decennial or a moving average cast further doubt on the reliability of the index. Real wages did rise in the 1880s and 1890s for organized skilled workers, but later studies revealed that low wages for common labor and chronic unemployment pulled the average down. But the BLS did little before 1915 to study the effects of involuntary worklessness on the incomes and consumption habits of working-class families.[17]

[15]Senate Committee on Finance, "Retail Prices and Wages," *Senate Report* 986, 52d Cong., 1st Sess., 4 vols. (1893); Senate Committee on Finance, *Wholesale Prices, Wages, and Transportation, Senate Report* 1394, 52d Cong., 2d Sess. (1893). Frank Taussig, "Results of Recent Investigations of Prices in the United States," *Publications of the American Statistical Association* 3 (1892–3): 487–91, ascribed most of the change to monetary factors. The quotation is from Carroll D. Wright, "The Course of Wages in the United States Since 1840," ibid., 3 (1892–3): 500. The simple average increase in wages of all workers surveyed was 60.7 percent, whereas an average weighted to reflect the relative importance of different occupations rose 68.6 percent.

[16]Charles B. Spahr, *An Essay on the Present Distribution of Wealth in the United States* (New York: Thomas Y. Crowell, 1896), 95–118. Cf. Richmond Mayo-Smith, "Review of Charles B. Spahr, *Distribution of Wealth*," *Political Science Quarterly* 12 (1897): 345–8.

[17]Frank Taussig, "Results of Recent Investigations of Prices in the United States," *Yale Review* 2 (1893): 231–47; Charles Bullock, "Contributions to the History of Wage Statistics," *Publications of the American Statistical Association* 6 (1899): 187–218. For a

Instead of continuing and improving these data series immediately, Wright allowed these systematic price and wage studies, which had the most immediate bearing on the distribution question, and therefore on the fairness of the evolving capitalist order, to lapse through the entire depression decade of the 1890s. Apparently he was convinced that regular statistical chores belonged more properly to the state and federal censuses, which did gather some data on unemployment. Special BLS studies on hot political issues did sometimes shed some light on these matters. For the tariff debate, for example, the BLS annual reports of 1890 and 1891 compiled data on costs of production, wages, and living standards in the iron, steel, coal, textile, and glass industries, compared with those in Britain. And in 1895 Congress ordered the BLS to determine whether women and children were displacing men in manufacturing. The age classes were too gross—males and females under and over age eighteen—to reveal the full extent of labor by very young children. But the report demonstrated, though with little comment, that the fastest-growing class of workers was underage females, and the slowest, adult males. The number of employed women had doubled since the 1870 census. Between the mid-1880s and the mid-1890s, jobs for males over age eighteen grew by 63 percent, while employment of female minors increased 89 percent. The strongest motive for displacing male labor was economic. Men earned 32 percent more than women and 57 percent more than children doing the same job at the same level of efficiency. Unfortunately, the BLS neglected at this point to connect these findings to a larger, sustained analysis of total work force composition and wage and employment trends that would reveal trends in real wages, the incidence, duration, and causes of unemployment, and the growing fraction of essentially unorganizable workers.[18]

During the 1890s, the BLS focused its efforts in these lines largely on the problems of special groups—women, children, blacks, convicts, railroad labor, and the "dependent classes"—where, from the perspective of Wright's emerging corporatism, state protection and control might be warranted. A Civil War colonel who understood the tragedy of Reconstruction, Wright was blocked politically from obtaining special funds for a major study of Negro labor, but he managed to support nine reports on

---

response to these criticisms, see Roland P. Falkner, "Wage Statistics in Theory and Practice," ibid., 275–87.

[18]Bureau of Labor, "Work and Wages of Men, Women, and Children, 1895–96," *Annual Report* 11 (1896), *House Doc.* 341, 54th Cong., 2d Sess.

Negro life, including W. E. B. DuBois's pioneering study of the Black Belt Negro. A study of urban slums exposed the lives, habits, and employment of immigrants. The BLS was a quiet lobby for workers' compensation and other forms of income-maintaining social insurance, and promoted sweatshop and tenement regulation, child labor and safety laws. An important series by William F. Willoughby on labor laws in a dozen European countries informed Americans that welfare measures more advanced than theirs were becoming standard throughout the industrialized world; and one on industrial communities in Europe and America revealed oppressive as well as beneficent aspects of paternalism.[19]

Toward the end of his tenure at BLS, Wright began to appreciate some inconsistency between his macrostructural analysis and the limited role he envisaged for the state. In the late 1890s he extended his earlier analysis of the business cycle in a study of plant utilization and unemployment. He found that production in the highly industrialized state of Massachusetts ranged from less than 60 percent of the maximum possible in 1885 and 1896 to more than 70 percent in the prosperous year of 1890. Using estimates of national product and employment constructed from the eleventh census, Wright projected a national unemployment rate of about 5 percent for 1889–90, and concluded that an addition of 7 to 8 percent to the volume of business would mean substantially full employment in any normal year, "while, in the hardest times, from 10 to 15 percent added to the volume of manufacturing and mechanical production would have done away entirely with all evidence of depression."[20]

Wright's findings pulled him further toward an underconsumption theory of depression, similar to that advanced by John Hobson in 1889, and also toward the conclusion that voluntary cooperation alone would fail to solve the nation's economic problems. If underconsumption was mainly due to "unequal and defective distribution," as Wright now believed, even the slightest rise in the "consuming power" of families— perhaps $1.00 to $1.50 a week—would "overcome the margin between actual production and productive capacity." And if a stable equilibrium

[19]For a complete list of investigations of the Wright era, see *Index of Reports Issued by Bureaus of Labor Statistics in the United States Prior to March 1, 1902* (New York: Johnson Reprint Corporation, 1970). See also Moye and Goldberg, *First Hundred Years*, Chapters 2 and 3.

[20]Wright, "Relation of Production to Productive Capacity," Parts I and II, *Forum* 24 (1897–98): 290–302, 660–75. See also H. L. Bliss, "Census Statistics of Unemployment," *Journal of Political Economy* 6 (1898): 250–3. On the Massachusetts data, see Alexander Keyssar, *Out of Work: The First Century of Unemployment in Massachusetts* (Cambridge, Eng.: Cambridge University Press, 1986).

actually required expansion of the *home* market, tariff revision alone would miss the mark.

Yet, torn between an institutionalist's appreciation for structural imbalances and the seductive logic of the emerging neoclassical system, Wright rejected directly redistributive measures such as a minimum wage or progressive taxation and public spending. Alternatively, he pinned his hopes on evolutionary changes like those predicted by corporatist economic writers such as George Gunton and Arthur Hadley, in which new desires impelled workers to greater effort and more, and more diversified, consumption, transforming the economy in the bargain and leaving them less vulnerable to cyclical unemployment. This "divine discontent" that would raise workers' aspirations and achievement Wright distinguished from the "unhappy, irrational discontent, which leads to riot and revolution." Thus, although the strike reports recognized that fair distribution depended on an "equal organization of labor," and Wright's macrostructural analysis revealed excess capacity and underconsumption, his policy recommendations were constrained by a habitual reserve regarding state action and the subjective individualism of the emerging neoclassical synthesis. Given the trend of prices and the staying power of unions through the 1890s, despite a concerted attack, especially on "general" and industrial unions, Wright's optimism was at least partially justified. In the coming era of labor relations, when the courts and the open-shop movement had done their work, it was not.[21]

The terms of class relations changed dramatically near the end of Wright's tenure at the BLS. Large employers such as U.S. Steel deserted the trade agreement formula for deunionization and undermined the structure of collective bargaining that the BLS considered essential to social harmony and economic stabilization. Frustrated by low productivity gains, capitalists attacked union resistance to scientific management in moralistic terms, as a drag on economic efficiency that harmed the com-

---

[21]This analysis of corporatist thinking on economic development is drawn from a more detailed discussion in Mary O. Furner, "Liberty Versus Efficiency: The Industrial Transformation and American Social Thought" (unpublished colloquium paper, Woodrow Wilson International Center for Scholars, December 1982), 18–66. As further evidence of Wright's evolutionary optimism, see Carroll D. Wright, "The Distribution of Wealth in the United States," *Independent* 54 (1902): 1021–4. On Hadley's and Gunton's conception of economic development, see Arthur Hadley, "Some Fallacies in the Theory of Distribution," *Economic Journal* 7 (1897): 477–86; George Gunton, *Wealth and Progress: A Critical Examination of the Labor Problem* (New York: D. Appleton, 1887). The most detailed study of union membership for this period is still Leo Wolman, *The Growth of American Trade Unions, 1880–1923* (New York: NBER, 1924).

munity. To deal with this highly politicized issue, Wright called in John
Commons, a labor economist and student of industrial relations.

Although much seemed to separate Commons and Wright, they shared
a high regard for trade unions, admiration for responsible capitalists, and
ambivalence about the proper role for the state in a liberal order. Commons accepted elements of marginal theory, but he rejected the idea of an
automatic equilibrating mechanism, and his works on distribution emphasized the importance of institutions—the law, in particular—as factors in
distribution. Like other institutionalists, Commons departed from a
Lockean view of government. He understood the state pragmatically, as a
historically evolved set of arrangements for the exercise of sovereignty, in
which power was gradually distributed to new social groups as they
became historically and politically conscious. Rejecting natural rights and
individualism for a collectivist approach, he located a new basis for political obligation in the "working rules" hammered out between capital and
labor.

In the 1890s, Commons argued, the division of power had not progressed very far; the state was usually on the side of the most advanced
classes, and legal privileges enabled corporations to capitalize the gains
from innovation that John Bates Clark described as "strictly temporary
profits," converting them into a permanent stream of income for the
capitalist class. A further development of the state might restrict such
privileges, or balance them with entitlements for other groups. Yet at the
turn of the century, fresh from service as an expert on labor investigations
for the Industrial Commission and a mediator for the National Civic
Federation (NCF), and impressed by these promising experiments in corporatism, Commons believed the most effective mechanism for tying
distribution to productivity was equal organization of both classes and
voluntary collective bargaining.[22] When the pattern of mediating institu-

[22]This summary of Commons's thought is drawn from Furner, "Liberty Versus Efficiency";
and Furner, "The Republican Tradition and the New Liberalism." The important Commons works on this theme are *A Sociological View of Sovereignty* [1899–1900] (New
York: Augustus M. Kelley Reprints, 1965); *The Distribution of Wealth* [1893] (New
York: Augustus M. Kelley Reprints, 1965); *Legal Foundations of Capitalism* (New York:
Macmillan, 1924). See also Clarence Wunderlin, "American Social Science and the Formation of a Corporate Liberal Labor Stabilization Policy, 1898–1902" (unpublished Ph.D.
diss., Northern Illinois University, 1986); John Dennis Chasse, "John R. Commons and
the Democratic State," *Journal of Economic Issues* 20 (1986): 759–84. Commons's
distribution theory in the 1890s was influenced by neo-Ricardian theories that explained
returns to all three factors in terms of rent, and by his reaction to the marginal productivity theories of John Bates Clark. To locate Wright and Commons in this developing
theoretical discourse, see Francis Amasa Walker, "The Wage-Fund Theory," *North Ameri-*

tions that he and Wright assumed would guarantee fair distribution came under fire, Commons agreed to head a BLS study of the revolutionary changes in shop management that threatened to destroy it.[23]

Scientific management, or Taylorism—with its component principles of subdivision, transfer of skill, and bureaucratic control—was the most significant innovation in management theory in our history. Charged with invidious assumptions about workers, it promised to revolutionize not only production itself, but business structure, class relations, and America's competitive position.[24] Commons's *Regulation and Restriction of Output* (1904) was the first official assessment of this application of the "visible hand" and the first attempt to define the public interest in relation to it.[25]

At one level, his BLS report conceded the case for scientific management: incentive pay undoubtedly raised productivity. In printing, for example, piece work raised the average composition rate 15 percent, and these gains were reflected in wages. The individual betterment argument

can Review (January 1875): 84–119; idem, "Source of Business Profits," *Quarterly Journal of Economics* 1 (April 1887): 265–88; Gunton, *Wealth and Progress;* John Hobson, "The Law of Three Rents," *Quarterly Journal of Economics* 5 (April 1891): 263–88; Sidney Webb, "The Rate of Interest and the Laws of Distribution," ibid., 2 (January 1888): 188–208; John Bates Clark, "Possibility of a Scientific Law of Wages," *Publications of the American Economic Association* 4 (1889): 36–69; Clark, "Profits under Modern Conditions," *Political Science Quarterly* 2 (1887): 603–19; Clark, *Distribution of Wealth* [1899] (New York: Augustus Kelley Reprints, 1956).

[23]John R. Commons, *Myself* (Madison: University of Wisconsin Press, 1963), 92–4. The National Civic Federation was a private planning and policy organization composed of prominent corporate, trade union, and public members, formed in response to the class conflict of the 1890s. See Weinstein, *Corporate Ideal;* Marguerite Green, *The National Civic Federation and the Labor Movement, 1900–1925* (Washington, D.C.: Catholic University of America Press, 1956).

[24]Frederick W. Taylor, "Shop Management," *Transactions of the American Society of Mechanical Engineers* 24 (1903): 1337–456; Taylor, *The Principles of Scientific Management* (New York: Harper and Row, 1911); Robert M. Hoxie, *Scientific Management and Labor* (New York: D. Appleton, 1915); Samuel Haber, *Efficiency and Uplift: Scientific Management in the Progressive Era* (Chicago: University of Chicago Press, 1964); Daniel T. Rodgers, *The Work Ethic in Industrial America, 1850–1920* (Chicago: University of Chicago Press, 1974), 53–7; Montgomery, *Workers' Control, passim.* For the best account of the motives and effect of scientific management, and its reception by capitalists, labor politicians, and economists, see David Noble, *America by Design: Science, Technology, and the Rise of Corporate Capitalism* (New York: Alfred A. Knopf, 1977), 267–320.

[25]U.S. Commissioner of Labor, *Regulation and Restriction of Output*, 11th *Special Report* (1904). The research methods involved were largely historical and institutional. BLS investigators visited hundreds of shops, studying work rules and trade agreements that governed introduction of machines, hiring and firing, apprenticeships, and methods of payment. Another BLS report, U.S. Commissioner of Labor, *Hand and Machine Labor,* 2 vols., 13th *Annual Report* (1899), had earlier assessed the impact of the introduction of machinery on labor, mainly with respect to the elimination and production of jobs.

supported by such results appealed to some workers, and even unionists showed mixed reactions. Union machinists rejected all forms of incentive pay as violations of craft mutualism, which undermined quality and led inevitably to speed-up. Yet many workers accepted reasonable performance standards if they included safeguards for older workers and union control of hiring, so that Taylorism was not an open-shop tactic in disguise. Workers engaged in "job-making" only in industries that deliberately harbored surplus labor at starvation wages, the report concluded. And although employers generally believed that reasonable quotas could hurry slackers without overstraining productive workers, many bosses, reflecting older, free-labor traditions, disapproved of piece work and did their best to preserve skills and defend unions.

At this second, cultural level of analysis, the Commons study revealed the disadvantages of a system that reduced workers to interchangeable cogs in the productive machine. In general, the study showed, unions opposed scientific management not only because of longstanding traditions of worker control, but also for humanitarian reasons, which the official report endorsed as valid public concerns. The short-term gains in productivity achieved by speed-up concealed heavy social costs in the form of workers' lives shortened by constant time pressure and a general demoralization of industrial labor. As for consumers' interests, Commons argued they were damaged more by capitalists in pooled industries such as coal mining, who collusively cut production and raised prices, than by workers attempting to protect standards and quality.[26]

As a policy statement, the report was balanced and judicious. The BLS frowned on unilateral dictation of work rules by unions but made a convincing social case against unrestrained imposition of highly stressful work demands. The economic argument was far weaker. The extent of restriction of output and its impact on the economy were as much matters for debate as ever. The great variety of products and conditions in different trades and shops made it hard to calculate economic costs of output restrictions, but the design and methods of the study also were at fault. There was no systematic effort to develop aggregates beyond the shop level—for manufacturing output by industries and for the nation as a

---

[26]On the congruence of workers' and consumers' interests in maintaining quality and standards, see David Thelen, "Patterns of Consumer Consciousness in the Progressive Movement: Robert M. La Follette, the Antitrust Persuasion, and Labor Legislation," in *The Quest for Social Justice,* Ralph M. Aderman, ed. (Madison: University of Wisconsin Press, 1983), 19–47.

whole—and to compare them over time, taking employment and investment levels into account, with worker output achieved by various methods as the standard for estimating the trend of productivity. And there were no precise estimates of the offsetting social costs of treating workers as commodities. BLS resources alone were insufficient to such tasks, but, for the economic issues at least, data from the Census of Manufactures and the BLS's own production studies of specific industries remained untouched. Concentrating as it did on the highly organized skilled crafts, the report served best as an indicator of current attitudes toward scientific management among contending unionists and capitalists, both of whom were at times unreasonable. The heads of national unions came off best—as judicious mediators who ended indefensible local restrictions, and simultaneously as class leaders who stood firm on work rules that benefited society at the expense of labor and undermined a union movement indispensable to social peace. This result coincided perfectly with the corporatist approach to industrial relations favored by Wright, Commons, and the NCF.[27]

But the trends toward unionization and collective bargaining that gave credence to that model had already ended, with important consequences for wages. In response to a dramatic shift in the determinants of income distribution that came with Taylorism and the open shop, after a hiatus of a decade in which there was no national study of wages and unemployment except the decennial census aggregates, the BLS resumed its work on wages and prices, with some improvements. In 1903, a retail price series based on quotations from 830 establishments covering the entire period from 1890 to 1903 was indexed to the average of 1890–9 and weighted according to a new BLS study of expenditures by 25,440 wage-earning families for the full range of household expenditures, including nonessentials such as books. Research on wages and hours also expanded to include more industries and occupations, indexed and weighted according to census aggregates for wages paid in each industry. In 1904, as Wright was leaving, the three series were merged in a report that showed hourly wages in 1903 up 16.3 percent from the average for the nineties, and retail prices of food (not including clothing, rent, and fuel) up 10.3 percent, "making the increase in the purchasing power of the hourly wage 5.4%," with weekly earnings up

[27]*Regulation and Restriction,* passim. For conflicting views on the role of conservative union leaders in the National Civic Federation, see Weinstein, *Corporate Ideal,* passim; and Montgomery, *Workers' Control,* Chapter 3.

2.3 percent after subtracting for a slight reduction in average working hours per week. Because the report ignored the fact that the panic of that year had produced a surge of wage cuts, strikes, and visibly high unemployment, it outraged labor spokesmen.[28]

Allowed to lapse in 1907 by Wright's successor, Charles P. Neill, a Roosevelt appointee who had received a doctorate in economics from Johns Hopkins University, the price reports were resumed in 1912 and linked up with the old index, confirming significant inflation. The wage series reappeared in 1913, reporting union and nonunion wages for selected industries indexed to a new base year, 1907. Unfortunately, at a time of unprecedented class violence, the BLS stopped reporting an index number for *real* wages.[29]

The reasons for this shift in emphasis are not entirely clear. The official historians of the BLS contend that BLS Commissioner Neill had two motives: taking the bureau's wage and price reports out of politics, and improving the technical quality of the statistical work. First he shifted the publication of the reports to nonelection years; then, when the bureau was heavily burdened with congressionally mandated investigations (of child labor, and of working conditions in the steel and mining industries that had provoked a sequence of disruptive strikes), he canceled them altogether for the five crucial years between 1907 and 1912. Undoubtedly the larger context for this decision—and for the allocation of all the BLS's resources during Neill's tenure—also related to his close association with the National Civic Federation and his general agreement with that body's corporatist approach to labor relations. Neill and his superior, Com-

[28]BLS, *Bulletins* 18 (1898); 27 (1900); 39 (1902); 45 (1903); 51, 53, and 54 (1904); BLS, "Cost of Living and Retail Prices," 18th *Annual Report* (1903); BLS, "Wages and Hours of Labor," 19th *Annual Report* (1904). Quotation is from *Bulletin* 53, 722–23. Cf. A. E. James, "The Dewey Report on Wages in Manufacturing Industries in the United States," *Publications of the American Statistical Association* 10 (1906–7): 319–44. In December 1898, when there had been no BLS wage and price studies since 1891, Wright told the United States Industrial Commission that "statistics prove absolutely the improvement in the social and economic condition of the wage earner during the past twenty years." USIC, *Report* 7:16. Cf. Samuel Rezneck, "Unemployment, Unrest, and Relief in the United States During the Depression of 1893–97," *Journal of Political Economy* 61 (1953): 324–45.

[29]Rumors circulated that the lapse in 1907 was prompted by criticism by noted economists of the statistical methods used in the BLS studies. Actually, Wesley Mitchell gave the BLS fairly high marks. In 1907 Congress ordered an elaborate study of female and child wage earners that consumed the BLS's time and resources until 1911. See I. M. Rubinow, "The Recent Trend in Real Wages," *American Economic Review* 4 (1914): 800; Moye and Goldberg, *First Hundred Years*, 38. The price and wage reports resumed in BLS *Bulletins* 105 (1912) and 128 (1913) respectively, and continued annually.

merce and Labor Secretary Oscar Straus, were NCF members. Neill in particular was keenly interested in the conciliation and welfare work that were the main emphases of the federation after 1904, when the open-shop movement undermined its trade agreement system, and in coopera-tive efforts between the NCF and the Roosevelt and Taft administrations to prohibit child labor, restrict immigration, and establish workers' com-pensation. Under Neill the BLS agenda not only paralleled the NCF's; it also mirrored the AFL's, including its emphasis on voluntarism, at a time when AFL leadership was increasingly unrepresentative of the labor movement as a whole, as attested by objections among member unions to AFL affiliation with the NCF, as well as by the rapid growth of labor militancy and the appeal of socialism.[30]

When the BLS stopped monitoring wages, private investigators could not resist filling the gap. The best contemporary example of these efforts was Isaac M. Rubinow's "Recent Trend of Real Wages" in 1914. Working entirely from BLS data, Rubinow stitched together a retail price index for the entire period and a continuous wage series for nine industries and six trades, and extended the index of working hours, which had also been dropped. In contrast to the latest BLS finding in 1904, he reported an index of real wages from 1890 to 1912 that showed a drastic decline in workers' purchasing power in the late Roosevelt and Taft years. Between 1907 and 1912, Rubinow found, hourly wages rose 9.4 percent, working hours dropped 2.2 percent, weekly earnings rose 7 percent, retail food prices surged 22.5 percent, hourly real wages fell 10.6 percent, and real weekly earnings were down 12.7 percent. BLS reporting had stopped in 1907, just when the tide had turned. To this decline in the living standard of the American worker and little else, Rubinow ascribed "all his strikes, boy-cotts, and riots," "all the picturesque I.W.W. [Industrial Workers of the World]-ism, new unionism, and the modish sabotage," of the period.[31]

Paul Douglas's impressive *Real Wages in the United States, 1890–1926* (1930), subsequently confirmed the trend, attesting to the dramatic recon-struction of manufacturing, the work force, and income distribution

[30]On Neill's background and BLS leadership, see Moye and Goldberg, *First Hundred Years,* Chapter 3; Greene, *National Civic Federation,* 74, 222–32, 239, 339, 346, 456–8. On trade union resistance to the NCF tie, see Montgomery, *Workers' Control,* passim.
[31]Rubinow, "Real Wages," 793–817. For a contemporary assessment of Rubinow's work that reached substantially the same conclusions, see F. W. Jones, "Real Wages in Recent Years," *American Economic Review* 7 (1917): 319–30. A similar conclusion based on a variety of public and private wage and price studies is in Henry Pratt Fairchild, "The Standard of Living—Up or Down," ibid., 6 (1916): 9–25.

achieved by increased mechanization and Taylorism. Working largely from BLS numbers and entirely from data available to the BLS, including cost-of-living data collected for war wage stabilization and a new family budget study done in 1918, Douglas found that, compared with the average for the 1890s, real hourly earnings for union labor in manufacturing had fallen significantly during the Progressive Era. Organized skilled workers earned 4 percent less per hour by 1914, and 8 percent less by 1920, than they had in the 1890s. By contrast nonunion "payroll" workers in manufacturing earned 6 percent more per hour in 1914 than in the 1890s, and 37 percent more by 1920. When union and payroll workers in manufacturing were combined, average real hourly earnings in 1914 stood a bare 2 percent above the average for the 1890s, although by 1920, reflecting wartime shortages and public policy, they were 13 percent higher.

Much of the apparent gain evaporated when Douglas made allowance for a reduction in working hours. On this measure, he found that real full-time weekly earnings of union members had fallen 13 percent by 1914, and 22 percent by 1920, from the average for the 1890s. Here, the skill and organization differentials were even more striking. Payroll workers' real full-time weekly earnings in 1914 were only 1 percent below those of the 1890s, and by 1920 payroll workers earned 16 percent more per week than the average for the 1890s. Average real full-time weekly earnings for manufacturing labor as a class stood at 95 in 1914, 97 in 1920, and 112 in 1926 (where Douglas's study ended), based on the 1890s index. For the 1899–1926 period as a whole, union workers showed an average annual *loss* of 8 percent, while payroll workers showed an average annual *gain* of 5 percent. Real *annual* earnings of all wage workers in manufacturing remained relatively constant in the Progressive Era, although there was a significant transfer of income within the reconstructed working class.[32]

The improvement that had occurred was attributed mainly to lower unemployment. For the entire labor supply "attached" to manufacturing and transportation, Douglas determined that unemployment after 1900 was lower than the average for the 1890s, except in the depression years

[32]Paul Douglas, *Real Wages in the United States 1890–1926* [1930] (New York: Augustus Kelley Reprints, 1966), Parts I–III. On Douglas's career, see Joseph Dorfman, *The Economic Mind in American Civilization*, 5 vols. (New York: Augustus Kelley Reprints, 1966) 5:526–34. See also Clarence D. Long, *Wages and Earnings in the United States, 1860–1890* (Princeton, N.J.: Princeton University Press, 1960); Albert Rees, *Real Wages in Manufacturing, 1890–1914* (Princeton, N.J.: Princeton University Press, 1961), both done for the NBER.

of 1908 and 1914–5. Steadier employment between 1900 and 1914 meant that annual real earnings of the entire working class were nearly 5 percent higher than in the 1890s. But the real earnings of all workers "attached" to manufacturing and transportation ran 5 to 8 percent higher than those of workers *actually employed* in those industries. As Douglas put it, "The gains that labor made during those years were therefore entirely due to the greater steadiness of work, rather than to any increase in the purchasing power of those who continued to be employed." Union workers lost ground while payroll workers gained, but the working class as a whole had not benefited materially from the increased productivity gained by mechanization and the dilution and transfer of skills.[33]

This was also true in comparative terms. According to Douglas, the wage laborers' share of value added by manufacturing remained relatively constant between 1899 and 1914, at something close to 41.5 percent, rose in 1921–3, and then fell back to slightly over 40 percent in 1925, a figure 1.5 percent below the 1899 level of 41.6 percent. Only after *salaried* workers were included along with wage labor did the distribution to labor remain above the 1899 level for the entire period; and on that basis labor's share peaked at 58.7 percent in 1921 and fell by 1925 to 51 percent. When rent, taxes, and capital depreciation were subtracted (because all these increased significantly), the results looked better; labor's share of total value added after these deductions rose from 54 percent in 1899 to 63 percent in 1919 (the latest year depreciation was available). Hence, referring to the new working class as a whole, Douglas concluded that labor's share of total product had not decreased during the first quarter of the twentieth century, although signs of slippage after 1921 suggested that workers would receive a smaller share, as management and capital became increasingly significant factors in production.[34]

[33]Douglas, *Real Wages*, Part IV, "Unemployment and the Real Earnings of the Wage-Earning Class as a Whole." Unemployment in transportation and manufacturing averaged 10.4 percent for 1890–9 and 7.5 percent for 1889–1926. After adding in the building trades and mining, plagued by seasonal fluctuations and excess capacity, the 1897–1926 average unemployment rate for all industrial workers rose to 10.2 percent, still 0.2 percent below the 1890s average. The quotation is at p. 490.

[34]Ibid. In fact, the relative purchasing power of a unit of manufactured goods declined 13 percent between 1899 and 1914, stood 10 percent below 1899 in 1919, and rose 5 percent in 1921 (mainly because of a drop in the value of agricultural products), before dropping back in 1925 to 9 percent below the level of 1899, according to Douglas. Because of gains in efficiency and reductions in marginal value, manufacturing workers produced less purchasing power and had less to offer in exchange in 1921 than in 1899, and real earnings in manufacturing rose more rapidly than value product per employee, confirming

On the policy implications of these findings, and particularly on the role of unions in improving earnings, Douglas was equivocal. A Quaker with an interest in social justice, he believed a union standard would prevent wage gouging by individual employers, but he thought unions would win substantial general gains only in newly organized industries, where pay scales had previously been exploitative. Thereafter, market forces would hold wages close to productivity, provided unemployment was not too high. When Douglas concluded, as Wright had earlier, that sustained employment was the crucial variable in labor's economic progress, he was pulled in a statist direction. Against the prevailing legislative and judicial mood of the 1920s, he advocated grants-in-aid to families and aid to education as a way of setting minimums and equalizing opportunities. Douglas blamed depressions on credit stringency and errors in monetary policy, not on inherent contradictions in capitalism; when unemployment reached an unacceptable level, he favored massive public works financed with fiat currency.[35]

Later research by the National Bureau of Economic Research (NBER) largely upheld Douglas's wage estimates for the early twentieth century, although it challenged some of his other findings. On the basis of fuller cost-of-living data, including retail prices for items other than food, these studies pointed to a modest steady rise, on the order of 1.3 percent a year, in real earnings in manufacturing—rather than no gain between the 1890s and 1914. Even this improvement was lower than the gain between 1860 and 1890, considerably lower than the rate of increase since 1914, and well below the increase in output per man-hour in manufacturing achieved during the Progressive Era. These later studies did not deny the redistribution of income within the working class, to the detriment of skilled workers, which coincided with the "homogenization" phase in the history of labor management strategies, detected by labor historians.[36]

the corporatist assessment that technological improvement would redound to the benefit of workers.

[35]See Douglas, "The Modern Technique of Mass Production and Its Relation to Wages," *Proceedings of the American Academy of Political Science* 12 (1927): 663–42; and idem; "Elasticity of Supply as a Determinant of Distribution," [1927], in *Economic Essays in Honor of John Bates Clark,* Jacob Hollander, ed. (New York: Macmillan), 71–118.

[36]Albert Rees, *Real Wages in Manufacturing;* John W. Kendrick, *Productivity Trends in the United States* (Princeton, N.J.: Princeton University Press for the NBER, 1961); Long, *Wages and Earnings in the United States, 1860–1890;* NBER, Conference on Research in Income and Wealth, *Output, Employment, and Productivity in the United States after 1800,* Studies in Income and Wealth, vol. 30 (New York: Columbia University Press, 1966). Parallel studies of the division of income—including Spahr's, already mentioned; Frank H. Streightoff, *The Distribution of Incomes in the United States* (1912); Willford I. King, *The Wealth and Income of the People of the United States* (1915); the first NBER

For our purposes, comparison of Douglas's wage work and the BLS efforts of that era is instructive. As an academic with a little foundation and university support, Douglas constructed a model of a working distribution system that included the entire working class, and, significantly, the implications of this model were statist. The BLS attempted nothing like this. The agency charged with monitoring labor's welfare could neither confirm nor deny the argument, supported by Rubinow and later by Douglas, that the gains normally expected for labor with the passage of time had been interrupted between the 1890s and the First World War. Thus, despite its many achievements, the BLS failed to provide the guidance necessary for truly informed discussion of what was arguably the most important economic question of that era.

Institutional constraints, bureaucratic inertia, and political interference played important parts in this pattern, as we have seen. The BLS operated in a partisan political system where the price of survival was avoiding controversy. Activist labor bureaus were under fire when Wright took office, and to establish credibility he stressed nonpartisanship and the neutrality of facts. Yet, as his role in the Pullman and Anthracite strikes showed, he was always an upright and sometimes a courageous figure who dared to chastise presidents and survived through five administrations.

In the last analysis, Wright's priorities were largely the product of his own commitments and assumptions, worked out in close association with the conservative union leaders and progressive capitalists of his day. His career reflected his faith in the moral power of information and the general progressiveness of the capitalist system. The transformation of the union movement from a diffuse and highly politicized labor republicanism to a more class-conscious but less overtly political trade unionism guided by Gompers's commitment to voluntarism, and the successful operation of the trade agreement system—albeit largely in older, less technologically advanced industries—reinforced his already optimistic assessment of economic structure and performance and his reliance on capitalist benevolence. Because official policy encouraged class accommodation in the McKinley and Roosevelt years, the expectation that a permanent, comprehensive structure of collective bargaining would come into existence, guaranteeing justice for workers while preserving

reports titled *Income in the United States: Its Amount and Distribution, 1909–1919*, 2 vols. (1921); and Willford I. King, *The National Income and Its Purchasing Power* (NBER, 1930)—provided an important complement to the early wage and price studies, but they are beyond the scope of this chapter.

the progressivism and dynamism of the market, was reinforced politically. Following the model set in its first decades, the BLS subordinated "routine" statistical investigations of wages and employment in the working class as a whole to a variety of special studies that reinforced this emerging corporatist vision.[37]

Unfortunately, the "managerial revolution" and antiunion policies undercut these assumptions. And, as Douglas found, a massive restructuring of business and industry left workers more dependent on the state for protection. At the turn of the century, when the coal owners and other corporate leaders refused to recognize unions, Wright acknowledged the limits of voluntary corporatism and moved in a statist direction. Had he continued at the BLS, he might have kept more distance from the NCF. As we have seen, his successor, Charles Neill (1904–13), accepted the NCF model wholeheartedly and poured his energies into mediation and promoting progressive legislation.[38]

All this skirted—or at least failed to confront directly—the fundamental question of distribution in a nonunion era. The BLS commitment to unions was a valuable official offset to judicial bias against them, but the model for American industrial relations that guided most of Wright's efforts and those of his immediate successors proved tragically ephemeral. Ironically, if the BLS had functioned as a "mere" statistical agency, rather than as an advocate for trade agreements and conciliation, it might have fostered fewer illusions, and the knowledge base for policy decisions in the era of deunionization, high unemployment, declining real wages, and unprecedented class violence after 1900 might have been better.

THE UNITED STATES INDUSTRIAL COMMISSION AND THE CORPORATIST VISION

Unlike more unitary state structures, the American system of fragmented power provides multiple access points for interests attempting to influence policy, and an array of public institutions capable of bringing knowledge to bear on decisions. In the Progressive Era, investigating commissions responsible to Congress paralleled, complemented, and sometimes

[37]There was no central location for gathering labor statistics. Some were collected at the Census Bureau, others at the Department of Agriculture, and still others at the Interstate Commerce Commission, in addition to the BLS. The only public agency doing national aggregates at this time was the Census Bureau; and as late as 1915, the best unemployment figures were the AFL's.
[38]Moye and Goldberg, *First Hundred Years*, 43–73.

competed with permanent agencies in the bureaucracy in the effort to marshal data and theory against the unfamiliar stresses of an industrial society and to endow the new social relations with meaning. Commissions produced a number of studies related directly or indirectly to the labor question. Among the most important were the massive Immigration Commission study, and a study of woman and child wage earners that provided statistical evidence used to win protective legislation and bureaucratic representation for "dependent classes" of workers. Because these studies addressed admittedly special cases, the conceptual approaches, findings, and recommendations they produced bore less directly on labor theory and policy than did the two more general investigations of the labor question, the labor sections of a comprehensive study of the turn-of-the-century economy by the United States Industrial Commission (USIC), and the work of the United States Commission on Industrial Relations (CIR), begun in 1913 after an explosion of labor violence and completed after Europe went to war.

A focus on these two highlights important differences between a permanent bureaucratic agency such as the BLS and the ad hoc investigations mandated by Congress in response to dramatic changes or events. Both types of investigations were increasingly penetrated by academic experts, but the special commissions gave greater scope to partisans in theoretical controversies, such as those regarding monopoly and wages, that had immediate policy implications. The congressional investigations were overtly ideological, policy-oriented, and aimed at producing legislation, whereas the labor bureau consistently avoided the appearance of political or class partisanship and an acknowledged policy agenda. Thus the commissions had a greater capacity to consolidate a new direction in official action, or to reverse a discredited trend in a time of crisis.

In the wake of a terrible depression and a capitalist assault on industrial unions, and in the midst of the merger movement whose full implications were as yet unknown, the USIC served to crystallize corporatist thinking about class relations. With interventionist Populism still reverberating politically, the USIC defended private, associative action over the more statist version of industrial government endorsed by labor radicals and statist progressives. In so doing, the commission helped to refine a model for industrial relations that had the backing of the McKinley administration, the newborn National Civic Federation, the American Federation of Labor (AFL), and leading labor economists and industrial relations experts at the turn of the century: the trade agreement—private bargaining between organized labor and trade associations—assisted where necessary by noncompulsory government mediation. This approach was compatible with the corporatism implicit in BLS research of the Wright era, and it directed government away from two other live options: legal individualism, involving the divisive and inflammatory reliance on injunctions that the courts had recently adopted; and the anticorporate, statist legislative proposals of democratic collectivists in the congressional labor committees of the 1880s and 1890s.[39]

On its way to this corporatist model of industrial governance, the USIC heard thousands of witnesses. Its staff compiled voluminous reports on the general condition of business in the new regime of concentrated capital; on the conditions of labor, with special reference to the South, new industries such as the largely female-staffed department stores that presented special problems, and railway labor, where the federal role was clearest; on immigration and the labor market; and on industrial education. The most elaborate attention was reserved for labor organizations per se—their history, membership, composition, methods, and legal standing, and the attitudes of capitalists and courts toward unions, and especially the sympathetic actions between them that bespoke class solidarity.

By far the most abundant coverage was devoted to labor relations in specific industries—in both the skilled trades, where organization had yielded strength, and in mass production industries such as textiles and printing, where mechanization and scientific management already demanded an alternative organizational strategy from both capital and labor—and to the successes and shortcomings of existing structures for mediation and arbitration. The nineteen-volume report devoted one entire volume to an analysis of foreign labor laws, highlighting differences between, on the one hand, state-corporatist industrial councils in Europe and Australasian compulsory arbitration-cum-wage boards that envisaged a mandatory, tripartite determination of income policy, and, on the other, the voluntary joint-agreement system emerging in Britain and the United States. As examples of the latter process at its best and worst, the USIC contrasted the machinists' strike of 1900, settled by a joint agreement that was taken as a model, with the Chicago building trades lockout

---

[39]Furner, "Republican Tradition and the New Liberalism."

of the same year, in which a hostile employers' association dictated a settlement that drastically curtailed union power.[40]

The USIC recommended, in addition to the trade agreement, state-level legislation to limit working hours for women and minors, end abuses by company stores, restrict immigration, and ban blacklisting and the use of private detectives as company police. Walking the line between the new collectivism and legal individualism, the USIC called for complete legalization of peaceful strikes but a total ban on secondary boycotts, which it described as "always illegal, sometimes criminal" violations of individual liberty. The commission majority strongly endorsed legislation recognizing labor organizations as parties to arbitration and recommended stiff penalties if either party initiated a strike or lockout without resort to arbitration. But the commissioners also condemned as class legislation recently enacted state laws outlawing yellow-dog contracts because they did not also guarantee the open shop.[41]

The USIC made valuable contributions to monopoly and price theory with important implications for distribution. From testimony wormed out of corporate leaders and his own original price series, the USIC expert on trusts, Cornell economist Jeremiah Jenks, documented as standard merger practice the capitalization of monopoly advantage that Commons had predicted earlier. Jenks showed that monopolistic combinations increased their profit margins but engaged in target pricing to maximize their profits and used entry pricing to avoid unwanted competition.[42]

The USIC's effect on wage theory was not only more modest but, in unexpected ways, misleading. Here the outlook of the commission's staff

---

[40]USIC, *Report,* 19 vols. (1900–2). Reports on the labor question are in vols. 7 and 14 on "Capital and Labor Employed in Manufactures and General Business," vol. 8 on "Chicago Labor Disputes of 1900 with Especial Reference to the Disputes in the Building and Machinery Trades," vol. 16 on "The Condition of Foreign Legislation on Matters Affecting General labor," vol. 17 on "Labor Organizations, Labor Disputes, and Arbitration, and on Railway Labor," and the labor section of vol. 19, "Final Report," 723–995. The building trades settlement ended most restrictions on output and outlawed sympathy strikes. By far the best account of the role of the USIC in the development of labor policy is Wunderlin, "American Social Science and the Formation of a Corporate Liberal Labor Stabilization Policy, 1898–1902." See also Richard T. Ely, "The Report of the Industrial Commission, I: Labor," *Yale Review* 11 (1902): 229–50. On the attraction of compulsory arbitration as it developed in Australia and New Zealand, see Peter Coleman, *Progressivism and the World of Reform* (Lawrence, Kan.: University of Kansas Press, 1987).

[41]"Recommendations of the Commission," USIC *Report* 19:947–55.

[42]Jeremiah Jenks, "Industrial Combinations and Prices," USIC *Report* 1:39–57. See also Maurice Robinson, "The Report of the Industrial Commission, V: Trusts," *Yale Review* 11 (1902): 278–96.

economists was controlling. The wage assumptions of Jenks, Commons, and E. Dana Durand were fundamentally at odds with the marginalist expectation of a market allocation of a wage corresponding to the efficiency of labor. Instead, the USIC staff economists assumed that union wage earners would receive a bargained wage that might approach, although it would never surpass, the product of labor, while individual wage contracts would reflect the unequal power of the parties. With appropriate caveats that extraordinary prosperity had ignited unusual competition for labor, Jenks observed that the new metal monopolies had raised wages as much as 50 percent. Labor leaders argued that these powerful employers were just as likely to cut wages in hard times, close plants selectively, and eliminate unions. But Jenks predicted, and Carroll Wright as a witness concurred, that these dangers would be more than offset by the trusts' tendency to steady employment. As market regulation gave way to managerial capitalism, corporate liberals expected that supply would be coordinated to anticipated demand, keeping both labor and capital more constantly employed. As dominant buyers, the trusts would force lower profits on the entrepreneurial capitalists who supplied their raw materials, and it was these small proprietors, not organized labor, whose ox they would gore.

Like the contemporary BLS, the USIC paid small attention to unemployment, deducing most of what it did say from first principles. The commission staff recognized two potential sources of unemployment: a business cycle that could be moderated by voluntary cooperation between competing firms, and new technology. Machines permanently eliminated some types of work, Jenks conceded, but he also argued, on the basis of his price studies, that the general cheapening of trust-made goods benefited labor as consumers. The USIC redrew the chart of American social structure, linking the consumer interest with the trusts, and setting it in opposition to collective actions by labor that artificially restricted output or raised prices above their "natural" cost.

The attitude of the trusts to unions was a major area of concern. Here the evidence before the USIC was conflicting. Where unions provided both motive and mechanism for removing the wage rate from competition, they were often indispensable to the formation of trusts and trade associations; and capitalists in these cartel-like combinations were highly favorable to unions. Where highly integrated, tight combinations concentrated power in one firm (a U.S. Steel or American Tobacco) and unions resisted elimination of outmoded skills, capitalists eliminated unions, while claiming to be friends of ordinary workers who cut the wages of labor "aristocrats" but raised the pay of the "average man." Drawing these conflicting strands together, the USIC called for legislation to protect consumers (e.g., from overcapitalization); restrict unions to their "proper" role (e.g., wage bargaining) but protect them, too; and legitimize mergers that met a common-law standard of reasonableness. Through its recognition of a growing segmentation of labor, a division between corporate and proprietary capitalists, and the consumer interest, this public investigation of class relations fostered a persuasive policy pluralism.[43]

Offsetting the crudeness of its wage work, the USIC report made more sophisticated contributions to historical-institutional economics and to the theory of "industrial democracy." Staff studies of the bargaining process suggested the desirability of separate machinery for determining future wage contracts through joint agreements and for settling disagreements over the terms of existing contracts. The latter were best handled, in the view of labor experts for the commission, Durand and Commons, by shop-level committees and locally constituted systems for arbitration of disputes. Inspired by American state boards of charities and various European systems for functional representation, Commons advocated another institutional innovation that eventually took root in Wisconsin— a tripartite labor council representing labor, capital, and the public to advise on labor legislation.[44]

Yet the USIC's handling of the labor question was ultimately misleading because, like the BLS, it assumed (or acted as though) the trend toward unionization would continue without state protection. In fact, of course, the BLS-USIC model of industrial relations soon collapsed, trade unionism stalled, and industrial unions virtually disappeared. Up dramatically between 1897 and 1904, total trade union membership leveled off and actually declined as a percentage of all workers until

---

[43]USIC *Report*, 1, *Trusts and Industrial Combinations*, "Digest of Evidence," 9–39, 105–11, 530–31, 542–3, 565; Testimony, 3–24, 959–6, 986–97, 1005–35, 1077–87, 1127–211; ibid., 7, *Capital and Labor*, "Topical Digest of Evidence," 9–17; Testimony, 5–26 (Carroll Wright); ibid., 13, *Trusts and Industrial Combinations*, cont., "Review of Evidence," v–xxv; Testimony, 448–77 (Schwab). See also Mabel Atkinson, "Trusts and Trade Unions," *Political Science Quarterly* 19 (1904): 193–223; Furner, "Republican Tradition and the New Liberalism."

[44]Wunderlin, "American Social Science and the Formation of a Corporate Liberal Labor Stabilization Policy," passim; [Durand], "Review of Evidence," USIC *Report* 7:v–xxxii; idem, "Collective Bargaining, Conciliation, and Arbitration," 17:lxxiv–cxiii; Commons testimony, ibid., 14:32–48; W. F. Willoughby testimony, ibid., 14:168–81.

World War I. Declining income, frustration, and outright oppression in that period raised the Socialist vote, fueled a growing syndicalism in labor, sparked violent union strikes, and triggered spontaneous rebellions on the part of unorganized workers, some belatedly led by the IWW, that shook the nation's confidence and impelled the Taft administration, after the *Los Angeles Times* bombing of 1910 and the frightening disclosure of sabotage by union leaders, to enlist the services of another industrial commission.

THE COMMISSION ON INDUSTRIAL RELATIONS AND DEMOCRATIC COLLECTIVISM

The state showed a different face in the investigative work of the CIR. Like the USIC, the CIR was tripartite in composition, giving heavy representation to NCF-type employers and conservative union leaders, and including neither Socialists nor Wobblies, despite its assigned mission of seeking the causes of industrial unrest. But the chairman appointed by President Wilson was Frank Walsh, a Kansas lawyer and social-justice progressive committed to industrial democracy; while John Commons, now secure in an academic job at Wisconsin and involved in work with the Wisconsin Industrial Commission that pulled him in a more statist direction, was one of the public members. The work of the CIR was divided between public hearings, reflecting the republican tradition of gathering information from the people, and empirically based investigative reports prepared by experts.[45]

Under Walsh's skillful direction, the CIR took mounds of testimony regarding conditions in the nation's industries and investigated on site, in the garment trades and department stores where women worked at inadequate wages; in the mines, docks, stockyards, lumber camps, wheatfields, and hopyards; in Paterson silk mills full of immigrants and southern textile mills full of poor white children, unprotected by unions or laws. Walsh's relentless questioning exposed heavy-handed, law-defying tactics by antiunion employers and feudal conditions in company towns. It culminated with a spectacular exposé of the complicity of John D. Rockefeller, Jr., in the brutal suppression of the United Mine Workers by Colorado Fuel and Iron and the subversion of state government that led to the Ludlow Massacre, where Colorado National Guardsmen caused the

[45]The most detailed account of the background of the CIR is Graham Adams, *Age of Industrial Violence, 1910–1915* (1966). See also Weinstein, *Corporate Ideal*, Chapter 7.

deaths of women and children, inciting retaliatory raids by strikers on scabs and mines all over Colorado.[46]

Behind the scenes, the CIR research staff undertook a massive empirical investigation of underlying conditions in American industry that might account for the accelerating tendency toward violence. Headed first by Charles McCarthy, and later—when Walsh fired McCarthy in a dispute over methods that disguised fundamental differences in ideology—by Basil Manly, a research staff of more than fifty persons was assembled. Most of them were young economists, trained in historical and institutional methods either at Wisconsin or by Jacob Hollander at Johns Hopkins, who displayed a hard-headed realism about the new industrial system, and recruits from state and federal statistical agencies. The CIR served as a training ground for a new generation of labor economists and social investigators who came to prominence during the 1920s and the New Deal. Among them were the young Selig Perlman, doing his pioneering accounts of industrial relations in the garment trade; George Barnett, Sumner Slichter, William Leiserson, and Leo Wolman, important figures in the emerging field of industrial relations; Robert Hoxie, author of a pathbreaking study of the effect of scientific management on labor; and W. Jett Lauck and Edgar Sydenstricker, authorities on conditions in American industries.[47]

Through its formative influence on these investigators, the CIR reoriented labor economics and paved the way for a reversal in official outlook and labor policy that would come to fruition in the New Deal. Taken together, CIR reports and analysis offered a devastating critique of the liberal-corporatist strategy for achieving economic stability and social justice through voluntary associative action. As we have seen, the NCF approach was not redistributive. It assumed that labor's gains would accrue automatically, as continuous expansion of an inherently progressive economic system yielded steady improvements in the general stan-

[46]CIR, *Final Report and Testimony*, 11 vols. (1916). See vols. 7–9 for the Ludlow-Rockefeller connection, and passim. An excellent, detailed series of analytical reports on the hearings also appeared in the *Survey*, vols. 30–35 (1913–6).
[47]The CIR Division of Investigation and Research divided work into nine categories: Legal and Legislative, Labor Organizations and Collective Bargaining, Employment, Hired Farm Labor, Education and Preparation for Life, Welfare Work, Public Agencies, Economic Causes of Industrial Unrest, and Women in Industry. The reports of the Investigative and Research Division were never published by CIR, although most of them were privately published almost immediately. CIR's funds were cut off by a congressional coalition dominated by southerners who wanted to prevent Walsh from holding hearings in the South. The staff reports have recently become available on microfilm, occupying, without the statistical appendixes, 15 reels.

dard of living. CIR research challenged these assumptions, and similar ones officially accepted by the BLS of that period, in reports that exposed structural weaknesses and inequities in the privately managed corporate economy, deunionization, deteriorating working and living conditions, and declining real income and living standards for a sizable segment of the working class. These conditions suggested a need for significantly greater state intervention, particularly through a mandated minimum wage, income-maintaining welfare programs, and public supervision of the investment system.

Reflecting its origins as a congressional response to public uneasiness about class issues, the CIR report centered its analysis on the economic causes of industrial unrest. The staff's attack on this problem was coordinated by W. Jett Lauck, a seasoned investigator trained at Chicago under Laughlin and Veblen. Lauck constructed a "commission view" that linked the corporate system to an abnormally violent type of industrial protest, very different from the normal striving for improved conditions that Carroll Wright had characterized as "divine discontent." The USIC, reflecting the corporatist tendencies of its staff and dominant members, had encouraged wage earners to expect economic stability as the product of a permissive trust policy that allowed larger, more efficient companies to dominate their markets, ending ruinous competition. In contrast, Lauck and his associates blamed the declining status of workers and industrial violence on the transgressions of those very corporations. Their investigations showed that monopolies reaped enormous profits from increased productivity, which they refused to share equitably with workers *or* consumers. Overcapitalization was routine; and redundant securities established streams of investment income that corporations pointed to as fixed costs, precluding lower prices or higher wages. Far from rationalizing the investment system, according to Lauck, unrestricted corporate capitalization of achieved and future gains in productivity had created unprecedented inequities in the distribution of income.

With his associate, Sumner Slichter, Lauck painted a Veblenesque picture of an industrial society in thrall to a pecuniary one. The two economists described a concentration in control of capital that placed six major banking and investment groups in charge of corporations that determined the income of nearly three-fourths of the country's railroad workers and more than a quarter of wage earners in manufacturing. Capital-intensive methods increased labor's productivity, but undermined the bargaining power of individual workers. Skilled craft unions lost ground because of

Taylorism, and industrial unions were undercut by immigration. Lauck noted that financial control over industry was causing increased segregation along class lines in America, and a new indifference to the conditions and problems of labor among the "controlling classes."[48]

Claims that American workers were losing ground were buttressed by extensive research on conditions in the principal industries. The Sydenstricker report attacked the problem of worker income from a point of view different from that of earlier official studies. Instead of merely tracking real earnings over time, Sydenstricker assessed the adequacy of worker income to support a decent standard of life. Fully one-fourth of adult male heads of families earned less than $400 a year, one-half less than $600, and four-fifths less than the $800 that reliable budget studies found necessary for barely adequate support of the average family of five. Because the major breadwinner's earnings were insufficient, women and children also labored to generate a family wage, and this pattern undermined the integrity of the working-class family and mortgaged the future by denying children education, in the view of the CIR investigators. Also, by creating a pool of easily exploitable workers, this practice encouraged industrial parasitism. Sydenstricker determined that nearly three-fourths of working women failed to earn the $8.00 a week considered necessary for their support, either independently or with a family. The average wage-earner's family spent from three-fourths to four-fifths of its income on subsistence, leaving little or nothing for unemployment or old age. Fully half the wage-earners' families in the United States lacked sufficient income for adequate subsistence and health.[49]

[48]W. Jett Lauck, "Economic Causes Underlying Industrial Unrest," and "Analysis of the Economic Causes of Industrial Unrest, with Accompanying Recommendation"; Sumner Slichter, "Report on the Concentration of Control of Industry in the United States"; idem, "The Agents of Concentration"; idem, "Control of the Railroads in the United States"; J. H. Bradford, "Tendencies in Labor, Total Conversion, and Capital Costs and Tendency Toward Overcapitalization in the Iron and Steel Industry"; F. P. Valiant, "Capitalization, Investment, and Earnings [of International Harvester, American Tin Plate, International Silver, American Sugar Refining, and Standard Oil Cos.]"; Ralph D. Fleming, "Overcapitalization and Monopoly"; idem, "Economic Effects of Immigration," *Investigative and Research Reports of the United States Commission on Industrial Relations*, 15 reels (State Historical Society of Wisconsin), Reels 2 and 3 (hereafter CIR Microfilm). These conclusions on concentration were based mainly on data drawn from the recent Pujo (Senate Banking) Committee investigations; studies of labor costs, output, and prices by the Bureau of Corporations; the U.S. Tariff Board, Internal Revenue Service records, and the Stanley Committee Investigation of U.S. Steel.

[49]Edgar Sydenstricker, "Conditions of Labor in the Principal Industries"; Francis P. Valiant, "Annual Earnings of Adult Male Wage-Earners and Their Adequacy to Support a Family"; Valiant, "Tendencies in Economic Consumption and Their Effect Upon the Cost of Living"; idem, "Trend of Prices and Wages from 1879 to 1912, as Indicated by Recent

The CIR linked the declining "American standard" to deunionization and unemployment. Leo Wolman's pioneering study of the growth of trade unions portrayed hostile employers' associations and the union-busting tactics of large corporations as major obstacles to organization. In fact, CIR studies indicated it was impossible to come to grips with the true conditions of American wage earners without first recognizing that American labor was for all practical purposes unorganized and unskilled, and thus dependent as a class either on corporate paternalism, which had conspicuously failed, or on state intervention.[50]

Unlike the earlier commission, the CIR gave top billing to the pernicious insecurity of employment that made wage earners the "residual sufferers" from seasonal and cyclical fluctuations. William Leiserson attempted to discover the nature and causes of work loss, whereas Sydenstricker assessed the impact of unemployment on worker income. Extensive field investigations and statistics from various sources convinced Leiserson there was no reserve army, or permanent labor surplus, in the United States. Yet the difference between maximum employment at peak production and the amount of labor needed in seasonal or cyclical lows could run as high as 50 percent. Thus, the CIR defined unemployment as an endemic structural problem, not confined to sick or special industries. Seasonal and unskilled workers obviously faced higher unemployment, with construction workers, for example, losing up to one-third of their working time. Yet four or five of every ten workers lost some time each year, and organized workers typically lost from 10 to 20 percent of the income they would otherwise have had. Substantially all workers lived constantly under the threat of unemployment.[51]

The urgency of this problem galvanized the BLS to undertake its first original research on unemployment since 1897. In 1914 the CIR, the BLS, and the Indiana Labor Bureau did a model collaborative study of female employment that focused on structural elements in women's work as causes of unemployment. The BLS then surveyed New York City, and in 1915 the entire country, revealing a jobless rate above 11 percent, with

Inquiries," CIR Microfilm, Reels 7 and 9. These investigations were subsequently published in W. Jett Lauck and Edgar Sydenstricker, *Conditions of Labor in American Industries* (1917).

[50]Leo Wolman, "The Extent of Organization in the United States in 1910," CIR Microfilm, Reel 10. See also idem, *The Growth of American Trade Unions, 1880–1923*.

[51]Leiserson, "Preliminary Report of Investigations into Unemployment and Unemployment Offices," CIR Microfilm, Reel 1; Sydenstricker, "Conditions of Labor," ibid., Reel 9; Lauck and Sydenstricker, *Conditions of Labor*, 71–111.

another 17 percent underemployed. The new Commissioner of the BLS, Royal Meeker, identified unemployment as

> the greatest evil in our competitive industrial system. We have been exceedingly slow to admit the actuality of involuntary unemployment. . . . Only in periods of industrial crisis and depression do we awaken to some faint realization of the fact of unemployment. . . . With the onset of good times, we . . . relapse into our normal state of profound indifference and speedily forget the unemployed. . . . We have never yet acknowledged that in the best of times there is in the United States an appalling amount of unemployment, even in our most stable industries.[52]

CIR research identified several causes of unemployment, including technological innovations, cyclical and seasonal fluctuations, deliberate management policies, and personal qualities that undermined the worker's capacity to take advantage of employment opportunities. In this part of the analysis, structural factors were mixed with more conventional, moralistic explanations. Vivid reports on casual workers showed how recurrent unemployment, low wages, and a subhuman existence eroded efficiency and self-esteem. And poignant accounts of joblessness in seasonal industries such as the garment trades pinpointed employers who refused to smooth out production, in order to maintain reserve labor for peak periods and weaken unions. Sydenstricker placed most of the blame on a system that encouraged employers to look upon workers as "so much productive power in the same sense as steam or electricity" and on a lack of public pressure for better performance.

CIR reports gave unemployment a definition and a context it had lacked in earlier official reports. For the first time, unemployment was officially recognized as a collective tragedy and a social responsibility, not a necessary discipline that could be kept within bounds largely by private, associative action. Defining a sphere for state action, the CIR staff proposed a variety of public measures designed to maintain income. Some— including a national system of labor exchanges, regulation of private employment agencies, free transportation of workers, vocational guidance, and labor colonies to retain casual laborers—were aimed at improving labor market organization and the mobility of labor. Others, such as Leiserson's proposals for national public works projects and federally

---

[52]BLS *Bulletins* 109, 160, 172, 192, 195; quotation in *Bulletin* 192 (1916), 5. The first BLS bulletin on unemployment since 1897, Frank Sargent's "Statistics of Unemployment and the Work of Employment Offices in the United States," *Bulletin* 109 (1912), reported statistics available from other sources without analysis. The first comprehensive BLS report on the national unemployment picture was "Unemployment in the United States," *Bulletin* 195 (1916).

coordinated unemployment insurance financed by industry, government, and wage earners, dealt with structural unemployment and cyclical factors at a macroeconomic level.[53]

The CIR staff explored the need for state intervention in other areas of social welfare. Selig Perlman, Sydenstricker, and B. S. Warren, the head of the U.S. Public Health Service, produced a number of detailed reports that contrasted the American practice of providing insurance against sickness, disability, and old age through private, company-based mutual funds with the publicly supported systems in other countries. Although these experts credited the benevolent motives that often inspired employers' "welfare work," they concluded that welfare capitalism all too often amounted to an "enlightened absolutism," controlled entirely by employers, designed primarily to increase labor's dependency, and therefore antagonistic to democratic values. Perlman and his associates defined a system appropriate for an "industrial democracy," in which employers, employees, and the public would cooperate in the collective provision of insurance against the misfortunes suffered by workers, with the state guaranteeing democratic methods, imposing decent standards on recalcitrant employers, and making special provision for the needs of the lowest paid. Although social legislation was largely beyond the reach of the federal government in the Progressive Era, the CIR staff prepared model programs for state sickness insurance and state oversight of pension plans, and even floated tentative plans for national old-age insurance.[54]

In overall conception, the CIR staff reports differed markedly from the earlier BLS-USIC approach to economic stabilization and welfare. Earlier government research had assumed, following neoclassical models of economic motivation, that, given equal bargaining power between organized parties to the labor contract, market ordering of the economy would be both efficient and equitable to labor. CIR research denied the validity of neoclassical assumptions and adopted a more critical approach to market discipline.

Although the staff reports never questioned the institution of private

[53]Leiserson, "The Labor Market and Unemployment"; Luke Grant, "Unemployment in the Building Trades"; Selig Perlman, "Seasonal Unemployment in the Garment Trades and a Possible Remedy," CIR Microfilm, Reel 5.

[54]For representative studies along these lines, see Selig Perlman, "Preliminary Report on Welfare Work and Social Insurance"; B. S. Warren and Perlman, "Tentative Plan for State Sickness Insurance," CIR Microfilm, Reel 1; "National Insurance and Old Age Pension— An Assisted Voluntary System," ibid., Reel 10; B. S. Warren and Edgar Sydenstricker, "Sickness Insurance," ibid. CIR social welfare experts were also enthusiastic supporters of the recently enacted state workers' compensation program.

property itself, their recommendations envisaged, in addition to restraints on monopoly, extensive socialization of the control of property, though it remained in private hands. The overall implications of the economic research done under CIR auspices were collectivist and statist, as was the version of the official commission report signed by Walsh and the labor members. On the basis of wide-ranging empirical research, CIR economists endorsed a mix of income-maintaining programs composed of private and public elements, and coordinated and supervised by the national government. Instead of seeking either a market wage or exclusively a bargained wage, which would decline with labor's bargaining power, allowing industrial progress to result in degradation of workers, CIR economists joined a number of reformist groups in calling for a national commitment to a "living wage," defined as one that would support a family in reasonable comfort without the labor of mothers or young children. To implement this recommendation, Jett Lauck proposed "a new theory or method of wage-payments and the abandonment of the idea of paying industrial workers on the basis of the supply of and demand for labor." This new method would begin with existing wage rates, and would tie advances to gains in productivity, allowing an ample profit margin to encourage new investment. Actual wages would be determined by industrywide collective bargaining or "protocols" such as those recently established in the New York garment trades; disagreements would be settled by arbitration or wage boards that would originate in the industry but would ultimately, as in the railroad case, come under the auspices of the state or federal government, reflecting the public interest in industrial efficiency and distributive justice. For such a structure to work, Lauck assumed unions would have to accept scientific management, and employers the desirability of unions.

The CIR program for economic and social stabilization included voluntarist elements, but it was based on a conception of social relations that differed markedly from corporate liberalism. As Lauck put it in a summary of principles on which reconstruction should be based, "Industry, as regards its control, its methods, and its treatment of workers, has too long been considered heretofore as essentially a private and individual matter." CIR investigators rejected the assumption that the enlightened corporate interest was identical with the public interest.[55]

[55]Lauck, "Economic Causes of Industrial Unrest," CIR Reel 2, 16–34. In addition to frequent demands by labor leaders, an early call for the living wage came in *Rerum Novarum,* a papal encyclical issued by Leo XIII in 1891 and incorporated into anti-

Like most of his co-workers, Lauck was not a socialist. His outlook incorporated elements of syndicalism, but he possessed a faith in the capacity of government to secure economic justice that labor leaders, whether AFL or Wobbly, generally lacked. Thus he outlined a larger role for the state in distribution than the nonsocialist labor movement traditionally had. Expressing the sentiments of Chairman Walsh and apparently most of his fellow investigators, Lauck anticipated a movement toward "industrial democracy and industrial constitutionalism" in which "the public through its governmental agencies will participate in industrial relations which in the past [have] been left almost entirely to employers and employees, and that the public will do this, not only for its own protection, but for the maintenance of those ideals in industry which it has already set up for itself in political affairs."[56]

This "CIR view" assumed that the reforms necessary to democratize capitalism were appropriate extensions of sovereignty, grounded in republican values. In rejecting the corporate liberal model of labor relations, the staff economists allied themselves with a reformist tradition in the profession, associated with Henry Carter Adams and Richard T. Ely, which, since the interregnum of the 1880s, had advocated extending constitutional principles to industrial government and subjecting corporations to legal control. Beyond a state role in wage determination, CIR reports advocated public regulation of corporate securities and mergers, to prevent excessive capitalization of monopoly, and to safeguard the interests of wage earners and consumers (which they saw as allied); decentralization and further supervision of the investment system; public control over the development of natural resources; taxation of land values; restriction of immigration; unemployment insurance; sickness and accident insurance; extension of the minimum wage for women; vocational education; and reductions in the cost of living through improved farm marketing and rural credit. From the legal division of the CIR staff, not discussed here, came resounding recommendations for ending abuses of the injunction and martial law, recognizing unions as

Marxist Social Catholicism, most notably in the intensely prolabor writings of John A. Ryan. See his *A Living Wage: Its Ethical and Economic Aspects* (New York: Macmillan, 1906; 1912; 1920).

[56]Lauck, "Economic Causes," 16–17. The AFL had actually initiated a tentative shift toward politics in 1906. See Montgomery, *Workers' Control in America*, 75–83; Adams, *Age of Industrial Violence*, 168–75, 219–26; Gwendolyn Mink, *Old Labor and New Immigrants in American Political Development* (Ithaca, N.Y.: Cornell University Press, 1986), 204–60. On industrial democracy, see Milton Derber, *The American Idea of Industrial Democracy, 1865–1965* (Urbana: University of Illinois Press, 1970), passim.

parties to contracts, and exempting all of labor's nonviolent collective actions from prosecution.[57]

In its staff research reports and the Manly (Walsh) report, which adopted many of the staff's recommendations, the CIR offered a vision of American New Liberalism that was more statist than corporate liberalism, more open to political participation by excluded groups, and more democratic. This conception incorporated corporatist elements, such as a Wisconsin-style system of tripartite advisory councils and centralized administration of labor policy advocated in the majority report signed by the two public members, Commons and Mrs. Borden Harriman. But it transcended the narrow basis in organized interests embodied in Commons's outlook by assuming public responsibility for overall management of the economy, including control of the investment system and a guarantee of equity in distribution.[58]

The CIR research effort had a slapdash quality traceable to its short life, short funds, and the youth of many of the investigators. At the same time, it achieved what the BLS had evaded between the 1890s and the midteens—a structural analysis of the determinants of wages, unemployment, and labor unrest. CIR economists accepted a fairly applied productivity theory of distribution, but they located structural elements in distribution that bore no necessary relationship to productive contribution. Reflecting the vibrant institutionalism of American economics, the CIR gave official recognition to industrial unionism—but more important, through the concept of the living wage, to a minimum guaranteed income as a vital factor in economic stabilization.

Although the staff reports were not published officially, they quickly found their way into print. Their goals had immediate policy significance when Walsh assumed the joint chairmanship of the War Labor Board and, in a fruitful working arrangement with former president Taft, used his authority to end a stalemate between the corporate and labor members of

---

[57]The Legal and Legislative Division did a number of historical and theoretical papers on labor, the Constitution, and the courts, as well as field investigations that revealed routine violations of workers' constitutional rights and amazing extensions of corporate power into the legal and police systems of communities. Papers by Edwin Witte and David Saposs were the most significant. CIR Microfilm, Reels 11 and 12.

[58]Despite important differences in tone and recommendations, the two official reports of the divided commission both identified insecurity of income as the major problem facing workers, and both called for social insurance, financed by redistributed taxation, and complete legalization of unions, accepting nonviolent collective actions recently disallowed by the courts. I am indebted to H. M. Gitelman for important insights regarding division in the commission.

the board, tied wage rises in war production to government cost-of-living studies, and encouraged unionization in the mass-production industries.[59]

The same concerns cropped up again in the Unemployment Conferences that addressed postwar economic planning; and they did much to set the agenda for private (albeit quasi-public) investigations in the 1920s such as those of the National Bureau of Economic Research (NBER). The earliest NBER studies included two volumes on *Income in the United States: Its Amount and Distribution, 1909–1919;* two studies of the business cycle, employment, and earnings, including Wesley Mitchell's first important volume on that subject; a study of labor and immigration entitled *Migration and the Business Cycle;* and an expanded version of Leo Wolman's CIR study on *The Growth of American Trade Unions, 1880–1923.* It might not be unfair to conclude that the CIR set the agenda for the privatized, Hooverian version of economic investigation that prevailed in the 1920s.[60]

IDEOLOGICAL SYSTEMS IN TENSION

The differences among the various forms of public investigation discussed here are partly institutional, reflecting, as we noted earlier, the different capacities of agencies housed in the permanent bureaucracy—and therefore responsible to a sitting administration—and the more independent congressional investigating commissions. The BLS under Wright and his pre–World War I successors promoted more equitable relations between organized labor and capitalists, and by countervailing against the courts it fostered a more constructive, less one-sided approach to labor on the part of the state. But as the American system of industrial relations moved toward deunionization during the Progressive Era, the BLS grew less effective as a guide to federal labor policy. Through its statistical work, the BLS set the stage for later development of the vital economic indicators it supplies today. Yet it would be inaccurate to conceive of the BLS (then or now!) as a "mere" statistical agency. Pro-union, essentially procorporate, and corporatist, the prevailing "BLS view" in the long progressive era reflected and reinforced the central role of trade unions in

---

[59]On Walsh's role in war labor policy, see Valerie Jean Conner, *The National War Labor Board: Stability, Social Justice, and the Voluntary State in World War I* (Chapel Hill: University of North Carolina Press, 1983).

[60]On ideological developments in the Hoover and Roosevelt years continuous from those described here, see Chapters 4, 9, and 13 in this volume.

early labor economics. It was close to the USIC view, but quite at odds with the CIR view, as well as with subsequent developments in the Isador Lubin era at the BLS during the 1930s, and in labor economics when a new generation of labor economists and a new view of industrial relations took hold. Especially in the years between Wright's retirement and World War I, the BLS was out of touch with the conditions and needs of the great mass of America's unorganized workers.

The state's contribution to economic knowledge—in this case to understanding of the labor question between the 1880s and World War I—changed over time, reflecting the stimulus of new social problems and changes in the larger political context, as well as persistent tensions in American liberalism. The fragmentation of power in the American system, and its greater permeability, compared with the situation in more unitary states, allowed opposing conceptions of an American New Liberalism to find expression within the institutions of government; and the resources that public agencies could command fostered development of the economic knowledge, both empirical and theoretical, that constructed and supported these different ideological perspectives. Investigating commissions such as the USIC and the CIR were directly linked to immediate social crises such as those related to the union movements of the 1880s and 1890s and the mass radicalism of the era of the Paterson strike and the Ludlow Massacre. Consequently, their efforts were more overtly politicized and adversarial than the regular work of permanent statistical agencies. But issues relating to class and distribution are never taken out of politics, not even by removing them to executive agencies. These same kinds of pressures eventually forced changes in perspective, a new focus of research, and an openness to different ideas in the BLS, where institutional imperatives favored greater ideological continuity and nonpartisanship. Yet, because of the crisis orientation and broader mandate of the investigating commissions under review here, they had a more immediate, visible impact on directing, and redirecting, both labor economics and labor policy.

The USIC and the CIR naturally reflected the theoretical and policy orientations of the complex of partisan, official, functional, and academic interests that gave them life and dominated their proceedings. Through their hearings, and especially through the work of their professional staffs, each of them gathered and integrated bodies of previously unconnected data and newly created knowledge into a comprehensive analysis that suggested major changes in liberal theory and policy. Although in the case of the CIR the commission itself was badly divided, the momentum was clearly with Frank Walsh, the labor members of the commission, and—more important, because their investigations helped to legitimize a new approach—the young economists and public officials who organized the research.

Just as the USIC established a direction for the corporate liberal era that opened politically with McKinley, providing a convincing rationale for a decisive departure from the republican past, so the work of the CIR both impelled and justified a shift in official attitudes toward labor in the Wilson years, when a more statist approach to social policy was invoked, in part to address the imbalance in class power and inequities in distribution that had destabilized the National Civic Federation system. The commissions came at major turning points in social relations, bringing inquiry to bear on the location of new roads, as in some fashion democratic politics must. And, in so doing, the scientific work of the USIC and the CIR helped to formulate, and to deploy politically, the opposing conceptions of the relation of the state to the economy—a resourceful, adaptive, and multifaceted corporate liberalism, and a statist, social activist, and egalitarian democratic collectivism—that marked the boundaries of modern liberal discourse down through the New Deal—and beyond.

9

Economic inquiry and the state in
New Era America: antistatist corporatism and
positive statism in uneasy coexistence

ELLIS W. HAWLEY

The rise of modern managerial states, most students of the subject agree, has been accompanied and to some degree shaped by the rise of modern economic inquiry. The two have helped to foster and justify each other, and this symbiotic relationship has found institutional expression in a variety of research and planning bodies linking economic inquiry and its fruits to the managerial process. Yet, just as managerial states differ in their structural composition and the accommodations reached with pre-managerial traditions, such states also differ in the mechanisms developed for bringing economic inquiry and economic management together. History has mattered, both in the sense that heritages from the past have been determinants of what could and could not be done and in the sense that choices existed and were made by historical actors. It has mattered both in the United States and elsewhere, and it is upon a period of history that helped to shape the arrangements characteristic of the American version of the managerial state that this chapter focuses.

More specifically, the chapter explores the forging of mechanisms that allowed the forerunners of modern managerial economics[1] to establish

[1] As used here, a managerial economics is one that views the economic system (or a sector of it) as in need of and subject to management and seeks to provide information and knowledge useful to persons undertaking the managerial task. A managerial economics differs in these respects from an economics that sees and studies the economic system as the workings of immutable natural law. Nor is it the same as an institutional economics that seeks understanding through a focus on institutional development and behavior. Although its developers were often institutionalists and the two were often linked, they were not necessarily so. Also excluded from the definition employed here is the use of the term to mean

new bases of societal support and link research to planning in the America of the 1920s. Such mechanisms, it is argued here, were difficult to forge, partly because the managerial impulses of the time coexisted with strong antimanagerial reactions and partly because the managerial apparatus that had been added to the American state during World War I could not be perpetuated or turned into a peacetime counterpart. But two routes to overcoming these difficulties did emerge, one exemplified in the rise of the Bureau of Agricultural Economics (BAE), the other in the similar success story of the National Bureau of Economic Research (NBER).

Most of what follows is concerned with how and why these mechanisms exemplified by the BAE and NBER emerged, what institutions and rival formulations of the "American way" were produced, and what the implications were for future developments. After a brief discussion providing necessary context and background, I want to focus on the story of the BAE, the alternative approach exemplified in the NBER, the clashes that developed between the two, the mechanisms at work in producing the *Recent Economic Changes* study of the late 1920s, and the need to understand both approaches if one is to understand America's subsequent arrangements for bringing economic inquiry and economic management together.

THE CONTEXT

In the United States, economic inquiry for purposes of managing the economic system as a whole had its real beginnings during World War I, at least insofar as it was done by credentialed professionals. One can, to be sure, find advocates of such economic inquiry in the prewar period, notably among the German-influenced institutionalist school and some heirs of Henry Carey's "Philadelphia school."[2] And bits of it had been

any economic knowledge of value to the operators of individual firms—except insofar as they are functioning as managers of the system or a targeted sector of it.

[2] See Robert L. Church, "Economists as Experts: The Making of an Academic Profession in the United States, 1870–1920," in Lawrence Stone, ed., *The University in Society,* II (Princeton, N.J.: Princeton University Press, 1974), 571–609; Joseph Dorfman, *The Economic Mind in American Civilization,* III (New York: Kelley, 1969), 160–88, 276–94, 434–73; Steven A. Sass, *The Pragmatic Imagination: A History of the Wharton School, 1881–1981* (Philadelphia: University of Pennsylvania Press, 1982), 40–4, 55–85, 91–126; Joseph Dorfman, "The Role of the German Historical School in American Economic Thought," *American Economic Review Supplement* 45 (May 1955): 17–28; A. W. Coats, "The First Two Decades of the American Economic Association," *American Economic Review* 50 (September 1960): 555–74; Mary O. Furner, *Advocacy and Objectivity: A Crisis in the Professionalization of American Social Science, 1865–1905* (Lexington: University of Kentucky Press, 1975), 59–124.

attached to the new investigating, regulatory, and developmental agencies spawned by progressive reformism and its interaction with managerial-minded business groups.[3] But it was the demand generated by the war-time administrative apparatus that brought dozens of trained economists into government service and put them to work producing the data, tools, and understanding needed for effective performance of the new manage-rial tasks. Research and planning bodies staffed by professional econo-mists and statisticians emerged in most of the major war agencies, and a number of them were eventually amalgamated into a Central Bureau of Planning and Statistics (CBPS) headed by Harvard economist Edwin Gay. Linked directly to the president and his war cabinet, Gay's organization was charged not only with providing accurate data for decision makers but with producing "conspectuses" intended to convey a moving picture of what was happening in and to the economy as a whole.[4]

The war experience also helped to change attitudes about the value and practical utility of the economist's product and potential product. Creden-tialed economic inquiry, a number of prominent government and business figures had come to believe, could greatly enhance a society's capacity for planning and purposeful management. Such inquiry could, if properly conducted and applied, turn "drift" into "mastery." Within the economics profession, a number of "activists" were also articulating a similar vision of its potential social contribution. They would concede that their wartime achievements had been limited—that the mobilization had revealed not only how much of a social need for economic knowledge there was but

[3]The most notable attachments of this sort had been to such congressionally authorized investigatory bodies as the Industrial Commission of 1898–1902, the National Monetary Commission of 1908–12, and the Industrial Relations Commission of 1912–5; executive branch agencies such as the Bureau of Corporations, Interstate Commerce Commission, Federal Reserve Board, Federal Trade Commission, Bureau of Labor Statistics, and Tariff Commission; private organizations such as the National Civic Federation and the Ameri-can Association for Labor Legislation; and state commissions and legislative reference services such as those established in Wisconsin and New York. The Federal Reserve Board is generally regarded as the first permanent agency of the federal government to have a trained staff of economic investigators. See Paul B. Cook, *Academicians in Government from Roosevelt to Roosevelt* (New York: Garland, 1982), 48–53, 62–79; Furner, *Advo-cacy and Objectivity,* 268–71; Daniel Nelson, *Unemployment Insurance: The American Experience, 1915–1935* (Madison: University of Wisconsin Press, 1969), 13–6.

[4]See Guy Alchon, *The Invisible Hand of Planning: Capitalism, Social Science, and the State in the 1920s* (Princeton, N.J.: Princeton University Press, 1985), 26–32; Herbert Heaton, *A Scholar in Action: Edwin F. Gay* (Cambridge: Harvard University Press, 1952), 98–129; Zenas L. Potter, "The Central Bureau of Planning and Statistics," *Quarterly Publications of the American Statistical Association* 16 (March 1919): 275–85; A. W. Coats, "The American Economic Association, 1904–1929," *American Economic Review* 54 (June 1964): 278–80; Dorfman, *Economic Mind,* III, 473–85; Gene M. Lyons, *The Uneasy Partnership: Social Science and the Federal Government in the Twentieth Century* (New York: Russell Sage Foundation, 1969), 26–9.

how little of it the credentialed experts possessed and could bring to bear on war problems. But given proper societal support, they argued, economists could develop their discipline and produce the kind of knowledge and information required. Such were the themes expounded at a joint meeting of the American Economic Association and the American Statistical Association in December 1918, and these same themes would remain prominent in the subsequent quest for societal support.[5]

One possibility for achieving the desired support lay in retaining some form of the administrative apparatus that had been added to the American state during the war. The United States, in other words, might be equipped with a permanent Peace Industries Board, Industrial Cabinet, or Council of National Progress, which would establish bureaus of economic science and divisions of research and planning to help them carry out their administrative assignments. This approach had its advocates, and for a time such advocates were relatively optimistic about the prospects for implementing their designs. But as it turned out, those with the power to create and fund new agencies could not be persuaded that such an apparatus was needed or that it could be fitted into America's design for balancing order with liberty. A political culture rooted in a mixture of Lockean liberalism and classical republicanism might concentrate power in the hands of temporary emergency managers but had yet to develop an accepted place for permanent ones. And a polity in which power had traditionally been lodged in parties, courts, local units, and organized interests also proved strongly resistant to the idea of a permanent managerial establishment, especially after it became clear that the postwar aspirants to membership in it could not command the deference and trust that an America at war had given the managerial elite it drew from the private sector. In the end, economists who had hoped to institutionalize their wartime position in this manner found that they could salvage little. A remnant of the Central Bureau of Planning and Statistics briefly survived, primarily by providing data for the postwar peace negotiators, but was then abolished.[6]

[5]Irving Fisher, "Economists in the Public Service," *American Economic Review Supplement* 9 (March 1919): 5–21; Wesley C. Mitchell, "Statistics and Government," *Quarterly Publications of the American Statistical Association* 16 (March 1919): 223–36. See also Alchon, *Invisible Hand of Planning,* 33–42; Dorfman, *Economic Mind,* III, 493–4.

[6]See Burl Noggle, *Into the Twenties: The United States from Armistice to Normalcy* (Urbana: University of Illinois Press, 1974), 46–65; James R. Mock and Evangeline Thurber, *Report on Demobilization* (Norman: University of Oklahoma Press, 1944); William Hoyt Moore, "Post-Armistice Industrial Developments, 1918–1920," Labor Department History Study #58 (1943), copy in Box 10, Edward Eyre Hunt Papers, Hoover Institution

Still, if government could not be equipped with a peacetime managerial establishment, there were many who saw the postwar economic gyrations and the accompanying labor turmoil and social distress as strong evidence that economic forces did need to be managed. And in the context thus created, there were other channels through which the war's legacy of managerial impulses and visions continued to find expression. It did so particularly in an array of designs for building a managerial capacity into society itself, partly through the formation of new institutions of economic self-government, and partly through the creation of a scientific informational base that could have both an enabling and an integrating function. Falling into this pattern, for example, were the projects being pushed by such organizations as the National Civic Federation and the American Association for Labor Legislation, by the promoters of a variety of private-sector "institutes" and "surveys," and especially by the engineering profession under the leadership of former war manager Herbert Hoover. As president of the new Federated American Engineering Societies, he persuaded his fellow professionals to support a much-publicized Waste Survey intended both to demonstrate the need for management and to stimulate appropriate institutional formation.[7]

Consequently, even in the absence of a managerial state, several possibilities of creating a new institutional base for a managerial economics existed:

1. Linkages could be forged between the universities and the new projects for equipping society with a managerial capacity—linkages that

Archives (HIA); Moore, "Dissolution of the War Industries Board and Release of Its Industry Controls," Labor Department Historical Study #56 (1942), copy in Box 9, Hunt Papers, HIA; Robert F. Himmelberg, "The War Industries Board and the Antitrust Question," *Journal of American History* 52 (June 1965): 59–74; Robert Cuff, "Harry Garfield, the Fuel Administration, and the Search for a Cooperative Order During World War I," *American Quarterly* 30 (Spring 1978): 39–53; Alchon, *Invisible Hand of Planning*, 35–7; Heaton, *Scholar in Action*, 131–6.
[7] John B. Andrews, "Unemployment Prevention and Insurance," *American Labor Legislation Review* 10 (December 1920): 233–9; Marguerite Green, *The National Civic Federation and the American Labor Movement, 1900–1925* (Washington, D.C.: Catholic University Press, 1956), 394–413, 436–49; Edwin T. Layton, Jr., *The Revolt of the Engineers* (Cleveland: Case Western Reserve University Press, 1971), 172–204; David W. Eakins, "The Origins of Corporate Liberal Policy Research, 1917–1922," in Jerry Israel, ed., *Building the Organizational Society* (New York: Free Press, 1972), 163–79; Alchon, *Invisible Hand of Planning*, 42–8, 63–7; Federated American Engineering Societies, *Waste in Industry* (1921); Ellis W. Hawley, " 'Industrial Policy' in the 1920s and 1930s," in Claude Barfield and William Schambra, eds., *The Politics of Industrial Policy* (Washington, D.C.: American Enterprise Institute, 1986), 64–6; William J. Barber, *From New Era to New Deal: Herbert Hoover, the Economists, and American Economic Policy, 1921–1933* (Cambridge, Eng.: Cambridge University Press, 1985), 2–5, 7–41.

might eventually be made strong enough to command regular university appropriations and to support continuing programs of research and disciplinary development.

2. Similar linkages could be developed for a professional organization, either the economists' own or one built on an alliance with engineering and management science, and then these could be strengthened in ways that would allow the organization to establish and maintain the needed institutional base.

3. The new managerial impulses could be linked to interest-group initiatives, and interest-group politics could be relied on to produce social scientific bureaus comparable to the bureaus of natural science that had already become established parts of such departments as Agriculture, Interior, and Commerce.

4. The managerial impulses could be linked to a philanthropic establishment increasingly concerned with social problems, managerial economics could be made part of the social science that philanthropic endeavor should now support, and then these connections could be used to create a privately funded but publicly oriented and scientifically minded institutional base.

To some extent, all these approaches would be tried in the 1920s.[8] But it was only the latter two—the interest-group route taken by the builders of the Bureau of Agricultural Economics and the privatism as an alternative approach exemplified in the founding and subsequent workings of the National Bureau of Economic Research—that succeeded in producing some semblance of the institutional base being sought. It was in these ways—despite the absence of a managerial state, the presence of strong antimanagerial reactions invoking traditional cultural values and orthodox economic postulates, and the ultimate failure of the projects for equipping society with a managerial capacity—that economic inquiry oriented toward purposeful management of economic forces continued to

[8]The efforts to develop university-based agencies included the Industrial Research Department at the University of Pennsylvania's Wharton School, the Committee on Economic Research at Harvard, the Institute for Research in Land Economics and Public Utilities at Wisconsin (later Northwestern), and the Food Research Institute at Stanford. An Institute of Economic Research under the auspices of the American Economic Association was proposed and debated but never established. See Alchon, *Invisible Hand of Planning*, 49–50; Coats, "American Economic Association, 1904–1929," 281–2; Fisher, "Economists in Public Service," 19–21; Dorfman, *Economic Mind*, IV, 198–9, 212; Sass, *Pragmatic Imagination*, 180, 208–13; Wesley C. Mitchell, "Institutes for Research in the Social Sciences," *Journal of Proceedings and Addresses of the Association of American Universities* (1930), 62–70.

be supported and to produce a body of knowledge that would be put to use in the 1930s and 1940s. It was also in these ways that the American state acquired new administrative capacities in some economic sectors while failing to acquire them in others, a development that would affect what that state could and could not do after 1929. And it is to a closer and more detailed examination of the BAE and NBER experiences that the remainder of this chapter is devoted.

THE BUREAU OF AGRICULTURAL ECONOMICS, 1922–1930

Officially, the Bureau of Agricultural Economics was born on July 1, 1922, its establishment taking place under the agricultural appropriation act of that year. But the roots of this action extend back to the prewar years, particularly to the prewar relationships that developed between the Office of Farm Management in the Department of Agriculture and the new departments and programs of agricultural economics that were then appearing in the land-grant colleges. Inherent in these relationships was the potential for departmental research in the social as well as the natural sciences. And it was by strengthening these relationships and training people for the office's new economic work that Henry C. Taylor, head of the recently established Department of Agricultural Economics at the University of Wisconsin and author of the first textbook in the field, made himself the logical choice to head a new Office of Farm Management and Farm Economics established in the wake of the department's war work. Once in government, moreover, Taylor became the key figure in carrying through on the implications of his assignment. It was largely through his initiatives that the reorganization plan finally implemented in 1922—the plan that would create the BAE and make him its first chief—became a project strongly supported by his fellow professionals, enthusiastically embraced by the secretary of agriculture (first E. T. Meredith, then Henry C. Wallace), and readily approved by Congress.[9]

[9]The origins of the bureau are traced in Harry C. McDean, "Professionalism, Policy, and Farm Economists in the Early Bureau of Agricultural Economics," *Agricultural History* 57 (January 1983): 64–82; Donald L. Winters, *Henry Cantwell Wallace as Secretary of Agriculture* (Urbana: University of Illinois Press, 1970), 109–16; John M. Gaus and Leon Wolcott, *Public Administration and the United States Department of Agriculture* (Chicago: Public Administration Service, 1940), 35–50; A. G. Black, "Agricultural Policy and the Economist," *Journal of Farm Economics* 18 (May 1936): 311–9; and Lloyd S. Tenny, "The Bureau of Agricultural Economics in the Early Years," *Journal of Farm Economics* 29 (November 1947): 1017–26. See also *B.A.E. News*, June 13, 1922; "Conclusions of Conference Held January 20, 1922"; E. E. Edwards, "Historical Background of the Bureau

On organizational charts the action in 1922 appeared merely as a bureaucratic merger between the Office of Farm Management and Farm Economics and the Bureau of Markets and Crop Estimates. But what the charts could not capture was the effect of the establishment of the BAE in elevating and providing a major institutional base for the work being done in a special branch of managerial economics with its own unique developmental history and disciplinary consciousness. Establishment of the BAE meant, as subsequent developments would make clear, that this work would now be given priority over the management and commodity work previously done by people whose professional credentials were in agronomy rather than economics. And it meant that a branch of economics that traced its roots to Germany rather than England, that had arisen in the context of state-supported practical education rather than traditional learning, that had early begun justifying itself as a provider of socially needed managerial tools, and that had drawn from its connection with the agricultural sciences an early penchant for and proficiency in using statistical techniques would now become the branch most directly and generously supported by the American state.

With this support, moreover, agricultural economics would by the late 1920s become a branch noted not only for its progress in data accumulation but also for its innovativeness and its increasing sophistication in research design and analytical technique. Although it might still be relatively low in the pecking order of economists as a whole, partly because it had emerged and become institutionalized outside the more prestigious departments of economics, it had moved into the vanguard of efforts to produce an economic knowledge that could be used for managerial manipulation.[10]

of Agricultural Economics," February 24, 1939, all in Records Relating to the History of Agricultural Economics, Record Group 83 (B.A.E.), National Archives.

[10]McDean, "Professionalism, Policy, and Farm Economists," 72–5; John D. Black, "The Progress of Research in Agricultural Economics in the United States," *Scientific Agriculture* 9 (October 1928): 69–79; Black, "The Development and Organization of Agricultural Economics in the United States" [1927]; Margaret Purcell, "A Quarter Century of Land Economics in the Department of Agriculture, 1919–1944" [1945]; T. W. Schultz, "Scope and Method in Agricultural Economic Research" (n.d.); and Merill K. Bennett, "Historical Development of Farm Cost Investigation" [1928], all in Taylor File, Record Group 83 (B.A.E.), National Archives; G. F. Warren, "The Origin and Development of Farm Economics in the United States," *Journal of Farm Economics* 14 (January 1932): 2–9; Henry C. Taylor, "Early History of Agricultural Economics," *Journal of Farm Economics* 22 (February 1940): 84–97; Mordecai Ezekiel, "The Broadening Field of Agricultural Economics," *Journal of Farm Economics* 19 (February 1937): 96–101; H. R. Tolley, "Recent Developments in Research Method and Procedures in Agricultural Economics," *Journal of Farm Economics* 12 (April 1930): 213–30; Sherman E. Johnson and Kenneth

Also evident in the action of 1922 and its aftermath was Taylor's application of a political formula that had allowed former scientist-administrators to become "bureau builders" and produce the network of scientific bureaus that made up most of the federal scientific establishment. As A. Hunter Dupree spelled it out in his classic *Science in the Federal Government,* the formula included adoption of a "problem approach," a "little constitution" expressed in an organic act, a cohesive corps of scientific professionals, a carefully cultivated group of congressional friends, an outside group interested in the bureau's welfare, a working relationship with one or more universities, and a yoking of the bureau's science to regulatory and routine service activities.[11] This was the formula that had worked for such "bureau builders" as John Wesley Powell, Harvey W. Wiley, Gifford Pinchot, and S. W. Stratton, both because it produced organizational forms superbly suited to the way power was distributed in the American polity and, as Don K. Price has noted, because America had no "administrative class" blocking the entry of credentialed scientists into the higher realms of its civil service.[12]

The formula was also potentially workable for social scientists; and just as agriculture had been the area in which it had produced the first bureaus of natural science, it now became the area in which it produced the first social scientific one. In the BAE economists became engaged not only in using their skills to provide informational services but also in developing their discipline and expanding the frontiers of knowledge, which in a major respect made them closer to the scientists in Agriculture's Bureau of Chemistry than to the technicians and economists used by agencies such as the Bureau of Labor Statistics and the Survey of Current Business.

Indeed, the situation in which Taylor's plan for the BAE was implemented seemed almost made to order for an application of the formula that had worked to produce the federal bureaus of natural science. A

Bachman, "Development of Production Economics in Agriculture," in James P. Cavin, ed., *Economics for Agriculture* (Cambridge, Mass.: Harvard University Press, 1959).

[11] A. Hunter Dupree, *Science in the Federal Government: A History of Policies and Activities* (Cambridge, Mass.: Harvard University Press, 1957), 158–61. See also Margaret W. Rossiter, "The Organization of the Agricultural Sciences," in Alexandra Oleson and John Voss, eds., *The Organization of Knowledge in Modern America, 1860–1920* (Baltimore: Johns Hopkins University Press, 1976), 211–42; Charles E. Rosenberg, "Science, Technology, and Economic Growth: The Case of the Agricultural Experiment Station Scientist, 1875–1914," *Agricultural History* 45 (January 1971): 1–20; and Don K. Price, *Government and Science* (New York: New York University Press, 1954), 14–16.

[12] Don K. Price, *The Scientific Estate* (Cambridge, Mass.: Harvard University Press, 1965), 59–67; Price, *Government and Science*, 22–5.

politically recognized "farm problem" existed, creating potential support for a social science properly oriented toward the problem's solution. A "little constitution" could be created under the established charter of a politically secure department. A cohesive group of credentialed competents could be assembled, thanks to the networks built earlier and a professionalization process that had recently produced the American Farm Economic Association. An "agricultural establishment" of intertwining government, interest-group, and educational institutions, an establishment to which the "bureau builders" in some degree already belonged, could, if properly cultivated, provide the requisite congressional friends, outside supporters, and university connections. And the recent moves of the Department of Agriculture into areas such as market news services and trade practice regulation provided a politically viable complex of regulatory and service activity to which the BAE's social science could be plausibly linked. The major difference was that the "bureau builders" were now asking the American polity to act as if social science were equivalent to the natural variety. But even accomplishing this was made easier by the statistical component and scientific posture that their particular social science had possessed from its very beginning.[13]

Structurally, moreover, the BAE quickly arrived at an organizational form that was relatively successful in combining a capacity for political survival with an ability to preserve the autonomy and respectability of those doing its social scientific work. Initially, Taylor and his associates had envisaged seven major subunits, concerned, respectively, with the economics of land, labor, capital, geography, organization, production, and living standards. But the structure of power within the "agricultural establishment" and the larger national polity meant that the plans for some units had to be modified and more attention paid to the inclusion of politically supported regulatory, educational, and service work. The geography and labor units, for example, became small subdivisions of the unit on land economics; those on organizational and living standards became a division of "farm life" studies; and instead of a single production unit, there appeared a number of production and marketing divisions specialized according to commodity or managerial functions.

As organized by 1924, the BAE had managed to establish what amounted to a public research institute, complete with research director, graduate school, and research projects. But this research organization

---

[13]McDean, "Professionalism, Policy, and Farm Economists," 64–5, 74–82; Henry C. and Anne Dewees Taylor, *The Story of Agricultural Economics in the United States* (Ames: Iowa State College Press, 1952), 80–98, 602–6; Lyons, *Uneasy Partnership*, 31–3.

was also linked to and integrated with a centrally coordinated complex of operating divisions, engaged in generally approved lines of production, marketing, financial, organizational, educational, regulatory, foreign relations, rural betterment, and land use work. It was a structure, as subsequent developments showed, that had a remarkable capacity to weather political and bureaucratic attacks while attracting and holding some of the best talent in the agricultural economics field.[14]

Eventually, under the New Deal, the BAE would also become the planning agency for a new managerial apparatus using government power for purposeful management of the agricultural sector. But in the 1920s, even though Taylor and some of his associates had few philosophical qualms about using the power of the state for managerial purposes, the BAE's impetus toward the New Deal form of positive statism could never break through the antistatist barriers associated with the retention of freedom and extolled by the period's most successful politicians. Instead, the BAE turned to its own distinctive version of the idea that managerial capacity could be built into the society itself, and proceeded on the assumption that it could turn the decision makers of the agricultural sector into a system-conscious managerial group for which it could then serve as an intelligence and planning agency. This was the assumption underlying its new Outlook program begun in 1923, a program that combined scientifically prepared outlook reports on farm markets and producer "intentions" with elaborate exercises in "production planning" and "continuous adjustment" carried on through national and local conferences, collaborating farm groups, and agricultural extension work. And even though the capacities and adjustments thus envisaged never really materialized, the links thus forged to the period's managerial impulses and projects worked to enhance the BAE's respectability and capacity for survival.[15]

[14]McDean, "Professionalism, Policy, and Farm Economists," 66–76; Gaus and Wolcott, *Public Administration and U.S.D.A.*, 51–3; C. W. Kitchen to C. H. Wooddy, April 8, 1932, listing old and new activities of BAE, in President's Research Committee on Social Trends File, General Correspondence, Record Group 83 (B.A.E.), National Archives; U.S. Department of Agriculture, *Agriculture Yearbook, 1924* (1925), 22–49; Gladys L. Baker et al., *Century of Service: The First Hundred Years of the United States Department of Agriculture* (Washington, D.C.: U.S. Government Printing Office, 1963), 107–8, 112–3.
[15]David E. Hamilton, "Neglected Aspects of the New Era Managerial Impulse: The Bureau of Agricultural Economics in the 1920s," paper presented at a meeting of the Organization of American Historians, April 4, 1987; Taylor and Taylor, *Story of Agricultural Economics*, 449–79; Winters, *Henry C. Wallace*, 119–23; Gaus and Wolcott, *Public Administration and U.S.D.A.*, 50–1, 311–2; Lyons, *Uneasy Partnership*, 55–63; John D. Black, "The Bureau of Agricultural Economics—The Years in Between," *Journal of Farm Economics* 29 (November 1947): 1027–42; H. R. Tolley, "The History and Objectives of Outlook Work," *Journal of Farm Economics* 13 (October 1931): 523–34.

Similar assumptions also underlay two other major research programs undertaken by the BAE, both of which, like the Outlook activities, were linked to an emerging theory of agricultural markets that recognized the perverse capacity of price declines to generate increases in production and the consequent inappropriateness of laissez-faire remedies for agricultural distress. One program produced the bureau's massive "type of farming" studies, aimed at determining what crops and livestock could best be produced in hundreds of different regions. In theory, these findings could be used to develop new farming specializations suited to the comparative advantages of particular regions, to facilitate a gradual regional readjustment in resources and their use, and thus to achieve the "order" and "direction" that a modern agricultural sector required if it were to perform the tasks being assigned to it.[16] The other program produced the BAE's equally massive "land use inventory," aimed at using the expertise of land economists to describe and classify all lands of uncertain value and adaptability. This inventory, it was believed, could eventually allow the BAE and the state extension services to provide "unbiased" information to prospective land buyers and settlers, thus transforming them into participants in a "land use planning" system that could correct the misuse responsible for the agricultural sector's current waste of both natural and human resources.[17] And again, even though these research programs never developed the sectoral capacities envisaged in their justifying theories, their general compatibility with the era's managerial designs and assumptions further enhanced the BAE's respectability and capacity for survival.

This is not to say, however, that the BAE experienced no political problems or political setbacks. It was troubled from the beginning by friction between the economists and employees originally trained in agronomy. The BAE became involved in clashes with southern cotton interests, with bureaus engaged in land reclamation and foreign service

[16]Bradford Smith, "The Adjustment of Agricultural Production to Demand," *Journal of Farm Economics* 8 (April 1926): 145–65; Hamilton, "Neglected Aspects of New Era Managerial Impulse," 8–9; Jesse Tapp, "The Principle of Comparative Advantage Applied to Farm Management Studies of Regional Competition between Farmers," *Journal of Farm Economics* 8 (October 1926): 417–26; F. F. Elliott, "The 'Representative Firm' Idea Applied to Research and Extension in Agricultural Economics," *Journal of Farm Economics* 10 (October 1928): 483–98.

[17]Hamilton, "Neglected Aspects of New Era Managerial Impulse," 9–10; L. C. Gray, "National Land Policies in Retrospect and Prospect," *Journal of Farm Economics* 13 (April 1931): 231–45; L. C. Gray, "Results of Research in Land Economics That Point the Way to a National Land Policy," *Proceedings of the Thirty-ninth Annual Convention of the Association of Land-Grant Colleges and Universities* (1927): 193–200.

work, and with proponents of "unscientific" or "special interest" solutions to the farm problem. It undertook to provide "ammunition" for the department's policy arguments, especially during the congressional session of 1924. And partly because of its role in these policy debates, it became involved in what amounted to bureaucratic warfare with Herbert Hoover's Commerce Department, a warfare in which the death of Secretary Wallace in late 1924 allowed Hoover to get the upper hand, influence the choice of Wallace's successor, and eventually secure the ouster of Taylor as BAE chief.

Yet even with its wings thus clipped and with the less-than-sympathetic hearing that its projects received from the new secretary of agriculture, William M. Jardine, the BAE's research activities and efforts to create new managerial and planning capacities continued to grow. Its budget expanded from less than $3 million in fiscal year 1923 to over $6 million in fiscal 1929; and by 1930 the BAE was clearly developing into one of the nation's foremost economic research institutions. By that time it was employing more social scientists than all other agencies of the federal government combined; among them were such distinguished economists as Howard Tolley, M. L. Wilson, Mordecai Ezekiel, Frederich Waugh, Louis Bean, L. C. Gray, and O. E. Baker.[18]

The BAE had not solved the farm problem. But its creators and developers had shown one way in which credentialed economic inquiry geared to managerial uses could be institutionalized in a government lacking any apparatus for national economic management. And both this institutionalization and the new knowledge thus produced would matter in the decade that followed.

THE NATIONAL BUREAU OF ECONOMIC RESEARCH,
1920–1930

The logical counterpart to the story of the BAE would have been the emergence, through similar processes, of a Bureau of Industrial Economics in the Department of Commerce. Yet no such bureau emerged, partly

[18]McDean, "Professionalism, Policy, and Farm Economists," 76–7; Winters, *Henry C. Wallace,* 120–1, 136–8, 222–6, 236–44; Hamilton, "Neglected Aspects of the New Era Managerial Impulse"; Tenny, "BAE—The Early Years," 1019–20, 1025–6; Department of Agriculture, *Bureau of Agricultural Economics* (reprint from Miscellaneous Publication No. 88, 1930), copy in Records Relating to the History of Agricultural Economics, Record Group 83 (B.A.E.), National Archives; Agricultural Appropriation Act, 42 *U.S. Statutes* 507, at 531–2, Public Laws, No. 217, 67th Cong., 2d Sess. (1922); *Report of the Secretary of Agriculture* (1929), 109; (1930), 93.

perhaps because of Herbert Hoover's antistatist proclivities, but also because of major differences in the institutional and cultural contexts involved. The Commerce Department, to be sure, had its counterparts to the problem orientation, the service and regulatory activity, and the efforts to develop managerial capacity that were parts of the BAE story. All were features of the "Hooverization" that the department was undergoing.[19] Also available was a managerial economics that was concerned with improving the performance of the industrial system—an economics that Hoover was eager to connect with his departmental machinery.[20] But there was nothing really comparable to the "agricultural establishment" that had given the creators of the BAE their bureau-building model, political standing, and highly developed sense of professional identity and solidarity. American business schools, unlike their agricultural counterparts, had emerged as privately supported institutions without much of a research function, either in the sciences or social sciences.[21] They reflected a business mentality that continued to fear a "politicization" of the market and to distrust academic input into "practical" matters in ways that mobilized agricultural groups had not. And the natural science used in industry, unlike that used in agriculture, had only a few outposts in the federal government. It centered instead in the laboratories supported by corporations, trade associations, and the research arms of business-supported private universities.[22]

One result of these differences was that the industrial branch of managerial economics, as developed by such economists as Wesley C. Mitchell and Edwin Gay, lacked the connections and attitudes necessary to estab-

[19]See Ellis W. Hawley, "Herbert Hoover, the Commerce Secretariat, and the Vision of an 'Associative State,' 1921–1928," *Journal of American History* 51 (June 1974): 116–40.
[20]In particular, he wanted Wesley C. Mitchell, the central figure in the field, to join the department as economic adviser. "If this Department is to become the economic interpreter to the American people (and they badly need one)," he wrote, "it has simply got to be stiffened up with stronger economic operators." Hoover to Mitchell, July 29, 1921, in Lucy Sprague Mitchell, *Two Lives: The Story of Wesley Clair Mitchell and Myself* (New York: Simon & Schuster, 1953), 364–5.
[21]Frank C. Pierson and others, *The Education of American Businessmen* (New York: McGraw-Hill, 1959), 35–49, 310–13; Sass, *Pragmatic Imagination*, 208–9. By the 1920s a number of business schools had bureaus of business or industrial research. But with the exception of those at Harvard and Wharton, these were small affairs; and the Harvard bureau was concerned mostly with providing case studies for teaching purposes. The traditional concern of business schools had been with transmitting knowledge for use in business careers rather than creating knowledge in a major area of learning.
[22]John Rae, "The Application of Science to Industry," in Oleson and Voss, eds., *Organization of Knowledge*, 249–68; L. P. Alford, "Technical Changes in Manufacturing Industries," and Henry S. Dennison, "Management," in *Recent Economic Changes in the United States* (New York: McGraw-Hill, 1929), 106–11, 499.

lish itself in a tax-supported Bureau of Industrial Economics. Its disposition, given the connections and models available to it, was to seek a new institutional base in the private sector. And although this produced a few university-based agencies, like the Wharton School's Industrial Research Department and Harvard's Committee on Economic Research, its major output was institutional arrangements through which credentialed members of the discipline were able to combine regularized tapping of the nation's philanthropic resources with credible claims of national service and effective preservation of their professional autonomy and respectability. In essence, the emergence of a professionalized philanthropic establishment and the rise within it of men who shared the postwar hopes for a new social science geared to managerial uses had made possible a privatist alternative to the route taken by the founders of the BAE.[23]

In time, the application of this privatist formula would produce a variety of "think tanks" specializing in "public service" forms of economic inquiry.[24] But the pioneer in this process, and the one that emerged at the center of an apparatus in which government officials helped to secure the private funding and make the new knowledge available to the intended users, was the National Bureau of Economic Research, which Wesley Mitchell and Edwin Gay helped to establish in February 1920.

[23]See Barry D. Karl and Stanley N. Katz, "The American Private Philanthropic Foundation and the Public Sphere, 1890–1930," *Minerva* 19 (Summer 1981): 236–70, especially 246–8, 266–8; and Alchon, *Invisible Hand of Planning*, 10–11, 75, 117–23. The Wharton and Harvard operations are discussed in Sass, *Pragmatic Imagination*, 180, 108–213, and in Dorfman, *Economic Mind*, IV, 199.

[24]The most prominent, aside from the NBER, was the Brookings Institute of Economics, established in 1922 under the direction of Harold Moulton. It did studies relevant to policy issues, especially in the areas of international economics, industrial relations, agriculture, the tariff, and the coal industry. But it never developed the connections to government projects or the apparatus of quasi-official sponsoring committees that became characteristic of the NBER. Hoover was one of the trustees initially, but resigned after a controversy over its tariff recommendations. Other organizations sometimes listed as "think tanks" were the Twentieth Century Fund, the Pollak Foundation for Economic Research, and the National Industrial Conference Board. But the first two were driven by the idiosyncratic visions of their founders, Edward A. Filene and Waddill Catchings, and the third was generally regarded as a "business" rather than a "public service" organization. In Harold Moulton's view, for example, it was a "very partisan organization supported by the manufacturing interests of the country." See Donald T. Critchlow, *The Brookings Institution, 1916–1952: Expertise and the Public Interest in a Democratic Society* (DeKalb: Northern Illinois University Press, 1985), 56–76; Eakins, "Origins of Corporate Liberal Policy Research," 174–5; H. M. Gitelman, "Management's Crisis of Confidence and the Origins of the National Industrial Conference Board," *Business History Review* 58 (Summer 1985): 153–77; Dorfman, *Economic Mind*, IV, 340–51; Critchlow, "Think Tanks, Antistatism, and Democracy: The Nonpartisan Ideal and Policy Research in the United States, 1913–1987," in Michael J. Lacey and Mary O. Furner, eds., *The State and Social Investigation in Britain and America* (forthcoming).

Again, as in the case of the BAE, the roots of the NBER stretched back to the prewar years. From 1914 on, Gay and Mitchell had been involved in efforts to establish an economic research institute modeled after the Rockefeller Institute for Medical Research and engaged especially in studies of the national income; and from 1916 on, they had been working with Malcolm C. Rorty, an electrical engineer and statistician with American Telephone and Telegraph, to develop an appropriate institute design. But not until 1920, in the context of the managerial visions and professional aspirations flowing from the war experience, were they successful in securing the funding, staff, directors, and endorsements to put the design into operation. The postwar context made it possible not only to interest other major economists and recruit an influential board of directors but also to secure a founding grant from the new Commonwealth Fund and begin an active endowment campaign.[25]

In designing the new organization, Mitchell, Gay, and Rorty had given careful thought to the kind of structural arrangements that would help to establish its output as authoritative and unbiased. It must be capable, they believed, not only of ascertaining the "facts" but of getting them accepted as such in the arenas where economic and political decisions were being made. And it must therefore combine mechanisms that would ensure professional competence and integrity with machinery for securing the testimony of the "interests" as to its neutral and "disinterested" status. Its board of directors, as finally constructed, was to include not only men of differing political views and representatives of the relevant professional organizations (i.e., those in economics, statistics, engineering, and law) but also representatives of organized business, labor, finance, and agriculture. Its composition resembled that of a corporatist "social unit" or "economic parliament"; and as such, it would deliberate on the research product, decide whether or not it should be published, and allow those who disagreed with a favorable publication decision to submit minority reports for inclusion in the publication.[26]

---

[25]The best and most recent account of the bureau's origins is in Alchon, *Invisible Hand of Planning*, 52–9. See also Eakins, "Origins of Corporate Liberal Policy Research," 166–7, 176–7; N. I. Stone, "The Beginnings of the National Bureau of Economic Research," in Wesley Mitchell, ed., *The National Bureau's First Quarter Century* (New York: NBER, 1945); and "The Origins and Function of the NBER" (a talk by George E. May), March 3, 1925, in Series X, Wesley C. Mitchell Papers, Columbia University.

[26]Alchon, *Invisible Hand of Planning*, 56–8. The ten directors representing different views were Mitchell, Gay, N. I. Stone, Harry W. Laidler, John P. Frey, Allyn Young, Thomas S. Adams, Elwood Mead, John R. Commons, and J. E. Sterret. The organizations having representatives were the American Economic Association, American Statistical Associa-

Initially, the NBER, with Gay as its first president and Mitchell as research director, concentrated its efforts on devising and carrying through a sophisticated study of national income that became, when finished, both a vindication of empirical methods and a milestone in the development of national income accounting.[27] But almost from the beginning, in view of the severe recession beginning in late 1920 and of Mitchell's established expertise in the field,[28] the NBER also became interested in mounting a major study of the business cycle. Such a study was under consideration in 1921, at a time when Mitchell and Gay were serving on the committees that helped to launch the Commerce Department's Survey of Current Business and implement Hoover's plan for a President's Conference on Unemployment (PCOU). And it was in the interaction of this project with actions establishing a PCOU Standing Committee to organize further studies of business fluctuations that the NBER's capacity to draw support from the state had its origins. In a pattern that would repeat itself in subsequent years, Hoover accepted a proposal from Mitchell and Gay that their organization serve as the PCOU's fact-finding body, worked with them to organize a sponsoring Business Cycle Committee that would carry the facts into "practical application," and accepted responsibility for approaching the foundations to secure the necessary

tion, American Engineering Council, American Bar Association, Chamber of Commerce of the United States, National Industrial Conference Board, American Bankers Association, American Federation of Labor, and American Federation of Farm Bureaus. Initially, there were also plans for having representatives from the Federal Reserve Board and the federal government's economics departments, but these were dropped when the Commonwealth Fund raised objections to "political" appointees. Subsequently, the NICB, Chamber of Commerce, and American Bar Association would be dropped from the roster of organizations represented, and the National Personnel Association (which later became the American Management Association) and Periodical Publishers Association (later known as the National Publishers Association) were added. Also, beginning in 1927, six universities (Harvard, Yale, Columbia, Chicago, Wisconsin, and the Wharton School) would have representatives on the board. See the "prefatory notes" to *Publications* 1 through 10 (1921–7).

[27] Alchon, *Invisible Hand of Planning*, 59–63; Arthur F. Burns, "Wesley Mitchell and the National Bureau," in National Bureau of Economic Research, *Twenty-ninth Annual Report* (1949), 32–3. The published results included *Income in the United States: Its Amount and Distribution, 1909–1919*, I (1921) and II (1922), and *Distribution of Income by States in 1919* (1922). The key figures in the research team were Willford I. King and Oswald W. Knauth.

[28] Mitchell was most noted as an expert on business cycles, a reputation based on his *Business Cycles* (Berkeley: University of California Press, 1913). In this work, he had broken from classical conceptions of cycles as equilibrium disruptions to argue that they were "systematically generated by economic organization itself." As he saw it, a theory of business cycles and their control, based on empirical study of cyclical behavior, could become a theory of capitalism itself and its control. See Burns, "Mitchell and the National Bureau," 23–6, 36–44.

funding. This became his way of combining "the prestige of the Unemployment Conference, the business judgment of large employers, and the technical equipment of the National Bureau" so as to create an American alternative to European statism.[29]

The first demonstration of what these arrangements could produce came in the resulting *Business Cycles* study and the accompanying exercises in seeking to develop a societal capacity for "stabilization planning" and business cycle prevention. Funded by the Carnegie Corporation, the study was conducted by a staff of NBER and collaborating experts under Mitchell's direction.[30] It was interpreted and given "practical application" by the PCOU sponsoring committee under the chairmanship of industrialist Owen D. Young,[31] and was then made the subject of an

[29]Burns, "Mitchell and the National Bureau," 36–7; Alchon, *Invisible Hand of Planning,* 71–85; Edward Eyre Hunt to Hoover, October 21, 1921; Hunt, "Study of Business Cycles," October 20, 1921, both in Unemployment—Business Cycles File, Commerce Files, Herbert Hoover Papers (HHP), Hoover Presidential Library; Hoover to Henry S. Pritchett, November 18, 1921; Hunt to Pritchett, December 21, 1921; Edwin Gay to Hoover, October 22, 1921; Mitchell, "Purpose, Scope, and Character of the Report upon Unemployment and Business Cycles"; Hunt to Owen D. Young, February 13, 1922, all in Unemployment—NBER File, Commerce Files, HHP; Mitchell to Hunt, February 28, 1922, in Unemployment—Mitchell File, Commerce Files, HHP. Hunt, who had been secretary of the Waste Survey and was now secretary of the PCOU Standing Committee, initially thought that the engineers should have a role in the investigation and that the NBER's economic experts should work with those at the Harvard and Wharton business schools, the leading banks, and the U.S. Chamber of Commerce, but he soon accepted Mitchell's plan.

[30]Committee on Business Cycles and Unemployment of the President's Conference on Unemployment, *Business Cycles and Unemployment, Including an Investigation Made under the Auspices of the National Bureau of Economic Research* (New York: McGraw-Hill, 1923). The principal investigators were Mitchell, Willford King, Oswald Knauth, and Frederick Macauley of the NBER, Leo Wolman of the New School for Social Research, Stuart Rice and Paul Brissendon of Columbia, William Berridge of Brown, Ernest S. Bradford of the American Statistical Association, John B. Andrews of the American Association for Labor Legislation, Otto Mallery of the Pennsylvania State Industrial Board, Julius Parmalee of the Bureau of Railway Economics, Mary Van Kleeck and Shelby Harrison of the Russell Sage Foundation, L. W. Wallace of the Federated American Engineering Societies, Thomas S. Adams of Yale, consulting engineer Sanford Thompson, and trade association lawyer Gilbert Montague.

[31]The other members were Clarence Mott Woolley of the American Radiator Corporation, Joseph H. Defrees of the U.S. Chamber of Commerce, Matthew Woll of the American Federation of Labor, and Mary Van Kleeck of the Russell Sage Foundation. Edward Eyre Hunt, the committee secretary, was primarily responsible for drafting and negotiating its report. To assist in this task, he asked the experts, who were to keep recommendations out of the technical report, to give him their ideas as to what should be done. See Hunt to Mitchell, July 19, 1922, and subsequent Hunt letters and telegrams to the principal investigators, July 20, 1922, in Unemployment—Mitchell File, Commerce Files, HHP; "Meeting of the Business Cycle Committee," July 18, 1922, and "informal" recommendations from the principal investigators, in Unemployment—NBER File, Commerce Files, HHP.

array of conferences and educational activities intended to stimulate appropriate action by business, labor, and public investment managers.[32] The whole operation was basically similar to the BAE's Outlook, regional adjustment, and land use activities. But in this case, the research center was in a corporatively structured private agency rather than a government bureau, and the apparatus for the stimulation of "planning" was a curious mix of the private and the quasi-official.[33] It was only through these kinds of arrangements, Hoover and his aides argued, that the nation could have an economic inquiry both "technically first-class" and of sufficient "weight" to meet its needs for improved economic decision making and new institutional formation. Even if it were possible to obtain government appropriations for such a study, it would be undesirable to obtain them because they would lower the quality and "disinterestedness" of the output and penetrate and help to break down the antistatist barriers and safeguards essential to the preservation of basic liberties.[34]

The *Business Cycles* study project, begun in 1922 and completed in 1923, was not immediately followed by similar operations. The NBER turned to several studies for which it secured its own funding and had no apparatus to connect the research with "planning."[35] And the Hoover

---

[32]These included conferences with trade association leaders and business periodical editors, a meeting with the nation's leading economists assembled at the AEA convention, an organized publicity campaign, and a "referendum" intended to stimulate discussion in the business community. Later, Hoover and his associates would see the operation as "the most important economic investigation ever undertaken," rivaled only by the work of the National Monetary Commission leading up to the Federal Reserve Act. They credited it with "flattening" a "dangerous boom" in 1923 and thus helping to produce a "sustained level of prosperity." Alchon, *Invisible Hand of Planning*, 85–111; "Meeting of Economists with Members of the Committee on the Business Cycle," December 28, 1922; Hoover to Owen Young, May 17, 1923, both in Unemployment—Business Cycles File, Commerce Files, HHP; Hunt to Hoover, August 18, 1922, Unemployment—NBER File, Commerce Files, HHP; Hunt, "Business Cycles and Unemployment," October 1, 1927, in Box 28, Hunt Papers, HIA.

[33]Hunt liked to stress the "private," "unofficial," and "non-governmental" character of the PCOU Standing Committee and its offspring. See, for example, Hunt to Henry Pritchett, February 11, 1922, in Unemployment—NBER File, Commerce Files, HHP. But the committee was quasi-official in the sense that it was not only a private organization but also a presidential agency, a functioning arm of the Commerce Department, and a body that Hoover chaired in both his official and private capacities.

[34]Hunt to Pritchett, December 29, 1921, Unemployment—NBER File, Commerce Files, HHP; and Alchon, *Invisible Hand of Planning*, 84–5.

[35]These continued to be concerned chiefly with what the NBER saw as the central questions, those relating to national income and business fluctuations. The published output included *Income in the Various States* (1924); *Migration and the Business Cycle* (1926); *Business Annals* (1926); *The Behavior of Prices* (1927); and *Business Cycles: The Problem and Its Setting* (1927). In addition, there were projects that led to *The Growth of American Trade Unions* (1924) and *Trends in Philanthropy* (1928). For reports on this ongoing work, see Mitchell to M. C. Rorty, December 10, 1923, Correspondence File,

apparatus went through a period during which it sought, without much success, to find a substitute for the NBER. It considered, for example, a similar relationship with the Brookings Institute of Economics, especially for a study of seasonal business fluctuations.[36] It designed but could not get funding for an "industrial disputes" study in which the Wharton School's Industrial Research Department was to serve as the fact-finding agency,[37] and it discussed on occasion the need for a private-sector "planning board" with an appropriate research arm.[38] But continuing contacts and shared assumptions about the efficacy of the 1922–3 operation kept alive the potential for reconnection. When talk turned to the need for a reliable picture of recent and ongoing economic changes, as it did in 1927, the potential for reconnection became reality. The NBER would become the directing center of a cooperative research effort engaged in "taking the pulse" of a "great industrial nation" for purposes of managerial action, an effort that its organizers liked to compare favorably with the "national surveys" being conducted at the same time by Britain's

Mitchell Papers, and "Current Work of the NBER," December 15, 1924, Series X, Mitchell Papers. For reflections on the coherence of the bureau's research concerns, see Burns, "Mitchell and the National Bureau," 31–44, and the NBER's Reports of the President and the Directors of Research (1932), 1–3; The National Bureau's Social Function: Twentieth Annual Report of the Director of Research (1940), 7–10; and Economic Research and the Needs of the Times: Twenty-Fourth Annual Report (1944), 8–17.

[36]Hunt to Mitchell, May 7, 1923; and Mitchell to Hunt, May 8, 1923, both in Unemployment—Mitchell File, Commerce Files, HHP; Hoover to Robert Brookings, May 9, 1923, in Unemployment—Seasonal Stabilization File, Commerce Files, HHP. Moulton was interested at one point, but no agreement was reached. Hoover eventually settled for a PCOU study limited to seasonality in construction, conducted by his Building and Housing Division in collaboration with the industry's trade associations, and funded in part by the Carnegie Corporation. The result was U.S. Department of Commerce, Seasonal Operation in the Construction Industries (1924). The earlier plans for a broader study using economic expertise from outside the department are apparent in E. E. Hunt, "Seasonal Stabilization," May 15, 1923; and Hoover to Ernest Trigg, May 28, 1923, both in Seasonal Industries Investigation File, Commerce Files, HHP. Hoover also tried without success to interest Moulton in a similarly structured study of governmental statistical services and their improvement. See Hoover to Moulton, September 12, 1923, Statistics File, Commerce Files, HHP.

[37]See Joseph H. Willits, "Bases of Settlement in Labor Disputes," January 22, 1924; E. E. Hunt, "Bases of Agreement in Industrial Disputes," October 8, 1924; Hunt to Willits, October 26, 1924; Hunt to Beardsley Ruml, October 31, 1924, all in Hunt File, Commerce Files, HHP; Hunt to Hoover, October 28, 1924; Hoover to Arthur Woods, January 13, 1925, both in Unemployment—Bases of Agreement in Industrial Disputes File, Commerce Files, HHP. An unsuccessful effort was also made to get the newly organized Social Science Research Council to sponsor the study and function as the NBER had in the business cycles investigation. See Hunt to Charles Merriam, January 29, 1924; Merriam to Hunt, February 21, 1924, Box 27a, Hunt Papers, HIA.

[38]E. E. Hunt, "National Planning Board," July 2, 1926, Box 18, Hunt Papers, HIA.

Committee on Industry and Trade and Germany's Commission on Production and Distribution in the Reich.[39]

Such projects proved incapable of really creating a managerial capacity that could "iron out" the business cycle, turn problem industries into
healthy ones, and prevent the coming of a major depression. But the
creators and developers of the NBER and its connections with private
and government power had shown another way in which support for a
managerial economics could be institutionalized in a nation that still
lacked a managerial state and was far from being completely sold on
managerial values and ideals. In the *Business Cycles* study project, they
had found a way to bring together and create mutually reinforcing inter-
connections between four basic kinds of economic knowledge,[40] those
grounded, respectively, in the discipline, in informed opinion, in cultural
values, and in practical experience. And in the NBER operation itself they
had found an institutional arrangement capable of coaxing enough "un-
tainted" income from the private sector to support an expanding staff of
economists (from four in 1920 to fifteen in 1930) and to finance research
programs costing several times more than the initial founding grant of
$20,000.[41] Just as in the case of the BAE, moreover, both the form that
the institutionalization took and the new knowledge thus produced
would matter in the decades that followed.

TENSION AND CONFLICT

At times the economists of the BAE and those of the NBER could collaborate and show mutual respect.[42] But the differing ways in which they had

[39]Mitchell continued to be consulted on PCOU study projects and was promptly brought in
when the planning for a national economic survey began in 1927. See Hunt to Mitchell,
April 2, May 7, November 8, 1923; and Mitchell to Hunt, May 8, 1923, all in
Unemployment—Mitchell File, Commerce Files, HHP; Hunt to Mitchell, January 30,
October 15, 1924; and Mitchell to Hunt, January 19, February 26, October 13, 1924, all
in Box 36, Hunt Papers, HIA; Hunt to J. C. Merriam, December 13, 1927, Box 27a, Hunt
Papers, HIA. On the comparison to studies abroad, see E. E. Hunt, "Taking the Pulse of
Three Great Industrial Nations" [1929], Box 21, Hunt Papers, HIA.

[40]Robert D. Cuff, "The State and the Growth of Economic Knowledge: A Commentary,"
Comments Made at the Woodrow Wilson Center Symposium on the State and the Growth
of Economic Knowledge, September 16, 1988; and Chapter 1 of this volume.

[41]NBER, *Publications* 1 (1921) and 13 (1929); NBER, *Reports of the President and the
Directors of Research* (1931); Alchon, *Invisible Hand of Planning*, 57, 138–9, 157–8.

[42]See, for example, the credits given to BAE or BAE-connected economists in Committee on
Recent Economic Changes of the President's Conference on Unemployment, *Recent Economic Changes in the United States, Including the Reports of a Special Staff of
the National Bureau of Economic Research* (New York: McGraw-Hill, 1929), xxvii–

gained societal support while maintaining their authority as disinterested experts tended to make them skeptical of each other's claims and inclined to challenge each other's output. In essence, they were parts of two coexisting and competing currents in twentieth-century American state building: the one tended toward a positive statism resting on interest-group politics and the close relationships such a politics could produce among administrators, members of Congress, interest-group representatives, and scientific experts. The other tended toward an antistatist corporatism resting on the notion that statism could be avoided by coaxing a substitute for it from the group life and power centers of the private sector. And as parts of these currents, they were also participants in the accompanying process whereby each kept trying to gain primacy over the other and in so doing helped to define and establish the boundary between them.

In the 1920s, the major efforts to establish an industrial counterpart to the BAE were in the future. They would come into their own in the planning agitation of the 1930s, the antimonopoly inquiry launched in 1938, and the schemes for reorganizing the Commerce Department in 1939.[43] But the apparatus over which Hoover presided had within it some potential for such a development. He had, after all, reassembled under his auspices certain elements of the wartime apparatus, most notably a parallel structure of business committees and councils linked to and sharing administrative responsibilities with the department's bureaus and divisions, a complex of community units intended to mobilize the support of local elites for departmental campaigns, a set of agencies for molding and managing public opinion, and an expanded Census Bureau seeking to function in ways resembling those of the statistical agencies of the war period.[44] In addition, he had managed to bring a substantial number of

xxx. Significantly, however, the "recent economic changes" in agriculture were surveyed and analyzed by Edwin G. Nourse of the Brookings Institute of Economics, not by one of the distinguished economists at the BAE.

[43] See Ellis W. Hawley, *The New Deal and the Problem of Monopoly: A Study in Economic Ambivalence* (Princeton, N.J.: Princeton University Press, 1966), 178, 180, 185, 412; George McJimsey, *Harry Hopkins: Ally of the Poor and Defender of Democracy* (Cambridge, Mass.: Harvard University Press, 1987), 126; and Chapter 4 of the present volume.

[44] On the nature of the Hoover apparatus, see Hawley, " 'Industrial Policy' in the 1920s and 1930s," 65–72; Hawley, "Hoover, the Commerce Secretariat, and the Vision of an 'Associative State,' " 120–39; Craig Lloyd, *Aggressive Introvert: Herbert Hoover and Public Relations Management, 1912–1932* (Columbus: Ohio State University Press, 1972), 123–42; Edward Eyre Hunt, "The Cooperative Committee and Conference System," December 14, 1926, Hunt File, Commerce Files, HHP.

people with professional training in economics and statistics into departmental operations, had proved adept at enhancing and solidifying the kind of interest group and congressional support that sustained the department's work in standards and minerals, and had worked with some success to expand the department's investigative role and claim for it work previously done by congressional committees or regulatory commissions.[45] There was, to be sure, nothing like the glue that held agricultural economists together. But the bureaus of Foreign and Domestic Commerce, the Census, and Standards employed a number of economists (among them Louis Domeratzky, Julius Klein, John Gries, Frank Surface, E. Dana Durand, and Grosvenor M. Jones) who might have been brought together to form an "industrial economics" unit. And in some of Hoover's economic investigations—notably the Seasonal Operations, Foreign Raw Materials, World Trade in Agricultural Products, and Domestic Market studies—they did show themselves capable of stepping into the role played by outside economic expertise in the *Business Cycles* study.

Such developments could and did generate discontents for which a central informational and planning body staffed with economic experts could be offered as a remedy. In this respect, they resembled their counterparts during the war; and potentially the discontents might have led to a new bureau with features corresponding to those of the war government's CBPS or Agriculture's BAE. Although there was nothing in the situation really analogous to the "agricultural establishment," one can at least imagine a scenario in which a Wesley Mitchell might have become Commerce's Henry C. Taylor; brought about a bureaucratic merger similar to that producing the BAE; urged public-sector action to defuse charges of trust building, conflict of interest, and unaccountability; and altered enough of the institutional and political context to permit the establishment of fellow professionals in another tax-supported economic research institute. Achieving all these things would have been difficult, but it was not unthinkable. And the fact that the potential involved remained so well contained indicated both the difference that Hoover

[45]See E. E. Hunt, "Notes on Economic and Social Surveys," paper presented to the Taylor Society, December 8, 1927; and Hunt, "Economic Investigations," May 19, 1927, both in Hunt File, Commerce Files, HHP; Winters, *Henry C. Wallace*, 231–6; Joseph Brandes, *Herbert Hoover and Economic Diplomacy: Department of Commerce Policy, 1921–1928* (Pittsburgh: University of Pittsburgh Press, 1962), 5–8, 71–8; Bureau of Foreign and Domestic Commerce, *Annual Report* (1925), 54–5. On science as established in the bureaus of Standards and Mines, the latter transferred from Interior to Commerce in 1925, see Dupree, *Science in the Federal Government*, 274–7, 281–3, 338–40.

himself made and the relative power at the time of the two competing conceptions of how managerial economics should be supported and put to work.

The other possibility, namely, that the Hoover apparatus would extend its jurisdiction and conceptions into the agricultural field, was by far the more realistic one. It was in conjunction with the efforts made to realize this possibility that battle lines formed and questions were raised about the formulas for combining disinterestedness with utility. For Hoover and his lieutenants, the BAE was a "political" and "special interest" agency rather than a scientific one capable of serving the public interest. Its scientific credentials, its claims of disinterestedness, and its economic work were all tainted and compromised by the special-interest politics that sustained its activities. And the real need, if the farm problem was ever to be solved, was for actions that would get the problem out of "politics," help farmers develop organizational counterparts to successful business structures, and entrust the needed economic work to appropriately structured research institutes in the private sector. But for the BAE economists and their political allies, it was the Hoover apparatus that was incapable of doing the truly scientific work that would benefit Americans as a whole. Invoking antitrust rhetoric and the antimonopoly tradition in essentially the same way that the Hooverites invoked antistatism, they insisted that the apparatus was in reality a cleverly disguised tool of dominant business-financial elites and commercial interests, who were engaged in the political work of retaining their private power and special privileges and did not want to see the farm problem solved.[46]

One of the fiercest exchanges of such charges came in 1924, when the Hoover apparatus and the BAE complex openly challenged each other's competence in the agricultural exports field and supported rival programs for stabilizing farm markets and stimulating production planning. The BAE saw the Hoover-supported Winslow bill, giving all agri-

[46]See, for example, William Steuart to Hoover, April 6, 1922, Commerce—Census File, Commerce Files, HHP; Hoover to C. B. Slemp, February 25, 1924, Commerce—Foreign and Domestic Commerce File, Commerce Files, HHP; Hoover to Henry C. Wallace, March 7, 1922, Agriculture Department File, Commerce Files, HHP; Hoover to C. C. Teague, December 1, 1924, Agriculture—Cooperative Marketing File, Commerce Files, HHP; Wallace to Coolidge, April 18, 1924, Agriculture File, Commerce Files, HHP; Henry C. Taylor to Wallace, April 18, September 19, 1923, Box 23, Taylor Papers, Wisconsin State Historical Society Library. See also James H. Shideler, "Herbert Hoover and the Federal Farm Board Project, 1921–1925," *Mississippi Valley Historical Review* 42 (March 1956): 711–6, 720–9; Russell Lord, *The Wallaces of Iowa* (Boston: Houghton Mifflin, 1947), 259–62; Winters, *Henry C. Wallace*, 217–42, 245–6, 275–7.

cultural marketing and investigative work abroad to Commerce, as an open attempt to organize "a Department of Agriculture within the Department of Commerce." The BAE strongly supported the rival Ketcham bill, under which such work would be kept in the Agriculture Department; and in the accompanying congressional consideration of the rival proposals, it functioned as an active and aggressive lobby intent on discrediting the Hoover initiative. At the same time the BAE was also helping to make a case for the Wallace-supported McNary-Haugen bill, a measure under which farm relief would take the form of price supports and export subsidies in order to restore an equitable balance between agriculture and industry. And in making this case, the bureau necessarily challenged the adequacy and purported intent of the rival Capper-Williams bill, a measure for which Hoover had provided the ideas and through which he hoped to implement his plan for fostering agricultural marketing associations.[47]

None of these measures passed in 1924. But the controversies that they had engendered persisted. And shortly after the adjournment of Congress that year, the BAE proceeded to prepare its famous "Encroachment of the Department of Commerce upon the Department of Agriculture in Marketing and Agricultural Economics Investigations," a document in which it publicly accused Hoover and his associates of bureaucratic aggrandizement, traced the path that this aggression had followed, and challenged again the competence and integrity of their investigative, analytical, and reporting machinery. Furious at the attack, Hoover saw it as a deliberate attempt to "smear" and mislead, as a grossly improper injection of external "politics" into cabinet and administration matters, and as the work of "socialists" and "petty bureaucrats" interested chiefly in preserving their jobs and domains.[48]

After the death of Secretary Wallace and Hoover's subsequent success

[47]See Winters, *Henry C. Wallace*, 236–41, 257–81; Louis G. Michael to Taylor, February 28, March 8, May 15, May 28, June 7, 1924, Box 15, Taylor Papers; Lloyd Tenny to Taylor, March 8, 1924, Box 2, Taylor Papers.

[48]"Encroachment of the Department of Commerce upon the Department of Agriculture in Marketing and Agricultural Economics Investigations"; Hoover to Howard Gore, November 24, 1924; Hoover to George Peek, December 19, 1924; Max Pam to Hoover, May 21, 1925, all in Agriculture—Dept. of Agriculture & Dept. of Commerce File, Commerce Files, HHP; Hoover to Teague, December 1, 1924, Agriculture—Cooperative Marketing File, Commerce Files, HHP; Winters, *Henry C. Wallace*, 241–2; Entry of February 12, 1925, Edgar Rickard Diary, Rickard Papers, Hoover Presidential Library. Following Wallace's death, Coolidge asked Hoover to become secretary of agriculture, but he declined. In private, he told Edgar Rickard that it "would take him at least two years to get any loyalty out of the bureau chiefs." See Rickard Diary, entry for January 23, 1925.

in ousting Taylor, a "tamed" BAE refrained from any further actions like that of 1924. But friction persisted as attempts to work out a division of labor in the agricultural exports field kept breaking down and as Hoover kept challenging the quality of work and thinking done at the BAE. His attitudes were apparent, for example, in his testimony before the Business Men's Commission on Agriculture in 1927 and in his subsequent remarks about the need for "sane" economists like those at the NBER and the Food Research Institute at Stanford.

In 1929, as Hoover moved into the presidency and put his ideas about agriculture into effect through the Agricultural Marketing Act, there was some doubt about whether the BAE would survive as a major center of economic research. The new Federal Farm Board, the agency that was to administer the new Hoover apparatus for fostering agricultural marketing associations, was set up outside the Department of Agriculture and equipped with a capacity for expansion through transfers of bureaucratic units from other agencies; and it was to have its own economic section linked to Hoover's "sane" economists. To organize the section, the new board called on Edwin Gay of the NBER and Alonzo Taylor, an economist serving as director of the Food Research Institute.[49]

Again though, even with Hoover in the White House, the BAE proved that it had developed a capacity for political survival. With Gay serving as the mediator, a deal was finally struck, one that called for the BAE to give up its Division of Cooperative Marketing but to get, in return, the support of the Farm Board for its foreign agricultural service and a promise that the board would endorse the BAE's other programs and rely on the BAE for most of the economic research and information needed in board operations. Neither Hoover nor the Commerce Department liked the deal, but they finally acquiesced in a congressional measure adding a new foreign division to the BAE. Subsequently, as the failure of the Farm Board under Depression conditions discredited the Hoover designs for agriculture, the BAE emerged in a strong position, and it was to play an important role in the coming of the New Deal version of "agricultural

[49]Memorandum re Taylor's Conference with Secretary Jardine, April 30, 1925; Jardine to Taylor, August 10, 1925, both in Box 2, Taylor Papers; Michael to Taylor, January 26, 1926, Box 15, Taylor Papers; Hoover's Testimony before the Businessmen's Conference on Agriculture, April 15, 1927, Agriculture—Legislation File, Commerce Files, HHP; Nils A. Olsen, *Journal of a Tamed Bureaucrat: Nils A. Olsen and the BAE, 1925–1935* (Ames: Iowa State University Press, 1980), ed. by Richard Lowitt, 31–6, 38–40, 51, 54–5, 59–60, 63–6; David E. Hamilton, "From New Day to New Deal: American Agriculture in the Hoover Years, 1928–1933," Ph.D. diss., University of Iowa (1985), 102–9.

economic planning" and the apparatus set up to administer it.[50] It would become a lasting part of the New Era legacy and a continuing demonstration of one way in which a social scientific discipline linked to instruments of socioeconomic management could be given an institutional home in the American state.

RECENT ECONOMIC CHANGES

Meanwhile, even as Hoover was criticizing the work of the BAE and trying to establish a rival apparatus for studying and reporting on agricultural conditions, he had also become concerned with using economists to provide another "conspectus" as to what was happening in and to the economy as a whole. The project had several purposes: (1) It was to follow up and expand the work begun with the *Business Cycles* study of 1922 and 1923. (2) It was to integrate into the larger picture the knowledge of particular industries and sectors that had been accumulating in congressional reports, operational research, and private research programs and institutes. (3) It was to be the American counterpart to the national economic surveys being done abroad, the American contribution to the study called for by the World Economic Conference of 1927, and the American answer to European speculation about the basis of economic growth and prosperity in the United States. (4) It would also be doing something similar to what Gay's wartime bureau had been attempting in 1918. But as envisioned, its product would be an aid and tool not for a managerial presidency or for a managerial elite entrusted with government power, but rather for the new managerial capacity that was supposed to be under construction in society itself. And this aid and tool would be provided in an American way, that is, not through a state-based research institute or through the kind of inquiry that accompanied legislative action, but through the kind of arrangements used in 1922 and 1923, the kind that could make it "technically first-class" and of sufficient "weight" for the purposes intended.[51]

[50]Hamilton, "From New Day to New Deal," 109–11; Olsen, *Tamed Bureaucrat*, 67–9, 72, 80–2; Lyons, *Uneasy Partnership*, 55–63.
[51]The thinking about the study is evident in Hunt to Hoover, October 25, 1927, with accompanying letter from Mitchell and draft of a letter to Keppel, in Business Cycles and Situation File, Commerce Files, HHP; and Hunt to Woods, December 23, 1927, plus Hunt's draft of a letter to members of the sponsoring committee, January 5, 1928, both in Committees—Economic Study, 1927–28 File, Commerce Files, HHP. See also Alchon, *Invisible Hand of Planning*, 129–31; Hunt, "Looking to the Future" [1935], Box 19,

The triggering event in the chain of developments leading to the *Recent Economic Changes* study was Hoover's response to a slackening of business and a decline in wholesale prices in the spring of 1927. Concerned about these, he decided to set up a departmental Committee on the Present Business Cycle, chaired by John Gries, the economist who headed his Building and Housing Division; and it was from the intersection of this committee's deliberations with those of the American delegation to the World Economic Conference and with thinking at the NBER that the project emerged. The need for something similar to the *Business Cycles* study was discussed in a series of departmental meetings in which Wesley Mitchell participated. Hoover aide Edward Eyre Hunt, who had been secretary of the 1922–3 operation and was a delegate to the World Economic Conference in 1927, then took over the task of exploring what could and should be done. And by October, mostly in conferences between Hunt, Mitchell, and Gay accompanied by consultations with Hoover, a detailed plan had been worked out and was ready for submission to funding agencies. Writing to Frederick Keppel of the Carnegie Corporation in late October, Hoover credited the *Business Cycles* study with making a "large contribution to our post-war stability and prosperity," argued that a similarly structured study of "recent economic trends" could reveal the "foundation of our prosperity" and show "how to maintain it," and asked for the corporation's support.[52]

Under the plan proposed and eventually funded, jointly, as it turned out, by the Carnegie Corporation and the Laura Spelman Rockefeller Memorial, the NBER was again to be the agency of credentialed inquiry. Again, too, it would have a quasi-public status, deriving from its special

Hunt Papers, HIA; Hunt, "Taking the Pulse of Three Great Industrial Nations"; and Hunt, "Recent Economic Changes" [1934] and "Planning: A Bird's-Eye View of Recent Experience," both in Hunt File, Commerce Files, HHP. The major congressionally authorized and funded economic investigations of the 1920s were those conducted by the Joint Commission of Agricultural Inquiry in 1921, the Federal Trade Commission (especially its investigation of public utility holding companies beginning in 1928), and the U.S. Coal Commission in 1922 and 1923. The Hoover people tended to see this kind of investigation as being politically tainted, in the same sense as the work of the BAE was. But they made an exception of the Coal Commission work, which had been organized by Hunt and done in part by Wharton's Industrial Research Department and the Brookings Institute of Economics. See Hunt, "Notes on Economic and Social Surveys."

[52]Hoover to Bureau Chiefs, March 17, 1927; "The Present Business Cycle," March 21, 1927; Hoover to Keppel, October 26, 1927, all in Business Cycles and Situation File, Commerce Files, HHP; "Outline of Fact-Finding Investigation," Committees—Economic Study, 1927–28 File, Commerce Files, HHP; Hunt to Mitchell, August 19, 1927; Hunt to J. C. Merriam, December 9, 13, 1927, all in Box 27a, Hunt Papers, HIA; Alchon, *Invisible Hand of Planning*, 131–8; Evan B. Metcalf, "Secretary Hoover and the Emergence of Macroeconomic Management," *Business History Review* 44 (Spring 1975): 78–9.

relationship with the Commerce Department, and it would be connected to a PCOU sponsoring committee responsible for carrying the findings into practical application.

In three respects, however, the arrangements differed somewhat from those in 1922:

1. The study was to be larger and more comprehensive, encompassing not only the workings of the business cycle and stabilization mechanisms but also the areas of technical progress, monetary flows, and performance in the economy's major functional divisions.[53]

2. It was, because of its size, more dependent on cooperating groups, with the NBER functioning more as the mobilizer, leader, and supervisor of a cooperative research effort. Involved, in particular, were the clusters of experts in such places as the Commerce Department; the Brookings Institute of Economics; the American Engineering Council; and university-based research agencies, especially those at Harvard, Columbia, Pennsylvania, Stanford, Cornell, and the Massachusetts Institute of Technology.[54]

3. The study's sponsoring committee, the Committee on Recent Economic Changes (CREC), was larger and more corporative in structure. To a core of business leaders, Hoover added several government officials (with himself as chairman) plus representatives of higher education, organized labor, and organized agriculture.[55]

[53]CREC, *Recent Economic Changes*, v; Alchon, *Invisible Hand of Planning*, 138–41; "Outline of Fact-Finding Investigation"; Department of Commerce Press Releases, January 26, February 11, 15, 1928, all in Committees—Economic Study, 1927–28 File, Commerce Files, HHP; Hunt, "Looking to the Future," Box 19, Hunt Papers, HIA. One significant change in the original outline was the decision to begin the report with an examination of consumption patterns and living standards and then to explain these standards in terms of techniques, labor relations, income distribution, foreign markets, price movements, and sectoral developments.

[54]CREC, *Recent Economic Changes*, xxvi-xxx; Alchon, *Invisible Hand of Planning*, 136, 138, 141–2, 145–6.

[55]In addition to Hoover and Hunt (who served as secretary), the committee consisted of Renick W. Dunlap of the Department of Agriculture, Julius Klein of the Bureau of Foreign and Domestic Commerce, Adolph C. Miller of the Federal Reserve Board, Lewis E. Pierson of the U.S. Chamber of Commerce, John S. Lawrence of the New England Council, Clarence M. Woolley of the American Radiator Corporation, Owen D. Young of General Electric, Arch W. Shaw of Shaw Publications, Daniel Willard of the Baltimore and Ohio Railroad, John J. Raskob of General Motors, Max Mason of the University of Chicago, George McFadden of the Penn Mutual Life Insurance Company, Louis J. Taber of the National Grange, William Green of the American Federation of Labor, and Walter Brown, soon to be Hoover's postmaster general. The list initially sent to funding agencies had not included government officials (except for Hoover) and had on it Henry Robinson, W. L. Clayton, and Alfred Sloan rather than McFadden, Shaw, and Raskob. Hunt suggested Mary Van Kleeck or another woman representative, but none was appointed. When asked about the nature of the agency, Hoover said that committee members were "named both in their personal and representative capacities." CREC, *Recent Economic*

The work of the NBER and its collaborators began in February 1928 and was completed with the publication in May 1929 of two massive volumes under the title *Recent Economic Changes in the United States*. In producing these, the NBER reserved for itself the shaping of general contours; the writing of the introduction and conclusion; and the technical work on population, living standards, price movements, national income, and business cycles.[56] After some deliberation, it also assigned the subject of labor to Leo Wolman, its labor economics specialist, and that of corporate organization and industrial structure to NBER staffer Willard Thorp.[57]

A number of other special topics became the responsibility of outside experts. Dexter Kimball and L. P. Alford of the American Engineering Council did the sections on technological innovation and changing industrial patterns. William J. Cunningham, Melvin T. Copeland, and O. M. W. Sprague, all affiliated with Harvard, studied and reported on transportation, marketing, and money. The sections on construction, foreign economic relations, agriculture, and business management were assigned, respectively, to John Gries of the Commerce Department, James Harvey Rogers of the University of Missouri, Edwin G. Nourse of the Brookings Institute of Economics, and Henry Dennison, the businessman-scholar who had been assistant director of the wartime CBPS and had subsequently become a prominent figure in the business regularization and scientific management movements. Dennison was assisted by experts at the Wharton School, MIT, and the National Civic Federation.[58]

The resulting study has been criticized for being too descriptive, hastily done, and unappreciative of the shakiness of New Era prosperity. But its organizers regarded it as a vindication of the "Hoover method"; and critics would concede that it had been strikingly successful in using historical perspective to provide a better understanding of changes under way and had given the United States more information about its economic life

Changes, v; Hunt to Hoover, December 2, 1927; Hoover to Keppel, December 3, 1927; Hunt to Hoover, January 30, 1928; Hoover to Max Mason, June 9, 1928, all in Committees—Economic Study, 1927–28 File, Commerce Files, HHP; Alchon, *Invisible Hand of Planning*, 140–1.

[56]CREC, *Recent Economic Changes*, vii–viii; Alchon, *Invisible Hand of Planning*, 145–8.
[57]Initially, Mitchell and Gay thought that outside specialists would be needed in these areas and that the person to study corporate organization might well be Adolf A. Berle, Jr. See Alchon, *Invisible Hand of Planning*, 142, 146. Wolman was also director of research for the Amalgamated Clothing Workers of America.
[58]CREC, *Recent Economic Changes* (note acknowledging assistance provided to Dennison, 495); Alchon, *Invisible Hand of Planning*, 146.

than was possessed by any other nation.[59] The study also stood as a long commentary on the fruits of the kind of empirical inquiry championed and spearheaded by the NBER, on the state of knowledge among those seeking to create a discipline of industrial economics that would enhance national and sectoral managerial capacities, and on the relative backwardness of this discipline compared with the progress being made in agricultural economics.

The developers of the new discipline, to be sure, were learning to think in terms of a system to be managed rather than one to be understood as the working of immutable laws. But in comparison with their counterparts in agriculture, they had accumulated less information on the system and its components and given less thought to how their knowledge could be made to serve managerial purposes. Although the accounts of their research findings were in many respects imaginative and effective, they had to admit, over and over again, that they still lacked the kinds of information, measuring sticks, and analytical tools that were necessary to answer some of the more interesting and important questions. For example, they lacked adequate measures of productivity, unemployment, and business income; adequate statistics of labor costs and social and family expenditures; adequate data on trading areas and business combinations; and adequate tools for bringing out the relationships between the parts and changes they could measure. If the goal of the NBER brand of economics was to lay a "scientific foundation" for national economic management, as some of the economists involved professed, then it still had a considerable way to go.[60]

Ignored in the study, moreover, both in the NBER work and in the accompanying CREC report, were those economists who were beginning

[59]Charles O. Hardy, "Recent Economic Changes in the United States," *Journal of Political Economy* 38 (April 1930): 213–27; Alchon, *Invisible Hand of Planning*, 146–51; Notes on Recent Economic Changes, July 4, 1934, Box 39, Hunt Papers, HIA.
[60]CREC, *Recent Economic Changes*, 14–9, 96–105, 181–8, 331–5, 445–59, 467–78, 766–74; Hardy, "Recent Economic Changes," 214–6, 220. Hardy suspected that the volumes would do less "to lay a more scientific foundation for national policy" than they would "to furnish illustrative data to be cited in support of preconceived doctrines." Also lacking, of course, was an authoritative numerical measure of the performance of the economy as a whole (i.e., the gross national product). But the NBER was already working to remedy this defect. Since 1926 Simon Kuznets, who had earned his Ph.D. under Mitchell, had been working on the subject and would eventually be the one to define and provide the missing measure. See Metcalf, "Hoover and Macroeconomic Management," 78; National Accounts Review Committee of the National Bureau of Economic Research, *The National Economic Accounts of the United States* (New York: NBER, 1958), 24; Dorfman, *Economic Mind*, V, 669.

to anticipate the theoretical achievements that would be credited to John Maynard Keynes in the 1930s. Fiscal policy, it was being argued by such economic heretics as William T. Foster, Waddill Catchings, John R. Cummings, and David Friday, was the real key to creating the capacities being sought—the key, in other words, to having a national economic management that could sustain prosperity while avoiding the kind of planning inconsistent with the retention of freedom. But even though the NBER economists were now thinking in terms of a national economic unit made up of interdependent aggregated variables and in need of continuous management, their search for a "technique of balance" was still focused on the private sector. It was only by incorporating social scientific knowledge and system-conscious perspectives into the daily decisions of business executives, so Mitchell implied, that one could have a "practical" economic management consistent with the freedom of enterprise that a capitalist economy required. And although problem areas were noted, the general treatment of developments since 1921 tended to encourage the belief that progress toward this goal had already been substantial. "Experts and committeemen alike," said Edward Eyre Hunt, agreed that the factor most nearly explaining the period's economic success story had been better management.[61]

The coming of the Great Depression would, of course, challenge and largely discredit such notions of managerial success. Indeed, by 1932 one trustee of the Carnegie Corporation was asserting that the NBER had "disgraced itself" by ignoring the prospects of disaster of which it must have been aware in 1929. Yet initially, the plans for continuing the CREC-NBER complex as a developer of managerial capacity remained operational. In late 1929 and early 1930, it carried on with a subsidiary study of the "planning and control of public works"; and later in 1930, after CREC chairman Arch W. Shaw had secured new funding from the Rockefeller Foundation and smaller contributors, another study group was formed, this time to examine the coming of "the recession of 1929–30," provide an account of "the whole organism and the interaction of its vital parts, now under pressure and strain," and thus contribute to the

---

[61]Dorfman, *Economic Mind*, IV, 337–51; V, 403–13; Richard P. Adelstein, " 'The Nation as an Economic Unit': John Maynard Keynes and the Progressive Ideal," Paper Prepared for the Seminar in Economic History, University of Munich, May 1988; CREC, *Recent Economic Changes*, xix–xxii, 862–7, 874–88, 909–11; Alchon, *Invisible Hand of Planning*, 148–50.

construction of a more effective "technique of balance."[62] In addition, the CREC-NBER complex attempted to improve government statistics; continued its work abroad, including participating in League of Nations efforts to coordinate the several national economic investigations then taking place; and could take some credit for the further progress made in the development of national income accounting. In 1932, when the Senate requested a national income report, the Department of Commerce borrowed Simon Kuznets from the NBER to supervise and direct the study. Later, it would establish its National Income Division to prepare continuing estimates and thus provide a basic measure of the functioning of the economy as a whole.[63]

The National Income Division, however, was not the Bureau of Industrial Economics envisaged in a variety of planning schemes proposed during the depression decade. Nor would it ever develop into such a bureau. Even though the "Hoover method" was now discredited, the privatism-as-alternative approach could take other forms that continued to make it politically viable. And if the NBER ceased to be the centerpiece of the approach, it would still be able to tap philanthropic resources while maintaining its professional integrity and reputation. And its economists would attune themselves to the new thinking about how a developing managerial economics could be put to use without creating a bureaucratic directorate or tainting the process with interest-group politics. Writing in 1933, the year of the New Deal's National Recovery Administration (NRA), Mitchell would see the answer in new types of politico-economic organization, among them "the quasi-governmental corporation, the government-owned corporation, the mixed corpora-

---

[62]Alchon, *Invisible Hand of Planning*, 152–8, 161–5; National Bureau of Economic Research, *Reports of the President and the Directors of Research for the Year 1930* (1931), 12–4, and *Reports of the President and the Directors of Research for the Year 1931* (1932), 5–7, 22. Shaw became chairman of the CREC following Hoover's election to the presidency. The Carnegie trustee, quoted in Alchon, was Russell M. Leffingwell.

[63]Hunt, "Planning: A Bird's-Eye View of Recent Experience," 47–61; Hunt, Memorandum of Meetings of Representatives of Economic Councils and Research Institutes, Geneva, March 2–4, 1931; and Hunt, "Miscellaneous Notes Made in the Sessions of the League Conference on the Course and Phases of the Business Depression, Geneva, March 2–4, 1931," both in Hunt File, Presidential Files, HHP; Alchon, *Invisible Hand of Planning*, 158–9; Dorfman, *Economic Mind*, V, 669; National Accounts Review Committee, *National Economic Accounts*, 24. The CREC became the agency through which the United States was to cooperate with a League investigation involving ten nations with national economic councils or parliaments. The participating bodies were to exchange information and collaborate on a study of the economic downturn. A preliminary conference met in March 1931 and a general conference in July of that year.

tion, the semi- and demi-autonomous industrial groupings in varying relations to the State."[64]

Like the BAE, then, the NBER would become a lasting part of the New Era legacy and a continuing demonstration of another way in which a social scientific discipline linked to instruments of socioeconomic management could be given an institutional home in the American system. After 1932, to be sure, it no longer had the kind of connections that had given it a quasi-public status during the 1920s. But it continued to have links with government activity, and it would continue to be a major center for developing and advancing the managerial economics drawn upon by the research and planning bodies created under the New Deal or as parts of another war government.

THE 1920S IN PERSPECTIVE

In the 1930s, as the Depression persisted and Hooverism gave way to Franklin D. Roosevelt's New Deal, there would be other ways for making economic inquiry and expertise a part of the expanding American state. For a time, there would be another emergency managerial apparatus, resembling that of World War I and providing a temporary home for the work of economists, especially in the NRA's Research and Planning Division and the Division of Industrial Economics that lingered after the NRA was overthrown. There would also be policy innovations in the labor and welfare fields, which provided the basis for bringing labor economists into government in somewhat the same way that agricultural economists had established themselves there in the 1920s. In addition, there would be efforts to establish and equip a managerial presidency, to forge a new and more scientifically grounded antitrust apparatus, and to expand and unify the government's statistical work, all of which would provide government positions for economists. And with the rise in the late 1930s of another branch of the "new economics," based on Keynesian theory and analysis, new units in the Treasury Department and the Bureau of the

---

[64]Mitchell is quoted in Dorfman, *Economic Mind*, V, 669. See also National Bureau of Economic Research, *Report of the Executive Director* (1937); and Alchon, *Invisible Hand of Planning*, 165–6. In early 1933 the NBER won pledges of renewed and continuous support from the Carnegie Corporation and the Rockefeller Foundation and by 1936 was engaged not only in its central work on national income, capital formation, and business cycles but also in cooperative projects involving New Deal agencies, the Social Science Research Council, and university researchers.

Budget began doing work that foreshadowed the coming of the Council of Economic Advisers in 1946.[65]

Yet what had taken shape by 1940 had come more through additions to the New Era legacy than through repudiation of it. The BAE became a major agency in the New Deal state, central to the agricultural planning and control operations that became a permanent feature of the American political economy. And far from repudiating the privatism-as-alternative approach exemplified by the pre-1933 story of the NBER, the New Deal initially adopted a program of industrial recovery that left its administrators highly dependent on the economic work and capacity of private-sector organizations. Throughout the 1930s, moreover, the institutional and political barriers against developing an industrial counterpart to the BAE remained strong, both because the New Era legacy had left no foundation for one and because the New Era notions of a superior privatist or corporatist alternative persisted in somewhat different form. Nor did the New Deal ever fully repudiate the antibureaucratic tradition shaping public policy in the 1920s. Although the state had expanded and the executive branch of the federal government had come to play a much larger role within this expanded state, there was still strong and effective resistance to either a managerial presidency or a public-sector managerial establishment resembling those in managerial states abroad. The halting steps taken in these directions still had to be fitted into a polity with large antimanagerial components and, as a result, were hedged about with constraints and compromises.[66]

A strong argument can also be made that these developments helped to shape the pattern of administrative capacity in the New Deal state and thus to determine the kind of economic interventions that the state undertook and the kind of policies it could implement. In the agricultural sector, the

[65]Lyons, *Uneasy Partnership*, 52–4, 64–5; Hawley, *New Deal and Monopoly*, 77–8, 159, 172–3, 399, 415–6, 432; Frederick C. Mills and Clarence Long, *The Statistical Agencies of the Federal Government* (New York: NBER, 1949), 71–4; Robert M. Collins, *The Business Response to Keynes, 1929–1964* (New York: Columbia University Press, 1981), 6–13; Herbert Stein, *The Fiscal Revolution in America* (Chicago: University of Chicago Press, 1969), 169–96.

[66]Richard S. Kirkendall, *Social Scientists and Farm Politics in the Age of Roosevelt* (Columbia: University of Missouri Press, 1966), 70–88, 133–92, 255–8; Hawley, *New Deal and Monopoly*, 53–71; Daniel A. Littman, "The Implementation of Industrial Policy," *Economic Review (Federal Reserve Bank, Cleveland)*, Summer 1984, 1–14; Ellis W. Hawley, "The Corporate Ideal as Liberal Philosophy in the New Deal," in Wilbur J. Cohen, ed., *The Roosevelt New Deal* (Austin: LBJ School, 1986), 85–98; Ellis W. Hawley, "The New Deal State and the Anti-Bureaucratic Tradition," in Robert Eden, ed., *The New Deal and Its Legacy* (Westport, Conn.: Greenwood Press, 1989).

Department of Agriculture had developed in ways that provided the tools and knowledge needed for administrative intervention in economic processes, built confidence in the effectiveness and workability of this intervention for the purposes intended, and eventually allowed the agricultural adjustment programs begun in 1933 to be permanently institutionalized.

But in the industrial sector, neither the Commerce Department, the Labor Department, the presidency, nor the independent regulatory commissions had developed in ways that allowed a similar set of industrial adjustment programs to be accepted as workable and eventually institutionalized. In this sector, the initial New Deal interventions rested on a combination of war analogies and the use of additional government resources to complete the managerial projects of the 1920s. And when this approach proved unworkable and politically unsustainable, the response was not a move toward planning mechanisms resembling those in the agricultural sector, but a retreat from the kind of planning attempted under the NRA and a search for strategic "levers" that could be operated with the kind of administrative capacity that the federal bureaucracy possessed or could easily acquire. The "levers" eventually found were fiscal, antitrust, and labor relations policy, and by 1940 the New Deal state was in the process of trying to develop mechanisms through which these could be managed in the interests of sustained prosperity, renewed growth, and optimal use of resources.[67]

By 1940, moreover, A. Hunter Dupree's characterization of the federal scientific establishment as one of bewildering diversity built up by different kinds of organizational activity taking place at different times might also be applied to the machinery developed for bringing economic inquiry and economic management together.[68] To the bits and pieces inherited from the Progressive Era had been added the peculiar developments of the 1920s that have been discussed in this chapter, and to both had been added the legacy that had come out of the government intervention of the 1930s, all adding up to a complex mixture that was difficult to understand without a knowledge of its organizational history. And just as in the case of the scientific establishment, the mixture was about to become

[67]For a persuasive argument along these lines, see Theda Skocpol and Kenneth Finegold, "State Capacity and Economic Intervention in the Early New Deal," *Political Science Quarterly* 97 (Summer 1982): 255–78. See also Hawley, *New Deal and Monopoly*, 270–80, 428–32; and Otis L. Graham, Jr., *Toward a Planned Society: From Roosevelt to Nixon* (New York: Oxford University Press, 1976), 30–5, 64–8.
[68]Dupree, *Science in the Federal Government*, 375–8.

even more complex. From World War II would come a national security state with its own distinctive machinery for the defense sector, its demands for continuing economic work in military and foreign assistance planning, and its contract system for government support and use of work done in the universities.

By the 1950s efforts were under way to rationalize and coordinate these historical accumulations, efforts that resembled the longstanding attempts to bring greater coherence and more powerful direction to the promotion and use of scientific research. But the organizational forms created by historical choices and processes would persist, and history would continue to matter for those who wished to understand how economic and other types of social scientific inquiry were promoted and used by the American version of the modern managerial state.[69]

CONCLUSION

Whether the organizational forms created during the 1920s were good or bad depended on one's view concerning the kind of managerial state that the United States needed and should have. For people who believed that the national government needed to develop the administrative capacity to implement an "industrial policy" and turn piecemeal planning into national planning, the legacy of the 1920s stood as one of the obstacles blocking needed and desirable institutional development. And for people who deplored the tendency of the organizational forms to serve the establishment and perpetuate existing power structures—people who kept asking "knowledge for what?" and "service to whom?"—the legacy stood as a contribution to the continuing triumph of social conservatism over impulses toward economic democracy. But for people who saw the containment and fragmentation of the American administrative apparatus as a way of preserving essential freedoms, the arrangements of the period stood as positive achievements in state building.

Nor could the capacity of the arrangements to advance economic knowledge and understanding be dismissed. As Wesley Mitchell would note in 1944, they had helped to convert economists from "onlookers" and "bystanders" concerned with the development and teaching of a

[69]Lyons, *Uneasy Partnership*, 81–3, 96–111, 136–67, 224–9, 269–86; Henry W. Riecken, "The Federal Government and Social Science Policy," *Annals of the American Academy of Political and Social Science* 394 (March 1971): 100–13.

branch of philosophy into gatherers of vital social information and developers of a behavioral science based on mass observations.[70] In any event, the organizational forms invented at this stage in the evolution of federal relations with social science continued to shape those relations in subsequent periods.

[70]Wesley Mitchell, in NBER, *Economic Research and the Needs of the Times,* 6–17.

10

Official economic inquiry and Britain's
industrial decline: the first fifty years

BARRY SUPPLE

Freedom of trade may be regarded as a fundamental axiom of political economy. . . . We may welcome *bona fide* investigation into the state of trade, and the
causes of our present depression, but we can no more expect to have our opinions
on free trade altered by such an investigation, than the Mathematical Society
would expect to have axioms of Euclid disproved during the investigation of a
complex problem.

W. S. Jevons (1883)[1]

No system of human politics or economics can be *absolutely* true: It can be true
only *relatively* to the circumstances and conditions of the society to which it is
applied. . . . No investigation, therefore, could in my opinion have been more
useful and none more profitable as bearing on our national industry than an
inquiry whether the circumstances of 1886 are in all respects equally appropriate
as those of 1846 to the adoption and application of free trade precisely as it was
then adopted and applied.

Member of Royal Commission on Depression of Trade and
Industry (1886)[2]

A century or more of economic turbulence and political cynicism has
obviously put paid to the very concept of theoretical axioms as the bases
of economic policy. As these divergent quotations exemplify, any period
of economic change inevitably involves a questioning as well as a reassertion of "established" doctrine. More than this, it exposes the symbiotic
relations between economic theory and political economy, between doc-

[1]W. S. Jevons, *Methods of Social Reform* (London: Macmillan, 1883) 181–2, quoted in J.
C. Wood, *British Economists and Empire* (London: Croom Helm, 1983), 105.
[2]G. Auldo Jamieson in *Final Report of the Royal Commission on the Depression of Trade
and Industry* (London: Parliamentary Papers, 1886, XXIII; C.4893, 1886), xxxiv–v.

trinal commitments and state policy. This chapter is concerned with the ways in which some erstwhile "fundamental axioms" of British industrial policy were scrutinized and challenged as the economy matured.

The story of that scrutiny starts in the 1880s, with the beginnings of modern forebodings about Britain's industrial decline. Admittedly, the country's industrial and commercial position in the 1880s was still strong, but an increasing number of observers shared the anxieties expressed in the *Final Report of the Royal Commission on the Depression of Trade and Industry* (1886) that unemployment and new competition threatened Britain's economic supremacy: "Our position as the chief manufacturing nation of the world is not so undisputed as formerly, and . . . foreign nations are beginning to compete with us successfully in many markets of which we formerly had a monopoly."[3] And in the hundred years since that report, the complaint about what a more recent inquiry—by the House of Lords Select Committee on Overseas Trade—called Britain's "vicious circle of uncompetitiveness and low growth"[4] has become a cliché.

My purpose in this chapter is not, however, to offer yet another assessment of the industrial performance of the British economy. Rather, I am concerned to see how far the principal issues—relatively slow industrial growth, flagging exports, structural frictions, unemployment—were taken to be important objects of official inquiry, what it was imagined might be done by the state to tackle perceived problems, and how far (and with what effect) systematic knowledge and analysis were deployed or generated in the course of the industrial inquiries that punctuated the years until World War II.

INDUSTRIAL PERFORMANCE AND ECONOMIC AXIOMS

The extent to which Britain's long-run industrial performance has given justifiable grounds for gloom is, of course, a matter of controversy,[5] but there is no disputing the *relative* decline. The rate of economic growth in Britain has been fairly consistently below that of most of the world's

---

[3] *Final Report of the Royal Commission on the Depression*, x–xi, xv, xx, xxiii.
[4] *House of Lords. Report from the Select Committee on Overseas Trade* (HL 238-I, 1985. London: Her Majesty's Stationery Office [HMSO], 1985), 25–6.
[5] For assessments of Britain's long-run economic performance, see R. C. O. Matthews, C. H. Feinstein, and J. Odling-Smee, *British Economic Growth, 1856–1973* (Oxford: Clarendon Press, 1982); "Long-run Economic Performance in the U.K.," *Oxford Review of Economic Policy* IV, no. 1 (Spring 1988).

leading industrial nations for a century or so; and Britain's share of world trade in manufactures has collapsed—from more than 40 percent in 1887 to about 33 percent in 1900, some 22 percent in 1937, and (after a brief postwar recovery) to less than 10 percent in the 1980s.[6]

Not surprisingly, therefore, official attention has been preoccupied with alterations in the world economy and with Britain's role and competitiveness within it. Britain's late-nineteenth-century supremacy, it is now clear, was related to a particular international commercial configuration and level of prosperity. As we shall see, changes in the international economy, as well as in the competitive standing of British industry, were therefore bound to affect the workings of the British economy and to excite the attention of the state.

Against this background, exports have always been seen as essential to employment and welfare.[7] Therefore, free trade for much of the time and low manufacturing costs throughout the last hundred years were predominant objectives of government policy. But the "problem of exports" involved more than a concern with commercial or industrial policy. The international role of sterling and of Britain's financial institutions also seemed to demand a commitment to an "open" international system and a stringently orthodox set of financial arrangements, designed to stabilize exchanges, prices, and capital markets and to encourage the mobile flow of investment funds and labor.

As implied by this description, until well into the interwar decades, the established ways of thinking about the role of the state in relation to changes in industry were determined by the corpus of classical and neoclassical economic theory—or at least by the version of it that was digested and regurgitated by politicians and civil servants. (See Chapters 2 and 7 in this volume.) Of course, there was considerable scope for government activity even in the prescriptions of orthodox theory. It has always been accepted, at least in principle, that the private and public costs and benefits of economic activity might diverge—and that free enterprise and competition could not necessarily be relied on to secure socially optimal

---

[6]Matthews et al., *British Economic Growth*, 435; *House of Lords. Select Committee*, 23.
[7]See *Final Report of the Committee on Industry and Trade* (Balfour Committee) (London: Parliamentary Papers, 1928–9, VII; Cmd. 3282, 1929), 12: "The twin problems of ensuring continuous employment and a satisfactory standard of life are inextricably bound up with the problem of export." Compare the opinion of the House of Lords Select Committee on Overseas Trade in 1985 that services were "no substitute for manufacturing because they are too heavily dependent upon it and only 20 percent are tradeable overseas." *House of Lords. Select Committee*, 43.

outcomes where matters of defense, justice, environmental evils, education, and even industrial research were concerned. Hence, in Britain's industrial maturity eminent economists like Marshall and Pigou deftly and without embarrassment analyzed the implications of unequal private and social returns and differing conditions of production in different industries—and found theoretical justifications for state intervention in industry and trade, in town planning and education.[8]

Nevertheless, for most of the nineteenth and early twentieth centuries such sophistications had not resulted in a *practical* advocacy of extensive public intervention in markets, pricing, industrial organization, or factor mobility. Free trade, competition, and laissez-faire were taken to be in Britain's economic interest; its industry and consumers would suffer from the imposition of customs duties or from government action designed to alter the structure or organization of industry or preempt the decision making of private enterprise. To the economists involved, this was partly because they acknowledged that (in the absence of more data about social and private marginal returns) their analyses were still largely exercises in "pure theory."[9] But beyond this, they judged that the ignorance and susceptibilities of politicians and civil servants would outweigh any possible benefits. As Pigou phrased it in relation to industrial regulation:

It is not sufficient to contrast the imperfect adjustments of unfettered private enterprise with the best adjustment that economists in their studies can imagine. For we cannot expect that any public authority will attain, or will even wholeheartedly seek, that ideal. Such authorities are liable alike to ignorance, to sectional pressure and to personal corruption by private interest. A loud-voiced part of their constituents, if organised for votes, may easily outweigh the whole.[10]

---

[8]Alfred Marshall, *Principles of Economics* (London: Macmillan; 1st ed., 1890; 8th ed., 1920; repr., 1930), Book V, Chapter 13; Alfred Marshall, *Industry and Trade* (London: Macmillan; 1st ed., 1919; 3d ed., 1920; repr., 1932), Book I, Chapter 5, Sections 3–4, Book III, Chapter 14, Section 9; A. C. Pigou, *The Economics of Welfare* (London, Macmillan; 1st ed., 1920; 4th ed., 1932), Part II, Chapters 3–5, 9–13, 20–22.

[9]Pigou, *Economics of Welfare*, 227. However, Pigou vigorously defended his analysis on the grounds that it facilitated the detection and exposure of "sophistical dogmatism" and that in time appropriate statistical data about industrial conditions might well become available. In 1930, Lionel Robbins wrote (approvingly) that "the so-called exceptions to the general presumption in favour of Free Trade have been regarded by economists as academic playthings—interesting as illuminating remote analytical points, but, from the point of view of practice, completely insignificant." See Susan Howson and Donald Winch, eds., *The Economic Advisory Council, 1930–1939: A Study in Economic Advice During Depression and Recovery* (Cambridge, Eng.: Cambridge University Press, 1977), 229.

[10]*Economics of Welfare*, 332.

Marshall had expressed similar anxieties about the further distortions that would arise from the adoption of protection for infant industries in search of the economies of scale ("those industries which can send the greatest number of voters to the poll, are those which are already on so large a scale that a further increase would bring very few new economies"),[11] as well as opposing a system of industrial bounties because of the "openings for fraud and corruption" and the danger that people "would divert their energies from managing their own businesses to managing those persons who control the bounties."[12] Like the gold standard, free trade and the absence of industrial regulation were imagined to be ways of making economic arrangements "knave-proof."

This viewpoint was also sustained by the dictates of practical politics. Powerful interest groups (producers as well as consumers) were naturally suspicious of measures that might increase the cost of imports, lead to further restraints on foreign purchasing power, hinder the mobility of domestic resources, raise the cost of domestic inputs, or restrict the operations of the international economy. Politically, even inquiry might be suspect: "A Free Trader who inquires is in the perilous position of a lady who hesitates."[13]

These theories and ideologies shaped political and policy assumptions until long after World War I and were critically influential until World War II. And although Keynes, Henderson, and some other economists were prepared, for example, to contemplate tariff protection in an emergency (in 1931–2 economic circumstances did force the government to abandon free trade), established figures such as Pigou and Robbins were still either highly skeptical about or ferociously hostile to tariffs.[14] Nevertheless, even before the dislocations of the international economy in the late 1920s and the 1930s threw serious doubt on the political acceptability of such theories, the advent of industrial "maturity" and competition in late Victorian and Edwardian Britain had generated the first serious challenge to theoretical convention and conventional "knowledge."

---

[11]*Principles of Economics*, 464.

[12] Ibid., 473.

[13]Quoted from the *National Review* 42 (1904): 674, in A. W. Coats, "Political Economy and the Tariff Reform Campaign of 1903," *Journal of Law and Economics* 11 (April 1968): 201n. The same source also quotes J. L. Maxse in the *National Review* 41 (1903): 702, as saying that the mere existence of an inquiry into free trade would be "fatal to the prestige of the hitherto accepted creed because it necessarily destroys its divine attributes."

[14]See the differing opinions in the Report of the Committee of Economists to the Economic Advisory Council (October 1930), reprinted in Howson and Winch, eds., *The Economic Advisory Council*, 202–11, 221–6, 229–31.

MATURITY, COMPETITION, AND FREE TRADE

The doubts about free trade that developed from the 1870s, if not before, were initially derived from anxieties about competition in specific industries. Ultimately, however, they were formulated around broad, and related, issues of economic power, industrial structure, unemployment, and occupational and geographic mobility.

This tendency was exemplified in the range of opinion expressed in the final volume produced by the Royal Commission on the Depression of Trade and Industry (1886). The majority report drew attention to two problems in particular: the structural changes within Britain, which had led to "insufficiency and irregularity of employment"; and the competitive implications of the industrialization of Germany and the United States, whose marketing skills and business tenacity contrasted with a decline in the reputation of British workmanship and a "falling off among the trading classes of this country from the energetic practice of former periods."[15] As far as commercial policy was concerned, the majority report was circumspectly reticent on the subject of free trade; but a few members of the commission were ready to insist that, as with every other political or economic system, its truth was not absolute, but relative "to the circumstances and conditions of the society to which it is applied." Empirically, the fact that a unique commitment to free trade did not prevent Britain from sharing depression with protected nations, while protection in Germany and the United States neither paralyzed enterprise nor stifled invention in those countries, was taken to disprove the supposed universality of the benefits of free trade and the disadvantages of tariffs.[16]

A subtler line was taken by another group of dissenting commissioners,[17] who warned of "the insufficiency of employment," due not only to the restrictions of foreign tariffs on Britain's overseas sales and the invasion of the home market by inexpensive imports, but also the growth in labor productivity resulting from increasingly sophisticated manufacturing technology. Technological unemployment might, after all, frustrate the beneficial effects of market forces in eradicating joblessness. Jobs,

---

[15] *Final Report of the Royal Commission on Depression*, xv, xx.
[16] Ibid., xxxiv–v. Note of Dissent by G. Auldo Jamieson. Jamieson signed the main report.
[17] Ibid., xliii–lxviii. The signatories were Lord Dunraven, W. Farrer Acroyd, P. Albert Muntz, and Nevile Lubbock.

rather than goods, might be scarce. Moreover, tariffs redistributed investment and employment away from unprotected economies.[18]

Finally, this analysis anticipated another familiar anxiety—concerning the structural balance of the British economy. The benefits of the adjustments posited by classical economists might turn out to be insubstantial, for, "in a country possessing vast foreign investments, and a great international buying, selling, and carrying trade," commerce and finance might flourish "whilst the earnings of its industries and the employment of its population are either stagnant or positively declining."[19]

The proposed remedy was a 10 or 15 percent duty on all foreign manufactures, which would resolve the problem of employment in a mature economy and in all likelihood lead (by means of larger and more continuous sales) to the attainment of economies of scale and lower, rather than higher, prices.[20] All in all, it was argued, the circumstances of the world economy had changed since 1846:

To buy everything in the cheapest market—though not permitted to sell in the dearest—may be the best policy, so long as we can find other full and equally remunerative employment for the home enterprise and industry which we displace in so doing. But no longer; for, from the moment in which the combined effect of protective tariffs abroad and foreign competition at home limits our market so as to cramp the free and full exercise of our industries, it begins to choke the living fountain of our wealth, our social well-being, and our national strength. We think the evidence is conclusive that during the past ten or twelve years this point has been reached, and that the adoption of a national policy suited to the changed conditions is imperatively demanded.[21]

Clearly, such arguments did not preclude the presence of special interests and special pleading; nor is there any reason to imagine that the commissioners were intellectually objective. But their comments raised issues that were of general and analytical significance. In particular, they addressed the "dynamic" implications of free trade and protection; their consequences for industrial organization, structural change, and the distribution of employment; and the frailty of the assumptions underlying the advocacy of free trade as a policy for maximizing wealth and employ-

---

[18]Ibid., lv.

[19]Ibid., lxiii–iv.

[20]Ibid., lxv. The minority report also urged the need for close ties with imperial markets for goods and capital.

[21]Ibid., lxvi. The thought that changes in international economic circumstances might involve a change in the basic principles of economic policy was, of course, widely discussed at the time.

ment. (Similar concerns about the deleterious consequences of structural change were expressed by bimetallists in the 1880s and the 1890s: Britain, they held, must not become a nation of "mortgagers and rentiers.")[22]

Such arguments had little effect on the dominant politics or economics of the day. Admittedly, the issues they raised came even more obviously to the surface of affairs in the renewed tariff reform controversy initiated by Joseph Chamberlain in 1903. Fierce as that controversy was, though, it was not characterized by any systematic official investigation of the subject. The government response was relatively low-key and indirect, and the only substantial inquiry into free trade was undertaken by the so-called Tariff Commission—a private group, assembled by Chamberlain's supporters and restricted in its membership to those who favored protection and imperial preference.

Not surprisingly, in view of its dependence on industrial witnesses, the Tariff Commission said little about the presumed competitive weakness of British manufacturing. Instead, protection was advocated principally as a counterweight to the unfair advantages enjoyed by foreign manufacturers in the form of government subsidies, cheap freight rebates, cartel organizations, the dominance of their home markets, and, above all, the tariffs that helped make all this possible.

In one respect, however, the Tariff Commission's evidence went beyond the question of fair competition to examine the "dynamic" effects of protection on organization and efficiency. Contesting the free traders' assertion that protection would increase prices, the Tariff Commission argued that foreign production costs were cheaper precisely because tariff barriers created bigger markets, which facilitated a larger scale of operations and more continuous production operations.[23] Hence, sanguine

---

[22] Although not directly concerned with industrial policy, the advocates of a bimetallic (as against a gold) basis for currency were, in the last resort, intent on supporting British industry and agriculture by a reflationary device. Although they acknowledged the general increase in Britain's wealth and income, they regretted the diminished importance of commodity production and the growing importance of financial services. They were averse to Britain's becoming a cosmopolitan, service-oriented economy. They argued that the basis of true national wealth could be found only in the production of goods, while the redistribution of private wealth resulting from the growing profitability of financial activity entailed a "national loss" through its harmful social consequences and the increased vulnerability of the labor force to unemployment. For this episode, see E. H. H. Green, "Rentiers Versus Producers?: The Political Economy of the Bimetallic Controversy, c. 1880–1898," *English Historical Review* CIII, no. 408 (July 1988): 588–612. Quotations from 600–1, 608.

[23] *Report of the Tariff Commission* (London: P. S. King & Co., 1904–), 1: *The Iron and Steel Trades*, paragraphs 45, 54–61, 77; 2, Part I: *The Cotton Industry*, paragraph 91; 2, Part II: *The Woollen Industry*, paragraph 1383. This point had already been made by

witnesses from the iron and steel and engineering industries claimed that British tariffs would so encourage investment, continuous operations, and larger units of production as, in all likelihood, to *reduce* costs and prices "probably below their present level."[24] The "want of enterprise among British firms," one manufacturer claimed, was attributable to

want of protection. . . . To adopt the newest things you must have a prospect of a reasonable return on expenditure. . . . The effect of a duty would be rather to encourage further expansion of trade and reduce the cost of production by keeping the works that are now going more fully employed. A trade that is liable to be cut into by foreign competition against it at any moment has not the heart to expand.[25]

Arguments about economies of scale were, however, peripheral to the main controversy. More influential in the tariff controversy before 1914 were arguments concerning the relationships between fiscal policy, on the one hand, and the geopolitical position and economic structure of the British economy, on the other.

At the broadest level, critics of free trade were worried that exposure to international market forces—even "successful" adaptation to them—involved a relative expansion of services and a relative decline of manufacturing industry that would reduce both the power of Britain on the world scene and the demand for labor in the British economy. They were little reassured by the obvious fact that Britain dominated the world's financial and commercial systems. The threatened weakening of the manufacturing base—Britain's *relative* decline as an industrial power—would reduce its authority "in the councils of the world."[26] The difficulty with a disproportionate growth in the service sector, it was held, was that "it may mean more money, but it means less men. It may mean more wealth, but it means less welfare."

The idleness of accumulated financial capital and the quaintness of traditional Britain, it was feared, would turn the country into a mere guidebook kingdom, dependent for its income and employment on tour-

some of the members of the Royal Commission on the Depression in Trade and Industry in 1886.
[24]*Report of the Tariff Commission,* 1: *Iron and Steel Trades,* paragraph 77.
[25]Evidence of the Hon. Charles Algernon Parsons on behalf of A. C. Parsons & Co., Mechanical and Electrical Engineers, in *The Report of the Tariff Commission,* 4: *The Engineering Industries,* paragraph 527. Neither the Tariff Commission nor its witnesses considered why a protected home market made it more likely that *any individual firm operating under competitive conditions* would achieve a larger scale of operations.
[26]Julian Amery, *Joseph Chamberlain and the Tariff Reform Campaign: The Life of Joseph Chamberlain, 1901–1903* (London: Macmillan, 1969), 548–9.

ists and the luxury expenditures of the rich—a lugubrious argument that bridges the decades, being used both by a representative of the woollen industry before the Tariff Commission of 1903:

> If something is not done—if we are to go on looking after the consumer in this country, and leaving the producer to take care of himself, I can conceive the time when this country will be the home of a great many millionaires, making their wealth abroad, and employing large numbers of servants and gamekeepers here, whilst many of the great productive industries we now carry on will be transferred to other countries.[27]

and by Lord Weinstock of GEC (Britain's General Electric Company) some eighty years later in his evidence to the House of Lords Select Committee on Overseas Trade:

> What will the service industries be servicing when there is no hardware, when no wealth is actually being produced? We will be servicing, presumably, the production of wealth by others. We will supply the Changing of the Guard, we will supply the Beefeaters around the Tower of London. We will become a curiosity. I do not think that is what Britain is about; I think that is rubbish.[28]

And in the first decade of this century the growing importance of money capital rather than manufacturing industry was held to be "a very bad thing for the workmen of this country. It perhaps accounts for the fact that, while we are so rich, while the income-tax is going up every day, there is more and more unemployment and thirteen millions of people are on the verge of hunger."[29]

Obviously, there was much special pleading and a certain amount of political deviousness in such arguments. But policy and political aims were not always independent of a reasoned analysis of Britain's contemporary economic position. The pessimists' sense of the future embodied a perception of the possible consequences of Britain's changing international role and economic structures, and of the painful maturity of its major staple industries.

Such anxieties also applied to structural changes *within* the manufacturing sector. Here, orthodox economics taught that in a mature country with mobile resources, the import of goods that could be produced at home did not displace labor, but merely changed the "direction of employ-

---

[27] *Report of the Tariff Commission*, 2, Part II: *Woollen Industry*, paragraph 1484.
[28] *House of Lords. Report from the Select Committee on Overseas Trade* (HL 238-I. London: HMSO, 1985), 42–3.
[29] Charles W. Boyd, ed., *Mr. Chamberlain's Speeches* (London: Constable, 1914), vol. I, 284.

ment."[30] But the social consequences of pressures to change the "direction of employment" were precisely what was feared by many tariff reformers. It seemed to them that unrestrained market forces might lead to the displacement of high-grade by low-grade labor and the consequent destruction of skills and the demoralization of social classes.

The low wages and unemployment resulting from the decline of a major industry were thought to have "a negative and degrading effect, far greater than the positive and elevating effect of a period of high wages and overtime."[31] Every great irregularity of employment, it was argued, "involves terrible wreckage of the capital fixed in humanity."[32] The process was fraught with social danger. In Chamberlain's well-known philippic:

Look how easy it is. Your once great trade in sugar refining is gone; all right, try jam. Your iron trade is going; never mind, you can make mouse traps. The cotton trade is threatened; well, what does it matter to you? Suppose you try dolls' eyes. . . . But how long is this to go on? . . . Why on earth are you to suppose that the same process which ruined the sugar refinery will not in the course of time be applied to jam. And when jam is gone? Then you have to find something else. And believe me, that although the industries of this country are very various, you cannot go on for ever. You cannot go on watching with indifference the disappearance of your principal industries, and always hoping that you will be able to replace them by secondary and inferior industries.[33]

Keen as all these arguments were, free trade and free markets prevailed: the sense that those who advocated protection represented vested

---

[30]Alfred Marshall, "Memorandum on the Fiscal Policy of International Trade" (1903), in *Official Papers by Alfred Marshall* (London: Royal Economic Society, 1926).

[31]W. J. Ashley, *The Progress of the German Working Classes in the Last Quarter of the Century* (London: Longmans, 1911), 116. Also p. 79: "Adam Smith, . . . relying on the transferability of capital, expected that the lessening prosperity of one particular home industry owing to foreign competition would result in the transference of capital to another home industry. But, as we have seen, it may lead to the transference of capital to the same industry in another country." For a modern analysis suggesting that Britain's exports were already significantly dependent on relatively less skilled labor, see N. F. R. Crafts and M. Thomas, "Comparative Advantages and U.K. Manufacturing Trade, 1910–35," *Economic Journal* 96 (September 1986): 629–45.

[32]H. J. Mackinder, *Money-Power and Man-Power: The Underlying Principles Rather Than the Statistics of Tariff Reform* (London: Simpkin, Marshall, 1905), 142. Compare Joseph Chamberlain: "Even if it could be proved in the long run that the country did not suffer in wealth, that there had been a transfer from one trade to another, still I should say, when you count up all the families that have been reduced to misery, all the heart-burnings, all the suffering that has been caused by these changes to the individual, when you think of all the honest men who have gone to the workhouse and can never be brought back again to the ranks of continuous labour—when you think of all these things, then I say, even if the country were enriched its wealth would have been dearly purchased." Boyd, ed., *Mr. Chamberlain's Speeches*, 224.

[33]Boyd, ed., *Mr. Chamberlain's Speeches*, 248.

interests was too strong; the business groups committed to abundant exports were too entrenched; the masses attracted by the prospect of continued cheap food were too suspicious. But the failure of the tariff reform campaign was not simply a question of political power. The fact was that the critics of free trade and markets had not yet succeeded in articulating a persuasive body of theory to justify their views. And the economic history of the prewar years implied that their apprehensions were illusory: the economy was buoyant and the opportunities for industrial change and adaptation appeared far from exhausted. The fear of structural unemployment, argued the president of the Local Government Board in 1908, embodied merely "lachrymose appeals and unstatesmanlike palliatives" at a time when wages and exports were both rising and pauperism was falling: "If we are a dying race, with a vanishing trade and disappearing industries, what comes of these remarkable figures?"[34]

Nor did the controversy lead to any elaborate government investigation: the prime minister firmly resisted proposals for a royal commission on the subject, and his promise of an official inquiry into the condition of British trade in the context of fiscal policy came to little more than an exercise internal to the cabinet. And at the Board of Trade there was official resistance to the analysis of the claim of the Liberal leader, Campbell-Bannerman, that protection would aggravate poverty. ("It is a waste of time," argued Llewellyn Smith, "to apply illusory tests to illusory guesses.")[35] Still, it was impossible to avoid some official empirical response.

In the end, the government's formal reaction to the tariff reform movement took the form of a series of parliamentary publications, most of them statistical, designed to provide reassurance on Britain's commercial performance and social and economic conditions, on which pessimistic comments had been bandied about in the controversy stimulated by the Tariff Reform Movement.[36] The principal exception was the belated publication, in 1908, of a paper by Alfred Marshall on the theory and principles of tariff policy, which had been originally composed at the request of the Board of Trade in 1903. This was a cogent presentation of the histori-

[34]*Hansard*, January 30, 1908, cols. 275–7, 333–4, 338.
[35]Quoted in R. Davidson, "Llewellyn Smith, the Labour Department and Government Growth, 1886–1909," in Gillian Sutherland, ed., *Studies in the Growth of Nineteenth-Century Government* (London: Routledge and Kegan Paul, 1972), 256.
[36]These were presumably the outcome of the rather indecisive "inquiry by the Cabinet for the Cabinet" announced by Balfour soon after the controversy began. Coats, "Political Economy," 201.

cal context of free-trade theory, an acknowledgment of the relevance of protection to relatively underdeveloped countries with infant industries—and a firm rejection of tariffs in Britain's case. Protection, Marshall argued, would deprive Britain's lackadaisical entrepreneurs of the stimulus to further effort and (even more serious) would be open to corruption and manipulation by powerful interests whose sole qualifications for protection would be their influence and voting power.[37]

The tariff controversy, therefore, did augment the supply of empirical information concerning the cost of living (the Board of Trade's inquiries were the origin of the modern retail price index), British and colonial trade, and long-run social and economic statistics. Such statistics aside, a controversy concerning fiscal policy, which had raised sophisticated questions about national economic structures and processes, failed to augment basic analytical knowledge or to lead the government toward a detailed empirical or theoretical examination of the workings of industrial evolution and tariffs.

THE AUDIT OF WAR

As in so many other spheres of government economic activity, the abnormal circumstances of World War I, together with anxieties concerning future commercial prospects, served to relax the inhibitions that had previously constrained official inquiry into Britain's trade and fiscal policy.

At a general level, this subject was most directly considered by a network of committees appointed by the Board of Trade to inquire into the prospects and needs of specific industries, and by a coordinating Committee on Commercial and Industrial Policy after the war (appointed in 1916 and chaired by the Unionist free trader, Lord Balfour of Burleigh).

The most immediately important issue to be considered related, naturally enough, to the fostering of those industries whose products were "essential to the future safety of the nation"—many of which turned out to have been controlled by Germany or by nations dominated by Germany. This inadequacy of British industry imposed a shock sufficiently great to overcome the constraints of economic ideology: it was now

[37]Marshall, "Fiscal Policy." For the history of Marshall's memorandum, see Wood, *British Economists and Empire*. Some of the government's empirical publications continued a series originally published in 1896, but most were clearly stimulated by the contemporary debate about trade and the social and economic conditions of the people.

considered vital that the government should foster "key" or "pivotal" industries by encouragement, subsidy, and if necessary protection[38]—a recommendation that ultimately led to selective "safeguarding" tariffs. The committee also recommended the creation of a Special Industries Board "charged with the duty of watching the course of industrial development" and framing detailed schemes for "the promotion and assistance" of industries of this special character. Industries receiving aid should be expected to maintain "efficient and adequate production at reasonable prices," failing which "the Government should itself undertake the manufacture of such articles as may be essential for national safety."[39]

All this was, of course, a strategic version of the infant-industry argument, which made the contamination of free trade easier.[40] But when Balfour of Burleigh's committee raised its eyes to general issues, it proceeded with greater caution and avoided the controversial question of protection. At the same time, however, it was adamant in its comments on the structural deficiencies of individual British industries (especially iron and steel and engineering). Basing itself largely on the rather dogmatic "investigations" by subsidiary committees, it criticized British entrepreneurs for their neglect of the economies of scale, their excessive individualism, and their inability or unwillingness to overcome the fragmentation of industrial and marketing structures.[41] The committee was also apparently sympathetic to the recommendations of the Departmental Committee on Iron and Steel that public funds be applied to building "large and well-designed new units for cheap production upon modern lines," and that tariff protection be given so as to encourage private investment. Nevertheless, nothing came of these proposals, and no wartime investigation was particularly eager to advocate state intervention to overcome the general deficiencies of market and individualistic decision making. Nevertheless, although exhortation rather than legislation remained the favored route to overall industrial reform, doubts about the efficacy of the market (and, by

[38]The committee investigated and specifically mentioned synthetic dyes, tungsten, magnetos, optical and chemical glass, hosiery needles, and limit and screw gauges.

[39]Commercial and Industrial Policy. Interim Report on Certain Essential Industries (Parliamentary Papers, 1918, XIII; Cd. 9032, 1918). Nothing came of the proposal for such a board.

[40]Even before the committee was appointed, the so-called McKenna duties of 1915 had imposed a duty of $33\frac{1}{3}$ percent to raise revenue, save shipping, and protect motor cars, clocks and watches, and musical instruments.

[41]Final Report of the Committee on Commercial and Industrial Policy After the War (Parliamentary Papers, 1918, XIII; Cd. 9035, 1918).

implication, laissez-faire) were obviously reaching serious proportions. Despite the absence of any new thinking on the larger analytical problems of industrial organization and performance, inquiries during World War I identified issues of "market failure." And it was as a result of this experience that during and immediately after the war some reform of the operation of the peacetime economy was at least contemplated.

The principal focus of this new thinking was the sense that larger-scale units of operation were essential to industrial health—and might have to be encouraged by state intervention in the marketplace. Such action occurred, for example, in relation to transport and public utilities, in which the potential weaknesses of private enterprise were thought to be inimical to industrial progress and in which, therefore, official inquiries served to advance the cause of centralized or public provision and managed amalgamation.

In the case of the railways, although nothing came of the hints of nationalization dropped by cabinet members in 1918–20, a Ministry of Transport was created in 1919, wartime controls were extended to 1921, and in that year legislation was introduced to merge more than 100 railway companies into four giant and noncompeting private systems.

World War I produced similarly radical thinking on the subject of fuel policy. The need for larger and more efficient electricity generating plants, for example, led to the establishment of a body of electricity commissioners in 1919. Ostensibly responsible for the reorganization of the industry, the commissioners were, in practice, denied the compulsory powers necessary to overcome the vested interests of private and local-authority supply companies. But this failure led a conservative government (in 1926) to create a public corporation (the Central Electricity Board) to construct a national "grid" for the distribution of electricity and effective regulation of the scale of operations and pricing of supply companies. Such an "extreme" step was made easier by the fact that the potential industrial beneficiaries of cheaper fuel had a far weightier political and ideological influence than the interest groups of the electricity industry. But the move was also justified by a "social benefit" model of fuel supply, even though the corporation had to raise its funds without a formal government guarantee.

The committee that examined the problem and produced a forthright proposal regarded the matter "from this view-point of the needs of the country as a whole" and criticized "the present system of individual generation and independent undertakings, each pursuing an uncoordinated and unrelated policy of development." It therefore proposed "not a change of ownership, but the partial subordination of vested interests in [electricity] generation to that of a new authority for the benefit of all."[42]

Coalmining was the object of similar discussions, underpinned by a full-blown inquiry in the form of the Royal (Sankey) Commission of 1919. But nothing came of the various proposals that emerged from the so-called Sankey Commission (or of the prime minister's offer, reflecting his original intentions, to sponsor large-scale district-based corporations).[43]

There were, of course, other wartime and postwar discussions of government-backed industrial change, but few were based on new knowledge. Their ultimate justification (beyond the strategic imperatives of war or the need to ensure harmony in industrial relations) lay in a relatively familiar, if mostly implicit, contrast between social and private costs and benefits. But they did illustrate the widening of "knowledge" in two senses: first, the perception that market forces might produce suboptimal results, that individual businesses were not always able to pursue policies that would have been in their *collective* interest, let alone in the interest of the economy as a whole; second, the incorporation of assumptions about the workings of industry, and justifications for intervention, into the realm of the intellectually respectable and the ideologically possible.

INDUSTRIAL STRUCTURES AND ECONOMIC PERFORMANCE
BETWEEN THE WORLD WARS

These developments became more critical between the wars as disappointment with the country's industrial performance came to be focused on the organization and efficiency of the staple and traditional industries. As if to fulfill the gloomy prophecies of the prewar tariff reformers, those industries began their crippling decline, unemployment appeared to have become endemic, and Britain's place in world trade was threatened. And even before the demise of the gold standard in 1931 and of free trade in the next year, these developments provoked an ever elaborated chorus of dissent on the subject of orthodox theory and policy.

Nonetheless, the interwar period seemed to witness relatively little

---

[42]Ministry of Transport, *Report of the Committee Appointed to Review the National Problem of the Supply of Electrical Energy* (London: HMSO, 1926).
[43]For Lloyd George's desire to avoid nationalization but willingness to contemplate restructuring within the industry, see Barry Supple, *The History of the British Coal Industry*, vol. 4: *1913–46: The Political Economy of Decline* (Oxford: Oxford University Press, 1987), 138–9; and Norman and Jeanne Mackenzie, eds., *The Diary of Beatrice Webb*, III (Cambridge, Mass.: Harvard University Press, 1984), 333–7.

amendment of the weight of official orthodoxy on the workings of the economy or the market bases of *general* industrial policy.[44] But depression and the manifest obstacles to industrial reorganization and factor mobility *did* come increasingly and explicitly to official attention, and led to a reallocation of policy priorities and a new orientation in the discussion of the industrial economy. In such an environment, microeconomic policies became more important and official investigations became increasingly relevant as political as well as intellectual devices.

One expression of all this—especially given the failure of deflationary policies in the 1920s—was greater emphasis on the structural deficiencies of British industry. Even orthodox opinion was ultimately persuaded that structural change to attain enhanced efficiency might be an unavoidable alternative to deflation, which carried unacceptable social and political risks.[45]

The view that an excessively small scale of business operations was one of the prevailing problems of British industry was widely held. In the case of electricity supply or railway services, the benefits of large-scale operations were so obvious and diffused us to allow little controversy. But the same could hardly be said of other industries, where "externalities" were less obvious, existing interests were more entrenched and suspicious, and the requisite industrial strategies and structures were more problematic. Hence, even though the "rationalization" of staple industries and the fostering of new industries were believed to be desirable—even essential—for Britain's industrial competitiveness, they were generally officially judged to be goals that private enterprise and market forces could best attain.

This was, of course, far from a consensus view, and dissenters undertook a number of important unofficial inquiries into British industry.[46] But

---

[44]Orthodox attitudes were reflected not simply in the weight of day-to-day Treasury opinion, but also, and hardly surprisingly, in the formal inquiries that punctuated the formulation of policy under political pressure as it related to monetary and exchange policy (the Cunliffe and Chamberlain/Bradbury committees) or to the presumed dangers of public-expenditure extravagance (the Geddes and May committees). None of these even assumed that there were viable alternatives to the traditional policies of financial and monetary rectitude that they had been appointed to advocate.

[45]For the Treasury's concern with industrial efficiency and organization in the context of unemployment policy, see Chapter 6 of this volume.

[46]*Coal and Power: The Report of an Inquiry Presided Over by the Rt. Hon. D. Lloyd George* (London: Liberal Party, 1924); *Britain's Industrial Future: Being the Report of the Liberal Industrial Inquiry* (London: Liberal Party Summer Schools, 1928). For a discussion of these developments, see Alan Booth and Melvyn Pack, *Employment, Capital and Economic Policy: Great Britain, 1918–1939* (Oxford: Blackwell, 1985), Chapter 3; L. Hannah, *The Rise of the Corporate Economy* (London: Methuen, 2d ed., 1983).

the fact that support for the idea of industrial rationalization came to be almost universal in the interwar decades did not mean that there was any significant amendment of *overall* government policy. Admittedly, some members of the Unionist administration in the late 1920s toyed with the idea of government encouragement of reorganization in the principal staple industries. But nothing came of this, and general "policy" was confined to exhortation, quiet argument, and "industrial diplomacy."[47]

It also happened that the overall competitive performance of the industrial economy, although it was perhaps the most pervasive problem, produced the least adventurous additions to official knowledge and the least radical official proposals. This situation was exemplified in the most comprehensive example of official investigation—that by the Committee on Industry and Trade (which was appointed in 1924, under the chairmanship of Arthur Balfour, and produced its final report in 1929). The Balfour Committee's scope was vast, for it was established "to inquire into the conditions and prospects of British industry and commerce with special reference to the export trade."[48] It published a number of individual industry surveys, as well as surveys of overseas markets, of industrial relations, and of the factors making for industrial and commercial efficiency; and altogether, in its five years of existence, it met 136 times and took evidence from 240 witnesses.[49]

In addition to gathering a huge amount of factual data about British industry, the committee considered the general determinants of efficiency and inefficiency. It also produced elaborate arguments in favor of rationalization and larger-scale productive units. But its prescriptions were formulated largely in market-based terms. It argued that the dangerous loss of Britain's competitive power could be redressed only by subjecting its industries to "a thorough process of re-conditioning," involving the reform of human relations and the rationalization of structures. In such a process, the majority of the committee implied, there was relatively little scope for government initiative. Rather, in a telling passage it insisted that none of the basic industries had been so weak-

---

[47]The term is Roberts's; see Richard Roberts, "The Administrative Origins of Industrial Diplomacy: An Aspect of Government-Industry Relations," in John Turner, ed., *Businessmen and Politics: Studies of Business Activity in British Politics, 1900–1945* (London: Heinemann, 1984), 93–104.

[48]*Final Report of the Committee on Industry and Trade* (Parliamentary Papers, 1928–9, vol. VII; Cmd. 3282, 1929), 234.

[49]*Committee on Industry and Trade.* The committee initiated special studies of the eight principal groups of exporting trades (coal, iron and steel, engineering and shipbuilding, electrical manufacturing, cotton, wool and worsted, chemicals, and clothing).

ened "as not to have the power within themselves to take the first measures towards their own regeneration, provided that they are thoroughly convinced that such measures are essential and unavoidable, and that they must be taken by themselves without reliance on any outside authority."[50] The Balfour Committee did little more than present a picture of market imperfections in a setting where the only feasible way of tackling them was by self-help.[51]

This verdict applies, of course, to the committee's *majority* report. The minority memorandum, signed by six of the members, challenged the view of the majority, that "private enterprise and free competition can be left, by themselves, gradually to right things." Instead, they argued in favor of collective methods of organization and control and the use of state power to effect "a rapid and general transformation in economic organization and industrial structure."[52] The investigations that provided an official platform for such minority opinions also provided information and impetus that helped in their formulation. And to that extent, the Balfour Committee's inquiry served to encourage and sharpen dissent. But, as with the majority opinion, rational investigation apparently had not transformed analysis or advocacy. It was publicity rather than insight that had been advanced. For the advocates of "coordinated" state intervention were unspecific as to actual policies and signally failed to tackle in any systematic way the knotty problems of how schemes for reorganization might be identified, assessed, managed, or financed—or how it would be possible for governments to overcome the lack of cooperation from those with the technical and managerial expertise.[53]

Hence, considered in terms of their influence or the cogency of their analysis, neither the majority nor the minority reports of the Balfour Committee represented much new knowledge (in the sense of policy-oriented understanding) about industrial performance in Britain and its putative decline. But the committee's extended inquiry did serve a num-

---

[50]Ibid., 297, 299.

[51]The committee was not, of course, opposed to all state intervention. Thus, it argued that the main obstacle to the advance of industrial research was "the imperfect receptivity towards scientific ideas on the part of British industry." It continued by accepting that, although the ideal solution was that industry should undertake its own practical research, such a change must come gradually and that in the interim state help for industrial research associations was appropriate. *Committee on Industry and Trade*, 218–9.

[52]Ibid., 303–4.

[53]The minority memorandum's only specific proposals were for the creation of two bodies (a National Economic Committee for broad strategy and a National Employment and Development Board for the execution of policy), together with the state control of land, coal mines, transport, electricity, and finance.

ber of unusual, even pioneering, tasks. It generated a substantial amount of *information* about the structure and performance of British industry. It activated and institutionalized subsidiary inquiries by various government departments, and thereby helped advance the modernizing, information functions of government ministries. It encouraged public discussion of industrial issues, helping to bring them to the forefront of the political agenda. And it attracted attention to critical problems of business enterprise and the presumed deficiencies of the British industrial system. Above all, and notwithstanding its reluctance to advocate government intervention, the Balfour Committee exposed the unstable character of industrial competition and survival where structures were determined by private decisions; and it drew attention to the economic importance, yet diverse nature, of occupational, geographic, and functional mobility.

INDUSTRIAL ECONOMICS AND STRUCTURAL DISLOCATION

During the 1920s and 1930s, with the principal exception of the Balfour Committee, the overall problem of industrial organization received relatively little systematic attention from government inquiries. Indeed, the discussion of political economy, even among unofficial groups, touched much less on the long-run, geopolitical, and large structural questions that had characterized prewar controversy. Even the final abandonment of free trade in 1931–2 came through the necessity of crisis and *force majeur*, rather than through the sorts of considerations that had moved men to such far-reaching thoughts in Edwardian England. Yet this result was hardly surprising: free trade was too sensitive to be the object of public and official investigation. As with devaluation, when drastic change was introduced it could most easily arrive unheralded.

Between the wars, then, the earlier anxieties about the country's international industrial standing were overshadowed by the differential impact of depression and structural change on the erstwhile staple export industries. Hence, it was in relation to coal, iron and steel, shipbuilding, and cotton that the intensity of social and economic crisis was sufficiently keen to overcome inhibitions and generate the sort of official inquiry that had been neglected before World War I.

Of all the staple industries, coalmining, by virtue of its critical social and political position, was subject to the most persistent official scrutiny. And although few of these inquiries produced new economic knowledge in the sense of novel or unorthodox analyses of the industry's operations, departmental and cabinet investigations, and public inquiries such as those chaired by Sankey (1919), Macmillan (1925), and Samuel (1925–6) played a vital role in disseminating information about the industry's plight, the deficiencies of its fragmented structure, and the essentially political nature of its industrial-relations problems. They therefore paved the way for the official enforcement of cartel arrangements that, from 1930, circumvented market mechanisms for the sake of social stability and a minimum of welfare.[54]

There were, of course, limits to the departure from a market-based industry. In particular, and despite the widespread view that only collective intervention to ensure mergers could overcome the mine owners' ability to improve productivity, the structure of coal *production* was left untouched. Nevertheless, public inquiry legitimized the drastic intervention embodied in the subsidies to coal (1919, 1921, 1925–6), the Coal Mines Act of 1930, the tightening of market controls in the early 1930s, and the Coal Act of 1938 (which nationalized the royalties and looked to greater administrative power to enforce the restructuring of production). Such experiments in political economy embodied administrative counterweights to perceived deficiencies of individualistic market forces and structures; but they were not based on any elaborate alternative theoretical "knowledge" of industrial structures and performance. Rather, they presupposed the factual knowledge, and sheer weight of sentiment, and the ritual displays associated with formal inquiry.

Like coalmining, the iron and steel industry was handicapped by fragmented structures, inadequate technology, and (apparently) excessively individualistic decision making, wary of the private costs and risks of extensive reorganization.[55] Its business leaders were reluctant to commit themselves to major programs of rationalization without the protection of the home market, and the government was reluctant to promise, let alone provide, the desired tariff protection without firm assurances of reorganization and improved productivity. These issues became manifest in an internal government inquiry (by the cabinet's Committee of Civil Research) in 1925, when the Treasury's view—that protection would not guarantee reorganization, would coddle inefficiency, and would create an

---

[54]Supple, *Coal Industry*, Chapters 4 and 6. The various committees did not all take the same line on major issues of political economy.
[55]For the following information about the interwar steel industry, see Steven Tolliday, "Tariffs and Steel, 1916–1934: The Politics of Industrial Decline," in Turner, ed., *Businessmen and Politics*.

uncomfortable precedent—won the day against an uncertain and woolly argument by the steelmakers. Indeed, both the inquiry of 1925 and another by the Labour government in 1929 concluded that protection would delay, not encourage, industrial reform. Moreover, in this case the role of formal investigation was ambiguous. While the 1925 and 1929 inquiries were ill-informed on some crucial technical questions, the government was understandably reluctant to delegate policy-making on the politically sensitive issues of protection to an independent committee whose recommendations would become public.

Finally, when protection became inevitable, as general free trade was abandoned in 1931–2, the government's reluctance to enforce ruthless rationalization on uncooperative businesses meant that the industry was, in effect, left to its own, inadequate, reorganizing devices behind a protective tariff screen. Knowledge of what the industry needed had, indeed, been transformed by investigation; but, as happened in the case of other staple industries, the "fundamental axioms" of laissez-faire were still sufficiently powerful, especially when intermingled with the practical and political problems involved, to prevent the state from taking the initiative suggested by that knowledge.

REGIONAL ECONOMIC POLICY

Although the predominant concern of interwar industrial inquiries was with individual industries, the problems that gave rise to such inquiries were also embodied in chronic regional disparities in the distribution of employment and resources. And these, too, attracted official attention and investigation.

Given the regional concentration of the stagnation in staple industries, by the late 1920s it had become necessary to pay much more political attention to the geographic and community aspects of industrial depression and to the issue of the imperfect mobility of economic resources.

In 1928, a year before the Balfour Committee's final report urged that economic salvation must lie within each industry, an Industrial Transference Board, staffed by senior civil servants, concluded that a chronic surplus of labor in some of Britain's heavy industries must be regarded "as a fact, and . . . too much reliance should not be placed on a reduction of this surplus by measures taken within the industries." Instead, the excess labor would have to be dispersed, with government help, away from the depressed areas.[56] The resulting modest schemes to subsidize migration and retraining did relatively little to affect the problems of regional mass unemployment; but this is less important than the fact that an official inquiry had accepted the imperfections of the labor market, reflected in chronic regional surpluses of labor, as "knowledge" both in the sense of empirical information and as the basis of feasible policy.

Indeed, once the government appreciated the extent (or, more often, the political dangers) of the problem of the depressed areas, it was logical that it should initiate other formal inquiries—either to explore the character of the problem or to manifest an apparent willingness to act. However, the state did little to gather information about the regional issues until 1930, when the Labour government's Board of Trade commissioned five industrial surveys of the worst-hit areas. But these essentially factual inquiries contained few analyses of possible policy; and their results—not published until after the fall of the Labour government—were in any case overshadowed by the widespread Depression, which reached its nadir in 1932.

It was only with the beginnings of cyclical recovery that the relative deprivation of depressed areas once more entered the arena of political controversy. In 1934 the National government was obliged to initiate four further investigations (of South Wales, Durham and Tyneside, Cumberland, and the Clyde Valley). Each of these regional inquiries was the responsibility of an individual politician or civil servant. But the extensive information gathered illuminated for the first time at a directly official level the complexity and desperation of the regional problem created by Britain's industrial maturity and the structural changes in world trade.

Symptomatic of the evolution of this sort of knowledge was the verdict of Evan Wallace, a junior minister in the National government, assessing conditions in the Durham and Tyneside coalfield. Past prosperity, he acknowledged, had been based on British industry's ability to find "continually expanding markets overseas"; but such markets had not only ceased to expand: their contraction was likely to continue and then be replaced by stagnation. This transformation of the world economy, and of Britain's position within it, had serious implications for the use of resources in the regions formerly dependent on the export of such staples as coal, engineering products, and iron and steel. Against such a back-

[56]*Industrial Transference Board Report* (Cmd. 3156, 1928), 15.

ground, old shibboleths about the flexible operation of markets and the role of government policy were naturally open to challenge. As Wallace said of Durham and Northumberland:

If, therefore, it be admitted that the industrial depression and the heavy unemployment in this area are due to causes outside the control of those who reside in it, it is equally true to say there is no likelihood that the same forces which have created the present situation will automatically readjust it, except after a lapse of time and at a cost of human suffering and economic waste which no modern Government would care to contemplate. Durham and Tyneside can only escape from the vicious circle, where depression has created unemployment and unemployment intensified depression, by means of some positive external assistance.[57]

The very concept of "positive" external assistance opened new fields of policy as well as knowledge.[58] And the various reports on the depressed areas, and the ensuing public and political debates, provoked a (somewhat reluctant) change of policy in the form of "Special Areas" legislation, which provided for the appointment of two commissioners—albeit with inadequate powers—to try to encourage local development, under stringent rules and in circumscribed districts. The new measures were in part a belated recognition of a decisive change in Britain's role in the world economy—a change that had been implied by the stagnation of the staple industries in the 1920s and perhaps most dramatically signaled by the dropping of the gold standard and the adoption of protection in 1931–2. They were also, and perhaps in larger part, an acknowledgment of the political dangers of persistent neglect of the distressed areas. Once again, inquiry had served not so much to discover a hitherto unknown cache of factual or analytical knowledge as to bring that knowledge to the surface of political events and make possible the successful exercise of political pressure for a change of direction.[59]

There was, however, another side to the regional problem: *excessive* development and concentration of resources in the rapidly growing areas. The resulting industrial "congestion" was a "problem" that preeminently

[57] *Reports of Investigations into Industrial Conditions in Certain Depressed Areas* (Cmd. 4728, 1934).

[58] Wallace called for a program of local investment in social capital; reform of the coal royalties; the formation of an Industrial Development Company for Tyneside; the reform of local government in the region; improved transference; the dispersal of the excessive concentration of industry in and around London; and the appointment of a local commissioner or small board to coordinate development projects.

[59] By the same token, the subsequent reports of the commissioners helped create the knowledge and environment within which extensions of the legislation (and the commissioners' powers) became possible and even inevitable.

lent itself to inquiry. Indeed, it had of necessity been mentioned in some of the investigations of the distressed areas. The 1934 report on Durham and Tyneside, for example, criticized the "waste of social capital" involved in the large-scale movement of population into London, and urged that the government could no longer regard industrial location with indifference, but must exercise "a measure of control" through "some form of national planning of industry."[60] And the commissioner for special areas (England and Wales) in his report of 1936 advocated government intervention to disperse the congestion of industry in and around London.[61]

The government accepted some of these principles. New legislation allowed the commissioner to offer modest financial incentives to new plants in depressed areas. And in 1937 the Royal (Barlow) Commission on the Geographical Distribution of the Industrial Population was appointed to investigate not simply the economic implications of concentration, but much wider questions of health and welfare, communications, and the vulnerability to air raids. With the appointment of this commission, the possible tension between social costs and individual economic benefits became an explicitly political issue insofar as it affected industrial policy.

The most obvious clash of opinion concerning industrial location before the Barlow Commission was exemplified by evidence from two government departments. On one side, the Board of Trade defended both "individual choice" and the economic rationality of private enterprise. The market, it was claimed, worked well. Resisting arguments that social costs of an explicitly economic sort might arise from individual choice, the Board of Trade's spokesman warned of "the dangers to the economic interests of the country which must be guarded against in any attempt to direct industries away from particular localities." He also asserted that the actual distribution approximated to the economically optimum from the viewpoint of business and the country as a whole.[62]

On the other side, however, and reinforcing a strong line of questioning from sympathetic commissioners like Patrick Abercrombie and Ernest Bevin, the principal witness on behalf of the Ministry of Labour, Humbert Wolfe, was much more alert to the possible social costs involved in the

[60]*Report of the Royal Commission on the Geographical Distribution of the Industrial Population* (Parliamentary Papers, 1939–40; IV; Cmd. 6135, 1940), 107.
[61]Quoted in ibid., 3.
[62]*Minutes of Evidence Taken Before the Royal Commission on the Geographical Distribution of the Industrial Population* (London: HMSO, 1937–8), I, 93–4.

unequal distribution of industrial populations. Wolfe pointed out, for example, that, even for the industrialist, economic considerations were not always decisive in determining location (personal preference or the accident of original location also played important parts). It was also necessary to take account of "considerations of a social nature closely affecting the welfare and contentment of labour." Indeed, led by persuasive questioning from Abercrombie, he acknowledged that the concept of economic costs and benefits (to which the Board of Trade had ostensibly confined its evidence) was itself ambiguous: to modern economists, "economic" considerations were not confined to a specific industry, but might equally be relevant to the overall environment of industry. In an admission that could have far-reaching consequences for the knowledge base of official policy, Wolfe accepted that "there are really two types of economy, the economy to the industrialist and the economy to the community."[63]

In its report, the commission did not deny that the rapid changes and high financial risks of modern industrial and commercial activity "represent emphatically a field of energetic individual initiative rather than of cautious Government control." Yet the fact remained that intense industrial concentration involved economic as well as social "handicaps and even in some respects dangers to the nation's life and development, and we are of the opinion that definite action should be taken by the Government towards remedying them."[64]

In the event, the commissioners, although all of the opinion that a regulatory authority was needed "to protect the national interest,"[65] were unable to agree on the exact powers that needed to be exercised by the state, or whether those powers should be applied generally or only in "congested" areas. Nevertheless, their inquiry had demonstrated that some substantial increase in powers was indisputably needed. These, they agreed, should be exercised through a strong National Industrial Board, which would curb the influx of resources to already crowded areas.

These conclusions were muffled by the advent of World War II (the Barlow Commission's report was not signed until the end of 1939). But, in the long run, the war also served to give greater momentum to the

---

[63]Ibid., 274–6.
[64]Ibid., 192–5.
[65]The Barlow Commission's emphasis of the gap between private and public costs, of the drawbacks of relying on market forces to determine industrial structure, of the national welfare, and of the scope for government policy were all reminiscent of strains in the argument of the minority reports of the Royal Commission on the Depression in Trade and Industry of the 1880s.

revision of knowledge and the advocacy of market amendments represented by this latest inquiry into the workings of industrial society. During and after the war the exercise of government power to influence the location of industry—and therefore to shape the course of industrial development—became a virtual orthodoxy.

INDUSTRIAL MATURITY, POLITICS, AND ECONOMICS

During the first fifty years of Britain's industrial decline or maturity, public perception had focused on a limited number of "strategic" issues: free trade, the balance of services and manufacturing, the organization of industry, and regional imbalances in the distribution of production. The terms in which free trade was debated before World War I had relatively little effect on orthodox economic knowledge, although the debate undoubtedly helped diffuse the idea that tariffs might be advantageous as well as respectable. The most interesting contribution of the protectionists—the concept of the "dynamic" effects of free trade or protection on the balance and organization of economic activity and the quality and distribution of employment—was not embodied in particularly rigorous theory, and rested more on assertion than demonstration. But it, too, set the scene for a reappraisal of Britain's position in the international economy. That reappraisal, however, owed more to the pressure of events than to the ratiocination of committees of inquiry. Protection, like the abandonment of the gold standard, when it came, was a practical response to forces beyond the economy's control—that is, to the steady reduction in the importance to Britain of the world economy and exports and the abrupt impact of a severe depression.

Formal inquiries—at general and industry-specific levels—also shed new light on the deficiencies of the market in terms of industrial organization. They suggested what seemed obvious to the casual observer, namely, that in Britain's principal industries, competitive forces failed to produce units of production of an optimum size. With rare exceptions, however, no industrial crisis was sufficiently severe to prompt governments to intervene extensively to reorganize a major industry.

In contrast, the economic and political experience of regional stagnation and congestion did stimulate new views of individualism and new industrial policies. In this last respect the most far-reaching changes came in the 1940s. And these policy changes were undoubtedly facilitated by the investigations that had been the initial response to political pressure.

Yet the fact remains that the most powerful stimulus came from the experience of the Depression and structural change between the wars, which had served to accustom people to new ideas, even if they were not instantly accepted or yet translated into effective policies.

Moreover, beyond the dislocation of slumps in industrial activity lay a longer-term experience—the change in the international economy, in the presumed vital role of exports, and in the character of a maturing industrial society. The fact of a permanent reduction in the world market for Britain's erstwhile staples had been acknowledged (even semiofficially) after the "economic blizzard" of 1929–32. With the Barlow report, the reduced importance of railways and steam power, the end of the era of "the unimpeded division of labour" in the world economy, and the decisive transformation of Britain's position had all become starting-points for policy. In this sense the Barlow report marked an important stage in the heightened perception of the structural and regional implications of growth as well as decline. It was in many ways the culmination of the 1930s spirit of political-economy inquiry.

What are we to make of the spate of contemporary investigations? Certainly, they helped legitimize and justify analyses, ideas, and proposals that were increasingly widely held and that, though resisted by those in authority, would ultimately be reflected in novel policies. Hence, although government departments accepted the new assumptions with varying degrees of enthusiasm after the Depression and the disjointed recovery, as a result of World War II (which engendered even more far-reaching and radical government inquiries) and the sociopolitical changes that accompanied and followed the war, the transition to political action became relatively effortless. Once again, therefore, it was crisis or the threat of crisis, whether in war or in the depths of the Depression and of social dislocation, that provoked new thinking and therefore new knowledge, and enabled that thinking to be incorporated into established institutions and policies.

Insofar as Britain's industrial "decline" was the stimulant or the object of inquiry and readjustment, it was only when that "decline" was manifested in dramatically painful terms that the pursuit of "knowledge" and legitimacy through official investigation became an important element in the development of political economy. Indeed, from the current perspective, it is significant that the focus of inquiry was less on general issues of national performance and power than on more immediate questions of employment and competitiveness. One might even hazard the generalization that in terms of the evolution of the political economy of industry, experience proved more important than inquiry, the rationalization of imperatives more important than rationality, and politicians more important than economists. Consequently, in the last resort, the function of inquiry was the pursuit of "knowledge" as political acceptability, and the negotiation of policy transitions at times of stress. For all the clamor and effort of private discussion and investigations, when governments did not wish to change (or see the need to justify) policies, official inquiries were otiose.

11

Economic ideas and government policy on
industrial organization in Britain since 1945

LESLIE HANNAH

The liberal argument is in favour of making the best possible use of the forces of
competition as a means of coordinating human efforts, not an argument for
leaving things just as they are. It is based on the conviction that, where effective
competition can be created, it is a better way of guiding individual efforts than
any other. It does not deny, but even emphasises that, in order that competition
should work beneficially, a carefully thought-out legal framework is required and
that neither the existing nor the past legal rules are free from grave defects.

F. A. von Hayek, *The Road to Serfdom*
(Chicago: University of Chicago Press, 1944), 36

Common-sense economics may indeed be all that anyone must use in the end. But
it takes the most uncommon sense and wisdom to know just which part of the
filing case of muddled notions that men call common-sense is relevant to a
particular problem.

Paul Samuelson, *Problems of the American Economy: An Economist's
View,* Stamp Memorial Lecture (London: Athlone Press, 1962), 15–16

INDUSTRIAL POLICY

This chapter is concerned with industrial policy not in the currently
fashionable sense of government policies toward planning for industrial
"winners" (or, to put it less charitably, for covert protectionism) but,
rather, in the sense of policies to be adopted toward the forces of competition in the economy. These issues are conjured up in the British mind by
terms such as *monopolies, restrictive practices,* or (in the public sector)
nationalized industry guidelines, and in the U.S. mind by the terms *anti-*

I am grateful to Denys Gribbin, to the conference participants, and to the editors of this
volume for helpful suggestions. They should not be held accountable for any deficiencies.

trust and *regulation*. The thesis here is that economists in Britain have played a restricted but nevertheless significant and increasing role in the determination of policy in this field since World War II, and that their influence has been largely in the direction of promoting competition as an appropriate object of public policy.

In attempting to substantiate that view I draw on two major examples: policies toward nationalization and privatization in the electric utility industry and policy toward monopolies, restrictive practices, and mergers in the economy more generally.[1] The generalizations I make from these cases can, I believe, be substantiated for a much wider range of government policies relating to industry. I also, although less confidently, suggest that the real impact of policies devised by economists on business policy was somewhat greater during the first decade after the war and in the 1980s (when "irregulars" were particularly dominant in this area) than in the intervening period, which might be characterized as a period of emerging professionalization in the Government Economic Service. This finding may suggest to the cynic that governments pay economists to bless what they would do anyway, rather than that economic science contributes to government enlightenment, but I hope to show that the picture is not quite so bleak.

These generalizations are made on the basis of somewhat sketchy evidence. Although the official archives on the decade or so after the war are open, those for most of the period under consideration are closed, and what is said here may well be drastically amended or even falsified when the official records become available.

BRITISH ANTITRUST POLICY

The development of antitrust policy in Britain (and indeed in most other industrial economies) came much later than in the United States. There are three milestones in that development. In 1948 a Monopolies (and Restrictive Practices) Commission was established to report on private sector cartels or monopolistic firms. In 1956 the Restrictive Trade Practices Act created a separate Restrictive Practices Court, which effectively outlawed cartels. Finally, in 1965 the Monopolies and Mergers Act ex-

---

[1] L. Hannah, *The Rise of the Corporate Economy* (London: Methuen, 1976); L. Hannah, *Engineers, Managers and Politicians* (London: Macmillan and Johns Hopkins University Press, 1982); R. Cohen, L. Hannah, and J. A. Kay, *Electricity Privatisation and the Area Boards: The Case for 12, A Report Commissioned by the Twelve Area Boards of England and Wales* (London: London Economics, 1987).

tended the work of the Monopolies Commission to include investigation of mergers that were likely to restrict competition. Other acts have extended the power to new sectors (services, nationalized industries), made the law more precise (the abolition of resale price maintenance), and established an enforcement agency, the Office of Fair Trading, which is free from ministerial control. But the legal framework of British antitrust policy was established by 1965.

The Monopolies and Mergers Commission investigates monopoly situations that are referred to it by the independent director general of fair trading, or, in exceptional cases, the secretary of state for trade and industry, while merger proposals are referred exclusively by the secretary of state. If the commission concludes that a monopoly situation or a proposed merger is against the public interest, it may make remedial recommendations. In the case of a merger, the commission's recommendation could permit the merger to go ahead on conditions designed to safeguard the public interest. The implementation of monopoly policy is now not controversial, and has no de facto political input, but the secretary of state has a political role in the implementation of merger policy.

This process for mergers contrasts strongly with the rule of law rather than men in the restrictive practices field. Here the Restrictive Practices Court in clear, early rulings virtually outlawed all cartels and limited the scope for legal loopholes to develop. However, recent developments of political bargaining and the growing influence of European competition law appear likely to undermine that simplicity.

From the start, economists within government were a pressure group for the development of some form of antitrust policy in Britain. Denys Gribbin has shown that the economists recruited to Whitehall as temporary civil servants during the war had the effect of focusing attention on the problem of cartels and monopolies in the 1940s.[2] Their proposals were watered down by administrators, industrialists, and politicians, but American pressure on the British to move toward an antitrust policy (particularly in attacking international cartels) meant that something had to be done. Thus the antimonopoly briefs of men like G. C. Allen, Philip Chantler, Lionel Robbins, John Jewkes, Henry Clay, and Hugh Gaitskell contributed to the establishment in 1948 of the Monopolies Commission.[3]

[2]This account draws heavily on unpublished papers by Denys Gribbin. I am also grateful for advice from Helen Mercer, whose Ph.D. thesis on this topic at the London School of Economics will shortly be completed.
[3]E.g., G. C. Allen and H. Gaitskell, "The Control of Monopoly," Public Record Office (P.R.O.) BT 64/318, July 17, 1943.

Government economists did, of course, represent a variety of political traditions, but it is remarkable that these men with an economics training, whether politically on the left or the right, generally registered views in favor of competitive forces and against reestablishing in the postwar world the prewar monopolistic arrangements in international trade, among domestic competitors, or in single-firm monopolies. There were, naturally, differences among the economists of the 1940s.[4] For example, traces of the modern neo-Austrian/Chicago position on antitrust can be seen in the views of Henry Clay, who argued that positive government action against monopolies was less important than government abstention from support of monopolies. Clay saw such support as virtually the sole reason why monopolies might come into being and persist; thus laissez-faire rather than vigorous antitrust enforcement was Clay's prescription.

Economists like Hugh Gaitskell, by contrast, saw Labour's nationalization program for public utilities and other natural monopolies as a major part of the answer to the monopoly problem, with a residual problem in the private sector once the state sector had been expanded. Nonetheless, the belief in markets, and an explicit recognition that competition was the principal justification for, and the best disciplinary force on, the private sector, separates the British economists in the decade after World War II from many of their administrative colleagues in the civil service, and, indeed, from the weight of business opinion.

Moreover, there was much greater unanimity in basic approach among economists at this time than among other professional civil servants or politicians on these questions. A striking corroboration of this unanimity came in 1948 when industrialists had lost their battle against antitrust legislation and a Monopolies and Restrictive Practices Commission was being formed. The Federation of British Industries then successfully lobbied against the appointment of a professional economist as the chairman of the Monopolies Commission (a victory that has been consistently recognized in the appointment of a lawyer ever since), on the ground that economists had a built-in bias against restrictive practices that incapacitated them from fair-minded adjudication.

Nonetheless, economists were among those appointed to the new Monopolies and Restrictive Practices Commission in 1948, and they provided much of the meat of the reports that followed. G. C. Allen, who

[4]See, for example, Robbins's note of dissent to the Report of the Steering Committee on Post-war Employment, R(44)6 in P.R.O. CAB 87/63.

had earlier advised the Board of Trade on monopolies and cartels legislation, was made a member of the commission, and the first six industries referred to the new commission in March 1949—dental goods, cast iron, rainwater goods, electric lamps, electric cables, matches and matchmaking machinery—were chosen from among those that he and his colleagues had earlier singled out as justifying public intervention to promote competition.[5]

The commission's most influential report, published in 1955, addressed not a particular industry but the general issue of collective discrimination to enforce price agreements and other restrictive practices through exclusive dealing, aggregated rebates, collective boycotts, and the like.[6] The report of the commission concluded unequivocally that these practices operated against the public interest and that they should be generally prohibited; and the two economists on the commission—G. C. Allen and Arnold Plant—were, significantly, on the majority side. Of the twenty reports the commission issued, only three found that the monopolies or restrictive practices they investigated operated in the public interest.

By the mid-1950s industrialists were more divided about the merits of these developments. Some of the larger firms saw the merit of increasing competitive pressure on their smaller competitors to increase their own market share, although they feared the impact on their own cartel agreements. Small businessmen themselves did not have any of the delusions of their earlier U.S. counterparts that antitrust laws would act as a protection for them against the large corporations. In general, business accepted the new developments, in some cases as politically necessary to establish the case for liberal capitalism, in some cases because they saw the opportunities created for corporate growth, but most often reluctantly and without great interest.

The most vociferous protests about the inquisitorial nature of commission inquiries came from the victims themselves. Reports of the Monopolies and Restrictive Practices Commission had added to the public pressure for further action in this field, and counterpressure from industry was confined to deflecting the imminent, new legislation (from a Conservative government otherwise considered favorable to business) toward a

[5]J. D. Gribbin, ed. *Survey of International Cartels and Internal Cartels* (1944 and 1946, reprinted by the Board of Trade, 1976), introduction, 17.
[6]Monopolies and Restrictive Practices Commission, *Collective Discrimination* (London: HMSO, Cmd. 9504, 1955).

judicial rather than administrative process. The Federation of British Industries again thought that the judiciary would be less influenced by the procompetitive prejudices of economists.

The Restrictive Trade Practices Act of 1956 established a Restrictive Practices Court, with judges presiding. Again, however, the federation's strategy backfired. The court, far from being easier on restrictive practices, showed a remarkable propensity to take harsher decisions than the Monopolies Commission,[7] and very few restrictive agreements were approved under the various "gateways"—such as benefits to the consumer, the promotion of exports, or countervailing oligopsony—which the act specified. After the early cases, few industrialists held out much hope of winning approval for cartels and restrictive practices, and price agreements and other restrictions were quietly abandoned or conducted more secretly.[8] Both lawyers and economists derived little employment from this legal clarity, certainly not in comparison with the bloated ranks of their American counterparts. This legislation, plus the revival of import competition with the recovery of continental Europe and the reduction of tariffs under the General Agreement on Tariffs and Trade, exposed British industry to a wave of competitive forces that decades of restrictive practices left it ill-prepared to meet.

In the late 1950s and in the 1960s, managers found it difficult to come to terms with this situation; one of their strategies was to seek the alternative route to monopoly power by merger. From the court's establishment in 1958, British merger activity—including several vigorously contested takeover bids such as Imperial Chemical Industries' 1961 bid for Courtaulds—accelerated. The Conservative government responded to the growing concern, and in a white paper published in March 1964 proposed the control of mergers that would create or intensify a monopoly as legally defined.[9] Labour's manifesto in the 1964 election also committed that party to new legislation to control mergers, which was implemented in the 1965 Monopolies and Mergers Act. The Monopolies Commission was strengthened, and the Board of Trade (now the Department of Trade and Industry) was authorized to refer mergers to the commission, delay them while a

[7] For example, in the *Linoleum* case, the Court found against restrictive practices with safeguards for the public interest which had been recommended by the Monopolies Commission.

[8] R. B. Stevens and B. S. Yamey, *The Restrictive Practices Court: A Study of the Judicial Process and Economic Policy* (London: Weidenfeld and Nicolson, 1965).

[9] *Monopolies, Mergers and Restrictive Practices* (London: HMSO, Cmnd. 2299, March 1964).

report was being prepared, and dissolve them if they were found to be against the public interest.

In practice, few mergers were referred. Between 1965 and 1973 the Board of Trade mergers panel considered 833 mergers within the terms of the act; 20 were referred to the Monopolies Commission for investigation; 7 were abandoned voluntarily, 7 were allowed to proceed, and only 6 were found to be against the public interest and duly prevented.

Nonetheless, the threat of these procedures acted as a mild deterrent against mergers.[10] The government's attitude toward most mergers remained benign: indeed, Labour in 1966 established the Industrial Reorganization Corporation (IRC), one of whose aims was to promote industrial efficiency by encouraging mergers. Some of Britain's largest industrial groups, including British Leyland and GEC (Britain's General Electric Company), were put together in the late 1960s with IRC help, and without reference to the Monopolies Commission.

If, as we have argued, there was a broad consensus among economists in government in the 1940s and 1950s in favor of extending competition policy, this view had mellowed somewhat by the late 1960s. It was difficult, given rising imports, to sustain the view that British industry *generally* was subject to no competitive pressure, because the contrary appeared to be the case. Increasingly in academic circles, too, the quiescent neo-Austrian theories, which suggested that government had better merely abstain from supporting monopoly and that it was quite unnecessary for government actively to promote competition, were gaining ground.

Nonetheless, Margaret Thatcher's government, which has in general been heavily influenced by such laissez-faire argument, has broadly maintained the monopolies and mergers policy it inherited intact, rather than taking an extreme laissez-faire position. But the archival record of the interaction of academics, professional economic advisers, and politicians in policy-making for this period is not yet available, and it would be premature to conclude firmly that economists were as important an influence on the government's position as they had been earlier.

THE ECONOMIST CLASS

What is clear is that whether they influenced recent policy or not, far more economists are participating in policy-making now than in the

[10]J. D. Gribbin, "The operation of the mergers panel since 1965," *Trade and Industry*, January 17, 1974, 70–3.

decades immediately after World War II. The influence of economists on the evolution of British government antitrust policy between the 1940s and the mid-1960s is largely a history of the influence of "irregulars." There was in this period no separate class of economists in the civil service hierarchy. Pivotal figures trained as economists, like G. C. Allen or James Meade, moved out of their temporary wartime civil service jobs into academe; Allen served also as a part-time member of the Monopolies Commission while in his university post. Other wartime economist irregulars who had been influential, like Harold Wilson and Hugh Gaitskell, became M.P.'s in 1945 and were soon ministers influencing policy discussions more directly.

There were a few official posts for economic advisers within Whitehall,[11] mainly in the Cabinet Office Economic Section, which had been created in 1941 and was transferred in 1953 to the Treasury. These advisers were concerned mainly with macroeconomic policy issues, although in times of government physical planning of output, their work sometimes took them close to microeconomic issues and individual firms. A few economists did work in the ministries with responsibilities for sponsoring the interests of specific industries within Whitehall, where the ambitious ones often saw their career progression, after a period of service in a specialist professional post, was within the administrative class.

One example was Philip Chantler. Born in 1911, he had lectured briefly at Manchester University before the war and had specialized in gas tariffs. After a period in industry and war service, he joined the War Cabinet secretariat. He was made an economic adviser in the Cabinet Office in 1945 (where he influenced the monopolies policy discussions), and transferred to the same grade at the Ministry of Fuel and Power in 1947. After a period in 1955–7 on secondment as economic adviser to the government of Pakistan, he saw his next career move as within the administrative class and became an undersecretary in the Electricity Division of his ministry in 1960.[12] Chantler was one of a rare species: when he ceased to be an economic adviser in 1960, there were barely a dozen similar appointees in Whitehall.[13]

---

[11]Civil Service Commission. *Posts in the Civil Service for University Graduates* (London: HMSO, 1951), 33: "There are openings in the Economic Section of the Cabinet Office and in the Treasury; and there may be occasional posts in other Departments."

[12]*Who's Who 1982.*

[13]Civil Service Department, Statistics Division, *A Statistical Review of the Economist Class and the Employment of Economists in Government Service: Pre-1960 to 1969* [Statistical Review Series:5–69] (London: HMSO, 1970). For a more personal view of the work of

This position was transformed during the well-known expansion in the Government Economic Service under the Labour governments of Harold Wilson between 1964 and 1970.[14] The economist class was finally established in 1964 (a measure of its backwardness is the contrast with the psychologist class within the civil service, which had been established in 1950). Its members then totaled only 22, but by 1969 there were as many as 194. Universities, particularly Oxbridge, were temporarily denuded of economics teachers as well as finding their economic graduates in high demand.

For example, Wilfred Beckerman was an economic consultant to the Department of Economic Affairs in 1964–5 and economic adviser to the Board of Trade 1967–9; and Michael Posner was director of economics at the Ministry of Power 1966–7 and economic adviser at the Treasury 1967–71. Many of these new recruits were on temporary contracts, but, nonetheless, this expansion proved to be an enduring change. Economists in the ministries that recruited them heavily, notably the Ministry of Transport, have remained a strong professional group with a clear separation from the administrative class (although transfers between classes of course remained possible). At the same time as central departments were busily recruiting economists, the quangos (quasi-autonomous governmental organizations) and other special bodies, from the Monopolies Commission to the National Board for Prices and Incomes, were also recruiting economists on the fringes of Whitehall, and arrangements for secondment and transfers meant that the effective size of the Government Economic Service, including these people, was larger than the basic official statistics suggest.

Although many participants in this transformation have pronounced views on their benign influence,[15] the archival record and the long-term perspective on these results may produce a less rosy view. The jury on that question is still out. Certainly the role of professional economist became more established, and economic ideas were increasingly likely to be used in a "justificatory" way by ministers, to bolster their case and overcome contrary argument.[16] In the case of antitrust policy, the in-

---

government economists in the 1950s, see P. D. Henderson, "The Use of Economists in British Administration," *Oxford Economic Papers,* 13 (February 1961), 5–26.

[14]W. Beckerman, ed., *The Labour Government's Economic Record 1964–1970* (London: Duckworth, 1972).

[15]Ibid.

[16]For similar arguments, see Chapters 7 and 14 in this volume.

creased professionalization went further to produce a strong and coherent professional line that ministers broadly respected.

This is not to say that the professional economists in the Board of Trade (later the Department of Trade and Industry), or at the Monopolies Commission or the Office of Fair Trading in the 1970s, changed the fundamentals of policy against ministers' wishes. By questioning the increasing concentration of industry, of which merger was the major component, however, they provided the basis for a more active monopoly policy, and provided solid arguments for any minister who did wish to stop a merger on the ground that excessive market power would be created. In that sense they were following the procompetitive traditions of earlier irregulars, but they were also, like professionals in the antitrust division of the American Federal Trade Commission, increasingly shaping the development of policy. Two important reports produced in the late 1970s by Hans Liesner, the chief economic adviser of the Department of Trade and Industry, have had a great influence on toughening monopoly and merger policy in the 1980s despite the laissez-faire instincts of many government ministers.[17]

ELECTRICITY: NATIONALIZATION AND PRIVATIZATION

My second example of the role of economists in policy-making shows a similarly remarkable adherence if not strictly to procompetitive policy, at least to a similar set of precepts derived from general equilibrium theory. Britain's nationalized sector was greatly expanded and transformed when the Labour government of 1945–51 took over road, rail, and air transport; coalmining; the Bank of England; and the gas and electric utilities. Nationalization was, as many commentators have stressed, in one sense Britain's equivalent of the U.S. antitrust authorities. At least in political terms, public ownership was a populist response to the alleged dangers of big business and monopoly.[18] Economists advising on Britain's policy toward monopolies and restrictive practices saw it in these terms also, so much so that it is only recently that nationalized corporations have been

[17] *A Review of Monopolies and Mergers Policy* (London: HMSO, Cmnd. 7198, May 1978); *A Review of Restrictive Trade Practices Policy* (London: HMSO, Cmnd. 7512, March 1979). Cf. E. V. Morgan, *Monopolies, Mergers and Restrictive Practices: UK Competition Policy 1948–87* (Edinburgh: David Hume Institute, 1987).
[18] R. S. Neale, *The Antitrust Laws of the USA* (Cambridge, Eng.: Cambridge University Press, 1960).

brought within the purview of monopolies legislation. It was quite widely accepted before this that, as government-controlled entities, their behavior as monopolies need not be controlled in the manner appropriate to the private sector.

The economic input into the discussion of nationalization in 1945–51 was minimal. "Economist" is not an entry in the index of Sir Norman Chester's exhaustive survey of the subject.[19] Moreover, it is clear that on the one issue on which the Economic Section of the Cabinet Office expressed a clear view, it was clearly overruled by the framers of the nationalization legislation.[20] Most of the nationalization statutes required the public sector corporations they created to break even in conventional accounting terms taking one year with another, implying that prices should be set at historic average cost. The Cabinet Office economists were adamant that merely meeting the requirement would, in many cases, lead to underpricing, and that setting their prices at the marginal cost of incremental supplies would send signals that would be more conducive to efficient resource allocation. This initial disagreement between economists and administrators (which the administrators won) concerned the central issue that was to dominate (the nonbeliever would perhaps say distort) the thinking of most professional economists in government on the issue of nationalized industries for decades to come.

On the other immediate issues of policy structure, control, and organization of nationalized corporations raised in the 1940s and early 1950s, however, the influence of economists was peripheral. In the energy field (where, with transport, subsequent experience suggests their influence might perhaps have been greatest) economists were confined to adding to the pressure for more rational pricing (which, at the time, meant higher prices) for fuels, and particularly for electricity. On the Ridley Committee on National Policy for the Use of Fuel and Power Resources, for example, Arthur Lewis argued for higher coal prices, while Philip Chantler at the Ministry of Fuel and Power exercised a similar influence and argued for sensible peak pricing of electricity.[21] Although such arguments were, perhaps, ahead of those being advanced by official economists responding to energy utility regulation in the United States before the era of Alfred

---

[19]D. N. Chester, *The Nationalisation of British Industry 1945–51* (London: HMSO, 1975).
[20]Ibid., 565.
[21]Committee on National Policy for the Use of Fuel and Power Resources, *Report* (London: HMSO, Cmnd. 8647, 1952). L. Hannah, *Engineers, Managers and Politicians*, 34, 198.

Kahn,[22] they at first evoked little response from administrators and politicians, except where ministers like Gaitskell (with a sympathetic training in economics) made their influence felt.[23]

Matters were transformed when the pricing and investment policies of the nationalized industries moved to the center stage of Treasury concern in the later 1950s. Spurred by financial losses in the coal and railway industries and by concern that expanding public corporations in industries like electricity were "crowding out" desirable investment in the private sector, the Treasury's Padmore Committee by 1959 was fundamentally reappraising the pricing policies and rates of return of the nationalized industries. The public-sector corporations themselves preferred the old, average–cost pricing rules and low profits, which most of them thought were prescribed by the nationalization statutes. But two seminal white papers in 1961 and 1967 shifted the ostensible objectives of the public corporations to pricing at something nearer to marginal cost and to making a rate of return nearer to that earned on comparable private sector projects.[24]

The suggestion that the best rules of behavior for public corporations were essentially to ape the behavior to which they would have been constrained in a competitive private market—policies such as marginal cost pricing—flowed naturally from the economist's tool kit. The Treasury economists were strong exponents of the changes in 1961, and in the Ministry of Fuel and Power, these ideas attracted support from economists such as Philip Chantler, an earlier advocate of competition policy and of marginal cost pricing in the energy sector.[25] In the nationalized enterprises themselves these ideas evoked the warmest response from those, like the chairman of the Electricity Council (Sir Ronald Edwards), who had an academic economics background.[26] The 1967 white paper

[22]R. H. K. Vietor, *Energy Policy in America Since 1945: A Study of Business-Government Relations* (Cambridge, Eng.: Cambridge University Press, 1984), 89–90; T. K. McCraw, *Prophets of Regulation* (Cambridge, Mass.: Harvard University Press, 1984), 222 ff. On Tugwell's lack of receptivity in the United States to British ideas on marginal cost pricing, see Chapter 4 in this volume.

[23]For example, in the implementation of the Clow Committee recommendations on peak-load pricing differentials for electricity in 1948–9, albeit on a temporary and unsuccessful basis because of electricity industry sabotage of the proposals, see Hannah, *Engineers, Managers and Politicians*, 35–7.

[24]*Financial and Economic Obligations of the Nationalised Industries* (London: HMSO, Cmnd. 1336, 1961); *Nationalised Industries: A Review of Economic and Financial Objectives* (London: HMSO, Cmnd. 3437, 1967).

[25]This account is based on the Treasury Historical Section Survey of the making of the 1961 white paper, shortly to be deposited in the Public Record Office.

[26]L. Hannah, *Engineers, Managers and Politicians*, 204 ff.

was strongly influenced by the influx of able university economists recruited on secondment by the new Labour government.[27]

To the man in the street—and most public corporation chairmen came in this category rather than being professional economists—the rules were accepted with eyebrows distinctly half-raised. If all that economists could say was that these industries were to ape the actions of private companies in competitive markets, then why were the industries in the public sector at all? There were, of course, perfectly respectable arguments relating to natural monopoly for treating them differently (whether by public ownership or by regulation). Nonetheless, the resigned view of most chairmen—that they were in the public sector because politicians wanted them to behave *differently* from the private sector—proved all too true in the period after the white papers. Indeed, one study of the electricity industry found that, far from conforming more closely to private sector norms of investment behavior, they performed less closely to those norms after 1961 than before.[28] The economists had won the war of words in white papers, but they had completely lost the battle for policy implementation at the crucial level of the ministers and chairmen who actually took decisions in the 1960s and 1970s. As the chancellor of the Exchequer is reported to have said when told by a cabinet colleague that the 1967 white paper was a poor one: "What does it matter? It's only read by a few dons and experts."[29]

The reasons for this failure go far beyond the flawed framework established, under the influence of economists' perceptions, in the 1961 and 1967 white papers. The quality of nationalized industry management was severely compromised by low salaries and persistent ministerial intervention in their affairs; and even the better managers had low morale as this intervention increased rather than decreased in the 1970s. In order to support employment or reduce inflation, nationalized industries were permitted, encouraged, or compelled to accept overmanning and underpricing, with the result that financial deficits emerged in most of the public sector during the 1970s.

[27]See, e.g., M. V. Posner, *Fuel Policy: A Study in Applied Economics* (London: Macmillan, 1973); Wilfred Beckerman, ed., *The Labour Government's Economic Record 1964–1970* (London: Duckworth, 1972).

[28]D. Targett, "Testing Whether the Annual Capital Investment of Nationalised Industries Can Be Replaced by Private Sector Investment Models: A Working Paper," *Applied Economics*, X (1978): 233–50.

[29]R. Crossman, *The Diaries of a Cabinet Minister* (London: Hamish Hamilton, 1976), II, 524.

By 1974–5 nationalized industries received £1.7 billion of revenue support from the government, £1 billion of which was paid to the electricity and gas industries and the Post Office, with large sums going also to coalmining and railways. This was in addition to the £1 billion paid by the Exchequer to finance their normal capital expenditure. Although the Labour government, under pressure from the International Monetary Fund, then made some attempt to stem the deficits and tighten financial controls, ministers like Tony Benn placed a large premium on increasing inefficiency in order to preserve jobs and keep the public sector unions sweet. Richard Pryke, who had made an optimistic survey of the nationalized industries' performance relative to that of the rest of the British economy for the 1958–68 period, reported that the performance of those industries had slipped back to an inferior level by the 1970s.[30]

The Treasury policies of the 1960s had held out a hope that when the public corporations were subject to political intervention to modify their goals—as, for example, when an uneconomic rural railway line was preserved, or the electricity industry was forced to burn high-priced British coal, or prices were held down as part of the government's anti-inflation policy—explicit compensation would be paid to the corporation in question. This was done in a few cases, but the practice was too patchy for the incentive and monitoring structure implicit in it to work effectively. By the end of the 1970s, there was general agreement that the existing relations of government and nationalized industries bore little relation to the ideals of the white paper and that new approaches were required.

Disappointment at the practical results of the initiatives to establish a proper financial framework in the 1960s helped change the climate of opinion by the 1980s toward privatization. Objections to privatizing natural monopolies remained powerful, but in some areas such as telecommunications and electricity generation, technical change was making their markets more contestable. Of course, the main thrust of the Thatcher government's privatization program has not been technocratic but ideological. Nonetheless, the failure to replicate competitive pricing in the public sector, or to find effective substitutes for competitive pressure to improve efficiency, certainly made economists outside government more receptive to the privatization program than they would have been two decades earlier. Within government, also, adverse reports by the

[30]R. Pryke, *Public Enterprise in Practice* (London: MacGibbon & Kee, 1971); idem, *The Nationalised Industries: Policies and Performance Since 1968* (Oxford: Martin Richards, 1981).

Monopolies Commission (now charged with investigating public as well as private monopolies) also drew attention to inefficiencies in water, coal, electricity, and railways, which had eluded the scrutiny of sponsoring departments whose civil servants were at least as prone to "capture" by their industries as the regulatory authorities for utilities in the United States. A significant number of British economists were now inclined to give privatization two cheers on the sidelines, while reserving the third cheer for the introduction of genuine competition in the few cases where that appeared to be in prospect.[31]

The relations of the Thatcher government with economists in general can nonetheless easily be painted as unhappy. A total of 364 economists, including most of the top brass of the Royal Economic Society, and 5 ex-government chief economic advisers signed a collective condemnation of Margaret Thatcher's "monetarist" economic policy in 1981.[32] They were reviled by Conservative politicians at the time and are still derisively referred to by ministers, now confident that the economists have been proved wrong. Yet economists are clearly in British government under Thatcher in all the senses established by the precedents of earlier decades: as ministers, as "irregular" advisers, and as permanent professional civil servants. The use by the Thatcher government of its own favored economists has been intensive. This use is not, moreover, confined to the adulation of Friedman and Hayek and the elevation of Sir Alan Walters and like-minded British monetarists to senior economic positions overseeing macroeconomic policies. The new commitment to "supply-side" solutions to the problems of slow British economic growth has also provided increased opportunities for the use of microeconomics.

Although some of this activity is impenetrable under the thirty-year closure of public records in Britain, several points are clear from published information. First, the microeconomists in government are now conventionally headed by the Treasury's deputy chief economic adviser (the chief being concerned mainly with macroeconomic advice) and are scattered in many departments directly concerned with privatization. They appear to have formed, initially under the leadership of Ian Byatt, a coherent and established professional group of economists, far more im-

---

[31]J. Kay, C. Mayer, and D. Thompson, eds., *Privatisation and Regulation: The UK Experience* (Oxford: Clarendon Press, 1986); J. Vickers and G. Yarrow, *Privatisation: An Economic Analysis* (Cambridge, Mass.: MIT Press, 1988).
[32]D. Blake, "Monetarism Attacked by Top Economists," *The Times*, March 30, 1981.

pressive in technical experience and in numbers than the microeconomists advising governments in the 1940s or 1960s.[33]

Second, a range of irregulars—university economists employed directly as consultants or on the traditional secondment basis—have been pressed into service by Thatcher's ministers, and they have been somewhat less dominated by Oxbridge economists than those in the previous influxes of the 1940s and 1960s. They include, for example, Steven Littlechild of Birmingham and Michael Beesley of the London Business School. Their presence symbolizes a more deep-rooted distrust of the Establishment consensus, which has generally been a hallmark of Thatcherism. The government has also drawn extensively on the services of the economics departments of major accounting firms and other economic consultancies, as well as on individual university economists for advice: another quite deliberate (and costly) move, apparently based on preferences for commercial service, rather than occasional and part-time advice. While the advice of consultants is shrouded in the confidentiality that is perhaps part of their service, it is not difficult to guess at the advice given by the academic irregulars. The influence of the neo-Austrian School, and the general preference for the new British style of price regulation rather than the American style of rate-of-return regulation, are clear, for example, from the published work of Littlechild.[34]

It appears that, as with antitrust policy, the general influence of economists—whether university irregulars or career civil servants—on the privatization program has been in the direction of promoting competitive solutions. Such solutions echo the government's aims of restoring competitive capitalism in the British economy, but the program of introducing competition has been severely compromised in the political and administrative processes. As a result, the government has been castigated for maximizing Treasury revenue from flotation by creating monopolies

[33] I. C. R. Byatt, deputy chief economic adviser between 1978 and 1989, was born in 1932, and holds a Ph.D. on the economic history of electricity. A lecturer in economics at Durham and London School of Economics 1958–67; he was also economic consultant, H. M. Treasury, 1962–4; senior economic adviser, Department of Education and Science 1967–9; director of economics and statistics, Ministry of Housing and Local Government 1969–70; director of economics, Department of the Environment 1970–72; and under-secretary, H. M. Treasury 1972–8.

[34] S. C. Littlechild, *The Fallacy of the Mixed Economy* (London: Institute of Economic Affairs, 1978); idem, *Controlling Nationalised Industries: Quis Custodiet Ipsos Custodies?* (University of Birmingham Discussion Paper No. 56, 1979); and idem, *Economic Regulation of Privatised Water Authorities: Report Submitted to the Department of the Environment* (London: HMSO, 1986).

rather than ensuring competition. For some of the smaller privatizations where the firms operate in competitive markets—such as Amersham International and Britoil in 1982, Enterprise Oil and Jaguar in 1984, and British Airways in 1987—there is a reasonable prospect of already existing competition providing an effective disciplining force. However, for some of the major utilities privatized—ranging from 51 percent of British Telecom (at an issue price of £3.916 billion) in 1984, through British Gas (£5.434 billion) in 1986, to the British Airports Authority (£1.225 billion) in 1987—the issue of creating competitive conditions was not squarely faced. The most blatant example was Peter Walker's privatization of British Gas, creating a virtual monopoly supplier with which the Monopolies Commission and the weak regulator, Ofgas, are now attempting to come to terms. British Telecom, also, was privatized with a far less ambitious competitive solution than the earlier breakup of AT&T in the United States: only one small fringe competitor, Mercury, has initially been permitted. By contrast, the smaller bus industry has been privatized in a manner that effectively opens it up to competitive forces.

It appears, though, that the economists (and others) who argue for competitive solutions have recently gained the upper hand. The large-scale privatization of the electric utility industries (for perhaps £20 billion) planned for 1990 onward will clearly provide a workably competitive structure. The English and Welsh electric utility industry, for example, is to be split vertically with twelve local distribution boards (having natural monopoly characteristics that will probably always require regulation) being privatized separately. These twelve utilities will jointly own the common carrier Grid transmission network, thus creating a market in bulk power supply. The power stations themselves are currently monopolized but need not be. The existing power station company, the Central Electricity Generating Board, is to be split into two and its monopoly ended. Already independent power station companies and the Scottish boards (which are to be separately privatized) are planning additional stations to serve the newly opened bulk power market.

There is a realistic prospect, then, that, in the longer run, competition will be established in bulk power supply, and regulation of, or Monopolies Commission inquiries into, this industry (except at the bulk transmission and the small and medium-size consumer levels) will be less necessary than in the privatization of gas and telecommunications. Consumer pressure and political discontent at the monopolistic behavior of privatized

British Gas and British Telecom have perhaps contributed most to this change, but the criticism of earlier privatizations by academic economists has certainly also played a part.[35] It is also clear that all the major actors—from the Department of Energy and the Scottish Office, through the Electricity Council, the Central Electricity Generating Board, and Area Boards, to the Scottish boards as well as some large electricity users—have found it necessary to appoint professional economic advisers.[36] Increasingly, then, professional economists in government are paralleled by an expanding market of consultancies like National Economic Research Associates and London Economics dealing with the public and private sector demand for professional economic advice to confront the economic problems raised by government policies.

CONCLUSIONS AND FURTHER RESEARCH

It is more appropriate in our current state of knowledge of economists' input to the microeconomic policy-making process to establish a research agenda than to present firm conclusions. Our examination of two issues does, however, suggest some working hypotheses.

The first is that when economists become involved in the microeconomic policy-making process, they have a tendency to favor competitive solutions to the problems of economic organization. That is not, of course, to say that they are blind to other arguments. Whether in the 1950s, when advising on the restructuring by merger of the aircraft industry, or in the 1960s, when advising on the need for the Industrial Reorganization Corporation, there were, no doubt, some economists who felt that the government's economic objectives were better served by suppressing competition and gaining economies of scale. Moreover, many economists in Whitehall have felt happier with the language of socialist planning than they have with the slogans of competitive capitalism. More generally, there have always been economists who favor the Socratic dialogue: while basically favoring competitive solutions, many economists in recent years, somewhat appalled by the simplicity of the

---

[35]See, for example, M. Bishop and J. Kay, *Does Privatisation Work?: Lessons from the UK* (London: London Business School, Centre for Business Strategy, 1988), for the most recent constructive criticism, and further sources cited in their bibliography.

[36]It is now the norm for parties to privatization to announce not only the appointment of merchant bankers, lawyers, accountants, and solicitors to advise on privatization, but also economic consultants who may represent independent consultancies or arms of accountancy partnerships.

procompetitive slogans of Thatcherism, have no doubt been writing judiciously worded minutes pointing to the dangers of overhasty transition, in the best tradition of the generalist civil servant reviewing the issues.

But whatever the rich variety of views of economists—which was and remains the point of everyone's favorite joke about economists—they remain, as a tribe, more wedded than the typical rider on the Clapham omnibus to the idea that competitive markets are conducive to the public interest. Even left-wing economic advisers spend a good deal of their time explaining to Labour ministers (and to Conservatives!) that markets may not be so bad a solution as the practical person might at first think.[37] The power of the central theorems of economics derived from general equilibrium theory—whether on competitive equilibrium or on marginal cost pricing rules—was certainly a major part of the training of the economists concerned with the development of competition policy and of nationalized industry policy—and it showed.

A second generalization is that the economist class in the civil service seems to rely much more on waves of irregulars for its substantial advances of influence than is perhaps the case with many other professional classes of civil servants. There appear to have been at least three waves of recruitment of "irregulars": during World War II and immediately after it, in the late 1960s, and in the 1980s. All of them heralded substantial policy innovations in the microeconomic sphere (and, as is better known and documented, in the macroeconomic sphere, too), although this phenomenon can be exaggerated. Our limited number of case studies indicate that economists have been more effective in influencing policy *implementation* (rather than formulation) in the 1940s and 1980s than they were in the 1960s, but this conclusion may merely reflect the particular case studies we have chosen. The 1960s policies on nationalized industry pricing, in which economists were influential, had an exceptionally rough ride, although the reason may be that they were riding professional hobby horses without having established a political market for their ideas.

Several further puzzles remain to be addressed in subsequent work on a wider range of cases. First, there is the question of the relations between developments in economic science and the nature of advice given to government by professional economists. If that advice does tend to favor competitive solutions, as I have suggested, it is at variance with develop-

---

[37]On the difficulties of confronting the "do it yourself" economics of politicians, see D. Henderson, *Innocence and Design: The Influence of Economic Ideas on Policy* (Oxford: Basil Blackwell, 1986).

ments of economic ideas over the past four or five decades. The general presumption of economists in favor of marginal cost pricing and competitive markets does, of course, derive its main justification from the propositions of general equilibrium theory. Yet the tendency of modern theoretical development has been to emphasize how special and contingent the assumptions of these central theorems are. They depend, for example, on quite implausible assumptions that are rarely encountered in the real world: that there are no externalities, that markets (including intertemporal markets) are complete, that information is instantaneously and costlessly available, that perfect competition reigns everywhere, or that there are no economies of scale.

Moreover, the elaboration of the theory of second best has explicitly denied the legitimacy of a simple commitment to increasing competition: if there is monopolistic distortion anywhere in the economy, the theory implies, then increasing competition elsewhere, far from improving allocative efficiency, may lead it to deteriorate.[38] The conditions for Pareto Optimality (on which the case for promoting competition as a welfare optimum usually rests) are not just occasionally, but quite routinely, violated. This body of theory was hardly unknown to the economists we have been describing; indeed, the fact that so many of them were "irregulars," recruited on temporary contract from universities, meant that the closeness of their links with contemporary theoretical developments in the universities was probably greater among economists than among other professional classes in the civil service. Yet the professors were not always pleased by their products; for example, Frank Hahn, in a Cambridge inaugural lecture, was driven (by those who routinely forget theoretical caveats such as those just cited) to expostulate that "practical men and ill-trained theorists everywhere in the world do not understand what they are claiming to be the case when they claim a beneficent and coherent role for the invisible hand."[39]

Is, then, the tendency of economists to parrot the virtues of competition just an ideological simplification to which the ill-trained are prone? A more detailed study of the theoretical stance of advisers and of the practicalities of the situations in which economists are asked to advise

[38]R. G. Lipsey and K. Lancaster, "The General Theory of Second Best," *Review of Economic Studies* 24 (1956): 11–32; and M. Boiteux, "Sur la gestion des monopoles publics astreints a l'equilibre budgetaire," *Econometrica* (1956): 22–40, inaugurated the extensive literature on the theory of second best.

[39]F. H. Hahn, *On the Nature of Equilibrium in Economics: An Inaugural Lecture* (Cambridge, Eng.: Cambridge University Press, 1973), 15.

would, I think, produce a kinder verdict. The presumption in favor of competition by staff of the Monopolies Commission and Office of Fair Trading, for example, was derived from detailed econometric work that confirmed presumptions of the effect of industrial structure on behavior and performance—which, in turn, owed more to commonsense observation than to general equilibrium theory. Whereas such studies might not please the theorist entirely, and were certainly subject to various alternative rationalizations, they did attempt to move beyond opinion to researched conclusions as a basis for policy-making.[40]

Government economists did not seek perfection in their science; they were all too aware that "in the land of the blind the one-eyed man is king." The practical men with whom they dealt—politicians and administrative-class civil servants—were all too prone to assume that market competition was a flawed form of economic organization needing administrative intervention that they were ill-equipped to give, and the economists' advocacy of competition was often simply in reaction to this view. Moreover, some of the economists, especially in recent years, denied that their faith in competition was based on general equilibrium theory and explicitly espoused the alternative neo-Austrian doctrines.[41] Thus, economic opinion was richer and had a more catholic theoretical basis than has been sketched here.

A second puzzle is the varying degree of influence of economists in different fields. In principle, one might have expected the influence of economists on policy implementation to be greater after 1964 when the Government Economic Service established a professional niche for economists, increasing the probability of successful implementation of policies for which they had gained cabinet approval. The example of marginal cost pricing in the public utilities hardly supports this optimistic view, but it may be atypical. What is obvious is that a variety of other factors— from industrial pressure through political ideology to economic conjunctural factors—also determine the success or failure of policy initiatives. To unravel these factors more systematically, we will need much more research on the formulation of microeconomic policy as the archives become available in the next three decades.

---

[40]For a review of the recent research on workable definitions of competition derived from modern developments in oligopoly theory, see J. S. Cubbin, "Market Structure and Market Performance: The Empirical Research" (London Business School, Centre for Business Strategy, Working Paper no. 40, January 1988).
[41]Littlechild, *The Fallacy of the Mixed Economy*.

A final puzzle concerns the varying roles of microeconomists in government in the United States and in Britain, and the reasons for apparent leads and lags. It seems clear that developments in economics affect policy, but equally clear that policy changes induce developments in the subject. The greater development and sophistication of applied microeconomics and the economics of industry in the United States, for example, presumably owe something to the early development of antitrust laws, and to the consequent growth of a market in economists, whether as expert witnesses or as policy analysts. Much the same development occurred in Britain later, partly in response to the development of government policy on monopolies, mergers, and restrictive practices. Yet in other fields, notably, the literature of marginal cost pricing, U.S. economists were behind their British (and French) counterparts. It is not obvious why regulatory authorities in the United States were more dilatory in applying these principles (at least before the era of Alfred Kahn) than their counterparts responsible for regulating the nationalized public utilities in Britain.

What is clear from this preliminary survey is that, in the relatively underresearched area of the influence of microeconomists on microeconomic policy, the lessons learned from the better-developed macroeconomic field need to be learned. Economists are not repositories of pure "professional" knowledge, whose influence derives only from the automatic application of "scientific" laws. They are participants in political and bureaucratic as well as intellectual processes; and understanding the market for their ideas and what their "clients"—whether civil servants or politicians—wanted from them (and why) is as important in explaining their function as is the content of the economic knowledge they purveyed.

Part IV

Economic knowledge and social action

12

Economic knowledge and British social policy

JOSE HARRIS

THE PROBLEM

Social policy is perceived sometimes as a subset of economic policy, some-times as its antithesis. The accumulation of data about the economic basis of social problems has been portrayed sometimes as the indispensable prerequisite of purposive social change, sometimes as an exercise in ma-nipulating knowledge in favor of the status quo.[1] The empiricist emphasis of the British "social science" tradition has frequently been seen as a radical solvent of abstract economic axioms, but more recently the lack of a discrete body of social policy "theory" has been identified as a critical source of weakness in relation to other disciplines, notably economics.

Some authorities see social welfare policies as serving primarily to buttress the efficient working of the economic system, while others see them as repairing the damage that economic life leaves behind. Some might claim that the apparent link between economics and social policy is a false one because they belong to two categorically different spheres: the former to the "natural" order of things, the latter to acts of political will. Social service provision clearly intersects with both micro- and macroeco-nomic considerations at many points; yet, paradoxically, the advance of what came to be known as the "welfare state" systematically removed many areas of social provision from the ambit of "welfare economics," in that it reduced or eliminated considerations of consumer choice.[2]

---

[1]See O. R. McGregor, "Social Research and Social Policy in the Nineteenth Century," *British Journal of Sociology* (1957): 146–57; and Roger Davidson, *Whitehall and the Labour Problem in Late-Victorian and Edwardian Britain: A Study in Official Statistics and Social Control* (London: Croom Helm, 1985), especially 241–9.

[2]I. M. D. Little, *A Critique of Welfare Economics* (Oxford: Clarendon Press, 1950; Oxford paperback edn., 1960), 259.

Often the relationship between social policy and economic thought is perceived as changing over time: a familiar model is one in which nineteenth-century makers of social policy are portrayed as having been confined within a corset of orthodox classical thought, while their twentieth-century successors either shifted to a more liberating "Keynesian" paradigm or were able to assert "social" priorities as ends in themselves.[3]

A pessimistic version of what is fundamentally the same model has been traced to the transition from an "age of principle" to an "age of expediency." Social policy before 1870 was rooted in a set of coherent and preordained economic principles; thereafter, so it has been claimed, it was increasingly the random offspring of democracy, pragmatism, and sectoral self-interest.[4]

These generalizations tell us little, however, about how makers of social policy have actually used economic theory and economic data in specific contexts. They leave unanswered the following questions:

- Have promoters of social welfare schemes systematically flouted economic laws and ignored economic constraints (as it is now fashionable in some quarters to believe), or has the relation between the two spheres been symbiotic?
- What did ministers and public officials in social policy departments know about economic functions and economic data, and where did they acquire their information?
- Was "fact" or "theory" a more important influence on policy formation, and how far, if at all, did the two interact?
- Did the "modernization" of departmental structures result in improved economic information, or was it the case, as a distinguished public committee claimed in 1946, that the official collection of social and economic data in the mid-twentieth century was markedly inferior to that of the mid-nineteenth century?[5]
- Was the growth of statistical information about economic and social functions a sine qua non of the growth of "rational" social policies (as was believed by reformers in the mold of Chadwick and the Webbs and has since been claimed by historians like Oliver Macdonagh and Macgregor),[6] or was the relationship

---

[3]R. Skidelsky, *Politicians and the Slump* (London: Macmillan, 1967), ix; K. J. Hancock, "The Reduction of Unemployment as a Problem of Public Policy 1920–29," *Economic History Review*, n.s. 15 (1962): 328–43.

[4]P. Atiyah, *The Rise and Fall of Freedom of Contract* (Oxford: Oxford University Press, 1979).

[5]*Report of the Committee on the Provision for Social and Economic Research* (chairman, Sir John Clapham) 1946 (Cmd. 6868, 1945–6, XIV, 655), 4–5.

[6]S. E. Finer, *The Life and Times of Sir Edwin Chadwick* (London: Methuen, 1952), 23, 157–8; S. and B. Webb, *A Constitution for the Socialist Commonwealth of Great Britain* (Cambridge, Eng.: Cambridge University Press, 1975), 244–5, 352–4; O. R. McGregor,

between knowledge and the growth of the "administrative state" largely oblique and accidental?

• Were the economic assumptions that guided Edwardian "New Liberals" in the 1900s or the framers of the "welfare state" in the 1940s fundamentally different from those that inspired the Poor Law in the 1840s, or was there some degree of continuity between all three phases?

This chapter cannot provide a comprehensive survey of the "knowledge" basis of social policy over two centuries, but an attempt will be made to sketch possible guidelines for interpretation and to suggest potentially fruitful areas for more detailed research. It should be stressed that what follows relates primarily to British experience. A very different pattern might emerge from reviewing the social policies of a political culture with a more historicist tradition of economic theory or with a more mercantilist perception of the state.

DEFINITION, CONVERGENCE, AND TENSION

Why should any connection between social policy and economic thought be assumed in the first place? Some preliminary and perhaps obvious answers may be suggested. At a general level, social policies are predicated on the very existence of prior economic resources (or their pathological absence), and the level and character of such resources necessarily react to changing social perceptions of human need. Poverty itself, to take the most striking example, was firmly categorized as "not a problem" by generations whose average per capita income was at or below the level of subsistence; it became defined as a "problem" only in an era when resources were beginning to be at least notionally available for some kind of socially mediated cure.[7]

Second, despite their differences of content and emphasis, both economics and social policy developed from a common tradition of moral and political philosophy, which revolved around such issues as the just distribution of resources between individuals and classes, public and private property rights, the form and content of rational behavior, and the nature of the good life. Debate on social policy never achieved the preci-

---

"Social Research and Social Policy in the Nineteenth Century"; and O. MacDonagh, "The Nineteenth Century Revolution in Government: a Reappraisal," *Historical Journal* (1958): 52–67.

[7]Michael E. Rose, *The English Poor Law, 1780–1930* (Newton Abbott: David and Charles, 1971), 47–8; Gertrude Himmelfarb, *The Idea of Poverty* (London: Faber and Faber, 1984), 41, 77–80; and *Official Papers of Alfred Marshall*, ed. J. M. Keynes (London: Macmillan, 1926), 233, 247–8.

sion and analytical rigor of economic thought—not because economic knowledge was "hard" while social knowledge was "soft," but because the goals of social policy and of social life generally were inherently more multifaceted, more varying, and, therefore, less easily abstractable than those of economic policy. Social well-being was never seen as wholly reducible to economic well-being, and the "economic" dimension of social policy always had to jostle for position with priorities derived from other sources, such as public order, social discipline, moral duty, physical survival, or the sheer pressure of political will.[8] (How far these other priorities were themselves ultimately reducible to economic factors is, of course, a matter for opinion and debate.)

A major tension between the two spheres—even in the era when the hegemony of economics was supposedly at its height—was the fact that the mainstream of British economic thought always assumed an impersonal *Gesellschaft* model of society, while both the theory and practice of social welfare always retained traces of a more traditional familial and communitarian *Gemeinschaft*.[9] Nevertheless, few spheres of social policy were wholly lacking in economic import or content. Even areas such as child care, prison reform, treatment of lunatics, or reclamation of prostitutes, which, overtly at least, raised no major economic principle, were nevertheless "economic" in the sense that they made potential demands on both public and private expenditure. And at the other extreme were policies like the statutory limitation of working hours and the provision of work or maintenance for the unemployed, which impinged on major issues of both macro- and microeconomic theory. (What was the optimal ratio between profits and costs? Was there a full-employment equilibrium? At what point did public welfare benefits erode saving and incentives to work? Did public expenditure subvert or stimulate provision through the private market?)

Issues such as these were never far removed from the concerns of political economists. Economic writers from Smith and Malthus to Keynes and Hayek wrote about poor relief and transfer payments gener-

[8]On the practical limits to purely economic perceptions of public policy, even when belief in market forces was most powerful, see Lionel Robbins, *The Theory of Economic Policy in English Classical Political Economy* (London: Macmillan, 1952); and Boyd Hilton, *The Age of Atonement: The Influence of Evangelicalism on Social and Economic Thought, 1785–1865* (Oxford: Clarendon Press, 1988).
[9]This tension was clearly expressed in Nassau Senior's desire on the 1834 Poor Law Commission for a national poor rate and abolition of the settlement laws, and the subsequent rejection by government of both these proposals.

ally as though they were integrally related to wider economic theory; and all of them addressed the policy issue of the proper balance between public and private expenditure. Moreover, from Alfred Marshall onward, economists were concerned with social welfare as an aspect of "human capital": certain kinds of social policy (particularly education and health) were seen as reacting on economic performance by enhancing industrial efficiency and skills and as consolidating the wider infrastructure of a modern capitalist economy.[10]

The writings of Sidgwick greatly expanded the concept of a utilitarian no-man's-land, within which no private individual had an interest in taking actions from which all would benefit.[11] At the same time the injection of "marginalism" into economic thought and the formulation of Fabian and New Liberal ideas about the "rent of ability" and "organic surplus value" began to supply a theoretical rationale for policies of redistribution.[12] And never strongly represented among academic economists, but an important part of popular economic debate, was the argument that the inherent malfunctioning of a capitalist economy was responsible for social problems and hence for social policy in the first place; that without expropriation there would have been no "reserve army of labour," no "wounded soldiers of industry," no "submerged tenth."

How far were such concerns represented within government and public administration, and how far was the "economic" dimension of social policy an important constraint on policymakers themselves?

THEORY AND POLICY: AN ERRATIC RELATIONSHIP

One point that immediately strikes the historian of social policy is the extreme haphazardness and uncertainty of policymakers' access to economic advice and information. No social policy department in British government employed any practicing economists as economic advisers at any time between 1834 and 1964 (though, as will be suggested later, the significance of this fact is perhaps deceptive). Occasionally, administra-

[10] Alfred Marshall, *Elements of Economics of Industry* (London: Macmillan, 1892; 1920 edn.), 404–15.
[11] Henry Sidgwick, *The Principles of Political Economy* (London: Macmillan, 1883, 3d edn. 1901), 399–418.
[12] F. Y. Edgeworth, "The pure theory of taxation," *Economic Journal* 1897, reprinted in F. Y. Edgeworth, *Papers Relating to Political Economy* (London: Macmillan, 1925), 100–16; John Allett, *New Liberalism, the Political Economy of J. A. Hobson* (Toronto: University of Toronto Press, 1981), 70–7.

tors in such departments practiced economic theory as an intellectual sideline, but never in relation to questions of "social welfare." (Robert Giffen, for example, wrote extensively on economic questions, but his areas of expertise bore almost no relation to the nascent social policy functions of the late-nineteenth-century Board of Trade.)

In the great debates of the Edwardian period on methods of financing the social services, economic ideas were mediated to ministers almost exclusively through administrative civil servants; the issues of poverty, redistribution, and the taxable capacity of different classes of the community were not seen as requiring professional economic advice. The new social policy departments that emerged during and after World War I (Ministry of Labour, Ministry of Pensions, Ministry of Health) were all concerned with major questions of economic and financial management, yet none of them had access to independent sources of economic advice (which may help to explain the degree of their subordination to Treasury control).[13]

The postwar movement to improve official research facilities (inspired by the Haldane Committee on the machinery of government) was initially concerned not with exclusively economic matters but with "how to render more effective every form of social organisation: how to make more socially fertile the relations among men."[14] Yet the work of the Economic Advisory Council, which was partly the fruit of this movement, hardly touched on the social welfare field.[15]

Lack of formal reference to economic advice was almost equally apparent in the great public inquiries into social policy issues. In the early Victorian period, economists had frequently sat on select committees and royal commissions, the most famous example being Nassau Senior's role in constructing the 1834 Poor Law Report. Later, in the Victorian period and in the early twentieth century, however, economists were more often than not conspicuous by their absence. The great Victorian housing and public health inquiries, the Interdepartmental Committee on Physical Deterioration (1904), the Select Committee on Homework (1907), the Royal Commission on the Income Tax (1920), the Royal Commission on National Health Insurance (1926), and the Royal Commission on Work-

---

[13]Rodney Lowe, *Adjusting to Democracy: The Role of the Ministry of Labour in British Politics 1916–1939* (Oxford: Clarendon Press, 1986), especially 210–14.

[14]S. and B. Webb, *A Constitution for the Socialist Commonwealth of Great Britain* (Cambridge, Eng.: Cambridge University Press, 1975), 354.

[15]S. Howson and D. Winch, *The Economic Advisory Council 1930–1939* (Cambridge, Eng.: Cambridge University Press, 1977); and Chapter 2 in this volume.

men's Compensation (1939)—all were examples of major public inquiries that dealt with central issues of economic as well as social policy
(property rights, wage theory, maintenance of incentives, public expenditure) but included not one economic expert among their members. And of
these inquiries, only the Royal Commission on the Income Tax sought
evidence from economic experts.[16]

Moreover, when economic experts did sit on or submit evidence to
social policy inquiries, it was often not qua economists but because they
were deemed to possess some other kind of relevant administrative or
philanthropic experience. When Marshall gave evidence to the Royal Commission on the Aged Poor in 1893, for example (evidence that symbolized a
major turning point in the application of economic theory to social welfare
practice), his views were sought not because he was a professor of economics but because he and his wife were active members of the Cambridge
Charity Organisation Society.[17] And when Sir Leo Chiozza Money gave
evidence to the Select Committee on the Income Tax in 1906, he did so
initially at least not as a fiscal expert but as a Liberal MP.[18]

The nature and limits of the kind of advice sought from economists
can be plainly seen in the Royal Commission on the Poor Laws of 1905–
9. The two economists who sat as members of the commission, Lancelot
Phelps and William Smart, were both chosen because of their experience
of local and charitable administration rather than because of their economic expertise. William Beveridge, who was the commission's main
witness on the problem of unemployment, was selected not because he
was writing a theoretical treatise on the labor market, but because he was
chairman of the Labor Exchanges Committee of the Central (Unemployed) Body.

The same was largely true of other economists who gave evidence to
the Poor Law Commission; their views were sought not because of their
academic expertise, but because they happened incidentally to have been
actively involved in local philanthropic schemes. William Ashley, head of

---

[16]The contempt, verging on personal abuse, with which economist witnesses were treated
by some of the members of this commission makes it perhaps the exception that proves
the rule. (*Royal Commission on the Income Tax*, Minutes of Evidence, Cmd. 288, XXIII,
1919, QQ. 6,923–53, 10,597–11,024.)
[17]*Official Papers by Alfred Marshall*, 217.
[18]The Select Committee on the Income Tax was unusual in that it did make serious inquiries
into aspects of contemporary economic opinion, and with the help of Arthur Bowley spent
an afternoon grappling with Pareto's theory of distribution: but, unsurprisingly, none of
this appeared in the Select Committee's report (P.P. IX, 1906, H. of C. 356, QQ.1152–
1320, and appendixes 6, 7, and 9).

the Department of Commerce at Birmingham University and a leading
expert both on tariff reform and on Mill's *Principles,* specifically declined
to comment on "social welfare" questions on the ground that he had no
practical experience of English charity or poor relief. Ashley's reticence is
particularly surprising, because it is clear from other sources that he *was*
actively involved at this time in supplying social policy advice to the
Conservative party, and a few years later was to act as the leading economic expert on the Unionist Social Reform Committee.[19]

It is worth noting that the Poor Law Commission, which is often seen
as a crucible of Edwardian social reform ideas and a harbinger of subsequent welfare state thought, did not take evidence from any of the prominent "New Liberal" economists of the period, nor were their ideas referred to in any substantial way in either of the commission's reports.[20]
The commission also received a memorandum from the Cambridge
economist A. C. Pigou, which sought to provide an objective yardstick
for measuring social welfare and to construct a theoretical framework for
the concept of the "national minimum." But although the "national minimum" was central to much current social welfare thought, Pigou was not
cross-examined by the commission and his arguments were ignored by
both majority and minority reports.[21]

A similar detachment from formal economic advice was apparent in
the setting-up of the Beveridge inquiry into Social Insurance and Allied
Services more than thirty years later. Cabinet and Treasury sources reveal
that from the start of Beveridge's inquiry there was much political alarm
that Beveridge's proposals were going to prove financially and economically unrealistic; but it occurred to no one to staff the Beveridge Committee with trained economists. Apart from Beveridge himself, all members
of the committee were administrative civil servants (and the Treasury
representative, Sir Edward Hale, was wholly inexperienced in the Treasury's fiscal and budgetary departments). As it happened, Beveridge was

[19]*Royal Commission on the Poor Laws,* VIII (Cd. 5066 XLVIII, 1909), appendix no. 4, p.
504. E. H. H. Green, *Radical Conservatism in Britain c. 1899–1914* (unpublished Ph.D.
dissertation, Cambridge University, 1986), Chapter 4, passim; Jane Ridley, "The Unionist
Social Reform Committee, 1911–14; Wets before the Deluge," *Historical Journal,* 30
(1987): 397, 406.
[20]Hobson received one minor passing reference in the minority report, as a source for the
view that it was difficult for men to find work after middle age (*Royal Commission on the
Poor Laws,* Minority Report, 1168).
[21]*Royal Commission on the Poor Laws* (Cd. 5068, XLIX, 1910), appendix lxxx, pp. 981–
1000. This memorandum anticipated part of the argument in Pigou's *Wealth and Welfare*
(London: Macmillan, 1912).

able to employ the services of Keynes, who was a personal friend and fellow diner at the Gargoyle Club; and Keynes's support was to prove an inestimable source of strength in buttressing the budgetary and actuarial aspects of the Beveridge Plan against its critics.[22]

But the Beveridge Committee was very unusual among social policy inquiries in being able to call upon that kind of high-level economic advice; it was typical in that provision for such advice was highly fortuitous and idiosyncratic. Moreover, Keynes's influence on the Beveridge Plan was almost entirely confined to limiting its costs. Despite his assumption of "full employment," Beveridge in 1942 had almost no familiarity with Keynesian ideas on unemployment policy, and there is not the slightest evidence to support the commonly held view that the Beveridge report was a social welfare complement to Keynes's general theory. Moreover, Beveridge himself was notably resistant to the idea, proposed by economists attached to the Offices of the War Cabinet, that social security spending should itself be used as a device for economic stabilization.

THE "SOVEREIGNTY" OF FACTS

So far I have considered the impact of economic knowledge mainly in terms of policymakers' access to grand economic theory. Was the position any different in relation to the collection of economic facts? Was the emergence of modern social policy rooted in that "rational accounting" approach to government familiar to students of Weberian sociology?

The making of social policy since the early nineteenth century has been closely connected with the accumulation of social and economic data, and no student of nineteenth- and twentieth-century British history can be unaware of, or ungrateful for, the vast tracts of primary data collected in the publications of the Poor Law Board, the Local Government Board, the Home Office, the Privy Council, the Board of Education, and the Board of Trade (and in their institutional successors, the Ministries of Pensions, Labour, and Health).

Many of the great heroes of modern social reform movements held highly ambitious views about the ultimate possibility of formulating scientific laws (and thereby solving social and administrative problems) through a process of collecting and sifting empirical social and economic data. Edwin Chadwick, Florence Nightingale, Octavia Hill, William

[22]Jose Harris, *William Beveridge: A Biography* (Oxford: Clarendon Press, 1977), 408–12.

Beveridge, and Sidney and Beatrice Webb, although differing widely in other respects, all adhered to a philosophy that saw precise, positivistic, scientific knowledge as the only rational basis for social action, and rigorous inductionism as the only basis for that knowledge.

The crucial importance of the accumulation of such data has been stressed both by historians who have seen social policy as primarily the product of ideological commitment (Utilitarianism, Fabianism, New Liberalism, etc.) and by those who have seen it as a primarily functional response to structural and environmental change. Census data and the registration of births and deaths have been portrayed as the logical predicates of the nineteenth-century public health movements; and the institutionalization of routine processes for collecting regular industrial, economic, and cost-of-living data has been invoked to explain the dominance of the Board of Trade in the social reform movement of the Edwardian era.[23]

By contrast, the limitations of Poor Law statistics, and the fact that such statistics were designed mainly as a means of auditing public expenditure rather than as a tool for analyzing poverty, have been used to explain the relative policy inertia of the Local Government Board.[24] Early-twentieth-century plans for the functional reconstruction of government (such as the Haldane report on the machinery of government, the Webbs' proposals for a "socialist commonwealth," and Beveridge's plans for an "Economics General Staff") all laid great emphasis on the indispensable role of regular social and economic statistics. Indeed, Beveridge to his dying day was convinced that his accumulation of price data over seven centuries would make a much greater contribution to the understanding of social processes (and thus to ultimate social welfare) than all his writings on social insurance.[25]

How far can this emphasis on the role of data be sustained? Whatever may be the possibilities of sophisticated economic data collection in the future, so far as the history of social policy in the past is concerned, I confess to a certain skepticism. Indeed, of the large number of modern

[23]Roger Davidson, "Llewellyn Smith, the Labour Department and Government Growth 1886–1909," in Gillian Sutherland, ed., *Studies in the Growth of Nineteenth Century Government* (London: Routledge and Kegan Paul, 1972), 227–62. It is worth noting that the highly positivistic account of labor statistics presented in Davidson's article is diametrically opposite to that given by Davidson in his *Whitehall and the Labour Problem*, cited earlier.

[24]John Irvine, Ian Miles, and Jeff Evans, eds., *Demystifying Social Statistics* (London: Pluto Press, 1979), 5.

[25]Harris, *William Beveridge*, 468.

monographs that have put the making of social policy under the historical microscope, few seem to lend support to the view that economic and social data were the indispensable tools of "rational" government that protagonists supposed.

Mark Blaug's studies of the 1834 Poor Law Commission have reconstructed a picture of policy formation almost wholly opposite to that which Chadwick and Senior claimed to espouse; in other words, both men framed their report around a series of axiomatic principles, and largely ignored (except for purposes of random quotation) the data painstakingly accumulated by the Poor Law Commission's regional investigators.[26] Edwin Chadwick grasped the relevance of fertility and mortality statistics to public health policies only *after* the introduction of civil registration of births and deaths; and Florence Nightingale's famous dictum that "facts are everything—doctrines are nothing" was conveniently set aside whenever the facts failed to support lines of action she knew to be correct.[27] The ubiquitous Victorian "social science" societies purposefully sought to ground public policy on a basis of empirical data. Yet recent studies of these societies have shown that their work was almost wholly taxonomic, rather than analytic or genuinely prescriptive; for all their amassing of detail, they by and large failed to generate coherent explanations of pathological social conditions.[28]

Indeed, in certain circumstances, exhaustive gathering of facts could be a substitute for, rather than a prerequisite of, thought and action, as was notoriously the case with the Royal Commission on Labour in 1893–4.[29] The accumulation of data by the Board of Trade's Commercial, Labour, and Statistical Department undoubtedly improved the board's standing and "clout" vis-à-vis other departments, including the Treasury (a clear example of the principle that knowledge is a form of political power). Nevertheless it is difficult to see any of the board's research as the logical prerequisite of the social policies it so successfully promoted in the late 1900s. On the contrary, statistical data on which to

[26] Mark Blaug, "The Myth of the Old Poor Law and the Making of the New," *Journal of Economic History* 23 (1963): 151–84; and "The Poor Law Report Re-examined," ibid., 24 (1964): 229–45.
[27] S. E. Finer, *The Life and Times of Sir Edwin Chadwick*, 155; F. B. Smith, *Florence Nightingale. Reputation and Power* (London: Croom Helm, 1982), 99–100.
[28] Laurence Goldman, "A Peculiarity of the English? The Social Science Association and the Absence of Sociology in Nineteenth Century Britain," *Past and Present* 114 (February 1987): 133–71.
[29] Peter Hennock, *British Social Reform and German Precedents: The Case of Social Insurance, 1880–1914* (Oxford: Clarendon Press, 1987), 60.

base the board's most important policy innovation—unemployment insurance—were almost wholly lacking before the insurance system actually came into operation in 1912.[30]

The same was true of legislation against low pay. Empirical information (as opposed to abstract reasoning) about the impact of statutory minimum wages upon employment and price levels only became available *after* the introduction of the Trade Boards Act of 1909.[31] In other words, economic information in both these cases was a consequence rather than a cause of policy innovation—clear examples of the process whereby state action often generates rather than responds to economic facts.

Moreover, the apparent precision and objectivity of routine data could mask a highly erratic process of fact gathering that was ridden with interpersonal relationships and subjective meaning. When, for example, the 1905 Poor Law commissioners urged that the Local Government Board's Poor Law reports should be made more factual and statistical, the board's chief inspector replied: "That might be all very well for us who are living in London, but the inspector has got to live among his boards of guardians and it may be an indiscreet thing for an inspector to be too frank."[32]

Arthur Bowley, in his evidence to the Select Committee on the Income Tax, complained that the use of data by public inquiries was almost wholly arbitrary and unscientific. Economic experts were used to express off-the-cuff opinions or to give rough statistical estimates that then passed into administrative folk wisdom with no further scrutiny. "The round number given rather hastily is not examined but is quoted again and again, and presently this round number is received as one of the standard measurements of our national welfare, when, in reality, it has no basis. There are many instances of that."[33] Even where there was a direct sequential relationship between acquisition of knowledge and formation of policy, the relationship was not necessarily strictly logical. Late-nineteenth-century housing and public health policies, for example, were closely predicated on the correlation perceived by William Farr between residential overcrowding and high death rates; but, as was later shown, the correlation was in fact a false one.

Moreover, policy advice often bore little relation to empirical data,

[30] A. C. Pigou, *Unemployment* (London: Williams and Norgate, 1913), 19.
[31] R. H. Tawney, *Studies in the Minimum Wage*, Nos. 1 and 2 (London: G. Bell and Son and Ratan Tata Foundation, 1913 and 1914).
[32] *Royal Commission on the Poor Laws*, Minutes of Evidence (1909, Cd. 4625, XXXIX, QQ. 1917–19).
[33] *Select Committee on the Income Tax, Minutes of Evidence*, Question 1158.

even when such data were available. When Alfred Marshall challenged the orthodox view that old-age pensions were liable to depress wages and suggested instead that they might boost wages by stimulating consumer demand, he based his claim not on comparative study of local variations in Poor Law practice and wage statistics, but on a mixture of imaginative speculation and gossip with his wife about local clients of the Charity Organisation Society.[34] This is not, of course, to say that his argument was therefore false, but that it was an intuitive, not an inductive, one. When in 1942 the Beveridge Committee considered the problem of poverty among deserted wives, Beveridge commissioned a large-scale empirical study of single parenthood as a cause of poverty; yet he ultimately left provision for unsupported mothers out of his scheme, not because of these empirical findings but because of sensational exposés of collusive-desertion scandals published in the *Evening Standard*.[35]

The Beveridge Committee also carried out extensive statistical inquiries about the impact on poverty of individual and regional variations in liability for rent, and Beveridge was advised by B. S. Rowntree and others that no subsistence-level social security scheme could be effective without allowing for variation in rent. Yet such provision was wholly left out of the eventual Beveridge insurance scheme, in this case because of Beveridge's overwhelming prior commitment to certain conceptions of freedom and equality (e.g., freedom in spending benefit income on more or less expensive accommodation was one of the citizen's "essential freedoms").[36] The whole "Beveridge Plan" was supported and illustrated by an impressive array of statistics and citation of expert and lay evidence. Yet archive sources make it clear that the structure of Beveridge's scheme was fully worked out before a single item of evidence was gathered. Number-crunching and expert opinion peformed an important political and rhetorical function in enhancing the plan's attractiveness and plausibility, but it would be quite wrong to suggest that they determined its fundamental shape.

THE CULTURE OF POLICY: FOUR EPOCHS

Up to this point I have put forward a largely negative or agnostic view of the relationship between economic knowledge and the making of modern

[34]*Official Papers of Alfred Marshall*, 217–8, 225, 248–9.
[35]Harris, *William Beveridge*, 403–7.
[36]Ibid., 396–9.

social policy. I do not wish to press this view too far, and I certainly do
not share the view of those who see social and economic data as nothing
more than cultural artifacts, logically incapable of determining or changing the course of rational social action.[37] Indeed it seems obvious that
there are many spheres in which the relationship between economic perception and social policy has been an active one.

Thus, just as in 1834 the belief that high levels of Poor Law expenditure were depressing rents and profits and thus contracting employment
led to dramatic cuts in social welfare provision, so at the end of the
nineteenth century, evidence of rising national income and rising real
wages put forward by Giffen and Arthur Bowley was specifically invoked
to legitimize more extensive welfare provision.[38] In both cases economic
knowledge was an important part of a policy-enabling process, rather
than merely epiphenomenal to what was going to happen anyway. In a
similar way, Nassau Senior's claim that profits were made in the "last
hour" of daily work was strongly invoked by factory owners in their
resistance to Ten Hours legislation[39] (although this is an interesting example of a piece of economic theorizing that ultimately *failed* to determine
policy, not because it was logically or empirically refuted but because it
simply gave way before the superior weight of humanitarian indigna-
tion). And Pigou's classic study of welfare economics, published in 1920,
identified the maintenance of a proper balance between national dividend
and transfer payments to poorer income groups as the key problem of
social policy. Although policymakers disagreed among themselves about
the exact fulcrum of this proper balance, few would have disagreed with
Pigou's general formulation. The "welfare economics" language used by
Pigou, ignored in 1909, was much more pervasive by the 1920s.[40]

At a more specific and practical level, growing realization among Local Government Board officials of the "poverty trap" impact of the Poor
Law on personal saving was a major stimulus both to the growth of
interest in social insurance schemes and to the introduction of "statutory

---

[37]For example, see Karel Williams, *From Pauperism to Poverty* (London: Routledge and
    Kegan Paul, 1981), passim.
[38]See, for example, *Royal Commission on the Poor Laws* (Cd. 4499, XXXVIII, 1909),
    Majority Report, 48–9.
[39]Derek Fraser, *The Evolution of the British Welfare State* (London: Macmillan, 1973), p.
    17.
[40]A. C. Pigou, *The Economics of Welfare* (London: Macmillan, 2d edn., 1924), especially
    Part IV. The ideas of Beveridge, for example, seem to me now to be imbued much more
    with Pigou's thought than I realized when I wrote my biography of Beveridge a decade
    ago.

disregards" into the system of poor relief.[41] And the whole tenor of late-Victorian and Edwardian social policy was affected both by awareness of international economic competition and by the discovery that poverty was not just a result but a cause of physical, environmental, and moral deterioration.[42] The construction of the welfare state in the 1940s was linked initially to the growth of wartime economic controls and, slightly later, to a shift from supply-side to demand-side economic analysis (a transition that is not discussed in detail here, as it has been dealt with so thoroughly in other chapters). And although I have just argued that there was no specific *theoretical* connection between Beveridgean social policy and Keynesian economic analysis, there was clearly a practical one (because, as Beveridge himself acknowledged, social security was financially inconceivable without prior attainment of the goal of full employment).[43]

But the impact of economic knowledge has typically been much more diffuse, erratic, and informal than historians of policy have sometimes suggested. Rarely has it consisted of the direct application of economic theory and data to specific societal problems; far more often it has consisted of gradual and often scarcely perceptible shifts in the wider climate of economic and political culture. Even the famed 1834 Poor Law Amendment Act was much less the result of the direct application of political economy (the act, after all, rejected many prevailing tenets of economic thought) than of a much wider intellectual ambience, within which political economy was merely a part.

In other words, economic thought and Poor Law thought were both derivatives from a prevailing moral philosophy of rationalistic hedonism, and from many other influences besides. Boyd Hilton's wider studies of early-nineteenth-century social policies suggest that, although the influence of economic thought was not wholly negligible, its intellectual role was largely subsumed under the much more powerful and all-embracing influence of evangelical theology. Eighty years later there was a marked congruence between many aspects of Edwardian social policy and New Liberal economic thought; but historians have so far singularly failed to find direct evidence that departmental policymakers consciously absorbed and applied, for example, Hobsonian ideas about unemployment

---

[41]Jose Harris, *Unemployment and Politics: A Study of English Social Policy 1886–1914* (Oxford: Clarendon Press, 1972), 245–6.

[42]See particularly, Hennock, *British Social Reform and German Precedents,* and the *Report of the Interdepartmental Committee on Physical Deterioration* (Cd. 2175, 1904).

[43]*Social Insurance and Allied Services* (1942, Cmd. 6404), 163.

and underconsumption. There was no Eureka effect in the discovery and application of economic knowledge, but a more humdrum and complex process of gradual intellectual penetration. Acknowledgment of the legitimacy of redistributive taxation, of the practical limits to private saving among the very poor, and of the existence of involuntary unemployment all fell into this category.

Coupled with this process was the fact that, for much of the period under review, "economics" was rarely viewed by policymakers as a discrete area of genuinely "expert" knowledge. As already noted, social policy departments and public inquiries employed or took advice from experts in other fields, such as law or medicine, but knowledge of political economy was regarded as part of the all-round intellectual equipment of the administrator or public notable, in much the same light as ethics and political science.

This was particularly true after the mid-Victorian civil service reforms, as highly educated "generalists" replaced the piecemeal and ramshackle appointments of an earlier era. Ministers and public officials in the reformed Home Office or Local Government Board would no more have thought of employing a permanent economist than they would have thought of employing a tame moral philosopher. Some degree of familiarity with both applied economics and economic thought was part of the elite culture of the age; and politicians and administrators were themselves not infrequently members of such bodies as the National Association for the Promotion of Social Science, the Political Economy Club, the British Association for the Advancement of Science, and the Royal Statistical Society.[44] Others, who were not members of these self-consciously quasi-academic bodies, learned their political economy on the job (like David Lloyd George, who, as chancellor of the Exchequer, picked up the theory of social insurance partly by lightning visits to Germany, partly by listening to the speeches of backbench MPs).[45]

One consequence of this widely diffused "lay" economic literacy was that, despite a lack of reference to trained economic expertise, social policy debate throughout the Victorian and Edwardian periods was deeply imbued with economic language and economic considerations.

---

[44] S. E. Finer, "The Transmission of Benthamite Ideas 1820–50," in Sutherland, ed., *Studies in the Growth of Nineteenth Century Government*, 11–32; Laurence Goldman, "The Social Science Association 1857–1886: A Context for Mid-Victorian Liberalism," *English Historical Review* 101 (1986): 95–134.

[45] Hennock, *British Social Reform and German Precedents, the Case of Social Insurance, 1880–1914*.

"Generalist" public administrators, government inspectors, and members of royal commissions widely assumed that there was a given framework of economic laws that social policy must not transgress; such an approach was omnipresent in the Poor Law, medical, and public health reports published by the Local Government Board, and the evidence given by the board's inspectors to royal commissions.[46]

Doctrinal "folklore," of the kind pinpointed elsewhere in this volume, was often apparent. Ideological differences between Edwardian social reformers were transcended by the fact that both conservatives and progressives looked back on the period before 1834 as an object lesson in the evils of divorcing social policy from economic constraints; and the main criticism of "labor" and "socialist" policies in administrative circles was not that they aimed to substitute an alternative system of economic analysis, but that they threatened to ignore economics altogether.[47]

Another consequence was that the temper of government debate on social questions tended to be endemically "conservative," in the nonpartisan sense of that term. It reflected not the most advanced mode of contemporary economic thought, but that of a generation earlier;[48] and the judgments of economically minded administrators on the economic fantasies of such folk as J. A. Hobson and J. M. Keynes tended to be sterner than the judgments of their academic counterparts. Thus "marginalism," which emerged in political economy in the 1870s and '80s, did not penetrate government thought until the 1900s and even then only peripherally. And notions about what later generations defined as the "multiplier" effect of social services expenditure, sighted though not mapped by Marshall in the 1890s,[49] did not make much specific impact on social policy until World War II. The diaries of Sir Edward Hamilton, permanent secretary to the Treasury at the outset of the "progressive taxation" revolution, suggest that his mind was firmly set in the economic paradigms of forty years earlier.[50] The Royal Commission on the Poor Laws may have ignored Marshall and Pigou, but it continually cited Aristotle, Malthus, and Ricardo. The power of long-standing economic ideas was perhaps most apparent in relation to free trade: both the collection of data about poverty and working-class living standards and the substan-

[46]See, for example, *The Evidence of J. S. Davy to the Royal Commission on the Poor Laws* (1909, Cd. 4625, XXXIX, QQ. 2358, 2413–48, 2769–85).
[47]Harris, *William Beveridge*, 88–9, 94–5.
[48]*Official Papers of Alfred Marshall*, 225–6.
[49]Ibid., 224–5, 248–9.
[50]Hamilton diaries, Add. Ms. 48642–83, passim.

tive content of social policy in the Edwardian era were heavily influenced by the prior goal of legitimizing and shoring up a threatened free-trade system.[51]

Nevertheless, it would be wrong to assume that the relationship between economic thought and social policy was unchanging. Within the public culture of lay political economy identified earlier, trends in the application of economics to "social welfare" can be divided into four distinct though intermeshing periods.

Between the 1820s and 1840s debate over the Poor Law, working hours, factory conditions, and public heatlh engendered heated government and popular controversy about what were the economic causes of distress and about which of a number of competing economic models was most applicable to the framework of public policy. At the start of this period there was little consensus or orthodoxy about economic or social policy goals, and the ideal of a self-activating market system was still locked in combat with the ideal of a traditional moral economy. Social policy departments were tiny, often ad hoc, bodies with little continuity or intellectual tradition; a great plurality of "theories"—economic, political, moral, and theological—rolled around government inquiries and commissions like a tide of molten lava.[52] Public discussion of social policy in this era was nothing if not theoretical (although, as mentioned above, the extent of any causal relationship between theory and policy may be questioned).

After the dust had settled over these early conflicts, however, and after civil service reform was under way, reference to economic theory largely died out of official social policy debate—not because it had ceased to be relevant, but because it had ceased to be controversial. Most mid- and late-nineteenth-century makers of social policy simply assumed a high degree of coherence between private and public welfare and between social and economic laws. What was deemed to be rational for the individual was deemed to be rational for the community as a whole (not so much because of an "unseen hand," but because, except in certain limited

[51]The Board of Trade's cost-of-living studies of 1908 and 1912 were known respectively as the Bible and New Testament of Free Trade: Walter Layton, *Dorothy* (London: Collins, 1961), 29–30.

[52]Finer, *The Life and Times of Sir Edwin Chadwick*, Books 2–7. Hilton, *The Age of Atonement*; and Boyd Hilton, *Corn, Cash and Commerce: The Economic Policies of the Tory Governments 1815–1830* (Oxford: Oxford University Press, 1977); William Lubenow, *The Politics of Government Growth. Early Victorian Attitudes toward State Intervention 1833–1848* (Newton Abbott: David & Charles, 1971).

spheres, the community had no autonomous existence separate from that of its members). Apart from these narrowly designated spheres, there was no question of a clash between the values governing the well-being of the individual and those governing the well-being of the whole of society; and political economy, as its name implied, did not contravene but subsumed questions of social policy.[53]

This belief in the natural unity of social and market concerns began to fragment around the turn of the century. Theorists as diverse as Henry Sidgwick, Alfred Marshall, A. C. Pigou, the heterodox New Liberals, and the neomercantilist tariff reformers became increasingly aware of a possible tension between collective and individual well-being,[54] while empirical studies of poverty and unemployment by Booth, Rowntree, and Beveridge implicitly challenged the equilibrium model of classical political economy. Politicians and administrations became much more conscious of Continental and colonial welfare systems (generally much more étatist and less market-oriented than their British counterparts).

These shifts of emphasis did not, of course, invalidate or displace older styles of economic thought and economic decision making; but they did suggest that the norms of economic efficiency and those governing the treatment of individuals—even able-bodied, productive, choice-making individuals—might not always be the same. The sum of rational choices was no longer seen as necessarily identical with "social justice" (itself a neologism of the Edwardian period); and studies of the "submerged tenth," the "residuum," and the "unemployable" called into question earlier Victorian assumptions about individual capacity for rational calculation.

Between 1900 and 1920, therefore, the semantics of "welfare" subtly changed, and what had previously been a strictly individualist concept became increasingly an organic and metaphysical one (or, in popular parlance, simply a synonym for the "social services," wholly devoid of any theoretical meaning).[55] Edwardian theorists and reformers responded

[53]This view is clearly expressed in the subtitle of Mill's *Principles of Political Economy* ("with some of their applications to Social Philosophy").
[54]See, for example, Sidgwick, *The Principles of Political Economy*, 403–8; J. A. Hobson, *Problems of Poverty* (London: Methuen, 1899); and Pigou's memorandum to the Royal Commission on the Poor Laws (Cd. 5068, XLIX, 1910, appendix LXXX, 981–2).
[55]The shifting terminology of "welfare," "economic welfare," and "social welfare" deserves a study in its own right and cannot be considered in detail here. On the early language of welfare economics, particularly in the writings of Pigou, see Donald Winch, *Economics and Policy: A Historical Study* (London: Hodder and Stoughton, 1969), 28–46; and T. W. Hutchinson, *"Positive" Economics and Policy Objectives* (Cambridge, Mass.: Harvard

to these new challenges in a variety of ways. Some, notably Pigou, tried to devise objective standards for judging the welfare of the whole community, while others looked to more normative disciplines, such as "social philosophy" or "social administration" rather than to "political economy" to provide an alternative (or at least a supplementary) frame of reference for social policy.[56]

Social policy tacitly moved away from the nineteenth-century view that the economy was self-regulating, although both theorists and policymakers continued to adhere to certain classical propositions about individual behavior (to Beveridge and to Pigou, no less than to Chadwick and Nassau Senior, the principle of less eligibility was not an outdated piece of Gradgrind Victoriana, but an inexorable fact of life). This third period produced much of the thinking that was to give rise to the emergence of the "welfare state" (although, paradoxically, "social philosophy," with all its organic and idealist overtones, had begun to disintegrate as an intellectually fashionable mode of discourse by the time the welfare state came to fruition in the 1940s).

During the fourth period, which began in the mid-1930s and has lasted more or less until the present day, a range of both disparate and interlocking factors threw all kinds of normative and prescriptive discussion in the social sciences into a state of confusion. The advance of linguistic positivism discredited the "organic" and "idealist" formulas that had supplied the Edwardian critique of political economy with a legitimizing framework,[57] and the integrative function that organicist theory performed earlier in the century was largely taken over by various forms of vulgar Marxism, whose protagonists could not make up their minds whether "social welfare" was pro- or anticapitalist.[58] Welfare economics of the kind pio-

University Press, 1964), 143–7; and *A Review of Economic Doctrines, 1870–1929* (Oxford: Clarendon Press, 1953; 1962 edn.), 280–302; and Edmund S. Phelps, *Economic Justice, Selected Readings* (London: Penguin, 1973). The use of the term *welfare* to imply either *social policy* or *social service agencies* seems to have been unknown in Britain in the nineteenth century, but arrived in the 1900s from North America. (A correspondent in the *Westminster Gazette*, January 28, 1905, claimed that "The home of the 'welfare policy' is the city of Dayton, Ohio.")

[56]Jose Harris, "The Webbs, the Charity Organisation Society and the Ratan Tata Foundation," in Martin Bulmer, Jane Lewis, and David Piachaud, eds., *The Goals of Social Policy* (London: Unwin Hyman, 1989).

[57]T. D. Weldon, *The Vocabulary of Politics* (London: Pelican, 1953); and idem, *States and Morals. A Study in Political Conflict* (London: John Murray, 1946; 1962 ed.), especially 166–86, 235–9.

[58]For example, Victor George, *Social Security and Society* (London: Routledge and Kegan Paul, 1973), 1–36.

neered by Pigou was attacked on all sides—dismissed by some as "crass materialism," by others as covertly metaphysical.[59] The disciplines of psychology and sociology increasingly challenged more traditional economic and philosophical ways of looking at welfare, and often came up with arguments diametrically opposed to those of economic thought (for instance, behavioral studies of low pay suggested that people who were deterred from working by the lure of welfare benefits were vastly outnumbered by those who refused or neglected to claim benefits to which they were entitled).

In this last period, the enormous expansion of officially generated data, itself a consequence of earlier state policy formation, facilitated a pinpointing of specific problems that was far more precise than had been possible a generation earlier. Yet it may not be fanciful to suggest that the sheer volume of data made synoptic understanding more elusive than it had been in the past. And at the same time all the social sciences became increasingly specialized and less accessible to the lay political and administrative mind. By comparison with earlier periods the inner logic of the various social science disciplines "took off" and became much less subordinate to the functional, rhetorical, and legitimating requirements of the administrative state. The result was that policies for the alleviation of poverty and other forms of social need became increasingly fragmented both from economics and from systematic moral discourse. Economics survived and indeed expanded as a technical tool for the analysis and measurement of social problems, but it rarely constituted or contributed to the kind of general intellectual framework for social policy that had been sought in earlier periods.

Postwar thinking about social policy within the inner circles of the British government remains an area largely unexcavated by historians; but in public and academic debate there was a widening gap between "economic" and "social welfare" perspectives. With certain notable exceptions, much writing on social welfare (particularly in the 1960s) was largely innocent of reference to the possible economic consequences of social legislation, and highly skeptical of the validity of such factors as pricing and consumer choice. More recently, government attempts to "recommodify" certain well-established areas of "welfare" have forced protagonists of social policy to reconsider the links between social policy

[59]Little, *A Critique of Welfare Economics,* 76–83; Hutchison, *A Review of Economic Doctrines,* 289–93; Hutchison, *Positive Economics and Policy Objectives,* 155.

and economics, and there have been efforts to recover the more synoptic "political economy" perspective of the nineteenth century.[60] It remains to be seen whether "economic knowledge" and "social welfare" can reintegrate with each other, or whether they will be permanent victims of the epistemological fragmentation of thought about modern society.

[60]Gordon Graham, *Contemporary Social Philosophy* (Oxford: Basil Blackwell, 1980); Albert Weale, *Social Policy and Political Theory* (London: Macmillan, 1983).

13

Economists and the formation of the modern tax system in the United States: the World War I crisis

W. ELLIOT BROWNLEE

As the federal government has enlarged its economic roles in the twentieth century, it has struggled to enlarge its understanding of the economic environment. At times, systematic economic learning has been a routine part of the emerging regulatory state. Implementing regulatory initiatives often demanded enhanced capacities to study and analyze economic impacts. The instability of politics, however, has been a more important factor in stimulating the quest for economic information. Because political contests over economic policy have been characterized by sharp conflict, and because their outcomes have been highly uncertain and contingent, political factors have placed a premium on deliberate economic investigation. The contestants have promoted the advancement of economic knowledge as an instrument of power designed to further their causes. The state itself has been one of those contestants, and it has often promoted economic knowledge in order to mediate on behalf of social order.

Through the resulting process of state-sponsored economic investigation, the modern state has shaped and molded the development of professional economics. Government agencies and their needs have contributed to setting the agenda of economists, influenced their definition of economic problems, and shaped the structure and conduct of economic investigation and analysis. And through this influence over economic knowledge, the state itself, as distinct from the various interests represented there, has played a major role in determining the course of public policy.

The adoption and expansion of income taxation in the United States during World War I provide an opportunity to explore how policy initia-

401

tives augmented the capacity of the federal government to describe and understand economic life. This is so because World War I was the first of the two great transitions in the development of federal taxation, and because it was the first major war in which the modern economics profession had an opportunity to address issues of public finance.

During World War I, the federal government, as it pioneered in the financing of modern warfare, dramatically expanded its participation in the production of economic knowledge. Part of the reason was the need for operational information; the government needed to predict future flows of revenue from a tax base that had been poorly understood or measured. But far more was required. The process of tax reform had become highly disorderly, and it produced dramatic, almost overnight shifts in tax policy during wartime, which was already a period of intense economic instability. Furthermore, the clash of conflicting claims with regard to the effects of taxation on economic growth, stability, and distribution—claims that economic instability intensified—had increased demands for better economic knowledge.

TAXATION AND ECONOMIC KNOWLEDGE
BEFORE WORLD WAR I

Even in peacetime, the need of the federal government for reliable information has perhaps been greatest in the area of taxation. This need has been exceptionally powerful in the United States, where republican sensitivities to the incidence of taxation—the distribution of the real tax burden—have often been exquisite. In 1788, in the wake of "taxation without representation" issues, and of Shays's Rebellion, Alexander Hamilton commented that "no part of the administration of government . . . requires extensive information and a thorough knowledge of the principles of political economy, as much as the business of taxation." Hamilton explained, "There can be no doubt that in order to [achieve] a judicious exercise of the power of taxation, it is necessary that the person in whose hands it is should be acquainted with the general genius, habits and modes of thinking of the people at large, and with the resources of the country."[1] Nonetheless, until World War I, the federal government made no sustained effort to obtain systematic information about taxation.

Until World War I, the federal government was able to satisfy its need for knowledge of the incidence and effects of taxation by relying almost

[1] Alexander Hamilton, "The Federalist No. 35," *The Federalist* (New York: Modern Library, 1937), 215–6.

exclusively on the collective and conventional wisdom of public officials, especially legislators, and their advisers from business and the legal profession. The limited need for systematic economic information resulted in large part from the success of republicans, through Article I, Section 9, of the Constitution, in denying the federal government the power to impose property taxes—the taxes whose incidence and effects have tended to be most controversial. Moreover, the federal government generally recognized and avoided those extremely unpopular taxes that have been constitutional. For example, during the early days of the Republic, the federal government eschewed uniform "head," or "poll," taxes, and after the Whiskey Rebellion of 1794 it avoided excise taxes, or internal taxes on the manufacture or sale of commodities. As a consequence of this tax sensitivity, until the Civil War the federal government relied almost exclusively on tariffs for its revenues and, given its limited responsibilities, was able to keep those tariffs rather low and, in fact, consistently reduce them during the 1840s and 1850s.

With the Civil War, the federal government's revenue machine grew permanently more substantial, but that growth did not produce a sustained demand for sophisticated knowledge of the sources and the effects of taxation. Until World War I, the only systematic studies of the tax system sponsored by the federal government were those of Commissioner of Internal Revenue David Ames Wells, whose responsibility it was to advise the Grant administration on the peacetime conversion of the complex, hastily constructed Civil War revenue system. Surprisingly, the retention of the high Civil War tariffs, and the controversy they generated, did not lead the federal government into careful analysis of the economic implications of its tax policies.

Federal officials chose to address tax issues without benefit of systematic study because the two powerful political parties, which were largely responsible for determining federal economic policy, developed vested interests in discussing the tariff issue as a matter of faith rather than science. The Republican party used the tariff issue in building its powerful coalition of interests around a program of national aggrandizement, and successfully maintained the tariff as the cornerstone of national revenue policy until World War I.[2] Responding to the Republicans, the Demo-

[2]The Republicans bound up in their symbolic invocation of the tariff a variety of concrete economic benefits. Thus, the Republicans used the tariff as an instrument to ease repayment of private and public debts to Europeans, to increase the nation's savings rate, to fund pensions and disability benefits for Union veterans, to pay for the "pork barrel" internal improvements provided by the annual rivers and harbors bill, and to protect American industry and labor from foreign competition.

crats extended their support among farmers, southerners, middle-class consumers, and small businessmen by challenging the tariff with calls for a reassertion of republican and Jacksonian values. Harkening back to a simpler era, Democrats attacked the tariff as the "mother of trusts" and the primary engine of a Republican program of subsidizing giant corporations. Thus, at the national level, the two competing political parties based their identities on sharply conflicting, ideological views of the tariff, and neither party believed that systematic data would usefully enhance the popular appeal of their programs.[3]

Even the movement led by the Populists to enact an income tax that might replace some tariff revenues and simultaneously assault monopoly power did not immediately increase the demand for the services of economists. The income tax movement progressed too slowly and cautiously for that. Democrats generally preferred small government and were reluctant to propose taxes to replace the tariff. The party embraced the tax only after the Supreme Court ruled in 1895, in *Pollock* vs. *Farmers' Loan and Trust Co.*, that the very modest income tax of the Wilson-Gorman Tariff of 1894 violated Article I, Section 9, of the Constitution.

The Democratic and progressive Republican proponents of income taxation did not make a breakthrough until 1909, when Congress approved and sent to the states the Sixteenth Amendment, authorizing federal income taxation. It was not until 1913 that ratification prevailed, carried forward during its critical phase by the presidential campaign of 1912, in which popular enthusiasm for federal policies designed to attack monopoly power reached an all-time high. Even so, the income tax that followed Wilson's election to the presidency was little more than a token measure, and required hardly any professional analysis apart from that provided by lawyers. Virtually no proponent of the tax within the government believed it would become a major source of revenue. The Underwood Tariff of 1913 established the income tax at the "normal" rate of 1 percent on both individual and corporate incomes, with a high exemption excusing virtually all middle-class Americans from the tax.

Meanwhile, the economics profession as a whole showed little interest in the national debate over taxation. Nonetheless, between the 1880s and

---

[3]Reflecting the ideological function of the tariff issue was the extraordinarily low quality of the economic content of the congressional tariff debates in the late nineteenth century, and the sharp decline in quality since the early days of the Republic. On this point, see Richard C. Edwards, "Economic Sophistication in Nineteenth Century Congressional Tariff Debates," *Journal of Economic History* 30 (December 1970): 802–38.

World War I, some economists were developing a lively curiosity about state and local tax issues, and, after 1900, increasingly served state and local governments as consultants and members of tax commissions. In 1907, to enhance their status and influence within both the public and private sectors, those economists with an interest in tax issues joined with state and local tax administrators, and with accountants and tax lawyers, to organize the National Tax Association. The organizers declared that their intention was to "formulate and announce . . . the best informed economic thought and ripest administrative experience available for the correct guidance of public opinion, legislative and administrative action on all questions pertaining to taxation." Through their analysis of public finance and of the general property tax in particular, these economists, on the one hand, assisted state and local governments in capitalizing on their property-tax base and, on the other hand, worked with corporate and individual taxpayers to establish a more predictable and equitable system of state and local taxation.[4]

In contrast with political discussion of property tax issues, however, the debate over the tariff carried great risk for the emerging economics profession. Most economists disapproved of high tariffs, but relatively few, like Frank W. Taussig, sustained active opposition. The leaders of the profession were too preoccupied with building respect to maintain visible stands on a highly divisive issue like the tariff, particularly because free-trade views ran afoul of many of the conservatives they were seeking to impress. Only when significant bipartisan support emerged for tariff revision and the adoption of income taxation did economists take and uphold leading positions on national issues of taxation.

The economist who led his profession beyond state and local tax issues to address national issues of taxation was Edwin R. A. Seligman, a professor at Columbia University. At the same time, Seligman contributed significantly to building the professional status of economists within important centers of conservative power by lending a hand to protect the investment system against radical threats. Thus, beginning in the 1880s and continuing to World War I, he worked for moderate reform of general property taxation and against replacing the property tax with Henry George's "single tax"—the program of an "unscientific" amateur.

[National Tax Association Proceedings, 1908, 617. On the approach of the National Tax Association to state and local reform, see Ferdinand P. Schoettle, "The National Association Tries and Abandons Tax Reform, 1907–1930," *National Tax Journal* 32 (December 1979): 429–44.

Seligman was committed to more, however, than the protection of property. He sought to develop, through slow but steady experimentation, institutions of public finance that could reduce economic inequality and win popular confidence—over the objections of narrow-minded capitalists. Consequently, as early as 1893 he supported a progressive inheritance tax, and he even supported the short-lived income tax of 1894. But he insisted on moving slowly, in part to protect himself against the charge of political partisanship. He highly qualified his positions. Even though he supported progressive taxation and provided a novel theory—the "faculty" theory—to justify it, he opposed progressive income taxation in 1894 on the grounds that administrative problems would doom it to failure. Only in 1910, after Congress had sent the Sixteenth Amendment to the states and after Britain had embraced progressive income taxation, did Seligman admit that it might be practicable in the United States. Even then, he argued that a long period of experimentation with proportionate income taxation would be necessary before the federal government could work out appropriate definitions of income and devise effective methods of assessment and collection.[5]

The crisis of World War I, however, accelerated the pace of tax reform far beyond the leisurely rate that Seligman preferred. In mid-1915, the Wilson administration concluded that it was necessary to increase taxes substantially to replace falling tariff revenues and to establish a preparedness program. Two years of experience in collecting progressive income taxes led Wilson and Secretary of the Treasury William G. McAdoo to be optimistic about the revenue potential from increases in the income tax, including both its individual and its corporate components. Moreover, they decided to shape the new taxes in close cooperation with a powerful group of insurgent Democrats who opposed preparedness but supported redistributive taxation.

The insurgents, led by Congressman Claude Kitchin of North Caro-

---

[5]Seligman's most elaborate discussion of his position on the income tax is found in his book *The Income Tax* (New York: Macmillan, 1911). Seligman had even more severe reservations about the ability of state governments to administer income taxes. However, in 1915, his fear of single-tax radicalism, which had acquired a new impetus from the financial resources of Joseph Fels, changed his mind. Along with economists Charles A. Bullock and Carl C. Plehn, Seligman had become convinced that its adoption was the way to defeat the movement to exempt improvements from property tax—a movement they regarded as the thin edge of the single-tax wedge. Seligman became a leader in drafting New York's 1916 income tax legislation. On his New York strategy, see Seligman to Alfred E. Holcomb, September 7, 1915, Edwin R. A. Seligman Papers, Butler Library, Columbia University, and W. Elliot Brownlee, *"Progress and Poverty:* One Hundred Years Later," *National Tax Association Proceedings, 1979, 230.*

lina, who chaired the House Ways and Means Committee and served as majority leader of the House, carried forward nineteenth-century antimonopolist, redistributionist traditions. Focusing on issues of taxation, they merged Populist and single-tax hostilities toward concentrations of wealth and power. They shared with the advocates of more aggressive antimonopoly policies among Wilson's closest advisers—Secretary of the Treasury McAdoo and Louis Brandeis, for example—the belief that an income tax could discipline corporations and promote a more competitive economic order. The product of the collaboration was a potent measure of tax reform, the Revenue Act of 1916, and, less than a year later, the Revenue Act of 1917.[6]

ANTICORPORATE, STATIST TAXATION AND THOMAS S. ADAMS

The 1917 act rejected both high taxes on domestic consumption and a mass-based income tax (an income tax falling most heavily on wages and salaries because of low exemptions and high rates on lower income brackets). Instead, the 1917 act dramatically advanced progressive personal and corporate income taxation by raising the rates on personal income to a maximum of 67 percent (on incomes over $1 million) and, most important, by expanding the taxation of excess profits. In contrast with Britain, which taxed "war profits" with a tax on the excess of wartime over peacetime profits, the United States, through the Revenue Act of 1917, imposed a graduated tax on all business profits earned above a "normal" rate of return on invested capital of between 7 percent and 9 percent. The act set the tax rates in a range from 20 percent to 60 percent, the maximum applying to net incomes providing more than a 33 percent rate of return.

The goal was to tax the profits accruing to monopoly power. As one Treasury staff member put it, the excess-profits tax had "the manifest advantage . . . of becoming a permanent part of the Government's revenue system, and can be used, if need be, as a check upon monopolies or trusts

---

[6]This act, in one stroke, broke the dominance of the tariff over the federal revenue system, transformed the experimental income tax into the foremost instrument of federal taxation, introduced federal estate taxation, initiated the first significant taxation of corporate profits and personal incomes, and introduced the concept of taxing corporate "excess-profits" (applying it to munitions manufacturers) and that of taxing corporate surpluses and undistributed profits. For an account of the Revenue Act of 1916, see W. Elliot Brownlee, "Wilson and Financing the Modern State: The Revenue Act of 1916," *Proceedings of the American Philosophical Society* 129 (1985): 173–210.

earning exorbitant profits."[7] The architects of the tax believed it would control monopoly power by attaching penalties to bigness and concentrations of wealth—characteristics assumed to be the major source of high rates of return. By 1918, corporations were paying over $2.5 billion in excess-profits taxes—more than half of all federal tax revenues, which in turn amounted to about one-third of all federal wartime revenues.[8]

Excess-profits taxation thrust the federal government into the financial structures of corporations to a degree, and with a complexity, that was without precedent in the United States. While drafting the Revenue Act of 1917, Secretary McAdoo and Commissioner of Internal Revenue Daniel C. Roper concluded that the problems of defining excess profits, assessing the taxes, and understanding their economic effects were sufficiently daunting to require the services of economists. Furthermore, they agreed, professional economic expertise was necessary to frame legislation that accomplished the goals of the excess-profits tax, to convince legislators that the new tax would be feasible, and to persuade the business community to accept the tax. Consequently, they hired a Yale University economics professor, Thomas S. Adams, as their principal tax adviser.

The Treasury singled out Adams for a variety of reasons. He was one of the most distinguished economists specializing in the study of taxation. But far more important to the Treasury was Adams's record of success in developing and refining methods of assessing and collecting progressive income taxation. Adams was among the second generation of professional economists, having received his doctorate in 1899. As was typical of the public finance economists in that generation, he had immersed himself in the practical problems of tax administration. In fact, Adams had a stronger interest in such problems than any other economist at the time, including Seligman.

The part of Adams's extensive career in public service that was most impressive to the Treasury was his success as a member of the Wisconsin Tax Commission in developing the means for administering the state's income tax, which was, at the time, the most ambitiously redistribu-

[7] I. J. Talbert, Head of Law Division, Commissioner of Internal Revenue to George R. Cooksey, Assistant Secretary of the Treasury, August 8, 1917, William Gibbs McAdoo Papers, Library of Congress.

[8] For a survey of the financing of the American efforts during World War I and of the relationships among that financial history, social investigation, and the development of the modern state, see W. Elliot Brownlee, "Social Investigation and Political Learning in the Financing of World War I," in Michael J. Lacey and Mary O. Furner, eds., The State and Social Investigation in Britain and the United States (forthcoming).

tional tax in the nation. In so doing, Adams had single-handedly confounded public finance orthodoxy, represented by Seligman, which held that a state income tax, particularly a progressive one, could not be administered.

In addition, Adams had played a critical role in drafting New York State's income tax law in 1916. Before American entry into World War I, state income taxation appeared to many progressives to have more redistributional potential than federal income taxation, and Adams, as early as 1911, had warned economists such as Seligman that their opposition to state income taxes would prove to be as shortsighted as the opposition of political economists to the trade union movement during the early nineteenth century.[9]

The Treasury also recognized that Adams, like Seligman, had cultivated a reputation for caution and objectivity. In the National Tax Association, he had worked closely with Seligman in steering the organization away from advocacy that might impair its reputation for objectivity. And he admitted that he had initially regarded Britain's program of wartime taxation as "revolutionary." Furthermore, in early 1917, Adams had gone public with criticism of excess-profits taxation. If the Treasury could manage to persuade him to support the tax, as Wisconsin progressives had led him to support Wisconsin's radical income tax, he might well persuade fence-sitting progressives and businessmen to favor or accept the excess-profits tax.

Two facts suggested that Adams might convert: (1) he was a Democrat, sympathetic to the Wilson administration's approach to the mediation of class issues; and (2) in the process of studying with Richard T. Ely at Johns Hopkins and then pursuing a secondary academic interest in labor relations, he had become more accepting than was Seligman of the influence of class issues on tax politics. Indeed, throughout his career as public servant, Adams recognized that issues of economic class were inescapable in matters of tax policy. Moreover, he rejected as politically naive, and wrong, the extreme answer of classical economics: there are no class issues; the market has solved all distributional problems.[10]

[9]Thomas S. Adams, "The Place of the Income Tax in the Reform of State Taxation," American Economic Association, *Papers and Proceedings* I (April 1911): 303–21. Privately, Adams told Seligman that the Wisconsin tax was "an experiment which I . . . thoroughly believe is well worth trying." Adams to Seligman, August 9, 1911, Thomas S. Adams Papers, Sterling Library, Yale University.

[10]In 1912 Adams agreed to be secretary of the NTA and then recruited Seligman for the presidency because, as he told Seligman, "The Association was in danger of being used as

Once in the Treasury, Adams worked to advance the objectives of the Wilson administration while attempting to avoid directly addressing the ideological issue at the heart of the excess-profits tax debate: what stake does society have in corporate profits? The question, one of the most fundamental and sensitive of issues in the modern economy and one that Populists and single-taxers had first raised, asked whether the modern corporation was the prime engine of productivity, which tax policy should reinforce, or an economic predator, which tax policy could and should tame. Adams believed that his expertise, and that of his profession, could help sharpen the definition of the question, but that it had little to offer in the way of answers. If he addressed this question directly, his answer, like those of the central political actors, would necessarily be more ideological than scientific. Adams, and his profession, simply lacked adequate data or analytical tools to address even preliminary matters such as the statistical relationships between scale of production and productivity.

Worried about jeopardizing his reputation and at the same time seeking to advance the influence of economics over tax policy, Adams attempted to steer a course between the procorporate and anticorporate arguments that characterized the discussion of the tax. His approach in 1917 was to support the tax, thus changing his position from what it had been before he joined the Treasury, but to say as little as possible about the nature of corporate profits. In July, he privately analyzed the tax situation, urging the Treasury to distribute tax burdens according to the principle of "equality of sacrifice," which he took from John Stuart Mill. Adams argued that "sacrifices of the food, clothing, fuel and shelter necessary to maintain physical vitality are more keenly felt than is the abandonment of the more refined forms of consumption," and that "inroads upon small savings are as a rule more grievous than proportionate inroads upon the large surpluses." Before taxing small incomes and consumption, the Treasury should exhaust "the possibilities of all other less burdensome taxes." Of these, Adams advised, the least burdensome was the excess-profits tax, and it was, therefore, the most desirable of wartime taxes.

Adams continued to avoid reaching a judgment on corporate profits,

a device for propaganda work which however sound and desirable in itself was an unsuitable function for an association like the National Tax Association." Adams to Seligman, September 6, 1912, Seligman Papers. For the first reactions of Adams to the British tax program, see Roy G. Blakey, "The War Revenue Act of 1917," *American Economic Review* 7 (December 1917): 809.

finessing the issue of whether the tax would become a permanent part of the revenue system. He did so by proposing an administrative solution that, he argued, would make it irrelevant what basis the Treasury used to calculate "normal" profits. He argued that there was no theoretical conflict "between the pre-war and invested-capital bases." Either basis, properly applied, would produce "normal" rates of return. What was needed to implement the law was "a maximum of administrative discretion"— and the scientific conduct of that discretion. In particular, the creation of a "board of referees" could investigate and determine *"normal rates of profit* for different classes of business."

Adams's approach proved compelling to progressive members of Congress who had reservations about excess-profits taxation. In fact, Adams generated the critical margin of support for excess-profits taxation in Congress and, largely as a consequence, won the key administrative role in the resulting Excess Profits Advisory Board. Under his leadership, the board institutionalized a process of investigation and learning, one in which experts within the Treasury interacted with taxpayers to refine excess-profits taxation. Adams found the process exciting, and, buoyed by his victory, began openly to embrace excess-profits taxation as a permanent feature of the tax system. The tax offered promise, he said, as "a liberal and democratic financial policy during the reconstruction period which must follow the war." Adams's political success had encouraged him to move away from his exclusive emphasis on administrative technicality and express publicly his agreement—as a responsible member of Wilson's Treasury more than as an economist—with the broad social goals of the Wilson administration.[11]

SELIGMAN VERSUS ADAMS

In lending his support to the excess-profits tax, Adams moved beyond most of the other leading economists of public finance. In fact, led by

---

[11]On Adams's initial statements regarding excess-profits taxation, see his "Defects of the Excess-Profits Tax," *The Annalist* (June 4, 1917): 750, 756; "The Income and Excess-Profits Tax," *Financial Mobilization for War, Papers Presented at a Joint Conference of the Western Economic Society and the City Club of Chicago, June 21 and 22, 1917, 10–125*; and Adams to Seligman, March 30, 1924, and April 28, 1924, Seligman Papers. Adams's change of mind was most fully developed in July in his memorandum "The Fundamentals of War Finance," July 1917, in the Adams Papers. His later appraisals include Thomas S. Adams, "Principles of Excess Profits Taxation," *Annals of the American Academy of Political Science 75* (January 1918): 147–58, and "Federal Taxes upon Income and Excess Profits," *American Economic Review 8* (March 1918): 18–26.

Seligman, the senior public finance economists generally opposed the excess-profits tax, regarding it as a tax based not on Mill's "equal sacrifice" theory but instead on a flawed "benefit" theory of taxation, one that directed the tax toward those who benefited most from the war effort.[12] Moreover, they described the tax as ill-designed to discourage consumption and reduce inflationary pressures; as incapable of fair, predictable administration; and as likely to penalize initiative, destroy business confidence, and compromise the war effort. For these critics, campaigns to defeat or repeal the excess-profits tax offered an opportunity to resume the campaigns they had waged against the single tax and other programs of radical redistribution.

Seligman and his supporters joined with bipartisan business opposition (including not only Republicans but also the leading business supporters of the Wilson administration) in arguing that the excess-profits tax posed an extreme threat to corporate autonomy and to the efficiency of capital markets. Beginning in 1917 and extending throughout the war, Seligman energetically promoted his tax ideas among businessmen, particularly Wall Street investment bankers, and sympathetic members of Congress, both Democrats and Republicans. And some of these opponents of excess-profits taxation in turn promoted Seligman's analysis—and his career. Banker Thomas Lamont recommended Seligman as a consultant to Senator Henry Cabot Lodge, telling Lodge that Seligman was "not a theorist, but a sound student of economics." Seligman and business leaders promoted wartime tax policies that they regarded as acceptable. They sought replacement of the excess-profits tax with a combination of war-profits taxation, a mass-based, progressive income tax, and a variety of consumption taxes.[13]

Seligman's position was politically more sophisticated, however, than a straightforward defense of business interests. With Adams, he hoped to help the national government steer a middle course between socialism

[12]Adams and Seligman both rejected "benefit" theories as the basis for progressive taxation but were at odds over the proper formulation of "ability" theories. Adams preferred Mill's formulation and Seligman favored his own variant of it, the "faculty theory," through which he claimed to be able to incorporate power as well as sacrifice in determining "ability to pay." However, the daunting difficulties in quantifying either "equality of sacrifice" or "faculty" meant that neither Adams nor Seligman went beyond theoretical statements of these criteria. A useful analysis of Seligman's views on the basis of progressive taxation is found in Harold M. Groves, *Tax Philosophers, Two Hundred Years of Thought in Great Britain and the United States* (Madison: University of Wisconsin Press, 1974), 39–47.

[13]Thomas Lamont to Henry Cabot Lodge, May 12, 1917, Thomas Lamont Papers, Baker Library, Harvard University.

and unmediated capitalism. While Adams looked for ways to moderate socialism through the democratic statism favored by Secretary of the Treasury William Gibbs McAdoo, Seligman tried to civilize rampant capitalism through what he described as "progressive capitalism."[14] Thus, although he sought to ensure private control of capital markets and placed more emphasis on that goal than did Adams, and although he tended to believe, in contrast to Adams, that corporate bigness reflected economic efficiencies, he, too, became committed to making the tax system more progressive.

As Seligman implemented that strategy, he argued more vigorously for a shift of the tax base toward incomes. Moreover, Seligman, and the other economists who opposed excess-profits taxation, did not slavishly adopt all the arguments of business opponents of excess-profits taxation. In particular, Seligman never agreed with the businessmen who claimed that corporations could pass the tax forward to consumers or backward to suppliers and argued that the tax fueled price inflation. An important implication of Seligman's earlier pioneering study of the incidence was that the burden of the taxation of net corporate income could not be shifted and would, therefore, fall on stockholders, and Seligman held fast to his position. Indeed, this position contributed to Seligman's worry that excess-profits taxation would discourage investment in corporate activity.[15]

In their theoretical economics, Seligman and Adams were in substantial agreement. Adams shared Seligman's concern about the potential disincentive effects of the excess-profits tax. And Seligman was willing to grant Adams that excess profits were "the result, in part at least, of the social environment" and that, therefore, "it is entirely proper that a share of the profits should go to the community." It was their working assumptions about economic life, however, that distinguished the two. Whereas

---

[14]In his frequent discussions of what he called "progressive capitalism," Seligman emphasized the leavening of capitalism by progressive income taxation and, more important than any state interventions, by philanthropic support of private welfare initiatives. See Interview with Eustace Seligman, January 14, 1975, Columbia Oral History Collections, Butler Library, Columbia University.

[15]For the disagreement between Seligman and investment bankers over the shifting of excess-profits taxation, see Otto Kahn, *Our Economic and Other Problems, A Financier's Point of View* (New York: George H. Doran, 1920), 168–74; Seligman to Otto Kahn, November 1, 1920; and Kahn to Seligman, November 17, 1920, Seligman Papers. After Kahn had published his charges that the tax increased costs of production and prices, Seligman wrote to Kahn that "recent detailed statistics, studies by [Josiah] Stamp and others in Great Britain, as well as [David] Friday, [Carl] Plehn, and others in this country, have supplied an entire confirmation of the principles laid down by me a generation ago in my book on 'The Shifting of Taxation' as to the essential nonshiftability of the tax."

Seligman presumed that excess profits tended to reflect "individual ability and inventiveness," Adams acted as if he believed the contrary. And whereas Seligman presumed that the administration of excess-profits taxation would introduce "a deplorable uncertainty in administration," Adams devoted himself to proving the opposite.[16] Until 1917, however, Seligman and Adams had little interest in either identifying or resolving these issues. The war, however, playing on the political differences between the two economists—differences that had little to do with their economics—drew them, and many other economists, into determined and significant efforts to expand the boundaries of their profession. In 1917, Seligman and Adams extended the range of the professional analysis of taxation and confirmed their reputations as the leading students of public finance.[17]

The excess-profits initiative had proved to be the first time in which the federal government enlisted economists in the service of tax reform. Part of the reason was that, perhaps for the first time, economists who studied public finance had demonstrated that they had something to offer the federal government. Their success at the state and local levels in assisting the development of complex new forms of taxation—formulating valuation procedures for ad valorem railroad taxation, for example—had shown that their services could be of value to government and to private interests.

Also, public finance economists had become more willing to plunge into national controversy. The scale of wartime taxation had made national issues unquestionably significant, and the breakdown of party lines in the discussion of wartime taxation reduced the political risk from such involvement. Proponents of Wilson's wartime program included both Democrats and progressive Republicans; opponents included both Republicans and conservative Democrats. Even though wartime debates over taxation, particularly excess-profits taxation, were heated, they lacked the symbolic edge of the nineteenth-century tariff debates, which were so firmly rooted in political party identities. Nonetheless, the wartime debates led the public finance economists into terrain that was new to them,

[16]Edwin R. A. Seligman, "The War Revenue Acts," *Political Science Quarterly* 33 (March 1918): 29.
[17]Seligman and Adams have been the only two economists ever to serve as presidents of both the American Economic Association and the National Tax Association. Seligman was president of the AEA in 1902–3, Adams in 1927. Seligman was president of the NTA in 1912–5, Adams in 1922–3.

and highly sensitive—a serious discussion of the meaning of corporate profits.

THE STATE INVESTIGATES

The breach in the economics profession, and the scope of intellectual debate, widened further in 1918. Paralleling and supporting an attack on the excess-profits tax by the business community, Seligman and other more orthodox economists intensified their assault on T. S. Adams and the Treasury. The criticisms of the tax by business and economists converged in an extensive economic investigation conducted outside government—a study of the economic impact of excess-profits taxation in Britain and the United States.

Beginning in the spring of 1918, a group of businessmen in New York, Boston, and Philadelphia, led by Jesse I. Straus of R. H. Macy & Co. and including Thomas Lamont and other investment bankers, organized the financing of this study, which Seligman supervised as chairman of the War Finance Committee of the American Economic Association (AEA). (The AEA had formed the committee in 1917 to organize advice on a wide range of wartime fiscal issues.) Since the passage of the Revenue Act of 1917, Seligman had continued to play an active role as a critic of excess-profits taxation, publicly ridiculing Adams for his shift of position and vigorously recruiting support for his AEA study. In April 1918 he reported to Irving Fisher, the president of the AEA, "We have already received offers of assistance amounting to several thousands of dollars from a few friends" and the study "may become a very important investigation, calling for the expenditure of many tens of thousands." Despite the fact that Seligman had already made up his mind on the merits of the tax, he assured Fisher, "We shall not in any way compromise either the dignity nor the standing of the Association."[18]

---

[18]Seligman attracted attention with a "Comment" on Adams's support of excess-profits taxation, *American Economic Review* 8 (March 1918): 42–5. The Straus group raised a fund designed to cover any deficit up to $50,000 incurred by Seligman and the War Finance Committee. Straus to Lamont, May 1, 1918; Seligman to Lamont, June 5, 1918; Lamont to T. DeWitt Cuyler, June 6, 1918, Lamont Papers. See also Seligman to Charles J. Bullock, who chaired the War Finance Committee's subcommittees on income and excess-profits taxes, April 29, 1918; Straus to Mortimer L. Schiff, May 16, 1918; Straus to Lamont, May 16, 1918; Straus to Seligman, August 2, 1916, Seligman Papers. For Seligman's understanding with Irving Fisher, see Seligman to Fisher, April 20, 1918, and Fisher to Seligman, April 30, 1918, Seligman Papers.

Meanwhile, the Treasury moved to develop its own independent base of information, and an investigatory competition developed that went beyond a straightforward exchange of ideas. Despite Seligman's investment bankers, and their fund to support a study, the Treasury was better supported and more powerful.

Under the general supervision of Assistant Secretary Russell C. Leffingwell (who was in charge of fiscal affairs) and the direction of Adams, the Treasury conducted its own investigation of tax options—one that was unprecedented for its depth and range—and made recommendations for new revenue legislation. As the Treasury study progressed, T. S. Adams watched the AEA effort closely and lent some encouragement when it touched useful technical issues. But he resisted Seligman's efforts to exert peer pressure, and he kept the investigation at arm's length. He gave Seligman some general advice with regard to the legislative timetable but refused an appointment to the AEA War Finance Committee, scrupulously avoided revealing the development of Treasury thinking, and rejected Seligman's offer to use the study as a means of testing Treasury ideas. Also, he may have played a role in Secretary McAdoo's refusal to provide the support of AEA investigators needed to acquire passports for their British research. Seligman was informed that the Treasury did not want to appear to give "official sanction to the mission." In part as a consequence, the AEA study moved too slowly to have any direct influence on legislation in 1918 or even on the Revenue Act of 1918 (passed in February 1919).[19]

The critical part of the Treasury investigation was an assessment of the excess-profits tax. Adams conducted the study with the assistance of Robert M. Haig, whom Adams drafted from Columbia University in April, perhaps in part to ensure that the credibility of the Treasury within the community of economists would match that of the War Finance Committee. Adams certainly realized that Haig was Seligman's most prominent and productive student and that co-opting him would set back the Seligman investigation. Moreover, Adams viewed the investigation as

[19]Adams to Seligman, April 6, 1918; Adams to Seligman, April 11, 1918; Seligman to Adams, May 29, 1918; Adams to Seligman, June 1, 1918; Seligman to Adams, June 3, 1918; Seligman to Adams, June 12, 1918; Seligman to Bullock, June 12, 1918, July 5, 1918; Adams to Seligman, July 16, 1918, Seligman Papers. On the denial of the passports, see L. S. Rowe, assistant secretary of the Treasury, to Seligman, June 26, 1918, Seligman Papers. The AEA report on the workings of the American excess-profits tax did not appear in print until March 1919. See *Report of the Committee on War Finance of the American Economic Association, American Economic Review* 9 (March 1919).

a way of advancing fundamental economic knowledge regarding the sources and nature of corporate profits.

The Treasury study provided the first systematic findings regarding the effects of excess-profits taxation. The results were, however, troublesome for proponents of the tax. First, the Treasury analysts found that the difficulties of accurately determining capital investment and rates of return on capital had actually contributed to "profiteering" through tax avoidance. Most important, some corporations had increased their capital issues to reduce their rates of return and slip into lower tax brackets under the excess-profits tax. Second, the analysis of the distribution of excess-profits taxes by size of company demonstrated rather conclusively that the highest rates of return on capital, and thus the highest tax rates, were found among the smallest corporations. Third, the Treasury concluded that numerous war contractors were earning large rates of return yet were taxed at relatively low rates under the excess-profits tax. The clear implication of these findings, at least for Assistant Secretary Leffingwell, was that the federal government must replace excess-profits taxation with the British-style taxation of "war profits."[20]

The results of the Treasury's study of excess-profits taxation were especially discouraging, and potentially embarrassing, to Secretary McAdoo, who remained committed to redistributional ideals that focused on taxing bigness and restraining monopoly power. But McAdoo was reluctant to lose face by embracing the British concept of taxing "war profits" that he had rejected in 1917. Adams, however, had not accepted Leffingwell's logic and, just as he had a year earlier, Adams offered McAdoo a compromise. He suggested adopting a "dual-basis," under which corporations would pay the higher of an increased excess-profits tax or the British-style war-profits taxation.

Adams, who had begun the war with a preference for the British-style tax before he endorsed excess-profits taxation, had now changed his

[20]On the drafting of Haig, see Adams to Seligman, April 6, 1918, and Adams to Seligman, April 1, 1918, Seligman Papers. On the report, see Russell C. Leffingwell to Paul Warburg, April 7, 1918, Russell C. Leffingwell Papers, Library of Congress (LPLC). See also Leffingwell to McAdoo, May 18, 1918; Leffingwell, "Tax Legislation," May 20, 1918; and Thomas S. Adams, "Table Showing 7899 Representative Corporations Classified According to Amount of Invested Capital and Ratio of Net Income to Invested Capital," 1917, McAdoo Papers. Within the Treasury, Leffingwell was a sharp critic of excess-profits taxation. In 1920, Leffingwell told his successor at the Treasury, Parker Gilbert, that "the trouble" with the excess-profits tax was that it "carried to an extreme Kitchin's desire to throw the burden on the profiteers and the rich." See Leffingwell to S. Parker Gilbert, November 1, 1920, Russell C. Leffingwell Papers, Sterling Library, Yale University (LPYU).

mind once again. The reason was his quest for tax equity far more than political expediency. Six years later, Adams told Seligman that he had supported the shift to the hybrid "dual-basis" tax because to have provided tax relief for either Standard Oil, which would have fared better under a pure excess-profits tax, or the Ford Motor Company, which would have paid lower taxes under a pure "war-profits" tax, "would have been absurd." Adams had concluded that the Treasury had not yet been able to define "normal" profits under the excess-profits tax administration and that a hybrid tax would be more successful in reaching true excess profits.[21]

Adams defeated Leffingwell in the bureaucratic clash. Relieved to keep the excess-profits tax but persuaded that the "war-profits" basis would place a relatively heavier burden on the largest corporations, McAdoo quickly recommended that the president endorse a "real war-profits tax" that would be "super-imposed upon the existing excess profits tax in such a way that the taxpayers should be required to pay whichever tax is the greater." A few days later, after complaining to the president about the monopoly power of J. P. Morgan and "the financial bosses of Wall Street," McAdoo told him, "A proper war-profits tax will have a salutary effect upon these gentlemen."

McAdoo won Wilson's vigorous support in May and then recommended to Congress a *doubling* of federal taxes in fiscal 1919. He proposed raising the normal income tax on "unearned income," imposing high luxury taxes, and, most important, shifting corporation taxation from an excess-profits to a "dual-basis." McAdoo suggested raising the rates to a flat rate of 80 percent of profits, the rate employed by Britain.[22]

McAdoo then struggled to persuade progressive members of Congress, who generally wanted to defer any tax increases until after the November elections, that they should enact his proposal for dual-based corporate taxes and then attack war "profiteering" during the 1918 congressional

[21]Thomas S. Adams, "Suggested Memorandum for the Secretary," May 10, 1918, National Archives, Record Group 56; Adams to Seligman, March 30, 1924, Seligman Papers. For Adams's comparison, in 1918, of the taxes of the Standard Oil and Ford Motor companies, see his testimony, U. S. Congress, House of Representatives, *Hearings before the Committee on Ways and Means on the Proposed Revenue Act of 1918, June 7 to July 17 and August 5, 14, and 15, 1918* (Washington, D.C.: U. S. Government Printing Office, 1918), 102.
[22]McAdoo to Woodrow Wilson, May 23, 1918, and May 31, 1918, McAdoo Papers; Woodrow Wilson, "An Address to a Joint Session of Congress," May 27, 1918, Arthur S. Link, ed., *The Papers*, vol. 48 (Princeton, N.J.: Princeton University Press, 1985), 162–5; McAdoo to Kitchin, June 5, 1918, McAdoo Papers.

elections. McAdoo cooperated with Senator William E. Borah, who was launching his own attack on corporations that had exploited the war and were not paying their fair share of taxes. The Treasury agreed to produce for Borah a list of all corporations that had earned more than 15 percent on their capital stock in fiscal 1917, and by July, in barely more than a month, Adams and his staff had produced an extensive compilation of critical data on more than 30,000 corporations. Then, in August, McAdoo placed on the record more of the Treasury's analysis—estimates by Adams that the 80 percent tax on war profits would bear more heavily on a great many of the largest corporations, including all the steel companies (producing $100 million more in revenues from U.S. Steel alone) and the Standard Oil group ($60 million more).[23]

Claude Kitchin and other Democratic leaders in the House, however, refused to break with excess-profits taxation. Kitchin focused on the postwar world, and feared that any erosion of the excess-profits concept would limit the ability to deal with *long-run* distributional issues through the tax system.

In August, Adams once again played a crucial role in breaking the deadlock. In the hearings before the Ways and Means Committee, Adams was able to persuade Kitchin that accepting the "dual-basis" compromise would not prevent excess-profits taxation from becoming permanent and would, in fact, be a more effective means of taxing corporate profits. At the conclusion of Adams's testimony, Kitchin remarked, "I used to think I was a radical until we got on this bill, but now I find I am a conservative." With Kitchin's support for the compromise, the House cleared the bill in September.[24]

The victory in the House capped Adams's formidable wartime politi-

[23]George R. Cooksey to McAdoo, June 6, 1918; Thomas S. Adams, "Memorandum on the Differences Between a War Profits Tax and an Excess Profits Tax," July 27, 1918, National Archives, Record Group 56; McAdoo, "War Revenue Act, Memorandum, August 14, 1918," McAdoo Papers. U. S. Senate, 65th Cong., 2d Sess., *Corporate Earnings and Government Revenues, Senate Documents 15*, no. 259 (July 5, 1918).

[24]Wilson's intervention was arranged by Leffingwell, who, while McAdoo was on a Liberty Loan speaking tour, explained the principles of war-profits and excess-profits taxation to the president and Joseph Tumulty. In contrast with McAdoo and Adams, Leffingwell emphasized the argument that "war-profits" taxation would stimulate business enterprise. See Leffingwell, "CONFIDENTIAL: Memorandum concerning War Profits Taxes and Excess Profits Taxes," July 31, 1918, Leffingwell to Tumulty, July 31, 1918; Leffingwell to Wilson, August 2, 1918; and Leffingwell to McAdoo, August 3, 1918, LPLC. On Adams's persuasion of Kitchin, see Adams to Seligman, March 30, 1924, Seligman Papers. For the crucial exchanges among Adams, Kitchin, and the Ways and Means Committee U. S. Congress, House of Representatives, *Hearings Before the Committee on Ways and Means on the Proposed Revenue Act of 1918 . . .* , 87–119.

cal accomplishments. He had made possible a shift in responsibility for initiating revenue legislation from the legislative to the executive branch; he had increased the range of executive discretion in the implementation of tax policy; and within the executive branch, he had led the economists in gaining significant intellectual responsibility for shaping both legislation and its administration. Furthermore, working to implement the social vision of the Wilson administration, he had helped win what the administration and congressional progressives regarded as a major victory for vertical equity in taxation.

In the process, Adams had an important impact on the agenda of the economics profession. He led the profession into the analysis of tax options—particularly with regard to the taxation of corporate profits—that it had not previously considered. In particular, he had brought into the professional analysis of public finance the question of the social setting of corporate profits. In so doing, he had begun to develop data and refine arguments that could help economists analyze the sources and nature of corporate profits.

Events in late 1918, however, threatened the wartime accomplishments of Adams and the Treasury, and placed in jeopardy plans to institutionalize the wartime changes as permanent features of the nation's system of public finance. The electoral defeat of the Democratic party in November, the relief of the acute fiscal emergency by the armistice later that month, and the need to rebuild a Democratic coalition for 1920 led Democrats to consider reduction of wartime taxes on business. In November, Secretary McAdoo warned of the possibility of a postwar depression and urged Congress "to look ahead to the future of American business and industry." Taxation, he told Congress, "should be devised as to encourage and stimulate rather than to burden and repress them."[25]

Nonetheless, McAdoo, assisted by new studies conducted by Adams, continued to support the main element of the Adams compromise—the dual "excess-profits" and "war-profits" formula—and support for excess-profits taxation remained strong among both Democratic and Republican progressives in Congress. Consequently, the Revenue Act of 1918, passed by Congress in February 1919, included the Adams formula; Congress thus kept open the possibility that the excess-profits tax might become permanent.[26]

---

[25]McAdoo to Furnifold M. Simmons, November 14, 1918, McAdoo Papers.

[26]In October, a close study by Adams of what more than 600 corporations would pay under the "dual-basis" tax led him to emphasize that an excess-profits option "would bring

McAdoo left the Treasury at the end of 1918, however, and doubts mounted as to whether the federal government would continue the emphasis on progressive equity in taxation and the commitment of the Treasury to analyzing systematically public finance and its economic setting. Would these wartime accomplishments be institutionalized as permanent parts of the American state?

THE VICTORY OF "PROGRESSIVE CAPITALISM"

Under the leadership of McAdoo's two Democratic successors at Treasury, Carter Glass and David Houston, some signs pointed toward long-run continuity.[27] Glass had been a major architect of the Federal Reserve System and consulted closely with McAdoo after he took over the Treasury. Houston, a former chancellor of Washington University with professional training in business and finance, had a deep faith in the benefits of systematic economic knowledge. But there were counterindications, particularly with regard to the most progressive elements of the wartime tax program. Glass deferred to Assistant Secretary of the Treasury Leffingwell, who was the Treasury official closest to Wall Street and the investment bankers and had been a consistent critic of excess-profits taxation. Leffingwell continued in his post through Glass's Treasury year and then into Houston's term. Houston, in turn, also relied heavily on Leffingwell and then on his understudy and former associate at the law firm of Cravath & Henderson, S. Parker Gilbert. And Houston quite explicitly regarded his Treasury service as the means of advancing a career in the corporate sector.[28]

under the tax a large number of very prosperous organizations which ought to contribute to the expenses of the Government, and that the tax would not be excessive." Thomas S. Adams, "Corporations Paying War Profits and Excess-Profits Taxes," October 17, 1918, National Archives, Record Group 56.

[27] McAdoo supported either Glass or Bernard Baruch as his successor and then was heavily involved in the selection of the successor to Glass, who entered the Senate in 1920. McAdoo preferred Commissioner Roper, while Glass favored Assistant Secretary Leffingwell. Wilson, however, apparently wishing to avoid appointing a secretary associated with either Wall Street or southern interests, settled on Houston instead. McAdoo to Edward M. House, November 29, 1918, McAdoo Papers; McAdoo to Carter Glass, December 8, 1919; Glass to McAdoo, December 11, 1919; McAdoo to Glass, December 13, 1919; and House to Glass, December 15, 1919, Carter Glass Papers, University of Virginia Library.

[28] On Houston's ambitions for a corporate career, see Charles W. Eliot to Houston, February 20, 1920; Houston to Eliot, February 24, 1920; and Eliot to Houston, February 26, 1920, David F. Houston Papers, Houghton Library, Harvard University. After leaving the Treasury in 1921, Houston became vice-president of Bell Telephone Securities Company and board chairman of the Mutual Life Insurance Company of New York. After resigning his Treasury post, Leffingwell rejoined the Cravath firm and, in 1923, became a partner in

A major goal of the Glass-Houston leadership was, in fact, to move the Treasury away from McAdoo's anticorporate, statist policies while preserving an important role for economists in the formulation of tax policy. In striving to establish what Leffingwell later called a "non-partisan" Treasury, Glass and Houston placed heavy emphasis on professional economics. Their concept of economic "science" was exactly that advocated by Seligman and his colleagues in the late nineteenth century. Economics, in addition to enhancing the government's comprehension of the surrounding economy, would help steer government away from the shoals of radical experiments and, ideally, lift tax policy above politics—which, to Glass, Houston, and Leffingwell, meant class politics.

They described what they meant by contrasting what they hoped would become the process of determining internal revenue policy with that which governed tariff policy. Leffingwell noted that tariff making "has been lamentably the football of politics for several generations." Furthermore, they sought a Treasury that worked against intervention in corporate decision making. Taxation would become part of a larger Treasury effort to protect corporations as the major engines of economic progress, and would itself influence tax policy. To implement tax policies that provided mediation of class conflict and yet reinforced corporations, the modern Treasury would work to retain income taxation as the federal government's primary revenue instrument but to broaden its incidence to reduce the tax burdens of corporations and the wealthy. In essence, Seligman's approach to taxation had triumphed.[29]

Nothing represented Seligman's victory better than the decisions of Glass and Houston to press for the repeal of the excess-profits tax. They were responding to business pressure, which became even greater in 1919 and 1920. As inflation mounted during 1919 and the early months of 1920, businesses found their tax rates, under the progressive excess-profits tax, increasing even more rapidly than were prices. Business attacks on the tax became ferocious, constituting what one economist described as a "crusade." Near the end of 1919, Glass denounced the tax as one that "encourages wasteful expenditure, puts a premium on overcapi-

J. P. Morgan & Company. In 1948, Leffingwell became chairman of the board. Gilbert, after leaving the Treasury, returned to the Cravath firm as a partner in 1923, served as agent general of reparations between 1923 and 1930, and became a Morgan partner in 1931.

[29]Leffingwell to Glass, March 16, 1925; Leffingwell to Carter Glass, February 20, 1924, Glass Papers.

talization and a penalty on brains, energy, and enterprise, discourages new ventures and confirms old ventures in their monopolies."

Glass even supported the claim of the National Association of Manufacturers, unsubstantiated by any evidence and disputed by Treasury analysts, that the excess-profits tax "pyramids its burden and adds to the price from raw material to finished product." Glass declared that the tax was often "added to the cost of production" and was "a material factor in the increased cost of living." With the onset in mid-1920 of the nation's sharpest depression, before or since, business blamed the excess-profits tax and, more generally, the antibusiness policies of the Wilson administration, for the demise of prosperity. By the time of the 1920 elections, business had won massive middle-class support for abolition of the tax.[30]

Despite the hostility to excess-profits taxation, Glass, and then Houston, kept T. S. Adams on as the Treasury's principal tax adviser. The retention of Adams reflected the strength of their commitment to basing Treasury policy on economic analysis, their desire to establish a capability for economic analysis within the state—in the permanent bureaucracy of the Treasury—and their knowledge that Adams had by far the most successful record in bringing economic knowledge to bear on revenue policy. Houston underscored the importance of economic research by creating, in 1920, the Section of Statistics, which gathered together all the activities in the Treasury related to economic research.[31] In addition, Adams critically enhanced his value to the "non-partisan" Treasury by having yet another change of heart, his third, with regard to excess-profits taxation. In December 1919 he emerged as a leading opponent of continuing any form of excess-profits taxation.

It would be reasonable to suspect that Adams's change of position had more to do with his desire to follow the policy objectives of the post-McAdoo Treasury than with "scientific" conviction, and to conclude that his shift provided another example of the force of political contingency, exerted through the agency of the state, in shaping informed economic

---

[30]Roy G. Blakey and Gladys C. Blakey, *The Federal Income Tax* (London: Longmans, Green, 1940), 190–1; *New York Times*, December 4, 1919, "Platform for American Industry," *Proceedings of the National Association of Manufacturers, 1920*, 234.

[31]Previously, no formal organization existed to provide sharp focus for the research activity of the Treasury. In 1866 a Bureau of Statistics had been created in the Treasury Department. As the revenue system stabilized around the tariffs, the bureau languished until 1903, when it was transferred to the new Department of Commerce and Labor. In 1927 the Section of Statistics became the Section of Financial and Economic Research.

opinion. Indeed, such a suspicion is reinforced by the fact that by the end of 1919 the scrutiny that professional economists had been giving excess-profits taxation had persuaded more of them to favor continuing the tax into the postwar era.

The fracture in the economics profession had widened, with the forces behind excess-profits taxation actually gathering strength. To be sure, the AEA's Committee on War Finance, led by Seligman and Charles Bullock, a professor at Harvard University, had condemned the tax a year earlier, during the December 1918 meetings of the AEA.[32] But other economists had come to the support of the tax. David Friday, an economist and accountant who joined the Treasury in 1918 and worked closely with Adams in the analysis of income, savings, and government revenues, was most enthusiastic. He argued that "a tax on differential profits" could correct the fact that "the workings of the price system played queer pranks when it came to the distribution of incomes and of wealth." He recommended that the excess-profits tax be embraced as such a tax and, in fact, "substituted for all other taxes, except the tax on land." In effect, Friday had explicitly attempted to bring Henry George's ideal of a tax system focused on the expropriation of economic rent into the realm of acceptable discourse.[33]

Even Robert Haig, Seligman's student, supported the tax. After his work with the Treasury, Haig had joined the continuing investigation of British excess-profits taxation by the AEA and the New York financiers, telling Seligman that the tax "should, of course, be repealed as soon as the financial demands of the Government diminish to a point where it is no longer required, or as soon as some more satisfactory substitute is available."[34] But, as Haig surveyed the workings of the British tax for the AEA, and particularly when Josiah Stamp confided to him that "the Government has elaborated a new profits tax exactly along the lines of

[32] *Report of the Committee on War Finance of the American Economic Association*, *American Economic Review* 9 (March 1919).

[33] David Friday, "The Excess Profits Tax—Discussion," *American Economic Review* 10 (March 1920): 19–22.

[34] Seligman, his financial backers, and the AEA continued their investigations of the American and British taxes as they had originally planned in the hope of eventually shaping excess-profits taxation. See Seligman to Straus, May 23, 1918; Seligman to Bullock, January 31, 1919, Seligman Papers. On Haig's views, see Robert M. Haig to Seligman, March 10, 1919, Seligman Papers. Seligman knew that Haig was more favorably disposed to excess-profits taxation during the period of reconversion—a position he had held since late 1918—than the other members of the AEA War Finance Committee, but Seligman's prime goal was to defeat the tax as a permanent measure. See Seligman to Bullock, November 25, 1918, Seligman Papers.

our own old law, using invested capital as the test of excessiveness of profit," he began to change his position.[35] In December 1919, just when Adams was shifting toward favoring repeal, Haig made public his conclusion that retention of the excess-profits tax was distinctly preferable to either an increase in the normal income tax (favored by Secretary of the Treasury Carter Glass) or the adoption of a general sales tax, which business representatives increasingly proposed. A year later, Haig further explained his findings in the final report of the AEA on the British excess-profits tax.

Haig's proposal for continuing the excess-profits tax was explicitly part of his version of a long-term strategy for steering a passage between unregulated capitalism and socialism. Haig emphasized that "in the principle of special profits taxation there may exist a practicable method of arriving at a solution of the problem of monopoly profits against which the American public has steadfastly set its face, and of seizing some of the promised advantages of socialized industry without incurring the risks and disadvantages of socialism."

Haig, however, set a condition on his support: it was necessary to have "radical action in the direction of the improvement of our administration." He worried that, without significant administrative improvements, excess-property taxation and income taxation in general would degenerate into the chaos that characterized general property taxation. Haig recommended that Americans learn from the British: "Especially should we strive to secure for our country their system of original assessments by skilled, permanent, responsible civil servants and their system of appeal and review conducted on the principle of arbitration by persons not connected with the Treasury." Haig concluded, "We cannot have just taxation under the complicated conditions of modern life unless we prove ourselves equal to the task of establishing a skilled and permanent civil service."[36]

Haig had, in fact, pointed to a serious deficiency with the excess-profits tax and, more generally, with the Wilson administration's wartime tax program. As early as mid-1918, McAdoo had complained that the

[35]Haig to Seligman, July 30 and August 26, 1919, Seligman Papers.
[36]Robert M. Haig, "British Experience with Excess Profits Taxation," *American Economic Review* X (March 1920): 1–14; and idem, *The Taxation of Excess Profits in Great Britain: A Study of the British Excess Profits Duty in Relation to the Problem of Excess Profits Taxation in the United States*, *American Economic Review* 10 (December 1920), especially 173–6. This was the full AEA report on the British tax.

Treasury lacked a "sufficiently large and competent corps of expert audi-tors or accountants" to keep up with the review of excess-profits returns. Administrative problems became even more acute after the war when increasing inflation compounded the normal difficulties of the assessment process, when corporations became more recalcitrant in disputes over assessments, when large corporations rapidly increased their employment of accountants, and when trained assessors became even more scarce. From October 1919 through June 1920, for example, nearly 1,000 em-ployees, many of them skilled technicians, left the revenue service for more lucrative jobs. In February 1921, Secretary Houston complained privately of the "great difficulty we have in getting and retaining compe-tent people." Arguing for more adequate compensation, Houston com-plained that "we no sooner get a man trained than business takes him."[37]

It was, in the last analysis, the failure to acquire the resources to provide adequate administration of the excess-profits tax that led to the shift in Adams's position. Adams never changed his theoretical support for the tax, which had hardened during the war, and he never agreed that the tax was inherently flawed. But by December 1919 he had concluded that the tax could no longer succeed without a massive, politically impos-sible, augmentation of administrative capacity in the Treasury. The great-est difficulty was in determining a "normal" rate of return. "Whether normal return be computed upon the basis of past profits, invested capi-tal, or both," Adams wrote in late 1919, "it can only be determined safely after close study of individual cases." But "the government cannot secure the requisite number of trained auditors to keep pace with the multiply-ing assessments." Without enrichment of administration, the tax could be neither effective nor just.[38]

In short, Adams had not sacrificed his intellectual integrity for the sake of career advancement. It was the practical knowledge he had accumu-lated during his Treasury career, joined with his assessment of political realities, that led him to abandon excess-profits taxation. Nonetheless, the strength of his commitments to public service did have an effect on his intellectual agenda that went beyond his conversion to opposition to excess-profits taxation. In particular, he dropped any interest in conduct-ing research on the tax. Meanwhile, the Treasury abandoned any system-

[37]McAdoo to George R. Cooksey, June 4, 1918, McAdoo Papers; Randolph E. Paul, *Taxa-tion in the United States* (Boston: Little, Brown, 1954), 127; Houston to Charles W. Eliot, February 10, 1921, Houston Papers.
[38]See Adams's "Immediate Future of the Excess Profits Tax," *American Economic Review* 10 (March 1920): 15–18.

atic effort to analyze the economic effects of the tax. David Friday, in particular, regretted this. He had wanted to see the excess-profits tax continued, in part "for the sake of its statistical by-product." With the data, he had looked forward to formulating "a relevant and adequate theory of profits." He had concluded that "it is farcical to pretend that we have an adequate explanation of the distribution of wealth and income when we know so little about the underlying principles which determine this share."[39]

Regardless of Adams's motivation, his conversion did exemplify the power of the state over the agenda of economists, particularly economists like the students of public finance, who worked in a field of applied economics, focusing on the analysis of public policy. Once Adams, and then Friday and Haig as well, had accepted the impossibility of funding adequate administration of the excess-profits tax and had concluded that the demise of the tax was necessary, they ignored the tax as a topic for further research. Only Friday continued the analysis of profits, becoming an important innovator in applying the microeconomics of the firm to an understanding of macroeconomic behavior.

The excess-profits tax survived into the Republican administration elected in 1920. But Secretary of the Treasury Andrew Mellon continued the policy of Glass and Houston to seek repeal of the tax. He enlisted Adams in this cause, retaining him as the Treasury's principal tax adviser. Adams responded in 1921 by sharpening even further his criticism of the administrative inadequacies of the excess-profits tax.[40] Whatever the advances in tax administration during the war, he concluded, the Bureau of Internal Revenue lacked the administrative elasticity that Haig had found in Britain and believed necessary for excess-profits taxation in the United States. But even if Congress immediately granted the adequate discretionary powers to Treasury officials, Adams lamented, administrative problems would remain. In fact, the chaos of the general property tax would result. This was so, Adams believed, because the American state was too weak. "The ultimate source of American administrative weakness," he concluded, "is found not so much in Congress or the executive department as in our legalistic traditions and our system of government." Also, Adams

---

[39]David Friday, "The Excess Profits Tax—Discussion," *American Economic Review* 10 (March 1920): 22.
[40]For a suggestion of the importance of the Treasury advisers, like Adams, whom Mellon retained from the Wilson administration, see Benjamin G. Rader, "Federal Taxation in the 1920s: A Re-examination," *The Historian* (May 1971): 419–21. These advisers included S. Parker Gilbert, whom Mellon elevated to the position of under secretary in 1921.

recognized that under Andrew Mellon the ambitious wartime administrative program faced curtailment, not consolidation and expansion.[41]

In 1921, Adams proceeded to play a visible and effective role in assisting Congress in eliminating the tax, which the Revenue Act of 1921 accomplished. In that year, his work on behalf of eradication of the tax had an edge that it had lacked in 1919. This was so because the Revenue Act of 1921, and Secretary Mellon's tax program, involved much more than a repeal of the excess-profits tax, and the program posed new challenges to Adams's ideals of tax equity. Despite Mellon's claim that his recommendations "were in line with similar ones made by Secretaries Houston and Glass," Secretary Mellon expanded the attack that Glass and Houston had begun on the most redistributional parts of the wartime tax system. Mellon also vigorously promoted "supply-side" tax policy, calling for tax cuts that would stimulate the economy and, he claimed, tax revenues. Consequently, the Revenue Act of 1921 not only abolished the excess-profits tax but also made the individual income tax substantially less progressive, and installed many devices favoring capital, such as the preferential taxation of capital gains.

Under this pressure, Adams became convinced that he, and similarly minded progressives, were faced with a cruel choice: if they did not abandon excess-profits taxation, they would jeopardize progressive income taxation. The nation's administrative capacity under the Mellon regime, Adams concluded, could support only one of the two. "A lengthy campaign of education, research and reform on the part of the taxpayer, the tax gatherer, Congress, the courts and the experts, including economists, must be carried on," he wrote, "not only before the installation of a permanent excess profits tax would be justifiable, but even before the practical right of the income tax to endure can be assured." But, Adams believed, "No Federal administration . . . is capable during the next five or six years of carrying with even moderate success two such burdens as the income tax and the excess profits tax." His clear preference was for the income tax as "an essential part of financial democracy" and as a more efficient revenue producer. For Adams, with his strong sense of historical contingency and his sensitivity to class issues, the future of federal income taxation had become highly insecure. It was largely this concern over the conservative threat—the threat of a Republican-sponsored alignment of corporate and

[41]On Adams's position in 1921, see his "Should the Excess Profits Tax Be Repealed?" *Quarterly Journal of Economics* 35 (May 1921): 363–93; and Adams to Seligman, March 30, 1924, Seligman Papers.

middle-class groups—to its very survival that had led him to abandon excess-profits taxation.[42]

TAX REFORM UNDER "PROGRESSIVE CAPITALISM"

Adams's strategy succeeded, at least in part. The pressure from progressives like Adams helped persuade Mellon to stop short of trying to eradicate progressive income taxation. As part of a sophisticated strategy of protecting corporate wealth, Mellon urged business not to press for a national sales tax, which many corporate leaders favored, and, instead, to accept *some* progressive income taxation as a way of demonstrating their civic responsibility and defusing radical attacks on capital. To the public at large, Mellon claimed that he was rising above class interests.

Thus, in 1924, in *Taxation: The People's Business,* Mellon declared that he would approach taxation from "a non-partisan and business viewpoint." Using language that evoked the ideals of both Alexander Hamilton and Edwin R. A. Seligman, Mellon explained that "tax revision should never be made the football either of partisan or class politics but should be worked out by those who have made a careful study of the subject in its larger aspects and are prepared to recommend the course which, in the end, will prove for the country's best interest." Thus, a central element in Mellon's political economy was economic science, steering the Republic away from the shoals of class politics and radical experiments, just as Seligman, for nearly four decades, had been claiming it could.[43]

Mellon's appeal to economists did, in fact, win the support of leaders of public finance such as Seligman, who believed Mellon to be embracing his concept of "progressive capitalism." Seligman publicly embraced Mellon's "tax reduction" plan of 1924, offering special commendation for the lowering of the income tax rates, which he believed would increase tax revenues and initiate a chain of desirable events: enlargement of "the investment fund," an increase in "enterprise," increases in wages, and reduction of interest rates. Although the plan would entail some sacrifice of "the principle of individual ability to pay," it would result in "maxi-

[42]Adams, "Should the Excess Profits Tax Be Repealed?" 363–93.
[43]Andrew W. Mellon, *Taxation: The People's Business* (New York: Macmillan, 1924), 10–11. T. S. Adams attributed "the greater part" of Mellon's book to Under Secretary of the Treasury S. Parker Gilbert and to Assistant Secretary Garrard Winston. See Adams to Seligman, May 5, 1924, Seligman Papers.

mum social advantage." Thus, Seligman reinforced Mellon's promotion of popular acceptance of the axiomatic assumptions that corporate profits were central to the advance of productivity and that taxation should reinforce the private investment process.[44]

Mellon's retention of progressive income taxation and his cultivation of economists also appealed to Adams, who remained a Treasury adviser until his death in 1933. And because Adams had dropped excess-profits taxation and the related issues of corporate profit from his intellectual agenda, his approach to public finance more closely resembled Seligman's than had been the case during the war. But important differences remained, largely as a consequence of Adams's stronger commitment to vertical equity in taxation. For one thing, Adams was a more vigorous protector of the progressive income tax from the conservative reaction of the 1920s. For another, he took the position that analysis of the effects of a tax system on productivity should include consideration of the impact of the spending that tax revenues made possible. Adams reminded Seligman that public expenditures could be an economic "tonic" that could reduce interest rates.[45] And, most important, Adams actively tested the outer perimeter of possibilities for change that conservatives had defined under the Mellon regime.

In this testing, Adams demonstrated that he remained committed not only to the promotion of institutional learning and the advancement of practical knowledge and systematic information about taxation, but also to seizing politic moments of opportunity when his powers of analysis and persuasion might win victories for vertical equity. The first of these moments came in 1919, when he advocated a radical new tax as a replacement for excess-profits taxation. This was a tax on the profits that corporations did not pay out in dividends to their stockholders. Adams's idea, in part, was that this tax would place corporations and partnerships on a more equal basis.

In 1921, and again in 1924, he made a very different kind of proposal: to establish a more comprehensive, simplified, uniform, and even-handed

[44]Seligman to Andrew W. Mellon, February 2, 1924, Seligman Papers. Seligman also joined the lobbying group, "The National Citizens Committee in Support of the Mellon Tax Reduction Proposal," organized by the Institute of American Business. Among the other members of the committee were Otto Kahn and nineteen university presidents or ex-presidents, including Charles W. Eliot. See Bronson Batchelor to Otto H. Kahn, December 26, 1923, Otto H. Kahn Papers, William Seymour Theater Collection, Princeton University Library.

[45]For example, see Adams to Seligman, April 28, 1920, Seligman Papers.

income tax within the context of the lower rate structure preferred by Andrew Mellon. Among his proposals were the elimination of favored treatment for "unearned income" (by which he meant income from property) and the "drastic elimination" of deductions (coupled with "drastic" rate reductions) under the corporate income tax.

In these two years, Adams also proposed a dramatic transformation of the basis of progressive taxation: maintaining high individual surtaxes but applying them to personal spending rather than net income. Reviving the idea first advanced by John Stuart Mill, Adams proposed a progressive tax on spending, one that would tax "unnecessary or surplus consumption." Meanwhile, he criticized the Mellon "tax reduction" plan as containing "incurable inequalities and inconsistencies." More generally, he concluded that the income tax was "not merely defective." It had, he declared, "reached a condition of inequality the gravity of which could scarcely be exaggerated." The weakness of the American state compounded inequalities, just as it had during wartime. Thus, "the evil goes back not to administrative inefficiency or personal dereliction, but to the complexity of the law and the fundamental conditions of public service in the United States."

Adams found, however, that his effort to attack the Mellon tax loopholes and challenge the prevailing configuration of class politics was too extreme for the 1920s. Neither liberals who championed high rates of progression nor conservatives like Mellon saw long-run, strategic advantages in Adams's formulation. His approach to tax reform did not win support from these diverse quarters until 1986.[46]

Meanwhile, the postwar victory of Seligman's "progressive capitalism," represented by the demise of excess-profits taxation, meant a narrowing of the scope of economic investigation. The federal government had acquired greater influence over the agenda of public finance during World War I, but after the war it emphasized its commitment to studying public finance within the context of conservative assumptions about the state and corporate power. At the same time, the reputation of economists who did "pure" research grew, relative to that of those in government service, just as Seligman's disdain for economists in the service of government had grown stronger in the course of his competition with

[46]Thomas S. Adams, "The Economic and Social Basis of Tax Reduction," *Proceedings of the American Academy of Political Science* 11 (March 1924): 24–34; "Mellon Plan Finds Champion and Foe," *New York Times*, April 16, 1924; Adams to Senator James E. Watson, April 11, 1924, Adams Papers.

Adams. Seligman had associated Adams's departures from sound economic science with his having given too much of himself to public service. In 1920, Seligman warned his leading student, Robert Haig, who had slipped over into heretical support for excess-profits taxation, that "you must not allow yourself to go the way of Tommie Adams." Seligman explained, "It is all very well to help in accomplishing things; but our chief duty after all is to Science, and you must not neglect that jealous mistress."[47]

It is hardly surprising, in light of the force of the postwar victory of "progressive capitalism," that the substantive influence of the economists who followed Adams in the Treasury was not so great or in the same direction as Adams would have wished. Many of the experts who remained in the Treasury into the New Deal era resisted the early efforts of Franklin D. Roosevelt and his secretary of the Treasury, Henry Morgenthau, Jr., to resume Woodrow Wilson's effort to shift the tax burden to the wealthiest individuals and corporations. The Keynesian Revolution and the crisis of the Great Depression pushed economists even further away from questions of progressive equity to issues of short-run economic stability, and World War II mobilization focused public finance specialists on designing mass-based income taxation and on minimizing popular resistance to it.

Since World War II, the interest of the federal government in maintaining an expansive revenue program and the interest of corporate America in minimizing its taxes have encouraged public finance economists to focus on the development of taxes to stimulate economic growth. As Robert Collins has suggested in Chapter 5 of this volume, the Kennedy-Johnson Council of Economic Advisers (CEA) was committed to "growthmanship"; the CEA sanctioned the 1964 tax cuts, which were especially generous to corporations and marked a distinct reorientation of the post–New Deal Democratic party's attitude toward corporate taxation. Sounding very much like Andrew Mellon, Kennedy and Johnson argued that cutting capital gains taxes and allowing more generous depreciation allowances would accelerate investment and forestall economic recession. In 1957, corporations had accounted for 37 percent of federal tax payments; by 1983, with Mellon-style tax cutting winning new victories in 1978 and 1981, the corporate share had shrunk to 11 percent.

Nonetheless, there have been important, albeit rare, moments for tax

[47]Seligman to Haig, May 11, 1920, Seligman Papers.

reform of a democratic-statist nature—and for economists who were committed to using public policy on behalf of economic democracy—to shape the course of events and confound economic determinism. During such opportune moments Adams's ideas have fared well. During the latter part of the New Deal, when progressive redistributive taxation again rose to the top of the nation's political agenda, the focal point was on the tax that Adams had proposed in 1919: a graduated tax on undistributed corporate profits. In fact, it was Adams's legacy that had been responsible for placing the undistributed profits tax on the agenda of the New Deal Treasury.[48]

And, during the 1970s, Adams's idea of a comprehensive, uniform tax gathered increasing liberal support. Some tax experts objected that the proliferation of loopholes had destroyed the progressivity of the tax by allowing widespread tax avoidance by wealthy Americans. They also complained that these loopholes introduced massive "horizontal" inequities by providing special advantages to some individuals while taxing others with the same income at higher rates. Stanley Surrey and Joseph Pechman exposed the extraordinary subsidies—"tax expenditures"—buried in the tax code and criticized its inequities and economic inefficiencies.

By 1986, the search for uniformity, which Adams had begun in 1924, formed one of the central elements in a successful reform coalition. This coalition made possible the passage of the Tax Reform Act of that year, and confuted forecasts based on dismal assessments of pluralism.[49] Congressional liberals agreed to a compression of the rate structure, drastic cuts in the top individual income tax rates, and a slash in the corporate rate in return for increases in the personal exemption and the standard deduction, which took millions of the nation's poorest families off the income tax rolls, and the elimination of important "tax expenditures"

---

[48]For evidence of Adams's New Deal influence, see Louis Schere, assistant secretary to the Treasury, to Robert M. Haig, March 6, 1936, Robert Murray Haig Papers, Butler Library, Columbia University.

[49]Two other key elements help explain the difference between the 1986 act and the tax cutting of Andrew Mellon. First, the Reagan administration was more interested in improving economic incentives for entrepreneurship than in protecting corporate bureaucracies. This approach, described by Assistant Secretary of the Treasury Richard G. Darman as "tax populism," led the administration to accept a shift of more than $100 billion in taxes from individuals to corporations as part of the reform package. See Richard G. Darman, "Populist Force Behind Tax Reform Suggests Future Culture Shifts," *Financier* X (December 1986): 23–32, and "Beyond Tax Populism," *Society* 24 (September/October 1987): 35–8. Second, the 1986 act was written with substantial Democratic cooperation. For an excellent account of the politics of the act, see Jeffrey H. Birnbaum and Alan S. Murray, *Showdown at Gucci Gulch: Lawmakers, Lobbyists, and the Unlikely Triumph of Tax Reform* (New York: Random House, 1987).

favoring middle- and upper-income groups. The result may well turn out to be an income tax with a substantially more uniform, and perhaps even progressive, cast. The contingencies were favorable for liberals to succeed in 1986 with the program, and with the tactics, that Adams had outlined in 1924.

ECONOMIC KNOWLEDGE AND THE MODERN STATE

The World War I debate over excess-profits taxation and, more generally, over all aspects of wartime finance illustrates several critical points that should inform the general discussion of the relationship between economic knowledge and the development of the modern state. Most important, we should remember to use a broad definition of economic knowledge when we try to link it with the formation of the modern state.

A broad definition is necessary, in part, because the implementation of policy has often stimulated the growth of practical economic knowledge and the accumulation of economic data. The wartime Treasury economists—T. S. Adams, most notably—played their most important role by using their skills to enhance administrative effectiveness of policy and to expand the store of basic economic data. Often the new data, like the income data developed by T. S. Adams and the savings data mobilized by David Friday, became important foundations in building a professional understanding of the nation's economic life.

Such a definition is necessary also because the politics surrounding the expansion of the modern state has influenced how economists have drawn the intellectual boundary between the economy and society at large. If we simply accept the boundary conventionally drawn by neoclassical economists, we exclude much that is important in the story of the evolving relationship between economic knowledge and public policy. For example, because the World War I crisis pressed excess-profits taxation to the fore, economists debated wartime tax issues within a context that included consideration of the fundamental assumptions of a capitalist society. By the same token, because of the victory of "progressive capitalism" after World War I, the economics profession narrowed the discussion of tax policy to exclude consideration of the social underpinnings of the economy. Indeed, the revealing World War I experience suggests that the impact of government on the fundamental agenda of economics, on the questions economists pose, and on the structure of the profession may well be the most important ways in which the state has influenced the development of formal economic knowledge.

Including in a definition of economic knowledge the assumptions that economists make about the relationship between the economy and society at large recognizes that political considerations, including the development of the modern state, have heavily influenced the development of the discipline. If we can use the history of the economics profession in addressing issues of taxation during and after World War I as a guide, the development of modern economics has had much less to do with the internal logic of the discipline than with historical contingency, with the political orientation of economists, and especially with their culturally based assumptions regarding the proper relation between the investment system and the modern state.

14

Population, economists, and the state: the Royal Commission on Population, 1944–1949

JAY M. WINTER

It is a commonplace that during and after World War II economists came to play a leading part in the formulation of virtually all aspects of government policy in Britain. This chapter examines one exception. In the development of British population policy, economists were marginal figures, whereas on the Continent the opposite was true. In the brief space available, I shall explore this contrast in the period between 1935–50.

The Royal Commission on Population, which sat from 1944 to 1949, was established in order to discover the causes of, and remedies for, population decline. This phenomenon was understood as the secular decline in fertility, constituting not an absolute decline of present numbers but a "failure" of the current population to reproduce itself, which in turn would lead in several decades to an absolute decline in population. By the time the Royal Commission had reported, the problem appeared to have solved itself. In 1949, the birthrate in England and Wales stood at 16.7 per 1,000, a figure well above the prewar level. Both the gross and net reproduction rates exceeded 1.00,[1] and the total fertility rate stood at 2.26,[2] which meant that the population was above the replacement level.

---

[1] The gross reproduction rate is the sum of the age-specific fertility rates to yield the expected number of girls or boys produced by women or men in their reproductive lives. The net reproduction rate (usually limited to females) corrects this figure to take account of the mortality of children before they reach child-bearing ages and of adults thereafter. A rate of 1.00 signifies that each adult is replaced in the next generation.

[2] The total fertility rate is the composite of all the age-specific rates for each group within the reproductive life span. Replacement fertility requires approximately 2.1 children per woman, to allow for the facts that a small number of girls die before reproductive age and that somewhat more than half of all births are male and hence excludable from the net reproduction calculation.

This apparent reversal of prewar trends was an international phenomenon, registered in countries both directly affected by military operations and in those remote from the theaters of warfare. It was also substantially different from the short-term recovery of marriages and births that had occurred after the 1914–18 war. In effect, a new demographic era—which we now call the "baby boom"—had begun in the years surrounding World War II, at precisely the time the Royal Commission undertook its task.

One common objection to royal commissions is that they take too long to report. This instance is a particularly good illustration of the tendency for events to bypass such cumbersome instruments of policy formulation. The Royal Commission on Population was set up when the expectations of and anxieties about population decline dominated discussion of future economic and social policy. It concluded its work and made its recommendations at a time when those assumptions no longer corresponded to demographic reality.

Changed economic conditions added to the anachronistic quality of the Royal Commission's report. One of its key objectives was to examine the economic implications of population decline. But the coincidence of full employment and rising fertility rates after 1945 made it no longer necessary to dwell on the prewar arguments, advanced by Beveridge, Keynes, and a number of those on the Royal Commission, that demographic decline and economic decline were in some sense related. By 1949, this issue was no longer relevant to policymakers. Instead, population policy, outlined in the Royal Commission's report, focused on the social and demographic implications of family allowances, tax relief, housing policy, and maternity benefits. Demography became a matter primarily, although not exclusively, of social, not economic, policy, which is where it has rested by and large to this day.

The workings of the Royal Commission on Population reflect, therefore, the perils of public inquiries undertaken in periods of social upheaval and economic instability. But this episode also tells us much about what economic experts do for royal commissions. Other experts—statisticians, physicians, biologists, and demographers—advised the Royal Commission. They provided facts and adopted an inductive approach to the effects of fertility and mortality on population trends. Economists offered arguments and followed a deductive approach in analyzing the effects of population trends on economic policy and (broadly speaking) the economic fortunes of the nation. The collection of data was not their business. Once their report was ready in early 1946, their work on behalf of the Royal Commission was largely over. Thereafter they awaited the outcome of the empirical studies of medical statisticians and demographers. Three years later those inquiries were concluded and the official report published. Given the delay, the economic analysis in the Royal Commission's final report was bound to have a musty air about it.

Economists provided logic and rhetoric rather than new data or evidence in support of the Royal Commission's mildly pronatalist position. They acted as rhetoricians, whose expertise was of value both in establishing the case presented by the Royal Commission and in dismissing objections to it. This instance of the application of economic knowledge to public policy provides an excellent illustration of economics as the art of public persuasion. Keynes may have been the master of the art, but he was not alone among its practitioners.

The special features of this episode limit its representative value. By the late 1940s there was relatively little disagreement among economists on demographic issues. Unlike the famous confrontations between Keynes and the Treasury in the interwar years, the Royal Commission was not the scene of economic polemics or of a clash between temperaments or schools of thought. Most economists spoke with one voice. They gave their blessing to measures that were intended to provide a stimulus to the birthrate and quieted fears about the economic implications of population trends. They added their prestige and common sense to an already existing consensus. Economists sitting on other royal commissions, or less exalted committees, dealing with more contentious issues such as unemployment or economic decline, were not so lucky. They had to swim against the tide. But even when they did so, they frequently played a more significant part in the formulation of policy than did the economists on the Royal Commission on Population.

This paper examines parallel developments in Europe, the background of the Royal Commission on Population in Britain, some of the workings of its Economics Committee, and the nature of its recommendations. It concludes by suggesting that the Royal Commission was a failure, and that its anachronistic character was a function both of the time-consuming nature of the investigation and of a radical change in both the economic and demographic environment in which population issues were discussed. The fact that the Royal Commission was born in one era and reported in another consigned its recommendations to the margins of social and economic policy. No alternative leadership or vision could have prevented this from happening in the British case.

POPULATION DECLINE:
SOME EUROPEAN INITIATIVES IN THE 1930S

The Royal Commission on Population addressed problems that preoccupied economists, demographers, journalists, and politicians in many European countries in the 1930s. Two European examples provide an insight into the kind of work undertaken by economic and demographic experts to mobilize social and economic policy to raise the prewar birthrate. Both the Swedish and the French cases were well known to those who sat on the Royal Commission and suggested precedents that could be followed. The fact that the British inquiry was less influential in the area of social policy than either the Swedish or French initiatives was a result both of the accident of timing and of different political and economic contexts.

Sweden and fertility decline in the interwar years. Let us consider the Swedish example first. The Swedish campaign to raise the birthrate provided a model of how a carefully planned campaign to educate the public on population questions could prepare the ground for major advances in legislation aimed at reducing the economic burden of parenthood.

The central figures in this campaign were Gunnar and Alva Myrdal. Both were to become Nobel laureates, for work in economics (Gunnar in 1964) and peace (Alva in 1968). The key to the Myrdals' position was their acceptance of the defense of the family as a primary social democratic objective. Indeed, the Myrdals exemplified a social democratic approach to population problems, in which patriotic pronatalism and a commitment to social reform went hand in hand. It was essential to their enterprise that demographic policy was phrased in nationalist as well as in socialist terms. To maintain the vitality and international standing of that state, the Myrdals argued, a revival of fertility was necessary. Parenthood had to be freely chosen and the state had to relieve some of the economic impediments that stood in the way of family formation. This is the form in which their approach to population policy as family policy emerged in the 1930s.

At that time the total fertility rate in Sweden had dropped to the then all-time low point of 1.67, a full 20 percent below replacement.[3] The result was a major review of population questions, in which the Myrdals played a decisive part.

Their first intervention in the debate was a book titled *Crisis in the*

[3] J. M. Winter and M. S. Teitelbaum, *The Fear of Population Decline* (New York: Academic Press, 1985), appendix A.

Population Question (1934). Its originality was in its blending of socialist egalitarianism, pronatalism, and feminist arguments about the right to contraception and abortion. The Myrdals accepted the thesis that fertility levels well below replacement reflected a crisis in family life. Not only were most families unable to command an income or find housing suitable for rearing children, but it appeared that perhaps 50 percent of the dwindling number of Swedish births were unwanted. The future was gloomy indeed: a stagnant economy, an old, conservative society, an increasing number and proportion of immigrants in Swedish society, even the possible dissolution of Swedish culture itself.

To produce an estimated 40 percent increase in native births, the Myrdals presented a bold program of social reform, incorporating many measures that as socialists they supported on grounds of natural justice. They advocated tax relief for large families, rent and housing allowances, free health care and schooling for all children, and maternity benefits. In effect, it was difficult to see where their socialist principles ended and their pronatalist zeal began.

Perhaps this was the secret of their success: they found a patriotic way to use demography as "the most effective argument for a . . . radical socialist remodeling of society."[4] This ambitious project could mobilize support precisely because it appeared to be a necessary precondition for the demographic revival of Sweden. The country was, Gunnar Myrdal believed, on the "threshold of a new epoch in social policy . . . which will most naturally and necessarily be directed at the family and at the children who are the people of the future." Population policy was thus a form of investment in human capital, by far the most important kind of investment, for "the principal wealth of a nation always lies in the quality of its population."[5] Here we find encapsulated the Myrdals' approach: to link population, family, and the nation together in an inextricable (and socialist) embrace.

The chief vehicle for this political program was the Swedish Royal Commission on Population, set up in 1935 with the backing not only of the ruling Social Democratic government but also of all other major political factions.[6] Gunnar Myrdal was its dominant intellectual figure.

[4]Gunnar and Alva Myrdal, *Kris i Befolkningsfragen* (Stockholm: A. Bonnier, 1934), 117, as cited in A. C. Carlson, "The Myrdals, Pro-Natalism and Swedish Social Democracy," *Continuity*, VI (1983): 75.
[5]Gunnar Myrdal, *Population: A Problem for Democracy* (Cambridge, Mass.: Harvard University Press, 1940), 100.
[6]H. Gille, "Recent Developments in Swedish Population Policy," *Population Studies* II (1948): 3–70.

He succeeded in bringing like-minded people onto the commission's staff; he managed to handle the complex business of a wide range of subcommittees; and he had a central voice in drafting most of the sixteen major reports produced by the commission between 1935 and 1938.

It is important to note that Myrdal and his colleagues used the mechanism of a royal commission, with all the authority it conferred, as a device, first, to elaborate previously determined policy conclusions and, second, to devise and study means to attain those predetermined ends. The Swedish Royal Commission was not a fact-finding body; data gathering was not its aim. Its purpose was to move an already existing political consensus in a direction known at the outset. Political knowledge overlapped with economic analysis in a way that made the scientific findings of the Royal Commission a function of prior policy commitments.

The Myrdals kept up public interest in the work of the commission— and in that of the similarly pronatalist Social Housing Commission, on which Gunnar Myrdal also sat—through newspaper articles and radio broadcasts. Alva Myrdal even appeared on newsreels that preceded feature films in Swedish cinemas. What they were doing was what Lenin termed "all-sided political agitation."

The result was first to rally support for their ideas both from the radical camp and from some more cautious elements within the Social Democratic party. But the Myrdals also succeeded in demonstrating that socialist family policy had real party political appeal.

The latter should not be ignored. In 1936, the ruling Social Democratic–led coalition resigned and went to the country on a reform platform. Its entral theme was the need to return to power a government dedicated to restoring the Swedish family and thereby the Swedish nation. The Myrdals campaigned actively for the pronatalist reforms on the agenda of the population commission.

The result was a sweeping success for the Social Democratic party and a mandate for legislation in the field of family policy. This body of measures dominated the 1937 parliamentary session, familiarly known as the "mothers and babies" session. The range of reforms was impressive, encompassing family allowances, prenatal financial assistance, marriage loans at low interest, and measures to improve midwifery and hospital delivery services.[7]

The Myrdals' pronatalism was not an argument to return women to the home and restrict their right to control their reproductive lives. On

[7]Carlson, "The Myrdals," 86.

the contrary, time and again they repeated the claim that only by helping women to combine paid work outside the home with childbearing would the birthrate rise. They both reaffirmed women's right to work and pointed to the need for "a large number of social reforms, adjusting housing, supervision of children, and working conditions, et cetera, in such a way as to allow women to have both work and a family." Herein lay the most salient "radical possibilities" disclosed by the debate over the population problem. These were issues that enabled feminists—perhaps for the first time, in Gunnar Myrdal's opinion—to find a common language with other radicals in the development of policy on population questions.[8]

Alva Myrdal's detailed study of these matters, aptly titled *Nation and Family*, written during World War II but reviewing their prewar work, dealt with other aspects of the politics of reproduction. She, too, started with the premise that "marrying must be encouraged" in order to revive the nation's fertility, and pointed out that the best ways to ensure increased marital fertility were to defend the married woman's right to work and to equalize the burden of child support throughout the population. But the climate in which an increase in the birthrate would occur had to be created through education as much as through transfer payments and statutory regulations. To this end she advocated mandatory sex education in schools, free access to contraceptive information and devices, and (as a last resort and only under certain conditions) the right to abortion.[9]

In 1937, some of the Myrdals' ideas on liberalizing the law relating to contraception were translated into law. Parliament passed a series of measures on contraception and abortion, which substantially followed their arguments. The 1910 anticontraceptive statutes were repealed, and abortion was legalized on some—but not all—medical and social grounds.

Further measures were advanced by the commission in 1938, but by then the clouds of war had gathered, and population questions were no longer at the center of political debate.[10] A second population commission was set up in 1941, without the Myrdals' participation. It consolidated the gains made in the previous decade.[11]

The political achievements of the Myrdals' work as socialist demographers should not be underestimated. Basically, they translated demo-

[8]Gunnar Myrdal, *Population*, 102ff.
[9]Alva Myrdal, *Nation and Family: The Swedish Experiment in Democratic Family and Population Policy* (Cambridge, Mass.: Harvard University Press, 1968), 117ff.
[10]Carlson, "The Myrdals," 87–8.
[11]Gille, "Swedish Population," 7.

graphic analysis into a sound political strategy and showed that in framing and enacting family policy, Social Democrats could demonstrate their patriotism and concern for the future welfare of the nation as a whole. In effect they showed that socialist demography made good political sense.

France and the politics of dénatalité. The second example of pre-1939 population politics that anticipated the British Royal Commission was that of France. There has been a pronatalist consensus in France since the 1870s. Indeed it was (and remains today) one of the most salient features of French political culture that all parties tend to express their patriotism in terms of a desire to increase the birthrate.

That conservatives should rally round the family, patriarchy, and procreation should cause little surprise, but it is important to note how wide an appeal on the French left such ideas had in the 1930s. Pronatalism was part of the language of the Popular Front. Its commitment to bolster the family, and with it the population of France, was rooted in the patriotism of the left. Socialists repeatedly drew on the traditions of the *levée en masse* in the French Revolution, the defiant resistance of the Paris *communards* after the debacle of the 1870 defeat, and the force of *union sacrée* in the 1914–18 war to demonstrate their commitment to the nation. Indeed, the socialist discourse on the national "family" provided a rallying point for all "progressive" elements in French society. To call for the restoration of France through the reversal of *dénatalité* was to provide a way to draw all classes into the center-left coalition of the mid-1930s. Such an appeal for consensus politics was an attractive alternative to the language of class antagonism and class struggle that marked the early history of the French Communist party.[12]

By the mid-1930s, the Communists, too, joined the pronatalist camp. It is no accident that this action followed Stalin's sudden discovery of the virtues of motherhood, after the appalling losses of the period of forced collectivization and the purges. On May 4, 1936, Stalin addressed the Academy of the Red Army on the subject of "Man, the Most Precious Capital." His intention was to urge all Russians to celebrate the joys of maternity and the pride of paternity, home, and marriage. A carefully orchestrated series of meetings and newspaper articles announced the new policy, which led to the passage of a new law in

---

[12]J. M. Winter, "Socialism, Social Democracy and Population Questions in Western Europe, 1870–1950," in M. S. Teitelbaum and J. M. Winter, eds., *Population and Resources in Western Intellectual Traditions* (Cambridge, Eng.: Cambridge University Press, 1989).

June 1936 banning abortion and substantially increasing maternal and child welfare schemes.[13]

The French Communist party soon saw the light. Numerous echoes of Stalin's voice were heard among the party leadership, which, in any event, followed a very traditional line on questions of sexuality and the family. Rallying around the nation thus became a Communist slogan, which was translated into support for pronatalist measures.[14]

The French center and right campaign for a rise in the birthrate emphasized the danger of German rearmament. In January 1937, Paul Reynaud, soon to become minister of justice and later minister of commerce and then finance in the Daladier government, told the Chamber of Deputies that "There is one factor that dominates all: the demographic factor." Because of France's lower birthrate, rearmament had to be accelerated to enable the small French army to fight a mechanized war, the only war France could win. Other deputies supported this argument, and the same voices were prominent in the elaboration of the French family policy in the late 1930s.[15]

The centerpiece of this legislative program was the *Code de la famille*, promulgated on July 30, 1939. This measure was the culmination of a long series of provisions, initiated during World War I by individual firms, to provide family allowances for French industrial (and later, agricultural) workers. On February 23, 1939, Daladier appointed an *Haut comité de la population* to oversee the reform of population policy. One of the most important members of this group was the economist Alfred Sauvy, who performed in France some of the same academic and political tasks that the Myrdals had undertaken in Sweden. He was a committed pronatalist, who wrote tirelessly of the desirable consequences of rising birthrates and the disastrous future, both economically and politically, that awaited France should that country be unable to shake off the curse of *dénatalité*.[16]

The report of this committee of experts—pronatalists all—was submitted on June 30, 1939, and adopted without discussion by the Chamber of

[13]H. Chambre, "L'evolution de la législation familiale soviétique de 1917 à 1952," in R. Prigent, ed., *Renouveau des idées sur la famille*, INED Cahier no. 18 (Paris: Presses Universitaires de France, 1954), 206–27; R. Schlesinger, *The Family in the U.S.S.R.* (London: Routledge and Kegan Paul, 1960), 251–74.

[14]F. Delpla, "Les communistes français et la sexualité (1932–1938)," *Mouvement Social*, no. 129 (1984): 7–28.

[15]Winter and Teitelbaum, *The Fear of Population Decline*, 55–75.

[16]Of many publications, the following should give a taste of Sauvy's approach: A. Sauvy, *Richesse et population* (Paris: Payot, 1943).

Deputies on July 12, 1939. Just as in the case of the Swedish Royal Commission, the French committee was less interested in studying demographic phenomena than in changing demographic behavior. The presumption was that demographers knew why fertility was low; it was the turn of politicians to demonstrate their political will in supporting a remedy in law. Aims were not in question; the French case (like the Swedish) was about means and the political legitimacy needed to enact them.

The most important features of the report of the *Haut comité de la population* were the universalization and equalization of family allowances and the shift of catchment area for grants from the place of work to the place of residence. Three separate schemes were set up to administer allowances for salaried urban workers; for employers, professionals, and self-employed people; and for rural workers. To finance the scheme a tax was to be levied on unmarried, divorced, and widowed people and on childless couples.

Allowances increased progressively with family size. There was no allowance for the first child, but 10 percent of the average daily wage was payable for the second, and 30 percent of the average daily wage was payable for all subsequent children. In addition, mothers received a grant toward the cost of child care, the *mère au foyer* allowance. This allowance provided 10 percent of the average daily wage for mothers of a first child to the age of five, and to age fourteen for the second and subsequent children. In addition, a marriage loan was made available to help rural people start families and run farms. Part of the debt would be eliminated each time a child was born; a family with five children thereby discharged the debt entirely.[17]

THE BRITISH DEBATE IN THE 1930S

These developments were closely monitored by a broadly representative group of economists, demographers, politicians, and civil servants in Britain who saw the need for government action on population questions in the 1930s. There appeared alarming (and woefully inaccurate) estimates of the effects over one or two generations of declining fertility in

---

[17]C. Watson, "Population Policy in France: Family Allowances and Other Benefits. I," *Population Studies* 7 (1954): 263–74; A. Prost, "L'evolution de la politique familiale en France de 1938 à 1981," *Mouvement Social*, no. 129 (1984): 7–18; J. Doublet, "Family Allowances in France," *Population Studies* 2 (1948): 219–39; P. Laroque, ed., *The Social Institutions of France*, trans. by R. Evans (New York: Gordon and Breach, 1983), Chapter 5.

England and Wales. Grace Leybourne published a paper in 1934 predicting that, in accordance with then current trends, the population of Britain in 1976 would be about 28.7 million.[18] (The actual figure was 56 million.) Another demographer, Enid Charles, forecast a British population of 31 million in 1975, 17.7 million in 2000, and 4.4 million in 2035.[19] These wildly inaccurate predictions were based on a fundamental misinterpretation of the components of population growth. They failed to appreciate the force of inertia in population change, which moves much more slowly than the alarmists believed, and the greater significance for projections of cohort (as opposed to period) fertility rates. But these errors were not exposed until after the projections they had produced had helped amplify a chorus of concern that had been raised about the future of the British race.

Such views were expressed on the left, right, and center of the British political spectrum. Just as in Sweden and France, there emerged a political consensus to investigate the problem of below-replacement fertility and to try to formulate measures to reverse the secular trend. In addition the nascent discipline of demography added the authority of science to the campaign. Expert and activist worked hand in hand to mobilize opinion in Britain as on the Continent.

Many of the experts were based at the London School of Economics (LSE). Perhaps the most important figure was Alexander Carr-Saunders, who came from a chair at Liverpool to be director of LSE in 1937, on the retirement of Sir William Beveridge. Two years earlier, Carr-Saunders had set out the agenda for a British demographic research institute. In February 1935 he addressed the Eugenics Society and pointed out the need to escape from the unfortunate associations of negative eugenics. Those interested in population policy had to work for positive eugenics, which was not "an attempt to breed a race of supermen, but to raise the fertility of those who are not definitely subnormal until at least they reproduce themselves."[20] To do so required detailed research, more on

---

[18] G. G. Leybourne, "An Estimate of the Future Population of Great Britain," *Sociological Review* 26 (1934): 130–8.

[19] E. Charles, "The Effect of Present Trends in Fertility and Mortality," *London and Cambridge Economic Service*, Special Memorandum No. 40 (1935); and idem, *The Menace of Underpopulation: A Biological Study of the Decline of Population Growth* (London: Watts, 1936).

[20] A. M. Carr-Saunders, "Eugenics in the Light of Population Trends," *Eugenics Review* 37 (1935–6): 12 and passim; and L. Wallach, "The Problem of Maternal Health in Britain During the Second World War," M.Phil. thesis, Cambridge, 1982.

social processes than on policies, based on statistical information then available.

The Eugenics Society sponsored a Population Investigation Committee (PIC) to provide this expertise. Carr-Saunders saw its purpose as lying "in the enlargement and dissemination of the knowledge that is required in order that policies may be formulated. It is a scientific and not a political body, and therefore it leaves to others the task of devising practical measures."[21] Its founders carefully distanced themselves from the Eugenics Society and played down its role in the formation of the PIC.[22] Members of professional bodies, such as the British College of Obstetricians and Gynaecologists, the Medical Research Council, and the Royal Economics Society, were invited to join. The first chairman was Carr-Saunders. C. P. Blacker, a stalwart of the Eugenics Society, became honorary secretary, and a young demographer, David Glass, became full-time research secretary.

In the first year of its existence, the PIC helped broadcast the issue of population decline through a series of well-publicized publications. Carr-Saunders produced a survey of world population trends; Glass explored contemporary policy initiatives to raise population; and the LSE demographer R. R. Kuczynski added his voice to those calling for further scientific and official inquiries in this field.[23]

In 1936–7 the volume of journalism on population questions grew substantially. Readers of *The Times* and other newspapers digested numerous articles on "the dwindling family" and similar themes. The *Standard* reported on November 12, 1936, that the "heavy fall in the birthrate has become a matter of serious concern to the Cabinet," which (the newspaper predicted) would "make an appeal to childless couples, and couples with small families, to give consideration to the national interest." The *News Chronicle* told its readers two days later that the "ugliest fact to be faced by the new Investigation Committee . . . is that we are already failing to reproduce ourselves." PIC members used the letters-to-the-editor columns to similar effect, and helped nurse along the idea that official action to promote research in this field was essential for the nation's future. The purpose of research was to provide the data from

[21] A. M. Carr-Saunders, "Memo on the Work of the PIC," in LSE, Department of Population Studies, PIC minute book, 1936.

[22] Wallach, "Maternal Health," 18–19.

[23] A. M. Carr-Saunders, *World Population: Past Growth and Present Trends* (Oxford: Clarendon Press, 1936); D. V. Glass, *The Struggle for Population* (Oxford: Clarendon Press, 1936); R. R. Kuczynski, *Population Movements* (Oxford: Clarendon Press, 1936).

which later political action would flow. In contrast to the Swedish and French cases, the British example lies solidly within the empiricist tradition, and reflects a strict separation of knowledge and policy.

Just as in Sweden, though, PIC members went to the airwaves to reach the public. A series of discussions on "our dwindling population" were broadcast in the spring of 1937. Among the commentators were T. H. Marshall of the LSE, Carr-Saunders, Kuczynski, and the Liberal economist H. D. Henderson, then a fellow of All Souls College. These discussions were published in 1938 under the title *The Population Problem: The Experts and the Public.*[24]

The government's response to this campaign was to introduce a Population (Statistics) Bill. Sir Kingsley Wood, minister of health, accepted the view that declining fertility was a national danger. In recent years, there were signs, he noted, that the decline was slowing down, thus providing hope "that continued decline was not irresistible or inevitable . (Cheers)." If additional information were gathered, it might identify the forces exerting "an upward tendency" on the birthrate and thereby inform future policy. Britain was behind other European countries, as well as Australia and New Zealand, in the range of information obtained from vital registration on reproductive behavior. Only with such data could systematic "research of a scientific kind" proceed effectively. The government brushed aside some Labour and Liberal objections as to the intrusiveness of the intimate questions asked about sexual behavior, and even rode out the laughter accompanying a poem on population decline in 1937, introduced into the debate by the Independent MP A. P. Herbert, which ended with these lines:

> The world, in short, which never was extravagantly sane,
> Developed all the signs of inflammation of the brain;
> The past was not encouraging, the future none could tell.

(Here the honorable member, to the amusement of the House, pointed to the Minister of Health.)

> But the Minister still wonders why the population fell.

(Loud cheers and laughter)[25]

---

[24]"Cabinet Anxious about Low Birth-Rate," *Standard,* November 12, 1936; "The World This Morning," *News Chronicle,* November 14, 1935; the interviews with Carr-Saunders and with H. D. Henderson were published in the *Listener* on March 10 and 17, 1937. These clippings were found in the Titmuss Papers, in the possession of Dr. Ann Oakley. I am grateful to her for permission to cite material in this valuable archive.

[25]"Fall in the Birth-Rate," *Times,* November 30, 1937.

POPULATION AND WORLD WAR II:
THE ORIGINS OF THE ROYAL COMMISSION

The issue of reviving the birthrate took on a new urgency during World War II for two reasons. The first was the popularity of wartime pronatalism, which flourished in all combatant countries; the second was the linkage of campaigns to raise fertility with efforts to lower infant, child, and maternal mortality.

Here again, the group of activists drawn to the PIC played a fundamental role. Many had other wartime responsibilities but continued to draw public attention to the importance of demographic questions. One such figure was Richard Titmuss, who published a series of studies in the late 1930s on the persistence of inequalities in health. In light of declining fertility, Titmuss argued, it was a national scandal that more was not being done "to safeguard the younger generations from premature death." Under conditions of below-replacement fertility, public health improvements were essential for the nation's future.[26]

After the war, in his contribution to the official *History of the Second World War*, Civil Series, Titmuss himself showed how the military, political, and cultural atmosphere of wartime provided a unique background for the spread of reform opinion in the field of public health.[27] During the war, he was one of many who continued the prewar campaign to inform and direct public opinion on the parallel questions of fertility and mortality decline.[28]

The key political difference between the prewar and wartime campaigns was that by 1940 these experts had the advantage of working with and for a Coalition government in which the Labour party had a prominent (though not decisive) voice. As the war went on, the government was prodded into action on matters of postwar social policy. The story of the Beveridge report is perhaps the best known of these ventures.[29] The

---

[26]R. M. Titmuss, *Poverty and Population: A Factual Study of Contemporary Social Waste* (London: Macmillan, 1938).

[27]R. M. Titmuss, *Problems of Social Policy* (London: HMSO, 1950).

[28]See for instance, his *Birth, Poverty and Wealth* (London: Hamish Hamilton Medical Books, 1942), which was given extensive coverage in the national and local press, as well as the book he wrote with Katherine Titmuss, *Parents Revolt: A Study in the Declining Birth-Rate in Acquisitive Societies* (London: Secker and Warburg, 1942). Press clippings may be found in the Titmuss Papers.

[29]The *locus classicus* for all students of this question is Jose Harris, *William Beveridge: A Biography* (Oxford: Oxford University Press, 1977).

creation of the Royal Commission on Population is a less well-known part of the same story.

Even though the PIC temporarily disbanded in 1940, with the evacuation of LSE to Cambridge, many of the central figures continued to work through press and Parliament to highlight demographic questions. By late 1942, a war emergency committee of the old PIC met to consider its future role. It chose to model itself on the Medical Research Council and thereby to "include in its activities a study of population policies without committing itself to one policy in preference of another." It also agreed to launch a new set of inquiries on a broad range of issues, including housing, maternity services, and child welfare programs.[30]

Such work was overshadowed, though, by the government's announcement of its intention to set up a Royal Commission on Population. This was the opportunity for which the PIC had waited ever since its inception. Carr-Saunders wrote to *The Times* in support of the idea on the day the measure was announced in the Commons.

Just as in Sweden and France, the measure was greeted with patriotic enthusiasm in the House of Commons. The Independent MP Eleanor Rathbone, a champion of family allowances, spoke for the majority when she said that the statistics of fertility decline were "surely sufficient to terrify anyone who has the intelligence to grasp them and patriotism enough to care for the future as well as the present of this country." After some grumbles by the Scottish militant Jimmie Maxton that "it was the aggressor nations who started the idea of stimulating the growth of the population" and objections to speaking about people as if they were "Ayrshire cattle," even he joined in the consensus that the demographic factor made social reform, of kinds to be determined, a political and national necessity.[31]

THE ROYAL COMMISSION AND ITS ECONOMICS COMMITTEE

The Royal Commission got down to work in March 1944.[32] Its membership included nonexperts as well as experts. But as is usually the case with such bodies, the real work of the commission was done by its specialist

[30]LSE, Department of Population Studies, PIC Minute Book, "Memorandum by the War Emergency Committee," December 24, 1942.
[31]*Hansard's Parliamentary Debates*, July 16, 1943, vol. 391, cols. 545ff.
[32]Public Record Office, London Papers of the Royal Commission on Population, Record Group (hereafter RG) 24/2, Minute 1, March 3, 1944.

committees, representing professional opinion. The first was the scientific and medical profession, led by the distinguished pediatrician A. W. M. Ellis. He chaired the commission's biological and medical committee, which co-opted experts including the distinguished physiologist E. V. Adrian, and Sir Eardley Holland and Dugald Baird, both physicians intimately involved in prewar campaigns to improve maternal and child health. David Glass also served on this committee, in part because of the project, jointly sponsored by the PIC and the Royal College of Obstetricians and Gynaecologists, to study the nation's maternity services. This investigation published its findings in 1946.[33]

The second was the statistical and demographic profession. Here the PIC was well represented. Carr-Saunders chaired the specialist committee dealing with statistical questions. Among those assisting him in this task were the omnipresent David Glass, as well as Edward Grebenik and R. R. Kuczynski, both active PIC researchers. (Kuczynski died in 1947.)

The third group within the Royal Commission was the Economics Committee, chaired by Sir Hubert Henderson, who, after the retirement of Viscount Simon in 1946, was also chairman of the commission as a whole. As we have seen, Henderson, too, was active in the work of the prewar PIC. Joining him on this committee were W. B. Reddaway of LSE, the author of a study of *The Economics of a Declining Population*;[34] Alexander Gray, professor of political economy at Edinburgh and the author of an economic evaluation of family allowances;[35] J. R. Hicks, then professor of political economy at Manchester and formerly lecturer at the LSE; E. C. Ramsbottom, director of statistics at the Ministry of Labour from 1929 to 1945; and the Cambridge economist Joan Robinson.

For the purposes of this discussion, let us consider the report of the Economics Committee in some detail, and then relate it to the work of the Royal Commission as a whole. This is not to suggest that the contribution of the other two committees was less intrinsically interesting or important; on the contrary. Indeed, the weight of evidence taken into account by the Royal Commission as a whole shifted away from the Economics Committee as time went on. Economic considerations, strictly defined, mattered much more at the outset of the Royal Commission's

---

[33]RG 24/5, Minutes of Biological and Medical Committee; *Maternity in Great Britain* (Oxford: Oxford University Press, 1946), and Wallach, "Maternal Health," passim.
[34](London: G. Allen and Unwin, 1939).
[35]A. Gray, *Family Endowment: A Critical Analysis* (London: Ernest Benn, 1927).

work than they did in the report stage. The major reasons were that both the economic environment and the demographic situation leading to the formation of the Royal Commission had changed.

In addition, there was a shift in the nature of the work of the Royal Commission itself. Initially, the commission intended to issue its report within two years, but by the summer of 1945, it became apparent that it could not do so.[36] The problem was that both the Medical and Biological and the Statistical Committees believed that their work was hampered by lack of relevant data. The medical problems of infertility, obstetrics and gynecology, and infant and maternal mortality required detailed statistical and other research. For instance, a special analysis of all legitimate births in England and Wales in 1939 was undertaken to provide data on abortion, stillbirths, and infant mortality.[37] Such research took time and inevitably set back the timetable of the Royal Commission.

The Statistical Committee caused a much more substantial delay. It decided, not without serious disagreement,[38] to postpone its report until it could collect new data on the strategies of family formation of British women. Without such data, they felt there was no firm basis for conclusions on the nature and causes of the trend in the birthrate. The last fertility census was taken in 1911, and, as R. R. Kuczynski put it, "The solution to the problem of the motives for family limitation is the taking of a fertility census at which each married woman would be asked to state her age, date of marriage, and number of children."[39]

The Royal Commission approved the planned family census, and with the blessing of the Treasury, a questionnaire was framed and information was collected in January and February 1946 on the fertility behavior of more than 1 million women.[40] Then came the arduous task of tabulation and analysis, which produced more than a few headaches and further delay. A preliminary report was promised first for 1946, then for 1947;

[36]RG 24/2, Minute 25, June 22, 1945.
[37]RG 24/2, RC 76; RG 24/5, Draft Report on Reproductive Wastage, Minute 13, March 12, 1946; Report on Involuntary Infertility, Minute 14, January 8, 1947.
[38]RG 24/6, Minutes of Statistical Committee, Minute 9, July 12, 1944; RG 24/2, RC 18, objections of Stocks, Derrick, and Kyd to the taking of a fertility census, September 1944. These difficulties reflected tensions between the General Register Office, where these statisticians worked, and the PIC.
[39]RG 24/10, Written evidence, EV 1, R. R. Kuczynski, June 1944.
[40]RG 24/2, Minute 8, September 15, 1944; Minute 13, November 24, 1944; Minute 15, January 5, 1945; see also, RG 24/16; Fertility census: note for the Lord Chancellor, September 18, 1944, and RG 24/6, Statistical Committee Minute 9, September 12, 1944.

drafting the full report dragged on into 1948 because of "unexpected difficulties on the statistical side."[41]

This delay held up the final report of the Royal Commission until June 1949. The scientific and statistical work of the two specialist committees of physicians, biologists, statisticians, and demographers determined the pace and the character of the report. Without any data to collect, or substantial investigation to undertake, the members of the Economics Committee of the Royal Commission in effect waited around for their colleagues to finish their work. In part this accounts for the dated character of the economists' report.

At the outset of its work, the Economics Committee was set a specific task. Its terms of reference, set out on February 25, 1944, were "to formulate for the assistance of the Royal Commission on Population the economic factors relevant to the Commission's inquiry and generally to advise the Commission on the economic aspects of the inquiry."[42] This task was interpreted to mean the preparation of a paper for the committee on the "Economic Consequences of the Trend of Population." The trend in question was the prewar fertility decline, rather than wartime oscillations in demographic behavior. The committee worked on two premises, specified in its first meeting of March 15, 1944. The first was that "the present population trend increases rather than diminishes the difficulties of maintaining full and steady employment, but that these difficulties need not be insuperable." The second was that with full employment, and with a low but positive rate of population growth, the chances of improving the standard of living will increase.[43]

Sir Hubert Henderson stated the objectives of the Economics Committee in a joint discussion with the Statistical Committee. Henderson "said that he had aimed not so much at elucidating the economic arguments for and against a policy of raising the birth rate as at suggesting the consequences for various fields of public economic policy of the change in the population trend (given that this must to some extent be taken as

[41]RG 24/2, Minute 39, May 10, 1946; Minute 52, May 23, 1947; Minute 60, January 16, 1948; RG 24/1, Note on Progress, April 8, 1948; see also, RG 24/6, SC 81, Progress Report on the Fertility Census, by D. V. Glass, May 27, 1946; RG 24/6 Statistical Committee Minute 34, December 18, 1946; Minute 37, May 13, 1947, and Minute 48, April 27, 1947.
[42]*Papers of the Royal Commission on Population, Report of the Economics Committee,* February 1, 1950 (London: HMSO), p. 1.
[43]RG 24/8, Minutes of Economics Committee 1, March 15, 1944.

inevitable). In this context he proposed to give a wide scope to the word *economic*."[44]

The initial draft for discussion was prepared by Joan Robinson in April 1944. Further drafting went on through the summer and fall, with a debate on the notion of an "optimal population" sparked by James Meade's *Economic Analysis and Policy*. Reddaway drafted the sections on the balance of trade, and the chairman penned the section on external consequences. By January 1946, the draft report was ready for comment by Whitehall. Friendly comments were received from R. W. D. Clarke and R. G. Hawtrey of the Treasury, from R. L. Hall and A. K. Cairncross at the Board of Trade, and by an unnamed official at the economic section of the Cabinet Office.[45]

On June 22, 1945, Henderson told his fellow commissioners that the Economics Committee report was in its final stages. On February 1, 1946, the report was considered, and on the whole approved, by the commission. Some suggestions were made about the desirability of incorporating discussions of migration and defense, but these were minor criticisms. The report was accepted and then frozen. The reason was clear: "Because of the difficulties in isolating economic from other considerations in assessing the consequences of the trend of population, it would be undesirable to publish the Economics Committee's report in advance of the main report of the commission."[46]

And there the report rested, with only minor modifications, for three years. It is obvious that the delay was in no sense the fault of the report's framers. The family census was taken just as the Economics Committee had completed its work, and everyone waited for the demographers to get on with the job. The longer the delay, the more dated the economic arguments became.

The delay undermined the utility of much of the report. In its final draft, dated February 1, 1950, the Economics Committee admitted that, if there had been time for a full revision, an entirely new perspective would have been adopted. First, the "present" trend of population in 1945 was not that of 1950. The fundamental demographic assumptions

---

[44] RG 24/8, Minute 3, July 5, 1944.

[45] RG 24/8, Minutes of Economics Committee 2, April 26, 1944; Minute 4, July 19, 1944; Minute 5, September 20, 1944; Minute 6, May 16, 1945; Minute 7, May 31, 1945; EC 2, Joan Robinson's paper; EC 3, revision; EC 6, Robinson note on Meade's "optimum population"; EC 15, comments by Clarke, Hall, Cairncross; EC 16, comments by Hawtrey; EC 17, comments by Economic Section of Cabinet Office.

[46] RG 24/2, Minute 25, June 22, 1945; Minute 34, February 1, 1946.

on which the Economics Committee report rested were inaccurate. The postwar period of demographic growth was clearly not a continuation of the prewar trend. Similarly, the analysis of economic issues was based on the situation in 1945, not that of 1950. The discussion of unemployment rested on the memory of the 1920s and 1930s, which was an equally unsteady guide to developments in the labor market in the late 1940s. Assumptions about the growth of the housing stock rested on wartime plans to increase the construction labor force to 1.25 million, in order to provide 350,000 new houses per year. The actual figures were much lower: fewer than 1 million workers were producing 200,000 new houses per year in 1949.

But it was not only what the Economics Committee got wrong that vitiated its findings. It was also what it neglected. There was no rigorous discussion of the mechanisms of the labor market, labor shortages, postwar migratory flows, or inflationary pressures. The new international economic environment was not seriously discussed. To have anticipated such issues in 1944–5 would have required prophetic talents that economists rarely if ever possess.

By leaving its report in its original form, the Economics Committee admitted that, in effect, it had largely wasted its time. It is not clear why a new version of the report could not have been written in the four years between its drafting and its publication. All those on the committee were busy academics, but that was no excuse.

The suggestion, just barely hinted at in the introduction to the Economics Committee report, must be entertained that the purpose of the exercise was not to provide a full economic analysis of the meaning and significance of population trends. Its aim was rather to show that professional economic opinion was in favor of a *moderate* increase of the population of Britain.

This agenda required the refutation of two alternative and time-honored positions. The first held that the demographic trend of the 1930s, usually referred to as "population decline," had no deleterious effects on the workings of the economy. Indeed, the popular form of this argument asserted that there were too many people and too few jobs before the war. Under these conditions, who would want a revival of the birthrate? The second position to be contested held that population growth was undesirable on economic grounds. This modern form of Malthusianism maintained that Britain could not afford to feed its home population, and that, given high rates of unemployment in the interwar period and a serious wartime and postwar balance-of-payments problem, it was irresponsible to accept government policies that would, over time, add more people to the labor force and consuming population.

In effect, the first question addressed by the Economics Committee was this: Do population decline and economic decline go hand in hand? Their answer was basically yes, if the demographic decline were steep and precipitate. The second question was this: Is population growth undesirable? Their answer was basically no, although rapid growth under unfavorable terms of trade would depress the living standards of the population. The implications were clear: a slowly growing population was preferable to a rapidly growing or swiftly declining one. Population policy, it followed, had to aim at encouraging a *modest* rate of growth, through either natural increase or immigration.

Anyone familiar with the classic debates on population and resources since the seventeenth century will see that the Economics Committee of the Royal Commission followed well-trodden paths. We should hardly be surprised that the committee did not provide much in the way of original reasoning or conclusions. Indeed, the discussion went little farther than the positions sketched out by Beveridge and Keynes in the 1930s.[47] It may therefore stand as a statement of the wartime and postwar liberal consensus on questions of population and economic growth. When its report was received in 1949, it provided another instance of the extent to which a socialist government implemented liberal ideas in the sphere of social and economic policy.

Basically, the economists' role in this story was as advocates rather than initiators. The Economics Committee favored a mildly pronatalist policy, but not solely on academic grounds. It had definite political objectives. First, its arguments served to reassure politicians, civil servants, experts, and the public that social policies adopted to raise the birthrate over the levels to which it had fallen in the 1920s and 1930s were not a danger to the economic life of the country. The economic analysis presented was not central to the scheme, but rather calmed fears that it was something the country could not afford. In effect, economic analysis was reduced to a lawyer's brief that measures to be taken by the government might not do much good, but certainly would not do much harm. Perhaps the logical

---

[47]For Beveridge, and for the evolution of Keynes's ideas, see W. H. Beveridge, "Population and Unemployment," *Economic Journal* 33 (1923); 447–75; J. M. Keynes, "A Reply to Sir William Beveridge," *Economic Journal* 33 (1923): 476–86; and J. M. Keynes, "The Economic Consequences of a Declining Population," *Eugenics Review* 29 (1937): 13–17.

format used in the Economics Committee's report reinforced this impression; this format contrasts to the more inductive, perhaps more scientific, presentation of the data on family limitation and fertility decline in the contributions of the statistical and medical committees.

A balanced tone was maintained throughout the committee's report, which pointed out the dangers of rapid population growth when the terms of trade were unfavorable to Britain.[48] But equal emphasis was placed on the deleterious effects of declining population on the aggregate volume of home investment activity.[49] Given a smaller population, both the supply and the demand for labor would diminish. The consequences for the postwar economy were clear:

In an environment of rapidly growing numbers, a revival of the rate of investment could be expected sooner or later in order to supply the capital goods required for the increasing population. In this way, the growth of numbers acted as a fundamentally expansionist influence, which served to lift us out of the rut of depression. With stationary numbers, this particular remediable influence will be lacking; and at a later stage, when numbers are declining, the effect of the demographic trend will be positively inimical to the revival of investment. It is possible that depression may be more prolonged in consequences.[50]

Population decline thus presented a threat of chronically deficient aggregate demand, or, in other words, a return to the interwar slump. Stationary or declining numbers were, therefore, a barrier to a full-employment policy.

The committee's view was indeed that population decline and economic decline went hand in hand. But when dealing with the other side of the coin, that of food imports and living standards, the committee was perfectly prepared to recognize that "the balance of economic advantage is strongly" against a rapid increase of numbers.[51] The logic of their argument therefore led the committee to support on economic grounds the pronatalist measures that others advanced on social and ideological grounds.

The final report of the Royal Commission contained many of the arguments found in the report of the Economics Committee. The proposals, though, rested on their own merits. Basically, they called for financial aid to all parents to help improve the economic position of the family.

[48] *Report of the Economics Committee,* 15.
[49] Ibid., 29.
[50] Ibid., 43.
[51] Ibid., 53–5.

The government was to pay family allowances of seven shillings per week, and for children aged eleven or over, ten shillings per week, with the exclusion of the first child. Home help, both for emergencies and for the normally running household, also was to be provided.

Other forms of state aid also would help bolster the British family. The new National Health Service was to provide contraceptive advice to all women who wanted it and to coordinate and improve the maternity service as a whole. Housing policy had to take account of the effects of shortages and maldistribution of housing units on family formation. A more prominent place would be given to preparation for family life, including sex education, in school curricula.

Finally, the commission called for further research and for extension of the role of the Statistical Division of the General Register Office to enable a regular census of fertility to be conducted. Throughout this document, the hand of the PIC can be detected. The report, and its specialist papers, provided the most sophisticated analysis of demographic developments undertaken to that date and has served as a model for research in the subsequent generation.[52]

CONCLUSIONS AND IMPLICATIONS

Two conclusions may be drawn from the workings of the Economics Committee of the Royal Commission on Population. The first relates to the role of economists in providing a public body with economic "knowledge" and analysis. The second relates to the political uses to which such information was put.

We have briefly considered three independent ventures in population policy in the 1935–50 period. In the Swedish, French, and British cases, economists were central figures in the formulation of policy and, on the Continent, in its implementation. Alfred Sauvy and Gunnar Myrdal exploited their position as leading economists to initiate bold experiments in population policy. On the Economics Committee of the British Royal Commission on Population were men and women of equal professional distinction; Hicks, too, was to win a Nobel prize, and Henderson was in the 1940s one of the most eminent economists in Britain. In Joan Robinson, the committee had a young and influential scholar, in some ways the economic counterpart of David Glass, who played such an active part on

---

[52]*Report of the Royal Commission on Population* (London: HMSO, 1951), paragraphs 658–85.

the other two scientific committees. Why then did the British "experts" fail to leave a legacy in policy terms that compared even partially with that of their Continental colleagues? The answers lie in two different spheres, which may be described as the analytical and the political.

First, the British economists treated the population factor as a secondary, exogenous variable in their discussion of economic trends. They refused to follow French or Swedish suggestions that population questions were paramount; in Britain, they weren't. Instead, demography formed an adjunct to the development of Keynesian economics, and the general questions of manpower planning in wartime and a full-employment policy in peacetime. Their discussion of population was therefore the elaboration of a subtheme in a more important text, that of demand management in the postwar world. As we have noted, they had no independent data or evidence. What they offered was an analysis of the impact of demographic trends on economic affairs and policies.

Second, the economists never formed a group with identifiable policy interests. In contrast, the Population Investigation Committee, whatever its pretensions to academic neutrality, was a successful pressure group and fashioned much of the final report of the Royal Commission, which is a statement less about population policy than about family policy. The influence of the PIC rested in part on its membership in the other key committees and in part on Glass and Grebenik's pioneering family census of 1946, the first fertility census since 1911. The demographers and social scientists of the PIC were, therefore, able to mobilize science, in this case demographic science, in the service of social reform that most of the group supported on grounds of social justice, as well as demographic necessity. It was pleasing that the two went together, and as the Myrdals had shown, the mixture could yield political rewards. In a way the PIC used both the Royal Commission and its Economics Committee to advance a particular view of the population that Britain needed to survive in the postwar world. Economic knowledge and argument were useful in this effort, but economics was not essential for it. The Economics Committee helped it along, but only in a direction that was determined by considerations other than economic ones. In this case, the balance suggested by the term *political economy* was no balance at all. Population policy became family policy, and economic analysis and demography went their separate ways.

In effect, the demographers associated with the PIC wanted to foster a population policy—more precisely, a family policy—that was mildly pronatalist. This was presented as timely, in the light of contemporary fears of population decline, which, in turn were reinforced by the "fact" that fertility trends in the 1930s seemed to be inimical to a healthy environment for both domestic life and economic activity. The demographers emphasized the need to generate knowledge before entertaining policy options, hence the campaign to pass a Population (Statistics) Act in 1938 and to conduct a fertility census under the auspices of the Royal Commission itself.

Medical statisticians and demographers provided the Royal Commission with evidence; economists offered not knowledge but arguments about the likely effects of below-replacement fertility on Britain's economic prospects. They explored the links between economic decline and population decline and were attracted to a compromise solution, ruling out both rapid population growth and rapid population decline as undesirable economic options. They reached this conclusion on logical, not empirical, grounds. There is no indication that the economists gathered new evidence or explored new interpretations of these options; instead they relied on the "received wisdom" of Keynes and Beveridge to create their own essay in persuasion. It was persuasion, no doubt, but persuasion on behalf of a case for social reform that by and large stood without it.

About the authors

━━

WILLIAM J. BARBER is Andrews Professor of Economics at Wesleyan University. His recent scholarly projects include *From New Era to New Deal: Herbert Hoover, the Economists, and American Economic Policy, 1921–1933,* and *Breaking the Academic Mould: Economists and American Higher Learning in the Nineteenth Century,* of which he is editor and principal author. He serves as President of the History of Economics Society in 1989–1990.

W. ELLIOT BROWNLEE is Professor of History at the University of California, Santa Barbara. His publications include *Dynamics of Ascent: A History of the American Economy* (2d ed., 1979) and "Woodrow Wilson and Financing the Modern State: The Revenue Act of 1916," *Proceedings of the American Philosophical Society,* June 1985. Currently he is writing two books, one a history of the financing of World War I in the United States and the other called *Taxation and Social Choice in America: A History.* He is a former fellow at the Woodrow Wilson Center.

PETER CLARKE is Reader in History at the University of Cambridge. Among his recent works are *Liberals and Social Democrats* (1978) and *The Keynesian Revolution in the Making, 1924–1936* (1988).

ROBERT M. COLLINS is Professor of History at the University of Missouri—Columbia. He has written *The Business Response to Keynes, 1919–1964* and is currently at work on a study of American attitudes regarding economic growth since 1880.

MARY O. FURNER is Associate Professor of History at Northern Illinois University. The author of *Advocacy and Objectivity: A Crisis in the Professionalization of American Social Science, 1865–1905* (1975), she is currently coediting with Michael J. Lacey a companion volume to this

461

one entitled *The State and Social Investigation in the United States and Britain* and writing a book entitled *Redefining America: The Industrial Transformation and the American New Liberalism*. She is a former fellow at the Woodrow Wilson Center.

LESLIE HANNAH is Professor of Business History at the London School of Economics. His publications include *The Rise of the Corporate Economy; Engineers, Managers, and Politicians;* and *Inventing Retirement*.

JOSE HARRIS is Tutorial Fellow in Modern History at St. Catherine's College, Oxford University. Her publications include *Unemployment and Politics, 1886–1914* (1972) and *William Beveridge: A Biography* (1977).

ELLIS W. HAWLEY is Professor of History at the University of Iowa. He is the author of *The New Deal and the Problem of Monopoly* (1966) and *The Great War and the Search for a Modern Order* (1979), a coauthor of *Herbert Hoover and the Crisis of Modern Capitalism* (1973) and *Herbert Hoover and the Historians* (1989), editor of *Herbert Hoover as Secretary of Commerce* (1981), a coeditor of *Federal Social Policy in Modern America* (1988), and a contributor of shorter pieces to historical journals and volumes of collected essays.

JOHN LAURITZ LARSON is Associate Professor of History at Purdue University. His publications include *Bonds of Enterprise: John Murray Forbes and Western Development in America's Railway Age* and several recent articles on economic development in the early republic, including "A Bridge, a Dam, and a River: Liberty and Innovation in the Early Republic," *Journal of the Early Republic*, Winter 1987.

GEORGE C. PEDEN is Reader in Economic History at the University of Stirling. He is the author of *British Rearmament and the Treasury, 1932–1939* (1979); *British Economic and Social Policy: Lloyd George to Margaret Thatcher* (1985); and *Keynes, the Treasury, and British Economic Policy* (1988). He is currently writing a book on the British Treasury from 1906 to 1958.

BARRY SUPPLE is Professor of Economic History at the University of Cambridge. His publications include *The Royal Exchange Assurance: A History of British Insurance, 1730–1970* (1970) and *A History of the British Coal Industry, 1913–46* (1987). He has edited collections of essays on economic growth and on British business history. He is a former guest scholar at the Woodrow Wilson Center.

DONALD WINCH is Professor of the History of Economics at the University of Sussex. His most recent books are *Adam Smith's Politics* (1978); *That Noble Science of Politics* (1983), written in collaboration with Stefan Collini and John Burrow; and *Malthus* (1987).

JAY M. WINTER is Lecturer in History at the University of Cambridge and has published *The Great War and the British People* (1985), *The Fear of Population Decline* (1986), and *The Experience of World War I* (1988).

Index